Language Barrier

"You see here in Champagne," Tim sat back as though he were completely at home, not only in the countryside, but in her car, "there are certain things you can't change . . ."

"But things *have* changed." Sandra stamped her foot.

"Unlike the others, I know more about you, Sandra O'Neill," he said very softly. "I know that you are a woman with a soft heart, a loving nature that for some reason, perhaps I know what it is, you have repressed. I know . . ."

"For heaven's sake, Tim!" Sandra said, sharply switching on the key in the ignition. "Do you know what year this is? Do you think *I* am going to be seduced by these tactics?"

"Sandra . . ." Tim's expression was less certain now. "I only meant to help."

"You can help me by getting out of the car." Sandra paused, her face now lit by a mischievous smile. "You see, Monsieur, the road is quite clear now and I want to be on my way."

Champagne

NICOLA THORNE

Harper Paperbacks

Harper & Row, Publishers, New York
Grand Rapids, Philadelphia, St. Louis, San Francisco
London, Singapore, Sydney, Tokyo, Toronto

This is a work of fiction. The characters, incidents, and dialogues are products of the author's imagination and are not to be construed as real. Any resemblance to actual events or persons, living or dead, is entirely coincidental.

Harper Paperbacks a division of Harper & Row, Publishers, Inc.
10 East 53rd Street, New York, N.Y. 10022

A hardcover edition of this book was published in 1989 by Bantam Press, a division of Transworld Publishers Ltd.

First Harper Paperbacks printing: January, 1990

Printed in the United States of America

10 9 8 7 6 5 4 3 2 1

CONTENTS

AUTHOR'S FOREWORD ix

PROLOGUE 1

ONE
Strange Inheritance 7

TWO
The Rules of the Game 187

THREE
The Walls of Troy 271

FOUR
The Sands of Time 411

FIVE
Voice from the Dead 567

EPILOGUE
More Sinned Against Than Sinning. . . . 629

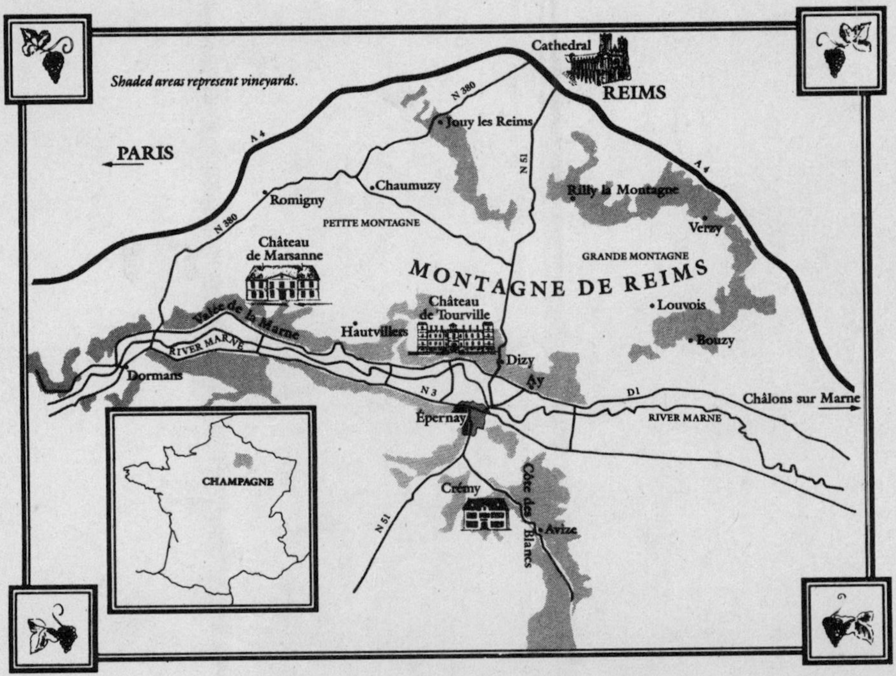
Shaded areas represent vineyards.
PARIS
A 4
N 380
Romigny
Chaumuzy
Jouy les Reims
Cathedral
REIMS
N 51
Rilly la Montagne
Verzy
PETITE MONTAGNE
GRANDE MONTAGNE
Château
de Marsanne
MONTAGNE DE REIMS
Château
de Tourville
Louvois
Bouzy
Hautvillers
Vallée de la Marne
RIVER MARNE
Dizy
Ay
Dormans
N 3
D1
Châlons sur Marne
Épernay
RIVER MARNE
Crémy
Côte des Blancs
Avize
N 51
CHAMPAGNE

AUTHOR'S FOREWORD

The story of the book *Champagne* was originally the brainchild of the Marquis d'Aulan, President of the famous house of Piper-Heidsieck.

Eventually, by various unusual routes, I came into the picture and was invited to write a novel based on this original outline. After many discussions in France and England and after writing two extended synopses, I embarked on the story which now unfolds in the following pages.

François d'Aulan has given me much help and advice. He also had very strong ideas about characterization, appearances, locations and so on, as well as the story line and I am most grateful to him for his meticulous help. I certainly felt rewarded when finally he gave the book his seal of approval, and I would like warmly to thank him and his wife Sonia for their hospitality and also their kindness to me in putting everything I needed at my disposal to assist me in my research. I am also grateful to Jean-Patrick Flandé and Luiz Williams of Tropix Ltd. for their assistance and to John Parkinson and Peter Janson-Smith of Booker PLC for putting the whole project together.

N.T.
London, 1988

PROLOGUE

As the plane left the rolling Tuscan vineyards behind and headed toward the mountains, the telephone in Georges Desmond's cabin rang and the pilot said:

"Your son is calling you, Monsieur Desmond."

"Which son?" Desmond said gruffly, putting the headpiece to his ear. "Hello?"

"Hello, Father. It's Zac. How were the vines in Tuscany?" There was a note of concern, almost of sycophancy in his son's voice which seemed to irritate Georges.

"How would you expect them to be at this time of the year?" snapped Georges. "You should know better than to ask me that question."

He gave an exaggerated sigh and stared out of the window.

"Sorry, Father. Look," Zac paused as if carefully choosing his words so as not to offend his awesome parent. "I want to meet your plane. What time do you arrive in Reims?"

With a flick of his wrist, Georges consulted his watch.

"At about fifteen hundred hours. Any special reason for meeting me, Zac?"

"I just wanted to talk to you, Father, before dinner tonight. I have some plans to discuss with you." Zac sounded excited. "I've got great news for you, Father. Great, great news."

"I can't wait to hear it," Georges said, but his tone was laconic. "Until three this afternoon, Zac. *Au revoir."*

"Au revoir, Papa. Bon vol."

Georges abruptly replaced the receiver and leaned back in his seat, gazing through the flimsy, wispish cloud at the towering peaks of the Alps below. Such grandeur never ceased to move even a man who had made the most of his life, achieved the highest goals. Or some people thought he had. As Chief Executive of the Desmond Group which, from small beginnings, had grown into a world-wide corporation, he was one of the most important men in France.

But Georges Desmond was a troubled man and at the root of his trouble, his unease about the future, was his eldest son, Zac. Memories of Zac as a child, willful, obstinate, yet strangely unsure of himself, came vividly to his mind as the executive jet banked steeply and began to turn toward France: his small children playing on the lawn of his great château on the banks of the Marne; his English wife, poised and serene, her large picture hat shading her eyes from the sun, sitting under a tree gazing fondly at them. Dreamlike, nostalgic, it was a familiar scene, but in many ways the happiness was illusory. Georges was restless, mercurial, hard to please . . . and Zac, poor Zac, tried so hard to please him.

Now yet again he had a great idea . . . another one. The last one had cost the Group fifty million francs and it was then that Georges had made his momentous decision. . . .

The vision of the children at play was replaced by another, even more vivid: a tall, blonde girl growing into womanhood, walking thoughtfully along the sandy beach at beautiful, remote Agay in the South of France. He would watch her progress from the terrace of the villa in the hills that he and the girl's mother—his mistress Hélène—rented for the peace and seclusion they so seldom had.

The girl fascinated him, despite the little he had seen of her. She was bilingual, she was beautiful, her intelligence was amazing. Georges delighted in teasing her, but she could solve every conundrum he ever posed. Their wits matched each other's with startling reciprocity. In time she grew up to be the woman who had fully achieved her earlier promise.

The aircraft lurched and dropped several hundred feet. Georges nervously seized the phone and demanded what was happening.

"Turbulence, Monsieur Desmond," the pilot said, "nothing to worry about." But his voice sounded strained.

And then the small aircraft shook again, losing more height, and the mountains seemed very, very close. . . .

ONE

Strange Inheritance

1

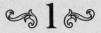

The day Georges Desmond died France was *en fête.* It was the fourteenth of July, a national holiday, a day of rejoicing, except perhaps for those who mourned; for the Desmond family, for instance, who, besides the pain of his death, had to suffer the anguish and humiliation of dispossession.

For Georges Desmond, one of the richest men in the world, had left the bulk of his vast fortune to an unknown woman.

News travels fast; it literally flew around the world in minutes; but it escaped the notice of a certain young woman whose normal domicile was California. At the time she was vacationing on a small yacht somewhere off the coast of Florida with her brother Bob and some friends.

Her name was Sandra O'Neill and while, thousands of miles away, she was quite unaware of the fact, it was a name that was soon on everyone's lips.

The Desmond family, thrown into disarray and confusion at the news, which scarcely gave them time to grieve the sudden departure of a husband and father, went to ground. After the funeral, which was a hurried affair in the circumstances, despite the eminence of the deceased, the gates of Tourville were firmly shut. A gendarme was stationed outside and paparazzi with telephoto lenses tried desperately to get a shot of some members of the family strolling in the extensive grounds. They climbed trees, scaled the massive brick wall, and hung onto railings. But no one appeared. The great house remained immersed in sorrow, solitude and mystery and it was left to the spokesman for the family, Paul Vincent, to try and explain to a wondering public and, in particular, a puzzled business community, what had happened, and why.

He mumbled his way through the explanation, reading parts of the will with hands that shook, especially the parts referring to the woman of whom no one had ever heard—the bequeathing of the bulk of this vast estate "To Sandra O'Neill," he read unsteadily, "whom I have adopted legally according to French law in recognition of the bonds linking me for so many years with her mother . . . I believe her to be entirely capable of managing energetically and ably the champagne business as well as the other extensive activities of the Desmond Group, and with the same success as myself.

"I ask my family to respect my choice . . ."

Sandra O'Neill, who had left Los Angeles as a normal member of the public, unknown to all but a few, returned to find herself a celebrity. The paparazzi, who had spent days clambering up and down the trees surrounding the park of Tourville, wandering through the extensive forest surrounding it and trying unsuccessfully to bribe the servants, knew a lost cause when they saw one. They made haste to board jets for California and were there poised with their cameras, their zooms and wide-angled lens, when Sandra, mystified, returned home to find her house in Beverly Hills in a state of siege, her Filipino maid a virtual prisoner.

Bob had been driving his Red Rabbit convertible as they left the Santa Monica Boulevard to climb up the short stretch of road to the house which was tucked attractively away in the trees. Sandra was listening to music on the radio. They had heard no news for nearly two weeks, but neither cared. For a woman whose fast-moving life was dominated by world crises and their effects on the various leading currencies, it was bliss indeed to get away from it all, and for several weeks every year she did. Bob had just spent his first year at college and it was mostly with his friends they had shared the yacht: fishing, swimming, diving, eating large meals mainly cooked by Sandra—a novelty for a busy woman.

"There's some—" Bob began as the house came into sight. "There's something going on. . . ."

Sandra looked up in alarm.

"My God," she said. "There must have been a fire. Maria—"

"There's no sign of smoke," Bob said. "No fire trucks. I hope to God nothing's *happened* to Maria."

Maria was not merely a servant. She was part of the family, almost like a warm and protective mother toward her employer.

"Drive straight past . . ." Sandra began, but it was too late. Even the make of her car was known and the reporters and cameramen who had been encamped for days streamed across the road to block her way.

"Miss O'Neill—could you—this way please Miss O'Neill. Miss O'Neill is that your brother, or your boyfriend?"

Bob was a tough and agile young man with the build of a quarterback. He stopped the car, got out and began strenuously to clear a path through the throng to the short drive that ran up to the house. He did it quite forcefully and a few of the more timid souls fell back. The hardier squatted on the back of the car for close-ups of Sandra.

"She's a looker . . ." they called to each other in some amazement. Who, after all, would have thought that someone of her ability had the cool blonde looks of a younger Catherine Deneuve? They knew she was half French. By now they knew almost everything about her.

"How long did your mother know Georges Desmond?"

"Did you get along with him?"

"Was the will a surprise to you?"

"Now wait here," Bob said, returning and getting into the

driving seat. "What on earth is happening? We've been on vacation. What has this to do with Georges Desmond?"

"You mean you don't know . . . ?" The reporter from NBC was ecstatic. "Your sister is an heiress . . . one of the richest women in the world. . . ."

Two hours later the house was still surrounded. None of the reporters had gone or, perhaps, a few had slipped away to telephone their news. The TV reporters were being interviewed in front of the still shuttered house and it was from the news bulletin that Sandra eventually found out what everyone else had known for a week.

Georges Desmond was dead. Not only that: he had made her his heir; heir to a vast fortune based on the prestigious firm of Desmond champagne, a hundred years old; to an empire built up on the profits of that champagne which now embraced newspapers, supermarkets, aeronautics and various businesses almost too diverse to mention.

Sandra hardly smoked and rarely drank. But now she reached for a cigarette and asked Bob to pour her a half-inch of whisky.

"I simply can't believe it," she said. "There must be some terrible mistake. We shall have to telephone Uncle Henri."

Bob, who had been sorting through the mail handed to him by an anxious but now greatly relieved Maria, who had various horror stories to tell about attempts to bribe her, or invasions of the house, held up a cable.

"No need," he said. "Uncle Henri is on his way. He flew back to France for the funeral; but cabled . . ."—Bob glanced at the date—"yesterday that he will be here"—he glanced at the clock—"today. In fact," as they heard a fresh commotion outside, "that could be him now."

Sandra quickly got up and ran with Bob into the hall. Outside they could hear an argument going on.

"But I tell you I am expected. I am an emissary from the family of Monsieur Georges Desmond. . . ."

Henri's charmingly accented voice was uncharacteristically pleading. "I promise you as soon as I have seen Miss O'Neill there will be a statement . . . no maybe not tonight, but certainly tomorrow. You must allow her to collect herself, you know. She has had a very big shock."

"You can say that again," Sandra murmured as, arms outstretched in welcome, she waited for Bob to let him in.

Henri Piper was Georges Desmond's brother-in-law, the husband of his only sister, Sophie. He was an elegant, cultured man who concealed considerable business acumen under a veneer of languid charm. Like Georges he had been born to money through champagne and, like him, enjoyed the kind of lifestyle it had inevitably enabled him to lead.

But the two men, though close, differed in temperament. Henri had been content with his inheritance, with adding only slightly to his riches by the cultivation and marketing of his business, particularly in California, where he had broken new ground in introducing a marketable champagne. Piper Champagne was a *marque* as old and distinguished as that of Desmond and the families had been friends for generations. The Pipers lived in some style at the Château de Marsanne near Épernay. It did not compare in size to the grandeur and magnificence of the Château de Tourville, but it possessed its own comfort and dignity, its own quiet and restrained air of tasteful opulence.

To Sandra, Henri, though no relation, had been like a wise and kind uncle; the only real contact she had had with Georges and the mother who had left her when she was still a small child to become his mistress and live in France.

As quickly and as briefly as he could, he told her the circumstances of the crash in the Alps and its extraordinary aftermath.

"It was a terrible shock to the family." Henri turned from his contemplation of the view of Los Angeles from the poolside to a study of Sandra and her brother who was sitting, head slumped on his chest, beside her.

"I can imagine," Sandra said. "It is a shock to me."

Restlessly she got up and, picking a strawberry from a large bowl on the white poolside table, examined it carefully. "Of course I can't accept. . . ."

"But—" Henri moved swiftly toward her, careful to avoid falling into the pool.

"You know I can't." Sandra put the strawberry into her mouth and picked up another. "The whole thing is absolutely absurd. I know nothing about corporate finance, nothing about business on a global scale. No one will take any notice of me. Moreover I know nothing about the Desmond family and I know they will hate me."

Henri strolled silently along the length of the pool, hands clasped behind his back.

"It *is* very difficult for them to understand . . . especially Zac. He is completely shattered by the whole thing."

"Well there you are. It is his birthright, not mine. I can't accept."

"I agree with Sandra." Bob stretched his legs, resting his head on arms linked behind him. "She should not accept this bequest. It sounds like a lot of hassle to me."

"Hassle . . . ?" For a moment Henri looked furious. *"Hassle* did you say? This is one of the biggest jobs in the world."

"And I don't want it." Sandra's voice sounded final. "I'm sorry you came all this way. . . ."

"I had to come back to California in any case. We have some delicate negotiations going on here. Sophie is staying behind with the family."

"Sophie will be upset."

"Sophie doesn't really understand, like everyone else; but, yes, I suppose she is upset on account of the hurt Georges has caused. He left no hint of his intentions, no explanations, nothing. . . ."

"And my mother . . ." Sandra paused, gravely regarding Henri across the width of the pool. "Did *she* know anything?"

"Ah!" Henri Piper shrugged his shoulders at the mention of Sandra's mother. "No one has yet inquired of her what *she* knew . . . poor soul."

"Poor soul!" Sandra gave a brittle laugh. "First she took him away from his family, and then he left his fortune to her daughter. . . ."

"That's not fair," Henri said quickly. "Your mother was *very* discreet as his mistress. Even the Press, try as hard as they may, have not fully grasped what her status was. Lately I understand she has not been well, an old occurrence of bronchial trouble. She has retreated to her country house. She must have taken this very badly. Personally I doubt if she was behind it. Georges was a law unto himself. However, you can find all this out, when you come to France."

"Sandra isn't going," Bob said in his deadpan voice. "She told you. The whole thing is fantastic. Sandra's place is *here.* She's doing well. She likes her job, her friends, her life. . . ."

"Bob's quite right." Sandra sat down again, leaning back in the wicker chair. "I have a lifetime of misery ahead of me if I accept this."

Henri crossed to her side of the pool and, standing in front of her, leaned over so far that his head nearly touched hers. She was aware of his pale blue eyes only inches away.

"You *must* give this a chance, Sandra. Georges Desmond was no fool. He never did anything without a reason. This was no whim, no sudden impulse. He must have planned it carefully, perhaps for years. . . ."

"Yet he told no one, not even you?" Sandra looked incredulous.

"Not even me, or Vincent or Laban the lawyer, though, of course, Laban knew because he drew up the will just over a year ago. Now, about eighteen months ago something quite interesting happened." Henri straightened up. He was a tall, lean man with a casual air of aristocratic nonchalance that some people have whether of noble birth or not, and he put his hands in his pockets as if sniffing the fragrant evening air. "His son Zac purchased behind his back a chain of supermarkets. It was not the first time he had acted without consulting his father but, as the head of the Desmond Bank, he often felt he could make decisions on his own. Many of them were not wise. Georges was very angry about the supermarket chain because when he looked into it he saw that the company had not been well run; it was obviously a bad investment showing poor judgment on the part of Zac."

"Asset stripping?" Sandra said immediately. "Maybe they were on prime sites which Zac felt he could sell. . . ."

"Aah," Henri said delightedly, pointing a finger at her. "The nose of a good businesswoman. See how quickly you react? That is exactly what Georges thought, but no, there was no value in them at all and the Desmond Group lost about fifty million francs." Thoughtfully Henri sank into the chair beside Sandra.

"I think, at that moment, Georges began to mistrust his son. And soon after that he decided to adopt you—a fact you did not legally need to know—and changed his will. He felt the empire he had so carefully and skillfully built up would not be safe in Zac's hands."

"But why should it be safe in *mine* for heaven's sake? He hardly knew me."

"Ah, but he took a close interest in you, much closer than you realized. After all he knew a lot about you. He paid for your education, studied your examination results. He knew Doug Hammerson, who thought so well of you at the Hammerson Trust. Hammerson judged you a high flier with an excellent record and a brilliant future and so did Georges."

"Did he talk to Doug about me?"

"He talked to him, I'm sure. But not about the will. Why don't you ask Doug? You will have to, anyway, if you are to quit your job."

"I'm not quitting," Sandra said, rising again and restlessly pacing the cool blue tiles around the pool.

"Ask Doug," Henri said. "Then see if you change your mind."

Some people said that Doug Hammerson Jr. was the smartest businessman on the West Coast, maybe the East as well. From small beginnings he had made the Hammerson Trust into a group almost the size of Desmond and, like Desmond, it included a prestigious merchant bank, Hamco Incorporated. In four years Sandra had become one of the chief analysts working for the bank; her job was to assess the potential and risks of any company approaching the bank for money. In time Doug Hammerson had come to place her judgment before that of more experienced people. She had an unusual knack of sorting chaff from wheat, seeing true from false and judging where the truth lay. She had saved the bank from some disasters and helped substantially to increase its revenue.

Sandra's forte was math and economics which she had majored in at Berkeley. She did a year in Business Studies at the Harvard Business School and after that she was vigorously head-hunted; there was no shortage of job offers.

Consequently she had commanded a large salary, her own office overlooking Los Angeles City Center, a company car and such fringe, but legitimate, benefits that Hammerson considered executives of her caliber and potential were entitled to: medical care, long vacations, school fees for children where applicable and so on.

"Of course you'll have to go," Doug said, sitting back with his crinkly smile, a pencil stretched between his fingers. "Though I hate to lose you I can't keep you. It's a challenge you simply can't refuse and"—he tossed his pencil on his desk—"there's always a job here for you if all else fails."

"Failure would be terrible," Sandra said.

"Is *that* what you're afraid of?" Doug's eyes were kind, concerned for someone for whom he not only had a high regard but who had become a family friend.

"One's always afraid of failure." Sandra reached over and finished the coffee Doug's secretary had brought when she came in. Then she shuddered and, standing up, went to the window and gazed at the ground far below. "I wish those fellows would stop following me about. I feel hounded. I'm not Madonna."

"Maybe you'll wish you were. I don't think there will be a lot of glamor in your life, Sandra, though there will be much power and prestige." He came from behind and put his hands gently on her shoulders. "You know I had a very high regard for Georges Desmond. I only met him half a dozen times but we did a lot of business, we spoke often on the phone. He always asked about you. He asked about you a lot."

"Yet he never told you. . . ."

"Never." As Sandra turned, Doug shook his head and in his wise gray eyes she saw the truth. "Never a whisper. I knew nothing about Georges' private life, his plans or intentions."

It was a wet August day when Sandra O'Neill, accompanied by Henri Piper who had met her at the airport, arrived at the door of the Ritz in Paris to be greeted by the usual bevy of photographers who had squatted in the place Vendôme since her arrival the day before.

But now there was a spokesman, Georges Desmond's invaluable factotum, Paul Vincent who, in a few short weeks, had rapidly mastered the art of dealing with the Press. In fact he rather liked it, enjoyed his power and, with his pince-nez halfway down his nose, he looked about him with an air of profound disapproval. With one long lean arm he barred them physically from getting any nearer to their prey.

"Mademoiselle O'Neill will *not* be making a statement today," he said as Sandra, knowing that they were either for her or against her, smiled all around. She looked particularly charming in a shirt-style dress of yellow silk belted at the waist, a closely pleated skirt which suited her slim form. She was very tall for a woman and always wore shoes that were either flat or with heels of medium height. She had honey-blonde hair, bleached by the California sun, which was brushed back from her forehead without parting, swirling with a slight natural wave just above the level of her shoulders.

Her deeply tanned skin complemented perfectly the color of her dress which was one such as any young California girl of good breeding and good taste might wear for a day's outing with her family, for shopping in town or visiting friends.

She seemed to be letting the world know that she was going nowhere in particular; but she was.

She was going to Tourville, the family home, *her* family home and, deep inside, she was afraid.

But her clear blue eyes and sunny, broad smile gave no hint of the fear lurking inside her as, hands in the pockets of her open raincoat, she smiled under the umbrella held high by the doorman before getting into the Phantom VI Silver Rolls which had been sent from Tourville to pick her up.

After some final shots of her waving and smiling she settled back against the soft leather upholstery of the luxurious car as the Press gathered around Paul Vincent who, with his glasses even farther down his nose and perspiring slightly, was giving details of her itinerary which carefully excluded any mention of Tourville. In fact it was an itinerary intended solely to deceive. But later in the week he promised them an interview, if they were very good, and if they were naughty and followed Mademoiselle everywhere she went, which she was beginning to find very tiring—after all she was not a film star—they wouldn't get one.

For some of them, what with the rain and the tiring, relentless rather fruitless pursuit, this was enough. They stuck their cameras in their bags and went off in search of liquid refreshment in the nearby bars.

"He's sweet isn't he?" Sa[illegible] said with a backward glance as the car circled the place Vendôme and eased into the rue Saint-Honoré making for the Porte de Bercy and a westerly exit from Paris along the main autoroute to Reims.

"He's a clever man," Henri agreed, settling comfortably in his seat.

"I don't *really* know who or what he is. Was he something to do with Georges?"

"He was Georges' right-hand man. A kind of confidential secretary. But the odd thing is that he didn't know a thing about you. He was as mystified, as surprised as anyone else. Yet for the last thirty years or so he has known almost everything there was to know about Georges Desmond."

"And my mother?"

"He knew her very well." Henri paused. "As Georges' secretary she worked closely with Paul."

"Did they get on?"

"Hélène made it her business, I think, to get on with everyone. She was the *eminence grise,* kept very much to the background, by choice and by natural tact and discretion. She was, and is, a very discreet woman. I hope you will change your mind and go and see her. She has retired to Crémy in, I hear, very poor health, shocked by the abruptness of Georges' death and the attitude of the family who, of course, will have nothing to do with her."

"You can't complain about that," Sandra said, crossing one leg over the other. "She may have been a good friend to Georges and Paul Vincent and you and others for all I know;

but she was a wretched mother to me and Bob. I don't think I've heard from her for two years."

"She says you never replied to her letters."

"I don't think that's *quite* true. Never mind . . ." Sandra tapped her fingers on her knees and looked at the cars streaking past on either side of the busy *périphérique* around Paris.

"Paul Vincent is important for another reason," Henri said with a cough that caught her attention. She looked sharply at him, observing something rather unusual on that equable countenance: a trace of nerves.

"What reason is that?" Sandra said. "You look quite worried, Henri."

"There *is* something I didn't tell you." Henri spoke in English so that the chauffeur would not understand, the glass slide between him and his passengers being half open. "I suppose I should; but had I, I don't think you would ever have come."

Sandra didn't say a word but waited for him to continue and momentarily, under that compelling gaze, he wilted as if realizing, if he never had before, the reason for her astonishing success. She had a presence, an aura that was distinctly fearsome. She was one of those people who knew she could get more by what remained unsaid, rather than what was said.

"In his will," Henri said with another cough, "Georges stipulated that you were to be helped and guided by a Council which had the power to dismiss you if it found your conduct of the affairs of the Desmond organization unsatisfactory."

Now, finally, he felt the full impact of Sandra's silence. Only a muscle in her cheek rippled and there was a tightening of the lips, a swift lowering of those beautiful, hooded eyelids.

"It is only meant to help and guide you," Henri repeated, "to be at your beck and call any time you wish; to do nothing if you do not need it; but . . . well, there it is." He gestured helplessly with his hands. "It *is* a kind of tribunal. . . ."

"Why was I not told?" If words could cut, Sandra's would have penetrated steel.

"As I said . . ."

"You were right, I should not have come. A council, to control *me?"*

"No not *control,* not at all. You have completely the wrong idea. But, in his wisdom Georges realized that, for all your abilities, you were, are, an *ingénue* as far as many things were concerned. Paul Vincent knows all there is to know about the Desmond organization. That is why he is controlling the Press, and doing it very well. Incidentally, he likes you already."

"Who else is on the 'Council'?" Sandra resumed tapping her fingers on her knee, a movement which now seemed to have a hint of menace.

"Well I am." Henri glanced at her again. "Maître Laban, who is the family lawyer and . . . the members of the Desmond family."

"The members of the Desmond family!" Sandra swiftly leaned forward and, for a moment, Henri thought that she was going to order the chauffeur to turn around and go back to Paris. However, she was merely closing the window between them. Perhaps she didn't want him to hear that they were having an argument.

"Zac is an expert on all aspects of the business too."

"Then why didn't Georges Desmond leave it to him?"

Henri ignored the question. "Belle also is very able. Claire and Tim, well," he screwed up his nose, "the lightweights of the family, if you like. Lady Elizabeth a formidable matriarch; but you can get her on your side, if you're clever."

"I don't think I want to try." Sandra's voice was still steely. "I feel that I could really sue you for deception on this."

"I only meant well. I really did. I think that you and Desmond are made for each other and I want you to be a success. I know you will."

Henri felt her taut, stiff body relax a fraction and stealthily allow his hand to steal comfortingly over hers.

By the time they left the motorway an hour later the sun had come out. And it was from under a brilliant blue sky, framed by dark clouds, that Sandra first saw her inheritance: the countryside of the department known as Champagne which had given its name to a glorious, unique wine.

The vineyards of Champagne covered about 27,000 hectares of land planted mostly in the valley of the Marne, the Côte des Blancs, beyond Épernay, and the Montagne de Reims through which they were now driving, and on whose gentle undulating slopes were situated both the chateaux of Tourville and Marsanne.

The Montagne was not a very high mountain in the sense that one thinks of mountains. Although, rather grandly divided into "la grande montagne" and "la petite montagne," it was more or less a gentle slope—its highest point the Forest of Verzy—rising from just outside the ancient city of Reims in the north, to Épernay and the Valley of the Marne in the south along which its principal vineyards were gathered. They stretched for mile upon mile, as far as the eye could see, in neat, orderly, carefully tended rows interspersed with colored flags, which denoted whether the grapes were the Pinot Noir or the white Chardonnay with the name of the owner.

Beyond and above the vineyards was La Forêt de la Montagne de Reims which provided acres of tall trees, sometimes, like the vines, in straight disciplined rows through which the sun, when it could, slatted onto the thick, verdant undergrowth. Parts of the forest were very dark, but suddenly one chanced upon stretches of woodland, shrubs and bushes, drenched by rain and sparkling in the sun which seemed to give the whole area through which they now passed an almost primeval freshness.

"It *is* heavenly," Sandra said at last, having spent some time silently watching the landscape.

"It is." Henri sensed that she had relaxed even further. "And a lot of it is yours. . . . Wait, any minute now, you will see Tourville. Look, the river!"

Henri shouted with the excitement of a schoolboy, and Sandra leaned forward eagerly as he tapped the glass and told the driver to stop.

"If we get out here," Henri explained, "you will see a unique view of Tourville through the trees."

Sandra realized her heart was beating rapidly as the chauffeur held the door open for them. At that moment the sun penetrated once again through cloud showing her, in all its glory, the valley of the Marne and the place that from now on, if she accepted it, was her home.

From the plateau onto which Henri led her she saw a house that almost eclipsed in its magnificence, its grandeur, its sheer size, anything she had ever seen. It was also totally out of place in its environment yet, somehow, paradoxically, the more she gazed at it the more suited to it it appeared.

She knew something of its history. It had been built in the middle of the nineteenth century by René-Zachariah Desmond, the great-grandfather of Georges and great-great-grandfather of Zac who had been named after him. The first René-Zachariah had been the founder of the great champagne house which now bore the Desmond name.

It had been built in the English style by an architect whose imaginative skills had captured the fancy of the first René-Zachariah who, perhaps, had wanted to outdo his rival, the widow Clicquot, who was also building a magnificent château in the Renaissance style on the other side of the Marne. Sandra now saw a rectangular white stone building; it was two stories high with two square towers at each end, and on either side colonnaded balconies that ran from one tower to the other. Each of the towers gave an extra story, so that the tower rooms would be much sought after, affording, as they did, a view of the Marne across the high red brick wall which surrounded the Château, protecting it from the gaze of summer trippers, the curious and, fortunately on this occasion, reporters. From the road that ran up from the banks of the Marne a pair of ornate iron gates led to a short drive and an impressive porch with a massive front door. On the other side Sandra could see an ornate staircase leading from a grand colonnaded porch surmounted by twin cupolas that led out to gardens, and a formal lake, most of which was lost to her view in the forest that, descending the slopes of the Montagne, surrounded it.

On either side, surrounded by the high brick wall, were extensive formal gardens designed in the style of Le Nôtre, full of the rare and beautiful trees that had been imported by the son of René-Zachariah, Georges' great-grandfather, Jean-Timothée, who had indulged in gardening as a rich man's hobby.

"It is like a pearl," Sandra whispered. "A pearl set in a perfect shell." She gestured toward the river, the valley of the Marne now bathed in the splendid light of early afternoon. "I never imagined anything half as magnificent."

"Many people regarded it as a folly and it *is* very expensive to run and maintain. There are thirty-five bedrooms; but, of course, it is a rich family who lives there and you will share it with them."

Sandra got slowly, thoughtfully back into the car which resumed its journey down a steeply winding hill, again affording here and there exquisite views of the river flanked by trees. The Château was now lost from sight as the car descended slowly, though clearly visible across the banks was the town of Épernay, a bustling center of the champagne industry.

"How can we *share* that place?" Sandra mused as the car emerged onto the even road at the end of which she could see that high brick wall, those huge, costly wrought-iron gates.

"In French law Georges had to leave it equally to his heirs. Each has a share; but as he adopted you, made you his daughter, you have inherited the greater part of the rest of his fortune. Georges always loved the idea of his family gathered together under one roof in peace and harmony. Alas, it was not always like that, largely due to himself. He was a restless man and as we know"—he glanced at Sandra, who seemed still lost in thought—"he had a mistress for many years who all the family knew about. That alone certainly did not make for harmony."

"It will not make for harmony now." Sandra's voice was scarcely above a whisper, her fists tightly clenched in her lap. "You have no idea how I dread this."

Then, as the car halted, the gates swung open almost miraculously and Tourville, and her future, lay before her.

2

"Mademoiselle O'Neill, Madame . . ." Pierre the butler, an imposing man, bowed and withdrew through the narrow doors of the greenhouse with as much dignity as he could muster in the circumstances. The greenhouse was large and very hot, filled with the exotic plants, shrubs and flowers that would otherwise not have flourished even in that temperate part of France.

Lady Elizabeth Desmond was a tall slender woman, rather formidable in appearance, wearing a curious gray, long-sleeved ankle-length monastic-type garment over her day dress to protect it from soiling. On her head was a yellow straw hat bound with a long chiffon scarf which was tied under her chin. Her gloved hands held a pair of secateurs and, as she rose to greet Sandra, she had the indefinable air of a medieval abbess about to chastise a young postulant. In a way she seemed a caricature of what an elderly, aristocratic lady should look like in similar circumstances.

It was certainly unnerving, as it was meant to be, yet Sandra wasn't deterred. Her entry to the home of the Desmonds was one which she hadn't expected to be easy. After driving through the gates leading up the short drive toward the magnificent house, she had been greeted on the steps by the stately butler to be informed that Lady Elizabeth would like to see her privately, and that Monsieur Piper should wait in the main salon with the rest of the family.

A footman had then appeared, as if at some prearranged signal, to escort Henri indoors. Sandra had followed the majestic form of Pierre around the front of the vast house before finding herself in the greenhouse, among the tropical plants and the various species of camellia draping the whitewashed walls. But it was the fragrant *Polyanthus tuberosa* with its creamy-white funnel-shaped flowers whose cultivation was a special hobby of the gifted horticulturist, the châtelaine de Tourville.

If Lady Elizabeth had thought that by greeting her thus she would daunt her unwelcome guest she was mistaken.

She was obviously taken aback by the appearance, the apparent self-assurance, of her husband's heir and slowly drew her gloves off before offering Sandra her hand.

"How do you do, Miss O'Neill?"

"How do you do, Madame?" Out of respect to the older woman, but without the least trace of obsequiousness, Sandra inclined her head as they shook hands, aware of the firm clasp of the person whose children she had supplanted: a formidable adversary indeed.

Lady Elizabeth passed her hand across her forehead and beckoned her to the door.

"You may find it too hot in here, Miss O'Neill. I have to maintain this temperature for the orchids and tuberoses which are my specialty. I have asked Pierre to have tea brought into the garden."

Even as she spoke a footman appeared bearing aloft a silver tray, followed by a maid with another. Whatever other objective Lady Elizabeth had she was certainly setting out to try and impress her guest. But Sandra's grave yet pleasant expression seemed to indicate how perfectly at ease she was, how accustomed to grandeur on this scale. Or, if not accustomed, she seemed to be saying, certainly she was not overawed by it. Henri had warned her that the Desmonds would try to intimidate her and his prediction was being proved correct.

To their right was a side of the house with its colonnaded balconies and, in front, the lake beyond which one could see deep into the forest.

Sandra took in all the beauty around her yet aware, all the time, of Lady Elizabeth who, if she wanted to impress her, had not dressed for her. Perhaps her gardening attire was coincidental or, maybe, it was intended as an insult. Who could tell from the impassive features of this mysterious, imperious woman?

Maybe, surreptitiously, she was studying Sandra too . . . perhaps a little surprised by her chic, the absence of stockings on bare legs, the low-heeled white calf shoes, the lack of ornament. But perhaps, more than anything, she was impressed by her striking looks. Hélène O'Neill had never been a beauty; the haughty Englishwoman had been unable to understand her husband's attraction to a member of the bourgeoisie from the provinces, and yet . . .

Glancing at Sandra, she led the way toward a table and chairs that had been placed under a large oak whose heavy branches caressed the roof of the greenhouse. Sandra was aware, nevertheless, that her hostess was at pains to conceal her nerves, fidgeting ceaselessly as she took her seat, pointing to Sandra to do likewise. The effect on Sandra was to make her feel unexpectedly at ease, cool and graceful, and she sat back in the upright chair watching as Lady Elizabeth dismissed the hovering servants and began to pour.

"I do hate those reporters," she said with a gesture of her hand, as though brushing away a fly. "Vulgar people. They swarm all over the place."

"I hate them too." Sandra's eyes, unflinching, met the severe gaze. "They are like pests."

"Certainly *we* didn't want them."

"Nor did I . . . you can be sure of that."

Sandra's tone seemed rather to surprise her ladyship who, as if to change the subject, said peremptorily:

"Milk or lemon, Miss O'Neill?" Her precise English vowels were unchanged despite years of living in France.

"Milk please, Lady Elizabeth."

"I thought it would be better if we got to know each other before I introduce you to my family, Miss O'Neill. I need not tell you what a shock my late husband's will was to us all."

"You, as well, Lady Elizabeth?" Sandra tilted her head.

"Good gracious me yes!" Eyebrows raised, Lady Elizabeth paused in the act of passing Sandra her cup. "Me most of all, even though it was no secret that, for many years, my husband had a liaison with your mother."

"I had no idea of the will either."

"So I understand." Lady Elizabeth's tone suggested that, though she might have understood this, she did not necessarily believe it. She had already decided in advance to be as polite and as bland with her guest as she could. In this way, she had told her children, they might achieve more than by showing outright hostility.

"In fact I scarcely knew Monsieur Desmond," Sandra said suddenly, realizing they were on delicate ground. "I met him only a few times, and briefly."

"Strange, then, that he should have selected *you* for his heir." Lady Elizabeth could scarcely keep the disbelief out of her voice. "My eldest son has worked for years and years in the family business. He is, naturally, very disappointed indeed, a very bitter man. I wanted to prepare you for this."

Lady Elizabeth leaned forward and gazed searchingly into Sandra's eyes. "Is it not possible, Miss O'Neill, that the task my late husband has entrusted you with is too daunting? Gifted and capable you may be, but you are so young, so inexperienced . . ."

"I can understand all your reservations," Sandra said, an immediate sympathy entering her voice, "as well as your despair, even revulsion, at what your husband has done. I can also understand your eldest son's anger and hostility and I will do all I can to take him into my confidence and make a friend of him. He will still be a man of great power and importance."

Lady Elizabeth sighed and, leaning back, tapped her fingers impatiently on the white painted wrought-iron table.

"But, believe me, that is not enough. Have you quite, quite made up your mind to accept? We hoped . . . we had all hoped . . . if it's a question of money . . . you can have all you need without the responsibility of running a business you know absolutely nothing about."

A note of bitterness now entered Lady Elizabeth's voice as if at her husband's betrayal not only of their children but, more especially, of her. It was, indeed, a humiliating experience to be confronted by the daughter of her husband's mistress and to know that it was she whom he had appointed as his heir. It was rather like proclaiming to the whole world how much more he loved his mistress than his wife. Just then, in Sandra's eyes, Lady Elizabeth seemed a very sad and unhappy figure, not the *grande dame* at all and she wanted to take her hand in hers and comfort her. But it was impossible. One day, maybe, but not now. Instead she said gently:

"I realize, Lady Elizabeth, what resentment you must feel not only about me but toward my mother. I will do all in my power to make this trying time as easy for you as I can. I wish in no way to interfere with you or your family affairs and as for this"—she gazed over to the huge house, the legendary home of the Desmonds—"I will do my best to live in it as happily as I can with all of you."

"That was the unkindest, the cruelest thing of all." Lady Elizabeth rose with an agility belying her years and began to pace the lawn in front of Sandra. "This has been in the Desmond family for generations. It *is* the Desmond family home. To share it with someone who is not in any way related to us . . ." She paused and gazed solemnly at Sandra. "At least I do not *think* you are in any way related, are you?"

"How do you mean?" Sandra raised her eyes, confronting those staring down at her.

"It has occurred to me that you might be my husband's natural child."

"It occurred to me too," Sandra said frankly. "But so far as I know, I am the daughter of John O'Neill whom my mother married in England."

"So far as you know. . . ."

"There has never been any reason to doubt it. My father was a ne'er-do-well who slipped out of our lives and I've no idea now where he is. But, to my knowledge, he never disputed the fact that he was my father."

"Anyway your mother could put you straight on that," Lady Elizabeth said, her mouth curling slightly as if she found the whole conversation distasteful. "Only I understand you are not on good terms with her?"

"Does that surprise you?" Sandra leaned back in her chair, the expression in her eyes hidden by the shadow of the tree. "My mother left me and my brother to be brought up in institutions. We were each sent to boarding schools in America—the best, maybe—but we had no settled home life. It wasn't until I was fifteen that my mother bought the house in Beverly Hills that I now consider my real home. I understand that even that was bought with Georges Desmond's money, and my education was paid for by him . . . but solely because of my mother, not on account of me. It is a home I have come to love and I am naturally reluctant to give it up."

"Then perhaps . . ." Lady Elizabeth interrupted hopefully, but Sandra continued as if anticipating what she was going to say.

"I don't want to give it up and I shall return there often; but in the meantime I want to try to fulfill the task Georges Desmond, for whatever reason, bequeathed to me. I find it a challenge. It intrigues me. I would be lying to you if I said it didn't."

"You had better meet my children," Lady Elizabeth said with a wry smile, "and see how you feel after that. I can assure you the way ahead will not be easy for you but"—she tilted her head to one side—"having met you I have little doubt that, if anyone can do it, you can."

From Sandra's suite on the second floor double doors led onto the balcony that overlooked the formal gardens. To the right of her was a pool house with a swimming pool.

It was that pleasant, tranquil time of day: sunset. The sun had already disappeared over the trees of the Forest of Tourville and the crickets had not yet begun their insistent chirping, the *click click click* that haunts French summer nights. Sandra had changed from her dress into a robe. She was relaxing before having dinner with the rest of the family to whom she had been briefly introduced after her meeting in the garden with Lady Elizabeth. What an ordeal that had been.

It was easy to see why the old lady had tried to pave the way for her, because the hostility that greeted her as she had walked into the huge salon was like some kind of invisible, magnetic wave. Anyone less determined might well have run, taken the first plane home; but not she. She had steadfastly maintained the same polite, gracious air that she had decided to adopt when she set foot in France, knowing that anything else would be impossible. In a way she must be as obdurate, as implacable, as she knew the Desmonds would be.

As the massive double doors had been thrown open, almost with indecent enthusiasm, by Pierre, she had been confronted by one of those daunting family portraits—the only difference being that this had been a live group—the men standing, the women seated stiffly on straight chairs. And there seemed so many of them. Even the benign, concerned face of Henri Piper had done nothing to dispel the sense of panic she had instinctively felt until she reminded herself that they also must be afraid of *her.* Perhaps more so, because she wielded the power.

Dominating the group had been Zac, whose presence seemed to fill the room. The formidable charm which his father had had in marked degree had clearly been inherited by his eldest son.

He was extremely tall, well built but not fat, clean shaven, and his hair though thick at the sides was receding slightly in front, which seemed to add to his air of almost awesome masculinity. His skin was dark, saturnine, and his brow overshadowed brown alert eyes which expressed a keen intelligence. He had a rather big nose and a firm, thin-lipped mouth which did not lack a certain sensuality. He wore a gray double-breasted pin-striped suit, and white shirt with a plain blue tie.

If she thought Lady Elizabeth formidable Sandra had to think again when she met her eldest son. How could she ever expect to be equal to, never mind in control of, such a man, so much her superior in power, experience, as well as years?

His eyes were on her from the moment she came in and, after being introduced by his mother, he politely shook her hand before introducing her, in turn, to the rest of the family.

"My sister Armelle," he had murmured. "Princess von Burg-Farnbach. We always call her Belle. Her husband Carl, their son Constantine is at home in Bavaria. My brother Tim, he is the sportsman of the family. You will surely have read about his heroic ascent of K2? It nearly cost him his life. Finally Claire; she is the baby, Countess de Saint-Aignan. Her husband, Armand. They have no children." Then, his arm outstretched, he waved toward him with an air of possessiveness a beautiful woman with striking titian-colored hair whose face Sandra instantly recognized from the covers of fashion magazines. "This is my wife Tara, Contessa Falconetti before our marriage. We have two children, little monsters, now with my sister's son in Bavaria for the holidays. Tara and Belle run the House of Jean Marvoine in the avenue Montaigne, you will surely be familiar with it. Their designer, Maurice Raison, was the toast of Paris at the collections this spring. Henri Piper you know. Now, is that all?"

Charmingly he had looked around as if to inquire of everyone present what on earth this apparently naïve girl from California could hope to accomplish against such a formidable array of talented, titled Desmonds?

It was Henri who, by a subtle nod of the head, had given her the courage to smile, shake hands and, in the end, make a little speech in French, whose fluency seemed to surprise them, saying how glad she was to meet them all.

Yet no one was deceived. Sandra O'Neill was not really pleased to meet them and they most certainly—despite the charm, the smiles, the bows, the little murmurs of appreciation of her excellent colloquial French—were not pleased to meet her.

But the menace that Sandra felt so keenly was only the tip of the iceberg.

3

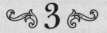

The Desmond family had married into some of the most aristocratic families in Europe. Lady Elizabeth, a Fitz-Caldwell, was one of the daughters of the tenth Earl of Broughton, whose family went back to the Conqueror. Lady Elizabeth was *une grande dame* par excellence, but Madame de Saint-Aignan, the mother-in-law of Claire, came a very close second. The Comtes de Saint-Aignan had been present at the meeting at the Cloth of Gold; and the in-laws of Belle, the von Burg-Farnbachs, traced their ancestry back to Charlemagne and the Holy Roman Empire. In the nineteenth century new Desmond money had chased old nobility when Jean-Timothée Desmond, Georges' grandfather, married Laeticia de Montecerboli, whose father, the Conte di Montecerboli, was a Chamberlain to the Royal House of Piedmont.

Then the old nobility began chasing Desmond money to prop up its crumbling baronial castles and restore the ruined splendors of ancient châteaux and domains. Zac's brother-in-law was the Marchese Falconetti, of a Florentine family which claimed not only a close relationship with the Medici but also with two sixteenth-century popes.

Georges had encouraged his children to acquire titles with which to adorn their vast fortunes, to lend a kind of spurious illustriousness to the Desmond name. When they failed to do this they were punished, which explained why Claire de Saint-Aignan had the dispirited look of permanent melancholia induced by once being forcibly deprived of her Italian lover because his origins had been in the gutters of Naples.

But by the middle years of the twentieth century the Desmonds, far from being bourgeois, had acquired the style and manner of the old aristocracy. The Château de Tourville was one of the great houses of France; there was a villa in Cap d'Antibes, a *hôtel particulier* in Paris, a yacht moored off Cannes, a chalet in Saint Moritz and a large estate in Tuscany which Georges had been visiting on the day of his fatal air crash. There was a private jet, two helicopters, a fleet of cars and more servants than were employed by the President of France.

Why then did Georges Desmond with his love, almost his passion, for old money and good breeding leave most of his wealth to a young American with no connections at all, whose origins were obscure and whose fortune was nil? Maybe he would now have enjoyed the spectacle of his family with all its illustrious names—de Saint-Aignan, von Burg-Farnbach, Falconetti, Fitz-Caldwell—dining with a woman who was plain Sandra O'Neill and who had claimed their inheritance. But why had he done it?

Why, indeed? thought Henri Piper as he gazed at the muted assembly sitting amid all the trappings of splendor they had grown up in. The evening meal was held in the family dining room known as the Italian room, because its walls were hung with red silk, and the dining table was the work of the leading cabinet maker for the House of Savoy, Carlo Piffetti. It had been brought from the Palazzo Reale in Turin by the then Marchese Falconetti and, subsequently, as a dowry by his great-great-great granddaughter Tara when she married Zachariah Desmond. Some other Italian pieces were attributed to Giuseppe Maria Bonzanigo, who had also worked for the House of Savoy; the Florentine Giovanni Battista Foggini, and the celebrated Venetian craftsman and sculptor Andrea Brostolon, who had produced a *credenza,* or side table, exquisitely carved which had come from the Palazzo Venier in Venice. Because of the inlaid marquetry of the exquisitely detailed slats which formed the backs, the severely rectangular set of dining-room chairs were thought to be the work of the Milanese classical designer Giuseppe Maggiolini.

The highly polished parquet floor was surrounded by black and white Venetian tiles and the silver candelabra and sconces on the glossy table had the ornate intricate workmanship of acanthus leaves, scrolls and mythological animals of the late classical Baroque.

At one end of the oval table sat Lady Elizabeth and Zac presided at the other, though he did not have Sandra on his right or left. Those places of honor were reserved for his aunt Sophie Piper and another aunt, Lady Broughton, his mother's sister-in-law who had remained after the rest of the family had returned to England following Georges' funeral.

Sandra sat opposite Henri Piper and next to her was Tim, a young man who, she decided, was the most pleasant member of the family, possibly with the exception of Claire who, however, gave few outward signs of friendliness besides a few shy glances. Claire's husband had returned to the family home in Berry shortly after meeting Sandra; but Carl von Burg-Farnbach had remained behind with his wife Belle and it was he who sat on the other side of Sandra, maybe because his French was poor and they could speak English.

The formality of the dinner, the ritual drinking of champagne beforehand in the Louis XVI salon had, naturally, impressed Sandra. It was similar to the kind of life that many wealthy Californians enjoyed; but, maybe, in not such style as the Desmonds to whom it was a daily occurrence whether there were guests present or not.

In their way, however, they were impressed by Sandra, and had been loath to admit it even to each other when she went up to change before dinner and take a brief rest in her room. Her height was impressive even to people who did not consider themselves diminutive. They agreed that her personality was natural, attractive and, despite the simplicity of the dress she had worn, there was an indefinable air of "chic." She could certainly not be called naïve. Now in her long white evening dress with a low, but not improper neckline and with a silver cord around the waist, that impression was carried still further. For the daughter of Hélène O'Neill she was uncannily beautiful; something they had not expected.

It was not just her California good looks of health and vitality; there was a quality, an aura that came from an almost perfect harmony of features allied to exceptionally good bone structure. The color of her eyes—aquamarine—was almost unique and seemed to illumine her entire face. She wore scarcely any make-up and a stylish and expensive diamond and emerald brooch drew covert glances of admiration.

She conversed well but not too much; she listened, appearing interested in everything they had to say. She had considerable presence and, in a curious way, she made them relax; though they knew that they would never be able, under any circumstances, to consider her part of the family.

As for Sandra, she was quite well aware she was under inspection, the family united against her, inevitably, despite their smiles and their charm; constantly on the lookout for faults, for lapses in taste, social gaffes of any kind. But these, she knew, would not occur. The only weapon against them was to be herself and as she knew she was fully in control this policy, as it happened, turned out to be the best one.

Ostensibly the family had set out to convey an impression, if not exactly of friendship, then at least of politeness. A smile was constantly on Zac's lips as he addressed her, which he frequently did—the master of the house at home as it were—but his eyes were wary. More unnerving, however, and undoubtedly intentionally so, was the expression on the face of the Princess von Burg-Farnbach, who was a tall slender woman of consummate elegance. Her chestnut hair, streaked with blonde, was swept up at the back and coiffeured into a clutch of curls just below the crown. She wore a halter-neck black dress with a very low neckline and the jewels at her throat, on her wrists and fingers, were probably from some of the most expensive houses in the world, collected over a number of years not only from her husband, her father but, maybe, a wealthy lover or two as a present for favors received.

Belle's impression was, and remained, one of studied charm. She had high cheekbones, carmine lips which smiled a lot and very deep brown eyes which did not. She had something of the looks, the hauteur, of a prima donna; an air about her that made those around her, even her family, tread warily.

By contrast her husband Carl von Burg-Farnbach was a genial, rather handsome man with a lean face and straight fair hair of about the same age as Zac. He spoke English well, having been educated at Gordonstoun in Scotland. He seemed to be doing his best to make Sandra feel at ease and asked about her life in the States, her hobbies and the way she spent her spare time.

"What I have of it," she said with her attractive low laugh. "I have been working very hard you know. An investment analyst is kept well occupied in the country that worships the dollar."

Carl seemed impressed.

"You are obviously no stranger to business."

"Not at all."

"It still must be very odd for you, this . . . inheritance." Carl glanced nervously at his wife.

"Extremely odd," Sandra said, following his gaze. "For all of you as well as for me."

She was suddenly aware that other talk had ceased and she was the center of attention. Dinner was almost over and the conversation suddenly came to a stop.

Sandra put down her spoon on her dessert plate, indicating that she had finished. The dining room was flanked by servants, one of whom immediately moved forward to offer her more, but she waved him aside with her hand and a polite shake of her head.

"I think we can all be frank with one another and say, at last, that this is a very difficult situation for us all," she said, looking at no one in particular, her eyes on the great silver centerpiece modeled by a pupil of Cellini.

"You have been very courteous in welcoming me among you and I can only say I am grateful. I realize the intolerable position that you have all been placed in, and I must say that I have no idea why the late Georges Desmond did what he did. . . ."

"I find that very difficult to believe," Zac said, making a signal to Pierre and looking at his mother. "Maybe we should continue this conversation in the drawing room?"

"And I don't think I should be part of it," Lady Broughton said, smiling awkwardly as she too rose. "This is obviously a family affair. . . ."

"And I . . ." Henri began but Lady Elizabeth said firmly:

"You *are* part of the family Henri. You can perhaps shed more light on this curious bequest than anyone else." She moved over to kiss her sister-in-law. "I know how tired you are, dear. I'll slip in and say good night before I go to bed."

Tim stood up and gallantly held back Sandra's chair, smiling at her:

"After you," he said. "Or perhaps I should show you the way? After all you must get to know your inheritance."

Sandra smiled her thanks just as Belle swept up to Tim and whispered to him, loudly enough so that Sandra could hear:

"What a stupid thing to say!"

"Yet it's true," he whispered back, also loudly.

"Not for long. Not if we have anything to do with it." Belle seized her brother firmly by the arm and drew him through the door ahead of Sandra, who found herself beside Uncle Henri.

"I told you it wouldn't be easy," he said comfortingly. "But you did well." He put his lips close to her ear. "Now comes the crunch."

"How do you mean?"

"You'll see, but continue as you have been doing at dinner . . . polite, charming, noncommittal. You were superb."

When they reached the salon Pierre was directing the uniformed maids who were serving coffee. A footman was offering liqueurs from a silver tray and another was dispensing cigars and cigarettes. Sandra had never expected to see so many servants in a private European home in the 1980s. In America such a phenomenon was rare. Lady Elizabeth had told her the staff had been much reduced and she wondered how many there had been before: now there was a butler, footman, maids, chambermaids and, assuredly, a vast kitchen staff she had not yet met, to say nothing of gardeners, chauffeurs, grooms, nannies for the small Desmond and von Burg-Farnbach children, and other personnel.

She took the coffee held out to her and the chair indicated by Henri who remained by her side like a faithful bodyguard. Lady Elizabeth and Sophie Piper sat together on the gilt wood Louis XV sofa whose tapestry seat and back, after the style of Boucher, had been designed at the Gobelin factory.

Next to them his beautifully gowned wife, Tara, was selecting a chocolate from a box on an ebony table before languidly draping herself over one of the upright Louis XV chairs. Everyone's attention was on Sandra.

"You were saying," Zac said, "that you had no idea why my father disinherited us. . . ."

"No idea." Sandra shook her head. "And I realize what a very difficult situation it is for us all. . . ."

"For *us,*" Belle said evenly, "for *us,* not *you.* For *you* it is a very *fortunate* situation." She emphasized almost every word with the greatest care.

"I don't think it is a 'fortunate situation' for me at all," Sandra protested. "Like you I am bewildered but also, like you, I am prepared to abide by the decision of Georges Desmond. . . ."

"That's quite understandable," Belle said with a malicious laugh.

"Am I to believe then that you are not? That you will fight the will?"

Sandra gazed questioningly at Henri Piper who shook his head.

"On the contrary." Zac caught the glance between Henri and Sandra. "We have no intention of seeking the unwelcome publicity that such a gesture would give our family. Besides which it could last for years and result in the destruction of the Desmond empire. No, Miss O'Neill, it is not our intention to fight our father's will. It is our hope that we shall dissuade you from accepting. . . ."

"Oh." Sandra felt the pulse in her throat beat faster. "And how do you propose to do that?"

"By inviting you to go home," Belle said as if brother and sister had carefully rehearsed the conversation. "By inviting you to take the share of his fortune that you are entitled to as my father's adopted daughter; by accepting the very generous settlement *we* are prepared to make, in addition, and by asking you to sign a declaration that you will never show any interest in the Desmond family or its business again."

"And if I don't . . . ?" The pulse now had taken up a steady rate, real fear threatening her at last, as she gazed at the faces that seemed suddenly to have become so hostile, even Uncle Henri's—or was she imagining that? But she realized, at last, that among the people here she did not have a real friend: not kind Uncle Henri and not dear Aunt Sophie, who had entertained her so often at their California home; not charming Prince Carl who had made her laugh with stories about the hunt, or handsome Tim Desmond who had taken her breath away with an account of his latest expedition to the Himalayas; not shy Claire with her gentle smile, and certainly not Lady Elizabeth, that polite and austere matriarch whose mouth had, even through dinner, remained set in a cold, forbidding line.

Implacably, inevitably, all the Desmond family were ranged against her, bound together by blood, bonded by hostility and desire for revenge.

"My father made a stipulation," Zac continued in a pleasantly different, almost conciliatory tone of voice, "that if you should prove yourself intellectually and socially unworthy of the confidence he has shown in you, his will becomes null and void." Zac paused, glancing around at his family who all, silently and with various small gestures, seemed to give their approval to what he was saying. Then he raised a finger and pointed it straight at her as though it were a gun taking aim, a deadly weapon from which there was no escape. "Do not be deceived by our apparent geniality because I can assure you, Miss O'Neill, that if you do accept my father's bequest your head will never for a moment rest easy on your pillow; there will never be a day when you will feel free from one of us watching you, waiting for you to make a false move, take a wrong step here, a wrong direction there, to prove that intellectually, socially and from every point of view you are utterly and completely unworthy of the trust that Georges Desmond was mistaken enough to place in you.

"From this moment on, until you decide voluntarily to return to the place from whence you came, you are a marked woman and we, the Desmond family, are pledged never to leave you in peace."

There was a moment of utter silence, then Sandra slowly rose, aware of every eye in that room on her.

"Thank you for being so frank, Monsieur Desmond," she said in an icy tone, "I appreciate your candor and your honesty. At least we know where we are. If I may, I shall go to my room now as I've had a tiring day. You can do me one favor—if you're capable of that. I should like a car to take me back to Paris, first thing in the morning."

Henri Piper waited until Sandra could decently have had time to reach her room and then he jumped from his chair and, striding over to Zac, pointed a finger at him.

"*You* have killed that girl!" he said. "What an intolerable, monstrous way to behave after appearing so friendly."

"I just wanted her to know," Zac said with a pleased smile, clipping the end of one of his rare Havanas which he would probably toy with rather than smoke. "I think another glass of champagne is called for?"

As if with evident satisfaction he smiled at his family. The mask of Belle's face also relaxed in a pleasant smile and she gave a polite handclap.

"Why not? Well done. If you ask me she will be on the plane back to Los Angeles tomorrow night." Then she turned to Henri and her brittle smile was replaced by that familiar look of hauteur.

"You say *we* have killed her, Henri; that is what we meant to do. It is not the Desmond way, as you know, to take an enemy other than by surprise. Mother would never have permitted us to greet her with outward hostility and nor did we wish to. By lulling Mademoiselle O'Neill into a false sense of security we have enabled Zac to get his shaft home. She can be in no doubt now as to how we really feel and what our intentions are."

"It's a pity," Claire said from the depths of her chair. "I rather like her."

"You *what?*" Belle rounded on her younger sister, who was her antithesis both in nature and looks. "*Liked* did you say?"

"Another time, another place . . . maybe. I think I'm going to bed too."

Claire rose and went over to kiss her mother who, clasping her arm, looked rather anxiously up at her.

"I think you should have gone home with Armand darling. All this business is very unpleasant."

"But Sandra is going tomorrow, Mother. Maybe she *will* go back to America. I prefer to be with you until you feel the shock of Father's death a little less severely."

"Sweet child," Lady Elizabeth murmured, kissing her brow and wiping a tear from the corner of her own eye. "It is really all too much, coming at this time. Sometimes I think your father must have hated us all to behave as he has. Inflicting a *stranger,* someone who is not even French, upon us to share our house. . . ."

"To run the business. . . ." Zac said angrily. "*That* is far more to the point. As for you, Henri," he paused and stared at Henri Piper who had gone to the window as if gazing sightlessly into the dark. "Just whose side are you on?"

Henri slowly turned. He was a handsome man, tall, thin and with the face of an aesthete. Despite his years, his graying hair, he had an air of vigor, youth and urbanity. He could easily have passed for forty or forty-five. By nature he was a gentle person yet his family, or rather his wife's family, had never daunted him. He had the full measure of Zac, or any of them if it came to that.

Hands in the pockets of his well-cut dinner jacket, he gazed nonchalantly at his nephew by marriage.

"I am on the side of the law, Zac. Your father has willed the Desmond Empire to someone else, whether you like it or not. Why he did not leave it to you is something you should be asking yourself. Instead of fighting Miss O'Neill you could try cooperating with her. She has a lot to learn, but maybe she can teach you a few things too.

"In Los Angeles she is considered brilliant. She has a first-class mathematical brain; she is an acknowledged wizard with figures. She has gifts lacking in capable people twice her age.

Doug Hammerson was desperate at the thought of losing her. He respected your father's judgment, and so do I."

"I can't believe you're talking like this, Henri!" Sophie, who had been sitting quietly at the side of the room since dinner, heatedly intervened. "Zac is your nephew. Sandra, I must say I have always been fond of, but she is *not* a Desmond. I can't understand why my brother did what he did and I'm surprised you can. Your admiration for Sandra seems to me to border, if I may say so, on the ridiculous."

"Aunt Sophie is quite right." Belle glanced approvingly at her aunt. "Sandra has turned your head. If we are not careful she will turn Tim's too. I saw the besotted way you were looking at her, Tim Desmond. Please remember who she is and who *you* are."

Tim's handsome face went scarlet. He was a man of thirty but had retained much of his boyish charm and youthful good looks. Tim had never aspired to running the business, having neither the interest nor the need since he always had all the money he wanted. His weakness was to be overfond of women who found him extremely attractive. His sun-bleached brown hair and tanned skin combined with the deep blue eyes he'd inherited from his once-beautiful mother, gave him the air of a film star. He had excellent teeth and a wide generous mouth, which was usually smiling. He looked like the kind of man one could trust, who would be useful in a difficult situation, say in some tricky moment in a climb; some stormy passage at sea. But looks could be deceptive. He was, besides, very much in awe of his elder brother, intimidated by him. He started to mumble but his mother came to his rescue.

"Please don't start on your brother, Zac. Leave Henri alone too. Confine your remarks to Miss O'Neill. Personally I agree with Claire. At another time in another place I too should have liked the girl. She did her very best to make us like her and, in a way, I'm sorry for her. I think Henri is too and that is at the root of his defense of her. But Henri dear"—she looked up at him with a smile that still had the power to charm—"*Please* consider if it is not in her own interests that Miss O'Neill returns home. For her sake as well as ours. No one in Champagne will *ever* accept her. I find it hard to believe that, however gifted she may be, she can manage to run the Desmond Group. For her own sake try and persuade her to return home. There's a dear. Tell her we wish her no harm. It is for her own sake. You can do it, I know. You can do it and—"a note of determination entered the voice of his formidable sister-in-law—"and you *must.*"

The head office of the Desmond Group was in the place de L'Étoile overlooking the Arc de Triomphe. It was once the home of a French nobleman who had built it for his family when Haussmann began to redesign the square in 1854.

Jean-Timothée Desmond, the one who loved trees, had first bought it as the Paris home of the family; but after the First World War his son Charles-Louis, father of Georges Desmond, began to have thoughts of expansion outside Reims and the champagne business. He developed an interest in the fast-growing automobile industry, in medical research and in numerous other activities most of which, fortunately, proved profitable. He shrewdly avoided the effects of the Depression caused by the Wall Street crash a few years before his own unfortunate death in a road accident, and thus left his son a very wealthy young man indeed, heir to a potentially vast empire. Georges Desmond energetically lost no time in supplementing his fortune after the interregnum, during which his capable mother, Camille d'Argentan, controlled the fortunes of the firm on his behalf.

It was Camille who fancied a *hôtel particulier* in the rue de Varenne because of her friendship with the noble de Comblis family, and other well-off members of the nobility or *haute bourgeoisie,* who had their town houses there, drawn perhaps by the fame of a previous inhabitant, the sculptor Rodin.

The Desmond family moved to this elegant address in the thirties and it remained the family home until Georges Desmond decided to give it over entirely to Zac, at that time the presumptive heir to his empire, as a wedding gift. Georges had already formed his liaison with Hélène O'Neill, for whom he had bought a large apartment in the rue de Seine, and his wife had always preferred the comfort of Tourville where she had raised her children, and where she had her hobbies and the garden which she loved.

Georges had never flaunted his mistress—he had had affairs before, but it was not difficult to realize that his relationship with his secretary was one of intimacy. He spent little time at home, appearing with his wife only on formal family occasions.

The *hôtel particulier* in the rue de Varenne could be used by any member of the family as he or she wished, but Tara, who soon established herself as a personality of some strength and determination, tended to discourage this.

Few modern-day families could afford the upkeep of such a large town house. But Zac Desmond could, and did. He felt that his position as his father's heir demanded it and his wife, of noble Italian birth, was quickly spoiled by a style of living to which she had not been accustomed before her marriage.

She and Zac had the *hôtel* lavishly restored in keeping with their station as near neighbors of the Prime Minister of France at number 57, farther down the street. On his father's death, Zac, an acquisitive man, had quickly removed some of the best pieces from the offices in the Étoile and from Tourville for his exclusive use.

From her office window Sandra overlooked the huge Arc, surrounded by cobblestones and trees now in their full summer foliage, as was the rest of the Champs Élysées up which she now drove every morning from her suite at the Ritz.

These had been hectic, unsettling days. In the office there was an air of unreality as Sandra struggled to familiarize herself with everything that was going on and to decide in her own mind, once and for all, whether she was capable of it, or whether, as everyone assumed, she had taken on too much.

People were helpful but distant. Paul Vincent came in every day and gave the impression that he was trying to be useful, though Sandra thought that, in reality, he was keeping an eye on her.

Her secretary, Edith Huelin, had worked for Georges and, to her surprise, was the first to offer congratulations and support. Maybe Edith, shrewd woman that she was, and not so young, realized who would be signing her paycheck from now on. Sandra also suspected it was because Edith was no lover of Zac, though she was careful not to inquire. She had to be very careful, very discreet, in those early days at the office.

Henri Piper had told her of the talk at Tourville after she had gone to bed. The family would oppose her, he said. They were determined to squeeze her out. As for himself . . . (there had been a pause over the phone) things were very difficult. Sophie was on the side of the family. He mustn't too openly ally himself with Sandra . . . it was not in her best interests.

Sandra felt very lonely. Lonely, insecure and a little frightened. Was it worth it?

There were times when head said "yes" and heart said "no"; and times when one overruled the other. There were lonely evenings by herself in the Ritz, with her dinner sent up to her room while she tackled the volumes of reports and accounts that she brought home for closer inspection.

Very badly she wanted an ally, a friend; but where was one to be found? How she missed Bob, whom she telephoned frequently, and the moral and physical support of motherly Maria. Gradually she had the feeling that she was being isolated, edged out . . . made to feel that there was no place to go but home.

The phone connecting her to her secretary rang and she answered it:

"Yes, what is it, Edith?"

"Monsieur de Lassale wondered if he could have an appointment to see you this afternoon, Mademoiselle. He said it is urgent."

"Who is Monsieur de Lassale?"

"He is the head of the Banque Franco-Belges, Mademoiselle. That is part of the big Heurtey Corporation of America. They also own Tellier Champagne."

"Have you any idea what he wants?"

"I think it is not merely a *social* call, Mademoiselle," Edith said tactfully.

Sandra consulted her diary, bare of any engagements other than to do with meeting staff connected with her business. She was still groping in the dark.

"Could he come at three?"

"One moment Mademoiselle . . ." A pause and then Edith's voice came back. "Monsieur de Lassale will look forward to meeting you at that time, Mademoiselle."

Sandra sat back, hands in the pockets of her white linen suit. She then went over to a cabinet containing private files which she was slowly putting together, but could find nothing about the Banque Franco-Belges. Nor could she find anything about the Desmond bank, a fact that disturbed her. It was as though all references to it in the files at Head Office had been removed. Even Edith had been puzzled. She was just about to ask Edith to look again in central records when there was a tap at her door and Paul Vincent put his head around, the usual smile on his face.

But it was not a friendly smile. It was a Desmond smile—on the mouth but not in the eyes. Paul Vincent liked her no more than any member of the family and she felt that, in a way, he was doing his best to do their will; to edge her out, slowly, so that she appeared to be going of her own accord.

Vincent had enjoyed his brief moment of power as spokesman for the Desmond organization, his appearances on TV, his face on the front page of *Figaro.* Perhaps he had hoped that she would make him her, as it were, *chef de cabinet.* But she had no intention of doing that to an old and trusted friend of the Desmond family; someone to whom not even Georges had confided his intentions.

Paul Vincent was somewhere in his sixties; a long, lean man with the look of a clever ferret, someone used to sniffing things out. He had been around for years: a kind of personal assistant to Georges Desmond. Sandra had not particularly taken to him, even though he had tried to assure her that his intention was only to help her.

But when she asked for actual help it was not forthcoming. If anything he was obstructive. Everything was so hard, so difficult; how could he explain, where could he begin . . . ? Many a sigh, shake of the head, shrug of the shoulders which Sandra found irritating.

He wasted so much of her time that, little by little, she began to be openly impatient with him. Yet he was an important man; a member of the Council. Why him?

"Monsieur Vincent," she said with a smile as artificial as his. "Do sit down. And what can I do for you today?"

"What can I do for *you,* Mademoiselle?" Vincent said pleasantly enough, taking his usual seat opposite her desk and folding his arms. In his hand he had a packet, but he didn't put it down or tell her what its contents were.

"What do you know of the activities of our bank?" she asked abruptly, watching him closely.

Vincent frowned.

"Our bank, Mademoiselle?"

"The Banque Pons-Desmond."

"But Monsieur Desmond is the head of the bank, Mademoiselle." His voice sounded reproachful.

"I know that." There was a trace of impatience in Sandra's voice. "But I can get no cooperation from him about its affairs."

"That is hardly surprising, Mademoiselle." Vincent pursed his thin lips. "Monsieur Desmond is quite competent to run it himself."

"But it's the only file I can't find!" Sandra threw up her arms in despair. "I can find absolutely nothing about the bank at all. Isn't that odd?"

"But why should you *need* it?" Vincent looked about him with an air of disdain.

"Because I must know everything to do with the Desmond Group, don't you see . . . ? If I am to stay, I must know . . ."

Paul Vincent's eyebrows arched sharply over his eyes.

"*If* you are to stay, Mademoiselle? It is not a certainty then?"

"I am finding my way around, Monsieur Vincent. I am seeing if I can do what Georges Desmond wanted me to do. If I can't . . . It isn't easy. . . ."

She shrugged and angrily tugged the glasses she used for her work off her nose. Badly in need of a friend, she felt suspiciously close to tears.

When she raised her eyes again the packet which Vincent had clasped in his hand lay on her desk before her. On it was her name typed and nothing else: "Mademoiselle Sandra O'Neill."

"This is for me?" she inquired unnecessarily.

"As it says, Mademoiselle."

"But what is it?"

"Look and see," Vincent said encouragingly. "Perhaps it will be of assistance to you. I know, Mademoiselle, how difficult all this has been for you. Believe me, I know this organization like the back of my hand, and it was not made for you. I tell you that, if I may be so bold, as a friend.

"It was created over a century ago by Desmonds *for* Desmonds. The rightful person in your place is the true heir to the Desmonds, Monsieur Zac, and in that envelope you will find a little encouragement to help you make up your mind."

He folded his arms again with a satisfied smile and sat back as Sandra slit open the envelope with a paper knife and slowly drew out a thin piece of paper and an airline ticket.

The paper was a check for five million American dollars. The airline ticket was from Paris to Los Angeles . . . one way.

Philippe de Lassale had the air of an absent-minded professor as he came into Sandra's office, looking around him as though he expected to see someone else.

"How do you do?" Sandra stood up and held out her hand. "I am Sandra O'Neill."

"I'm very pleased to meet you," de Lassale said and, for one of the few times since she had arrived in Paris, Sandra was aware of a warm, sincere handshake.

"May I have coffee sent in?"

"Nothing thank you." The professorial air vanished immediately and de Lassale became businesslike, looking around him for somewhere to sit. "I have just had lunch." Then, taking his seat, he sat back and stared at her.

He was a distinguished-looking man, not tall, but confident and clearly someone at ease in most company. He could have been a diplomat, a member of the legal or medical professions, an academic. His face was relaxed and smiling and, together with his balding head, gave him a friendly, paternalistic look as he studied her. He wore an exceptionally well-cut gray suit, white shirt and a tie with some kind of emblem. As he crossed his legs she saw highly polished black shoes, possibly handmade.

Sandra felt that she liked Monsieur de Lassale immediately

and that he liked her. She was a woman who always felt at a disadvantage with her looks. They tended to make people think she was something she was not and maybe the frequent use of glasses was to make her image more grave, more studious, more like the person she was inside.

"So *you* are Sandra O'Neill," Philippe de Lassale said after his inspection. "Well, well."

"I suppose it surprises you to see me here, Monsieur de Lassale?" Sandra said, boldly resuming her glasses and gazing at him.

"It does indeed," de Lassale said. "I thought it was something that Desmond would never do . . . but I'm glad he did."

"You're *glad?"* Sandra leaned forward as if unable to believe her ears.

"Definitely I'm glad. Of course I am sorry Georges is dead—he was a most gifted man—but I am glad there is someone else here other than Zac Desmond."

"You astonish me."

"Do I?"

De Lassale got up and moved his chair closer to her, his eyes glancing surreptitiously over his shoulder toward the door. "I sense you are having a bad time."

"Very. Some things I can't even get files on."

"It was inevitable." De Lassale shrugged nonchalantly. "The Desmonds were shocked, shocked . . . we all were. But I, for one, was extremely pleased when I knew the contents of his will. Of course I knew nothing about you personally; but I have friends in New York, Los Angeles." De Lassale looked at her shrewdly. "Douglas Hammerson is *also* a very good friend and business acquaintance of mine. You may not know it and I didn't until recently—I spoke to him only last week—but a warning from you some months ago prevented us from providing a collateral for a very unfavorable loan. . . ."

"Indeed?" Sandra's eyes lit up.

"Nantucket Securities. You may recall it. They were trying to raise a billion pounds sterling. Even Hammerson thought they were blue chip . . ."

"Oh yes." Sandra dropped her eyes. "Nantucket appeared very persuasive, a fine record, undervalued, some people said. But when I looked into it closely I found they were grossly *overvalued,* and they were heavily committed to other creditors. They had not been honest. Clever, but not honest. I was lucky to find out what I did in time."

"Exactly." De Lassale nodded. "Imagine my joy when I heard you were to be in charge here."

"Joy? I can hardly believe it." Sandra looked around. "If I had some champagne here I would open it. You are my first real friend."

"I can believe that, Mademoiselle." De Lassale rose and, going over to her desk, leaned across it. "They are suspicious of you, the Desmonds. You are not wanted . . . with good reason. Zac Desmond knows quite well that if you find out what he has been up to, what his father only began to suspect . . . he would be out on his ear. That is why you are finding it so difficult to get files, cooperation."

De Lassale drew himself up and joined his hands neatly in front of him.

"At this moment in time the Banque Pons-Desmond owes *my* bank alone more money than it has assets. In effect it is bankrupt and should not be trading. Now Mademoiselle, what do you think of that?"

At midnight that day, or some time after, Zac Desmond drove through the doorway of his home in the rue de Varenne, greeting the concierge who had opened the outer door to let him in.

He parked in the courtyard of his house, which was flanked by tall poplar trees swaying in the night breeze, and he shivered as his butler opened the front door with a bow. The rest of the house was in darkness except for a light on the mahogany staircase which rose nobly up from the central hall.

"Is Madame at home, Gaston?" Zac said to the butler who maintained his usual air of lofty impassivity.

"Madame retired to her room an hour ago, Monsieur Desmond. There is a letter for you."

It was Gaston's practice never to do anything in a hurry and Zac impatiently tapped his foot as he walked slowly over to a silver tray on the hall table and, taking from it a long envelope, presented it to his master. "It came by hand just after nine o'clock, Monsieur. Will that be all?"

"You may go to bed, Gaston," Zac said, noting the Desmond name on the left-hand corner of the envelope as he went into the salon on the ground floor in search of a paper knife.

He put on a lamp and, finding what he wanted, sank into one of the exquisite bergère chairs he had recently had sent from Tourville and slit open the envelope.

Inside was a check for five million American dollars, a single ticket to Los Angeles and a note from Paul Vincent.

Dear Monsieur Desmond,

I am officially informed by Mademoiselle O'Neill that, as from this evening, she considers herself the de facto *President of the Desmond Group according to the will of your late father.*

She asked me to tell you that during the past week or so she many times had doubts as to the wisdom of accepting her inheritance; but now she has no doubt whatsoever. Something has happened to make Mademoiselle change her mind, but I can only guess what it is.

I am sorry to bring you news which, I know, will distress you. Believe me, I did everything in my power to dissuade her. Maybe in time we shall get what we all earnestly wish and actively seek: her resignation and departure for America.

But I must tell you, however, that now that Mademoiselle O'Neill has made up her mind I shall feel bound by my duty, not only to you but your late father, to do what I can to assist Mademoiselle in the affairs of the organization, as your father was good enough to trust me as a member of his Council.

Mademoiselle has made known her formal acceptance of the will to your father's notary, Maître Laban, and has applied, also according to your father's wishes, to have her name changed to Desmond.

With every good wish,

Paul Vincent

It was almost dawn before Zac Desmond rose from the chair in which he had remained slumped for several hours, and slowly dragged himself up the stairs to bed. For one of the first times in his life, Zac had an overwhelming, shattering sense of defeat.

4

Below the ground it was bitterly cold and Sandra hugged her tweed coat tightly around her. There were twenty-five kilometers of caves which they had reached by climbing down 170 steep stairs. These had probably been hewn into the rock many hundreds of years before, when the Romans excavated a network of cellars for storage—a kind of ancient form of refrigeration.

"You aren't too cold, I hope?" Étienne Legrand bent toward her solicitously. Yet, she noticed, he was wearing only a suit. Maybe his hardiness was due to the long apprenticeship he had served, first in the caves as a worker, then as a member of management, and finally as Director General of the Établissement de Champagne Desmond.

"I'm cold, but it doesn't matter," Sandra said briskly. "Obviously you are used to it."

He tugged at his lapels and merely smiled.

"Half my life has been spent underground. It is true that one does, in time, become acclimatized. May I compliment you on your excellent French, Mademoiselle O'Neill?"

"Thank you." Sandra smiled briefly. She supposed it was common knowledge that the mistress of the late Georges Desmond was her mother. Yet since she had been in France she had never once heard her name mentioned. Momentarily Sandra experienced a brief spasm of pity for the woman who had lived for so long in the shadow of a great man and now appeared to have been forgotten by everyone. But not by her daughter. She, Sandra, would never forget and it would be very difficult to forgive.

But she was sure that Monsieur Legrand was being polite rather than inquisitive, and they continued their walk through the long cold corridors which seemed to wend their way endlessly beneath the chalky subsoil that had proved so beneficial to the cultivation of the grapes from which, in the course of many hundreds of years, the manufacture of this incomparable wine had slowly, patiently, painstakingly been evolved.

The long galleries were lined with thousands and thousands of dusty unlabeled bottles arranged in an assortment of positions, each of which was a distinct and important part of the champagne-making process. Those which were undergoing the slow process of second fermentation after bottling lay on their sides *sur lattes,* on the wooden lathes separating the rows. Those in a slanting position, necks down, were resting in *pupitres,* large slanted boards with holes in them, a bottle to each one, so that it could be vigorously riddled, or shaken, each day and turned to allow the sediment to gather at the base around the cork. A splash of white paint at the bottom of each bottle enabled the riddler, or *rémueur,* to know at what angle he had left the bottle the day before. Finally at the end of the riddling *rémuage* (a process taking from three weeks to six months) the bottles would be resting upside-down, with all the sediment collected around the cork. In this position the bottles were then stacked again, *sur pointes,* that is with each resting on its cork in the punt of the one underneath. There they remained gathering dust until they were needed for consumption and a process known as *dégorgement,* or the expulsion of the sediment, took place and the bottles were recorked, "dressed" and ready to be drunk.

In time Sandra would get to know all these complex, delicate processes even if she would never be as familiar with them as the man beside her, who had worked in the caves all his life, a loyal servant to the Desmonds. Would he be to her? However, she had one attribute that probably he did not: a remarkable facility for learning new facts quickly and retaining them, a talent which had undoubtedly drawn her to the attention of Georges Desmond in the first place.

"Much of the *rémuage* is now done by mechanization," Monsieur Legrand said, stopping and pointing to *pupitres* which were slightly different from the ones where the bottles were riddled by hand, and which revolved slowly at an angle governed by a computer.

"It was a process first invented by the grandmother of Monsieur Georges and he added many refinements to it when he transferred most of our day-to-day functions to the computer, one of the first champagne manufacturers to do so." Monsieur Legrand gave a smile as he gently took her by the elbow and drew her in a new direction. "It caused many an eyebrow to be lifted in Reims I can tell you."

"Not quite the thing." Sandra nodded. "I can well understand how people resist change. Even here," she stopped and looked around in the gloomy corridors which stretched for as far as the eye could see on every side, "I am sure there are ways you could improve methods of storage and retrieval. It must be backbreaking work laying down all these bottles and removing them by hand."

"There is *some* mechanization here," Monsieur Legrand said cautiously. "But we have to be careful. We are not making Coca-Cola."

"Of course not." Sandra sensed a reprimand in his words. "I wouldn't dream of interfering before I knew the facts."

As they continued their tour sometimes she stopped to make notes; but mostly she listened attentively to what Monsieur Legrand was saying, storing it all carefully at the back of that computerlike mind of hers at some stage to retrieve it, study it and use it to bring about the changes that she knew were needed, and that Georges Desmond must have known were needed too.

Sometimes they would stop and, gazing upward, were able to see the sky at the end of a long chalky-white tunnel. It was a most curious experience and something that was unique to the cellars below Reims. Many of these tunnels, or *crayères,* which had been constructed by the Romans, were up to ten feet in diameter at the top but grew wider when they reached the gallery at the base so that they seemed to form a kind of anteroom. In some places these "rooms" had been decorated with sculptures in relief and it was almost impossible not to admire the skill of the nineteenth-century artist working not only in cramped conditions but in the freezing cold with only candlelight for illumination.

"They were well fortified with champagne," Legrand said as Sandra paused to admire yet another of the huge sculptures which were mostly carved around some bucolic theme after Bacchus, the god of wine.

"But still they are remarkable." Sandra gazed up to the tiny pinpoint of light protected by a wire mesh hundreds of meters above them. "Tell me why *exactly* did the Romans dig these pits? To cool the wine only? Surely not?"

"You're right, Mademoiselle," Legrand said respectfully. "Appreciating the preservative quality of the cold combined with the chalk, they stored perishables here, maybe oil and wheat too, for they were far from home and not always welcomed by the local population, as occupiers of our country seldom have been. Incidentally, in both the wars of this century, these galleries were used not only by the Resistance but to help Allied escapees on their way to safety out of France. Monsieur Desmond himself, as a young man, became a legend for his work in the Resistance in the last War. The Desmonds have always been great patriots, Mademoiselle."

Yet if so, Legrand seemed to be saying, turning his face from her with a look of bewilderment, why did he give his empire to a stranger? Would she ever be accepted here? Sandra wondered as, falling silent once more, they resumed their walk past the bottles which seemed now like mute witnesses, a silent reproach to the fickleness of a man of the soil, a true *champenois,* who could leave his patrimony to someone not of his family.

As they walked they were saluted politely by dungareed workmen, many of them driving small yellow trucks followed by trolleys on which there were layers of cases or empty bottles. To Sandra, each interconnecting corridor was alike, and it was a marvel to her how anyone ever found their bearings in this maze lit only by dim lights to preserve the character of the wine.

Finally the number of people grew and she found herself in a large room full of modern machines linked by a conveyor belt on which wine bottles rattled along. The scene was one of great activity as workmen bustled about doing everything at great speed.

"You see," Legrand explained, pointing to a long metal trough which ran the length of the room, "the deposit at the top of the bottle is frozen, the cork removed and the bottle recorked. This process is known as *dégorgement.* Some firms occasionally do this by hand, 'a la volée' as we call it, but we freeze it in this machine so that it becomes a pellet of ice." He pointed to a piece of apparatus that looked like the kind of cork extractor that is seen in most bars. Only it was larger and more efficient, being mechanized to receive each bottle as it arrived on the conveyor, remove the cork, and expel the pellet of frozen sediment that had collected beneath it during its long rest in the cellar. Then the bottle was "topped up" before it was recorked.

"This is the *dosage,"* Legrand explained, moving on. "It consists of a little cane sugar dissolved in the wine which is now very dry because the process of fermentation will have consumed all the natural sugar. We have five categories: *Brut,* which is dry or about two percent sweetening; *extra brut* about one point five percent liqueur; *sec,* or *demi-sec,* four to six percent of liqueur; finally *doux,* which is more than six percent or a really sweet wine, such as some ladies prefer."

He saw Sandra's grimace and laughed. "But not *you* I think, Mademoiselle. I can see you are a lady of taste. Our *Centennaire* vintage is perhaps the one for you. That was especially created for our centenary year."

"Now that is delicious." Sandra nodded her head. "We had it for dinner the night I first arrived to meet the family."

She stopped as she saw the look of interest on Legrand's face. Obviously he wanted to know how that had gone and, equally obviously, he knew she wouldn't tell him. Quickly he moved on as the recorked bottles rattled along the line.

"Now what happens, once the deposit is removed and they have been topped up and recorked?"

Legrand took her over to another machine where, yet again by automation, the newly inserted corks were being fitted with a metal disc bearing the name *Desmond* and rewired.

"Now," he explained, "they are given a final shake to ensure that the *dosage* is well mixed and then rested again, but only for a short time, and lastly, dressed, or labeled with gold foil placed over the cork, packed and dispatched. The bottles lie in the cellars until they are needed, always on the first cork, and the second cork is applied just before consumption. We allow our nonvintage bottles at least three years and our vintage five—some firms allow shorter or longer periods—all in all the manufacture of champagne is a very expensive business."

"And something I'm going to look into very carefully," Sandra said, frowning, remembering yet again, always with a fresh shock of surprise, that she was now the head of this extraordinary and important business operation.

"You, Mademoiselle?" Now Legrand seemed surprised.

"Oh yes, me," Sandra said decisively. "I am now the director of the whole group. . . ."

"But Monsieur Zac Desmond . . . ?"

"Is the head of the Bank," Sandra affirmed. "As he always was."

"But he has an excellent palate. And so has the Princess."

"Well, I can assure you that I'm going to be very dependent on their wise counsels when necessary," Sandra said with that sudden, charming smile that could transform her expression. "I do have an excellently qualified staff to advise me here on the premises, I assume?"

"A little lunch now, I think, Mademoiselle? It is ready upstairs in the boardroom." Legrand seemed anxious to avoid answering the question.

Sandra took one look around at the busy scene noting that, although the continuous process went on, the number of workers was fewer—probably as others went to their own lunch. Legrand led her through a room where yet another conveyor belt was taking the "dressed" bottles to be packed into cases, stamped with the letters DESMOND, which then remained in batches on fork-lift lorries to be stored in the vast shed they now entered. This too was packed high to the ceiling with cases, many of them being loaded onto larger fork-lift trucks and trundled to a slow-moving conveyor belt which was taking them out to a waiting lorry.

Sandra walked slowly along with Legrand observing everything, saying little. But she was thinking very deeply about the whole process, time-honored methods that were now, perhaps, a little wasteful, a little old-fashioned. She was thinking as a businesswoman, and as a consumer, for it was the people who drank the champagne who were ultimately behind the Desmond fortune.

The headquarters of the Desmond Champagne business in the center of Reims had been constructed since the War. It was an attractive, low, two-storied modern building, its walls covered by green trellis work which in the summer were covered with vines bearing small, sweet grapes. In front of it was a graveled courtyard and facing it were the assembly of old buildings which had formed the original Desmond firm founded in 1840 by René-Zachariah, who bought a small champagne firm with his wife's dowry and renamed it *Desmond.*

They had come through the original old neo-Classical building which had been built in the middle of the nineteenth century by René's son Jean-Timothée and which now housed the offices. All the champagne firms in Reims were fiercely competitive and tried to outrival each other in the opulence and splendor of their headquarters. These were, naturally, the front for each individual *marque,* vital, particularly in modern competitive times, to impress would-be purchasers. There was a highly polished marble entrance hall with gleaming marble walls which housed an exhibition of memorabilia unique to the Desmonds, including the coach in which René's nephew, Christian Desmond, traveled to Russia in order to sell the family product. There were old wooden casks where champagne used to be stored for the first fermentation before the company adopted the more modern, and easier-to-clean, vats lined with glass. The various bottles containing priceless vintages, particularly the *Centennaire,* stood in alcoves along the walls, tastefully illuminated by concealed lights.

To the left of the main entrance was a lecture theater, again adorned with bottles of champagne, where the many visitors and groups, which were welcomed by each champagne house, were entertained and given a lecture before being driven around the underground caves, in the case of Desmond by small electrical trolleys. Sandra, however, with typical thoroughness, had preferred to walk so as to be sure that nothing escaped her keen eye.

From the main hall a lift led to the first floor on which were the executive offices including that of the late Georges

Desmond, with which Sandra had already spent some time familiarizing herself. There was also the boardroom where the senior staff were now waiting to receive her.

Among them, to her surprise, was Zac, who came over to her with a smile on his face, a glass of champagne already in his hand. It suddenly occurred to Sandra that Zac had taken the initiative to appear to be the titular head of the company by using his superior knowledge.

Zac was an extraordinary man, Sandra thought, as a uniformed maid came forward to take her coat. Since she had returned his insulting bribe and the ticket that went with it, they had not met. Yet she knew from Maître Laban, the Desmond notary, that everything was going smoothly; there was no overt objection from the Desmonds, and Zac had signed all the papers that had been put in front of him, effectively signing away his birthright. Apparently, despite what had been said, they accepted everything.

Yet it was difficult really to know what went on behind that charming exterior, that welcoming smile as she held out her hand and said:

"How nice to see you again, Monsieur Desmond."

Zac shook her hand and then brought it briefly to his lips.

"I hope you will forgive me, Miss O'Neill, but as this is your first full day here I popped in to see if there was anything I could do to help. You have had an extensive tour around the caves I hear."

"Yes, I have." Sandra accepted the flute of champagne offered her by the maid who had returned. "And I saw the *dégorgement,* the rebottling . . ."

"It is a very good time to be here," Zac said. "Because soon we shall have the harvest and then a whole new process begins all over again!"

Zac took her gently by the arm and steered her toward the window as if helping her to see, in her mind's eye, the acres of vine-covered fields which even now were bearing the, as yet, tiny bunches of grapes which would soon grow and finally be turned into wine. "You know the main vines from which we make champagne are the *Pinot* which is black and the *Chardonnay* which is white. There are of course many subvarieties of the Pinot in existence—it makes some of the renowned Burgundies—but here, in Champagne, we grow mainly the Pinot Noir and the Pinot Meunier.

"The black Pinot grapes cluster tightly together on the bunches while the white grapes hang rather more loosely." Carried away by his own enthusiasm, Zac gestured once again in front of him as if toward some imaginary slope on the Montagne de Reims and, in the background, his audience, as experienced as he if not more so, listened as attentively as Sandra. "When the harvest begins you will see how we pick and select the grapes, a process called *épluchage,* and how we press them, which is very important. The first pressings yield the finest quality of juice, two thousand liters known as *vin de cuvée.* This is used only in the production of the best champagne. The later pressings are known as *première taille, deuxième taille* and *troisième taille.* It is all very complex and governed strictly by regulations which control the industry."

"Still, I see you do have a lot of mechanization." Sandra turned to draw Legrand into the conversation together with Raymond Jourdan, the *Chef des Caves,* and René Latour, the head cellarman, who were standing nearby. "The conveyor belt needs only a very few people to man it. Have you had time-and-motion experts to look over the work to see if the labor force can be reduced any further?"

Everyone appeared momentarily shocked by her words.

"But we have to offer work to the people of Reims," Raymond Jourdan said. "Over the years the work has been whittled away enough as it is."

"Yes but this is not a charity," Sandra said. "And the harvest? How many people do you employ for that?"

"Oh, we can do nothing about the harvest," René Latour

protested. "That is one of the events of the wine-making season."

"But I believe that you could mechanize the picking of the grapes," Sandra insisted. "I was talking to a time-and-motion expert in Paris who says that a grape harvester, although expensive, is already available. I believe it is used quite extensively in some vineyards in the south."

"But not in Champagne," Zac said with lofty disdain, leading the way to the table, as if he were the host, and offering Sandra a seat. It was as though a gust of cool air had blown in and settled over the company.

"We do not accept such practices here. It is not permitted. Grapes must be picked by hand and sorted by hand. You will suggest mechanizing *épluchage* next."

Sandra unfurled her crisp white napkin and put it across her lap. She knew how sensitive the French were on the subject of their wine and that she must go carefully. Despite Zac, she wanted these people to be her friends, not her enemies. She needed them.

The French also enjoyed their lunch and this was a good one, beginning with a delicious mousse made of pimentos, accompanied by a glass of vintage champagne. She broke into her crisp, freshly baked roll.

"But why should there *not* be more mechanization?" she asked, looking around. "Who forbids it?"

"The body that controls the making of champagne," Zac replied sharply. "The Comité Interprofessionnel du Vin de Champagne, known as the CIVC. It was established during the First War and my father was a distinguished founding member of it."

"But you can't resist progress forever," Sandra observed, almost to herself. "I believe that you yourselves here in the House of Desmond were the first to automate the process of *rémuage* which many houses still do by hand."

"It was invented by my great-grandmother," Zac said

proudly. "Camille d'Argentan, who married my grandfather, was widowed at the age of twenty-seven and, as the Veuve Desmond, ran the company until my father came of age, my grandfather having been killed in battle in 1917. My grandmother invented the *table de rémuage* which you will have seen today and which saves the endless hours that so many men used to have to work who did it by hand. To say nothing of saving them the tedium of the job. One man could riddle up to forty thousand bottles in a day. Imagine, what a boring routine."

"And a machine could pick up how many bunches? Is it not the same principle?"

"We have the *vendangeurs* to consider," Raymond Jourdan said sternly. "For generations they have come to help in the harvest."

"But have you not to maintain, feed and house them? Does that not all add to the price of the wine?"

"It is traditional . . ."

"It *was* traditional to spin by hand at one time," Sandra reminded them. "Progress has always been resisted. What happened here in the Desmond cellars when the Veuve Desmond introduced her riddling frame? I believe it is now activated by computer. How many cellarmen were thrown out of work, then?"

"It is not the same thing at all," Zac said gravely as he finished his mousse. "People were not as aware of the socio-economic aspect as they are today. I daresay that one day we could make excellent champagne merely by pressing a button, maybe employing half a dozen people from start to finish." He made a sweeping gesture with his hand. "One machine runs along the rows of vines collecting grapes, another presses it instead of the old-fashioned *maie,* or wine press, we use now. The liquid is automatically poured into vats, the *dosage* is automatically added, the wines flow into bottles, stored on moving trolleys and so on. . . . Besides," he added, looking at her intently, "the mechanical harvester might work for vineyards situated in the plain. Here in Champagne most of the vines are on the hillsides which it would be very difficult, and perhaps dangerous, for a harvester to climb."

Zac suddenly stopped as he saw René Latour laughing.

"I assure you, Latour, even you will be out of a job if Mademoiselle O'Neill has her way."

It suddenly occurred to Sandra that Zac's real intention was to alienate her from the senior employees. He was certainly not here to make her feel at home. His masterly exposition of the manufacture of champagne, the vines and the methods used, served merely to emphasize the gap between his knowledge and hers. He was a Desmond, steeped in the tradition of an old, wine-producing family. She was a newcomer, an upstart. Once again his presence was not an encouragement but a warning.

"If Mademoiselle O'Neill has her way . . ." Sandra protested. "Indeed, Monsieur Desmond, you do exaggerate. I was only drawing the lessons learned from history to their logical conclusions. In this case, in theory, I don't see why the wine process cannot be automated. If you say it can't, then we shall see."

"We don't even like plastic corks," Legrand said dismissively. "You can be sure we won't take to automatic grape pickers."

At that point a manservant entered with the second course, tournedos and green salad accompanied by a fine bottle of Bouzy, one of the few, but excellent, red wines of Champagne. Sandra decided that enough had been said about mechanization and the talk turned to generalities, to the weather and the prospects for the harvest.

It was a good meal but, after all that had been said, it was not a jolly one. Sandra felt that here in the heart of the champagne country she was not only a woman but a stranger.

In Champagne women were historically acceptable. There

had been a number of distinguished *veuves* of whom among the most famous were the widow Clicquot whose name still graces a *marque* of champagne, the widows Heidsieck and Pommery. However, Sandra was not a *champenoise* as the others had been; nor had she married a *champenoise.* But her worst fault was not that she was a woman, that was tolerable, but that she was a foreigner, an American. What on earth were the Americans supposed to know about champagne?

She realized from that moment on that her task in Reims, among the *champenois* who had grown up within the sight of the vineyards, would be even more formidable than it had been in Paris. There she had been getting to grips with the other formidable ramifications of the Desmond Empire—the press, the cosmetics, the aircraft industry, the food and, not least of all, the bank—Zac's bank. And, as with champagne, she had found in every sphere a proliferation of outdated methods that cried aloud for cost-cutting economies.

More and more she realized why, from his grave, Georges Desmond had called on her. His empire was slowly disintegrating.

After lunch Sandra asked Zac if he could spare her some time and, thanking those who had attended the lunch, especially Étienne Legrand who had shown her around the caves, and promising to call on their expertise often, she drew him into the office that had once been his father's.

Zac stood momentarily on the threshold of the room and then, taking a deep breath, preceded Sandra into it as though he were claiming his own territory, oblivious of her presence. Although he was a hard man and she was a strong woman, Sandra felt a spasm of pity for him as he stopped in front of his father's huge desk and ran his fingers along it, saying, as if to himself:

"This desk was made especially for my great-grandfather René-Zachariah, after whom I'm named, by an *ébeniste* in the rue Vivienne in Paris. You see it has knee holes on both sides?" Zac turned for a moment with almost childlike pleasure, to smile at Sandra who remained in the doorway gazing at him. "The story is that it was a present from my great-grandmother, Agathe Perthois, who was extremely jealous of the handsome René who had something of a reputation as a flirt. So, while he did his business she sat opposite him embroidering, keeping a watchful eye on him!"

"What a charming story." Sandra came quietly into the room, sensing an opportunity for *rapprochement* with Zac. "But what a trial for poor René."

"Oh, he didn't mind. He was very much in love with her too and, doubtless, there were occasions when"—Zac paused and smiled thoughtfully to himself—"he could slip off quietly if he so wished, although they were reportedly a very devoted couple. Eventually after her children were born she became preoccupied with them and allowed him to work by himself. But I hear he missed her and would invite her back to the office just for company. My father was extremely fond of this desk. He . . ."

"Then you must have it," Sandra said impulsively. "I would not dream of taking it from you. I shall have it moved to your own office in Paris. . . ."

Immediately the expression of nostalgia vanished from Zac's face and he straightened up, shaking his head. "Oh, no; no, thank you, Mademoiselle O'Neill. This desk was made for this room and it belongs here. Besides . . ."

He looked at her as she motioned for him to sit down on the long leather couch that faced the desk while, purposefully, she took her place behind it. There is something, perhaps intentionally, rather intimidating about a person behind a desk and Sandra O'Neill knew this. Had she wanted to indicate to Zac that they were friends she would have sat alongside him on the couch, or next to him in one of the easy chairs. But, sensing that they were involved in a game of domination, she sat at his father's desk in his father's chair and folded her hands in front of her.

"Besides you intend to come back here. Is that what you wished to say?"

"Something like that." Zac looked at her without smiling. "I only regard your occupancy as a very temporary one, I can assure you."

As if sensing his disadvantage, Zac immediately got up and began to pace the floor in front of her.

"You can see, quite clearly, that it is a ridiculous situation my father has placed us all in, Miss O'Neill, including yourself. For instance I have grown up in the champagne business. To me it was, literally, like mother's milk. I know almost everything there is to know about the manufacture of champagne; a lifetime's art, I can assure you. Whereas you, it is quite obvious, are completely ignorant. You are not even very subtle. You came storming in here talking about mechanization. The harvest is sacrosanct to those who take part. I can almost imagine riots if we discontinued it. I could tell from your remarks over luncheon that you intend to regard this business as though we were manufacturing"—he looked around as if searching for the right word—"ball bearings, say. No we are not." He went up to her and thumped the scarred leather-topped desk. "You can no more mechanize champagne than you can the creation of a painting or a piece of music. . . ."

"But you can, and you have," Sandra said gently. Rising, she joined him, leaning against the side of the desk, her arms akimbo. "Not so very long ago you had glasses with long hollow stems so that the deposit from the champagne went to the bottom while the person was drinking it. Now, in the process of *dégorgement,* the deposit is frozen and expelled by an automatic process. I believe that there are very few of the original *dégorgeurs* about who can unclip the *agrafe* and ease the cork out by hand, retaining sufficient strength and having the requisite skill to prevent the entire contents gushing out." As Zac was about to speak, she hurriedly continued. "Once upon a time the corks were secured with string, now you have corks automatically fastened in place by wire. Everything I have seen today in your cellars has been automated, even the riddling process invented, as you proudly said, by your grandmother Camille d'Argentan. No, I do not want to destroy the methods of producing champagne even though, nowadays, your great-grandfather would not have recognized them. I want to improve them, especially the methods of production and distribution; not the quality, for I know that is perfect. Tell me what *is* wrong with a mechanical harvester if it does the job properly?"

As Zac once more groped for words she went quickly on.

"I tell you what, it destroys tradition; for years, generations of families have been coming to take in the harvest. It was the same in England at hop-gathering time. These customs are very quaint and time honored and I, for one, would also hate to see them go, and yet, if we are to be competitive . . . In England the Desmond champagne is hardly known. In America you would be hard put to find your champagne in one of any twenty liquor stores. Is that what you call successful?"

"Nevertheless we do very well," Zac said haughtily. "I need not regale you with the names of the famous people who are said exclusively to prefer our champagne."

"But that doesn't mean that other less famous people may not be able to buy it," Sandra said patiently. "And the more people who buy it the more we can spend on improvements in technology, the richer the company, and we, can all become."

"I should have thought we were rich enough." Zac slumped into the leather chair and threw one leg carelessly over the other.

"I'm surprised to hear *you* say that, Monsieur Desmond."

Sandra resumed her place behind the desk once more and carefully folded her hands, clearing her throat before she spoke.

"We have not met or communicated since I returned the bribe you tried to offer me, Monsieur Desmond. . . ."

"Bribe . . . ?" Zac exclaimed uncomfortably, his hand automatically rising to the knot of his tie.

"Bribe is exactly what it was. You should, even after a short acquaintance, have known me better. I suppose you thought I was not above accepting five million dollars and going back to Los Angeles?"

"In *addition,*" Zac said, "to the inheritance you still have as my father's adopted daughter. It was merely a symbol of more to come, a percentage of profits from the business. Vincent handled it stupidly."

"*You* handled it stupidly," Sandra said sharply. "Besides you should have come yourself. You could have explained to me exactly what was going on at the Desmond bank."

"And why should I do that?" Zac maintained his aggressive air but she could sense his unease like a tired fox sensing the hound at his heels.

"Because I cannot find a single file pertaining to its affairs in the whole of the Desmond headquarters. Isn't that extraordinary?" She paused. "However, more of that later."

Sandra bent her head as if marshaling her thoughts and then, once more fixing her eyes firmly on him, continued:

"Please never, for as long as you know me, try to bribe me again or insult me by offering me money. If you do you will make a very serious enemy of me indeed. But"—her hand played with some papers before her—"there are other matters besides the affairs of the Bank that disturb me. Since I have been looking into the activities of the Group, I have made a very careful study of the balance sheets of all the major Desmond holdings and most of them are failing to maximize their profits. In particular the estate agency group is actually losing money. I understand that you were responsible for its acquisition. . . ."

"That was a few years ago when it was quite profitable," Zac said hastily.

"Then it should be even *more* profitable now. I intend to sell off the chain of shops and utilize the money we shall receive for the valuable sites on which many of them are placed; to inject more capital into more profitable aspects of the business: aerodynamics, machine tools and the aerospace industry, all growth industries. As for your supermarket purchase"—Sandra sat back and tapped her fingers sharply on the desk—"a very unwise move if I may say so. You must have sustained quite extraordinary losses."

"That is all over now. . . ."

"Because your father came to the rescue." Sandra regarded him solemnly for a few moments and then said slowly, "Maybe that was the time your father began to think about changing his will. . . ."

"What on *earth* do you mean?" Zac jumped to his feet, staring furiously at her.

"Maybe he thought your judgment was suspect; that his business wasn't safe in your hands." Sandra paused then concluded in a lower tone of voice: "And maybe he was right."

Zac looked as though he were about to have an apoplectic fit; his cheeks bulged and the veins stood out on his forehead. Rapidly Sandra got up and rounding the desk came over to him.

"Please Monsieur Desmond, Zac, *don't* let's continue like this. I didn't mean to speak quite as I did and I see I have upset you. I didn't intend to. But you upset me. You were *very* rude to me, very cruel on my first night at Tourville and your crude attempt to bribe me deeply disturbed and distressed me.

"When I saw you here today for luncheon I was very pleased and your manner to me, if a little peremptory, was helpful. I was touched by your expression as you looked at your father's desk, and, believe me, Zac, I do feel very sorry for you. You say you find it hard to believe." Instinctively she placed a hand on his arm. *"Please* don't say it again. It is true I am a businesswoman, but I am not a hard, faceless bureaucrat. I too have known much disappointment in my life, believe me, and it has not left me without sympathy for others. I am not a ruthless, ambitious woman determined to succeed at all costs. . . ."

"Then give up your inheritance—it is quite simple really." The color left Zac's face and, as if appeased by her words, he resumed his seat. *"That* way you will make us all happy, maybe even yourself, who knows? And still you will remain a very wealthy woman. You are not wanted here. You are not liked and you are not welcome. The senior staff will never accept you, particularly here in Reims at the House of Desmond. You came here talking about time-and-motion experts. I'm afraid they will laugh at you behind your back. It is my family they respect and me, in particular, they look up to. You will never succeed and your best plan, before you lose more face, is to take the next plane home."

"I can't do it, Zac," Sandra said, seating herself next to him on the broad leather sofa. "You know that. I am not ruthlessly ambitious, but I *am* ambitious. I see in what your father left to me the opportunity of a great challenge. To anyone trained in business it is irresistible. And much of what I have already seen has convinced me that the company has not been well run, that it does need considerable pruning and, maybe, what your father wanted was a fresh new approach. Many family firms fail for the same reason: they go from father to son and then they sink. Maybe your father, in his wisdom, thought that might happen to Desmond. Well," she crossed her arms again, "I intend to see that it does not happen. But I would like you with me as an ally, a friend and partner. Obviously your father had a high opinion of you or he would not have made you head of the Desmond bank. It is a position of awesome responsibility. Yet even there I would like to go over the figures with you and discuss some new ideas, new potentials for investment, for diversification of funds you might not have thought of." She stopped and smiled at him, encouraged by a new and pensive look on his face. For the moment she decided to say nothing about the visit of Philippe de Lassale. Then she leaned toward him, hands extended. "Come Zac, please let us be friends, partners. Show yourself a man of generous spirit and I promise you, you will never regret it."

Zac looked at the ceiling, closed his eyes and appeared lost in thought. He stayed that way for several moments and so powerful was his attitude of concentration that Sandra could almost see the many mixed emotions that warred within him. Then she would have liked to reach out and grasp his hand in friendship. He was a solitary person; so was she. They had both been betrayed, deceived, let down. Maybe they were both victims of a cruel fate; parents who had rejected them. She as a girl, he as an adult. Which, after all, was worse?

René-Zachariah Desmond was not a man who particularly appealed to her, for whom she felt an instinctive sympathy; but they did have something in common: each needed the other.

Finally he opened his eyes and gazed at her, his expression not an unfriendly one. She felt a moment of hope.

"We'll see," he said softly. "We'll just have to see."

5

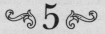

For the harvest the pickers came from all over France but mostly from the Ardennes, Lorraine and Northern France because the south and southwest has its own harvest. Many factory workers brought their families from the great smoke-filled cities of Lille, Amiens, Longwy or the industrial towns of the Saar and the Massif Central. The traveling people, gypsies, turned up in large, windowless caravans; and a vast army of itinerant workers, peddlars, students and layabouts seemed to appear from nowhere to be present for the ten days or so that constituted the harvest time, approximately one hundred days after the first flowering of the vine.

For townsfolk it was the chance to get some pure country air into tired lungs, color into pale faces, especially for the children, growing up in the shadows and pollution of vast smoke-laden chimneys. It was a treat to see how complexions and general well-being improved despite the hard labor of the work in the vineyards because the pickers had to stoop to remove the bunches from vines trained low to the ground. It was not a job for slackers, and the layabouts, the drunkards, or those who simply hoped to have a good time with plenty to drink soon sloped off, or were sorted out by the serious workers in the same way that bad grapes are separated from the good.

Some of the *vendangeurs* had been coming to the fields owned by Henri Piper on the Montagne de Reims for generations, sons and daughters following mothers and fathers, and so on. Whole families came as part of the season's ritual. The Piper *marque* was one of the most prestigious of Champagne but, as a House, it was not as large as some others, as Desmond for example. Consequently Henri could use mostly grapes from his own vines in the manufacture of the exclusive Piper champagne which, before the First World War, had graced most of the royal tables of Europe.

The *vendangeoirs* that housed the pickers had been built by Henri's father between the wars. These long huts were built among the vineyards and kept in perfect condition throughout the year even though they were only in use for about a fortnight. Henri had installed central heating in each one after the War, and his vineyards were much sought after by those pickers who valued their comfort as well as good food, good pay and the chance of a job well done.

On the other hand the House of Desmond made only ten percent of its champagne from its own vines and, although the *vendangeurs* were equally well looked after, there were fewer of them. Thus the harvest, especially its ceremonial climax, was not the event it was at the Château de Marsanne when, on the final evening of the vintage, a great feast or *cochelet* took place which was attended not only by the pickers in the Piper vineyards but by those from round about, by Henri Piper, his family and his friends.

The main grape grown in the Piper vineyards was the pale-green, delicately scented Chardonnay grape which had to be cut early in the morning when the vines were cool to prevent fermentation in the hot sun on the way to the press-house. Each skilled picker, known as a *hordon,* carried out his or her task with a pair of *epinettes,* a sharp instrument that resembled both a pair of scissors and secateurs, and a small plastic basket. The *porteurs* would take the full baskets from the *hordons* and give them empty ones. Then they would tip the ripe contents of the laden baskets into huge *mannequins,* or oval-shaped baskets, which could hold 176 pounds of grapes.

The *mannequin* was based on a basket used in Roman times and Henri Piper was one of the few *vignerons* still to keep them in his vineyards. Many growers now preferred to use flat boxes to save space and ease the task of the *colporteurs,* the men who loaded the carts and lorries, as the *mannequins* were very heavy to lift.

Henri was also one to maintain the practice of *épluchage,* or sorting out, if there was any doubt as to whether or not his grapes were in prime condition. Sharp-eyed elderly women who had perfected the same task over many years sorted through the grapes which had been tipped out on large osier trays known as *clayettes* propped between the *mannequins.* Unsound or unripe grapes would be placed to one side to be made into *vin de détour* and consumed locally.

During the days of the harvest Henri was up at dawn with his workers, wandering in the vineyards among them, sometimes accompanying the carts to the press-houses and supervising their pressing in the huge *maie,* or champagne press, which was made of oak and could hold 4,000 kilos of grapes. These were pressed down by a heavy lid known as a *mouton* suspended from a huge oak beam above it. The *maie* was about ten feet in diameter but not more than two feet deep to ensure that the juice extracted from the grapes, particularly the black Pinot Noir, never remained for too long in contact with the skins for fear of tinting the "must" or juice.

Champagne intended to be pink was allowed to remain for longer in contact with the black skins, from which it got its delicate coloring, though this was also blended after the Christmas following the harvest, by the addition of red wines, after which it underwent the normal processes used in the manufacture of champagne.

Because Sophie Piper was particularly fond of the delicate, deliciously perfumed pink champagne Henri had done much to modernize its manufacture. In the old days cochineal and a tincture of elderberries was sometimes used to give it a rosé color but this was now forbidden by law. Henri used a still red wine, either Bouzy, Rilly or Cumières, but even then there were years in which he had some failures though his best vintage pink champagne was without equal in the region. Piper Rosé was justly celebrated throughout the world.

Almost every evening in Champagne while the harvest lasted there was a party, a fête or a fair. Great quantities of food and red wine were consumed during the day by the hungry and thirsty workers and these, as well as the preparation of the evening meals, were supervised by Sophie and some of the younger members of her family.

Claire Desmond, especially, loved to come over for the harvest because it was such a special time at the Château de Marsanne. There, as in the days when she was young, she would throw off her inhibitions and some of her sadness and become a girl again, laughing and joking with her Piper relations and their friends.

As soon as the harvest had begun Sandra had arrived at the Château de Tourville to take up residence in Reims and to carry out a personal examination of the work and the methods used. She was accompanied by two time-and-motion experts from Paris, whose activities were regarded with great suspicion not only by the family but by her employees at the Desmond headquarters, and even by Henri Piper who, for once, did not approve of what she was doing.

He could sense the unrest and agitation the spectacle of the two time-and-motion men with their stop watches and clipboards was causing both at the headquarters and in the cellars and the fields. Above all he knew how angry Zac felt about the whole thing and, for once, he shared not Zac's anger exactly but his concern that Sandra, a woman for whom he had the greatest admiration, for whom he even felt a degree of love that he liked to think was purely paternal, should appear to be hurrying the pace too fast. Of all people who had surrounded the late Georges Desmond Henri guessed, perhaps, the reason for his extraordinary bequest. The Desmond empire was not keeping up with its competitors. It was too diversified and, in some spheres, too sluggish; too many parts of it were barely making a profit.

It was also true that Georges' great love had been the jewel at the heart of his empire: champagne. That tiny jewel from which had grown not only wealth, influence and prestige but which remained the pivot of what the name Desmond really stood for: quality, reliability, a touch of luxury.

The Desmond champagne was world class; every bottle they made they could sell. But costs were high; the wine had to rest for many years before it could be sold, vintage wine a lot longer.

The law governing the making of the wine, which had been formulated to maintain quality, also made it a very expensive commodity to produce. By law only 2,000 gallons of juice per acre could be made into champagne, whereas in the south of France it was 3,000 gallons of juice per acre.

The amount of capital sunk into those bottles as they lay in the caves was huge, distribution costs were enormous and yet . . .

As he watched Sandra in the cool of the late September evening circulating among the *vendangeurs* at the last meal of the harvest Henri's admiration was mixed with concern. Among her many assets were her beauty and charm. Yet this was still a man's world so far as business was concerned and if she went too fast, or made too many wrong steps, she would certainly fall; and Zac would be only too pleased to hasten this process.

Happily the time-and-motion men had been sent back to Paris and what their conclusions were not even Uncle Henri yet knew.

The meal had been laid out on enormous trestle tables: *char-*

cuterie, pot au feu, the delicious cheeses of Champagne, Marolles, Brie and, of course its sweet wines. The success of the vintage had been toasted many times, and half of those who were now dancing around a fire that had been lit well away from the tables and the vines were more than a little drunk. One of the traveling men, probably a Spaniard from Andalusia or Saratoga, had a violin and his woman companion a pair of castanets which she clicked as she energetically twirled and swirled among the dancers encouraging them to dance too. The smoke rising from the fires against the sunset in the background, the acrid smell of burning wood, induced a heady, almost sensuous, atmosphere tempered with nostalgia, with sadness that the harvest was over for another year. In the next few days all those who had taken part—the *vendangeurs,* the *hordons,* the *porteurs* and *colporteurs*—would pack their bags and be on their way, some of them in modern cars, some by bicycle, some by cart, or caravan or overladen lorry; but the majority thronged the station in Reims for trains which would take them to the far corners of France and beyond.

Sandra was wearing white again, a belted dress of soft wool which was suitable for the chilly evening. Around her shoulders was a white mohair coat and at her throat a single brilliant splash of color: a royal blue silk scarf. Many glances of admiration were cast at her—something about her style was inimitable—but most people didn't know who she was and treated her as a guest of Monsieur and Madame Piper. Her easy familiarity, her idiomatic use of the French language made her a welcome and popular member of the group and some of the men, emboldened by the wine, asked her to dance. She accepted cheerfully, her slim, lithe body twirling with some skill to the rustic sounds of the Spanish fiddler.

It made a very beautiful spectacle as the night wore on: the many dancers outlined against the flames and in the background the gracious house of the Piper family.

The Château de Marsanne owed much to the inspiration

of Louvois, some twenty kilometers to the east, which had been built by Mansart for Louis XIV's Minister, the Marquis de Louvois, and subsequently occupied by the daughters of Louis XV. Marsanne was an elegant, classical building of mellow sandstone with twin gables, the whole enclosed by a small but beautiful park. Behind the Château rose the Forest of Marsanne and to either side, on the slopes of the hill, were the vines stretching upward and outward on this, one of the prettiest, most varied parts of the Montagne de Reims.

Marsanne shared a frontage onto the River Marne with Tourville some ten kilometers away and it was only a short drive along the river road between the two châteaux, although overland through the hilly, winding roads it took much longer.

Sandra had been brought over from Tourville the longer, prettier way, and her first sight of Marsanne, so much smaller than Tourville and closely protected by the trees, was of fairy-tale turrets gradually coming into view as she was driven down the steep, narrow road toward it. Around its walls was a cluster of white stone houses, the cottages and dwellings of the *vignerons* or servants of the Château, all of whom worked for Henri.

Owned by the Piper family for so long, the Château had the well-worn, though comfortable appearance of a family home. The Pipers had acquired it from the impoverished aristocratic family who, having built it in the eighteenth century, had subsequently lost everything in the Revolution and thus the means to support it. At the time that René-Zachariah Desmond was entertaining much more grandiose thoughts of building on a large and luxurious scale, Henri Piper's great-great-grandfather, Luc, was thinking along different, more conventional lines. At that time, of course, it is probable that the families, beginning to develop their extensive champagne interests, had never met.

The village of Marsanne with its Château was very much

a community and it was thus all the more unfortunate that Henri and Sophie had no children to whom to bequeath it.

However, on this mellow October evening after a good summer the Piper family and their guests had come down to take part in the celebrations, eating with the *vendangeurs* and the local people. Among them were Tim and Claire and a bevy of friends and relations not only from the Piper and Desmond families, but also from most other champagne families in the area because so many of them over the years had intermarried and were related.

Next to Henri was the Baron Charles Havet sitting in his wheelchair to which he had been confined since the onset of Parkinson's disease several years before. The Baron, however, thanks to excellent medical treatment but mostly due to the care and devotion of his wife, kept in good spirits. As a considerable producer of champagne himself he had been a close friend not only of the Piper but of the Desmond families for many years.

The Baron, knowing much about her history, had been watching Sandra all evening, fascinated by the vagaries of fortune as well as the quirks in the character of his old friend Georges Desmond that had made him leave his empire to the daughter of his mistress. He watched her now dancing with a handsome young *vendangeur* who lifted her in the air and whirled her about in tune to the music of the Spanish fiddler. Sandra seemed to love it. Surrounding them was the crowd of appreciative onlookers, many of whom had stopped their own dancing to clap and stamp to the beat of the music.

"Your Sandra has many talents," the Baron mused. "No wonder Georges was fascinated by her. I find her fascinating myself. Did you see how she immediately made herself at home with the pickers of both sexes, to say nothing of charming the younger ones?"

"Georges wasn't fascinated by her," Henri hastened to correct his old friend. "He *admired* her."

"Ah, but there was something else, wasn't there?" The Baron's eyes twinkled as he took a pinch of snuff from a silver case.

"How do you mean?"

"The mother . . . his mistress? I bet she had a big say in the way Georges left his estate."

"There I think you are wrong," Henri mused, sitting back in an old *fauteuil* brought down from the house by a thoughtful servant. "I think she was as much surprised by Georges' bequest as any of us. He never discussed it with me and it is my opinion that he didn't tell her about it either. He came to this decision all by himself."

"Extraordinary." The Baron shook his head.

"Quite extraordinary," Henri agreed.

"And resented by all the family, only two of whom, I see, are here tonight."

"Claire and Tim are not very interested in the politics of the situation and nor, I think, is Lady Elizabeth; but Zac and Belle as you might imagine are absolutely furious. Sometimes I fear for Zac's mental health he says such wild things. . . ."

"Such as?" The Baron looked up, concern on his face.

"Oh getting his own back, that kind of thing . . . all nonsense of course. He'll have to accept it. She has already firmly assumed control."

The Baron shook his head, his face grim.

"Zac was always unpredictable. Nothing I hear about him surprises me. He is violent, too. Do you remember how he nearly pummeled Guy's face to a pulp when they had that argument about Marie-Louise Flore?"

"He lost his head that's all. He was very jealous, and still is. He watches Tara like a hawk."

"Yes, but that is not simple jealousy. Guy, who was at school with Zac, has always disliked him intensely. He says as a boy he delighted in doing cruel things to the younger boys and to animals . . ."

"To animals?" Henri looked surprised.

"Oh yes, he once . . ." The Baron paused, then waved a hand dismissively. "But I won't go into all that. It happened such a long time ago." He leaned closer to Henri.

"If you ask me, *mon vieux,* it was *because* Georges knew the limitations of his own son that he felt he couldn't trust him with his empire. But to leave it to a stranger, well . . ." The Baron once more shrugged and both men fell into a ruminative silence.

As darkness fell many of the workers, tired from their strenuous days of effort among the vines, began to think about retiring. The little ones still up were taken, protesting, off to bed by their mothers; but some of the young people decided to go into the town where a fair was currently in progress.

Sandra protested that it really was too late for her to go and, laughingly, said goodbye to her partner who gazed at her, crestfallen. He tried to seize her hand and, as he did, another equally strong hand came down on his wrist, removing it from Sandra's slender one.

"Please don't do that," Tim said sharply. "Don't you know who Mademoiselle is?"

"I . . . please . . ." The young *vendangeur* backed away, slightly drunk but nevertheless still sober enough to feel mortified.

"Oh I really, *Tim . . ."* Sandra looked apologetically at her partner who, mumbling something unintelligible, turned his back and moved out of the light of the fire. "You shouldn't have done that."

"I can't have you manhandled by that lout. You're the head of the Desmond Group."

"Yes, but he didn't know that."

"You mustn't be too familiar, Sandra," Tim said, leading her out of the range of the light. "The country people will not respect you. We may have had equality here since 1789 but, believe me, people still know their places."

* * *

Now the family and guests were moving across the field in which the dancing had been held. As Tim and Sandra arrived at the gate they found it held open by Henri so that the Baronne Havet could push her husband's chair through. Tim immediately went to assist her and Sandra stood back watching them negotiate the narrow opening.

It was not until they were on the other side that Henri turned to her and said:

"May I introduce you to the Baron and Baronne Havet, my dear Sandra?"

"We have heard *so* much about you." The Baron held up his hand and, as she bent to take it, his wife said:

"So very much."

"Delighted to meet you." Sandra took her proffered hand as Tim steered the chair up the slight hill toward the terrace at the back of the house.

"Have you enjoyed this evening?"

"Very much. I've enjoyed everything about the harvest, in fact everything about Reims and Champagne."

"I'm glad to hear it," the Baron said as Tim negotiated the last couple of steps onto the terrace. "It must be very difficult for. . . ." He paused and Sandra interjected quietly:

"Someone like me to take on something like this."

"Exactly, a very big task for anyone. And you, Tim." The Baron seemed anxious to change the subject. "You have been in the Himalayas, I hear?"

"I was there when they brought the news of Father's death to me." Tim steered the chair across the broad terrace.

"And will you go back?"

"Not . . ." Tim glanced at Sandra who was standing on one side listening, "not for a while. Not until everything's settled."

"But I thought everything was settled now?" Sophie Piper

looked at him anxiously as with the aid of a servant he negotiated the final steps into the brightly lit salon of the Château.

"There is still opposition to Sandra," Tim said. "Zac is far from happy. . . ."

"It was quite understandable that Zac would be unhappy; but does he not, in fact, accept what Georges has done, and that Sandra has now claimed her inheritance?"

"Reluctantly." Claire, who had followed them into the Château, took a seat, her eyes on a fat bunch of grapes she held in her hand, ripened after the harvest.

Claire was aware that everyone was watching her, waiting for her to speak as she carefully, deliberately studied each fat grape on the bunch before selecting one and popping it into her mouth.

"Reluctantly?" echoed the Baron Havet encouragingly.

"You all know that Zac will never accept Father's will," Claire said at last. "He has told Sandra that and he means it."

"Naturally none of the family can completely understand why Father did what he did." Tim, making sure the Baron was comfortable and his chair secure, sat down next to Claire and began to help her eat the ripe, golden-tinted grapes. "But we, the two younger ones, were less concerned at the outcome than Zac or Belle, who is also very ambitious. Personally I am very sorry for Sandra." He sat back and looked over to where she sat, perched now rather precariously and nervously on the edge of a chair. "I think Sandra had a very awkward job and has done what she had to do well and gracefully. But she needn't feel the trouble is over; that it is all plain sailing from now on."

Indeed she didn't. Sandra glanced up at Henri, who knew too well what she was thinking. Only to him had she confided what he had already guessed: all was not well in the Desmond organization; many of the smaller companies were poised on the edge of bankruptcy. Even the great Banque Pons-

Desmond had allowed itself to be used by a Swiss bank in some doubtful enterprises and was heavily in debt.

Sandra had slumped now into her chair, her coat still over her shoulder, her hands on the arms as though she were tired; but she was listening very carefully to what was being said and as Tim had mentioned the words *plain sailing* she suddenly smiled.

"Don't think for a moment *I* think it is all plain sailing. It is far from that. The trouble with your brother is that he is so unpredictable. He is hostile one moment, disarmingly friendly the next. I even thought he was going to come tonight but he changed his mind and made your mother change hers."

"That was because Belle was coming," Claire interrupted her, "and, believe me, Belle . . ." She paused and looked thoughtfully at the half-eaten bunch of grapes, shaking her head but saying nothing else.

At the mention of Belle's name Sandra felt her heart involuntarily freeze. Zac was an irritation and an annoyance, but there was something about Belle—a curious chilling quality which reminded one that the female of the species was, sometimes, more deadly than the male.

Sandra got down early to breakfast the next morning hoping to make her exit before the others came down but Belle was there before her dressed in jodhpurs, hacking jacket and riding boots. It was only seven o'clock but obviously she had already been out riding; her face glowed and her appetite was hearty. Lady Elizabeth always took breakfast in her room but, from seven o'clock onward, the staff were alert to serve coffee, croissants, brioches, fruit and jams to those who wished to make an early start. The breakfast was always served not in the grand dining room, but in a small morning room on the ground floor which gave an air of intimacy to the occasion.

Belle smiled as Sandra came in and pointed to the sideboard and the silver dish of croissants resting on a hot plate.

"They're all quite fresh. They've only been there ten minutes; but do ring if you want them heated up. The servants will bring in coffee."

Belle appeared unusually cheerful and smilingly indicated a place for Sandra to sit opposite her. "Sorry I missed the party at Henri's last night. It's always a lot of fun."

"It was," Sandra said guardedly, pouring herself black coffee and glancing at her watch. She wanted to go to the office in Reims before leaving for Paris, where she had a Board meeting in the afternoon.

"Henri is such a darling; but then you knew him very well already, didn't you?"

"I knew him better than anyone," Sandra said, gazing at Belle over her cup. "He came regularly to California to oversee his property there."

"I suppose Father made sure he kept an eye on you?"

"I suppose he did." To Sandra the coffee tasted bitter but it may have been her imagination that made her see in Belle's expression something akin to portraits of Lucrezia Borgia.

Belle was a very beautiful woman, her skin healthy and tanned from the many outdoor pursuits she enjoyed. Her hair, now brushed smoothly back from her brow without parting, curled naturally and neatly over her ears. It was thick, luxurious hair, easy to style in a variety of coiffeurs. She looked like a princess, and her arrogant gaze, as she stared across the table at Sandra, bore all the insolence of an aristocrat contemplating a peasant.

"How many times did you actually *meet* my father?"

"Not more than half a dozen," Sandra said carefully, "and never for very long. You must understand, Princess, that it was a relationship that had as little favor with me as it did with you."

"So you said." Belle gazed thoughtfully at her cup. "Still,

I find it all very strange. Have you seen your mother since you came to France?"

"No." Sandra wanted to go but, somehow, felt compelled to stay, mesmerized by the power of those apparently innocuous but strangely viperous eyes.

"That seems to me the strangest part of all," Belle said before sinking her perfectly formed teeth into a fresh brioche covered with apricot jam. Then as Sandra didn't reply, she eventually continued. "There is no need to call me 'Princess' and I shall call you Sandra. We may not particularly like the relationship that has been forced on us but, at least, let's be civilized. Besides," she smiled mischievously, "I understand my brother is quite taken with you."

"Your *brother?*" Sandra said with a gasp.

"Oh not *Zac.*" Belle quickly rectified the misunderstanding. "Poor Zac, you can quite understand *his* feelings. No, my younger brother, Tim. But I must warn you he is extremely vulnerable. However, it would be unfortunate, wouldn't it. . . ." She left the sentence unfinished.

Sandra got up and took her bag from the floor beside her chair, not even bothering to reply. In everything that Belle said she managed somehow to insinuate innuendo or menace. If anything Sandra thought she liked her less than Zac, and, in that strange way, she feared her.

"Goodbye," she said with a brief nod and went immediately into the hall where Pierre was waiting with her briefcase and coat.

"Your chauffeur isn't here, Mademoiselle O'Neill."

"I'm driving myself, thanks, Pierre. André will pick me up in Reims to take me to Paris."

"Very good, Mademoiselle." Pierre, well aware of who now paid his salary, grandiloquently threw open the wide doors. "And when shall we have the pleasure of seeing you again?"

"I will telephone Lady Elizabeth."

Pierre stood back and Sandra was just about to run down the steps when she remembered that a dress she had to wear to a dinner the next day was still in her wardrobe.

"Un instant, Pierre," she said. "I have forgotten something." She threw her coat and briefcase onto the ornate carved bench in the hall and went quickly up the marble staircase to the second floor. She ran lightly along the carpeted corridor to her room, surprised to find that the door, which she had shut, was slightly open. Doubtless one of the maids. She pushed open the door and then stopped as, to her surprise, she saw Claire standing at the far end of the room gazing out of the window which overlooked the drive.

Hearing her, Claire turned and her hand went to her mouth. The opposite of her sister, she was no beauty; her looks were pallid in comparison. But much of Belle's attraction was due to artifice: to skillfully applied makeup and the adoption of certain mannerisms. Claire had brown hair, very pale skin and almost bloodless lips. Her large blue eyes lacked sparkle and, altogether, the impression she gave was of someone who not only had little concern about her appearance, but was also in the grip of some hidden illness, or, perhaps, a secret sorrow. The night of the harvest she had been animated, almost pretty but now, still in her dressing gown, her hair tousled, she looked as though she hadn't slept well. Also her expression, which she didn't attempt to disguise, was of someone caught out in a misdemeanor.

"Oh! I thought I'd missed you. . . ."

"I'd forgotten something," Sandra said, going to her wardrobe and rapidly running her hand along the clothes hanging there. "Is there anything I can do for you?"

"It's what I can do for *you,*" Claire said, rapidly recovering and, crossing the room, she firmly shut the door. "I wanted to talk to you last night but it was too late. Before, there was no opportunity. You see"—she sat heavily on the unmade bed, the weight of her body resting on her hand—"I heard my brother and sister talking about you last night in the salon, after you had gone to bed. I should have been in bed too, but I was restless and went downstairs to look for something to read. I couldn't help overhearing. . . ."

"Really I don't think you should be telling me this." Sandra looked nervously at the door. "Belle was at breakfast. Her room is only next door. She may soon be up. I . . ."

To her amazement and alarm Claire leapt off the bed and running over to her seized Sandra by the hand.

"Sandra, I like you. I do really. Despite everything that has happened. I like you and I'm sorry for you because you don't know what Zac and Belle are like . . ."

"I'm beginning to have some idea . . ." Sandra began but Claire shook her arm urgently to stop her talking.

"They are evil, really evil," she hissed. "Not only to you but to everyone who crosses their path. When they were small, Zac so much older than I, they were always together. Belle was so easily influenced by him. They used to 'pretend' in their games, but to me much of it was real and they frightened me. They tormented me because I was the youngest. . . ."

"But your parents . . ." Sandra said, aghast.

"They never knew! Or if they did they pretended not to—but our nannies knew, and the servants knew."

"Just childish tricks . . ." Sandra said helplessly.

"*Not* childish tricks," Claire urged. "Some people are evil from birth. You know that, don't you?"

Sandra said nothing but remembered her own discomfiture on hearing that Belle had arrived at the Château.

Claire went on in the same breathless tone of voice. "We once had a nursemaid who told me that Zac and Belle were children of the devil. Shortly after that she was found dead, floating in the river at the end of the park. I have been terrified of them ever since. And years ago, a man I loved very much called Mario was almost drowned while we were yachting off the coast of Greece. He fell accidentally off the side of the boat and no one saw him except Zac and Belle, who were fishing. He says, and I believe him, that they just watched him, made no attempt to rescue him or call for help as he floundered in the sea. . . ."

"Maybe they didn't really see him." Sandra felt lost for words.

"Oh they saw him. They even turned their heads as the boat ploughed on through the sea, perhaps expecting to see the last of him. He could recall it quite vividly."

This was the secret sorrow, the reason for the insipidity, the pallor. Sandra gazed at her compassionately.

"What happened to him?"

"One of the crewmen saw and jumped in to rescue him. . . ."

"So, how did you end up marrying Armand?"

"Oh . . ." wearily Claire stroked her brow, "that's another story. I'll tell you some day. Mario was a painter. Basically my father thought he wasn't good enough for me, socially inferior . . ."

Suddenly she stopped, cocking her ear toward the door.

"I told you," Sandra whispered as Belle's voice rang out clearly from the other side.

"Sandra, are you there? I thought you'd gone."

"Just going," Sandra said, pointing silently to the side of the room so that Claire would be out of sight of the door. She then flung it open, a smile on her face, the forgotten dress over her arm.

"This is what I left," she said brightly.

"I thought I heard voices." Belle attempted to poke her head around the door.

Sandra shook her head firmly, closing the door behind her, and gesturing for Belle to precede her into the corridor, she gazed at her watch. "I really must run." Then, with a wave, and a prayer in her heart that Belle would not go back and find her sister, she called out in English, "Have a good day," and ran down the stairs to the hall where Pierre was still waiting for her.

Belle watched from her window as Sandra drove away in her Mini-Metro then, returning to the corridor, she walked swiftly back to Sandra's room and threw open the door. She was perfectly sure she had heard her sister's voice, but a careful search of the bedroom, the sitting room next door and the bathroom showed no sign of her. Those precious minutes which elapsed when she'd waited to be sure Sandra left the house had meant that her suspicions had to remain unconfirmed.

Belle left the room and, passing her mother's room, stopped outside Claire's and knocked at the door. There was no reply and she knocked again. She tried the handle but the door was locked.

Then thoughtfully she went along to Zac's room, tapping her riding crop against her knee.

"Come in," Zac called as she knocked at the door and when she threw it open she saw he was dressed, his eyes puffy as though he had woken late.

"I'm terribly late," Zac said. "There's a bank Board meeting this afternoon and I want to be sure I'm there."

"She's already gone." Belle walked slowly into the room, jerking her head in the direction of Sandra's.

"Yes, I heard her drive off," he said. "She's got to go into Reims first."

"I swear that Claire has been talking to her," Belle said, still swinging the riding crop between her knees as she sat on his bed.

"What makes you think that?" Zac looked appraisingly at himself in the mirror.

"I don't *think,* I know. I heard her talking to Sandra as I was about to go to my room."

"Is that so terrible?"

"Supposing she heard us last night?"

"You're worrying about nothing," Zac said. "Claire was very tired when she came in and went straight to bed. You know how badly she sleeps." He looked severely at his sister. "You're letting your imagination run away with you, Belle."

"But *why* should she be talking to Sandra who was already preparing to leave the house? I'd just had breakfast with her."

"I have no idea." Zac impatiently shrugged himself into his coat. "You know what an odd girl Claire is." He tapped his forehead. "Sometimes I think she's not all right there. She seems determined to befriend Sandra, just to spite us. Let her." He laughed unpleasantly. "Mademoiselle O'Neill will not, after all, be with us for very long."

"I still don't like it." Belle's eyes narrowed, fixing on the highly polished toe of her riding boot. "Too early in the morning. Too surreptitious. Sandra insisted Claire hadn't been there. Why? Only to hide something. But I *know* she was there. I sensed it. Sandra practically route-marched me to my room! Why would she do that?"

"I have *no* idea, my sweet sister."

Zac briskly patted after-shave on his cheeks and flicked a speck of dust from his shoulder. Then he gazed once more closely into the mirror, adjusted the carnation in his buttonhole, seeming pleased with what he saw: a man of affairs ready for a day's work.

What he couldn't see but what he knew were there, lying heavily on his heart like a stone weight, were the rage, the hatred and revenge that festered continuously, ready to erupt, like an exploding pustule, against the woman he hated more than anything else in life; she who had deprived him of his birthright.

Sandra O'Neill.

The Château de Tourville was twenty kilometers or so from the city of Reims and, whichever route one took, the way was invariably a pretty one, lined with trees, or fields of wheat, or vines. Past neat villages, their white-painted houses bright with flowers—geraniums, petunias, lobelia—the walls festooned with bougainvillaea and clematis. On the way there were also many military cemeteries; mute, sad witnesses to the century's wars that had scarred the Valley of the Marne and its environs.

But not only recent wars. It was an area that had been fought over again and again for hundreds of years by the English as well as the Germans; by Frenchmen locked with one another in internal strife. All that was left of Dom Perignon's beautiful abbey at nearby Hautvillers was the church with his tomb before the high altar, the memorial to a master cellier, the "father" of modern champagne.

But Sandra bypassed Hautvillers on her steep climb out of Tourville through the vineyards that stretched in the sunshine on either side as far as the eye could see. Below was the Marne and she could just glimpse to her left the steeple of Dom Perignon's church through the trees.

Some of the vineyards were still full of stooping *vendangeurs* gathering in the harvest, though for all the local *vignerons* this would be the last few days. In front of Sandra trundled a cart laden with grapes, a bunch of flowers and vines tied behind, which rocked from side to side as the horse slowly and contentedly trotted on its last journey, toward the press-house.

Long ago, Henri had told her, it had been the custom for the last carts leaving the vineyard to be adorned thus as a sign that the harvest was over. Now the lorries had taken over and this custom was retained by only a few. For this particular *vigneron* tonight there would be a party and, perhaps in some nearby village, a young man would be crowned with vine leaves as *roi des vignerons,* just for the night.

Henri had told her that a lot of the old customs which were prevalent everywhere in his youth had been abandoned because of increased mechanization and the general quickening in the pace of life. Many of the *vendangeurs* were using annual holiday leave to come to the vineyards and had to depart on time to be back at their factories. Soon harvesttime in Champagne would be but a fragrant memory that would perhaps return from time to time during the year as, through the din of machinery, the clatter of the workbench, the hurly burly of the shop floor, they thought back with nostalgia to those mellow, wine-filled, halcyon days of autumn.

Sandra's car slowed down to a crawl along the narrow road as the laden cart filled with bunches of white succulent grapes and driven by a solitary driver, who seemed to have all the time in the world, took up most of it. She was aware of more horse's hooves behind her and, thinking she had unwittingly become part of a convoy, looked in her car mirror. There, to her astonishment, following her on a large roan without a care in the world was Tim Desmond! Seeing her look at him he waved and, as a clearing appeared, she pulled to one side of the road and stopped. As she opened the door Tim drew alongside her and gave her a wave.

"Morning! Lovely morning."

"Lovely morning, Tim." Sandra crossed her arms and leaned back in the seat. "And what are *you* doing, may I ask?"

"I am following *you,* Mademoiselle. I might even pass you if the cart keeps up its slow, laborious crawl."

"Are you following me intentionally or by accident?"

"Oh by *accident* of course," Tim said with a disarming smile. "I must say I espied you leaving Tourville and thought it would be fun to see if I could keep up with you. Happily I was able to, thanks to our friend in front. Isn't it a charming sight?" Tim put his head to one side and his horse impatiently whinnied and pawed the ground. "What would your time-and-motion men say to that, Miss O'Neill?"

Sandra sighed, leaned forward and switched on the engine of her car.

"Oh that again."

"No, really." Tim jumped off his horse and came over to her. "It was just a joke."

"You simply don't understand do you? You don't *want* to." Sandra engaged the first gear, her foot on the accelerator. Deftly, and taking her completely by surprise, Tim leaned across her and switched off the engine. Then, before she knew what he was doing, he went to the other side of the car, his horse obediently following him, and got into the seat beside her, the horse's reins held loosely in his hand.

He was really a very attractive man, Sandra thought despite herself, never having seen him at such close quarters before. He had Lady Elizabeth's fine bone structure and, like her, blue eyes. His thick hair was a much lighter color than Zac's. Tim didn't have quite Zac's strength or physical power, or his studied charm, but he had a lot more appeal, at least to Sandra. He had the litheness and elasticity of an athlete kept in perfect trim. He exuded good health and, as he gazed at her, Sandra remembered what Belle had said at breakfast: "My brother is quite taken with you. . . ."

Sandra quickly looked away, but he put a hand firmly on her arm:

"It is *you* who don't understand, Mademoiselle O'Neill, and I wanted to warn you because, believe it or not, I like you very much. You are an attractive, beautiful woman, and I don't like to see you misunderstood and hurt. *I* know you mean well. I know that you couldn't help my father's bequest. But you see when you bring time-and-motion people to the harvest . . ." Tim shrugged in that way that was particularly Gallic, a hunch of the shoulders, a twitch of the lips. "It was a *very* stupid thing to do, and you are certainly not a stupid woman."

"I didn't think." Sandra bit her lip. Henri Piper had said the same thing, so she had sent the men back to Paris.

"You see here in Champagne—" Tim sat back as though

he were completely at home, not only in the countryside, but in her car. His natural charm was immense. "—time has stopped still in many ways. In your mechanized automobile you are held up by a horse-drawn cart. Nothing you can do will enable you to pass it. It is as though they, horse and driver, are trying to show you that you cannot hurry things too far; there are certain things you can't change. . . ."

"But things *have* changed." Sandra stamped her foot on the floor.

"Over a period of many many years," Tim interrupted her gently. "Oh I know we have computers in the Desmond offices and there are many things we have done and are doing which slowly will change the way we make champagne. But—" Tim gazed at the back of the rustic, vine-covered cart which had taken a path down toward the *pressoir*—"can you see the mechanized harvester making quite such an impression as that dear old horse winding its way slowly along the lane with a bunch of flowers and vines tied behind it? Doesn't it move your heart? Doesn't it bring a lump to the throat?"

"It does," Sandra said, laughing rather shakily. She was too aware of Tim's presence for comfort; his very masculinity seemed like a threat to her . . . every bit as much a threat as the malevolence of his brother and sister. She was a woman who, for a long time and for good reasons, had kept careful guard on her emotions. She tried to retreat from him, to withdraw, but he moved closer. Then with a hand he touched her brow and began to smooth her hair back from her forehead.

"Unlike the others I know more about you, Sandra O'Neill," he said very softly. The expression in his eyes was now a curious mixture of desire and compassion, almost of tenderness. "I know that you are a woman with a soft heart, a loving nature that for some reason, perhaps I know what it is, you have repressed. I know . . ."

"For heaven's sake, Tim!" Sandra said with some force, pushing him away from her and sharply switching on the key in the ignition. "Do you know what year this is? Have you never heard of women's liberation? Do you think *I* am going to be seduced by these tactics . . . ?"

"Sandra . . ." Tim's expression was less certain now, less confident. "I only meant to help."

"You can help me by getting out of the car and removing yourself and your horse from my side." Sandra paused as abruptly as she had exploded, her face lit now by a mischievous smile. "You see, Monsieur, the road is quite clear now and I want to be on my way."

The car roared into life and Tim looked first at her and then at his suddenly restless horse. He leapt from the car and drew the horse to the side of the road and the safety of the fence. Then he went back and, before shutting the door, he leaned toward her.

"You haven't finished with me yet, Sandra O'Neill. I like a woman with spirit but, you see, I never know when I've met my match."

Then he smiled politely, bowed elaborately, and slammed the car door firmly in her face.

6

Hélène O'Neill put down the paper she'd been reading and removed her gold-rimmed glasses. Then she gazed for a long time out of the long window of the house Georges had bought for her in the village of Crémy on a hillside of the beautiful Côte des Blancs, or Côte Blanche as it was sometimes called.

The vines in this area all bore the white Chardonnay grape and besides its use in the making of champagne, it was also the basis of one of the most prestigious *crus* of the area, "Blanc de Blancs." Like the Montagne de Reims, a few kilometers north on the other side of the Marne, the brow of the Côte des Blancs was covered with trees; but on either side, for mile after mile, stretched the carefully tended rows of vines, each one strung along on three wires except for the young, newly planted vines which were encircled with blue wire-mesh to protect them from the birds.

The cream-colored house at Crémy, previously occupied by a noted *négociant* in the area who had moved to another higher up the hill, was large. It was L-shaped with a wide terrace on which were tubs of flowers, pots of scarlet geraniums and an old wooden wine barrel in which the young wine used to mature before modern methods and the advent of plastic.

It was a family house used to children, dogs and plenty of activity; but now Hélène lived here alone, except for her maid. A few short months before, the love of her life, Georges Desmond, had suddenly left her.

Together with the large apartment in the rue de Seine which was now closed, its antique furniture covered with white sheets, the house at Crémy had been an exclusive gift to Hélène, and Georges Desmond's family had no part of it. In fact it was only in recent years, when an acquaintance *en route* to inspect a vineyard farther south, had chanced to see Hélène shopping in the small main street of Crémy, that they had got to know about it.

It was a typical house, such as many *vignerons* in the area had, with outbuildings and a *pressoir* no longer in use. In the days when the last family lived there the *vendangeurs* had brought in the grapes to be pressed by the large old-fashioned *maie* which still stood where it had for so many years, as though awaiting the call to work again.

To the villagers Hélène O'Neill was a woman of mystery; few had even known her name, and no one recognized her companion because he had usually swept in and out of the courtyard in a closed car and there was never the time to see his face. It is doubtful, however, that, even if they had, they would have recognized the owner of the Château de Tourville, though to most his name would have been familiar.

Now Hélène, tended only by a maid she had brought from Paris, bore her solitude and her grief, which never seemed to lessen despite the passage of time.

Hélène O'Neill was a comparatively young woman, only in her midfifties; but for the past few years her health had not been good. She had been seen less and less at the office in the Étoile when Georges was alive, leaving Paul Vincent to do most of the administration while she lived, as she preferred, in the manner of the wife of Georges Desmond with her large apartment in the center of the capital and her substantial home in the country.

She had for many years been a victim of chronic bronchitis

which had turned to emphysema and beside her bed was a cylinder of oxygen which her maid knew how to administer.

It was not a happy life now. Had it ever been? Had it ever been *really* happy, as the lives of other lovers were said to be? Now, more than ever, she wondered.

For whatever she told herself, or pretended, or liked to believe, she was a mistress: a member of the bourgeoisie who, from the life of an ordinary secretary—at one time a children's nurse and housekeeper to an American film star—had become the *maitresse en titre* of a man of substance and wealth.

She was socially his inferior, a kept woman and, in many ways, though she never doubted that Georges Desmond trusted her and needed her, he had never in twenty years allowed her to forget it.

Twenty years. Twenty years with one man; and now he had gone like a puff of smoke from her life—leaving only memories and a strange testament. A very strange testament. Carefully Hélène folded the newspaper at the spot where she had been reading over and over again the item about Sandra and, slowly getting to her feet, crossed the room and leaned heavily on the windowsill.

The harvest was over. The vines, carefully tended throughout the year, had been stripped. The *grapillage* had ensured that not a single grape remained on the vines, although the birds hopefully plucked them over for pickings and usually they were not disappointed.

She always thought the vines looked at their saddest at this time of the year after the harvest, denuded of their priceless burdens that would be turned, as if by magic, into the crystal of the Blanc de Blancs or the gold of champagne. By December they would all have been cut down and pruned right back, the soil tilled over for the winter to await that burgeoning again; that promise that came, at last, with the spring when the vines flowered, a sign that they would soon bring forth fruit. Within a hundred days or thereabouts of the flowering was the harvest—and then the cycle began all over again; like birth, like life.

Hélène often saw a counterpart of her life in this natural cycle of the vine: dying, bringing forth fruit, dying again. She had spent so many of her early years making new beginnings that it seemed, more or less, like a permanent cycle of death and rebirth. Yet when, at the age of thirty-five, she had met Georges, there had been no more dying, only perpetual life. It seemed too, that it would never end, and when it did the brutality, the suddenness of it, left her too almost bereft of life. That morning she'd spoken to him and by nightfall he was dead. Never to speak to Georges again, only in her memory. How did one come to terms with such a fact? Only painfully, very, very painfully.

For Georges she had forsaken her family. She had pulled up her roots and fled into the arms of the only man she felt could give her that continual light; warmth, peace, happiness, but, above all, security. It was the supreme selfishness, yet she hadn't realized it at the time because to serve Georges had seemed the very opposite. But Georges had blinded her to other more fundamental duties: it had seemed important to serve him, not them, and now, bitterly, she was paying for it.

Hélène O'Neill had been born Germond in a village, not unlike the one she lived in now, in the Limoges region of France. Both her mother and father had worked in one of the factories which produced the famous porcelain of the area and she had been an ordinary girl, with an ordinary upbringing, not expected to make anything special of her life. She had a brother and two sisters and at fourteen it was presumed she would leave school, destined to work in the same factory as her mother and father, her brother and elder sister.

But Hélène had never been quite like the others. She had always been considered bookish, different. Some people called her a snob and wondered where she got her airs from. The

Germond family had, as far as was known, been workers and artisans in the industrial city of Limoges for generations: why should Hélène, the second daughter of an industrious, working-class family, be any different?

But Hélène Germond undoubtedly was. She didn't want to leave school and neither did her teachers want this. They wanted her to take the Baccalaureat and make something of her life. So Hélène did what none of the members of her family—uncles, aunts, cousins however near or remote—had ever done. She stayed on at school, achieved success in her examinations and went on to Paris to take a secretarial course and perfect her study of the English language.

The War, of course, disturbed her life as it did that of everybody else; but during it Hélène stayed at school and, as soon as she could afterward she went to Paris, a city that was trying to pick up the pieces of normality again. She studied shorthand and typing and then perfected her English by getting a job with a British delegation trying to track down missing British personnel, especially those who had been on secret missions to occupied France.

It was there that she met John O'Neill, a staff captain with the delegation who, though an officer, was hardly a gentleman. But, at the time, the reserved, impressionable young woman from the provinces was mesmerized by his dark looks, his Irish charm and had no premonition of how faithless and feckless he would prove to be. In those days Hélène Germond, though too studious to be considered really pretty, had something about her which attracted John O'Neill as, much later, it was to attract Georges Desmond.

How to explain that quality which had captivated two quite different men? Perhaps it was an enigmatic air, a quality of self-containment that invited pursuit. There is a subtle flirtatiousness about such people that, perhaps unconsciously, they cultivate. Or perhaps they wish to be drawn out, in order to show they have something worth revealing.

In her later years, because she patronized the best *coiffeuses,* the discreet beauty salons of the rue des Pyramids and the rue de Rivoli, Hélène O'Neill came to be considered a handsome, clever woman who dressed well; but still that enigma remained, as if even she really did not know who she was. . . .

Hélène wandered back from the window and picked up the paper, rereading the paragraph that she had read so many times already:

MLLE. O'NEILL TO ASSUME
THE NAME OF "DESMOND"

Mademoiselle Sandra O'Neill, who so unexpectedly inherited the fortune left by the late Georges Desmond and the control of his huge business empire, has legally assumed the name of Desmond and so carried out the wishes of the testator. Monsieur Desmond had legally adopted Mademoiselle O'Neill, who was the daughter of his long-time secretary and personal assistant, Madame Hélène O'Neill, a Frenchwoman who had taken American nationality.

Little is known of the early years of Madame O'Neill except that she was born in midwestern France and went to America after the war with her husband, Captain John O'Neill, an Irishman serving in the British Army.

When interviewed yesterday Mademoiselle O'Neill, who speaks perfect French, refused to discuss her personal life or the whereabouts of her mother. It is assumed that they are not on good terms, though the reason for this is not known.

However, in the few months she has been in France, Mademoiselle O'Neill, who we must now call Desmond, has made a decided and startling impact on the fortunes of the Desmond Group, whose shares fell sharply on the Bourse with the death in an air crash in July of Georges Desmond, head of the large industrial empire.

Mademoiselle Sandra Desmond is an accomplished businesswoman despite her years. Again she is reticent about this but she is believed to be well under thirty. She studied at Berkeley in California and the Harvard Business School and it is assumed that her academic brilliance was the reason for the strange bequest of Georges Desmond.

Within weeks of her taking command, the shares in the Desmond Group rose sharply as she was seen to be tackling the problems which had begun to beset the Group before the death of Monsieur Desmond. It was well known in financial circles that things were not as good as they seemed; that the Group had diversified too much and unwisely. However, due to Monsieur Desmond's personality, the market in his stock remained firm.

There was much speculation about the reason for Monsieur Desmond's decision not to leave the running of the business in the hands of his son Zac who is the President of the Banque Pons-Desmond. There have been rumored troubles at the Bank, an unwise alliance with Helvetes Réunis, a company registered in Zurich. But this has been vigorously denied and Monsieur Zac Desmond is thought to enjoy the confidence of his adoptive sister whom the whole family has rallied to support. Still, rumors persist in financial circles which could still do damage to the Group as a whole.

Hélène threw down the paper with an exclamation. Rumors, always rumors. Rumors had dogged her own life with Georges, though there was nothing much for people to talk about. Ostensibly he had always been loyal to Lady Elizabeth, surrounded by her and his family on important occasions; pictured in the press at receptions, dinners, receiving the President of France at the Château de Tourville or important ministers and men of affairs in the rue de Varenne.

As his private secretary and personal assistant she, Hélène, had wielded enormous power; yet she was always self-effacing, seldom seen in public, content, as long as her health enabled her, to control his schedule, his routine, his public and private life from behind closed doors. Now she knew it was also rumored that it was her influence that had made Georges disinherit Zac; but she was the very last person to know about Sandra's inheritance. She had had to read it in the newspaper! The humiliation of this, coming so soon after the death of Georges, had worsened her health and the doctors had sent her immediately to the country and told her to stay there.

Now, still breathing badly, dependent on medication, she eked out her days, not short of money, but certainly not tranquil . . . a lonely, unwanted woman, completely shorn of her formidable power, whom not even Sandra wished to see.

Hélène sighed deeply and, not for the first time, tears stole down her cheeks.

If only Sandra knew.

Zac Desmond stood at the window of his office which overlooked the avenue de l'Opéra. Below him the Paris traffic plied busily between the Louvre, the bridges leading to the left bank of the Seine, and Garnier's flamboyant, extravagant monument to the Second Empire: the largest theater in the world. Zac's eyes moved restlessly, his finger playing with the carnation in his buttonhole which his valet renewed daily from a florist in the rue du Bac.

Behind Zac hovered Paul Vincent, looking a little anxiously at the man who, for so many years, he had assiduously cultivated and flattered in the expectation that one day he would be his employer.

No one was more shocked, or more hurt, than he by the contents of his late master's will. It seemed to undermine years of trust. No nose was more put out of joint and, ever since, he had endeavored with some desperation to cultivate Sandra while keeping a foot firmly in the camp of Zac.

For a man who was the same age as the late Georges Desmond at the time of his death such mental dexterity was not easy. Nervously he wiped his brow as Zac turned to gaze at him, eyebrows deeply furrowed.

"Then you must *ingratiate* yourself into the confidence of Mademoiselle, Paul. It is necessary to know *exactly* what is going on."

"Mademoiselle does not trust me." Paul Vincent tucked his handkerchief into the top left-hand pocket of his coat. "I tell her I am a friend but she does not believe me."

"Of course she won't believe you! I don't expect her to believe you. But, at least as long as you have an office there, you must get more information; bribe the staff, do anything you like. It is your duty to me as the lawful heir to my father."

"Mademoiselle has a filing cabinet in her office to which only she personally has the key."

"Then find a locksmith to make you another. It should not be beyond your capabilities. Go in there at night when the place is empty. Do anything, but find out *exactly* what she is up to. I must know everything and right now, because she doesn't trust me either, I know nothing."

Paul Vincent was a man of advancing years, not in the best of health and certainly not a thief. For so many years, as the trusted right hand of Georges Desmond, subterfuge had not been necessary. The idea of taking documents from anyone's private files appalled him.

He was everyone's idea of the perfect servant: a man of probity who respected his superiors, and exceeded himself in carrying out their orders with efficiency and docility.

But he was old-fashioned. Sandra even found him rather sly, and it was inevitable they would not get on.

"I want to know her exact position about aeronautics," Zac continued abruptly. "What is going on in negotiations with the Gulf States, what she intends to do about the supermarkets, the newspaper chain. I must have all this information because it won't be very long before I am where she is now." He paused. "Above all, I must know, *immediately,* what she knows about the true position of the bank."

"I can tell you," Vincent said, wearily slumping into a chair uninvited. "Mademoiselle knows everything. It is uncanny how she knows. She is thorough and demanding and keeps the staff on their toes. I am quite sure she knows the true position about the bank . . . about your debt to Helvetes Réunis and Franco-Belges. I am quite sure she will be moving in on you before very long."

"Get out of here," Zac said, pointing brusquely to the door. "What my father meant by making *you* a member of the Council I do not know. I'm absolutely sure, the more I know now, that my father was senile, out of his mind. He should have been certified, put in a home. Now, go back to l'Étoile and don't you dare come here until you've got something positive to show me."

Humbly, with the air of a longtime servant, Paul Vincent made for the door and slipped thankfully into the vestibule where the small private bank that was Pons-Desmond carried out its affairs.

Sandra O'Neill Desmond was an early riser. Sometimes she cancelled the car that came regularly for her at eight-fifteen each morning and walked along the rue Castiglione and the rue de Rivoli to the place de la Concorde, which she crossed to stroll at a brisk pace through the trees lining the Champs Élysées.

On this particular morning in late October she decided to walk to the office because it was fine, though chilly, and she was sadly short of exercise. For a woman who used to play tennis and swim regularly she knew she now did not exercise enough. Most weekends she went to Tourville, where she swam and rode; but, if there was time, on an autumnal morning a walk was pleasant and she strode up the Champs Élysées kicking underfoot the shiny horse chestnuts that fell from the trees.

Paris in the early morning was beautiful and she realized one missed a lot by seeing it merely through the windows of the car. She crossed the Rond Point, past the avenue Montaigne where she had yet to visit the Maison de Couture run by Belle and Tara, but largely financed by Desmond money. She was leaving that prickly, but rather small thorn, until a later date. There were much more urgent things to consider, and decisive action to take to divert disaster to the Group.

The Paris street sweepers in their green overalls with their curious plastic brooms were busy sweeping the gutters around the Étoile when, at just past seven, she let herself in through a side entrance and, avoiding the elevator, walked up the flight of stairs to her office. The stairs were thickly carpeted and it was not until she approached her door that she realized it was open.

Thinking that a cleaner was there, she didn't hesitate, but walked straight in to find Paul Vincent and a young man busy with some keys, both bending by the side of her mahogany private filing cabinet.

For a moment neither of them saw her and she paused abruptly on the threshold, breathing hard.

Then she said, in a quiet, controlled voice that surprised even herself, "Couldn't you sleep, Monsieur Vincent? Is there something I can do to help you?"

The young man bending by the side dropped his large bunch of keys on the floor and Paul Vincent swayed, clutching his heart as if in the grip of a seizure.

Momentarily alarmed, Sandra went up to him and took his arm as, slowly, he turned to gaze at her with horror.

"Mademoiselle . . ." he whispered, gasping for breath.

"Monsieur Vincent," Sandra said pleasantly, removing her fawn mohair coat and tossing it over the back of a nearby chair. "And Monsieur?" She looked interrogatively at the younger man stopping to retrieve his keys.

"Monsieur . . . this is Monsieur Becket . . ." Paul said hurriedly. "In charge of security, Mademoiselle."

"Security where?" Sandra continued in the same relaxed

tone. "I wasn't aware that we employed a security officer though perhaps we should. . . ." Frowning, she leaned over her desk and made a note on a pad as if to remind herself to look into the matter.

"Oh he's generally in charge of security . . . in the Desmond Group."

"Funny I never came across him before. I have made it my business to see the files of everyone employed here. Anyway what is he, or you, for that matter, doing in my personal office by my personal safe?"

Monsieur Becket gazed at her in alarm, switching the bunch of keys nervously from one hand to another, then looked at Paul Vincent who, a slightly better color, mopped his brow.

"Just checking, Mademoiselle."

"I didn't know there was anything to check, Monsieur Vincent," Sandra said with some asperity. "If Monsieur Becket could kindly leave us perhaps you can come up with a better explanation."

The young man looked thankfully at her and, at a nod from Vincent, went swiftly out of the door.

Sandra glanced at her watch. It was not yet seven-thirty. Outside her window in the place de L'Étoile the sun was beginning to illuminate the west side of the triumphal arch.

"I can only assume you were spying, or attempting to spy on me," Sandra said in a low voice, taking her place behind her desk after inviting the older man to sit down. "Was it on behalf of Monsieur Zac Desmond?"

"Oh no," Vincent said hurriedly.

"Because he has only to *ask* me anything he wishes to know."

"I think you are too secretive, Mademoiselle." Vincent's tone of voice was bolder, now that he had overcome his shock. "I have been associated with this company since the days of Monsieur Georges' mother, who ran it from his father's death in 1935 until after the War. I was an office boy starting work here at the age of fifteen. Over the years I became identified with the Desmond family, with the Group and its success. I feel it very much. It is in my blood. I have never married, Mademoiselle. I have no family and, personally, it is my life. I have felt very cut off, excluded, since you became President and Chief Executive. I feel I no longer have a place here. And yet the late Monsieur Desmond trusted me, in a way you do not."

Sandra bit her lip and turned her gaze away from scrutinizing Vincent's face, to studying the monument outside in the center of the oval.

It was indeed a very difficult situation and, though she did not like Vincent, she now felt sorry for him. In a way he was a nuisance, another thorn in her flesh. Yet he was getting old and, as he said, the firm of Desmond had been his life.

"That was the reason Monsieur Desmond did me the singular honor of including me on his Council, Mademoiselle, so that I could help and advise you. . . ."

Sandra turned to face him again, joining her hands before her on the desk.

"Monsieur Vincent," she said, "I wish I could believe you, but I find it very hard. I know the Desmond family does not like me and you, as you say, are closely allied with them. I have no doubt you were trying to break into my private files, perhaps on behalf of the family, perhaps for purposes of your own. I don't know; but . . ." Slowly she got up and came around her desk until she stood in front of him, arms folded. "I'm afraid I can no longer have you working in this building, and I would ask you to clear your office as soon as you can and let me have the keys. At the same time I realize you are an old and valued employee and friend of the Desmond family, and I do not wish to be too harsh on you. Perhaps it is time you retired to take a well-earned rest. I will make sure that you are amply compensated for your premature retirement and the arrangements for your pension will be honored.

"In the circumstances I think that is the best you can expect."

She turned her back on him and walked over to her file, making sure the lock had not been tampered with. It was a high-security device that she had had fitted on her own initiative and at her own expense. "Incidentally, who was that young man?" she said, turning around. "I sincerely hope he is *not* an employee here."

"He is a locksmith. He is blameless. I told him it was my cabinet and I had mislaid the key."

"Good day, Monsieur Vincent," Sandra said, holding out her hand.

But Paul Vincent, standing up, did not take it. Instead his expression was sullen and his eyes had a look of malevolence that she had not seen before. He had been a tiresome man, always nosing around, and she was glad of this pretext to get rid of him, often searching her mind for a way to do it.

"I should tell you, Mademoiselle O'Neill, that you will regret this." Vincent drew himself up to his full height, which made his eyes level with Sandra's. "Whatever you do to me, and whatever you say, I am a member of the Council appointed by Georges Desmond and, one day, you may need my help and come to regret your action now. I must warn you also, Mademoiselle, that if it comes to a vote of confidence I would not be on your side."

Sandra appeared to think for a moment, her gaze meeting his. "I assure you, Monsieur Vincent," she said slowly, "that I do not intend such an eventuality as you suggest will ever come to pass. I shall never need to have my responsibility in running the company called into question; you may be sure I shall take care I do not, and so I shall never, ever have need of your help. Good day to you now."

The relationship would never be an easy one, Sandra thought, watching Zac play with the flower in his buttonhole, a gesture which she had come to realize was a habit with him. It surprised her he didn't need more than one a day. In the months she had been at the Étoile Zac had only paid her two visits; one to welcome her on behalf of the family—and, by implication, wishing her a speedy return to the U.S.—and this meeting today to which she had summoned him.

Zac seemed to be telling her, like General de Gaulle during the War who maintained a lofty air toward the English, that he expected it to be only a short time until his return to power. What she did until then was of not much concern to him. He would not help her, but he would not hinder her. He inhaled the fragrance of his flower and studied his evenly pared, well-kept nails with a slight air of ennui.

"I assure you, Mademoiselle," he said, interrupting the account she had been giving of Paul Vincent's presence in her office, "it is of no interest to me at all, and certainly had nothing to do with me. I have all the information I want about the Group of which I consider you only a temporary custodian. I would never demean myself, and nor would any member of my family, by asking one of our servants to spy on you."

"Monsieur Vincent was hardly a servant."

"Oh he was." Zac raised his heavy-lidded eyes in surprise, his expression slightly sinister. "He used to be the office boy when my grandmother was in charge, after my grandfather's death. My family has always had a tiresome habit of advancing their servants who showed any merit, like Paul Vincent." He paused and stared at his fingertips again. "Or your mother, Madame O'Neill."

"I'm sure my mother never considered herself a servant," Sandra said heatedly.

"Well *we* did—" Zac's tone was deliberately insulting "—and we still do. It was not unknown in the old days for the master to sleep with his servants. I'm afraid that, in the case of Hélène O'Neill, that was exactly what my father did.

In time he came to depend on her, as he did on Vincent. It's a wonder he didn't make your mother a member of his Council! Thank heaven for that anyway."

Suddenly he looked at her sharply.

"I hope you have been kind to Vincent. He has lived all his life for us. . . ."

"I hope *you* will be kind to him too," Sandra replied, "seeing that I feel, still feel despite all you say, that he has lost his job in your service. . . ."

"I must say I resent . . ." Zac stood up, as if he were about to depart, but Sandra motioned for him to remain sitting.

"Please don't go," she said, "because there is something else, even more important, I wish to discuss with you."

She drew a heavy portfolio of documents from a drawer in her desk and placed them before him.

"I think you will find much of the material you were looking for is in here, an analysis of all the different aspects of a heavily diversified Group. I'm afraid some of it you will not find pleasant reading, but I have had every figure, every comment, verified by outside specialists." She inclined her head toward the file.

"I am sorry about this, I really am. None of it gives me any pleasure at all."

"I find that hard to believe," Zac said stiffly, not attempting to recover the papers from her desk. "I think you enjoy every minute of this, Miss O'Neill."

"I must remind you my name is now 'Desmond,' " Sandra said softly. "By the wishes of *your* father."

"I will never call you Desmond." Zac stonily looked her straight in the eyes. "Not as long as I have breath in my body. For me you are O'Neill, the Irishwoman, the upstart who has no business here," he pointed at his father's desk, "or meddling in my affairs." His eyes turned to the papers on the table. "My father must have been senile when he left everything to you. Senile, only we didn't know it."

"On the contrary." Sandra's voice shook slightly but with exhaustion rather than fear. "I think he knew exactly what he was doing, Zac. I have been here several months and I would never have believed a business could be in such a mess and yet continue to trade. There may even be some fraud involved if we go on as we have because a business, knowing it has insufficient assets to meet its debts, should declare that fact."

"We are far from bankrupt. Our assets . . ." Zac paused as if searching for the right words. "Our assets are certainly sufficient if not substantial."

"Our assets as a *group* may, just, exceed our liabilities," Sandra said with heavy emphasis on the words. " 'Just'; but, taken as a whole, we are broke. If it were not for electronics and aeronautics I feel we should be. The components business in the U.S. is booming thanks to the United States space program. But we shouldn't be using these profits to support the Banque Pons-Desmond, Aeronautics Desmond or the Bardot supermarkets in France. The *Gazette de l'Est* is viable and so are all our publishing activities, but what they contribute is a tiny portion compared to what you lose . . ."

"I lose . . ." Zac, who had remained standing as if on the point of departure, sat down heavily.

"I shall hold you personally responsible if the Banque has any more losses. . . ." Sandra paused and, leaning over the desk, picked up the dossier and appeared to weigh it in her hand. "I would obviously be loath to bring charges of fraud against you, as your father did not, Zac." She eyed him sternly. "Your father was aware, must have been, that you were fiddling the books, turning losses into spurious profits, lining your pocket and stealing . . ."

"Stealing! I protest!" Zac leapt up and struck the desk with the full force of his clenched fist.

"Stealing all the furniture from Tourville and this office. *My* home, and my office," Sandra said with heavy emphasis.

"The twin of that *fauteuil* you were just sitting on I believe is now in your house in rue de Varenne. That *armoir* in the corner has—"

"These were gifts while my father was alive," Zac said quickly.

"There I beg to differ." Sandra studied the top of the desk. "I have made inquiries and I am told that as soon as your father's will was read furniture removal men appeared here and at Tourville and took away most of the most valuable antiques. With difficulty you were persuaded to leave your father's desk." Sandra allowed her finger to run slowly along it.

"But it was all mine, mine!" Zac shouted, pointing a finger at his chest. "My father had no right to make you his heir. Can't you understand? No right . . . no right. . . ." Zac's voice began to falter, and Sandra's natural emotions of anger and indignation at so much deception and deceit were, as a woman, overcome by her pity for him as a human being.

Maybe his father had no right to do what he did without warning Zac; but that he had to do something was obvious. In every sphere she had looked into she found evidence of gross mismanagement which did, indeed, amount to fraud on a very large scale. Moreover the size of Zac's fortune was obvious judging by the scale on which he lived and entertained.

Sandra slowly got up from the desk and, coming around, leaned against it regarding him gravely. She wore a soft wool polo-necked dress by Yves Saint-Laurent, a heavy gold chain around her throat. Around her waist was a red leather belt and on her feet low-heeled red calf shoes. A red handbag lay against her desk. She looked very soft, very feminine, very chic; but only her appearance conformed to this stereotype. Inside she felt as hard as steel, as ruthless as any man and determined to carry out the task to which she had been called, and justify the faith of Georges Desmond in the girl he had made motherless.

"Zac," she said in a deceptively calm voice. "We, *you,* have been fortunate in that the Banque Franco-Belges, to which you are heavily in debt, has come to your rescue. One of the first people who ever came to see me was Philippe de Lassale to tell me of the predicament the Desmond Bank was in. He agreed to wait for some time because I promised to secure the loan then made to you from our emergency fund. I also hoped that *you* would wish to take me into your confidence, discuss everything with me. . . ."

"Hardly likely," Zac said with a sneer. "A woman, totally inexperienced . . ."

"As a matter of fact," she said gently, "this is something in which I *am* very experienced: analysis of marketing forces, wise and unwise investments, as you would have discovered if you'd tried to find anything out about me. The truth, that is. A woman I might be, but still not an idiot when it comes to money.

"As you know, the Banque Franco-Belges, as part of the large Heurtey Corporation, has tremendous reserves. They are willing to write off your bank's debt by securing a major share of the capital; but still leaving us with a very substantial share. It is even agreed that you will continue to be President of the Banque Pons-Desmond, but reporting to de Lassale who must personally sanction *all* loans. You will also retain your premises in the avenue de l'Opéra and will continue to trade as though nothing had happened so that confidence in the Bank will not be shaken. I, personally, consider it a very generous, magnanimous act which, I understand, is partly because of the respect Monsieur de Lassale feels toward your late father."

Zac, who had received the news with an air of incomprehension, started to splutter.

"But it's monstrous! Taken over? Part of the Heurtey Group which also controls Tellier Champagne? Soon they will get their hands on Desmond."

"Unlikely," Sandra said with a trace of sarcasm, "as *I* shall remain in charge there."

"I still think the idea is preposterous," Zac said, vainly spreading his hands as if in appeal. "How can *I* look Philippe in the eye with all this . . . ? God, I have known the man all my life."

"Then that should be a help to you," Sandra murmured, neatly putting the papers together. "You once told me the 'old boy' network was important. Monsieur de Lassale and I also get on well. We understand each other. When I discovered the extent of our debt to his bank, to say nothing of others who had foolishly underwritten your loss-making loans, I was aghast. And it is the result of several weeks of talks that we came up with this merger instead of the ignominy of liquidation. The Banque Pons-Desmond goes bust . . . very nice."

"Not very nice for *you,*" Zac spat at her.

"Nor *you,*" she spat back, riled, despite herself, by his attitude, his complete absence of gratitude for what she and de Lassale had achieved between them. "Don't worry, I wouldn't have taken the blame, nor would I have allowed your father to. I would have shown up quite clearly who had fiddled the books; who had sanctioned gigantic loans to companies without sufficient collateral . . . all on the 'old boy' basis, eh Zac? A favor for you, a favor for me. Well"—Sandra threw up her hand, a finger pointing toward the ceiling—"all that goes. For good. From now on I must sanction every single item of expenditure in every part of the group we retain. . . ."

"Retain . . ." Zac began to blink at her as though someone had just shone a very bright light in his face. Someone else, taking pity on him, might have thought him pathetic.

"Oh yes . . . but we shan't retain much." Sandra returned to her chair and, sitting down, withdrew a sheaf of papers from a drawer.

"We are going to sell the supermarkets, the chain of garages, all the estate agencies . . ." She put on a pair of glasses and stared at the papers she was flicking through. "God knows why we bought *them*. Ah—" her finger lingered on some lines heavily underscored—"through your friendship with Monsieur Lacoste . . . Victor Lacoste with whom you were at school."

"I thought it would be very profitable . . ."

"Well it isn't, and it won't be. You know nothing about real estate and nor I see," she glanced at the papers again then looked at him over the top of her glasses, "does Monsieur Lacoste, who I believe spends most of his time on the golf course. Anyway they're going to a group who does know something about the business and will even pay us quite handsomely for them. It's called liquidating our assets, by the way."

The telephone rang and Sandra answered it, still looking at him but speaking rapidly into the mouthpiece and making some notes on the pad in front of her. Then she replaced the receiver and folded her hands neatly in front of her, still looking at Zac.

"I'll be honest with you, Zac. You've been lucky. Lucky in your father and lucky in me. You may not be so lucky again. Philippe de Lassale is lunching here tomorrow and I would like you to join us. You know . . ." Sitting back, she continued her unnerving examination of him as though he were some biological specimen she was examining under a microscope. "It is hard to believe it but I think you really *are* a capable man. You have a good reputation among people who have not suffered as a result of your poor judgment. I have made a lot of careful inquiries about you." She got up and slowly came over to him again, her gaze never faltering. "*I* believe that if you could just overcome this tendency of yours to do things that are, how shall I put it? not quite above board, you could be really successful. That is my advice to you now and, if you are ever doubtful about anything, consult me, or de Lassale, or Antoin Dericourt of Aeronautics, both of whom I am putting on the Board of the Group. And I am keeping you, Zac . . ."

"You couldn't get rid of me," Zac snarled. "Nor would you dare."

"Oh yes I could and I would," Sandra snarled back, having decided that Zac must be dealt with without kid gloves. "I would summon the entire Board and the precious Council your father set up and show them exactly what you've been up to, chapter and verse: the tricks, the fiddles at their expense. . . ." She picked up the huge dossier and flicked through it with her fingers before tossing it contemptuously into the drawer. "And I would advise them to kick you out. I would *demand* they kick you out. I think even your mother would vote against you if she knew exactly what you were like. Now you must excuse me." She returned to her seat and picked up the phone, eyeing him warily as he slowly rose to his feet. "I'll see you here tomorrow, for lunch. Please be on time. Oh, and would you be kind enough to have the office furniture returned? Or shall I send round for it?"

As Zac turned his back on her she uttered the words "Good day" but, because of the heavy muttering that went on under his breath, she was not sure that he had heard her.

Henri Piper looked as though he had been in the Ritz bar for some time when Sandra, with a muttered apology, slid into the seat beside him.

"Sorry," she said, glancing at her watch. "I truly am. An hour late."

"It's all right, your secretary called me. Trouble with Zac, I understood?"

He signaled to the barman, who drew an open bottle of Piper champagne from a silver bucket and filled a flute for Sandra, who nodded her thanks.

"Well, Zac was there, and very angry. I had to remind him of the actual state of his business. I'll tell you about it later, but he's not a bit happy about it. Before that—" she sipped her champagne thoughtfully, gazing at Henri who, as family, she still did not quite know how much she could really trust—"I had to sack Vincent."

"Paul Vincent?" Henri exclaimed in some astonishment. "But he is almost part of the family. . . ."

"So much so he thought he could pry into my affairs." Then rapidly she gave Henri a résumé of the events of the last few days while he listened gravely, nodding from time to time.

"You see, Henri," she concluded, "I don't know how much I can trust anybody . . . even you."

"Even me?" Henri looked shocked and raised his glass toward the barman for a refill. "You can't trust *me?"*

"I don't know. When I needed you you couldn't come."

"I tell you it was very tough with the family. Even my wife was against me. I had to let things cool, my dear; but you know," cautiously Henri let his hand steal over hers, "I am *very* fond of you. You are to me like a . . ." He seemed to be groping for the right words and Sandra, very conscious of that hand, teasingly supplied it for him:

"Niece?"

"That's exactly the word I'm looking for." Henri appeared grateful. "We are not related but we, Sophie and I, have always been very fond of you and Bob; felt very protective toward you both."

"But Sophie now sides with the family."

"Well—" Henri shrugged—"she *is* more closely related to them than I am. Don't forget she is Georges' sister. Blood is stronger than water; always was. But no, my dear—" his hand pressed hers then he gently removed it—"I am on your side. You can trust me."

"I have to," Sandra said bitterly. "I need a friend."

"But Vincent . . ." Henri shook his head. "Was it wise? He is very powerful. He knows all their secrets."

"Well he doesn't know mine and he won't. I don't find him powerful but rather pathetic and Zac referred to him as a servant . . ."

"That *is* exactly Zac." Henri grimaced in disgust. "He is such a snob . . ."

"Also Hélène . . . my mother. He said she was a servant too, who slept with the boss . . . kind of *droit de seigneur* if I understood it correctly."

"Typical." Henri continued to shake his head. Then, his eyes suddenly wary and alert, he felt in his pocket and produced a rather crumpled envelope. "That reminds me," he said, extracting a sheet from the envelope, "I have had a note from your mother. She wishes to see you. Poor woman, I feel sorry for her."

"You're much too kind." Sandra rather nervously sipped her champagne. "Poor thing. If she knew that Zac had called her a servant . . ." She appeared even slightly amused by the idea so that Henri said rather reprovingly:

"Are you ashamed of the origins of your mother?"

"Of course not!"

"They think you are and that that's why you don't see her."

"You know that's not true!" Sandra's face, not so tanned now after months away from the California sun, turned slightly pink.

"I know why you don't see her; but maybe she will start talking to the Press too, if they find her."

"Oh I don't think so." Sandra smiled grimly. "I have gone quite thoroughly into my mother's affairs and Georges has left her very well off. She has a large flat in the rue de Seine which is closed and a substantial dwelling in Champagne where I believe she lives now."

"Don't you think you should see her? At least make the gesture?" Henri put down his glass and started to consult the letter.

"Why should I?" Sandra gazed at him defiantly. "Do you

know she has not been in touch with me for at least two years? Not even Bob has heard from her except at Christmas."

"I think she is too frightened to see you now. She thinks you have rejected her and because you have become so important . . ."

"Why? How do you know all this?" Sandra's tone was sharp.

Henri laid the letter between them on the table. "Read it."

Sandra took her reading glasses from her bag and adjusted them on her nose. Henri hadn't seen her wearing glasses and thought she looked attractive, but more businesslike, especially in her severely cut navy blue suit with a crisp white shirt.

"I didn't know you wore glasses," he murmured.

"You have never seen me working. I've worn them since I was at college." Sandra glanced at him and began to read the letter aloud:

My dear Monsieur Piper,

I hope you will not mind me getting in touch with you but there are so few people I can approach because of the difficult position in which I am now placed. It was very kind of you to write on Georges' death, one of the very few to do so, and I can't tell you how much I appreciated the gesture.

However, my dear Monsieur Piper, I have been far from well and I am afraid I did not feel strong enough at the time to answer it. You must think that is very rude of me and, perhaps, it is; but the terrible shock I suffered at Georges' death was compounded by the treatment I subsequently received.

Monsieur Zac Desmond asked me to leave the offices immediately, scarcely leaving me time to take away my things, and of course I was not invited to the funeral. Then I had the additional shock of hearing from the newspaper that Sandra had been appointed Georges' heir! Believe me, Monsieur Piper, I had no idea of this.

It was as much a surprise to me as I imagine it was to everyone else, or perhaps you knew about it. Did she?

Since then my health has rapidly deteriorated. My chest was never strong. I have had to leave Paris and live in this house which was so dear to me and Georges. I am surrounded by the vines he loved so much because believe me, dear Monsieur Piper, his vines and champagne were Georges' real loves, not his wife or his mistress. . . .

"Oh I can't read any more of this," Sandra said, angrily removing her glasses and throwing the letter on the table. "It is far too personal."

"I'm sorry." Henri got up and, retrieving the letter, studied it for a few moments. "Maybe I should have edited it for you. Here, let me read what she says at the end." Quickly he turned over a few pages and began to read aloud:

There is much about the past I regret, dear Monsieur Piper, believe me; but I do not regret my love for Georges Desmond or the years I gave him. He was not a happy man when I met him—I do not care to speculate why, though I think I know—and I believe that I gave him all the happiness of which I was capable. To this end I neglected Bob and Sandra. I know it and I am deeply ashamed of it. Now that I am alone I know what it is like to have forfeited the love of my children.

Do you think there is any way in which you could ask Sandra if she could forgive me, and if she could bring herself to come and see me . . .

Henri's voice trailed off and he looked anxiously at the woman who was staring at him with such intensity, unsmiling, her hands clenched in her lap.

"No!" Sandra said at last, thumping the table in front of her. "No. I can't bear to hear any more."

7

The sound of machinery, not very far away, never stopped: the whirring of drills, the whine of the car ramp, the roaring of engines being tested to their limits. Tara had long ago got used to the smells associated with the garage, but the noise she had never grown accustomed to. When the engines were going at full throttle it was deafening and the small attic room shook.

Still the noise drowned the sounds of their lovemaking. There was never any worry about that.

Émile Livio lay on his side, his mouth slightly open emitting a slight snore that Tara could only hear because she was near him. Beneath them yet another engine was revving up until it seemed that the screaming blast would tear off the roof. These were not ordinary cars that Livio and his men dealt with but racing machines; their fine precision-built engines being honed and tuned to perfection. The huge cars rattling through the narrow streets of Paris or carried on the backs of car transporters caused some sensation but Livio, who had driven in Formula Two races, had a reputation as a mechanic and many aspiring racing drivers had him check out their machines before they began that painful, arduous and often fatal climb to the top of Formula One.

Livio—he was always called by his surname Livio, even by Tara—had been born in Turin. His Italian father had been killed in the War and his French mother had brought her baby home to her parents when it was all over. They were not, it is true, very pleased to see her. It was hard enough for Parisians to exist in those years immediately after the War without an errant, unmarried daughter and her unwanted baby.

Livio had been an attractive, dark-haired urchin not dissimilar to thousands of his counterparts who littered the streets of the large Italian cities in the years after the War. He had very little schooling but he showed an interest in machinery and a talent for mechanics when he was quite young and he did have ambition. He had ambition enough to get himself away from the back streets of Paris, the poverty and degradation that had made him into a petty thief and his mother into a prostitute.

As soon as he could, when he was scarcely into his teens, he apprenticed himself to a garage owner and started the laborious climb from the very bottom to the very top.

But Livio was now thirty-nine and it was doubtful if he would ever make the top. He blamed his lack of success on money. He had the skills, he was a superb mechanic and a skillful driver, but he had never found anyone with money who had the same faith in him that he had and who would back him to the top. So he spent his time in the pits as the fabled cars driven by the racing heroes that he would like to have been went off with the laurels, the money prizes . . . and the women.

Tara lay on her back smoking, her eyes on the grimy skylight in the ceiling, and thought about Livio: how they had met. Even then he had deceived her into thinking that he was something he wasn't—a successful Formula-One driver. He certainly looked the part in his white suit and cream tie, his oily, jet black hair combed back from his forehead, a cigarette in his hand. She met him at a party given by Tim, who knew all kinds of people, particularly those who enjoyed the fast, dangerous sports like flying, polo, skiing and all forms of racing both on water and on land.

Tara remembered seeing Livio looking at her and she had understood immediately that it was not the casual sort of glance that one gives a pretty woman: there was something more intense, more passionate in it even then. His black eyes burned into hers as he edged slowly across the room toward her until, finally, he stood at her side just as Tim happened along to introduce them. Knowing Livio as she came to know him afterward Tara realized that the whole thing had been very carefully planned. The introduction that coincided with Tim being there too and Zac right at the other side of the room where he, in his turn, was talking to a pretty woman. That kind of thing went on all the time.

Whatever Livio was or was not he was a man practiced in the arts of seduction. He had such a quality of crude animality that even Tara, who had known a few men in her time, was knocked over by it even when she saw that he was not what he at first appeared to be, had briefly pretended to be, until he had her where he wanted her.

She, who was married to a Desmond, a champagne producer and banker, a man who had expected to inherit a huge empire, was completely overwhelmed by someone who lived by looking after other people's cars, following in the season the circuits from Monza, to Brands Hatch and Le Mans—but from the pits. He was taken on as casual labor during the racing season because he was such an expert mechanic. Yet in his field he was supreme and the great firms—Masarati, Renault, Ford, Alfa Romeo—valued his services.

One day Livio would like to set up in a really large well-equipped garage, away from the mean streets of Paris, where wealthy young Formula-Two, -Three and even -Four aspirants would come for his advice and, perhaps, ask him to build their cars. He was nearly forty and he was still ambitious. He was also bitter; and bitterness, anger and envy make admirable spurs.

Livio always looked as though he needed a shave and his

lean torso was covered with fine black hair. He was the most sensual man, the most accomplished lover Tara had ever had, and she had had quite a number. After the unsatisfactory nature of Zac's caresses Livio had been a revelation not only in his technique but in his tenderness, his thought, his concern. Tara wasn't used to this. She was used to rather cruel, violent men who gave little thought to her. Some women seem to attract nothing but sadists—perhaps they need them—and Tara was indeed one of these.

Only later did she realize that there was a reason for Livio's gentleness: when he began to ask her for money.

She could only give him a little, but what she had she gave him. Slowly she began to understand what kind of a man she had become entangled with, but by that time it was too late. She was heavily and deeply involved. She was obsessed.

Livio gave a sudden loud snore, an indication that he was about to wake up, and jerked his head up from the pillow, glancing at his watch as he did.

"What time is it?"

"Nearly three, my darling." Tara leaned over him and began to caress his silky hair which always smelled slightly of car grease. She couldn't tell whether it really did or whether it was the room. Car grease and Livio were always inseparable combinations. Sometimes when Zac was away they went for a meal in one of the nearby bistros where there would be no danger of Madame Desmond, wife of one of the most powerful businessmen in France, being recognized. And only then, when they were well away from the attic over the garage, did she realize that Livio didn't smell at all except of soap and the expensive after-shave she gave him along with many other presents: ties, belts, shoes once, even a ring, but he never wore it.

Livio, satisfied about the time, reached for her and drew her down upon him again. She sat astride his thighs and gently rose up and down to his rhythm. His long hand reached up and caressed her plump breasts, those long elongated nipples which, with a little more effort, he was able to take into his mouth until, sucking and riding together, they reached almost simultaneously the ecstasy of a mutual climax; in its intensity and brevity it was like a little liqueur after the main course which had been much longer, noisier and more profound.

Tara lay across his body and listened to the rapid beating of his heart. His chest was like a silk pillow and the smell of sweat compounded with the grease and the bodily odors that they had released seemed to linger in her nostrils long after she had left him.

Often she would wonder if Zac could smell it too; but by that time she had had a long bath and had covered herself with her own exclusive fragrances—especially made for her by Monsieur Guerlain.

There were two sides to Tara Desmond: on one side she was a fastidious woman, the daughter of the Marchese Falconetti whose family was older than the Medici whom they regarded as *parvenus.* In its time it, too, had produced princes and cardinals of the church, a couple of popes. It had been likewise rich and powerful but, perhaps, not as scandalous as the Medici. In time, like the Medici, the Falconetti had also gone into a decline, their greatness faded, and all that remained when the War started were a few tumbledown country houses, a decaying once-splendid palazzo in Rome near the Spanish Steps, and millions of lire in debts.

But in Italy after the War everyone had debts. The Falconetti were not unusual and they hung on to their villas, their ancestral home with its fading vestiges of the Baroque and Rococo—but anything of real value long since sold or put into pawn. Above all, they hung onto their sense of family pride. They were aristocrats. They were snobs; but they were very very poor.

Suddenly there was the screech of an engine followed by a loud roar that ended in what sounded like an explosion.

After that there was dead silence, one of the few moments of silence Tara ever remembered hearing in that noisy place.

"Merde!" Livio said, roughly pushing her off him and leaping out of bed. He bounded across the room, climbed into his underpants and jeans and, pulling his tee shirt over his head, opened the door, leaving it ajar.

Tara lay for a few moments listening to the angry babble of voices that came from below. This scene was not unusual either. The prestigious world of motor racing seemed almost as full of alarms and excursions as the business world occupied by her husband and, before him, his father. Only what went on there was all done with a lot less noise and mess but, probably, with a great deal more duplicity if not downright skulduggery.

Tara sighed, smoothed down the ruffled sheets and reluctantly got out of bed. These hours with Livio were like a drug to her, a necessary drug that was brought on by a psycho-medical problem: a serious, almost incessant need of sex and the total inability of her husband, or anyone else, to satisfy it.

After a session with Livio she was always in a better mood for the rest of the day.

Now she hummed a tune to herself as she began to dress, getting into her flimsy underthings: her little wisps of panties, brassière and girdle, her nylon tights, all of which inevitably in her eagerness to join him in bed, found themselves draped at various angles around pieces of the cheap ugly furniture in Livio's room.

Suddenly the babble below changed into the whine of the ramp, the incipient roar of machinery once more, and Livio appeared through the still open door rubbing his hands on a greasy rag.

"Fools," he said. "Idiots." He went to the basin and began roughly to scrub his hands. "It's always the same when I leave them too long." He glanced at her over his shoulder. "I think they do it on purpose."

"To separate us you mean?" Tara laughingly tightened a skirt belt, gazing at herself in the cracked mirror on the outside of his rickety wardrobe.

"Maybe they think we're having too much fun?"

"We are." Tara turned and ran a finger down his bare arm, causing it to ripple with her delicate touch. Then she put her arms around him and leaned her cheek against his, relishing the harsh, bristly texture of his skin.

"Not again, chérie, *please,"* he said, turning to dry his hands. "Enough is enough for today."

"Enough isn't enough," Tara said petulantly. "Once or twice a week is *never* enough for me. I wonder if it is for you."

"With you once or twice a week lasts a week," Livio said with a laugh. "Talking of 'enough,' chérie, could you lend me a few thousand francs?"

"A *few* thousand francs!" Tara exclaimed, sitting on the bed to fasten the straps of her elegant high-heeled shoes. "Where do you think *I* can get a few thousand francs from?"

"I should imagine you have a trivial sum like that in your bag." Livio sat next to her, running his hand up her thigh as she bent her leg. "I would really appreciate it."

Tara reached for her purse and began to count the notes in her wallet. She extracted all she had and placed them in his hands.

"Five hundred," she said. "It's all I have."

"Nonsense."

She opened the bag for him, revealing its contents, making him peer inside. "You can see for yourself. You know, Livio, Zac is becoming very suspicious of me. He wants to know where all the money goes."

"I bet," Livio said with a sneer, folding the notes and tucking them in his hip pocket. "What is a few thousand francs to a man like Zac Desmond? He's the head of a bank."

"You don't understand," Tara said, standing up and straightening her skirt in the long mirror, her critical, trained model's eyes on the swing of the pleats as she made a swift revolution on her toes. "Zac is in a very bad way at the moment. He is absolutely obsessed with rage against this Irish girl who is looking into his books with great care. She has found a number of irregularities. Zac is like a cat on hot bricks. Worse than usual . . ." Tara grimaced and started edging her lips with carmine, looking critically but admiringly at herself in her small compact mirror.

Livio watched her, a sardonic smile on his thin lips. Dark haired, with olive skin, Tara had the classical good looks both of an Italian aristocrat and the international model she had been before her marriage. She was an exceptionally beautiful woman, but she was thirty-three and those tiny tell-tale lines were beginning to appear at the sides of her eyes, along by her mouth. He noticed that over the years he had known her she applied more and more makeup; that her waist was thickening and her breasts growing more pendulous. The punishment for beautiful women was that their beauty soon, all too soon, faded. And when they were rich as well—and they usually were—it was very hard to endure. Tara was no more philosophical than the rest. By the time she was forty she would be finished. But he would be well finished with her by then too. He was discerning about women but not possessive and Tara was not the only one in his life by any means.

Livio had once been married and he had two children whom he never saw. He had been so scarred by the poverty of his childhood, the infidelities of his mother, that he was a man who had scarcely been touched by the spiritual gifts and graces of love. He hadn't loved his mother or his wife or children, and he had scarcely ever loved any of his girlfriends except in the carnal way of desiring them and the joy that came from possession.

Tara was still a beautiful woman, but he had a number of

beautiful women in his life and they all made love as well as she, some even better. Livio had no particular yardstick for measuring the accomplishments of the women he took to bed but he did like dexterity, variety and a certain inventiveness although no one could ever teach him anything he hadn't known or done before. It was much, much too late for that now.

No, his main interest, naked and unashamed—in both senses of the word—in Tara Desmond when he had first started the affair was that she would set him up in the business he'd dreamed of all his life. He'd assumed, then, that as the daughter-in-law of Georges Desmond the sums she had at her command were limitless.

But they were not. Were not and never had been. He found pretty soon that she had access to hardly any money at all and all he could get from her were a few thousand francs here, a thousand francs there—peanuts for a man of his tastes: drinking, gambling, racing and sex. Sometimes he paid for his sex although he never needed to, but he got a kick out of it: it was like sleeping with his mother and he treated the whores badly, paying them back for what she had been, what she had done to him all those years ago.

Tara finished making up her face, fluttered her eyelashes to make sure that her mascara was even and blotted her carmine lips. Then she smiled, showing her white even teeth but, also, the tell-tale crinkles by the side of her eyes.

"You must be careful of the makeup, Tara," he told her, enjoying the cruelty for its own sake. "It's beginning to show."

Immediately Tara stopped smiling, a look of fear clouding her eyes. She stepped back and glanced at her face again in the mirror above the washbasin, touching it with her hands.

"Cruel," she said. "Cruel, but then," she turned to him, all the dejection and misery of unrequited love showing on those mobile Renaissance features, "you never loved me, Livio, did you? All you wanted was my money."

"Money I never got," Livio said, angrily lighting a cigarette, extinguishing the match and tossing it into a tin wastepaper bin by the side of the bed.

"You've had *thousands* of francs from me . . . Millions maybe if you added them all together. . . ."

"Yes but not MONEY." Livio thumped the walls with his fist, eyes raking the ceiling as though he were in agony. "Not real, solid money. You don't know do you, Tara Desmond, with your airs and graces, your town house on the Left Bank, your château with its hundreds of rooms, what not having *real* money means. If I had money I wouldn't be here. I'd have the sort of place that you would like and the sort of life that you would like to lead. I might even have married you; but this—" He struck the walls again hard as though, if it were in his power, he would push them down as Samson destroyed the pillars of the Temple.

Yet she loved him. She would have done anything for him. She would have begged, stolen, probably prostituted herself, done everything except leave Zac. She needed the sort of things he had been able to give her, the sort of life the Desmonds lived and, even before them, the Falconetti. Even though she hated her husband, being married to him meant too much to her, was too important. She would never leave Zac, never; certainly not for someone with the lifestyle of Émile Livio. When she'd first met him three years before she had believed in his dreams; she urged him that it was not too late to make Formula Two or even One and that, one day, he would be on the race track and she would be there in the stands cheering him on, in the pits to welcome him with kisses and champagne.

But no . . . she knew now that as much as she loved him, wanted and desired him, Émile Livio would never make it to the big time. His importance to her was as an exciting sexual companion, who reminded her that she was a beautiful woman and rescued her from the boredom and fatigue of life with Zac Desmond.

But if she *had* had the money she would have given it to him, and if she could have she would have gotten it for him. She would have tried to buy his love and fidelity even though she knew such things could not be bought.

Looking at him now, thumping the wall, Tara saw a frustrated, desperate man and thought how unfair it was that Zac, who had nothing like the sexual powers of Livio, the ability to satisfy a woman, had everything while Livio had nothing.

"Zac is in the shit," she said, suddenly sitting on the bed. "If he's been doing something dishonest and Sandra finds out, she'll sack him."

"She can do that?" Livio looked at her with interest.

"Of course she can. She's the President of the whole Group. You don't realize just who this Sandra O'Neill is or what she can do."

"I didn't realize she had so much power over Zac," Livio said. "I thought he had the final power over her."

"That's what he thinks," Tara said, an edge to her voice. "*Theoretically* there is a Council that can deprive her of her power, but only if she does something really serious and injurious to the firm. If she finds out how dishonest he has been she can sack him just like that!" Tara clicked her fingers under Livio's nose and smiled.

"Really," Livio said after a moment's thought. "How very interesting." He turned and looked at her, clicking his fingers as she had. "Just like that eh?"

Tara always hated leaving by the garage but it was the only way to go. Self-consciously she opened the door that led from Livio's attic and, silently, unsmilingly, she walked past the cars, the men working underneath the bodies, some with head and shoulders hidden by the upturned bonnet, some by the fuel tanks, aware that as she passed each, momentarily, stopped what he was doing and stared at her. She knew what they were thinking: tart, whore—fancy going with a man like Livio. What sort of lady did *that?*

It was only at times like this that she cared; that the enormity of her behavior, the possible ruin of the reputation of the Desmond family, meant something to her but thankfully, at last, she got to the other side and escaped through the open double doors into the narrow street walking the few paces to where she had left her own car. She jumped in and drove off, glancing at her face in the mirror as she did so, to reassure herself about her looks. She always looked and felt better after making love. But how long would it last? For how long could it continue?

As she edged into the traffic, unseen by her a car, which had been parked on the other side of the road, slid into position behind her. But she didn't notice it and, if she had, nothing untoward would have occurred to her. She was too busy thinking about Livio and the rapture they had shared together that afternoon.

When Tara got home after stopping on the way to make a few purchases Zac was already there pacing up and down, glancing alternately at his watch or the glass-encased ormolu clock on the mantelpiece.

"Where have you been?" he said as she came in, looking at her with astonishment.

"I've been minding my own business," Tara said, glancing at the clock. "It's not late. What on earth are *you* doing home at this hour?"

"Have you forgotten Belle is coming to dinner?"

"Of course I hadn't forgotten," Tara said, pretending to yawn. "Everything is ready. You had only to go into the kitchen and you would have discovered that."

"Oh I knew the *kitchen* was prepared," Zac said with heavy

sarcasm. "What I wondered about was whether *you* were. Your behavior is very strange lately, Tara. You're out such a lot. Where do you go? Whom do you see? What do you do? I must say I'm curious."

His anxiety now somewhat abated by her appearance, Zac sat down in pretended good humor, crossing his legs and lighting a cigar.

"I can't think why you're curious," Tara said in a bored voice. "You lead your life and I lead mine. If you must know I spent the day in the avenue Montaigne. I saw several clients including an American film star who is over here to do a film. Her name is . . ."

"I don't care what her name is," Zac said with irritation. "I do know that you're telling a lie. I passed by the avenue Montaigne and none of the staff had seen you all day . . ."

"Serves you right, then, for being so nosy, doesn't it!" Tara shouted at him, leaning forward, hands on her hips in a manner of which the eighteenth-century Marcheses di Falconetti would never have approved. "Curiosity killed the cat."

Then she gathered up her parcels and was about to flounce out of the room when her husband seized her roughly by the arm.

"You're beginning to get on my nerves," he said, shaking her roughly, "with your lies and evasions."

"And you're beginning to get on mine," she shouted back. "With your suspicion and your paranoia."

"Paranoia!" Zac's voice rose even higher. "You think I am paranoic? That I am not actually persecuted by the Irishwoman, but that I imagine it all. . . ." His grasp on her arm tightened. "Well let me tell you this, my dear. Let me tell you this." With his other hand he pointed to many of the priceless pieces of furniture that had recently been installed at the house in rue de Varenne.

"All this is going back! That creature wants every bit of it back. Do you hear? She is reclaiming *my* birthright. . . ."

"Well you pinched it in the first place," Tara said and then screamed as his nails dug further into her arm.

"But it's *mine!* Don't you realize it is all mine? That the House of Desmond, the Desmond Group and all that belongs to it, is *mine,* not hers. And do you know what has happened?" He abruptly released her arm and she hastily moved away from him rubbing it. "She has gone over my head. She has sold my bank to another, without even consulting me. I am no longer even master in the tiny bit of my late father's empire that was mine. She has sold the Desmond Bank! I am answerable to a man who is not fit to wipe my shoes—Philippe de Lassale. I . . ." Zac shook so much that Tara gazed at him with an air of pretended concern.

"I don't actually care *very* much," she said, "but if you carry on like this, you'll have a stroke or a heart attack and Sandra will have no opposition at all."

The very thought of this had a calming effect on Zac but, still perspiring freely, he slumped in the one chair likely to remain, a charming but fairly undistinguished *fauteuil* in gilt wood from the reign of Louis XV, a wedding present to him and Tara from his mother.

"To have to report to de Lassale though I am still President," he said almost to himself. "Imagine the insult, a calculated insult to wound and humiliate me. No!" Zac thumped the arm of the chair once more. "Maybe her object is to try and drive me out. Well I will not be driven. I am a member of the Group's Board and there I shall remain until I have kicked *her* out and become what I should rightly be: President of the entire Group. . . . As for you, my dear Tara," Zac's eyes, which were quite large, an attractive and rather surprising feature, narrowed to mere slits and he drew a document out of his inside pocket which he proceeded to open, carefully smoothing it on his lap as he appeared slowly and deliberately to study the contents. "As for *you,* my dear Tara . . . let us have a little of the truth at last. Here I have the name of a man, a garage mechanic, it says," he raised his eyes swiftly to glance at her before continuing in the same unpleasantly unctuous tones, "but I see he has driven in Formula *Two* racing cars." Zac looked up again. "Imagine, Formula Two. Quite good eh? Not quite thc top but you never could get quite the best, could you my dear . . . ?"

"I don't know what you're talking about." Tara ferreted agitatedly in her handbag for her cigarettes, but the high color on her usually matte cheeks gave her away immediately and Zac smiled to himself with satisfaction.

"I see I scored a bull's-eye, ma chérie. Émile Livio, is it not?" Zac pretended to scan the page before him again but, in reality, he knew the contents by heart. "Émile Livio born in Turin—Turin! Maybe that's where he got his mechanical genius from, who knows? Anyway born in that industrial northern city in 1944, the son of a soldier, previously a worker in the Fiat factory, and a Frenchwoman, Marie Guitton." Zac paused. "I see that his father and mother were not married, so Livio must be a courtesy surname. As a bastard he would bear his mother's name. Émile Guitton—not quite so romantic, don't you think?"

"Do shut up!" Tara lit her cigarette, tossing her lighter on the sofa beside her. "What are you trying to prove by these insults?"

"Shh shh," Zac said, putting out his hand as if to calm her. "Gently, ma chérie. I am just going into the antecedents of Monsieur Guitton, sorry, Livio, to see if he is suitable as a lover for my wife. . . ."

"That's a lie!" Tara cried, but the color on her face deepened and her bosom began to heave against the tight, white organdy blouse she wore with a red skirt, giving her the air of a gypsy. She favored bright, primary colors which suited her, both her complexion and her personality.

"Anyway Monsieur Guitton," Zac continued unperturbed, "returned here after the war—his father having either disappeared or been killed, I'm not sure which—with his mother whose family lived in the Batignolles district (not a very salubrious area, I think you will agree). There poor Mademoiselle Guitton was forced to make a living as a prostitute, and her son . . ."

"I will not listen to any more of this." Tara clutched her handbag as she tried to rise. But Zac was before her, clasping her wrist and holding her down. The expression on his face was so frightening—a compound of lust and hate—that she remained as if paralyzed until slowly she fell back, her head resting against the back of the sofa.

"You will have to listen to it!" Zac snarled. "Whore! Madame Desmond consorting with a garage mechanic, a petty thief, a womanizer—or did you think you were the only one? You, Madame Desmond, making love, I understand, in a sordid *atelier* over his works and, doubtless, the laughing stock of all the mechanics who work for him. . . ."

"Someone is *lying* about me to hurt you." Tara's wrist ached from the clasp of his hand and she struggled to get up. "Whoever tells you these things is telling you lies . . . now, *please.*"

Zac let her fall suddenly and, bearing down on her, flattening her against the sofa, began to tear frenziedly at her clothes, tossing aside her wispy undergarments until he was able to crudely insert himself between her legs, his trousers around his knees, his hands on her stomach, mounting her quickly as a ram mounts a goat, or a stallion a mare. The copulation was as brief as that of the animals and, when he had finished with her, he hit her savagely across the face several times and left her as violently as he had entered her, defiled and bleeding.

He then adjusted his clothes, picked up the papers he'd been reading from and made for the door just as someone tried to open it.

"What is it?" Belle said, stepping back in alarm as he hastily shut the door behind him. "You look terrible. Why—" her eyes traveled downward—"your trousers are undone! What's the matter with you, Zac? What's happening?"

"Don't go in there," Zac cried as Belle tried to pass him. "I forbid it. Besides she wouldn't like it . . ."

"Ah. . . ." Belle's mouth curled. "I think I see what's been going on. And in your own house, Zac! Tut." She wagged a finger playfully at him. "What *will* Tara say when she gets in?" Belle looked at her watch. "She will surely be home quite soon. You'd better tidy yourself up and get your ladylove out of there."

"It's not what you think," Zac said thickly. Then seizing her arm he pulled her into a smaller salon, shutting the door of that firmly behind him.

"Tara is in there," he said, locking the door. "I . . . we lost control. Give her time to make herself decent. . . ."

"Oh dear, dear, dear." Belle's shapely mouth was still curled, only this time not smiling. "Swept off our feet by passion are we? I'm surprised at you, an old married man. Besides," she looked at him slyly. "I didn't think things were quite like that with you. . . . Nevertheless I'm glad to hear it. We all need a little excitement from time to time. The day Carl gets sent off by a frenzy of passion in our main drawing room I must say will be a red letter day for all concerned. . . . Anyway—" Belle glanced at some papers she too had in her hand—"here are the reports I have managed to get on Sandra's activities. I'm afraid not one black mark. It's whispered about that she's a genius, that her reforms were long overdue. . . ."

"I know that," Zac said irritably, conscious that the door of the room where he had raped his wife had quietly opened and shut again. "I know all about that. I am now number two in my own bank . . . I ask you! The bank founded by our great-grandfather a hundred years ago. Without any consultation with me Mademoiselle O'Neill has agreed to a merger with the Banque Franco-Belges which is to have a controlling share. Philippe de Lassale is to be over me, I tell you! Imagine when this gets into the papers. I shall be the laughing stock of all France."

"But it must be stopped," Belle said, appalled.

"I can't stop it. It's done, *fait accompli.* I—" Zac hesitated as a banging started on the door.

"Rapist, murderer!" Tara shouted. "I hope Sandra O'Neill reduces you to the gutter as you deserve. I hope she takes over everything that you ever loved, ever desired . . . I hope she destroys your whole family. I—"

Belle rapidly unlocked and then flung open the door, gasping as she saw the state her sister-in-law was in: her clothes crumpled, an ugly bruise rising on her left cheek, her left eye half-closed and blood dripping from beneath her torn skirt.

"Oh my God," she said, both hands to her mouth. "Oh my God . . . *Zac?"* She turned to her brother who was staring with similar stupefaction at Tara. "Did *you* do this? *You* . . . her husband?"

"Yes he did it," Tara shrieked. "Him, him, the man to whom I was married in the sight of God, before the altar of God, by the Patriarch of Venice no less. That great and good man, long the friend of my family, who is now our Pope. What would the Pope have to say about René-Zachariah Desmond, son of the great Georges Desmond—that he is a rapist . . . that he—" Tara on the verge of hysteria burst into a fit of uncontrollable tears, whereupon Belle, putting an arm around her, cast a withering look at her brother.

"Animal!" she spat at him then, gently, to Tara: "Come with me, my dear. It would be dreadful if your maid returned and saw all this. Thank heaven it is her day off."

Zac, very pale but otherwise in control of himself, bathed and changed into fresh clothes, sat upright at his carved mahogany bureau, a product of the English master furniture-maker, Thomas Chippendale, and soon to follow most of the furniture in the room to where it originally came from, the Château de Tourville. The report by Gomez was on the desk in front of him. As Belle entered the room he coughed in a rather shamefaced way and stood up beckoning her to a chair.

"How is she?"

"You may have to call the doctor later," Belle said curtly. "You have hurt her quite badly you know. If the bleeding doesn't clear up she'll have to see someone."

"Bleeding?" Zac looked puzzled.

"Yes, bleeding," Belle said meaningfully. "Something like a hemorrhage. How you *could* apply such violence to your wife, to any woman, I don't know. It makes me see you in a completely different light. I must say I am ashamed of you, Zac. . . ."

"She provoked me beyond endurance." Zac, still pale, flung the report of his spy Ignacio Gomez at his sister, who slowly sat down and began to read it, quickly flicking over the pages with their details of Tara's meetings as she did so. When she finished she stood up to hand the report back to Zac. Then she resumed her seat again. She thought for a while, studying the tips of her beautifully kept, elegant hands.

"Well, that explains something, I suppose." She looked up at him, but there was still a shadow of anxiety on her face. "Maybe it excuses you a little, I don't know . . ."

"It excuses me in every way," Zac said. "My wife is a whore, so I treated her like one. . . ."

Belle got up and, walking to the window, parted the curtains to look out onto the street. From a corner of the window the great dome of Les Invalides, burial place of Napoleon and other heroes of France, could be seen above the trees in the garden of the Musée Rodin. It was always a majestic sight. "Oh Zac she *isn't* a whore," she said at last. "She is just a very unhappy, frustrated woman. You know that you and she have never got on very well. Anyway why blame her for something you do yourself all too often? *I* know you have affairs.

However, nothing excuses what you did to Tara. It was a most savage attack. . . ."

Zac looked contritely at his sister.

"I agree. To be truthful I am ashamed of myself. I lost control, but it was not solely on account of this report. . . ."

Slowly Zac stood up and rejoined his sister at the window gazing into the street.

"I am at a loss exactly what to do. This report, coming on top of the news about de Lassale, did make me into an animal, did make me lose control of myself. What am I to do, Belle?" He turned and looked at her and on his face she saw the lost, hurt look of the small boy Zac had once been, anxious and insecure because the father he adored was indifferent to him. Someone who, despite being so much older, used to climb into her bed at night for comfort: a very frightened, insecure, frustrated boy grown into a frightened, insecure, frustrated man; a man on the brink of ruin. . . .

Impulsively she put her arm around him.

"It's like being on the battlefield here today," she said, "caring for the war wounded, mentally as well as physically. Well, how are you going to stop Sandra? Isn't there something we can do . . . ?"

"What *can* we do at the eleventh hour?" Zac said wearily, watching her as she slowly crossed the room and stood in front of his desk staring at the Gomez report. "The deal, as far as I know, is ready to be signed formally after lunch tomorrow. What can *I* do in less than twenty-four hours to stop it?"

Thoughtfully Belle picked up the report and idly glanced through the pages without really seeing the contents.

"Drastic deeds require drastic action, don't they?" she murmured in a low voice and Zac, reminded of the sense of menace that lurked, never far below the surface, in his sister, felt his blood run cold as she turned and looked at him.

"Impulsive people need to be stopped. . . . Tell me, Zac *mon cher,* what sort of man exactly is this Gomez?"

8

Sandra closed her notebook and put it in her leather briefcase together with the notes she had been discussing with Henri Piper during the evening—a hurriedly called business dinner at the Château de Marsanne because Sophie had the flu and Henri didn't want to leave her.

Henri was an expert on California wines, an area Sandra knew she neglected. She wanted to try and do some business through him, rather than having to make a visit herself. She would have liked to, but she hadn't the time.

Sandra looked appreciatively around the intimate salon with its predominantly blue motif: curtains, furnishings and carpet, all in exquisite taste, reflecting the flair of people who knew about fine things and could afford to have them. Gradually, painstakingly, the Pipers had built up a collection of treasures that lacked the salesroom value of the Desmond collection but which could nevertheless give greater pleasure because of the circumstances in which they'd been bought: with love and understanding, rather than for show.

"This is *such* a pretty room," Sandra said, putting the locked briefcase by her side on the floor. "I hate to go."

"Stay the night," Henri urged her. "There is always a room for you here. Or are you going to Tourville?"

"Oh no." Sandra looked at her watch and frowned. "I am going back to Paris tonight. I want to be at the office first thing."

Henri got up and, walking slowly across the room, pausing to adjust an object here, put his nose to a flower or a plant there, eventually stopped when he stood in front of her looking, she thought, rather sad.

"What is it?" she asked. "You have such an odd expression."

Henri sat beside her and reached for her hand.

"You know, my dear Sandra I am very fond of you . . . that is—" he hastily corrected himself lest his remark be misinterpreted—"Sophie and I are *both* very fond of you."

"And . . . ?" Sandra raised an eyebrow.

"You are overdoing things. You work too hard. You don't take enough rest, in fact I don't think you take any. You never give yourself time off. You never accept an invitation from us to the opera or the theater. I don't believe you relax in the company of men. A girl as beautiful as you should enjoy the admiration, maybe the love of a particular man. Though," he added hastily, "it is not for me to pry into your affairs."

"There is no one," Sandra said shortly. "That's no secret. There simply hasn't been the time. . . ." She was conscious of his warm hand encasing hers in an avuncular way.

"There is *always* time, if you make it. I don't think Georges meant you to kill yourself within a few years . . ."

"Oh, I won't do that." Sandra laughed and threw back her head. The soft light caught the exquisite line of neck to chin, a sparkle in those light, fascinating blue eyes with the dark irises, such an attractive and distinctive feature of this unusual woman.

"Nevertheless—" Henri's clasp tightened before he let her hand fall and, getting up, he started to pace up and down in front of her—"I think you work too hard and that may . . ." He paused and looked at her keenly as if judging whether or not it was the right time to say what he had to say.

Sandra said impatiently, "Go *on,* Henri."

"I don't think it's doing you any good, Sandra, I mean as a person."

"In what way, may I ask?" She swallowed, aware of a rebuff, and studied her hands, holding them out in front of the blazing fire though they were too far away to feel its warmth.

"I think, and I know you won't like my saying this, you're making some mistakes." He held up a hand as she sharply looked at him. "Oh not, I hasten to say, in business . . . or maybe they are mistakes, I don't know. Maybe it is a mistake to come down so heavily on Zac. . . ."

"But he would destroy me!"

"Would he?" Now Henri raised an eyebrow. "I'm not sure. Maybe he needs you as much as Georges realized he needed you. Maybe he *is* a man floundering; a man who, as a boy, was very insecure, felt himself unloved. Georges never hid the fact that Belle was his favorite and next to her, Tim. Zac used to do as much as he could to please his father; he tried very hard; he overdid it perhaps. . . ."

"Well he made some very silly mistakes toward someone he was trying to *please,*" Sandra said dismissively.

"Maybe he tried too hard because he wanted to impress Georges; people do you know. If they are overanxious they make mistakes. I think Zac was someone like that. His father mistrusted him from boyhood and then, very brutally and abruptly, without even a word or a letter, he disinherited him." Henri threw up his arms with an exclamation. "Just like that! And now *you* are depriving him too . . . just like that. Very suddenly and, if I may say so—" Henri lowered his voice and looked toward the door though he knew no one was about, his wife and the servants in their beds—"very brutally, my dear."

"Brutal? You call it brutal? Brutal toward Zac?" Sandra's brow puckered as if she couldn't believe the evidence of her own ears.

"I do call it brutal," Henri said still firmly. "I feel you

should have brought Zac in on the negotiations about the bank. Let him see what a state things were in. . . ."

"De Lassale wouldn't have him. It was with some difficulty that I have persuaded him even to retain Zac as President."

"Then you should have dissuaded de Lassale with your charm," Henri said gently, his eyes lighting up. "Oh you have such a lot of that. Even a man as shrewd as de Lassale you could have twisted around your little finger. . . ."

"I don't think so," Sandra said shortly. "I had to use a great amount of charm, a bit of bullying for him to agree to keep Zac at all. As it is he is to have no authority to make loans on his own account. Everything has to be approved by de Lassale or me."

"Well I've said what I have to say." Henri saw her glance at her watch. "And I know it is late. But the furniture, my dear. Was *that* necessary?"

"He'd stolen it!" Sandra raised her voice indignantly. "I *had* to make a claim on it."

"Maybe 'borrowed' it?" Henri suggested, his kind face puckered with concern.

"Stolen," Sandra replied stubbornly. "He had it removed once he knew I was the heir. It belongs to *all* the family, not just him. Luckily I can recognize a good piece of furniture when I see it and also a twin if it happens to be separate from another. He has denuded Tourville and the Desmond Group offices of fine, valuable pieces by established masters which Georges, no doubt, meant others to see and be impressed by. Although there is plenty left at Tourville, if I didn't lay a claim on it much of it would never be returned."

"That is because he feels that *he* will go back," Henri said softly.

"Well he won't." Sandra rose to her feet as if concluding the conversation and stretched her arms. "I can promise you that. As long as I have a breath in my body."

As he stood by the large double doors of the Château

watching her drive away Henri felt a heaviness in his heart he had not known before.

She was running before she could walk; leaping before she could jump . . . taking huge risks. Would she ever learn? Or would she learn in time?

Sadly, as the red lights of her car vanished out of sight, he turned into the house, shutting the doors behind him. He was just out of earshot when another car, which had been waiting in the lane beyond the gates, started up and began to follow the one in front of it driven by Sandra.

Sandra calculated she could save a few kilometers if she took the narrow country lanes as far as Passy-Grigny, which would lead her by a peripheral minor road onto the autoroute.

It was quite a steep climb through the trees and vineyards that surrounded the Château and when she was right at the top she could, by glancing down, just get a glimpse of its friendly lights.

After that the road was in darkness punctuated every now and then by the mezmerized eyes of a startled rabbit before it hurried out of the way. By day the countryside was of extraordinary beauty; but at night it was a little frightening, passing by the few darkened farm houses and cottages that sprinkled the route, the tiny villages of Trottef and Pereuil, the latter almost in ruins.

Sometimes she fancied she heard the sound of a car behind her, which added to her sense of unease and she wished she'd brought the chauffeur.

But, maybe her apprehension of danger was, in a wider sense, because she was angry not only with Henri Piper but with herself. She knew she was beginning to resent any criticism and that if she allowed this to continue she would be surrounded by yes-men as Zac had been, men who had shielded him from unpleasant facts. Probably, too, as Georges

Desmond had been, which was why his business had deteriorated to such an alarming extent.

The price of power was, sometimes, that those at the top considered themselves incapable of error. She had known many of them in her short business life and despised them. She didn't want to be like them and she should be grateful to Henri for warning her against her own weakness: malice, maybe revenge against Zac for making life so difficult for her; maybe a subconscious wish to discredit him so that she got rid of him altogether.

Suddenly in her mirror she saw twin points of lights still some distance behind and knew that her sensation of being followed was a real one. But "followed"? Surely that was absurd? Who would wish to follow her and why? It was rather too late for members of the Press to be on her trail and these days they mostly left her alone.

But she had been foolish to drive on her own. After all she was a wealthy, increasingly important woman and even in civilized France and Europe kidnap was not unknown. What would the Desmond Group be prepared to pay for her? She would rather not know; forced to wait in some mountain cave or underground cellar to find out, while she was subjected to the indignities of the involuntarily imprisoned.

She was tired and, yes, she was frightened. But it would not be long before Passy-Grigny and the autoroute and then she would allow the car behind to speed past her and her fears, hopefully her foolish fears, would be put to rest.

Maybe Henri was right. She was not taking enough rest. Her nerves were frayed. She was due to go to New York and, after that, she would try to go to California and spend a few days in the sun with Bob. She . . . The road began to widen and the lights of Passy-Grigny appeared on the horizon.

Suddenly the spotlights of the car behind her flashed full on, the driver gave a terrifying blast on his horn and Sandra, now frightened out of her life, crouched over the wheel, attempting desperately to keep her car on the road. But relentlessly the monster behind crept up until it appeared to be almost on top of her, dazzling her with its lights. Then she heard the terrible crunch of metal on metal; the wheel slithered out of her hand as her car left the road under the impact and rolled over and over. . . .

Already by two-thirty the atmosphere in the room was tense. Philippe de Lassale kept on rising to look out of the window and Antoine Leriche, who was Director of the Desmond Press and Editor-in-Chief of the influential *Gazette de L'Est,* went once or twice to the door in agitation.

"It's very unlike Mademoiselle to be late," he said, glancing at his watch. "She is known for her punctuality. Does *anyone* have any idea where she is?"

Dericourt, Director of the Aeronautics Group, gazed expectantly around. His eyes lingered on Zac who, head bent over some papers before him, was apparently oblivious to the consternation of the others.

Suddenly there was a commotion in the anteroom and only then did Zac raise his head, his face registering surprise as the door burst open and Sandra entered. At once the men in the room rose to their feet to greet her. She paused before them.

"I'm *so* sorry I'm late," she said. "You all know it's most unlike me." The expression on her face was strained, her smile forced, her pallor most noticeable. "In fact," she continued, "this meeting nearly did not take place at all."

"Indeed? How is that?"

Philippe de Lassale left his chair as, for the first time, she displayed the bandages around both her wrists. With difficulty, she removed her coat slung around her shoulders. Solicitously Philippe de Lassale took it from her and held out a chair.

"I'm perfectly all right, I assure you." Sandra smiled around at the circle of concerned faces. "Just a flesh wound, as they say. No bones broken; no serious injury; light concussion. I spent the night in the hospital and—" she glanced at her watch—"shortly I have an interview with the police."

"The police?" Zac exclaimed, his face pale and his eyes puffy, as though he had had too little sleep.

"The police want to look into the nature of the accident." Sandra carefully, painfully shuffled her papers together. "If accident it was."

"What on earth do you mean, Mademoiselle?" Antoine Leriche looked at her with concern.

"I had a car accident," Sandra said, "and I have the feeling that what happened to me was deliberate. Some madman determined to get me off the road."

"You think it was done on purpose?" Dericourt could hardly conceal his concern. "That, I find incredible."

"I do too," Sandra replied. "I didn't think I had been in France long enough to make any enemies. . . ."

As she looked around the group which constituted the directorate of the newly constituted executive board Sandra's eyes rested, perhaps, a fraction longer on Zac's preoccupied face than any other.

"Certainly you have *no* enemies, Mademoiselle," Dericourt said gallantly. "Only admirers." Of all the directors he was the youngest and, perhaps, the most ambitious. He was not yet forty and yet he was not only in control of the expanding aeronautics side of the Desmond Group, but had been made an executive director thanks to the perceptiveness and initiative of Sandra O'Neill. He had never got on particularly well with Zac and had been quite sure when Georges Desmond was killed that he would soon be removed to be replaced by one of Zac's cronies of whom there were many; people of little talent always toadying up to the boss's son for the chance of promotion. Zac was a man who craved, and thrived on, flattery. This was well-known and he was accordingly loved, or feared, by those who expected to do well but knew they could not without his patronage.

Sandra sat back listening with gratification to the testimonials of her directorial board, mindful of her thoughts the night before. One or two voices were muted, maybe out of deference to the presence of Zac, who was remarkable for not adding to them. Not only did he not comment during the entire discussion, but he kept on looking at his watch as though to indicate that the whole matter of Sandra's welfare or otherwise was of considerable indifference to him.

Finally Sandra thanked them for their confidence in her and then, leaning forward, toyed with the long silver Cartier pencil with which she made her notes.

"The reason we are here is to formally announce that the Banque Pons-Desmond is to have a friendly merger with the Banque Franco-Belges of which Philippe de Lassale is President." She smiled at Philippe, who acknowledged her with a bow of his head.

He listened as Sandra succinctly went through the conditions of the merger thinking, as many had before him, that he had never in his life met a young woman of such ability. Such wisdom and perspicacity would have sat more easily on someone of about his age, certainly someone in her forties. That a woman could behave in this way, have the capacity for logical analysis that she had was a source of perpetual astonishment to a man who, because of his age and the nature of his business, was perhaps chauvinistic in his attitude to women; but, in reality, he had never come across many in executive positions, and none at all as senior as this. At first he had been skeptical when approached by Sandra, thinking that the Desmond Group was done for, doomed. He had quickly changed his mind.

Moreover that she was now able to marshal all the facts, including figures of astronomical amounts of money, with only the aid of a few pencilled notes, was all the more remarkable considering the gravity of her accident; a near fatality apparently, from which she had been very lucky to escape not only with just a few scratches but with her life.

It was noticeable that Zac scarcely looked up during the recitation, which Sandra kept as impartial as possible, never once referring to him by name or touching on the many mistakes directly attributable to him which had made this merger necessary.

As soon as Sandra had finished—the effort had obviously exhausted her though she tried hard to hide it—Philippe spoke to give her a rest.

"Mademoiselle Desmond has admirably outlined the substance of our discussions and may I compliment her on the clarity of her exposition, her mastery of the facts and her undoubted grasp of what has, to all of us, been a very complex and difficult matter."

Sandra, her face very pale as though she were in pain, nevertheless managed to smile and Philippe noticed how, under the table, she was trying to massage her wrists.

"I think we should soon stop for lunch," Philippe said anxiously, "and give Mademoiselle Desmond the chance to rest. I think she is suffering more than she cares to tell us. However, there is one thing I would like to add . . ."—he shuffled his papers in front of him carefully as though weighing a decision—"I would also like to thank Monsieur Zac Desmond for his graciousness in concurring with these suggestions which came, in the first place, from myself, once I had time to read the special report my colleagues had drawn up on the affairs of the bank and realized the predicament it had gotten itself into on account of unwise loans." Philippe coughed and smiled deprecatingly in Zac's direction. "It could happen to any of us. Those of us engaged in international finance know the dangers of risk capital, speculative ventures that at first seem so attractive. However I, as I am sure is the case with all around this table, have a great respect for Zac Desmond, not only as the son of his father, a member of a distinguished family," he paused while everyone, except Sandra, murmured their agreement, "but, as a man of flair, a man of business, a respected member of the community.

"I would like to suggest and I have not discussed this with Mademoiselle Desmond"—he glanced apologetically at her—"as she was unavoidably not here at the time; but I would like to propose that Zac Desmond should also join the Board of the Banque Franco-Belges as Vice-President. Thus it would not for a moment appear to the public that he was in any way—how shall I put it?—demoted as a result of our reorganization. But simply that he had assumed new, and very important responsibilities."

Sandra involuntarily shut her eyes and inwardly cursed the fate that had sent her into a ditch by the side of the road the previous night. However, she said nothing but gave a faint smile which was not meant to indicate her concurrence with Philippe de Lassale's decision. On the contrary she abhorred it.

She knew he was a kind man, kind and, perhaps now, a little foolish. To try and save Zac's face might well result in the ruin of the Banque Franco-Belges. But who was to know? Only she so far was aware of the ruthlessness of Zac, the depths to which he alone, it seemed, was able to sink. Only she knew the full extent of the near ruin he had brought on his father's business; his cynicism, intolerance of criticism and criminally poor judgment. She knew it and Georges Desmond had known it—but what neither of them had known was how much he had feathered his own nest in the process.

But only she, alone, suspected that behind those bright lights that bore down on her, dazzling her as she turned onto the motorway, might have been the face of an emissary of René-Zachariah Desmond. It was not inconceivable.

From now on she knew she had to be on guard, not only for her business, but for her life.

* * *

Zac was not displeased with the outcome of the events of the day. When de Lassale had come up with the totally unexpected announcement that he was being placed on the Board of the huge Franco-Belges Bank with all its resources, and made Vice-President, he felt a surge not only of pride but of revenge. The surprise to Sandra had been obvious and even that consummate actress, that hypocrite, who, in his eyes, would make the antics of a Sarah Bernhardt look like amateur theatricals, had been unable to conceal not only her dismay, but her rage.

Even before he left the office the joint press departments of Desmond and Franco-Belges were at work on a release the effect of which would be to proclaim that Monsieur Desmond had not been sacked as President of the Desmond Bank but had been elevated to a much more important position: that of Vice-President of a bank whose influence and assets were vast compared to that of Pons-Desmond, though the Desmond Group as a whole was larger and infinitely more diversified. The Press and the world would be bamboozled into thinking that Zac had bettered himself and, in a way, Zac had; though that had not been the intention. Instead of being made to look small he appeared in the guise of a new giant on the financial horizon, and the whole concept was a profound irritant to Sandra and the source of great satisfaction to Zac as he let himself into his house with his key and shouted that he was home.

There was an ominous silence about the hall which, at that time of evening, was unusual. It was true he hadn't expected Tara to run out and fling her arms around him after the events of the day before but usually his two children, Giada or Robert, were about and, especially, his daughter, whom he adored, would fly into his arms to welcome him. Studious little Robert even at his tender age was usually in his room doing his homework, a habit that had been instilled in him with the idea of one day succeeding his father as head of the Desmond Group. Well one day, Zac was sure that was exactly what would happen.

Zac rang a bell in the hall to summon one of the staff and when the maid, Nicole, appeared he gave her his coat, saying:

"Where is everyone, Nicole? It is very quiet for this time of the evening."

"Oh . . ." Nicole looked perplexed as a door at the end of the corridor opened, was abruptly shut and Madame Louise, the children's governess, came rapidly over to him.

"Ah, Monsieur Desmond," she said, arms outstretched. "Forgive me for not being here to receive you . . ."

"What *has* happened, Madame?" Zac said with some irritation, checking his hair in the hall mirror. "Where are my wife, my children? The place is very quiet."

"It is Madame," the governess said in some agitation. "She had to leave suddenly and was unable to contact you. She asked me to tell you—"

"Leave!" Zac boomed in the thunderous voice which terrified all and sundry when they heard it but particularly servants, secretaries, and minions of all kinds, as it was meant to do. A sudden eruption of bad temper is notoriously bad for the nerves. "Leave for where?"

"Madame has flown to Rome. It was something to do with her brother. She had an unexpected phone call. . . ."

"Oh was it indeed?" Zac snarled. "Was it indeed? If there was a phone call, which I doubt, I can't understand why Madame Desmond was unable to contact *me.* I am the most contactable man around. I have secretaries everywhere, a phone in my car, in my plane. My assistant Monsieur Strega *always* knows my movements. I . . ."

"Please, Monsieur, don't blame me," Madame Louise pleaded with a tremor in her voice. "It was just the message I had from Madame. I—"

Zac brushed her to one side and, rapidly entering the drawing room, made for a tray on which there were a number of decanters, glasses and a bucket of ice. Nervously, hesitantly, Madame Louise followed him and stood obsequiously in the doorway, clutching and unclutching a handkerchief which, once white, had grown rather grimy in a remarkably short space of time.

"I . . . Monsieur . . . The children have gone out with their aunt, the Princess . . ."

"She had no *right!*" Zac thundered, his eyes almost bulging from their sockets.

"She thought you wouldn't mind, sir. I think she has taken them to Tourville to visit their grandmother. They are to spend the night there. . . ."

"No right at *all.*" Zac downed his whisky in one gulp and poured another. "My wife gone, my children . . . what sort of place is this?"

"I am sure the Princess did it for the best, sir. She came specifically to see you. She left a note for you. I . . ."

"Then give it to me!" Zac peremptorily held out his hand, causing the poor, elderly lady to sway as she fumbled in her adequate bosom for an envelope which she had tucked for safety's sake into the folds of her bodice. "Now please leave me alone," Zac said, promptly turning his back and taking the letter over to the light. "Shut the door after you," he called.

"Of course, *sir.*" Madame Louise who, in a blameless life, had never been so harshly treated, having been protected from the master of the house's tantrums by its mistress, was by this time trembling so much and her hands were so damp with fear that her clasp on the door handle was slippery. Once she heard it click she leaned against it, her other hand on her heart which was fluttering as unevenly and faintly as that of a wounded bird. Not for the first time she vowed she would give notice.

My dear Zac," [the letter read in Belle's familiar large handwriting,]

"I came here to find that Tara has gone to see Marco. Undoubtedly it is after what happened last night. Perhaps she has left you. I am surprised she has found the strength to make the journey because Nicole said she looked most unwell. Doddery old Madame Louise—I can't think why you hang on to her by the way—was frantic: about you not knowing, about the children, about the interruption to her routine. So I decided the best thing was to take them to see Mother who always complains she doesn't see them enough.

I hear the Irish cow is still alive! Tant pis! Next time we shall have to be more accurate.

Dearest brother I embrace you. I know what a difficult time this is for you.

Belle.

"Idiot," Zac muttered, screwing the paper into a ball and throwing it in the fire, making sure that it burnt to ashes. If this had fallen into any other hands it was tantamount to an admission of attempted murder. Just suppose that he had failed to return home and that geriatric old woman had opened it? He put a hand that shook slightly over his face, trying to calm his fantasies, his fears; not for the first time in their lives had he and his sister taken a step over the border between legality and a criminal act. One day fate might, perhaps, catch up with them. Then, after a few seconds, he went to the telephone and dialed a number, instinctively looking around as if fearful that anyone would hear or see him.

Ignacio Gomez, long-time con man and petty criminal, cringed in his chair.

"Of course I won't use him again, Monsieur. It was a botched job."

"Botched!" Zac hissed at him. "We could all have been in prison by now. Even *she* thinks it wasn't an accident. Luckily she can't convince the police, who think it was a drunken driver."

"Thank God for that," Gomez said, scratching his head and looking out of the window of the cafe in one of the less salubrious parts of Paris, just beyond Montmartre.

"No thanks to you," Zac said, reaching into his inner pocket for an envelope which he threw on the table. "A bargain is a bargain, so I'll pay you this time; but next time—"

"Next time it will be done properly, Monsieur Zac. I promise you that," Gomez said unctuously, his nicotine-stained hand sidling toward the tempting envelope which lay on the plastic-covered surface of the table. Fingers grasping it at last, he gave a deep sigh of satisfaction and palmed it into his side pocket. "You didn't give me enough time, Monsieur. Twenty-four hours is not enough time to arrange to have somebody killed. . . ."

"I didn't want you to *kill* her," Zac said sharply, "but mess her up; give her a shock, incapacitate her if you like. I never mentioned the word *kill.*"

"I thought you meant that, Monsieur," Gomez said in the whiney voice he could so easily conjure up and which so infuriated Zac. However, the Gomezes of this world, though thick on the ground apparently, were hard to find unless one knew where to look: sleazy, immoral characters who could easily be bought for anything. "You *said* have a bad accident. . . ."

"Accident. I meant accident, not slaughter. . . ."

"That 'accident' should have been enough to accomplish the task." Gomez appealed to his benefactor. "Molinier said the car went right off the road and spun over several times. He had no doubt that he had succeeded, luckily with only very little damage to his own car. . . ."

"Being repaired now I hope?" Zac said, a tremor of unease showing at last in his voice. Gomez spread out his hands with an air of satisfaction and shook his head.

"No doubt about it, Monsieur. Already it is a new car; new

paint, new license plate. No questions asked." He patted his pocket. "This should take care of everything nicely."

"Creep," Zac thought, finishing his *café filtre* before getting up. The trouble was that in unsavory business one had to use unsavory characters. There was something, however, inherently weak about Gomez which he particularly despised. Perhaps he had been the wrong man to entrust such an important task to.

He got up and nodded.

"Next time no mistake, Gomez."

9

The park around the Château de Tourville was, if anything, even more beautiful when winter approached than it had been when Sandra first saw it in the height of summer. Now the autumn tints had turned to the stark browns, grays and blacks of December, though there were still leaves on many of the great trees that had stood there since before Tourville was ever dreamt of.

From the window of the Louis XV salon on the second floor, Belle stood watching Sandra as she walked slowly around the lake in the distance, head bent in thought, occasionally kicking the damp leaves with her sheepskin boots.

Behind Belle, legs stretched in front of a fire, Tim idly turned over the pages of a magazine. He was dressed to go riding. Tim had a private polo ground at Tourville and kept many of his best ponies in the stables there where he could frequently exercise them.

Weekends were always spent at Tourville by any member of the family who was within distance. Lady Elizabeth lived there permanently; Claire came when she could; Zac and Tara usually drove over from Paris; but this weekend they were absent. Tim, if he was in the country, was almost always there at weekends, and so was Sandra who was determined to claim her share of the family home. There was so much space it was not necessary to meet any of the others except at mealtimes.

Still it was beautiful and, after Paris and the many trips she had to make abroad, restful.

Belle, Princess von Burg-Farnbach, preferred the Château de Tourville to her husband's family seat in the Bavarian Mountains—a huge stone schloss set in the foothills of the Alps. Belle was a city woman. She loved Paris, the bustle of the boulevards, the excitement of meeting friends at smart places to eat and drink—the Tour d'Argent, Fouquets in the Champs Élysées, Brasserie Lipp in Saint Germain or the bar of the Plaza-Athenée in the avenue Montaigne.

But Belle was not merely a socialite, though she loved society. She was a clever, ambitious woman whose goal in life had been as frustrated by her father as had Zac's. Georges Desmond would never contemplate a woman in his business so near the top, which was odd seeing that, ultimately, he had left it to one. Belle used her considerable energies in building up the House of Jean Marvoine, the Maison de Couture which had, as its designer-in-chief, one of the cleverest couturiers in France. In many ways it ran itself. Besides its shrewd Directrice, Louise Riboux, it had a devoted staff both on the floor and behind the scenes, seamstresses sewing away for the collections that followed one another so rapidly throughout the year.

All Belle's restless energies seemed to have coalesced at the bequest in her father's will of the bulk of his estate to a strange woman. Like Zac she regarded Sandra with a bitter, personal hatred, one that appeared sometimes to border on mania; a hatred that would not stop at killing.

Yes, she would kill Sandra if she had to, she thought, watching that elegant, solitary figure reach the far end of the lake and disappear momentarily between the tall coniferous pines that bordered it. One way or the other she would get rid of her.

"You like her, don't you?" Belle said without looking

around and Tim, not really concentrating on the pages of the society journal he was flicking through, looked up.

"Are you talking to me?"

"Who else?"

"And of *whom* are you talking?" Tim said, thankfully putting the magazine aside and crossing the room to join his sister.

The second-floor salon was a room of great beauty and charm with its views of the lake, of the forest and the surrounding vineyards that stretched on one side nearly to Épernay and on the other past Hautvillers to the banks of the Marne.

It was not only a place where the family gathered but the scene of most of the important occasions for the past hundred years. Its exquisite decoration, the intricate plasterwork on the ceiling and walls was the work of the celebrated interior designer Eugene Lami, engaged by the first René-Zachariah when he realized the fortune his champagne would bring him. The brocaded chairs and sofas had gilt-lacquered frames, cabriole legs and a floral motif on the backs exquisitely embroidered in silk.

The carpets on the highly polished parquet floors were Aubusson, and every other item in the room had been made by skilled *ébénisties* and craftsmen in the reign of the King whose name had been given to the salon, Louis XV, and whose daughters had lived at nearby Louvois.

It was a sumptuous but restful room and, on reaching his sister's side, Tim casually put an arm around her shoulders, following the direction of her eyes.

"Are you talking *about* Mademoiselle O'Neill?"

"Who else?"

"What do you mean do I 'like' her?" Tim placed a casual emphasis on the word *like.*

"You know what I mean!" Belle turned and Tim was surprised to see that her brilliant eyes blazed with malice, despite the smile on her face, as she gazed up at him.

"You mean 'like' sexually speaking? Yes, she is a pretty woman. More, she is beautiful. I would fancy a fling with her any day."

"Then why don't you try?"

"Are you serious?" Tim's expression turned to one of amazement. But then Belle was like that. Unpredictable.

"Perfectly serious," Belle insisted.

"But I thought you hated her?"

"I loathe her; but I would very much like to see her entangled with you. What a come-down for 'Mademoiselle' when you ditch her as you have ditched all the others."

"Oh come now!" Tim backed away from his sister as if in protest, removing his arm. "That is a *very* cynical thing to say."

"At least it's harmless."

"But why should you want something like that?"

"Because I want to see her humiliated. I want there to be a series of 'events' and 'episodes' that make Mademoiselle so nervous, so insecure she will be glad to leave France."

Tim's eyes narrowed and he felt uncomfortable. "Episodes? What do you mean 'episodes'? What sort of 'events'? I hope you weren't behind the attempt to kill her the other night. . . ."

"Oh good God no!" Belle gave a high, artificial laugh. "Besides I don't believe there was an attempt to kill her. She was probably speeding, driving dangerously and the cause of the collision in the first place."

"But . . ."

"I mean," Belle continued, eager to change the subject, "little episodes such as you pretending to fall in love with her and then dropping her abruptly. We will think of others, just as harmless, just as much fun for us, tormenting for her."

"What makes you think I will drop her?" Tim said with an edge to his voice.

"Because you have never been faithful to any woman once

you have conquered her, *mon cher frère.* Why should 'Mademoiselle' be any different?"

Tim didn't reply for a minute, thinking that, as it happened, his sister was right.

There are some men whose pursuit of women amounts to a disease and Tim Desmond probably fell into this category. He was unable to resist them and then, when he had gotten what he wanted, he couldn't put them aside fast enough. In this way he had broken the hearts of some of the most well-born, wealthy and attractive women not only in France but in the world. For Tim Desmond, international athlete and playboy, was much sought after. Not only did he have a dangerous element of attraction, but he was rich and, perhaps, in most women there was the hope that one day the man she fell in love with, however much of a reprobate, however bad his reputation, would change.

"Mademoiselle O'Neill would never look at me," he replied, watching Sandra reappear from the trees and continue her tour of the lake. She walked with such extraordinary elegance that even at a distance he was aware of her allure. "I have tried."

"Oh you have?"

"Just a little. I followed her once on horseback after the harvest and tried to kiss her. I've sent her flowers and asked her to dine. I . . ."

"You *rogue,"* Belle said in a mocking tone. "I should have known, and yet you never said a thing to us."

"Why should I tell you everything?" Tim bent to touch her cheeks with his lips. Tim's only regret all his adult life had been that one of the acknowledged beauties in all of France was his sister and out of reach. "Of course I want to go to bed with Sandra; but not for the reasons you suppose. She is a challenge. She would, I am sure, be very good in bed. There is a sensuality about her that I find challenging. If you ask me she has had many lovers. Of course I wouldn't mind a romance with Sandra; but don't think I would drop her so easily. You never know, I might become attached."

"That's what you say about them *all,"* Belle said with a smile. "You have great hopes, but I can tell you that the Irish-woman would be no luckier than the rest."

"I'm not so sure." Tim's eyes narrowed. "I'd like to give it a try though. Will you help me then?"

"Of course," Belle said with a crystal clear, delighted laugh. "If she is so difficult why don't you hire a room at Versailles?"

"Are you mad?"

"No, perfectly serious. It's one of the little ploys I already had in mind. Look, I'll tell you how you go about this scheme. . . ."

As she came back to the house from her walk Sandra saw Tim, dressed in riding jacket and jodhpurs, waiting on the main staircase for her. In his hand was a riding crop and as she came toward him he raised it, hailing her, and then ran lightly down the steps toward her.

Sandra pretended not to care and walked on, but it was very difficult. Tim was an extraordinarily attractive man and, though she knew his reputation, she had as much difficulty as many another woman in finding the idea of a romance with him resistible. Despite his charm and his looks he had such an air of deceptive honesty, of candor, that it was hard not to hope that, somehow, one might eventually be able to change him. . . .

However, he was a Desmond and it was that above all, not his looks or his reputation, that made him forbidden territory.

No. Never trust a Desmond. Never get involved with one.

"I wondered if you would like a ride before lunch?" Tim held out his hand invitingly as she approached the steps. "I've had two of my polo ponies saddled just in the hope. They can do with the exercise."

"Well that's very kind," Sandra replied with a smile. There

was no harm after all in a horse ride. Nothing much could happen there. "Didn't Belle want to ride?"

"Belle has already had her ration for the day. She always rides before breakfast."

"Of course." Sandra returned his gaze. "I'll just go and change."

"See you at the stables in twenty minutes," Tim said, his heart rising. He watched her run eagerly up the steps and then, as she vanished through the open doors, he raised his hand toward the second-floor window and gave the thumbs-up sign.

His sister Belle, looking down on him like some predator, waved her hand and smiled back.

Sandra had a good seat on a horse and she rode well. But her wrists still hurt from her accident and Tim saw how loosely she held the reins in her hands.

"I'd forgotten about your wrists," he said. "I'm sorry."

"Don't worry. I can still ride. It's much better."

"Must have given you a nasty shock."

"Horrible." She shuddered as they turned from the road to the path that led toward the river and would then follow for some distance in the direction of Cumières and Damery.

"You're quite sure it was deliberate?"

"I'm quite sure." Sandra glanced at him. "But I know your family doesn't think so."

"I believe you," he said. "If you said it was deliberate, I believe you. But why?"

"I can only think of one reason and I can't tell you," Sandra replied. "Could we change the subject?"

"I'd gladly change the subject," Tim reined his pony across the path so that she couldn't proceed any farther, "if I didn't think you implied *my* family might have had something to do with it."

"I have no other enemies that I know of." Sandra's gaze was unsmiling.

"But they would *never* do that. I assure you that no one would ever think of anything like that."

"Then I'm glad to have your reassurance." Sandra's tone lacked conviction. "Shall we ride on? I'm getting a bit cold."

Tim obediently nudged his pony and, together, they rode along the frosty path until they reached a bridge over the river when they decided to turn back.

They were nearly at the Château, its turrets clear above the surrounding high walls, when Tim stopped again, pointing his crop toward the house.

"The family home for a century," he said. "You can understand why they feel uneasy about you."

"Of *course* I can; but do you expect me to stay away? I have taken the name of Desmond. From now on I must think of myself as a Desmond too. Your father left a very strange will, but I now know the reason for it."

Sandra's pony began to whinny but she stroked its neck and murmured softly into its ear and it grew quiet again. Tim thought that she had a way with animals as well as people and he rather envied the pony.

"Your brother Zac made too many mistakes," Sandra went on. "He was going to bring Desmond to its knees. Your father knew that."

"But why didn't Father say anything? *That's* what I don't understand. He didn't even tell our mother."

"I don't really understand it either, and I do feel sorry for her. But I don't feel sorry for Zac because I think a lot of what he did was reckless, lacking in judgment. As your father's son he thought he could get away with anything and maybe your father didn't feel strong enough to stop him."

"Zac was always headstrong."

"Well, there you are."

"He never thought Father loved him. He thought he loved

me best and I think he did. Zac and Father were too alike; they got on each other's nerves. Father and I never had to compete and Father loved sport and was proud of me."

"You must miss him very much," Sandra said, nudging her pony in the flanks as they approached the Château by a side gate in the wall near the stables.

"I do miss him very much. I have been very lonely since he died. Sandra, I—"

"Please, Tim." Sandra's smile was gentle as she briefly put her gloved hand on the neck of the pony. "Please, not again. I've had your flowers and thank you very much, they're beautiful. Thank you for your invitation to dine; but I can't honestly believe that a man like you is short of friends, including women. I am much, much too busy and too involved with the affairs of the Group even to consider going out with you."

"But you must go out with *someone,"* Tim pleaded.

"But not you. Not a Desmond. No involvement with the family—please."

Tim seemed to regard her words as final and then paused as if having an afterthought.

"Well if you won't come out alone surely, surely you would agree to honor a dinner I am giving at the Château of Versailles for the International Olympic Committee? We expect to have many distinguished guests: Jean-Claude Killy, Niki Lauda, Nigel Mansell, Alain Prost. I am *hoping* you will agree. . . ."

"But I am not a member of the committee."

"No it is *for* the committee. I can have what guests I like."

"It sounds most attractive," Sandra said after a pause. "And at Versailles? How lovely." As she looked at him the severity of her expression relaxed. "Well there's no harm in *that* is there?"

"No harm at all," Tim said, his heart jubilant.

"Then I accept, with pleasure." Sandra inclined her head as she rode through the gate.

After all, it would have been churlish to refuse.

Sandra supposed that they dined every night like this at Tourville. Certainly whenever she was there they dressed for dinner, the men wearing black ties. Lady Elizabeth had a variety of exquisite dresses that all seemed to date from the time of the War, or maybe just before. In a way they were timeless, as she was, and pre-War fashions were coming back into vogue.

Sandra had found that since she came to France she had been very much more fashion-conscious. She had always been a neat and fastidious dresser, but it wasn't until she became President of the Desmond Group that ideas of wearing *haute couture* entered her head.

But now she was a familiar figure at all the famous couturiers and she had her own special favorites, some of them not yet well-known. With this had gone the apartment at the Ritz overlooking the garden, the Rolls-Royce, the private jet, the helicopter and all the accoutrements of celebrity and fame that Sandra would never have achieved, or even considered, as an all-American girl working for a bank, even in a highly paid executive position.

Yet Sandra was not conscious that she herself had changed. She didn't think these things mattered or, maybe, that was because they came so easily to her, so naturally now. Henri may have said she had become hard, but was that not just another name for practical good sense when confronted by a clan as hostile as the Desmonds, a business close to catastrophe? Uncle Henri in his sweet way was a dear, old-fashioned chauvinist. Who could expect otherwise?

Thus as she sat at the candle-lit table she was conscious that though it was an ordinary weekend, the table was laid as if for a feast and all the Desmonds were dressed for dinner. There were guests present; Sophie and Henri Piper and Monsieur and Madame Joffré, the former being one of the largest independent *vignerons* in Reims.

Monsieur Joffré was talking about the harvest and the quality of the grapes, predicting that the year would be as good as 1982 and that another vintage year would be declared. Only an exceptional year was declared a vintage year and Monsieur Joffré dwelled dolefully on the wines of 1980 and 1977 when neither year had been deemed worthy.

Belle talked a lot too; she seemed happy and relaxed, having brought her nephew and niece to stay with their grandmother while their parents were away. That day Sandra had seen a rare side of Belle, a charming, laughing, fun-loving side to her she would not have dreamt existed; a Belle dressed casually in jeans and a tee shirt playing with the children, swimming in the pool, joining her and Tim for a drink after their ride.

Now here was a vivacious, radiant Belle leaning over the table discussing, with all the knowledge of a serious oenologist, the vagaries of the harvest and the subtleties of the blend of cuvées which would take place soon.

"That is something you must see," Henri told Sandra, looking curiously at her. "Are you all right?"

"Perfectly all right." Sandra shook herself. "Daydreaming maybe. Slightly tired."

"Quite natural after the week you've had, including your accident," Tim said solicitously. "I think we went too far on our ride."

"We didn't go too far at all," Sandra said.

"Did they get that creature who tried to kill you?" Lady Elizabeth glanced sharply at her over her half-rim glasses. "They must surely have found his car."

"No one tried to *kill* Sandra, Mother," Belle protested. "It was an accident. It's nonsense to say anyone tried to *kill* her."

For the first time that day Sandra perceived that the sunny aspect of Belle had suddenly evaporated. It was as though a curtain had come down between that charming, happy, handsome woman and the person she considered slightly evil: a person who, with Zac, might easily one day try to dispose of her. It was an awful thought to have about someone; but with Belle it was quite easy. One could imagine a vicious, twisted side to Belle hidden behind the superficial glamor of her public persona.

"They haven't found anyone, Lady Elizabeth." Sandra shook her head. "No sign of a vehicle, nothing. Only tire marks that make them think it was some form of van or maybe a Jeep. They were heavy tires and the impression I had was of some much larger vehicle behind me deliberately bearing down on me. . . ."

"Imagination," Belle said shortly. "Are we playing bridge after dinner, Henri?"

"I hope so," Henri said, glancing at Sandra. "You don't play do you, Sandra?"

"No, but I don't mind if you do. I have some reading to do."

Somewhere in the depths of the large cavernous house the telephone rang and, shortly after, Pierre opened the door and quickly coming over, whispered in Lady Elizabeth's ear. Her eyes opened wide with surprise and then, excusing herself, she got up and followed him out of the room.

"I wonder what that is?" Belle mused, carefully selecting cheese from the laden board presented by a black-coated footman.

"I think I heard Zac's name mentioned," Claire said.

Claire had been in her room all day, pleading a headache. It was true she looked tired and washed out. Not a well woman, in Sandra's opinion.

"I hope everything's all right?"

"And why should it not be all right?" Sophie Piper inquired, looking around with her bright, alert eyes; but for a moment no one replied.

Sophie was not a beauty, but she was someone people took notice of. She had authority, probably acquired from the fact that she was a Desmond. To be born a Desmond, if you had the right frame of mind, was enough. The message had somehow failed to get through to Claire, but all the other members of the family had it; an instinctive air of authority that occasioned respect and obedience and for which one did not necessarily need to be beautiful.

Sophie was petite, rather skeletal, a thin, lined, angular face with large haunting, and haunted, eyes of a singularly attractive blue. She dressed well. In fact she spent an enormous amount on clothes to enhance the paucity of natural endowment. She was brittle, smart and rather selfish. She adored Henri and over the years had made him adore her; she needed flowers, presents, telephone calls perpetually to remind her who she was and what she was. If Henri had ever strayed or even wanted to stray she would have known it. In time they became part of each other; a mutual self-perpetuating kind of imprisonment cloaked by the veneer of love.

Sophie knew that the family was uneasy, but not why. Sandra knew too; but she could guess why. Already she had formed her own explanation for the nonappearance of Zac this weekend, so she felt that she too would be interested in the answer as to his whereabouts.

"Tara suddenly went off to Italy," Claire said to her aunt. "Telling no one. Belle found the children left on their own."

"Oh that's an exaggeration, Claire!" Belle corrected her sharply. "There *is* some minor matter to do with her family. She left the children in the care of their governess and with their father expected home that evening. There's no mystery about it at all, I can assure you."

Tim grimaced at Claire and then smiled. Sandra was aware of a bond between the two and was glad: in that family she perceived two good children waged against two bad ones. There was something solid, upright and trusting in Tim, the sportsman, and she rewarded him with a warm smile as though somehow willing across to him the good thoughts she found that, after all, she harbored about him.

Henri was just about to say something when Pierre opened the door and stood back to allow Lady Elizabeth to enter, which she did, her step far less sprightly than when she had hurried out to the phone.

Sensing her unease, Tim threw his napkin on the table and, getting up, hurried over to her, giving her his arm.

"What is it, Mother? You look awfully pale."

Slowly Lady Elizabeth sank into her chair and reached for her glass, bringing it to her lips with an unsteady hand.

"Tara is very ill," she said. "She nearly bled to death. . . ."

"Oh my God—" Belle's hand flew to her mouth. Instinctively she knew what had happened.

"She has had a miscarriage," Lady Elizabeth went on. "She began to hemorrhage on the airplane and was taken straight from the airport to a private clinic. That's why Zac left so suddenly. He phoned me from his plane; but she is expected to recover."

"Thank goodness," Sandra said in a heartfelt voice, aware that her hand, too, shook. "I'm terribly sorry to hear that."

"But why did she fly to Rome? She wasn't well . . ." Belle bit her lips and stopped. "In fact I knew she wasn't well the other day when I saw her."

"Did *you* know she was pregnant? I didn't." Lady Elizabeth sounded aggrieved. "I didn't *think* they got on. . . ."

"Mother please!" Belle said sharply. "Zac and Tara's affairs are nothing to do with us. Anyway . . ." Belle smiled around the table and aware that Sandra was listening attentively and, undoubtedly proud of her superior knowledge, was anxious, once again, to change the subject. She suddenly turned to Sandra, twisting the champagne glass in her hand to show the depth of mousse in the liquid that had just been poured.

"You don't understand any of this really, do you, Sandra?

I mean about champagne . . . not Zac and Tara. That's dreary . . ."

"I'm learning quite quickly." Sandra knew her tone of voice was defensive.

"But it takes a *lifetime* to learn about champagne. We were born into it. How can you possibly expect to learn in a short time what we grew up with?"

"Well I can't." Sandra looked to Henri for support. "You have that advantage over me; but I assure you that I can learn very quickly too, and I am learning . . ."

"But to think of you as the head of a champagne firm is ridiculous," Belle said, "and everyone else thinks so too. Desmond will soon become the laughing stock of the champagne world unless you put someone well qualified in charge. Papa really didn't know what he was doing. . . ."

"Please Belle." Henri's sudden anger showed in his voice. "Apart from the depressing news about Tara I was just thinking what a pleasant domestic evening this was."

"Oh were you?" Belle retorted. "Well I was too actually; but the thought of what poor Zac is going through now: worry about Tara, disappointment with the business . . . both these things are really too much for one person. Then to think of an *interloper* interfering in our affairs. . . ."

"Oh my dear . . ." Lady Elizabeth, who was very keen on form, good breeding and especially good manners, even in the most adverse circumstances, looked embarrassed. "It's not as bad as that," she hurried on before Belle could speak again. "But it *is* splendid news that Zac is to be Vice-President of the Banque Franco-Belges! I hear it is to be the headlines in all the financial papers. It is a great step *up* in the world, is it not?"

Sandra had difficulty once again in believing her ears and looked to Henri for confirmation. Silently he nodded.

"It is being put about like that," he said *sotto voce,* "to save face."

"And why not?" Belle, who was gifted with very sharp hearing, turned angrily toward Henri. "Just whose side are *you* on, Henri?"

"I'm on no side my dear," Henri said equably.

"Oh yes you *are.*" Belle pointed an accusing finger across the table. "It's quite obvious you're on *her* side. Sometimes I wonder if she paid you to act as a public relations consultant for her. . . ."

"I do object to that, Belle," Henri said sternly and Sophie quickly followed him.

"So do I. Withdraw, please, Belle. . . ."

"No I will not withdraw," Belle said. "I stick by every word! Zac has been very badly treated by his father. He needs his family. He is a man at the end of his tether and I, for one, will rejoice heartily if the Press see, as well they might, that the Vice-President of the Banque Franco-Belges is a very prestigious position. It is given in justification to a man who has been sorely wronged, a recognition of the esteem and respect in which he is held by his fellow businessmen. Where Sandra O'Neill has tried to drag him down, Philippe de Lassale has attempted to elevate him. He is preparing them, and us, for the time when Zac Desmond truly enters into his inheritance and is the rightful head of the Desmond Group."

With that Belle, despite being so well brought up, and to the horror of her mother, threw her napkin into the center of the table and, getting up abruptly, hurried out of the room.

Sandra half expected the tap at the door. One could imagine Claire like a little mouse scuttling along the corridors after dark so that no one would see her.

"Come in," she called and was not surprised when the Countess of Saint-Aignan shyly popped her head around the door and asked if she could come in.

"I was expecting you," Sandra said from the depths of the chair where she had been sitting reading by the fire.

"Were you?" Claire dropped on the floor beside her, her thin pale fingers plucking at the fine hairs of the rug.

"I thought somehow we might meet again tonight."

"I'm terribly sorry about dinner; but you should keep away you know."

"How can I keep away?" Sandra took off her glasses and put down the report she was reading. "Why should I? This is my home. Your father has left it to me too. I think it is important to establish it as my home as well as yours. I know he liked to keep everyone together: Tourville, the center of his business as well as his family life. I'd like to continue that tradition because, ultimately, I want to be considered part of the family."

"I know you do," Claire said sadly. "But you won't be. 'They' will never let you."

"Who are 'they'?"

"You know, Zac and Belle. They will do anything to stop you remaining as head of the Group. And I think they will win."

"Do you *want* them to win?" Sandra inquired softly.

"No. I like you." Claire's voice was clipped, rather breathless, and Sandra wondered if she had always been so timid, so insecure and what had made her that way. "I like you and I hate them. I wanted to warn you about them at the time of the harvest but I didn't get a chance. You see, Armand, my husband, is very dominated by his mother. He seldom leaves home, nor does he like me to leave home."

"Good heavens." Sandra threw back her head and laughed but Claire looked nervously at the door and then slowly turned back to Sandra, her finger to her mouth. "Be quiet. Belle could well be outside the door."

"She's playing bridge. I hear she's very keen. . . ."

"Still . . ."

"Well go and see." Sandra pointed to the door and Claire crept toward it and threw it open suddenly to satisfy herself that there was no one on the other side. She breathed a loud sigh of relief.

"You're right. It's my imagination. This house scares me. It always has. It's full of ghosts. At night the shadows on the walls frighten me. I—" Claire put her hands over her face as though to drive away the real, or imagined, fears that tormented her.

"There there," Sandra said kindly, bending over her. "There's really nothing to be afraid of. No one can hurt you unless you allow them to."

"Oh it's easy for you to say that." Claire let her hands fall by her side and sat back on her heels. She looked like a small frightened girl instead of a married woman of twenty-five with a husband, a home and responsibilities. "I can see you're very strong." Claire looked up at her, eyes glowing with admiration. "I envy you. I'm not. I never have been. When I was small I was very sickly. I adored my father but he despised me. He said I was a weakling. He loved Tim and Belle because they were always doing clever, dangerous things—in sport I mean. Belle was a marvelous horsewoman and Tim always excelled in any form of sport he attempted. I was always ill." Claire looked abjectedly into the fire as if living again those sad best-forgotten days of her childhood. "And then when I was seventeen . . . I told you about the man I loved . . ."

"You said you'd tell me more," Sandra said encouragingly. "Maybe now is the time for confidences."

"His name was Piero Borghi. He was a painter, a man of great talent and taste but he came from a very poor background and my family opposed him. They were quite horrified when I asked him to come with us on a yachting holiday and they made him feel out of place and ill at ease.

"He swore the day he fell overboard that Zac and Belle would have left him to drown. Anyway when we got back to Paris for an exhibition of his paintings the reviews were so poor that the gallery closed it almost immediately. He never had a chance."

"But you don't blame them for *that?*"

"Oh yes I do. They were both spiteful and my father had great power. He owned newspapers and he had only to tell an editor what to write and he would write it."

"You really believe that? That your *whole* family conspired against Piero? I find that incredible." Sandra sat back and gazed at her visitor. She was thinking of the car that had pushed her off the road only a few nights before. Unbidden, a suspicion as to who was behind the deed came again to her mind. It kept on recurring, however much she tried to banish it.

"The Desmonds would do anything to get what they want." Claire drew her dressing gown around her and shivered although the room was warm. "You must be very aware of them; very circumspect in everything you do. Be very watchful—tread carefully, very carefully indeed. Because what the Desmonds want they usually get."

For a long time, as the clock on the mantelpiece slowly ticked away, Sandra and Claire gazed at each other as if each were trying to divine what was in the mind of the other.

TWO

The Rules of the Game

10

In the great days of the family the Falconetti had filled every notable post in Rome from court chamberlain to reigning monarchs, to highly placed cardinals and prelates at the papal courts. They had sent members as ambassadors to countries all over the world and one youthful Falconetti had accompanied Marco Polo on his travels. There had been artistic, musical and scientific Falconetti, and a celebrated medical Falconetti who had worked with William Harvey in his discoveries concerning the circulation of the blood.

Nor had the women of the family been neglected. They had been almost regal heads of large households, had married into the very best Italian and continental nobilities—one had been a celebrated, and not always discreet, mistress of a mediaeval pope and had borne him several children. They had been gracious and beautiful and some were very clever, excelling not only in appreciation but in the execution of music and the arts. One was a notable scholar in the sixteenth century during that gracious and eventful epoch known as the Renaissance which Italy, in its flowering of precocity and talent, made so peculiarly its own.

But, alas, in the twentieth century the Falconetti stock had appeared, finally, to wear itself out. It became gradually more and more poverty-stricken. Either unaware of their decline, or refusing to acknowledge it, they continued to behave as though they were still one of the most celebrated families in

Italy with a fortune to match. Naturally they went on marrying one another, people in similar circumstances to their own, and continued to proliferate. Tara's father, Marchese Franco Falconetti, had thirteen children. His wife was a Principessa of the House of Gamborini whose history was very similar to that of the Falconetti, or any other noble Italian family since the end of the Italian monarchy.

However, there was something engaging and good-humored about Gabriella and Franco Falconetti. They became adept not only at making ends meet, but making the best of what small fortune was, inevitably after two wars, left. They sent their children to be educated by various better-off members of their respective families. Indeed there was something distinctly medieval and, indeed, rather admirable, about the way Gabriella and Franco made do with their enormous brood, managed to feed and educate them by sponging unashamedly off richer relations. Furthermore they kept their various houses, even if not exactly intact. Not a reputable painting remained hanging on the walls of most of them; and their plasterwork recalled the days of wartime occupation.

Tara Falconetti came somewhere in the middle of this large and, on the whole, cheerful and optimistic brood who, with their parents, resembled that legendary family created in English fiction by Charles Dickens who were always waiting for something to turn up: the Micawbers. Something often did, not least Zac Desmond who, at the time he met Tara, had been sent by his father to perfect his knowledge of the wine business in the vineyards of a distant, and more successful, relation of the Gamborini family. Chianti Gamborini was a most respectable product with not quite the éclat or fame of the House of Desmond but, among Italian wines, it occupied a high place.

Of all the Falconetti girls Tara had, perhaps, been endowed the most: with looks, with beauty, with character and personality. But she also had something of the characteristics of a magpie; she was acquisitive. She collected things: clothes, jewelry, handbags, people. She had become a very successful model before she was eighteen and her father, gracefully if ruefully bowing to necessity, had given permission for a contessa of the House of Falconetti to follow such a calling.

As a final accolade she had her photograph on the cover of *Vogue* and it was then that she met Zac Desmond who, perhaps, for the first and only time, was swept off his feet by an emotion as genuine as any he had ever felt in his life: love.

But Zac was a hard man to love, as Tara soon found out. He had enormous charm and a kind of fleshy attraction for women, based mainly on his apparent wealth and power, but he had never applied himself to the art of love, which is an art like any other. He was a selfish man in life and he was a selfish man in love; he took and he left other people dissatisfied. He soon lost the love, which had probably been rather superficial in the first place, of his wife who was selfish in her turn and hard to please.

Probably at whatever time they might have met the result would have been the same in marriage terms for Tara and Zac: two ill-matched people incapable of being happy or able to make each other happy.

Tara had soon turned to other men to give her what she craved and Zac could not. Not only sexual satisfaction, but a basic need to be constantly loved, admired, desired and praised; a tall order for any man to fill and, so far, no man ever had.

The exterior of the Palazzo Falconetti was one of the great glories of the Italian Renaissance; some said that the master Brunelleschi had a hand in its design in the middle of the fifteenth century but, whether he had or not, it was still considered of sufficient importance internationally to receive a grant from one of those American institutions which exist to bolster up European culture.

At the time that Zac arrived to see his wife it was in a reasonable state of repair and restoration. The great bronze gates, which were most certainly by Ghiberti, enclosed a magnificent courtyard and, as a disheveled servant emerged from the elaborate double doors it was *just* possible to imagine that the great days of the Falconetti family had returned.

However, inside it was a different story. Extravagant as always with other people's money, the present Marchese, Tara's elder brother Marco, had long exhausted the patience as well as the purse of the ever-patient and munificent benefactors. There was a distinct odor of damp as well as decay once inside, and it was many years since the grimy, encrusted walls had received the attentions of a decorator. The rugs and carpets with which a former marchese had endeavored to cover up the cracks in the floorboards were threadbare, and it was with some caution that Zac began to ascend the once grand marble staircase to the second floor, where his brother-in-law awaited him.

The fortunes of the Falconetti family might have been very different had the eldest son, Enrico, succeeded his father instead of his younger brother Marco. Enrico, born at the beginning of the War, had been a splendid almost Renaissance figure himself, blessed not only with good looks and a happy disposition—which all his family to a greater or lesser extent shared—but, in addition, some kind fairy had at his birth blessed him with two of the rarest of Falconetti attributes: energy and ambition. However, the same good fairy, or maybe it was a bad one also present at the time, had cursed him with a reckless love of speed, and that white hope of the modern Falconetti family, the glorious, gifted Enrico, dashed his brains out on the macadam surface of one of Mussolini's magnificent autostrada, on which he had been traveling at excessive speed, before he was nineteen years old.

Besides Enrico and Marco there were three other brothers: Lorenzo, Giacomo and Luigi, and they had all done well in their respective fields. The youngest, Luigi, had done the best, at least financially. He was the president of a large corporation manufacturing computers and word processors, living in Milan with a grand villa on Lake Como and a rich and intelligent wife. Of the two middle brothers, Lorenzo was a lawyer practicing in Turin and Giacomo a respected physician.

But it was the next in line to Enrico, alas, Marco, the black sheep of the family, who inherited the magnificent Palazzo Falconetti and what was left of the family fortune. Marco had none of the ability, drive, ambition or talent of any of his brothers; but he did have a love of the good things of life and, accordingly, a rapacious need of money, and not much concern as to where it came from.

He also preferred the company of men to women, but his parents in their grief at Enrico's quite unnecessary car smash had married him off, with Victorian determination and almost indecent haste, to another principessa of an even more distant branch of the Gamborini family, who now lived peacefully in the United States of America with her two children.

His wife, Mafalda, who was an alert intelligent woman, as well as attractive, had not been in the least bit vindictive—only thankful to obtain a papal separation from her husband. Certainly she had something to do with various benefactions that had been made to the Falconettis by wealthy Americans for the restoration of its palaces, but she could not stop Marco spending most of the money on himself. It was siphoned off, through crooked and indifferent builders, to indulging the tastes of Marco and his friends and when the good-natured benefactors eventually found out what was happening they stopped the source abruptly.

Not only flat broke, but heavily in debt, Marco had fled not once but several times to his brother-in-law, the wealthy Zac Desmond, to get him out of trouble. The rich and despotic Luigi refused to have anything to do with him.

But Zac never gave anything away. His motto, insofar as

he had one, was "an eye for an eye, a tooth for a tooth" and now as security on his loan he owned the deeds not only of a good bit of Falconetti real estate but of half the Palazzo Falconetti in Rome.

He looked around him with an air of disquiet, not to say disgust, as he climbed the stairs and greeted his brother-in-law in the long salon overlooking the via Falconetti, into which a pale, wintry sun cast a mellow glow on the dusty walls, the crumbling tapestries and the faded carpet on the floor.

"I am terribly sorry to give you such bad news," Marco said, holding out his hand to Zac, who formally shook it.

"Is she worse?" Zac inquired with the objective air of a doctor asking after the welfare of a patient, rather than a husband anxious for the health of his wife.

"She *has* lost the baby." Marco deprecatingly hunched his shoulders, at which point Zac noticed a young man comfortably ensconced in one of the armchairs pressed close to the meager fire that burned in the grate. The system of central heating installed by one of its more affluent members at the beginning of the twentieth century had long since gone the way of most of the water supply, gas and electricity, so that large areas of the huge palace remained unheated and unlit and, after dark in winter, it was a melancholy sight, a cold, sad place in which to be.

The young man waved his hand affably and Marco said, "This is my friend Fabio Fabbri. His father—"

"How do you do?" Zac cut him short, being not in the least interested in the antecedents of the Fabbri family. "How is she now?"

Marco spread those expressive hands once again.

"I think she's all right. I mean aren't you disappointed about the baby?"

"Not very," Zac said, "especially as I didn't know she was pregnant. It was not *my* child, but I would like to see my wife. . . ."

"Naturally . . ." Marco sighed and looked at Fabio, who stared morosely into the fire, but he made no move toward the door.

"Zac." Marco scratched his head and Zac, never very sympathetic toward his flabby and dissolute brother-in-law, found what little patience he had waning.

"What *is* it, Marco?" He tapped his foot impatiently on the floor. "Look . . . I am tired, I am fed up and," he rubbed his hands and looked pointedly at the fire, "and I am cold. Have you *no* heating in this place?"

"Well . . ." Marco continued to rub his head in a manner that irritated the already impatient Zac. It was noticeable too that the Italian had on a thick coat over a polo-necked sweater. "Unfortunately . . . funds being what they are . . . Zac, I wondered . . ."

"Oh please spare me any more of your begging speeches," Zac said loudly, "and take me at once to Tara."

"It's not only *that,* Zac." Marco looked toward the door, which remained closed. "She doesn't want to see you. I'm sorry, I shouldn't have telephoned. I didn't realize . . ."

With an exclamation Zac strode toward the door, flung it open to find the tired old servant apathetically cleaning the corridor outside the room, and no doubt taking in everything that went on inside it.

"Take me to the Contessa now!" he barked in his passable Italian, learned when he had been working for the Gamborini.

"All right, all right," Marco grumbled, bustling out of the room and elbowing the servant to one side. "I'll do it. There's no need to be so impatient; but please don't upset her. . . ."

"I upset her . . ." Zac said in a voice full of menace. "What do you think she had done to *me?"*

Without another word Marco, with more nimbleness than one would have thought he possessed, preceded Zac from the room, running up the staircase ahead of him, agitatedly waving his hands, and along the next corridor until he stood in front of the door of a room which stood half open.

"Tara . . ." He put his head around the door.

"I don't want to see him," Tara screamed in Italian. "I *know* he's here . . ."

"I'm afraid . . ." Marco began in the same language.

"Out of my way, Marco." Zac peremptorily pushed his brother-in-law to one side and strode into the vast room in the middle of which was a large canopied bed with the diminutive and rather frightened figure of Tara in the center of it. She seemed to shrink even more visibly as Zac advanced upon her and her brother, lacking the bravery of those legendary Falconettis who had fought over the centuries for the honor of their country, scuttled out of the room.

The chill of the malodorous room was not improved by the gloom in which Tara lay. The curtains were drawn and an even smaller fire than Zac had seen downstairs seemed to have given up any hope of producing flames and flickered dully. Even Zac felt some pity for this woman to whom he had given his name twelve years before, with whom he had briefly thought himself in love and who had remained an obsession with him, despite their gross mistreatment of each other.

With an exclamation he went over to the window and wrenched apart the curtains, one of which immediately came away in his hands amidst a shower of dust.

"Zut!" Zac stepped away with an expression of disgust, leaving one curtain hanging across the window and another lying on the floor. "What on *earth* made you come to this place?"

"Where else could I come?" Tara replied in a voice that Zac could hardly hear. "I was born in Palazzo Falconetti after all. It *is* my home."

"It is *not* your home!" Zac said, perching precariously on the bed as none of the brocaded or velvet-covered armchairs looked too safe. "Your home is in Paris with me and you should never have left it."

"You *raped* me," Tara said as though such a monstrous matter was something which Zac might have forgotten.

"Nonsense! A husband can't *rape* his wife . . . I was carried away by passion."

"I call it rape—against my will—violence . . ." Tara's voice grew stronger and she tried to sit up against the pillows piled behind her. "You raped me and you struck me. You brought about this miscarriage during which I nearly died. . . ."

"Thank God I *did* bring it about," Zac said without the slightest trace of contrition. "I wouldn't have wanted the bastard of a garage mechanic trying to pass as a son or daughter of mine."

"But you would have had to," Tara screamed, clearly beyond herself. "Imagine the scandal if you had tried to prove otherwise. . . ."

"I wouldn't have minded the scandal," Zac said loftily. "Divorce has no shame these days. . . ."

"Ah, but what about Miss O'Neill?" Tara's tone of voice became crafty and less shrill. "What about the *effect* on the Desmond Group and on your struggle to be its president?"

"That is of no importance now." Zac rose from the bed and, going over to the window, stared into the narrow street outside full, as usual, of the noise of cars and the little Italian motor scooters which, for many of the Romans, were their chief means of transportation. "Tara, you know that child could not have been mine. You and I have not slept together for many months." He turned toward her and stared down at her, his mouth in a grimace of distaste that might, possibly, have had in it an element of self-disgust. "I know that you have had lovers in the past but none, I think, as unworthy as Émile Livio . . . and the fact that you were carrying *his* child horrifies me. I know you would have tried to pass it off as mine, as you cannot have been many months gone.

Maybe if this miscarriage hadn't occurred you would have used that occasion the other night to foist the child on me. . . ."

" 'Occasion' you call it." Tara gave a laugh that seemed to lose itself inside the cavernous covers of her bed. "I like that word *occasion.* Why don't you call a rape a rape . . . ?"

"I was carried away I said." Zac paused and momentarily swallowed. "I must say now that I'm sorry. I was beside myself with anger and also—" he swiftly crossed the room and sat by her side again "—desire. I'll confess it to you. You know that I desire you and always have . . . yet you continue to spurn me, repulse me, mock me. . . ."

"Who wouldn't mock a man so bad at it?" Tara gave a derisive laugh and reached for a cigarette but Zac seized her wrist in a manner reminiscent of the way he had the week before and for a moment, recalling it, she felt herself tremble, and gazed at him with fear.

"Don't worry," he said. "I won't touch you; not yet, not now; but I want to serve notice on you, Tara, that this business with Émile Livio must stop. You must *never* see him again. My mother knows you were miscarrying and so now will all my family. It must never be known that it was not my child. It will be announced that I am heartbroken about it and that good relations have resumed between us again. I am having you moved again immediately to a clinic where you will be better cared for than in this awful place." Zac couldn't repress a shudder. "We shall be photographed together at the clinic, the picture given to the papers, the story of how united we are, how sorry to lose our third child bla bla bla. This miscarriage will be blamed on the fact that, as a former model, you were addicted to too severe a diet. After your recovery we shall foregather with all the family at the home of my sister for you to convalesce and enjoy the celebration of Christmas." He leaned over and looked into her eyes.

"Listen to me very carefully my dear Tara. The Desmond

Empire is in grave danger. The wolf has come into the fold. The Irishwoman would be delighted to know of your folly, the fact that your lover was a mere mechanic and that you were pregnant by him. I need all the prestige I can get not only in Champagne but in Paris and in the financial capitals of the world.

"I am going to use everything that I can to promote my image as a successful man with a happy, stable family life, and you are going to help me do it. Philippe de Lassale has played straight into my hands. Out of a misguided sense of pity, he has made me Vice-President and a member of the Board of the Banque Franco-Belges. I don't think he quite realizes what he has done, which shows the man's not as clever as I thought. In the eyes of the world I appear to have made an advance, not a retreat. I know that Sandra is furious about it, but she was too late to stop it. Philippe had a great regard for my father. He wanted to make a generous gesture toward me and it is one that, in time, he may well regret. Don't worry, I shall make full use of it for, henceforth, I shall have my sights not only on the Desmond Group but on the Franco-Belges Bank as well.

"I shall show the people who think they're in power that they can't fool about with me. . . ." Carried away by his own rhetoric, he stopped abruptly and looked down on his wife with an expression that was almost kindly.

"Now, my dear. You will be gone from here within an hour to the finest clinic in Rome. I want to make sure that you have the best of everything." Suddenly he leaned down and touched her hair, stroked her cheek. "You are a very beautiful woman you know . . . believe me, I need you for my image. From now on I want you constantly by my side and, like the wife of Caesar, you must be above reproach. Please remember," he shook a warning finger at her, "the rules of the game, and stick to them."

He then turned sharply and left the room, Tara's gaze following him in wonder.

Sometimes she seriously believed that her husband was clinically insane. Rules of the game, indeed! What game? She'd show him . . . and teach him too.

Zac said sharply:

"My wife will be leaving here within the hour, Falconetti. Kindly summon your doctor immediately and have arrangements for her to be transferred to the best clinic in Rome. . . ."

"Is she worse?" Marco, who had been standing very close to Fabio Fabbri when Zac came into the room, sprang toward him.

"No, but she will be if she remains here." Zac paused and looked around, a sneer on his face. "This place is disgusting, Falconetti. When I think of the ancient grandeur of your family. . . . A curtain came apart in my hand as I tried to draw it. It was like dust and ashes. Now listen carefully: I want it to be announced that my wife and I have lost the child we were expecting. . . ."

"But you said . . ."

"Forget what I said—" Zac pointed a threatening finger at him"—and you too." He turned to Fabio. "Tara has convinced me that the child was mine after all. She plays around too much. Corrupted by your family's past. But the dates were all right. I was mistaken. But if the papers come here they will not believe that the wife of a Desmond could *exist* for a second in such squalor. Call your doctor at once, Marco, because the smell in this place makes me ill."

"Really I think I should go." Fabio got nervously out of his chair, tossing in the fire the cigarette he had in his hand. "Be seeing you, Marco. . . ."

Marco looked up suddenly and shook his head as though he wasn't quite sure what was going on.

"Oh all right, see you. Call me this evening."

Fabio nodded and politely inclined his head to Zac. "Goodbye."

"Goodbye," Zac said coldly, turning his back on him in an insulting gesture of dismissal. "Are you making that phone call, Marco?"

"Pronto pronto," Marco said hurriedly and left the room in the wake of his friend.

Zac took up a stance by the side of the fire gazing sternly around him at the decrepit furniture, the crumbling walls, the large gaps where pictures had been carried off to the saleroom. He was still shaking his head when Marco came back and said:

"Dr. Luigi Seranno said it is not necessary for him to come. He attended Tara and knows what the situation is. He is making arrangements and an ambulance will be here within the hour. He says—"

"I'm not interested in what that quack says," Zac said curtly. Then indicating the room they were standing in, "But I am interested in the state of this palazzo. I own half of it, you know. Which half do I own? The dirty half or the clean half? The lit half or the unlit half? It is disgraceful and disgusting the way you have let it go, Falconetti. I'm surprised your brothers allow it. They're fond of you, I suppose, and have no use for a place this size. . . ."

"Oh please please *stop,* Zac!" Suddenly Marco flung himself into the chair vacated by Fabio and put his head in his hands. "If you had any idea of what I have been through even you, hard man that I know you to be, might have pity on me. My sister, whom I happen to love very much, arrived in a state near death. I have been very worried about her, about you, about your marriage. . . ."

"Don't give me that bilge," Zac said sternly. "Have you anything to drink in this hole?"

"Help yourself." Marco pointed to a table in the corner on which were glasses and bottles. "Take what you want. As you say, you own half of the place and the banks the rest . . .

have it all. But for God's sake, Zac," Marco looked up at him and, for a moment, Zac could have sworn he saw tears in his eyes, "I really *am* in a very bad way financially. I am in danger. . . ."

"*Danger* . . ." Zac's eyes narrowed. "What kind of danger . . . ?"

"From the people I owe money to. You know. I don't need to spell it out. All sorts of *types* here in Rome. One has to get money, and other things, where one can. . . ."

"*Other* things!" Zac instinctively lowered his voice. "Other things . . . you mean, drugs? Or is it simply boys?" He pointed his head derisively toward the door. "Incidentally you have very poor taste, if I may say so. . . ."

"Fabio is a very talented actor," Marco retorted defensively, but Zac waved a hand at him as if telling him to save his breath.

"No, I want you to tell me what this danger is you speak of." Zac poured himself a drink, recapped the bottle and came over to the fire, sitting as close to it as he could get. "It interests me very much."

"Why does it interest you so much?"

"Because I would like to know what or who you are involved with. After all you are my brother-in-law; your children are my nephews, poor little souls."

"It's none of your business," Marco said sulkily. "Let's just say I make mistakes. I am a bad judge of character."

"You can say that again," Zac said, laughing, but without mirth. "Why don't you go to Luigi? I hear he has plenty. Or Lorenzo . . . all lawyers have money."

"And *I* have my pride." Marco eyed Zac malevolently. "You may not think so but I have. I can ask you, or friends; but my blood relations . . . they would despise me. After all I am the eldest surviving brother. They still look up to me. I have to have some respect. . . ."

"Don't be too sure of that." Zac stuck a finger in the middle of his chest and Marco wriggled uncomfortably as though he had been pinioned on the point of a skewer. "I doubt if there is anyone left in the world who respects you. Anyway—" he appeared to think deeply for a moment or two as if savoring Marco's predicament all the more "—as you're in a spot and you're my brother-in-law, this time I'll pay your debts; but one day you'll turn over this palazzo to me completely and maybe I'll do something with it, or convert it into a hotel.

"Very soon I am going to be a big man, the Head of the Desmond Empire, and Palazzo Falconetti, ancient home of my wife's family, might suit me very well. *Buongiorno* Marco. . . ." And with an insulting pat on his brother-in-law's cheek he left, calling loudly for the ancient servant to get him a taxi.

It was going to be a large dinner party, Sandra thought, as her Rolls was stopped at the gate by a policeman who checked her driver's papers then saluted and signaled her through, directing him to the pavilion on the right. Immediately two lackeys dressed in eighteenth-century livery ran out of the main door, down the steps, sconces in their hands, one to open her door, the other to light the way. Sandra looked at her watch, surprise on her face. It was after eight o'clock.

"Surely I'm not the first? I thought I was rather late." She looked around. "Where are the other cars?"

"There *is* parking in a side garden, Madame," a flunkey replied, looking toward the great palace of the Sun King.

"But still . . . Oh well." Sandra shrugged, thanked her chauffeur and climbed the steps to that part of the huge Château where the lights were blazing.

Sandra, a francophile as well as half French by birth, had always loved French history. Maybe she had accepted an invitation she would otherwise have declined because of where it was to be held. A dinner party at Versailles! It was exciting enough, even for her.

But the hall was also deserted, the grand staircase of the Ambassadors empty. Maybe it was a joke. She stopped and looked about uncertainly as another flunkey, even more gorgeously dressed with powdered peruque and patches, appeared at the bottom of the stairs and bowed to her.

"If Madame will follow me," he said, starting to ascend.

Breathlessly Sandra followed him, relieved that she could now hear the sound of music in the salon beyond. She wore a black cocktail dress with a banded short skirt made for her by Emanuel Ungaro, who loved to add touches of luxury for his wealthy and choosy clients. He'd even been fussy about the jewelry that Sandra would wear to accompany his creation and, with her blonde hair adorned with a band of tiny diamonds to secure the bouffant style, she looked graceful, elegant and quite stunningly beautiful as she began to climb the stairs after the august servant.

"Where are the other guests?" she inquired of his back.

He didn't reply: perhaps he hadn't heard. They reached the top of the magnificent staircase and crossed the gallery adorned with statues, rich tapestries and fresh flowers massed in great silver urns. Yet still she could hear no voices.

She had a curious feeling of anticipation as the *maître d'hotel* flung open an ornate, elaborately carved double door and, standing back, bowed, indicating that she should precede him.

Catching her breath, she entered upon a scene of sufficient splendor to dazzle the Sun King himself. Hundreds of candles sparkled in sconces on the walls, illuminating the massive chandelier which hung from the center, its thousands of pieces of glass twinkling like the diamonds around her neck. From behind a screen in the corner came the sounds of a small chamber orchestra playing airs from concertos by Vivaldi. In the middle of the room was a table set for two people with gleaming silver and tall crystal glasses. The tablecloth and napkins were pink and a bottle of pink champagne lying in crushed ice could be seen in a silver bucket by the side.

The fragrance in the room from hundreds of flowers arranged in silver and porcelain vases mingled with the smell of the candles, the beeswax on the polished wooden floor, to produce an aroma at once mysterious and sensual. It was not unlike being in church.

Sandra momentarily closed her eyes as Tim appeared from behind the screen and came toward her, hands extended.

"Haydn, Vivaldi . . . just for us. For *you,* Sandra, the most beautiful woman in California, in the whole of France."

As he swept his arms around the room Sandra thought he must be drunk; but, in appearance and demeanor, he appeared perfectly sober.

"But where are all the sportsmen and women?" she demanded. "The International Olympic Committee . . ."

"Ah!" Tim hung his head like a small boy caught out in a naughty ruse. "That was just to get you here. . . ." He attempted to put his arm around her waist, but anger was already mounting in her breast.

"You mean we're *alone?"*

"How else could I have gotten you to dine with me? You never accept. I've sent you flowers, written you letters but—No!" Tim gazed at her with mock defiance, a hand before him. "So I had to resort to a ruse."

"Not a very funny one, or clever," Sandra said, looking behind her to where the door had been closed. "You've made an absolute fool of me, Tim."

"My dear, how can you say that . . . ?" Taking her arm, he steered her toward a chaise-longue placed in front of a roaring fire which only added to the charm, for on such a cold night the room was well heated by radiators. As he lowered her into a chair a waiter, expertly whisking the champagne from the bucket by the table, came toward them, and raised one of two fluted glasses that stood on a table to one side of them.

"Champagne, Madame . . . ?" he inquired, bowing and,

not waiting for her to reply, poured some of the liquid into her glass, a beautiful clear, rich rosé color, its fine, white mousse springing to the brim.

"Your favorite vintage," Tim murmured.

"Thank you . . ." At last, lest she be thought childish, Sandra smiled, though deep in her heart she felt a bitter chagrin at this joke, wondering how many other people besides the servants present here tonight knew of it.

"Oh, I see a smile," Tim said, excitedly taking the seat next to her. "At last! Don't you *like* surprises?"

"All right," Sandra said with a sigh. "What do we do now?"

Tim looked toward the table, extending a hand in the direction of the two waiters busily at work there.

"Caviar flown from Russia, *foie gras* from my brother-in-law de Saint-Aignan." He looked at her seriously, suddenly grave. "Tell me, how do you like that fellow?"

"I scarcely know him," Sandra said offhandedly. Occasionally she saw one of the waiters taking a sly peep at her and she felt increasingly foolish. Tim had obviously shared the joke with them beforehand and they were enjoying it enormously. Doubtless they thought she was a *"poule de luxe."*

Who else knew about it? Laughing up their sleeves from a distance?

"Oh he's difficult to know." Tim leaned over and offered her a *canapé* from a silver tray. "I don't really know him either. I don't think anyone does, not even Claire. She was never in love with him, you know. He was never her first choice, her first love." Tim sighed. *"That's* a sad tale and one which doubtless you will get to know one day. It shows neither my father, my elder brother nor my elder sister in a very good light. . . ."

"We're not here to talk about your family are we, Tim?" Sandra said sharply.

"No, we're here to talk about *us,"* Tim said, attempting

to take her hand; but when she refused to give it to him he ignored the gesture with the air of the practiced seducer that he undoubtedly was and poured more champagne instead. Nothing really seemed to upset Tim, Sandra realized. He had that uncanny gift of turning a rebuff, even an insult, to his own advantage.

"You see, my dear Sandra," Tim leaned toward her earnestly, "I genuinely want to get to know you better. I like you and I admire you . . . but you always resist me. You play with me; you don't take me seriously."

He *was* charming, she thought, looking at the shy deprecatory smile; but she still couldn't get over her anger. Worse, it was a feeling of humiliation, of being cheated and duped. To have had Ungaro rush her a special dress . . . for this! She looked around. Although it was magnificent, she couldn't help feeling Tim had deliberately made a fool of her. At last a Desmond had succeeded in doing what no one else ever had done: made her feel ridiculous!

Sandra put the champagne glass firmly on the table by her side and stared stonily at him, all traces of her smile gone.

"Please, Sandra, forgive me." He tried again to take her hand. "I did hope it would make you happy. A little game. Incidentally it cost a fortune, to say nothing of promises to the Minister of the Interior. . . ."

"There was absolutely no need for it, Tim." Sandra, to her added humiliation, was aware of tears springing to her eyes. "I dressed up for a party . . . this," she looked at her gown, "Ungaro's midinettes slaved for nights to get ready. My diamonds—" she fingered the jewels at her neck "—all to be made a fool of."

"A fool!" Tim sprang up, nearly knocking over the priceless ormolu table. "My dearest Sandra, that is the *last* thing I had in mind. . . ."

"Then what did you have in mind?" The steely voice, well-known to business opponents and dreaded by them, had returned; the tears had vanished.

"I'm being honest with you," Tim said earnestly. "I despaired of *ever* getting to know you better. You don't seem to understand." He paused, looking abstractedly at the ground. "I am in fact *extremely* attracted to you. As soon as I saw you walk into the grand salon of the Château de Tourville on the day you arrived I knew you were different from all the women I have ever known. . . ."

"I find it very difficult to take any of this seriously, Tim," Sandra said, beginning at last to relax, allowing maybe the excellent champagne to go a little to her head, a hint of mockery in her voice, enjoying the game at last. "I am, after all, a serious threat to the Desmonds, am I not? Hated by your brother . . ."

"But not by me. I'm not at all jealous of you. Anyone can run the business for all I care. . . ." He leaned toward her, his mouth an inch away from hers.

"Do you know the contour of your lips is terribly sexy . . ." Gently he caressed her cheek and Sandra allowed his hand, after all, to linger, his fingers gently to etch the outline of her mouth.

Well . . . why not? She lay back on the Recamier-style couch and the lips that he touched, so ardently wished to kiss, broke into a playful smile. Why not indeed? He had gone to an awful lot of trouble and expense, not to say worry. He must have known what her response would be. She might have walked straight out. He must want her very badly indeed to play such a risky game.

In the background the music played, the candles flickered, sending shadows dancing on the walls, and Sandra O'Neill realized she couldn't, didn't, want to be a businesswoman all the time. All work and no fun. Tim saw the acquiescence in her eyes and as one hand slid under the hem of her dress the other firmly cupped her breast and finally his lips rested first lightly, then passionately, on hers.

It was a long, lingering, loving kiss banishing all thoughts of hostility and resentment from Sandra's mind. Somewhere inside her a small voice said "never trust a Desmond," but that was banished too. His hand now rested on her naked thigh and the image of a nude, lustful embrace began not only to haunt her but to seem both urgent and desirable; but not here, not now.

Very lightly, almost playfully, she pushed him away, gazing into his deep blue eyes blazing with ardor.

"Not here," she whispered.

"Where?" he urgently whispered back.

"Where do you think?"

"This is the Cabinet Royal," he said suggestively. "I asked for it specially. It will surely have known of the love between Louis XV and the Pompadour." He raised his eyes langorously to the ceiling. "Do you see the arrow of cupid pointed toward the heart of the King? Look at the initials. AJP. Antoinette Jeanne Poisson, Marquise de Pompadour. . . ." His eyes slid toward her. "Certainly we can make love here if you like. The servants will be gone after dinner. . . ."

It was a sensational idea, at once primitive and exotic; a coupling in the Cabinet Royal at Versailles. . . .

"Then you *will?*" he repeated.

"I might." She had a mocking light in her eyes, and playfully tapped the wrist of the hand still under her skirt, murmuring, "Pas devant les domestiques."

"They're not even looking. After dinner, then. Here?" The tone of his voice was urgent.

Artfully her eyes slid toward the floor and he followed her gaze.

"I can't believe this," he said, sitting upright at last and rubbing his face.

"I'm not made of stone, Tim."

"I didn't think you were. I *knew* . . ."

He took her by the hand as a waiter approached and, with a low bow, started to refill their glasses. Discreetly he kept his eyes in front of him.

"Dinner in a few moments, Monsieur?"

Tim didn't answer, his eyes mesmerized by Sandra. The top of her breasts, exposed by the skillful design of the couturier, enhanced the elegance of her long slender throat. He could imagine undressing her very slowly, his hands caressing her body as, little by little, it revealed itself to him.

"I'm not a bit hungry," he said.

"Pity." Sandra smiled as if she could read his thoughts. "I, on the contrary, am starving."

"Let's eat quickly then."

"No, let's eat very *slowly* . . ." she spelled out the words teasingly, "and then slowly, afterward . . ."

"Make love . . ." Tim whispered, adding unnecessarily and, as it happened for him, fatally. "If only Zac could see you now."

"Zac?" Sandra sat up as if someone had stabbed her in the back with a sharp pin. "What on earth made you mention *his* name? I assure you Zac is never likely to see me like this." She crossed her legs modestly as if regretting the freedom she had allowed him.

"Does Zac know I'm here?" Sandra's air of dalliance had vanished, the lingering notion that she and Tim Desmond might actually make love gone, if not forever, at least for the time being.

"Of *course* he doesn't! *Darling. . . .*" Tim immediately realized his gaffe.

"I begin to think he does," Sandra said, looking around. "The caviar from Russia, family connections no doubt, *foie gras* from the Saint-Aignans. Is all your family engaged in feeding the silly goose until she bursts?"

"Nothing of the kind. Don't be preposterous! What makes you think they should?"

" 'If Zac could see you now' . . . what a thing to say to me! As if I'd let your brother near me in this way. The whole idea is nauseating . . ."

"Look, I'll tell you the truth." Tim sat up and straightened his tie. "I'll be honest, so that there are no secrets between us. I *did* need a little help. One can't hire the Palace of Versailles just like that. All I said to Zac was . . ."

"Enough." Sandra stood up, wishing she hadn't worn such a short skirt; maybe, unconsciously, she'd had seduction in her mind too.

"How else could I have gotten the Château . . . ?"

"Zac knew all about it?"

"A little . . ."

"That's quite enough. This, as we say in America, obviously suggests to me a setup. I see it now . . . 'Oh she was easy game; fell into my arms; all she needed was a few soft lights and sweet music. . . .' "

"Then what?" Tim said harshly.

"Then zut!" Sandra clapped her hands together, flicking her fingers. "Telephone the reporters, tell them the whole story. Show them what a fool Sandra O'Neill is; sex-starved probably . . . a mere, frail woman underneath it all. Maybe there would be an account by *you* of how easy it was to seduce me. Then the next plane back to California for me . . . set up . . . a fool." Sandra began to laugh a shade hysterically, but still perfectly in control. Inside her the fires of love had been stoked into rage. A servant began to walk toward them again, bowing low from the waist as though he had seen nothing.

"Dinner is served, Madame, Monsieur . . ."

"Your brother is my enemy, Tim, you know that," Sandra hissed, then, turning to the servant, said in a complete change of tone:

"Thank you, but please only serve Monsieur. Tonight *le roi* will be dining alone."

Then she turned her back on Tim, on the servants, the table groaning with delicacies, the candles, the flunkies, the orchestra—playing a little dejectedly now—and swept out of the room in a way of which the Marquise de Pompadour, one of its former *habituées,* most certainly would have approved.

11

As the helicopter hovered over the ancient fortress of Burg-Farnbach Sandra was able to see its extent even though, in comparison to the majestic grandeur of the surrounding Bavarian Alps, it looked quite tiny. Winter and summer the mountains were covered with snow but now, at Christmastime, the countryside was also white except for a forest of conifers: beautiful, tall, upright Bavarian conifers, the original Christmas tree, that stretched down into the valley and encircled a beautiful lake of clear, crystal blue water reflecting the azure sky above.

On all sides the high peaks and needles of the mountains stretched toward the sky, a kaleidoscope of muted pastel colors illuminated here or there by a jet of golden flame as the late afternoon sun caught a thick patch of icicles overhanging the cliffs. It was a spectacular sight.

Gradually, as the helicopter descended, the true dimensions of the castle became more apparent—a huge, monolithic, crenellated pile with tall Gothic spirals and picturesque gables reminiscent of one of the follies of King Ludwig, though this was much, much older.

Behind the castle, in a field where the helicopter was to land, a tiny crowd of people huddled together like pinpoints in an area that had been cleared of snow. Arms were raised to wave at Sandra or to shield eyes in order to view the giant mechanical bird as it slowly came in to land. Sandra, peering through the window in the seat next to the pilot, shook her hand excitedly toward the group below as faces became recognizable.

Sandra could make out Tim, Belle and Carl with their son, a figure that looked like Claire and one or two others she didn't know. There was no sign of Zac, though Sandra knew that he was to be present at the Christmas house party organized once again by that puzzling enigmatic brother and sister. Their motivations she found almost impossible to fathom, because their behavior, their attitude toward her, varied so violently from day to day, almost from hour to hour.

Sandra understood that Christmas was usually spent at Tourville and the New Year at Burg-Farnbach; but this year she had to be in New York early in the New Year and the family plans had been completely rearranged to accommodate her. Why? Yet, in the circumstances, she could hardly refuse. After what had passed it would have been churlish to throw back in their faces the offer of a flag of peace, or was it the white flag of surrender? Soon, possibly, she would find out.

Yet whatever happened, whatever they did, she knew she was not meant to feel comfortable: these were tactics to keep her on the hop; the fluctuations intended to produce in her a continual feeling of unease.

But they would not succeed; she was determined about that. To be forewarned was to be forearmed.

After the welcome in the shadow of the helicopter, the introductions made in the warm comfort of the castle, a hurried tour to show her the dimensions of the magnificent building and estate, Sandra was relieved to be shown her room, to which she was personally conducted by Belle, who flung open the wooden shutters letting in the bright afternoon sun.

"Naturally we have saved the best suite in the castle for you." Belle turned enthusiastically, inviting her guest to admire the view. "And over there you can just see the highest point in the Bavarian Alps."

"It really *is* beautiful." Sandra joined Belle by the window. "I don't know how you can ever bear to leave."

"Oh I can bear to leave all right." Belle gave a mirthless laugh, a shrug of the shoulders. "Don't forget it's terribly *boring* here all year round for a woman with an active mind and I have one, you know, Sandra." Wandering slowly back into the room, she sat in a wooden rocking chair and began to rock herself back and forth. "I hope you realize that our feelings for you, when you first came, were motivated by more than rage, jealousy . . ."

"Oh I understand *that.*" Sandra leaned her back against the windowsill, folding her arms. "I—"

Belle held out a hand.

"No, please, let me go on because I do think we owe you an explanation. We were not very nice to you and that is, in a way, the whole point of inviting you here for Christmas. We so want to try and make amends."

"I assure you. I—" Sandra attempted to calm their spurious fears. She, too, could play the game of bluff—if only they knew how well.

But Belle hurried on. "You see both Zac and I do care terribly about Desmond as a business *and* as part of our heritage. I would love to have had a hand in running it with Zac, but my father would never let me. In that way he was terribly old-fashioned, you know—the woman's place and all that kind of thing. He wanted me to marry well and be a princess, not a businesswoman. When, after I'd done my duty and produced an heir, I began to move around the world more, coming to Paris to stay with Zac, Father realized that being a wife and mother, the châtelaine even of a marvelous home such as this, wasn't enough for me.

"Tara, of course, by this time was bored too. Although we're not at all alike and don't, in fact, get on particularly well, we do have ambitions to have some role other than the purely domestic. She knows about fashion. I've got a good business head so, when the fashion house of Jean Marvoine was for sale, Father bought it for us with the intention of merging it in the Desmond Group. But it hasn't been very successful, I mean for us. Maurice Raison, our chief designer, doesn't like people interfering, understandably perhaps. By its very success we have put ourselves out of a job. Besides—" Belle spread her hands and looked wanly at her beringed fingers—"what *is* a maison de couture when you have ambition to be part of a huge company? I had hoped that Father would give me the champagne side to run by myself. I am known in the family as the one with the best palate, better even than Father's. My aptitude for marketing our *marque* of champagne is well recognized. I know all our representatives across the world. I say this without boasting, of course," she looked directly into Sandra's eyes, "but, believe me, I know my own worth. Oh yes."

"I'm sure you do." Sandra crossed the room and sat in a high-backed chair facing Belle. She knew she had to choose her words carefully. "I do wish we could have had this talk before. As you say your resentment was so obvious . . . I didn't know quite what to do. When I looked carefully into the affairs of the business I saw how bad things really were. Your father diversified too much . . ."

"Oh I know! He could never stay still for a moment."

"Then!" Sandra continued deliberately, "your brother didn't take enough care. Maybe he was too ambitious also."

"Oh he *was."* Belle leaned forward earnestly, as if discussing family affairs with a chum. "Zac's faults have been of omission rather than commission. Believe me, if Father had trusted us more, taken us into his confidence . . ." She paused for a moment frowning, as though in an effort to convince Sandra of her sincerity. "I would like us to put all that behind us now, if you can, and for us to be friends. After all, you are Father's adopted daughter. You must be like a sister to us and we like brothers and sisters to you."

"Willingly," Sandra said, rising and going over to take Belle's proffered hand. "I should like nothing better."

"Dinner's at eight." Belle rose too, a smile of satisfaction rather than pleasure on her face, as if at a job well done. "Please join us in the great hall when you're ready."

Preceding her to the door, Sandra opened it and then stood back, allowing her to pass. Some instinct made her want to reach out and kiss Belle on the cheek in true sisterly fashion; but another made her decide not to. On the one hand she wanted to trust her, on the other she knew that she couldn't. Not yet. Not, perhaps, ever.

Nevertheless—despite the air of mutual distrust—the days that passed were for Sandra among some of the happiest she had known since she had left the United States. Everyone seemed at pains to please her, to entertain and amuse her.

There was a moment of mutual embarrassment when she met Tim—having last seen him when she stalked out of the Cabinet du Roi—but he greeted her as though nothing had transpired, and she decided to play along with him. They kissed, with apparent affection, although Sandra tried not to think of that more intimate moment when she nearly succumbed, his hand caressing her bare thigh.

Thenceforward Tim aspired to be her squire. He was constantly by her side, a charming and attentive escort. He knew everyone and everyone knew him. He was as much at home at Schloss Burg-Farnbach as at Tourville. He and Carl took her on her first shooting party, which began well before dawn in the forest of Burg-Farnbach and around the lake where the birds were plentiful.

This was the least pleasant of Sandra's experiences. She was an animal lover, a supporter of wildlife, and she hated killing. But she knew that her friends, her newfound family, were apparently trying to please her and, for once, for their sake, she put up with the, to her, senseless slaughter of beautiful creatures.

For the rest it was more pleasurable: skiing with Tim, riding with Belle and Armand de Saint-Aignan, who was a much more interesting companion than Sandra had been led to believe. He was hardly amusing. He was a solemn man, obviously somewhat older than Claire, but he was courteous, kind and his air of old-fashioned nobility even more authentic than that of the Burg-Farnbach family, of whom there were several around the place, staying or making visits from homes—castles and shooting lodges—nearby.

Even Zac seemed to go out of his way to be polite, if not exactly pleasant, and his apparent attention to Tara, convalescing from her miscarriage, was almost too touching to be true. For, maybe, it was only Sandra who, in the silence of the night, heard the fierce arguments between them, voices raised in their suite which was directly above hers.

So, although it was a happy time, there was an undercurrent of unease; moments when it all seemed somehow not quite real. Christmas in Bavaria: Christmas with the fairy-tale trees, candlelit dinners and deer hurrying across the snow. Any minute one expected to see a genuine Santa Claus appear complete with reindeer and a sackful of gifts. No, none of it was quite real to a girl used to Christmas Day on Malibu beach in California.

Apart from the immediate family there were an assortment of guests, mostly old friends of the Burg-Farnbach family. Everyone was a count or a prince or a marquis. Georges had certainly known what he was doing when he married his daughter into one of the foremost families to grace the pages of the Almanac de Gotha. The pedigrees of most of their friends could also be found in the pages of that venerable reference book, the ancient bible of European nobilities.

Altogether there were about twenty guests staying in the

castle. Among them were one or two anomalies, people one could not quite place. These included a young French film star called Corinne Lalanne who was undoubtedly well acquainted with Tim.

As for decorations, absolutely no expense had been spared either in time or money to make it a magnificent spectacle symbolic not only of the spirit of Christmastime, but its pleasure too. At every mealtime the table groaned with food; not only the traditional fare—turkey, barons of beef, carp, foie gras and venison—but delicacies like oysters and caviar.

On Christmas Eve most of the house party and staff attended traditional Midnight Mass at the local church where the Prince and Princess occupied special places in the choir of the church, which was so tiny that the guests and castle staff formed half the congregation.

Afterward there was a magical drive back on sleighs in the snow and then German hot sausages and hot punch in the courtyard while the bells rang out to welcome Christmas.

On Boxing Day there was another shoot which began early and lasted all day and those who didn't take part in it—Sandra was one—met the participants for lunch at an inn, belonging to the Burg-Farnbach estate, by the side of the lake.

It was bitterly cold but the sun was strong and it was warm enough to sit out for those who wanted to eat by the side of the lake picnic fashion.

Rather to her surprise Sandra found that Tim virtually ignored her when he came in from the morning's shooting and went immediately to the side of Corinne, who was making rather a hit with one of the local landowners, an organizer of the shoot. Sandra had become accustomed to the idea, over this holiday, that Tim would always be attentively at her side, bringing her drinks, helping her off with her boots after an exhilarating morning skiing down the mountainside.

But Corinne had taken part in the shoot and had been out before dawn with the men. Now she was drinking beer from a mug, her pretty face flushed, her eyes sparkling, dark hair falling over the turned-up fur collar of her leather coat. She and Tim had obviously spent the morning shooting together, the landowner being one of the party.

Corinne turned to greet Tim, as if she'd been expecting him, her face alight with inquiry. Obviously he'd been on some errand for her and Sandra, briefly acknowledged by him, was aware of a sharp spasm of irritation.

Sandra saw for some reason now, and only now, that Corinne was, in fact, a very attractive, though rather vapid woman. The kind with little to say, who drape themselves over tables, around chairs and by the side of mantelpieces so that every aspect can be seen to advantage. She had flirted with all the men, none of whom appeared entirely impervious to her. But today with Tim she seemed to have scored a bull's-eye in the course of the morning's shooting.

Sandra knew it was illogical—and she accordingly despised herself for it—but she had a brief moment of instinctive, feminine jealousy and regretted the fact that she hadn't forsaken her principles for a second time and gone with them.

Tim served Corinne from the well-stocked buffet that had been set up on a long trestle table and then, commandeering a bottle of wine and two glasses, led her outside while one of the waiters carried a tray on which were the plates with the food they had selected.

Sandra felt rebuffed even though Carl von Burg-Farnbach immediately covered up for Tim and asked her what she had done in the morning and what she would like to eat.

"Actually I went for a walk with Claire and Armand," Sandra said. "I must say he's a very charming man."

"Away from his mother he is," Carl confided. "Don't you notice the difference when she's in the room and when she's not?"

"I can't say I have," Sandra said truthfully. "Maybe I'm not observant enough. I don't see a lot of them."

"He's dominated by his mother. That's the problem with him and Claire. I suppose you know they sleep in separate rooms. . . ."

"Oh . . . I didn't." Sandra looked nonplussed. "But don't you think we should change the subject?"

"You're quite right," Carl acknowledged a little shamefacedly. "As the host I, especially, shouldn't gossip. But, of course, we regard you as one of the family."

"Do you?" The light in Sandra's eyes was challenging. Carl, after all, was married to Belle and though certainly not as devious, one could hardly doubt where his loyalties lay.

"Indeed," Carl said encouragingly. "We all do. We have accepted Georges' will and you have made yourself exceptionally agreeable. I know you like Claire and I have always been very fond of my little sister-in-law."

"You're right, I'm fond of her too." Sandra smiled over to Claire, who was sitting with Count Otto Hardenberg, a diplomat on leave from the Far East. "In fact I like her. . . ." Her hand went to her mouth and Carl, who was selecting items for her from the buffet, stopped and looked at her quizzically.

"You were going to say?"

"Nothing. I like her, simply that!"

"Ah ah." Carl carried her plate over to a table just inside the door and then went back to get his own, asking one of the waiters to bring him a jug of beer. "You were going to say," he said sitting down beside her, "that you like her best of all the family."

"How do you know I was going to say that?" Sandra smiled uneasily.

"Because you left your sentence unfinished. 'I like her . . .' You trailed off. 'I like her better than her brothers and sisters' perhaps?"

"She is easier to understand." Sandra felt embarrassed and

was quite pleased that the heat of the room would explain the color in her face.

"Is she?" Carl wondered. "I personally find her a very complex young woman. But in their way all the children of Georges Desmond are complex."

"Did you like him?" Sandra asked suddenly and caught, fleetingly, an expression on Carl's face which was unexpected. He seemed taken by surprise by the candor of the question.

"Georges Desmond?" Carl played for time as he sorted through his things on the small wooden table. "Well he was not a man to *like,* really. He had enormous charm, but . . . if you were married to his daughter you knew what he was really like. And that—"

"Wasn't very nice?" This time Sandra finished the question for him, speaking quietly so that those next to and around them wouldn't hear.

"Oh no, no, no, on the contrary, not at all," Carl protested, also looking around perhaps a little nervously. "I see you and I are attempting to finish each other's remarks today. It's a bad sign. No." He wiped his mouth on a snowy linen napkin. "No, simply as his son-in-law I saw all sides of Georges Desmond, the good and the bad. That is what I meant when I said I knew what he was really like. Most people were mesmerized by him. I—"

"Carl," Belle, who had just come in, called at him from the door. "Have you seen Constantine?"

"He is with Christina," Carl said, referring to the nanny. "*She* said she thought he was with you."

"Oh my God—" Carl jumped up and suddenly the buzz inside the hut died down to be succeeded by the silence of consternation. Constantine, heir to the von Burg-Farnbach family and Belle and Carl's only child, was three years old and, as is often the way with the young, a handful. Constant vigilance was necessary to restrain his youthful ways, his constant high spirits, his impish mischievousness.

The harassed nanny appeared in the doorway literally wringing her hands and protesting to all who would listen that she had seen Constantine with his father walk into the hut.

"Constantinc was never with me and we didn't walk into the hut together," Carl said angrily. "Now get outside quickly and find him." He broke off to stare at the lake sparkling in the sun and, with an exclamation, Belle put a hand to her mouth and everyone tried at once to get out of the hut to help with the search.

As they all spread out toward the lake Lady Elizabeth called out to Sandra, who was the last about to leave the hut.

"No use you going, my dear. You'll get lost too."

"Oh he isn't lost *surely,"* Sandra said, aware of a feeling of apprehension.

"I knew that girl, that nanny, was no good," Lady Elizabeth said firmly. "She is too frivolous. Did you see her last night dancing with all the young men from the village one after the other, deciding, I have no doubt, with whom she would go to bed. . . ."

"Dear me, Lady Elizabeth!" Sandra felt amused but attempted to enter into the spirit of Lady Elizabeth's concern at the morals of present-day youth by trying to sound shocked. On the other hand she was genuinely rather shocked that the young boy's grandmother appeared so unconcerned about his whereabouts, especially in view of the proximity of the lake on the one side or the danger of exhaustion from cold while roaming through the forest on the other. "I feel I should at least try and help—"

"Find out where Tim is," Lady Elizabeth said knowledgeably. "Corinne is crazy about him. Also from the back Tim and Carl look rather alike; they have the same sort of jacket and similar-colored hair. It might have been Tim that Christina saw Constantine with. No harm in looking. . . ."

"But where is Tim?"

"If you ask me he is with that young woman somewhere. I must say she's pretty, don't you think so, Sandra?"

"Very pretty," Sandra said woodenly, having just decided that Lady Elizabeth was acting out of malice. As she was so observant she must have been well aware that Tim had spent most of the days of the holiday paying attention to her.

"She's just the kind of young girl I would like Tim to settle with," Lady Elizabeth went on, impervious to the commotion created by the disappearance of her grandson. "She's pretty, I believe she is of quite good family, and yet she's only nineteen. I would *like* Tim to settle down. He's the only one of my children not married."

"I don't really know why you're telling me all this." Sandra gazed back at the Desmond matriarch with the same frank expression with which she was looking at her. "Unless you're trying to give me a message."

"Why should I give you a message, my dear?" Lady Elizabeth seemed astonished by the remark. "Surely *you're* not interested in Tim . . . a Desmond, perhaps your half brother. . . ."

"By adoption only," Sandra said quickly. "There is no reason to think . . . there is no *doubt* that your husband was not my father."

"That's what they all say." Lady Elizabeth nodded and despite, or maybe because of, her anxiety about her grandson, spread butter thickly on a chunky piece of bread freshly baked that morning in the huge kitchens at Burg-Farnbach.

"He *couldn't* be my father . . ." Sandra began and then the complacent expression on the old lady's face started to anger her. "I think this is a ridiculous conversation, at this time anyway."

"It *is* rather ridiculous," Lady Elizabeth agreed but her expression when she looked at Sandra was unmistakable. "Now you go and look for Tim and you'll find my grandson. Back there," she pointed behind her to the rear of the hut away from the lake, "deep in the woods."

Sandra left her in the comfortable niche she had found at the back of the good-sized room of the hunting lodge, near the fire and with views of the mountainside from rear windows. Here she was well looked after and could see what was going on, both at the front and at the back. Lady Elizabeth wore tweeds—a skirt, thick sweater and woolen stockings and sensible brogues—and had been driven to the lodge via the lake by jeep accompanied by Countess Otto Hardenburg, Madame Schulz, wife of the Burgomaster of Burg-Farnbach and Carl's young niece, his sister's daughter Nora.

When she thankfully got outside Sandra could hardly see anybody; but the air was full of voices as they all fanned out calling for Constantine.

Sandra had a sickening feeling of fear, not only at the possibility that Constantine had fallen into impenetrable undergrowth or had drowned in the lake, but that she would find what Lady Elizabeth wanted her to find.

The holiday had, indeed, gone sour because she realized that the protestations of friendship on the part of the Desmond family were as false as she had expected; quite false. Lady Elizabeth had wanted her brood to succeed her husband and, possibly, she hated her more than the rest of them put together. Tim had led her to think he was interested in her, and Belle that she was her friend. Only Zac had been, perhaps, more honest in keeping his distance from her as much as he could except for the occasional civility: a drink brought, or something passed at table where the guests were rotated at each meal so that at some time they all sat next to one another.

Sandra took the direction indicated by Lady Elizabeth, choosing a narrow path that led from the back of the hut into the thickest part of the woods. Something warned her to abandon the search; there were enough people involved in it already who had the advantage of knowing the terrain much better than she did; but something else spurred her on: a perfectly human desire to find out the truth.

She was only a short distance along the track when she came across a shed in which peasants left winter food for the deer. It occurred to her that this was the perfect place for a young child to hide and she hurried around to inspect it. She was absolutely right.

The three-year-old was sitting contentedly on the floor chewing an apple, one hand still on the rope of a sled which he had obviously been leading through the woods, as if waiting to play.

"Constantine!" Sandra chided, kneeling beside him. "Your parents are *terribly* worried. You should never have wandered off. . . ."

Constantine smiled at her with equanimity and then pointed to a spot behind her back.

"Uncle Tim," he said, and tugged at his sledge.

Slowly Sandra turned but, oblivious of her, his back both to her and his nephew, was Tim. His body was straddled against that of a woman who, pressed against a tree, had her arms around him, her hands clutching his jacket, as they frenziedly embraced each other.

Corinne saw her first. She murmured something in Tim's ear and Tim clumsily sprang away from her, nearly tripping on a gnarled root in the forest undergrowth. Corinne, with great composure, merely tried to rearrange her long straight hair with both hands while she broke into a self-conscious, satisfied smirk.

Sandra was transfixed by the scene which left little to the imagination though both were fully clothed. She had interrupted a passionate embrace, not mere dalliance and, as the blood rushed to her cheeks, she tried to turn, one arm still protectively around the shoulders of the young child.

"Sandra . . . I . . ." Tim stopped, clearly nonplussed; not knowing what to say. "I . . ."

"Did you know everyone is frantically searching for Constantine?" Sandra demanded in a voice that, she knew, must have sounded slightly hysterical. "They think he's drowned in the lake."

"What?" Tim, appalled, looked at Corinne who, a triumphant light in her eyes, was staring insolently at Sandra. "But Christina, the nanny, saw him come away with me."

"She thought you were his father," Sandra said with more composure, removing her arm from Constantine's shoulder, and getting to her feet. "Apparently you resemble each other from behind."

"It's true," Corinne said helpfully, perhaps a little naïvely—perhaps maliciously—it was hard to know which. "They are the same height, they wear the same jacket. . . ."

"She's an absolute fool," Tim said angrily then turned to Corinne. "I'm sorry, I don't mean you. . . ."

"Perhaps you mean me . . . ?" Sandra's voice shook with anger, but also, perhaps, with rage, weariness and, dare one admit it? jealousy. "And now if you'd go and relieve the anxieties of your family, especially your sister who is almost distraught, I'm going back to the castle! I needn't say anything about the spectacle you presented to your young nephew. Personally I find it disgraceful!"

"He's only *three—*" Tim began, but Sandra turned on her heels, selecting a path at random which she desperately hoped would take her to her destination. At the same time the brisk walk, just conceivably, might enable her to clear her mind.

In front of the stables, which were lit by torches placed in brackets in the walls and also by the great fire that roared in the center of the courtyard, those who had taken part were assembled around the slaughtered pheasants bagged in the day's shooting. In addition to the light from the fires, the beaters and loaders who had assisted them held lighted torches in their hands and it appeared to Sandra that the atmosphere had an appeal that was quasi-religious. To one side a choir from the village, dressed in Bavarian costume, sang carols alternating with hunting songs.

Sandra stood behind the group, already dressed for dinner, which had assembled on the steps of the Castle. The ladies had fur wraps around their elegant shoulders but the men, who wore evening dress, were without their coats. It was bitterly cold and, in the night air, the icy breaths of the onlookers mingled with the smoke from the wood fire and the hundreds of wax candles.

In a way it was an attractive scene but one which Sandra personally found repellant. The killing of these beautiful birds, creatures of the woods, was the one thing that had spoiled her Christmas visit to Burg-Farnbach, now nearly over. Well it wasn't the only thing, there was something else and, it was true that now she would be glad to go.

Sandra was a woman with the normal vanities that women have, especially attractive ones used to the attention of men. She was accustomed to being admired; to men instinctively jumping to attention, especially since she had become powerful as well as beautiful, anxious to do her favors.

But there had been something special about Tim's attention because she knew that he wasn't interested in her power or money. He had both; he was rich, successful and independent, even if he did have a reputation. She felt flattered that, despite his family's disapproval, he had paid such singular attention to her.

Now, abruptly, he had transferred this to Corinne. Inevitably she felt spurned, but she was also instinctively jealous and frustrated; humiliated by his abrupt transference of his attentions to a younger woman.

Suddenly a hand slipped around her waist, interrupting her reverie, and also startling her, as a familiar voice whispered in her ear:

"Thank you for finding Constantine. I didn't realize his mother would be so worried."

"I find that hard to believe," Sandra said in a voice even chillier than the evening air. "Kindly remove your hand."

"We were going to play with his sledge . . ." Tim paused and his voice assumed a faintly mocking tone. "Poor little Corinne suddenly felt terribly cold."

"So I observed. You would *have* to be terribly cold to want to be embraced by you!"

"Oh come." Tim's hand around her waist tightened. "You liked it quite, once. . . ."

Finally she succeeded in breaking his clasp by ruthlessly prying apart his fingers and, with a quiet "ouch" Tim withdrew his arm. Had she looked, however, and seen his face she would have found his expression complacent.

"Maybe I did it to make you jealous," he whispered again, his mouth brushing her cheek. She impatiently flicked it away as though it were a fly.

"I find it hard to believe that *you* knew I would be the one to find you. . . ."

"I was hoping."

"Tim *Desmond,"* Sandra wrathfully turned to confront him and seeing one or two curious faces glancing at them, he put a finger to his mouth.

"I'll see you later," he murmured as the singing came to an end and one by one the candles were extinguished, then he suddenly slipped away.

The table that evening looked particularly splendid as though the servants had done their best to make what was the last day of the official Christmas period memorable. Some guests were staying on for the New Year and some were returning to their respective homes to make way for new ones arriving the following day.

Sandra was undecided as to what she should do. The Pipers were in California; the Desmond family would remain here for the New Year. Well, they were her family, weren't they?

Now? They had pressed her to postpone an American visit and she was on the verge of agreeing. After all, she was her own boss, answerable to no one except possibly the shareholders, and they were well satisfied with her performance so far.

She looked around the table at the expressions on the various members of her adopted family. Lady Elizabeth, *grand dame,* very much in command and enjoying herself, Sandra was now inclined to see as a woman who clearly relished intrigue. On the one hand she was the gracious lady of title, on the other the betrayed wife of Georges Desmond whose mistress's daughter had disinherited her children. No wonder she felt bitter. How could Sandra have expected otherwise; how could she ever have been deceived by that apparent graciousness?

In the center of the table was Belle gorgeously dressed in a magnificent red evening dress that Maurice Raison had made as part of her winter collection, for every night she had worn a different and more startling creation than the one before.

Across from her was Tara who had spent a lot of time in her suite officially convalescing but, probably, also because she didn't want to spend too much time in the company of her husband's family. Next to Tara sat Corinne talking animatedly to Countess Otto Hardenberg, who was a charming woman a few years older than her handsome young husband. Money there on her side, no doubt. Zac had entered into every aspect of the entertainment provided both day and night, leaving Tara pretty much to her own devices. Sandra was sorry that she had been unable to spend more time with Tara herself, anxious to understand and get to know a little better that rather interesting, yet tormented-looking woman. Clearly something had recently made her very unhappy. Her miscarriage? Only that?

Then there was Claire, who caught her eye now and smiled at her across the table. A very different Claire to the unhappy young woman she had previously encountered, usually on her own, at the Château de Tourville. Yet there was very little sign of any empathy between Claire and her husband even if she hadn't known from Carl that they slept apart. So what made Claire so happy here? The proximity of her entire family? The air of the Bavière? Claire was also, surprisingly for one who seemed so timid, a lover of the shoot and eagerly followed the guns, though she did not shoot, every day. An oddity, Claire. An enigma.

Farther down the table her husband Armand sat between two women Sandra didn't know, local people who had been invited to dinner that evening. These would be the local doctor, the priest, neighbors occupying the large houses, small castles or holiday homes in the vicinity. Those who stayed in the luxurious hotels in order to ski, but who knew the Desmonds in Paris, Rome, London or New York; there would be those who had hunting lodges and came for the pheasant shooting with their wives, and also the prosperous local tradesmen, yes even at the table of the Prince and Princess: for was not this the Federal Republic of Germany and were not all men and women equal now?

Next to her was Tim. A different Tim from the one she'd seen only at lunchtime entwined in the arms of another woman; an attentive, loving Tim, a Tim who never once looked in the direction of Corinne. That amorous young woman seemed to have found another unattached admirer, one of the young guns who was the guest of yet another neighbor. Really, there were almost too many people to count sitting around that vast table in this great hall which had been an original part of the castle that dated back to the thirteenth century.

Tim said, "A penny for them?"

Sandra decided to return flirtation with flirtation and smiled. Maybe that, alone, would surprise him.

"I was thinking about the age of the castle. Thirteenth century, I'm told."

"Oh at least." Tim's eyes were mocking her. "I hoped you would be thinking of me. Surely history isn't a specialty too?"

"Old things *do* attract me." Sandra entered into the spirit of their repartee.

"But not old men, I hope."

"There can be some very charming older men."

"Not Henri Piper, surely?"

Sandra inclined her head.

"Henri is certainly attractive; but not to me."

"Some people seem to think he is."

"Then some people are wrong," Sandra said, immediately turning to her neighbor, the Prince von Hohenbrugg, a man of great charm, a member of the Bundestag, who happened to be an older man too. Surely conversation with him was much more interesting than with a well-known playboy, a womanizer, a—

The Prince turned attentively toward her when she felt a hand placed on her knee. She sat upright, eyes bright with alarm, but the Prince looked the soul of innocence.

"Did you enjoy your day, Fraulein?" he inquired courteously.

"Very much." Sandra cautiously leaned forward to try and unclench the hand that held her. "It's absolutely magnificent countryside."

"Someone told me you don't much enjoy shooting?"

"Not much. Do you?"

"One is used to it from boyhood," the Prince said, looking rather curiously at Sandra. "Is your chair uncomfortable, Fraulein? May I do anything to assist you?"

He moved back as if to come to her help and immediately the hand of Tim Desmond was removed from her knee.

"That's better," she said, straightening up, smiling at the Prince. "I had a cramp in my foot. As you were saying . . ."

But Sandra had forgotten what he was saying, as though the impression of that hand on her knee remained, aware only of the rapid beating of her heart. It was true she was not made of stone. It was, moreover, a long time since she had had a lover . . . but Tim . . . ? Slowly she turned to him, allowing her gaze to rest on him. Tim was a Desmond . . . and could one *ever* trust a Desmond? Trust one's heart to one?

12

For a long time Sandra lay on top of her large double bed gazing at the ceiling which was adorned with a delicate plasterwork motif depicting the goddess Diana and the hunt. Vines, symbols of fecundity, seemed to be entwined with tiny figurines of charging bulls followed by Diana in her chariot, outstretched hand flicking her whip over the head of the leading horse. This deeply erotic motif was repeated all around the room: bulls, vines, the goddess of the hunt, as if to invite the practice of the symbolic chase.

Sandra knew that she was behaving like a young freshman during her first term at college. She was not the first woman to find Tim Desmond deeply attractive and undoubtedly she would not be the last . . . and that was the rub. She was the President of the Desmond Group, a woman of standing and fortune not only in France but in the world. Did such women throw themselves at men or allow themselves to be taken lightly?

Sandra had had few serious affairs in her life after she left Berkeley. The most important was with a fellow student on her course at the Harvard Business School. His name was Claudio Menendez and he was from a wealthy Argentinian family who farmed thousands of acres and bred horses. Up to that time her romances had been with men from backgrounds like her own, more or less. One took so much less notice of differences in class, and money, in America than in Europe.

But Claudio had been quite different. He was already thirty and had been in his family business for some years. He was experienced, a good and practiced lover. But he was also a South American and his ways were not her ways, his ideals not hers. He was serious about her and he loved her. He asked her to marry him and took her to Buenos Aires to meet his family.

And it was there she saw what her life would be like as châtelaine of a huge, gracious colonial-style house like the one his mother ran so efficiently and well. She would be the mother of his children, his partner and helpmate in life; but she would never be anything else, however exalted her position as the wife of Claudio Menendez. She would never be her own person, earning her own money, running her own life. She would be free, because there was no question of being enslaved; but, in a sense, she would be a slave to convention, to custom and what was expected of her.

Sadly she left Claudio with his family and came home, the course at Harvard over. It was the opening of a chapter. To marry Claudio would have been the close of one.

Sandra never regretted that decision taken five years before not to marry, but she often thought of Claudio Menendez. His family, too, had a bank and he occasionally came to San Francisco and looked her up. She'd heard now that he was married and had a year-old daughter.

But now she was the president of one of the world's great corporations and . . . she was waiting on a bed like a teenager for a rendezvous with a man whom she knew instinctively to be dangerous. Who was provocative, tantalizing . . . and she was sure he would come.

Sandra jumped off the bed, overcome with a sudden feeling of shame, of self-disgust. The two sides of herself were so uncomplementary that she had to make a decision one way or the other. It was not incompatible to be married or have a steady lover with the job she did; but one had to be single-minded and one's husband or lover would have to understand this and, preferably, be someone of a like mind.

Tim Desmond was after fun; everyone said so. That very day she had seen him having fun with a French starlet who had the air of someone who spent too much time in the beds of various casting directors in her efforts to claw her way to the top. She, Sandra O'Neill Desmond, didn't have to do that. She—

There was a tap on her door and she stood perfectly still, her heart racing like a schoolgirl. There was a low tap again and someone tried the handle of the door. Rather unsteadily she crossed the room and leaned against the door whispering, "Who is it?"

"You know who it is!" the voice whispered back. "Please open the door."

With trembling hands Sandra turned the key, realizing as she did so that she was listening to a rapidly beating heart, to the sound of the blood coursing through her veins and not to the reasoning that went on in her cool, clever head. As she unlocked the door the handle turned and Tim stood before her outlined by the soft glow of the light in the corridor outside as if there were an aura around him. Then, swiftly, he came in, closed the door and took her in his arms.

Sandra lay naked on the bed and Tim lay beside her, his eyes amorous, stroking her body as though she were a large cat.

"You certainly know how to get your evil way," Sandra said rather shakily. But it was too late for joking. Tim's answer was a tender smile.

"I knew it would happen," he said. "I saw it in the stars. Right from the beginning I knew. You resisted me too long, Sandra O'Neill. . . ."

He bent his head and she put her hands around his neck and brought his mouth down to hers.

"Get into bed," she whispered. "You're teasing me."

Tim lay on his side, fully clothed, only his tie undone and his shirt collar open. Sandra attempted to undo his shirt buttons but she felt too weak, too much in the thrall of a passion she couldn't control. From time to time Tim kissed her and she was aware of the soft velvety texture of his lips, the gentle persuasion of his tongue exploring the inside of her mouth.

"Please," she said when he freed her momentarily. It's all she seemed able to say.

Tim's hand slowly ran down her body, cupping her breasts, kneading her nipples, until it rested casually on her thick pubic hair. Then he raised his head and, in the soft light of the lamp by the side of the bed, looked into her eyes. She had felt no shame in his making love to her, no embarrassment at showing herself to him nude; in allowing him such freedom. She trusted him; she would be safe because he knew how to look after a woman and to please her. At that moment she craved him, her eyes begging him.

"Please," she said again.

He leaned down until his face was scarcely an inch from hers.

Suddenly the telephone rang by the side of her bed and Tim immediately put his hand on it to stop her reaching for it.

"No," he said firmly.

Sandra felt confused.

"We *have* to answer it."

"There's no need."

"It might be something important."

"Aren't *I* important?"

"Of course . . ."

"You're thinking of business, Sandra!" His tone reproved her.

"Of course I'm not . . . of propriety. There might be something wrong. After all the entire household is probably in bed."

She reached out, lifted the receiver, put it to her ear and listened.

"Yes?" she said in English, after a long pause.

"Is my brother there?" Zac Desmond's voice was noncommittal.

"Of *course* not . . ." She felt an immediate outrage.

"Should you see him," Zac replied blandly, "could you say it's something urgent. . . ."

"I *won't* see him," Sandra said and slammed down the phone. Her eyes were frightened, suspicious, as she gazed at Tim; her hands instinctively crossed over her bosom.

"It's your brother."

"My brother?" Tim, who had risen and begun to undress, looked around at her as if in amazement.

"Something urgent . . . you'd better go."

"But you *said* I wasn't here." He found it hard to suppress a smile.

"You'd better go and see. It might be something to do with your mother. I'd feel responsible. . . ."

"Oh very well. . . ." With every appearance of reluctance Tim slipped on his evening jacket and put his bow tie, which he had undone, in his pocket.

He got to the door and waved at her.

"Don't go away," he said.

"Tell him . . ." Sandra began but Tim whispered, "I *know* what to say . . . I'll see you very soon."

And then he was gone.

Sandra gazed for a long time at the back of the door. Then she got out of bed and went unsteadily into her bathroom where she doused her face with cold water. She splashed it all over her body which was burning, letting the cool water trickle down between her breasts, over her stomach, between her legs. She looked at herself in the full-length mirror which ran from the ceiling to the marble floor, and she tilted her head and saw the gleam of gold which came from the light shining on her hair. She had been too long without love, it was truc. She had no realization how much she needed this, how much she had wanted Tim to love her.

With that came the abandonment of responsibility, the rejection of reason. . . .

Then, swiftly, she washed her body in warm water all over, so that she would be sweet smelling and ready for him on his return. She brushed her teeth, her hair and, still naked, got back into bed to wait for that culmination she so urgently desired.

But he didn't come. Ten minutes passed quickly—those spent in the bathroom. Twenty minutes, forty, an hour, an hour and a half. She lay in the dark and began to feel foolish and angry; the passion for him evaporated and turned sour. He had made a fool of her, as one would expect of a Desmond. He had said something about her to Zac. He . . .

There was a tap on the door and immediately she forgot her foolish thoughts and called softly, "Come in."

She was aware of the shadow moving toward her and she held out her arms to receive that lover for whom her body was, quite literally, aching.

But instead of undressing quickly, as she expected, he stood by the side of the bed looking down at her, even though he could no more see her in the dark than she could see him. But gradually, as the anticipation became unbearable, the delay strange, she realized there was something about his shape, his stance, that suddenly terrified her. Calling loudly, "Tim?" she rapidly reached for the light and, in the sudden illumination that swept the room, she saw that most hated, most feared face, usually so stony and grim, now gazing down at her with a sneer that was also lustful. With one hand he reached for the sheet and jerked it away from her, exposing her nudity that had been intended for only one man.

"Whore!" Zac spat at her. "Did you expect my brother to fuck you too? Don't you know he's busy with Corinne? What a fool you are." Cruelly, insultingly, he ran his eyes over her as he said: "Your body actually isn't bad, not bad at all—but she's a sex kitten. I hear she's capable of multiple orgasms, so maybe he'll be there for quite a time."

"Get *out* of here," Sandra cried, reaching for the heaviest object at hand, the light by the side of her bed. "Get out and don't you *dare—*"

But as the lamp ricocheted against the door, breaking into a thousand tiny fragments, it had already closed behind Zac. And the humiliation, the ordeal of Sandra O'Neill was now complete.

Three to four hours later, just after dawn had touched the mountaintops in its particular effervescence of glory, a helicopter rose from the field behind the Castle of Burg-Farnbach, summoned by Sandra in the dead of night. The pilot had scarcely time to land before she was on it, and this time there was no friendly group to see her off.

As they climbed toward the sun and banked over the Alps the castle once more became a tiny speck as she had first seen it, surrounded by those beautiful, evergreen conifers stretching down to what now looked like a small pool, but which was the lake beside the inn where they had lunched. The helicopter pilot immediately headed toward Munich where jet Number One of the Desmond Corporation awaited Sandra. She settled back in her seat closing her eyes on a scene, a place, that she vowed she would never, ever see again.

Belle stood at the window of her bedroom, arms akimbo, watching the helicopter soar into the sky. From the depths of his warm bed Carl said, "What's the matter?"

"Just Sandra taking off." Belle didn't attempt to conceal her satisfaction.

But the announcement was enough to make Carl sit up, rubbing his tousled head.

"What? I didn't know she was going. I thought she'd decided to stay for New Year. She never even said goodbye."

"Maybe she'll write." Belle strolled back into the bedroom, taking a last, lingering look at the machine as it disappeared over the mountaintops.

"I still think it's very odd." Carl settled back against the pillows.

"Yes, but she's an odd girl," Belle replied. "Don't you think?"

"I thought you were beginning to like her." Carl, who had none of the complexities that seemed to afflict each and every member of the Desmond clan, looked puzzled.

"She thought I was beginning to like her." Belle sat on the bed stretching her arms. "That was the whole point of the exercise."

"What exercise, *mein kleine maus?"* Carl worriedly ran his hands through his hair again, looking thoroughly puzzled. "I don't understand a thing."

"Go back to sleep *mon petit lapin."* Belle bent over and fondled his hair—"and I'll explain it all one of these days."

Then, light of step, she went into her bathroom and ran the bath water singing a little song.

Two hours later everyone was once again in the courtyard assembling for the shooting party. Sometimes it began before dawn but sometimes it began later when they were after birds or rabbits, and this was the last one until the New Year. Most of the guests who remained were surprised to hear that Sandra had gone and Belle explained carelessly:

"She's like that. Here today and gone tomorrow. That's the style of a tycoon, isn't it, Zac?"

Zac, who felt extremely pleased with the night's work—a new man if ever there was one—nodded enthusiastically. "*Only* the new breed of tycoon. The old style had more manners."

"I must say I'm surprised." Tara stamped her feet on the snowy ground venturing, for the first time this holiday, to follow the shoot on foot. "She said nothing to me about it last night. I thought she looked very happy and relaxed. Did something happen?"

Zac smiled knowingly and looked in the direction of the stables where Tim was taking a practice aim through the sights of one of the guns being carried for him by a loader.

"I think you'd better ask Tim if anything happened. Maybe she got more than she bargained for."

"You don't *mean* . . ." Tara began to smile, her beautiful, sensuous mouth turning up slightly at each corner. "Oh I say . . . she didn't fall for *Tim?* I thought she had more sense."

"Well you see she hasn't." Zac took a sip from the flask of schnapps he carried in his pocket to keep out the cold. "And I never thought she had. We'll soon have her back where she belongs, in California. This is just the first mistake of many that she'll make in the next few months, you'll see. She's no judgment at all—in anything."

Finally everyone was ready and, accompanied by dogs, guns, gun loaders, beaters and hampers of food the party, much reduced, set out for the high grounds where from early morning beaters had been preparing to flush the birds out of their cover in order to be slaughtered. Tim walked ahead, his eyes to the ground and Zac had to run to catch up with him. Behind them Tara, Corinne and some of the women were strolling along together but Belle, who was a keen shot, was well forward with her gun talking to some new arrivals who had joined the house party for the New Year.

Zac clapped Tim on the shoulder, but Tim didn't stop and Zac quickened his step behind him.

"What is it, *mon petit frère adoré?* Too much activity . . . ?"

"Oh shut up," Tim said roughly without turning his head.

Zac frowned, slowed his pace, and at that moment Belle turned. Seeing his expression, the shrug of his shoulders, she excused herself to the people she was with and waited for him.

"What is it?"

"Tim is very peculiar."

"That's what I thought. He avoided me at breakfast . . . well he's had a job to do"—she too shrugged her shoulders and gave Zac a smile full of meaning—"and he's done it. Very well I think." She then quickened her step and ran after her younger brother, hailing him until, hands in his pockets, gun under his arm, he stopped and looked at her.

"What is it . . . ?"

"I said 'well done.' "

"I said shut up," Tim growled and stalked ahead.

"There's no need to be like that," Zac called after him. "We all agreed . . ."

"We agreed that we Desmonds had to call the tune; that we would not have others call it for us. That we wanted *our* rights back and we would do anything to get them; but what happened last night—" Tim shook his head "—was not the act of a gentleman, of gentlemen. Our father would be ashamed of us." He looked solemnly at his brother who, however, was still smiling. "Don't you feel ashamed, Zac?"

"Not a bit," Zac said then, with a leer and a faraway look in his eyes, "I must say she has a wonderful body. Maybe one day you'll let me look at Corinne's too. . . ."

Zac reeled and fell against Belle as Tim hit him full on the mouth. The rest of the party behind them stopped and stared and then one or two came forward while Zac remained slumped in Belle's arms.

"Is there . . . ?"

"Please go away," Belle said sharply to Prince von Hohenbrugg who had been the first to reach them. There was a carefully rehearsed smile on her face, an attempt to reassure their distinguished guest, a member of the German Parliament. "Just a family tiff . . . Zac, pull yourself together," she hissed as the Prince, a scion of the old school, tactfully retreated but with an odd expression on his face. Zac, still a little groggy, got to his feet helped by Tim who said, "I'm sorry."

"A bit late for that." Belle looked angrily at the rest of the party who, with the innate good manners of the German aristocracy, were trying to avoid staring at them. "You made a spectacle of us."

"He shouldn't have provoked me. . . ."

"I'm sorry, *mon vieux,"* Zac said, still with a surprised look on his face. "I really didn't know you cared about her. . . ."

"I don't. . . ."

"Well then . . . as I said we got what we wanted. We humiliated her and she now knows what it is to cross the Desmonds. We shall never forget, or forgive."

"And she will never forgive me for what happened last night."

"But does it matter?"

"It matters now more than it did," Tim admitted, resuming his walk and, for the sake of appearances, taking his brother by the arm. "I felt it was a bit of fun; but I made love to her and she cared. I saw she trusted me and wanted me. I think it was something special for her. I lied to her. I don't care who she is or what she is or what she did to us, but she is a woman, a beautiful, proud woman and what I did last night was despicable."

"Well of course *I* don't see it like that." Belle, walking heartily in the middle of them, was still in the best of spirits. "A woman like her should have more pride than to throw herself at a man whose affections she knew were engaged elsewhere. Only at lunchtime yesterday she saw you with Corinne. What kind of person is that?" Belle pretended to shudder. "Desperate if you ask me."

"What kind of person are *you?*" Tim said, "to have forgotten what it's like?"

"Oh I haven't forgotten, don't worry about that." Belle looked at him askance. "But I assure you I would never behave as she behaved, never flaunt myself naked in front of a man. . . ."

"I don't want to talk about it anymore," Tim said. "Zac has obviously enjoyed telling you the whole story which is more than I would have done. As far as I'm concerned I have done what you asked me to do in the interests of the family and, as far as we know, we may have succeeded a hundred percent. She may go back to America and throw the whole thing up. But please don't ask me to do anything like that again. I can tell you it's a long time before I shall be able to look her in the eyes again."

"Or she you," Zac said, chuckling. "Or she you."

Claire didn't like shooting or killing birds, but she liked walking and the clear, crisp cold day was a particularly inviting one. Besides, if she stayed behind she would be forced into the company of her mother-in-law the Countess de Saint-Aignan who, despite being confined to a wheelchair, never left anyone in peace for a second. At Tourville and Burg-Farnbach one servant was permanently on duty to look after her capricious needs and when her son or daughter-in-law were there one of them always had to dance attendance on her.

Armand had escaped early each morning, a practiced and accomplished gun, to take part in the shoot and Claire, tired of being at the old lady's beck and call, usually hid or kept well out of the way.

Today, however, she'd decided to walk, maybe with the intention of slipping away to have some time in the woods on her own. Claire enjoyed her own company, her own thoughts. She was happiest thus but she also had a streak of gregariousness especially when she was on holiday. She had enjoyed the holiday and now she was depressed at the idea of going back to that dismal old home in Berry where life was passing her by.

Lady Elizabeth had a touch of rheumatism and decided not to accompany the shoot even by pony cart which was suggested. Instead she would keep the Countess company and thus free her daughter. So shortly, after her mother was installed at the Countess's side, Claire set out alone and soon caught up with the crowd walking in front of her. Well ahead were Tim, Belle and Zac and, eagerly, she ran after them just as there was an altercation between Tim and Zac and the whole concourse came to an' incredulous halt. Tim hitting Zac? Why? Though not close they got on; usually they were quite good friends.

Claire came up to them just as the Prince von Hohenbrugg passed her to rejoin his wife and brother, a disdainful look on his well-bred features. Belle, Tim and Zac, the latter obviously recovered, set on their way again without observing that she was behind them muffled in her coat but quite able to hear everything that was being said.

Claire had always been known as "the creep" by the family, not in the sense that it is normally used in English, as being someone sly or unworthy, but as someone who crept about: an eavesdropper. However, they thought she was relatively harmless and they usually ignored her. After all she was family; just to be a Desmond was protection of a kind. So the three older ones trudged on continuing their discussion and Claire listened, deducing from what she heard the reason why Sandra had so precipitously left the Castle, and a lot more besides.

After a while, as the strides of those in front lengthened, she drew back, wrapped in her own thoughts. Then there came the sound of gunfire and she knew the beaters had begun their work down by the scrubland at the lakeside.

She shivered and turned back toward the Castle, thinking about what she had heard, turning it over and over again in her mind.

As the long low Mercedes purred smoothly down the circuitous road that had been specially built, at vast expense, to take guests from the castle perched high in the hills to their destinations—whether it was train from Farnbach or to the airport at Munich—the Dowager Countess de Saint-Aignan gave a sniff and ordered the driver to put up the window.

"But, Mama, you know that Claire is carsick," Armand protested rather feebly.

"It's all right," Claire said, slumped in a corner next to her mother-in-law. "We'll soon be at the station."

"It seems as though you're glad," the old lady looked at her. "For once I thought you were enjoying yourself."

"That's why she looks glum," Armand said, "because she's going home."

"She could stay with the Desmonds all the time for all I care," his mother remarked brusquely.

"You sound as though you were talking about someone who wasn't here, *ma mère,*" Claire said. "When I am physically present and able to hear quite well."

"You wouldn't think it sometimes." The Countess sniffed and looked stonily in front of her. Then she poked the driver sharply between his shoulder blades with her stick. "Step on the accelerator young man. We'll miss the train."

Claire de Saint-Aignan hated her mother-in-law. Sometimes she wondered if she hated Armand too, the man her father had made her marry after the whole family had turned its back on Piero.

She'd married him then, it was true, to get away from home; but once she was away she wanted to go back. Anywhere was better than that stuffy, overheated ugly house that the de Saint-Aignans had built in the grounds when poverty had forced them to move out of their historical and gracious home, a jewel of the enlightened architecture of eighteenth-century France: Château de Saint-Aignan.

The de Saint-Aignans were an ancient and honorable family but they had never been any good with money. The Château had been bought by one of the post-First World War *nouveau riche* whose wealth came from the manufacture of armaments.

The old Countess could only just recall it as home; she had been very small when her family had to leave it, but she never stopped resenting the people whose family had owned it now for two generations. Two generations! The Saint-Aignans had fought at Crécy and a forerunner of the eighteenth-century architectural gem was standing then!

Madame de Saint-Aignan had hoped, when the marriage of her only beloved son was suggested to a mere Desmond, that the extensive dowry promised would enable the de Saint-Aignan family to reclaim their dynastic home. But the people who lived there now regarded it, with some justification, as their ancestral home too and, as they were large and extensive as well as very rich—the Second World War had made them even richer—it was unlikely they would ever wish to give it up.

The old Countess, who had been born in the days of the horse and cart, only barely tolerated anything as modern as a train. She abhorred motor cars and she refused to fly; so most of the dreary journeys taken in France and sometimes elsewhere in Europe, were taken by locomotion. Claire and Armand were always expected to accompany her visits. Mostly they stayed with relatives who had married into the many distinguished and, in most cases, similarly impoverished families scattered throughout Europe, Scandinavia and England.

The de Saint-Aignans were distantly related to the Fitz-Caldwells, and Lady Elizabeth and the Countess enjoyed a convivial chat but otherwise had little in common. The Countess was permanently warped by the misfortune that life had brought her and, indeed, it was true that she had not been spared. She had a degenerative condition of the muscles even when she was a young woman though this was not recognized at the time of her early marriage. The disease grew progressively worse, to the disappointment of her young husband, a handsome, attractive and somewhat selfish man. Accordingly he soon took a mistress with whom he spent dizzy holidays at Deauville, Biarritz and Saint Moritz and then he began to develop a passion for gambling and so, sadly for his wife, the thirties passed, until the Germans moved across the Ardennes in 1940 and invaded France.

Clement de Saint-Aignan was a patriotic Frenchman who wanted to fight for his country. He just had time to share a rare embrace with his wife before fleeing with the French army to join de Gaulle in England. Nine months later his son was born; a son he knew about but never saw. Clement was killed when the French forces invaded their own country to liberate it and was buried in an unmarked grave.

To blame his son for what had happened subsequently would hardly be fair; but Armand was a sickly, sensitive child brought up in an atmosphere of despair, grief and deprivation. He felt a morbid sense of obligation to his mother, a widow, an invalid and deeply in debt. Armand was a dutiful son, a good scholar and would have done well, say, in the Haute Administration or the Corps Diplomatiques. But his mother would never let him go and they lived a miserable existence on a pittance, the remnants of the once great Saint-Aignan family fortune.

Armand was seventeen years older than Claire Desmond when he married her. She was twenty and he was thirty-seven. He was only allowed to marry at all because his mother realized that the Desmonds might even make them comfortable and restore the family fortune as well as Château de Saint-Aignan which she stared at all day from her sitting-room window.

Madame de Saint-Aignan thought the alliance an inferior one, as far as her son was concerned. By the de Saint-Aignan book the Desmonds were *parvenus, nouveaux-riches* and their only claim to breeding had been provided by the genes of the daughter of the Earl of Broughton. However, as she knew full well, beggars could not be choosers and she bought a new hat for the wedding and managed a smile for the photograph afterward.

That was eight years ago and there had been no children, a little extra money, more comfort but not as much as they had hoped, mother and son. Gradually they had watched Claire, not a very happy girl when she married a man she didn't pretend to love, turn into a woman who gradually withdrew into herself and finally moved into her own room.

The Countess had screamed and raved. "You *cannot* have children if you sleep in separate beds!" But she knew it was no good and she thought the reason was that Claire was a melancholic, and Armand too weak. Perhaps, in a way, it was just as well they couldn't breed. Through the will of God the de Saint-Aignans, once a noble family, would cease altogether! Armand was the last of the line.

So now she could blame Claire for all that happened not only in the present but in the past.

It was not a very happy home to which to return.

Claire, however, was sorry for Armand. She felt that he had been deprived in the same way that she had; something for which neither of them quite knew who to blame. In a way they loved each other like brother and sister; they needed each other and they were kind to each other. But he would never allow anything to be said against his mother, though his mother could say what she liked about Claire.

Claire's bedroom also faced the Château on the hill, now grandly restored to what it must once have been when the de Saint-Aignans lived there. It was still called Château de

Saint-Aignan, a fact much resented by the dowager who, had she the money, would have gone to law to try and get it changed. So Claire, like her mother-in-law below her, had plenty of time to sit and brood about what might have been and when things got too bad she drank brandy until she fell insensible and then Armand used to creep in and, without telling his mother, put her to bed.

This time getting home was worse than usual. After the noise and gaiety, the excitement and bustle of Burg-Farnbach, the house, with its one melancholy maidservant clothed in black like the old Countess, still in mourning for the husband who had never loved her, seemed insupportable.

But something had happened at the Castle that concerned Sandra, something that had made her fly off in the morning without even saying goodbye and this upset Claire a good deal. Had she not supported Sandra against the family, and had Sandra at least not owed it to her to say goodbye?

For Claire, Sandra was the embodiment of glamor, success, happiness and good fortune: everything that she would like to be and was not. Also, unlike her brothers and sister, Sandra was kind to her, treated her like a friend and not an enemy. Nor did she patronize her as some people tended to do. Just because she was rather a withdrawn person people sometimes treated her as if she were an idiot and everyone knew or, if they didn't were soon told, that she and her husband slept apart. Even if Sandra knew this she was kind. They had gone on walks together in the snow and had several quite intimate conversations. She knew Sandra regarded her as an ally and, in a way, she loved her. Hero worship, a kind of schoolgirl crush, had been born the day infinitely glamorous Sandra first walked into the grand salon at Tourville to receive the frosty greetings of the family.

Now that Claire de Saint-Aignan knew the Desmond family was really out to get Sandra, and just how they would go about it, she longed to make an ally of her, to help her and spy for her. What a secret to have to keep to herself!

13

The Desmond Foundation had been formed in 1935 by that venerable lady, the last Veuve Desmond, Georges' mother Camille d'Argentan, in memory of her husband Charles-Louis who had been killed in a car crash when her children were still quite small.

The Charles-Louis Desmond Foundation was devoted to charitable works: the alleviation of hardship and illness and the betterment of peoples throughout the world, particularly the Third World.

Since the end of the Second World War it had grown to enormous proportions thanks to the expansion of the Desmond Group and the rapid increase in profits. A proportion of these every year went into the Foundation, whose headquarters occupied a building on the place Saint-Sulpice.

Georges was also a man who liked to be seen doing good and there was nothing clandestine about the Foundation donations; no operating under a cloak of secret benefactions for Georges. He saw charity as he saw his work: as a means of aggrandizement and power so, in his time, the functions held to promote the Foundation were always lavish and its donations on a grand and well-publicized scale.

Inevitably good *was* done even when the intention behind it was not strictly an honorable one. There were many causes and institutions devoted to the relief of human misery that could never get enough and were grateful for any sum, however large or small. There were many good, well-motivated and not particularly highly-paid people who worked for it. One of them was the Director, Jean-Louis Legris, who reported directly to the Head of the Foundation—Georges Desmond's brother-in-law Henri Piper. By instinct that good and charitable man was at the heart a philanthropist too and one, moreover, who liked to give by stealth, who didn't glory in the limelight of big, star-studded functions.

However, the control of the input of funds into the Foundation still rested with the Head of the Group and it was with these funds one morning that Sandra was wrestling, having had a plea from Jean-Louis Legris for more.

But this year, if Sandra's calculations were right, there would be hardly any surplus profits from the Group to spare for the Foundation. The well was drying up. Soon it would have to curtail its activities. As is quite common with charitable organizations the calls on its funds would never dry up, but would increase. Inevitably demand would exceed supply.

Sandra had already been in conference with the Director, whom she liked, and senior executives of the Foundation, some of whom had had to return home from abroad for an extraordinary meeting with the Group's new head. It was very hard for them to have the unpalatable facts about funds spelled out, and even harder to believe them.

Heads were shaken and after the meeting some of them expressed the opinion that Miss O'Neill was tight-fisted, mean-minded, lacking in the generous spirit that had activated the late Georges Desmond in carrying out the will of his mother. She was not a Desmond, not a true member of the family and, accordingly, she didn't really care.

But this was not true. Sandra did care and on her desk in front of her one morning in January, not long after the Christmas holiday at Burg-Farnbach, with its horrible memories, was a report from Uncle Henri, who was still in America, suggesting a function at the Metropolitan Opera in New York that would benefit the Desmond Foundation and others like it. Famous artists would give their services free and there would be an exhibition of the work of the Foundation and, particularly, its clever young Director, Dr. Michel Harcourt, who nowadays hardly ever left his fieldwork in Africa.

Sandra felt a bit like Henri about glitzy charity "dos" but there was no doubt that an occasion like this with world-famous stars like Domingo, Te Kanawa, Carreras and Baltsa, giving their services free, would raise a lot of money, now much needed.

Sandra pressed her intercom and asked her secretary, Edith Huelin, to come in and bring the Foundation file with her, but the voice of young Agnès Guyon replied instead.

"Edith is not in, Mademoiselle. She had to attend the clinic."

"Of course. I'd forgotten. Would you come in instead, please, Agnès, and bring the Foundation file and your note-book for dictation."

"Bien, Mademoiselle."

Sandra sighed and looked out of the window at the dank, wet day covering the place de l'Étoile in a fine mist. She felt depressed and it was not only because of what had happened at Burg-Farnbach. Edith was soon to leave her to have a baby and did not wish to return. She had come very much to depend on the woman who had served Georges Desmond so well and who, in her turn, had been loyal to her. Not only loyal, Edith had been a positive support against the machinations of the Desmonds, particularly Zac whom she knew well, and Sandra would miss her.

As she waited for Agnès to come in Sandra turned her attention to particulars about this bright young woman who, despite her youth, coped very well as second-in-command in the office. Promoted from the Group typing pool, she had quickly justified her selection as one of the secretariat of the

President. She was sharp, she was pretty, she was always well turned out. Above all, she was ambitious.

Sandra liked ambition and valued it. She had urged Edith to stay on after the birth of her baby; but Edith was going to settle, instead, for those interminable years of motherhood, something which would never have suited Sandra, who was sure they would not suit Agnès either.

Sandra already had the file concerning Agnès from the personnel department in front of her as she walked into the room. She was a small, neat person of twenty-three years of age with a good figure: trim hips and a firm bosom. She had dark curly hair which sprang from her head as if indicative of the kind of energetic person Agnès undoubtedly was. Her father was a miner from Clermont-Ferrand and she had made her own way to Paris and thence to the Desmond typing pool via a variety of jobs. Sandra liked her *curriculum vitae.* It reminded her of the background of Hélène O'Neill.

Shortly before Georges Desmond was killed Agnès, after working briefly for Zac, was given a job in the President's secretariat and accordingly so far had done her duties very well. Sandra had scarcely noticed her, as the entrance to her private office was dominated by the capable, rather formidable figure of Edith Huelin, who was almost past childbearing age, having decided to have a baby quite late in life.

Sandra greeted Agnès with a smile as she came up to her desk and pointed to a chair.

"Do sit down, Agnès, while I look through this dossier. Are you familiar with the work of the Foundation?"

"Only in so far as I have typed documents concerning it, Mademoiselle."

Sandra liked Agnès's manner, her firm way of speaking, and gazed at her approvingly. She was a neat dresser too; her clothes bought from the cheaper shops but, nevertheless, quite stylish and she wore them well. She had good legs which she showed off with very high-heeled shoes, adding inches to her height.

"Agnès, you know Edith is leaving at the end of next month?"

"Yes, Mademoiselle."

"I wondered how you'd like her job?"

Agnès started and there was a catch in her voice as she replied:

"Here, with you, Mademoiselle?"

"As my private secretary. To take Edith's place. I think you could do it, despite your lack of experience, don't you?"

Agnès moved to the edge of her chair, tucking one leg under the other to display her neatly turned ankle, her stiletto heels. Her little pink tongue nervously licked her lips with excitement and her trim bosom heaved. She was clearly in the grip of what, for Agnès, was a very strong emotion.

"I could be *your* private secretary, Mademoiselle? It would be a very great responsibility, but a very great honor."

"It's not a decision I have come to suddenly." Sandra leaned back, her hands in the pockets of her gray Chanel suit. "I discussed the situation with the director of personnel and he suggested that the post should be advertised for an older, more experienced woman. But I told him that I had observed you in my secretariat; that often when Edith was away, or indisposed, you have worked for me. I have read your *curriculum vitae* very carefully and I like what I know about you. You are a hard worker, you're ambitious and I approve of that. I'm ambitious too, Agnès, you know that don't you?"

"Yes, Mademoiselle." Agnès's dark eyes gleamed with excitement and tiny beads of sweat covered her forehead. "But I am only twenty-three."

"And I am only twenty-six," Sandra said, smiling and getting up, she held out her hand. "I think we'd suit each other, don't you?"

* * *

Later that afternoon when Edith returned from her visit to the clinic she and Sandra worked together on the documents concerning the Foundation, the financing of which was causing Sandra some concern. She approved greatly of its work and would like to have given both more time as well as money to it.

"It worried Monsieur Desmond toward the end, too," Edith said, sitting back thankfully on the easy chair to rest the bulk she was carrying. "But he had great faith in Dr. Harcourt. However, he is never to be seen."

"Why is that?" Sandra looked up with interest after carefully studying the papers.

"He is always in the field. He is said to hate office life."

"That doesn't sound very responsible," Sandra continued, leafing through the papers. "However, I suppose he doesn't necessarily have to be a good doctor *and* a good bureaucrat." She examined a photograph that was attached to the original *curriculum vitae* of the doctor when he applied to join the Foundation four years before.

"Does he still look like this?" she asked Edith who studied the photograph carefully.

"More or less, Mademoiselle."

"Nice," Sandra said approvingly, smiling as she tucked the document and photograph back in the portfolio and for a moment Edith paused too and gazed at her, meeting Sandra's eye.

"Oh don't worry." At once Sandra divined her meaning. *"I'm* not likely to fall in love . . . yet. Not with Dr. Harcourt anyway." She looked at Edith, knowing what she was thinking. "Now then, Edith, stop match-making. I'm a businesswoman. How can I be a wife and mother too?"

"But don't you want to, Mademoiselle Desmond?" Edith had always found it hard to credit the fact that a woman as attractive as Sandra would wish to remain single. But the relationship between Sandra and Edith was, and had remained, strictly a business one. This was the first time Edith could ever recall the introduction of a personal note. Mademoiselle guarded her private life jealously and Edith had no idea what went on outside the headquarters of the Group.

"Not yet anyway." Sandra pointed at Edith's stomach. "That's far too soon for me. Another five or six years, maybe."

"But that leaves it very late, Mademoiselle. I left it a little late myself." Edith sighed, massaging her stomach. "Sometimes I regret it."

"Soon enough for me, Edith . . . if it happens at all. Now." Sandra glanced at her watch. "Good heavens it's after six! You must be getting home or your husband will wonder where you are. You must look after yourself now that your time is so near. . . ."

Sandra put down her silver pencil and swung back in her chair, turning it this way and that as she considered the woman in front of her who in the six months she had worked with her had become necessary to her, not only a right hand but now a friend. Someone she trusted.

"I shall miss you, Edith," she said.

"And I you, too, Mademoiselle."

"I suppose there's no hope that you will come back, say, within six months of the birth of the baby?"

"None at all I'm afraid, Mademoiselle. My husband wouldn't like it anyway. He expects me to look after the baby and, maybe, in a short time to have another. . . ."

"Oh he *expects* it, does he?" Sandra grunted disapprovingly. "And is that what *you* want too?"

"Yes, Mademoiselle." Edith gave her a serene smile, knowing what she was thinking. "I am not like you, you know, Mademoiselle. I have no ambition now but to be a good wife and mother, to make up for lost time."

"But you're an excellent secretary. . . ."

"Nevertheless it doesn't keep you warm in bed at night. . . . No I have always wanted a family and when we had enough money put aside my husband and I decided I would stop work and we would have one. We live modestly, a small apartment—maybe we will move to the country. I know that I have done a good job for Monsieur Desmond and for you . . ."

"You've been invaluable. . . ."

Edith stood up and began to put her things together, clipping or stapling them in the neat methodical way she had. She was a good secretary and she would be a good mother too; the diapers would always be clean and the baby well cared for. Momentarily Sandra felt a spasm of envy, an emotion that she banished almost as soon as it had entered her head.

Even if her experience with Tim had not soured her, made her so bitterly ashamed of herself and contemptuous of him, she knew that it would be a long time before she felt broody like Edith, if ever; even if, at times, in the hurly-burly of her life a little house with a garden and the company of a devoted man seemed attractive. . . .

"Oh by the way, Edith," she said as the older woman was about to leave, "I thought Agnès Guyon might fill your place. She . . ."

"Agnès, Mademoiselle!" Edith turned sharply and looked at her. "Fill my place? She has hardly any experience. . . ."

"Still. What she does she does very well." Sandra saw the look on Edith's face and hurried on. "I mean not as well as you, but in time . . . don't you like her?"

"Oh I like her well enough, Mademoiselle," Edith said woodenly, "and it is *certainly* not my place to comment but . . ."

"But what, Edith?" Puzzled, Sandra sat back in her chair, hands still in her pockets, and gazed at her. "Do you know something detrimental about her? If you do you should tell me as I have practically offered her your job."

"Oh no, nothing detrimental, Mademoiselle," Edith, the perfect secretary, said quickly. "Nothing in fact that I could put my finger on and yet . . ." She paused and put a hand to her chin. "She is very pretty, Mademoiselle, very ambitious. . . ."

"So what of that?" Sandra laughed and got up, thinking, justifiably perhaps, that the woman who had chosen motherhood to a career was perhaps a little jealous, a little reluctant to relinquish such a position of responsibility after all.

"Well it is simply that such women usually prefer to work for a man, Mademoiselle. There is something coquettish about Agnès. I think she likes the men. . . ."

"I like the men too," Sandra said, reaching out a hand affectionately to touch Edith's arm. "And I know you do as well. Now don't get the Métro tonight but take a taxi home. Charge it up to expenses. Go on. I insist. I don't want your husband to be worried."

Edith shrugged her shoulders and, thanking Sandra profusely, hurried out to the anteroom. She was just in time to see Agnès, a smile playing on her lips, leap up from her desk, as if trying it out for size.

"It's a bit too soon for that," Edith said sharply. "I have another six weeks here, you know . . . and anything can happen in that time."

"What do you mean?" Agnès said in a tone of voice Sandra might have had difficulty recognizing and should, certainly, have been warned by.

"If you're not careful you may not get the job. I said nothing to Mademoiselle about your fondness for Monsieur Zac; but I might, and I can tell you, she wouldn't like that at all. She hates Monsieur Zac, and if she knew how much you liked him she wouldn't consider employing you."

Tossing her head, Agnès covered her own typewriter and, taking her handbag from her locker, flounced out of the room.

Zac said:

"This is really excellent news, Agnès. I felt I had to offer you my congratulations in person."

He lifted his glass of champagne and toasted her. Agnès, blushing prettily, responded. The bar at the Hôtel Meurice was full and the crush seemed to throw them together, shoulder to shoulder, in unaccustomed intimacy.

"That is very good of you, Monsieur Desmond. I never thought you would remember *me.*"

"Not remember you, Agnès?" Zac contrived to look astonished. "Come, come. I remember you very well from the days you worked for me."

"Only briefly, Monsieur."

"Long enough to make an impression," Zac said unctuously, carefully pouring some more champagne in her glass. "In fact I was thinking of offering you employment myself, but Mademoiselle has snapped you up."

Agnès could hardly believe her ears. After years of insignificance so much had happened to her, and all at once. Two very important people wanting to employ her at the same time! Incredible, as had been the invitation to meet Monsieur Zac Desmond in the bar of this expensive and elegant hotel on the rue de Rivoli.

Zac leaned toward her and she was aware of his piercing, slightly uneven eyes, noticed only if one looked at them for a long time. It was not exactly a cast, or a squint—it was a quality of unevenness that could, in certain instances, be very attractive. She had noticed them before when she had been seconded to him from the Desmond typing pool once, briefly, when his own secretary had been away. He had not looked such an unhappy man then.

"I suppose you haven't started to work for Mademoiselle yet, have you, Agnès?"

"In a few weeks' time, Monsieur," Agnès replied. "When Edith Huelin leaves, finally, to have her baby." Her tone of voice changed and Agnès heaved a big sigh. Zac moved even nearer.

"I gather you don't *like* Madame Huelin very much?"

Agnès shook her head.

"Nor does she like me. I'm surprised I got the job, Monsieur."

"Why doesn't she like you, Agnès . . . ?"

"She is very, how shall I put it? Close to Mademoiselle. She is a little jealous of me, I think. She knows there is no love between you and Mademoiselle." Agnès's wide blue eyes looked at him innocently. "And she knows that I liked you."

Zac looked rather puzzled, shook his head and scratched his chin.

Agnès knew many of the girls in the office thought Monsieur Desmond a very attractive man; old, but attractive. Some of them twittered a bit when Monsieur Zac had been around, but he was never seen now at the Desmond head office. It was a pity because the whiff of scandal that used to surround Monsieur Desmond gave the girls in the typing pool something to chat about during those tedious hours of office work.

He was known to be susceptible, notorious in fact. At one time the typing pool contained no less than three girls who had been taken to bed by him. Despite the age of women's liberation they thus enjoyed a status slightly elevated from the rest.

Now he had invited her . . . yet it was quite obvious he was after something other than her body. Agnès, working-class girl from the Massif Central, was no fool.

"I should tell you, Monsieur, that I didn't like what she said or the way she spoke. I also want to tell you that I am loyal to you even if I do become Mademoiselle's private secretary . . . just in case, well," she looked up at him again, with a slightly fey, appealing smile, "you come back."

Zac smiled and leaned back in his chair, his glass comfortably between his fingers.

"It's not impossible, Monsieur, is it?" Agnès hurried on. "I want you to know that if I am made Mademoiselle's secretary—and I would like to be because it is a tremendously important position for me—I am still loyal to the Desmond family. . . ."

"That is very, very good news, Agnès. I can assure you that your loyalty to my family will be rewarded because if one thing is certain it is that the days of Sandra O'Neill in that office, behind my father's desk, are very much numbered.

"Meanwhile, anything you can do to help that process . . ."

"Anything, Monsieur?" Agnès's smile disappeared. No one could be so naïve, Zac decided, as to feel she would simply be invited out for a drink by him—for nothing.

"If you can bring me some evidence of your loyalty, something to the detriment of Mademoiselle, anything like that, you will be rewarded ten-thousandfold. It would be not only in memory of my father, and for me, but for the whole Group. I would like you to keep your eyes peeled and your ears wide open; to be alert to all things and everything that goes on in that office, and outside it too if you can. I would like you—" he leaned forward, his face lit by a demoniac hatred "—to look at her private mail, read through her confidential files . . . I want you to be like the Trojan horse. You understand?"

"I *think* I understand your meaning, Monsieur Desmond," Agnès said with deceptive docility, producing a compact whose raised lid concealed her expression as she deftly powdered her face. But when she looked at him again her expression had changed. "But, believe me, I could never do as you suggest. Mademoiselle Desmond is much too sharp. She knows everything that goes on. I feel she would even see through my disloyalty." Agnès involuntarily shuddered. "She has such penetrating eyes, Monsieur."

"But Mademoiselle has her weaknesses I assure you." Zac laughed unpleasantly. "You would be surprised if you knew some of the things I know. Maybe you would not respect her so much."

"Really Monsieur? I find that incredible."

"You had better believe me, my dear. I know what I'm

talking about." Zac nodded his head wisely. "Moreover such weaknesses make me certain that Mademoiselle will not be there for very long; not where she is—in my seat, a position that was intended for me from birth."

Zac with an air of impatience studied the ticket left by the waiter.

"Well, if you can't help me. . . ."

Agnès was in a dilemma. To offend Monsieur Desmond was unthinkable; but to incur the wrath of Mademoiselle, by disloyalty. . . .

"Let me think about what you have said, Monsieur Desmond," she said with a new note of humility in her voice. "I will always be loyal to the Desmond family. . . ."

Zac put down the ticket and, producing his wallet, began to count out some notes, without looking at her.

"I think you will find it very rewarding if you do, Agnès. This is a number where you can reach me privately at any time."

And leaning forward, he put his thick embossed card between her nervous fingers, momentarily allowing his hand to close over them.

Lady Elizabeth leaned forward in her car and spoke to her chauffeur.

"You are *sure* this is the right address, Gerard?"

"Perfectly sure, Madame." The chauffeur nodded. "I have been here before. . . ."

"Oh."

Lady Elizabeth closed her mouth abruptly, wishing she hadn't spoken, thus inviting a familiarity from her husband's chauffeur she would rather not have had to endure. Of course Gerard had brought Georges here before, often.

She looked through the stone arch by which they had stopped in the pretty village of Crémy, to the large L-shaped house slightly obscured by a mist that rose from the valley.

As the chauffeur got out to open her door she thought she saw a light in his eyes, a smirk on his face. She looked at him sternly.

"Please turn the car around. I won't be long."

Gerard bowed as she got out of the car, his hat still in his hand, and watched her as she walked slowly up the graveled courtyard to the front door, stopping for a moment to admire what she could see of the view from the terrace. But almost the whole of the valley was cloaked by a fine drizzly mist. She turned her attention to the house.

She hadn't quite realized the size or sumptuousness of the place that her husband had bought for his mistress on the Côte des Blancs. However, knowing him, she should have realized it would hardly be a cottage.

She knocked sharply at the front door, which opened immediately as if she had been expected. A maid stood there dressed in black with a white pinafore.

"Madame O'Neill if you please," Lady Elizabeth said stiffly.

"Are you expected, Madame?" the maid replied, though Lady Elizabeth suspected she knew quite well who she was.

"You may announce Lady Elizabeth Desmond."

"Thank you, Madame."

The maid stood back and as she did Hélène O'Neill came to the door of one of the rooms on the ground floor and, for a moment, both women stared frostily at each other.

"I hope I do not inconvenience you, Madame," Lady Elizabeth said, "by arriving unannounced."

"Please come in, Madame." Hélène O'Neill stood back and it was then that Lady Elizabeth saw that she walked with the aid of a stick. For a moment she felt a sense of shock and wondered why she had been afraid of this prematurely aged, obviously sick woman and hated her for so long.

To break the ice she walked immediately to a high picture window that overlooked the vineyards.

"What an attractive view," she said in English, turning as Hélène gently closed the door and walked slowly over to her. "Of course this is the worst time of the year to see it."

"It is. In summer Georges—"

For a moment there was silence and then Hélène went on in a low voice.

"I must tell you I've been expecting you, Lady Elizabeth. Only I thought you would come sooner. Much sooner. It's about Sandra, isn't it . . . ?"

"Yes." Lady Elizabeth turned around just in time to see Hélène stagger into a chair, putting out a hand to save herself falling.

"Are you all right?" she inquired, crossing the room to the younger, yet at the same time, so much older, woman.

"I'm perfectly all right, Madame. It is only that my health at the moment—"

"I heard you were not well. I wanted"—Lady Elizabeth took a seat opposite her erstwhile rival, and sat upright in her chair, hands resting on her handbag, her head slightly tilted—"I wanted to tell you I was sorry."

"Sorry for what? That I am ill?" Hélène appeared confused and Elizabeth wondered again, as she so often had, what her husband had seen in that rather nondescript woman with her peasant origins—not particularly beautiful, even when she had been in good health. Maybe sympathy was what he wanted after all; sympathy, someone to warm his slippers and a kind and comforting breast.

Well hers had been kind and comforting once, and he should not have married the daughter of an English earl if he wanted home cooking and warm slippers placed in front of the fire every night.

"That, and the loss of Georges. I know you must miss him." Elizabeth paused awkwardly and hurried on. "We were all quite devastated, still are."

"Then it was *very* kind indeed of you to call, Lady Elizabeth." Hélène's voice took on a warmer tone. "I appreciate it."

"Please don't misunderstand me." The wife of the late Georges Desmond was at pains to make herself clear. "My husband also brought a great deal of unhappiness to me, his family . . . but I needn't go into that." She gazed around her at the comfortable chintzes of the attractive room that in the summer must have blazed with color. On the wall was an oil painting of Georges that she had never seen and she averted her eyes from it, aware of a sickening sensation in the pit of her stomach.

To have shared her husband with this . . . this menial. What misery he had brought on his family, indeed. How much, it is probable even Hélène would never know; never guess.

"As you say," Lady Elizabeth continued, "there is the question of your daughter's inheritance. It shocked us."

Hélène O'Neill sat upright in her chair, her face pale. Her graying hair was drawn tightly back from her forehead and her cavernous cheeks and prominent eyes made it difficult to imagine the young woman she had once been, emaciated now by ill health.

"It shocked me too, Madame," she said. "As did the attitude of Sandra who has never been near me since she came to France. That shocked me almost more than the death of Georges. I feel bitterly hurt."

"I can imagine," Lady Elizabeth said but, nevertheless, she felt a moment of quiet triumph. "She is, however, a very clever woman. Doubtless you must have known *something* about the will."

"I knew nothing. Nothing." Hélène stamped her stick rhythmically on the floor to emphasize the point. "Nothing. I would *never* have advised him to do what he did. Knowing your eldest son I am only too aware of the trouble it would cause, and could have warned him."

"Trouble indeed," Lady Elizabeth said, glancing at the

small watch on her wrist. "Well, that is really all . . . I came to ask. I'm sorry I troubled you."

"No trouble at all, Lady Elizabeth." Suddenly Hélène gasped and leaned forward, appearing to fight for her breath. Lady Elizabeth looked at her in concern.

"You really are *quite* ill, Madame. . . . Have you seen your doctor recently?"

"Oh yes I see my doctor and I have medicines." Hélène held up the sort of ventilator used by asthmatics. "I have suffered from this most of my life, you know, and Monsieur Desmond was so very good."

Strange, Lady Elizabeth thought to herself. Georges had always been a man who hated illness. Nothing got him out of the house more quickly than when someone other than himself needed a doctor. If it was him it was a very different matter. Yet to think that Georges had been kind to an asthmatic . . . the idea was almost incredible.

It occurred to her that she hadn't really known her husband very well at all.

"However, he has gone. . . ." Hélène sighed and gazed rather unnervingly at Lady Elizabeth without appearing to see her, as if she saw Georges instead. "I feel I shall go too, soon, to join him. I would like to see Sandra and Bob. She's pretty, isn't she?"

"Very. A beauty."

"I imagine Tim is impressed by her."

"Tim is impressed by anything in skirts," Lady Elizabeth replied icily. "But Tim has *no* trouble finding a woman, I assure you."

"Oh I know that. I follow the fortunes of all your family, but from a distance, naturally. If Sandra were only as kind as she is beautiful; but maybe she feels she has a lot to forgive."

She looked rather sadly at Lady Elizabeth.

"If you could *try* and persuade her. . . ."

"I will do what I can, Madame. But I have not much influence." Lady Elizabeth rose awkwardly and held out her hand.

Hélène, very slowly, rose too and took it.

"Have you *any* idea why Georges did what he did? Lady Elizabeth said abruptly and Hélène, who looked very tired, seemed puzzled by what she said. Then suddenly she gave a wan smile that appeared almost to give her pain.

"She was *not* his daughter if that's what you think. I can assure you of that. I . . ." She began to cough and once more looked around for a seat. The door opened and her maid came in as if she had been standing outside the door.

"Madame O'Neill . . ." she began.

"I will come for my oxygen, Blanche. Madame is just leaving. I . . ."

As Blanche held out an arm for Hélène to take, her mistress gazed once more at her visitor.

"I have something else I *would* like to tell you; but not now . . . later when I am better. It might help you a little to understand, and forgive."

THREE

The Walls of Troy

14

There on the desk, on top of a pile of letters that Edith would see when she arrived to sort through Mademoiselle Desmond's post, was the letter. Addressed to Sandra in handwriting, it had *Confidential Most Urgent* clearly written across the top.

Edith was due after all to leave prematurely and Agnès had been busily preparing herself to take over this important and onerous post. Already she had commended herself to Sandra by her willingness to work all hours, to come early and stay late.

Edith had developed a complication in her late pregnancy that was not uncommon: high blood pressure, and she had been advised to take things easy. Now she only worked in the office for a few hours a day and soon, soon . . . she, Agnès Guyon, would be sitting here right at the huge rosewood desk, an antique in itself, placed strategically just outside the door of one of the most important businesswomen in the world. In herself and in her own way she was to become a person of power and influence too.

Agnès sat there now, her hands on top of the desk, the pile of mail in front of her. *Confidential. Most Urgent.* She turned the letter over and over in her hands, smelling it for some reason as though it would afford her a clue as to its originator. The postmark was Bourges, a large town in the province of Berry. Who lived in Bourges? Agnès didn't know and she was about to put it to one side when she remembered those words of Monsieur Zac's, the look on his face as he asked her to let him have any information she could lay her hands on and intimated that her reward would be not only the gratitude of the entire Desmond family, but . . .

Agnès instinctively patted the back of her neatly brushed hair and studied the outside of the letter. It was only eight o'clock and no one would be in for at least half an hour. Mademoiselle had a meeting in Reims and had spent the night at Tourville. More and more the fortunes of the champagne firm were occupying her attention as the important time for blending the wines that would make the *cuvée* for the previous year drew near. A diligent student, she wanted to learn as much as she could before the Tasting Committee met to consider the blends, on the advice of the *chef des caves* and his assistants, at the Desmond office in Reims.

Champagne was, after all, the core of the Desmond business: a name synonymous with quality, luxury, an elegant, leisured style of living. The Desmond trademark might rest on other things: machine tools, airplanes, a newspaper, a bank, but to most people throughout the world Desmond meant one thing only: that exciting, sparkling, unique beverage which is only made in a single province of France situated some sixty miles southeast of Paris.

Mademoiselle was a good student and a keen one and, to her satisfaction, had been told that she had a good palate. She was concerned that her staff should not go out of their way to flatter or deceive her, and had made it clear all the time that in everything she wanted the truth. She had made this clear to Agnès too—an indication that she intended to take her into her confidence.

René Latour spent hours with her tasting wines blind, wines of all kinds and all vintages—still wines as well as champagne. His honest opinion was that, for a beginner, she was excellent.

So Sandra spent much of her time in Reims and Agnès assumed more and more control of her affairs at the Group headquarters while Edith rested to prepare herself for the birth of her baby.

Agnès Guyon was an ambitious girl and a smart one. If Mademoiselle was learning so was she; not about tasting wines and blending champagne, but about the smooth running of a large office where everything had to work in apple-pie order. Mademoiselle would not tolerate incompetence, sloppiness or inefficiency; lateness, sleepiness or error. She was a hard task mistress, driving others as she drove herself. Shirkers were quickly sent on their way.

Of the girls selected from the typing pool to work in Mademoiselle's secretariat, half didn't last the week. What was all right for the typing pool, whose standards were exacting enough in themselves, was, more often than not, not good enough for Mademoiselle, as she was known throughout the Group—Mademoiselle with the capital M implied—and only the very best were permitted to stay. And it was Agnès who, of them all, was to be promoted to personal secretary, a position that she had never dreamed of, not even when her elevation from typing pool to secretariat took place.

In a few days this desk would be hers. . . . She took the letter in her hands and smelled it again, studying the gummed flap. If it was anything interesting she could photocopy it; it would be easy to slip a knife under the flap, which had not been very well gummed, and return it to Mademoiselle's desk long before she arrived. But she would have to be quick. Edith used to get in at around nine and one thing she knew for sure: Edith did not like her. She did not like her promotion and she had made life as hard as she could for someone she didn't believe had the experience to succeed her. Had she, Edith, not worked personally for Monsieur Desmond for years; was she not a woman of considerable experience, whereas Agnès . . . ?

No, she made life hard for Agnès. She was not nice to her and she did not cooperate with her. What she did she did reluctantly, as if hoping that this would persuade Mademoiselle to change her mind.

But it was difficult to fault Agnès, who was meticulous in everything she did and it was also as though Mademoiselle, in her wisdom, had detected something spiteful in Edith's reaction to her successor, so she did all she could to pave the way for Agnès. In fact Agnès was beginning to like her very much; to respect her and appreciate her qualities, even if she was not a true member of the family. One couldn't help but admire a woman who was so beautiful, so powerful and yet so young; who, as well as being very competent and efficient, was also kind. A person who had seen that Edith was easily tiring, and was concerned enough about her health to have her own expensive private physician check her over and keep an eye on her until the birth. She was sent home every day in one of the company cars.

Some people did not like Mademoiselle. They were usually those whose dedication or attitude to their work left something to be desired. But others liked and admired her and these were invariably people who were as efficient and, in their ways, as ambitious as she was, though none of them would ever aspire to occupy the position she had.

This line was split right down the middle at the Group headquarters, not only in the secretariat and typing pool but among the executives, some of whom Mademoiselle was very skillfully beginning to ease out. For such a busy woman she had a grasp of detail, an eye for performance that was amazing.

Really it was a horrible idea to open a private letter addressed to someone one admired with the intention of showing it to a man who hated her. It was dangerous too. If Monsieur Zac thought he might return as Head of the Group she didn't really believe it. Nor was she particularly loyal to the name Desmond—why, after all, should she be? It was only a job.

Moreover Mademoiselle, not Monsieur Zac, was giving her her chance.

Agnès let the letter fall as if it had given her an electric shock. She was about to place it on one side, as she should have, and get on with the job of opening the rest of the mail when she thought of future rewards Monsieur Zac had hinted at as he escorted her from the Meurice to a taxi. He was a man and a susceptible, very attractive, commanding man and, with the right man, in the right circumstances, great things could happen that a girl who had been born into a mining family could never expect.

Everyone knew about Mademoiselle's mother, Madame O'Neill who, through guile, cunning and, undoubtedly, a very great degree of competence and efficiency, had succeeded in becoming the mistress of Monsieur Desmond. It had been a relationship which had lasted for years, until the time when both of them were no longer young . . . and look what had happened to Madame O'Neill (whom many in the Group clearly remembered with a mixture of respect and fear)? Her daughter had succeeded to this great empire . . . and Madame was living presumably, in comfort, security and luxury, for the rest of her life.

Agnès expertly parted the flap from the rest of the envelope with a deft flick of the paper knife as if she had been illegally opening private correspondence all her life. Then, very swiftly, her eyes ran over the contents and she gave a deep intake of breath. If Monsieur Zac saw *this*. . . .

She glanced at the clock. It was later than she thought but she still had time to make a copy. She rose from the desk and went swiftly to that part of the room which held the photocopy machine when she heard the whirr of the elevator outside and the sound of the door opening.

Very quickly, aborting her mission, she returned to Edith's desk and stuffed the letter with the envelope into her handbag.

As Edith came through the door, much much earlier than

expected; Agnès called out a cheery, and insincerely meant, greeting and vacated her desk . . . just in time.

It was very odd to lie in Livio's bed in the attic room and not be conscious of the whirring of machinery, the sound of drills, the whine of the car ramp. Instead, at night, it was very, very still. One could hear his breathing quite clearly, the noise when he snored; his cries, and hers, when they made love.

For to be together again was rapturous; rapturous and dangerous. In her weakness, after the miscarriage, she had given Zac her word that she would never see Livio again and as soon as they had returned to Paris she had broken it. She had fled to those familiar arms where it seemed that she got what she wanted, what she could never get from Zac . . . love and compassion, tenderness, even friendship.

For the Livio who welcomed her back had, in a way, been a changed man. Her experience had shocked him; her treatment at the hands of her husband revolted him. The fact that she had nearly died bearing his child seemed to bring an essentially vain and selfish man to his senses.

He had never thought to see her again and when he did he knew that his feelings for her had changed a great deal. He didn't just want her money or her body; he wanted her. At last he could call it love.

In the quiet of the night they would often discuss their feelings for each other. Because it was only at night that they could meet away from the prying eyes of his work force. They knew that someone had spied on them, but not who or how and now no one could be trusted. Having been the victim of his violence Tara knew quite well what could be expected of her husband if he found out that she had continued to be unfaithful to him. One time she had lost a baby; she didn't like to think what she might lose next: maybe her life or Livio's.

Tara had little doubt that she was married to a violent and

sadistic man. One who had always been rather narrowly balanced between sanity and madness, good and evil but who, since the advent of Sandra in his life, seemed to have gone over the top altogether. She knew now that his one consuming passion was to get rid of Sandra and, having personally experienced his violence, she had little doubt that one day he would, no matter how.

It wasn't, however, only physically that she knew Zac to be a violent man. He had always been an irascible man, quick to fly into rages, an unreasoning, vengeful and rather frightening man who had few, if any, close personal friends. In fact she couldn't think of one person Zac could call a true friend; he was surrounded by hangers-on, sycophants who wanted him not because they liked him, but for what they could get out of him. In a way maybe she had got what she deserved, for that was why she had married him. She was just as greedy in her feelings as the rest.

Tara herself had come to fear her husband over the years but also to despise him, and the one tempered the other. She wasn't frightened enough of him, for instance, not to see her lover when she wanted to, or to take other lovers as she had in the past. She was conscious of her nobility, always; of being a Falconetti, someone whose family had been powerful in Italy even before the Renaissance. Whereas who were the Desmonds? When one of her ancestors was Chamberlain to the Pope, Georges' great-, great-, great-grandfather was a foot-soldier in Napoleon's army.

It suited Tara to cling desperately to the idea of her innate social superiority over Zac whenever she felt that, just possibly, he was getting the better of her. His mother may have been the daughter of an earl, but his ancestors came from the petit bourgeoisie and, of the petit bourgeoisie, he remained.

Livio stirred and then jerked his head up; what time was it?

"Time for me to go," Tara said, aware of him turning to

her and knowing that he would want her again. That brief, final episode of their lovemaking was sometimes the best part of all . . . done with an eye on the clock as though, figuratively, they were looking over their shoulders. But tonight there was no time.

"It's nearly ten o'clock," she said.

"Where does he think you are?"

"With my friend Gina Heurté. Her husband is a bastard like Zac, spends all the time working and she is always at a loose end. We are supposed to have gone to the movies." She looked at the clock. "It will be finished in half an hour. . . ."

"And do you *know* which film you are seeing?"

"Oh yes . . . It is all rehearsed." She began to chuckle as his mouth closed over hers and, weakly, she started to struggle with him on the bed again, only this time not really wanting to win.

Dear Sandra, [the letter said].

"You might find it odd that I am writing to you in this way and I have given a lot of thought to what I am doing.

I feel, however, that you are in danger from my family and as I like you and even feel sorry for you I wanted to warn you to beware of them all, but especially Tim.

For I know you may think Tim is a friend but he is not. From what I heard after you abruptly left Burg-Farnbach at Christmas-time I gather that there may have been something between you and Tim and that you trust him.

Please don't. He and Zac and Belle are in cahoots with one purpose: to disinherit you.

Sandra, I do not lead a happy life. My past is sad and I am not happily married. My husband cannot give me the children who might make my life more bearable.

However, whatever my misfortunes are, I would not like you to be harmed in any way by the Desmond family who have done enough harm to countless people already.

If you want to know any more please get in touch with me, but do it discreetly. I know I can trust you. I will try and visit Tourville soon and perhaps we can have a chat there. But my mother-in-law has got the flu and I have been unable to leave home, so I thought the best thing was to write to you.

Believe me, I am very sincerely yours,

C de St-A.

"C. de St-A," Belle said with a sneer. "Did she think that would prevent anyone knowing who she was? Is it an anonymous letter do you suppose?"

"No one else was meant to see it but Sandra." Zac took the letter from Belle. "Now thanks to Agnès we know where we are with our little sister."

"Little viper," Belle snarled. "Do you remember how we always used to call her 'the creep' when she was small? Creeping around corners, along corridors, always listening in. She was behind us when we were walking in the forest the day Sandra left the Castle. I remember seeing her creeping along, but paid little attention to her. To think, our own *sister* betrays us to an enemy. . . ."

"Personally I'm not surprised," Zac said. "But thank God for Agnès, or the rest of our plan might have miscarried."

"As it is, it might miscarry already. Tim isn't at all keen to go on."

"Oh he will." Zac smiled. "I have promised him that the combined banks of Desmond and Franco-Belges will present a trophy and a fabulous financial prize to his favorite downhill ski competition at Verbiers next year . . . if he behaves himself. It will be known as The Georges Desmond Trophy and Tim is very keen . . . also he needs a little personal sub from me from time to time."

"Does he?" Belle looked up from the fireplace in front of which they were sitting, heads close together, locked in a discussion of their sister's treachery and their plan of operations. "I didn't know *you* had the means either."

"Oh things aren't too bad." Zac took a sip of port from his glass and winked. "Philippe de Lassale isn't quite as shrewd as I thought. I get away with quite a lot I can tell you. Frankly I think he is in awe of Sandra and the name Desmond."

"You do surprise me." Belle's tone was sarcastic.

"It's surprising the effect she has on people. They seem to think she is some wizard from another planet. Even that shrewd fellow, René Latour, says he has never come across someone who can learn so quickly, or develop such a palate. She has mesmerized even him." The expression in Zac's eyes grew mean. "She is a danger, that one, just because she *is* so clever."

Zac paused and, getting up from his chair, went over to straighten the painting by Watteau that his father had left him, intending him, in turn, to leave it with the Louvre. Zac, however, was the last one to be concerned by the gratitude of a nation and had rapidly taken it to his own house, especially after all the antique furniture was returned to Tourville or the place de l'Étoile.

Now he was slowly and laboriously reassembling a collection; purchases made at house auctions or in the salerooms and for that he needed money. Lots of it. He knew that the only way he would satisfy his lust for fine things, his need for acquisitions, his desire for the most gracious living possible, was by having at his command the almost limitless finances of the Desmond Group, mainly to channel into his pocket instead of reinvestment or good causes.

The picture to his satisfaction, Zac stepped back to admire it and then he went over to the side of his sister, pulling his chair even nearer to her, so that no eavesdropper at the door could possibly hear.

"You know," he said, his head close to Belle's, "it may not come off with Tim, who knows? He is going to try again in the Caribbean, but are we sure she will accept Carl's invitation to join your yacht after what happened? Is it really likely?"

"She told Carl she would."

"She was being polite. I'm sure of it."

"She doesn't know that Tim will be there."

"She won't take the chance. No, *ma chère,* I have a far far better plan." Zac puffed contentedly at his cigar, like a man who has done a good day's work and has a clear conscience. "It concerns the Tasting Committee which is due to meet at Reims a week from Monday."

"Of course, I shall be there," Belle said matter-of-factly, producing a diary from her handbag and turning the pages. "The previous Saturday I return from Burg-Farnbach, this time without Carl but with Constantine. . . ."

"No, no, my dear." Zac put a restraining hand on hers. "You will *not* be there."

"But why?" She looked at him with surprise. "You know I have the best palate in the family, possibly in the organization . . . unless one has now to take account of the 'superior' taste of the Irishwoman. Am I to be deprived of that one small privilege still left to me?"

"No, no, you don't understand." Zac lowered his voice even more. . . . "Let me explain."

Tara could hear voices in the drawing room as she came in, glancing rather guiltily at the clock in the hall. She would rather have hurried upstairs to bed, but it would be impolite not to say "hello" to Belle. So she knocked on the door and before Zac replied turned the handle and went inside rubbing her hands against the cold outside.

"Cold?" Belle inquired in a pleasant voice.

"Freezing," Tara said. "I hope you aren't going back to Tourville tonight? The roads will be icy."

"Yes, do stay here," Zac said. "You know there's plenty

of room and we'd love to have you. Besides," he smiled meaningfully at her, "we still have things to discuss."

"Oh all right." Belle didn't need much persuasion. "If you're sure I won't be in the way."

"You're never in the way," Tara said with the practiced ease of the habitual liar which was what one had to be to deal effectively with Zac and his family, to say nothing of having a love affair on the side. "I would also like to discuss business with you, perhaps tomorrow."

"Oh is there something wrong?"

"Not at all. Someone has told me of a new designer." Tara stifled a yawn as if speaking out of duty rather than enthusiasm. "I *suppose* we'd better look at his stuff."

"Very well," Belle said as Zac came over to offer her a refill.

"What do you think of this port?" he asked her as she held out her glass.

"Not much."

"I thought you'd say that, you with your excellent palate."

"I'll say good night then," Tara said. "Your usual room will be ready for you when you go up, Belle. See you tomorrow."

Belle rose and extravagantly embraced her sister-in-law savoring, for a moment, the delicate masculine fragrance of a well-known men's cosmetic. She stood back and looked at Tara with that air of surprise that people have who have detected something unexpected. Tara, however, unsuspicious, was giving nothing away except a friendly smile.

"See you tomorrow, darling," Belle said, "and we'll have a long, long talk about business."

Zac saw his wife to the door and gave her a peck on the cheek and a pat on the bottom.

"Off you go," he said. "I'll soon be up."

As he closed the door after her they could hear Tara calling to the maid to prepare the room usually occupied by the Princess. Then Zac selected a cigar and resumed his place by the fire.

"She looks better, don't you think?"

"She looks very well, *now.* You must take good care of her."

"Oh I do. I take very good care of her indeed. I see she is followed everywhere she goes."

"But is *that* necessary? After all, you warned her."

"I care who she associates with," Zac said testily. "I don't expect her to be virtuous for the rest of her life but she is a Desmond, and if she takes up again with that Italian Romeo I swear I'll kill him." He gazed menacingly at the door. "Fortunately I know where she was tonight; with Gina Heurté at the movies, someone who has as much time to be idle as Tara. There's no need to have her followed on occasions like that."

Belle looked at the floor, deciding for the moment to keep her own counsel. After all there was no need to share *all* her secrets with her brother, and a time might well come when the knowledge she had just gained about Tara might be useful. Also she didn't want to provoke a fresh war between them. There were more important things to do. Instead she said to Zac:

"To return to our business. Your plan, *mon cher,* will cost the company twenty million dollars. Is *that* wise?"

"Two hundred million dollars, minus twenty million. How much does that come to? That bitch has stolen from us *two hundred million* dollars and you hesitate to sacrifice a mere ten percent . . . are you mad?"

Belle appeared thoughtful for a moment and then nodded her head.

"If you think it will work. . . ."

"I *know* it will work. I will see to that personally. Meanwhile," he touched the letter that he had put in his breast pocket, "we have something else important to fall back on.

In fact we are building up a campaign which we cannot possibly lose."

Belle smiled and, looking at her tiny jeweled watch, gave a yawn. Then she stood up and tightened the belt around her attractive woolen suit, a superb creation from Raison.

"I hope you will reward the little Agnès," she said, an insinuating smile on her lips. "It seems she is an ally we cannot afford to lose."

"Oh don't worry." Zac drained his glass and, rising, stood beside his sister, his back to the fire, one arm around her shoulders. "I shall reward her very well indeed . . . for within the very walls of Troy we have a wooden horse of inestimable value."

One morning in February Sandra left the Château de Tourville early to drive herself to Reims for a meeting of the Tasting Committee. She took the road along by the side of the Marne past Damery, and Marsanne until she came to Verneuil and Cumières and joined the swift main road that marked the borders of Champagne with the Tardenois département. From here it was about thirty-five kilometers to Reims, a drive through pleasant, hilly countryside, sometimes wooded amid lush fields of wheat and maize and the vineyards which were the lifeblood of the region.

But this was a part that had seen much devastation during the Wars. Along the route were many of its sad testimonials: the military cemeteries housing the remains of veterans who had fought on both sides: French, British, Italian and German.

As she passed the great Italian cemetery the whole view of the plain around Reims stretched before her in the pale wintry sunshine and, in the distance, she could just discern the uneven twin towers of one of the greatest Gothic cathedrals in the world: Notre Dame, begun in the twelfth century which had taken three hundred years to complete.

The cathedral was a monument to its own survival, in keeping with the countryside in which it lay. Reims too had suffered atrociously and had the look of a city destroyed by war and carefully rebuilt. Inevitably on its outskirts were modern factories, high-rise buildings and, seen from this aspect, it could have been any industrial town in Europe. But, once inside the city, one became aware that some parts of it were very old: walls, battlements, tiny houses in narrow alleyways that had escaped the successive bombardments, the ravages of the German occupations of 1914 and 1940.

But much of Reims was new and carefully planned, a loving, painstaking copy of the old. But could anyone succeed in recapturing old Reims with its mellow buildings surrounding its ancient and massive church of Saint-Remi? Could anything recapture that pre-First World War Reims which, like so many other European cities, had vanished altogether?

Sandra bypassed the center on her way to the Desmond offices, keeping to the circular road which led her to the boulevard Henry Vasnier, built on a hill over the *crayères* where so many of the Houses constituting the *grandes marques* of champagne had their headquarters.

The Tasting Committee of Desmond Champagne met annually to consider one of the most important decisions that had to be made all year. It concerned the blending of the new champagne from the grapes collected at the previous autumn's harvest. Since September the juice of the grapes obtained by the various pressings in the *maie* had lain in large vats undergoing the process known as the first fermentation. The vats containing the fermenting wine had lain during the winter in *celliers,* not cellars, as the name implied, but wine stores above ground and maintained very strictly at a temperature of around twenty to twenty-five degrees centigrade.

During this hibernation the cellar master had kept an eye on the progress of the fermentation to be sure that it had proceeded at a regular rate. Toward the end of this period the vats were topped up every few days because of the shrinkage of the wines caused by evaporation and sometimes seepage, a process known as *ouillage.*

During the past winter Sandra had been frequently taken to see the process of the fermentation of the wine; the topping up of the huge vats and the precise maintenance of temperature which was done by computer.

The system worked so well that, having learned her lesson at the harvest, she didn't introduce time-and-motion study men into the *celliers* because there seemed to be no way this could be improved upon, though new methods were being considered all the time, particularly by the larger firms, those owned by the multinational groups.

Desmond wasn't owned by a multinational group but it was a very large, independent concern with vast resources to call on to modernize and improve on its methods.

When the deposits of yeasts and sediments that existed in the wine had fallen it was time to begin the process of drawing off and bottling the clear wine, a process known as 'racking' *(soutirage).* The lees that remained were often the color and consistency of mud (even these were sold off and used in the production of raw alcohol). The clear new wine was pumped into fresh clean vats and left there for a few weeks before undergoing a second *soutirage* to disperse any fresh lees that might have been formed and to air them.

After the racking which, at Desmond, took place just before Christmas, the wines were left in the huge vats to get rid of any remaining extraneous substances and to rest.

For weeks René Latour had been tasting samples of the wines lying in the vats and deciding how much of the wine to be used for the vintage *cuvée,* how much for the nonvintage *cuvée* and how much to be stored for the future. He had also to try and determine which of the new wines for the vintage *cuvée* would blend most happily with the old wines for the non-vintage *cuvée* and what proportion would be from red vines and what from white.

René Latour had been with the Desmond organization since he was a boy of eighteen when he had left the local High School with distinction. His father had been not *chef des caves* or anything so exalted but a cellarman, a *caviste* with the firm, working below ground for most of his life heaving and humping the barrels and bottles at the various stages of the complex champagne-making process. As the Desmonds had infected their progeny with a love of champagne, so had Latour *père* passed on his love of his work, which was a kind of vocation, to his only son.

René, naturally, was the apple of his eye and had proved a scholarly lad, but champagne was in his blood as it was in that of the Desmond children. His teachers wanted him to go to university but he wanted to work with champagne, maybe at a higher level than his father. However, like everyone else, he had to begin in the caves. René had always gotten on with Zac because when they were together they talked exclusively of that substance they loved and knew so much about: champagne. René knew nothing and cared less about the real character of his master's son. He only knew that he was an extremely good oenologist who had attended the same wine school at Montpellier as he had.

Like everyone else, René had assumed that Zac would succeed his father and that his participation in the selection of the blend and other aspects of the making of champagne would be a continuous one.

He was a man to whom a woman boss came as a great shock but he was also a dutiful employee and, like Pierre up at the big house, knew who would henceforth be paying his salary and looking after his and his family's welfare. Man or woman, it didn't matter to René. A woman in the champagne business was not all that unusual, except that they had invariably either been born into the business, or had married into it, and Sandra had done neither of these things but had been its head for only just over six months.

René had to acknowledge, and he did this frequently to his colleagues or, more often, to Madame Latour who shared his confidences, for he was a generous man, that Mademoiselle O'Neill for all the disadvantages she had started with, had acquired an exceptional grasp of the nature and manufacture of champagne. She had spent more and more of her time in Reims, staying at Tourville, so that she could be there any time René called her to show her a new process, a fresh development to the fermenting wine. And what a fascinating process it was, humbling to someone like Sandra who became increasingly aware that the manufacture of champagne was more of an art than a business. But unlike most art it was also financially rewarding and there were few, if any, poor champagne makers.

So now, on this day in February, Sandra sat at the round table in René's ultramodern laboratory in Reims as part of the Tasting Committee. She felt quite at home, wearing a white coat, as did the rest, and surveying the glasses set before them with the golden liquid which was soon to be the *cuvée,* or blend, for the year—an important one for Sandra; the first of her reign, so to speak. She wanted it to be a good one.

Latour checked his watch with the time on the wall, and then glanced toward Sandra.

"We can begin, Mademoiselle."

Sandra looked at him in surprise then around the table at the white-coated figures. All the places had been taken.

"Where are Monsieur Desmond and the Princess? They are part of the Tasting Committee, an important part. I don't think we can begin without them."

Latour shrugged his shoulders, adjusted his pince-nez and looked bewildered too.

"Alas, Mademoiselle, I understand Monsieur Zac is confined to his house in Paris with a bad attack of influenza. He rang only a few minutes ago to send his apologies. As for the

Princess she has not arrived from Burg-Farnbach; maybe she has been delayed by the weather."

"Then we must postpone it," Sandra said firmly. "I am very new here, Monsieur Latour, as you know. I cannot possibly be considered an expert on a committee as important as this. I cannot be responsible on my own for the *cuvée."*

One of the white-coated technicians leaned across the table, saying to her earnestly:

"You do not have to make any decision *yourself,* Mademoiselle, but be guided by Monsieur René and those of us," he paused and coughed modestly, "who have helped him to blend together the various wines and taste them. We have already formed an opinion of the *cuvée* and, of course, the opinion of Monsieur Zac and the Princess would have been helpful, but . . ." He shrugged his shoulders suggestively.

"Oh that's fine then," Sandra said with relief. "This is just a rubber stamp."

"In a *way,* Mademoiselle," the bright young technician, whose name was Charles, agreed cautiously, "in a way."

"However," René said sternly, "it is necessary to taste all the wines we have in these glasses before us, Mademoiselle. I do not wish to take responsibility alone for the *cuvée,* though my judgment has decided that these are the best blends to consider. It is always the head of the Group who signs the instructions for the final *cuvée.* He held a glass toward Sandra, who accepted it, put it to her nose, sipped it, twirled the contents around her mouth and then spat them neatly into a spitoon.

"The Pinot Noir is very tannic this year," Latour said, wrinkling his nose.

"We must sweeten a little the reserve wines," Charles said helpfully and another, much older man by the name of Marcel, nodded his agreement.

To Sandra most of this technical jargon was Chinese, though she listened carefully. Some of the blends that Latour had worked out so diligently over the weeks tasted unexceptional, with no hint of the great wine it would subsequently become after the *pris de mousse*. Before her was a sheet of paper divided into columns.

"Do we have to write on this?" Sandra asked. "I know I must seem awfully foolish."

"Not in the least, Mademoiselle," Charles said politely. "You are new. It is your first Tasting Committee. You cannot possibly be expected to know everything."

"I bet if the Princess were here she would make me feel an idiot," Sandra observed, wryly. "I do wish . . ."

"The Princess was, from birth, brought up to know and study champagne and fine wines, Mademoiselle," René Latour said kindly. "You cannot be expected to have such knowledge . . . yet; but I think the day is not far off when you will catch the Princess up."

"Oh don't say that!" Sandra laughed, pleased by the compliment. She thought she detected genuine glances of approval on the faces of the men around the table, the professional *champenois*. Unlike the Desmonds, at least her employees seemed to have accepted her.

Claire had remained at her home in Berry because of an illness of her mother-in-law.

And Tim? Tim, she thought bitterly, lifting a glass to her nose, wafting it gently back and forth in front of her to detect its subtle aroma. What sort of palate had Tim? She had seen neither Tim nor the Princess since the débâcle at Burg-Farnbach and very little of Zac either. This especially worried her. Zac was the kind of person one liked to have constantly in one's sights, to be sure what he was up to.

Sandra and Lady Elizabeth enjoyed—if that was the correct word—strained and rather silent weekends together at Tourville, each remaining, except for meals, in their respective suites.

There was a hollow in Sandra's life that work very neatly filled. It filled it completely and, thank God, it did.

Of course she would like to be part of the Desmond family whose name she now bore. Of course she would like to feel welcome and wanted whenever she visited Tourville. Instead the reception by Lady Elizabeth was invariably frosty and excuses were made so that, more often than not, she dined alone. With Uncle Henri and Aunt Sophie it was different. There was always a warm welcome at Marsanne for her. But they had been in California since Christmas and had not yet returned.

Aroma: limpidity: color.

She wrote her opinion of the blends which was, of course, purely her personal taste. In a way it was a little like an exam with no cheating or glancing at the paper of the candidate next to her.

Marcel finally lifted up a glass, holding it in front of him so that its clarity and limpidity could be seen by the assembled company.

"This is the *cuvée* of the past year. It was composed of eleven *crus* of the Montagne de Reims; seventeen from the Côte des Blancs. It was a very good mixture, and it would be very hard indeed to beat."

Sandra nodded and, tasting it, declared it excellent before she, with some expertise now, spat the contents into the leather spitoon in front of her.

Then with great solemnity, rather like a priest officiating at Mass, René Latour placed three glasses in front of her.

"Here are the three . . . which we propose to you, Mademoiselle, as the President of the Desmond Group. You should choose between three blends and perhaps modify them if you wish."

Sandra took each one of the three glasses and deeply inhaled the various bouquets, putting each glass to the light, tasting and then chomping the wine before spitting it out.

Then, after pondering a while, she finally put one aside from the rest and said, "*That* seems to me to be, how shall

I say? rounder. It would perhaps be more commercial than that one for instance." She pointed to the glass she had first tasted.

Charles now butted in and then René raised his voice rather sharply and two other men who had not yet spoken said their pieces. Sandra began to feel lost yet again even though she listened most attentively, making notes so that at the same time next year she would know better what was happening. She understood they were discussing an extremely complex and technical point: namely the exact kind and amount of yeasts to be added which would transform the natural sugar in the wine, plus the *liqueur de tirage,* which was added just before the bottling and consisted of still champagne wine and a little cane sugar, mixed with alcohol and carbonic gas.

The yeasts were either bought from a specialist or taken from the manufacturer's own wine. This process known as *levurage* was vital as the yeast enzymes were part of the process of second fermentation.

The carbonic acid gases trapped in the wine bottle by the cork became part of the wine and produced the sparkle, the *mousse,* the essence of champagne. The amount of sugar in the *liqueur de tirage* and the amount of natural sugar already in the wine would determine the degree of sparkle. The actual composition of the *liqueur* and the *levures* was a matter of mathematics—based on the pressure of carbonic gas in the bottle—as much as of the expertise and palate of a master blender, such as Latour.

At times the discussion became almost heated and at one point a glass spilled its contents on the table and the perpetrator of the outrage, though unintentional, was roundly reprimanded by René, whose normally aesthetic face was, by this time, quite pink.

Finally René put a piece of paper in front of Sandra with the air of one almost, but not quite, making a votive offering. After weeks of working out the blends, using complex mathematical techniques, as well as plumbing the depths of his oeneological knowledge and listening to the heated discussion today, he was casting his lot.

Sandra didn't know, though she could guess, that this same process happened every year in very much the same way—discussion, argument, decision, recommendation. It had the air of a time-honored routine and now the others around the table settled back with an air of agreement as Latour said:

"This is the choice, Mademoiselle. In fact it is *your* choice, as Chef de Maison. I think the choice is excellent. It will be a good bottle, perhaps a little fragile, but the wines of this year are difficult to control. Now if you will sign, Mademoiselle, I believe a little lunch has been prepared upstairs."

"And I hope you will all join me," Sandra said with a smile as she carefully appended her full signature "Sandra O'Neill Desmond" to the paper on which Latour still had his hand, as though he were delivering symbolically to her a child of their making which, in a way, he was.

All the atmosphere of strain vanished as soon as they met upstairs for lunch, which had been prepared with the usual care by the company chef.

Latour was particularly good-humored and chaffed his subordinates cheerfully about their opinions. Sandra, feeling content, watched them, taking care not to join in too much in what was really a masculine occasion, a kind of old boys' club.

What she couldn't quite understand, however, was why no other Desmond was present, no other director of the Group, apart from the curious omission of Zac and Belle, the acknowledged experts.

"Does Lady Elizabeth never attend the Tasting Committee?" she inquired. "Or Monsieur Timothée, or the Countess de Saint-Aignan?"

"Oh no, Mademoiselle," Latour shook his head vigorously,

savoring the champagne. "The late Monsieur Desmond was *very* particular that only experts should attend this function."

"But I am no expert," Sandra protested.

"Ah, Mademoiselle, but you are Monsieur Desmond's successor. His mantle, whether you like it or not, now rests on you and I am sure you do like it, if I may say so without presumption, Mademoiselle, because it fits you and you wear it well. It follows that you have to be there because it is your choice." He looked at her with rather a curious expression on his face, but one that was not unfriendly. "If anything should go wrong, Mademoiselle, the responsibility would be entirely yours . . . as it was Monsieur Desmond's before you."

"Oh dear." Sandra felt for a second a moment of anxiety. "I don't think I quite realized that."

"You signed the *ordre de tirage.* The instructions on that paper will now be fed into the computer and precisely carried out."

"Oh well in that case," Sandra said to a chorus of laughter all around, "if it is *computerized* I think we should have no fear at all."

Now they were in the best of humors not only because of the excellence of the lunch, the quality of the food and wines they were drinking but because the *cuvée* for the previous year had been chosen: the baby had been born, baptized and set on its way all at once. It was a mysterious process that would soon begin again with the flowering of the vines in the spring and reach its culmination at the same time next year.

It was an important moment in champagne making and one which engendered not only good humor and satisfaction but also a feeling of relief.

Sandra, who had her back to the door, was the only one to hear the loud knocking, as the staff had left the diners to enjoy the fine champagne with which they ended the meal.

She got up to answer the door herself, just as the handle turned and her secretary in Reims, a woman called Antoinette who had worked for the company for many years, put her head around the door.

"A call for you urgently, Mademoiselle. From America. . . ."

"From America!" Sandra momentarily felt some alarm, though she did not know why. Calls from America at all times of the day and night were common enough. "Excuse me."

She followed Antoinette into her office which was next to the boardroom where lunch had been held and took the mouthpiece held out to her, cradling it to her ear.

"Hello?" she said.

"Sandra!" It was Henri Piper's voice as clear as if he were in the next room; so clear that she could detect the air of concern in it. "Sandra, I am sorry to disturb the Tasting Committee. I know how important it is."

"That's all right," Sandra said, relief beginning to edge its way into her voice. "It's over. We have the *cuvée* for last year!"

"Sandra, I must interrupt you because this is urgent." Henri's tone of voice renewed her alarm. "I'm afraid I have bad news for you and you must get over here right away. Bob has been in an accident. . . ."

"Is he dead?" Sheer terror made her blurt out the awful question.

"No he's not dead. But he was found at the bottom of the swimming pool and is lucky to be alive. However, he *is* ill. . . ."

"I'll be over as soon as I can alert my pilot," Sandra said, looking over her shoulder to Antoinette. "But you're *sure* you're not hiding anything . . . ?"

"I'm hiding nothing, I promise you. There was a party of some kind; there were the usual high jinks; it was dark . . . but he *is* alive and he will recover. However, I think he needs you, Sandra."

"I'm on my way," Sandra said and after saying goodbye and putting down the phone, she began giving frantic instructions to Antionette, the business of the morning having fled from her mind.

15

Bob, his head swathed in white bandages, his leg in a sling and a drip from the bottle by his side feeding into his arm, looked near death. In fact they had told her as soon as she entered the hospital he was much better. He had come out of his coma, the deep unconsciousness that had worried them while Sandra was still flying over the Atlantic. Now, under medication, he slept around the clock and was fed by a tube.

As Sandra took his hand she imagined she could feel an answering pressure but, perhaps, she was mistaken. Then his eyelids flickered and his eyes briefly opened only to shut again as soon as he had seen her.

"He thinks he's in heaven," the doctor whispered with a smile and even the fact that he could make such a joke made Sandra feel better. She undid her coat and sat on the chair a thoughtful nurse had provided for her by Bob's side. Behind her was Henri.

"He really *is* better," Henri said. "At one time he had no color in his face at all and scarcely seemed to be breathing."

"Thank God *you* were here. I missed you in France but I'm glad you were here when it happened."

"So am I." Henri put a hand on her shoulder and, together, they stayed there for some time, aware of nothing but the quiet form of Bob and the noises of the various pieces of equipment measuring blood pressure, heart rate, carrying out their respective tasks.

Later, much later, they sat in the long, low-ceilinged room of the Piper ranch in the middle of the Sonoma valley. Sandra was tired. She was spending the night with the Pipers before seeing Bob's doctors again the following day. Then she would go to her home in Beverly Hills which, she knew, she was avoiding.

"You want to know exactly how it happened, of course?"

Henri stood before the fire. "In fact," he looked at his watch, "we may as well wait. A very nice policeman wants to talk to you about it too, and I have asked him to call and see us here. . . ."

"The *police—"* Sandra began but Henri held up his hand.

"No need for alarm. Naturally they have to investigate anything like this and there is no doubt it was an accident; but I feel I must warn you my dear, they're concerned about more serious aspects."

"What on earth do you mean?" Sandra, to whom the last year had delivered many shocks, thought she was inured by now; but Bob was Bob, flesh and blood, the person she most cared about in the world. Nothing had ever equaled the shock she received when she heard about the accident to her brother. What had happened to Bob had struck her hard because she felt responsible; she alone. As their mother had once left them she had left Bob for her own selfish motives. Everyone said he was nearly twenty, but still . . .

"There is another disquieting factor in which the police are more immediately interested, now that Bob is all right."

"You mean someone *pushed* him intentionally . . . ?"

"Oh, no, nothing like that. There were several witnesses. Bob just sank to the bottom of the pool and, in the dark, it was some time before anyone realized what had happened. . . ."

Sandra put her hands over her eyes and stared down at her lap. She could see it all: the beautiful California darkness with the lights of Los Angeles and Hollywood like a gem-encrusted carpet in the far distance. A happy party around the pool, a barbecue, maybe some drinking; splashing about in the water, a record player booming out the ceaseless rhythm youngsters were so addicted to . . .

"Drugs, my dear," Sophie said softly. "There were definitely drugs involved. . . ."

"Oh my God." Perhaps she'd known it. Perhaps that had always been the reason she had been reluctant to leave because she knew he smoked pot; she knew the prevalence of marijuana, cocaine and other illegal substances on the campuses of the American universities. Bob said pot was harmless; but it worried her. The drug scene in America worried her.

Bob defended the use of soft drugs every time she taxed him with the subject. Alcohol abuse was much worse, he said. But Bob liked a drink too . . . alcohol and hash.

"Oh my God!" Sandra murmured once more.

The young police lieutenant from the Los Angeles Police Department was familiar with the problem. He wasn't married but he had young brothers and sisters; maybe he smoked himself. He wore civilian clothes and seemed to know the Pipers and they sat in a relaxed group around the fire and the men drank canned beer. The police lieutenant was on his way home. It was almost like a casual, off-duty call.

"There's no question of *charges,* Miss O'Neill," the policeman said. "But I felt it was something you should know about."

"Of course," Sandra said quietly.

"If you're away and your house is used for parties like this it could get you in a lot of trouble and I understand that you occupy a high position. . . ."

"That's not what worries me," Sandra replied. "It's Bob being alone and subject to influences like this."

"There's nothing much you can do about that, in all honesty," the policeman said. "There's a lot of it about but we are cracking down hard. We know there was pot about that night and maybe some other substances, certainly cocaine, but we can't prove it. We could *smell* it, but you can't produce a smell in court, otherwise things might be more serious for your brother. Someone had cleaned up very well after he was taken to the hospital. But there is the point—" he leaned forward and looked at Sandra intently"—of your responsibility. *That* can't be taken lightly. It was your house."

Responsibility. Was she never to hear the end of the word? Only a couple of days ago it had been the responsibility for the blend, the new *cuvée.* Now, halfway around the world, it was responsibility for something else. The very word "responsibility" seemed to reverberate inside her skull with the persistent regularity and monotony of a nightmare.

"I'll take Bob back to France with me when he's better," Sandra said, looking the lieutenant straight in the eyes. "I don't take my responsibilities lightly, I assure you and thank you for the warning. I'll close my house and insist that Bob comes back with me."

"Can you do that?" Henri queried mildly. "Bob is very strong willed, you know."

"I'll *tell* him that if he doesn't come back, I'll get the police to press charges," Sandra said, looking from one to the other. "It's as simple as that."

In bed that night Henri whispered to his wife that Sandra had gotten harder.

"You'd never have heard her speak like that a year ago," he murmured.

"How do you mean?" she whispered.

"The way she said 'I'll close down the house . . . tell the police to press charges unless . . .' "

"That's not hard, it's decisive," Sophie said defensively. A man like her husband had no time for women's liberation, certainly so far as it applied to their wives. Henri Piper would never have married someone like Sandra, however much he

admired her. But he loved and respected his wife and he always paid attention to what she said.

"Decisive," he muttered. "I see."

"Yes, decisive. She has to be, because of where Georges put her. If Sandra hadn't changed she wouldn't still be there."

Bob came out of the hospital a week after Sandra arrived to be with him. He was young and the young heal quickly. There were no serious injuries or aftereffects once he recovered from the concussion and he was expected to make a full recovery.

Sandra called for him at the hospital and drove him back to their house. Bob said it was like old times and he'd missed her. Sandra had missed him too. She felt very emotional about the reunion with her brother, the circumstances of that reunion, and she was very apprehensive about the future. All day long as she waited for Bob, reacclimatizing herself to the Beverly Hills home, the telephone rang from France wanting a decision on this, that or something else.

Bob noticed it before he had been a few hours in the house.

"That damn phone," he said, jerking his shoulders with irritation. "It never stops."

They were sitting by the pool and Sandra went inside to deal with it. Agnès, her strong right hand, had a query for her that she answered quickly. Then followed the routine inquiry about how things were.

A lot had fallen on Agnès's shoulders during the week since she'd been summoned abruptly to the States, and Sandra could tell she was coping just as she had expected her to. The calls were brief, informative and to the point.

"I've got the most ideal secretary," Sandra said, returning to the poolside, donning dark glasses against the unaccustomed heat of the California sun. "She's only just taken over and she has everything under control." Sandra sighed and Bob looked over to her.

"Tough eh, Sis?"

"Tough what?" Sandra held out her hand to him, smiling. "Tough being at the top?"

"Tougher than I thought." Sandra squeezed his hand. "Do you realize this time last year I was here? We had no inkling of what was in store."

"None at all," Bob agreed, returning her pressure. "I really missed you, Sandra."

"If I'd have been here this wouldn't have happened." Sandra glanced sideways at him.

"The accident?"

"Yes. And there is something else. The police came to see me about your accident the night I arrived. I was with the Pipers . . ."

"But there was no mystery about my accident. I wasn't pushed. I slipped and fell . . . a bit under the influence, I'm afraid."

"Under the influence of drugs or booze—or both?" Sandra's tone, though concerned, was chilly. "The police had to be sure about the cause of the accident so they came up here to look around and make some inquiries. They said they knew drugs were involved. . . ."

"Only pot . . ." Bob said dismissively.

"Even that's illegal."

"Oh, Sandra, don't let's go into all this again. I probably smoke less pot in a year than you drink champagne."

"Drinking wine is not illegal. You know how I feel about it, Bob. Anyway I'm not here to argue or tell you off in any way. I want you to get well and to do that completely I want you to come to France with me."

"No," Bob said, sitting back and crossing his arms in a stance characteristic of him since he was a small boy. Stubborn. Stubborn and unbending. He hadn't really changed since the age of three. In a way he knew his sister loved him so much, was so protective toward him that he could twist her around his little finger. Sandra knew this quite well, but she realized again, now, how much she loved him. It was because he seemed partly her brother, partly her son. She had reared him, looked after him, fought his battles, stood by him. She would now.

"It's better, Bob, just for a short while. I'm anxious for you to come back to France with me. Please, Bob. . . ."

"But I've got my classes . . ."

Sandra took off her sunglasses and gazed at him.

"Look, darling . . . you're not really up to it. You had a nasty bang. I can't stay here. I have a huge business to run. The Pipers, too, are coming back soon so they won't be here to keep an eye on you. . . ."

"I'm *not* a baby . . ."

"But you're on your own, Bob. I hated leaving you last year and I don't want to leave you now. Besides I miss you. I want you with me, to help me. Please." She held out her hand and said, as Bob clasped it: "I need you. I really do."

"Well for that reason alone, and only that, I'll come."

Just then the phone went again, drowning Sandra's whoop of joy and Bob said, "Oh leave it, and let's have some lunch."

"I'll just answer this and then unplug it. It's an odd time to call if it's France. It's the middle of the night there." Sandra rapidly crossed the patio by the pool and went into the cool lounge.

"Hello . . ."

"Sandra *darling,* hello . . ."

"Oh Miss Wingate," Sandra said stiffly.

"Darling, I just heard you were here. It's in the papers. Do you know you're very famous now?" The voice, already throaty, dropped half an octave to denote rejection, disappointment and reproach. "Sandra, I *do* think you might have called."

"Bob's been ill, Miss Wingate. . . ."

Over the years she'd urged her to call her "Aunt Virginia"

but she never had. Nothing had ever come easily to her about this woman, nothing was ever simple or uncomplicated.

Virginia Wingate was a film star, celebrated in her time, for whom Hélène O'Neill had once worked. After her return to France Virginia frequently called to see how her children were, mostly out of a sense of duty, Sandra thought.

She had never really liked Virginia. The artificial life of a film star was reality for her, and Sandra detested it. Yet her mother's former employer was kind. She sent presents. She asked them for meals and even when they made excuses she asked them again. Yet, ever since she could remember there was that suggestion of reproach in her voice, the suspicion of a whine. "Sandra, *you* said . . ."

"If I'd known Bob had been ill," the voice went on, "I'd have been at that hospital. I wish someone had called me! I'm *always* here to help, you know that, my dear."

"I know that, Miss Wingate, and I'm grateful. Thanks."

"You don't *sound* very grateful, Sandra. I'm so longing to see you. Now I want you and Bob to come over here for dinner. I'm not going to take 'no' for an answer. . . ."

"There's so little time, Miss Wingate. We were talking of going back to France."

"When I think of all I did for you and Bob over the years, Sandra, I call your attitude rather ungrateful. Are you too important for me now? Can't you see that it would give an old lady like me great pleasure to see you and learn all about your new job?" Her voice became coquettish. "Quite a *cachet* too, to be able to say that I know you."

"We could come tomorrow," Sandra knew when she was defeated, "because probably the day after we leave for France."

"That would be *lovely,*" Virginia crooned. "See you at about eight, darling. I must fly now. I'm doing a TV commercial . . . imagine, fame again at my age! Bye."

"Bye."

"Silly old trout," Sandra hissed, slumping into her chair.

"By the way your temper has changed that could only be Virginia."

"The same. She wants us to go for dinner."

"I hope you said 'no.' "

"I felt I *had* to say 'yes.' I accepted for tomorrow night."

"Well I'm not going," Bob said. "You know how—"

"And *you* know how *I* feel about her." Sandra now felt very angry indeed, with herself and, leaping out of her deck chair, began to pace up and down. "I can't stand her and yet I can't say 'no' to her. Why?"

"Yes, why?" Bob gazed at her with interest. "I've noticed in the past if she ever asks you to do anything you do. Why? You say you don't owe her anything. She may say she was good to us, but she never was, really! She was always a selfish woman and age has made her worse. She treated us like objects of charity."

"That's because Mother worked for her," Sandra observed. "There's never quite equality with people you pay."

Sandra stopped her pacing and stood gazing down at him. "It's something to do with guilt on my part. I can't explain it. *And* I don't know the reason. She's just been around for so long, trying to do good, meaning to do good. In a way it's pathetic. I *suppose* I feel sorry for her."

"Sorry for Virginia, that *is* a joke!" Bob laughed and Sandra realized that he really was on the mend. She hadn't heard such gay, infectious, uncomplicated laughter from him since the previous year.

"You know," Sandra tried to explain, "people try and do good to please you and yet you can't stand them. That's why I feel guilty. I guess it is a legacy from Mother. . . ."

She paused and Bob inquired softly, "Have you seen her yet?"

"No." Sandra shook her head. "I can't."

"It seems a bit cruel, Sis."

"People say it's cruel. Henri Piper says it's cruel. But I simply can't face her. Especially after the will. I despise myself, but that's how it is."

"Couldn't you just pop in or invite her to lunch?"

"I suppose I could . . . but I can't. Do you know what I mean, Bob?"

"Not really." Bob gazed at the sunlight on the water. "You know, Sandra, you're a mystery to me. I know you very well and yet sometimes I think I don't know you at all. You're so determined and straight and upright . . . and yet somehow you seem afraid of Mother, of Virginia. It's not like you."

"I know it's not like me," Sandra agreed humbly.

"You've taken over a huge conglomerate—if what you tell me is true, and I'm sure it is, the papers confirm it. A task that would defeat experienced businessmen has been quite simple to you. . . ."

"Because I see things clearly."

"Exactly." Bob nodded vigorously. "You're so direct. Yet with Mother and Virginia—"

"*That's* because it's a personal matter. It's the same with you too. I can't help being very soft about you. I can't see straight about you either. You see, Bob, personal relations and business are quite different and at personal relationships I have never, ever been any good."

And suddenly, for no reason at all, she thought about Tim and she shuddered.

When the telephone went at three that morning Sandra lay for a while listening, feeling inclined to leave it. It could only be France and her staff there knew what time it was in California.

In that case . . . she jumped out of bed into her gown and ran lightly along the corridor and downstairs to the sitting room. Bob had a phone in his room—teenagers always needed a phone, everyone knew that—but when she had been an executive at the bank she had never felt a telephone in her bedroom to be necessary. The bedroom was the sanctum, the quiet place. As far as possible she liked it to remain that way. More practically she hadn't had time to have a telephone put in since her return to Beverly Hills.

"Hello," she said automatically in the French accent.

It was Agnès, as Sandra had expected, who apologized for telephoning at such an hour. Sandra stood patiently cradling the phone to her ear, an expression of bored irritation on her face. Maybe Agnès wasn't the paragon she thought she was. One of her functions should be to save her boss from calls in the small hours of the morning.

"I can tell you're annoyed, Mademoiselle," Agnès said with a slight stammer in her voice. "I mean, by your silence I can tell that . . ."

"Go on," Sandra said, her tone deliberately hard.

"I would only ring you because it is urgent, Mademoiselle. You know that."

"What *is* it Agnès?"

"It is Monsieur Zac, Mademoiselle. He has called an emergency Board meeting of the Group. A full Board meeting which, he says, he is entitled to call giving only twenty-four hours' notice in cases of urgency."

"And what *is* the urgency on this occasion, may I ask?" Sandra's irritation increased rather than diminished.

"It is something to do with the wine, Mademoiselle. There has been a disaster to the new *cuvée.*"

"The new *cuvée?*" Sandra's tone changed.

"The *cuvée* of this year, last year that is, Mademoiselle." Agnès began to stammer again and suddenly Sandra realized there was something serious afoot and felt sorry for her attitude. "Please be as explicit as you can, Agnès," she said in a gentler tone of voice. "Are you talking about the *tirage* we passed a few weeks or so ago?"

"That's exactly it, Mademoiselle. The authorization that

you gave me for the bottling to begin. Well, something is wrong with the wine. Monsieur Zac came to me in a terrible rage and demanded to have your telephone number." Agnès lowered her tone. "I made some excuse so that I could ring you myself, to warn you. The thing is that you should come at once, Mademoiselle, to attend the Board because if you don't . . ."

"Yes?" Sandra demanded.

"Monsieur Zac says you will be voted off it." Agnès's voice sank to a whisper. "He says that all the wine that has been bottled is no good . . . and that some twenty million or so dollars has gone with it down the drain."

Pale with lack of sleep, Sandra took her place at the head of the boardroom table next to her office in Reims. But she was carefully and meticulously dressed and, as she arranged her papers neatly in front of her, her hands were quite steady.

Her private jet had brought her swiftly from Los Angeles together with Bob and Henri. Aunt Sophie stayed behind to close both houses.

It was the first time that Sandra had seen Claire or Belle since Christmas and she gave them a perfunctory smile. Thank heaven Tim was out of the country and didn't want to return. Somehow the crisis of the moment seemed to eclipse, by its gravity, anything that happened at Burg-Farnbach. All Sandra had been able to discover from Agnès, who came to Reims airport to meet her and briefed her on the drive to the office, was that Zac said the wine was ruined. There had been an error for which she, Sandra, alone had to be held responsible.

By the time she got to her office the Board meeting was due to start and the members of the Board began to trickle into the room acknowledging her with self-conscious smiles. Only Lady Elizabeth inclined her head and didn't attempt to smile.

Sandra began to suspect a plot.

The last to appear was Zac in the company of Philippe de Lassale to whom he was explaining something with great care. De Lassale looked grave and kept nodding his head. He greeted Sandra with a bow, but no smile. She realized then that she was on trial.

Belle was talking to Antoine Dericourt in a manner Sandra thought overanimated and Claire had her head on her chest, as if sunk in thought. Sandra found it odd that she couldn't even raise a smile from her one known ally.

Her spirits sank even lower as, glancing at the clock on the wall, she called for attention.

"As this is an emergency meeting called under Article Eleven of the statutes I think it is not necessary to read the minutes of the last meeting. Am I right, Monsieur le Blanc?"

She turned to the secretary of the Board, a member of junior management who took the minutes. He nodded.

"I believe, Mademoiselle, that is correct."

"In that case, Monsieur Desmond," Sandra turned to Zac, "would you give the Board details as to why you requested this meeting?"

"With *pleasure,* Mademoiselle," Zac said, sweeping the space in front of him clear of papers. "With great pleasure, or rather, should I say, with sorrow? May I also say, Mademoiselle O'Neill, how sorry I am to have had to summon you back to France when I understand your brother is only just recovering from a near-fatal accident."

"My brother has recovered, thank you, Monsieur Desmond, and is with me. A car took him straight to the Ritz and he is resting. Please go on."

"Very well, Mademoiselle." Zac took a deep breath and then frowned as he considered those around the table one by one: his mother, his sisters, his sister by adoption, Vincent, de Lassale, Dericourt, Leriche, le Blanc and the Board's legal adviser Maître Laban to whom Zac pointed.

"I have asked Maître Laban to be here today because an

extremely grave fault of a professional nature has occurred which I am sorry to say, I must lay at the door of the President of this Group." He indicated Sandra with a brief nod of the head. "The *sole* responsibility of the President is the composition of the *cuvée*. . . ."

"If *you* will pardon me, Monsieur Desmond," Sandra interrupted him firmly. "The composition is decided by the *chef des caves* and his experts."

"Oh no, Mademoiselle." Zac shook his head, equally firmly. "It is decided by *you. You* give the order for the bottling, or rather my father did before you and I understood that was the case this year though, regrettably, due to indisposition," he coughed as though to indicate that the indisposition had been no trifling matter and still lingered, "I was unable to be present."

"Yes but the composition, the formula," Sandra explained patiently, beginning to feel some of the weight on her mind for the last twenty-four hours slowly lift, "is worked out by the experts whose advice I heeded. They presented me with a piece of paper on which was a formula written by them. I merely signed it."

"Excuse me, Mademoiselle." Again Zac seemed to be going out of his way to be punctiliously polite. "I understand that not to be the case, but I will go into that, if I may, in a minute. First let me explain what has happened, what terrible tragedy has occurred."

His voice as it rose also grew tremulous and Sandra sat back half-admiring, deciding that a great dramatic talent had been lost to the French stage.

"Mademoiselle O'Neill," Zac began.

"Desmond," Sandra murmured, but Zac ignored her and repeated. "Mademoiselle O'Neill, members of the Board, the new *cuvée* is ruined. As you know the bottling began about eleven days ago after the Tasting Committee had met.

"About three hundred thousand bottles a day are produced

and, as is natural after the wine has clarified, it is analyzed. As Mademoiselle was out of the country René Latour, horrified, brought the news personally to me at my home."

Zac again paused dramatically and once more looked around, fist clenched in front of him which he methodically and rhythmically started to bang on the table.

"There is no sparkle in the wine; there will never be a sparkle in the wine, the wine cannot sparkle for . . ." Zac again paused and Sandra felt a slight twitch in her mouth as she tried to suppress a smile. This was too ridiculous . . . some plot . . . whatever it was it could hardly concern her.

"For," Zac thundered, "the wrong *dosage* of yeast has been programmed into the computer. Without the proper action of the yeasts on the *liqueur de tirage* there is no fizz!" Zac thumped the table again in a passable imitation of a cork being drawn from a champagne bottle. "No champagne. It is a disaster!"

"Mon dieu, Zac," Lady Elizabeth murmured. "How on *earth* is that possible? René Latour is one of the most competent members of this company. He began work here as a young man. Your father—"

"Mother." Zac leaned forward as if to patiently explain something to a person who was feeble of mind. "The composition of the *cuvée* is fixed by the Tasting Committee. You know that, Mother. The order is signed personally by the President who gives the green light for bottling. That is exactly what happened in this case."

"I merely signed the paper presented to me," Sandra said with an air of boredom, making as if to rise. "I find this whole thing too ridiculous for words. Bringing me all the way back from California . . ."

Zac, still on his feet, his face mottled with rage, jabbed a finger at her.

"How can you treat it so dismissively, Miss O'Neill? Have

you no *idea* what this means? You have worked out the figures, have you not, Monsieur Vincent?"

Paul Vincent glanced at something held in his hands beneath the table, out of sight of those sitting around it, and mumbled inaudibly.

"Louder if you please, Vincent," Zac said, "louder so that *everyone* can hear."

"About three million bottles, Monsieur Zac . . . at fifty francs a bottle that is . . . er . . . one hundred and fifty million francs or over twenty-five million dollars, Monsieur."

"Exactly," Zac shouted. "*Twenty-five* million dollars of company money thrown away. That is a lot of money, is it not?"

"It is a lot of money," Sandra said, keeping her voice icy cool. "And we must find out who is responsible for it. I assure you it is not I."

"Oh indeed," Zac sneered, "do *you* blame your subordinates for your own mistakes normally, Mademoiselle?"

"No I do not," Sandra said, riled. "I certainly do not and would not. The wine that we tasted was perfect and the *dosage* of yeasts which were suggested to me were very similar, or so I understand from René who, after all, is the expert, to those used last year."

"Then let us ask Latour to be brought in by all means," Zac said silkily. "I would like very much to hear what he has to say."

"I'm sure you know already what he has to say," Sandra said under her breath and, as René was brought in as at a prearranged signal, she gazed at him searchingly. A man of such apparent simplicity, candor and honesty. Surely he couldn't be a rogue in the pay of Zac?

But Latour was avoiding her eyes and, instead, bowed to Lady Elizabeth, who asked him how his wife was and made him sit by her side as Zac continued.

"Latour, the Board would like clarification on one technical point regarding the composition of the *cuvée.* In asking Mademoiselle O'Neill to choose between the different samples of the *cuvée* have you looked for a mistake?"

"We explained to Mademoiselle the characteristics of each sample," Latour said stiffly, still avoiding her eyes. "Beside each was the necessary *dosage* of yeasts, together with the appropriate ones to choose. It had all been worked out very carefully and accurately, Monsieur Zac."

"So Mademoiselle tasted each sample and chose the one she liked best?"

"Yes, Monsieur."

"Then how was the mistake made?"

"I don't know, Monsieur, that is the truth." René looked at the table. "I can only think the mistake must have been made in the office."

"Then it *was* a mistake," Sandra said triumphantly. "Not a deliberate decision on my part to change the *dosage,* eh Latour?"

"I don't know, Mademoiselle." Latour's face was crestfallen, his voice expressionless. "I really can't say. All I know is that it was not my fault." He produced a piece of crumpled paper from his pocket, on which great effort had been made to smooth it out as though someone had rescued it from a waste-paper basket. "This was the composition I suggested to Mademoiselle at the meeting." In her mind's eye Sandra could see his capable hand resting on the paper as she signed it, and nodded in agreement. "But this, Monsieur . . ." This time Latour produced a typewritten sheet of paper from a folder he had brought with him, "this is the printout taken from the computer. It clearly states a different *dosage* from the one I recommended. Who did it I do not know."

"Operator's error, doubtless," Sandra said offhandedly.

"Ah, again you're blaming your staff, are you, Miss O'Neill?" Zac who, by this time, had whipped himself into a fury, grabbed the paper from Latour and shook it in front of Sandra. "See these figures," he said, thrusting the paper at her. "They are nothing like the original *dosage*; they are completely different. There is no computer operator's error here! It is my opinion, Mademoiselle, that you—a person who on her own admission knows absolutely nothing about champagne, who is here under false pretenses and because of the senility of my father—deliberately altered these figures to—"

"Yes to . . . *what* exactly, Monsieur Desmond? Why should *I* or anyone else alter the figures?"

"Because you don't know what you're doing, that's why," Zac shouted. "You're too clever by half. You're incompetent, a fool, a busybody, a know-all. Those figures should have been checked and rechecked. And that was *your* business . . . *yours,* President of the Desmond Group. As it is you have cost this company millions of francs and, worse, made us the laughingstock of the entire champagne business. No Desmond Champagne this year, imagine!" He appealed to the rest of the Board who were gazing at him with drawn faces as if in the process of beholding some unbelievable horror. "What would the ghost of my father say? My grandfather? His father? My namesake, René-Zachariah, founder of the business?" Zac raised his eyes to the ceiling as if addressing the departed and once more shook his fist. "Imagine me allowing such a mistake, me, trained in the business from boyhood. Or her . . ." he pointed to Belle, whose previous expression of consternation had turned to one of admiration. "With a true Desmond in charge, not someone who merely has the impertinence to call herself Desmond, such an error would have been inconceivable.

"I demand your resignation from the Group, Mademoiselle O'Neill, and if I do not have it at once I shall summon the Council my father wisely left to protect his legacy and have you thrown out. For you have shown yourself quite unworthy of the dignity which my father so unwisely thought fit to thrust upon you."

He turned to Vincent, who passed him a document which Zac in turn threw down in front of Sandra.

"I have taken the liberty of having your resignation drafted for you. If you would sign it we shall try and hush this unfortunate matter up as much as we can. Maybe some of the *cuvée* can still be saved. There is still a little wine in the vats, and we can make an excuse. But, first, it is necessary for you to go. . . ." He pointed sternly at the paper. "Sign," he commanded.

Sandra reached for her bag and briefcase which lay at her feet. Then, slowly, she stood up, straightening the jacket of her suit. She felt suddenly almost unbearably, overwhelmingly tired. Then she said quietly but firmly in English, her eyes not flinching from those of her persecutor:

"As we say in America, Mr. Desmond, you have got to be joking." Then in French, with a slight bow she turned to those around the table. "Excuse me, ladies and gentlemen, members of the Board."

And with that she left the room.

16

"I *hate* him," Sandra said, banging her hand upon a delicate antique occasional table. Unaccustomed to such treatment at the hands of a patron of the Ritz, it promptly collapsed onto the floor and Bob, retrieving it, tried to put together its shattered limbs.

The sight of Bob kneeling on the floor, the leg of the table in his hands, an expression of bewilderment on his face, brought Sandra to her senses. She clapped a hand to her brow:

"My God!" she cried, "what is happening to me? What am I doing?" She crouched by the side of Bob, frantically trying to take the leg from him, abjectly surveying the extent of the damage to the rest of the table. Bob put the remnant on the floor and took a firm grip on his sister's shoulder.

"Easy girl, easy. It isn't such a big job to put this right. A touch of super glue or something; but I'll have it done by an expert. It's no big deal. Don't *worry* about it. . . ."

Sandra sat back on her heels, the expression on her face rueful, the suspicion there of tears.

"I'm terribly sorry, Bob. I went over the top, didn't I?"

"I can understand it," Bob said, gently taking her by the hand and pulling her up. Then he led her over to one of the sofas in her room and, sitting her down, sat beside her.

"This man is getting you down. He sounds like a monster."

"He is, a sadistic monster. As if *I* would tinker with the

formula for the bottling! Did you ever hear of anything so absurd?"

Henri Piper had been sitting quietly in a corner, as concerned at the whole scene as Bob and admiring how well the younger man had dealt with the situation, while he, someone so much older, hadn't known what to do. Henri, however, was used to being protected, cushioned from life's blows which, happily for him, were few. Seeing that Sandra was calmer now, guilty about her most unusual outburst, he spoke up quietly:

"It's *obviously* absolutely absurd, the whole idea, my dear Sandra. I wonder no other members of the Board spoke up in your support. I'm surprised at Philippe de Lassale, or even Leriche, who has never been fond of Zac."

"I don't think any of them really knew what was going on. They were bewildered. As soon as it was over Philippe de Lassale did come to see me, but he said he knew absolutely nothing about champagne. He was sure, however, that if there had been an error it could not be laid at my door. I must say, though, I thought his manner stiff and he left as soon as he could. Everyone was quite mesmerized by Zac . . . oh how I *hate* him." She banged her fist again but this time into the palm of her hand and Bob said, "Steady there . . ."

"Don't worry, and I *am* sorry." Impulsively she laid a hand on his arm and gazed at Henri.

"Isn't he marvelous? Isn't he a wonderful brother?"

"He's a terrific chap," Henri said. "I think you need him with you, Sandra. You must find an apartment . . ."

"Oh I'm not staying, Henri," Bob said quickly. "I can't stay. I have my studies. I have my life in California, not in France."

"You can study here," Sandra said quickly, "and yes, I will find an apartment. Oh Bob, please . . . just to get me through this."

Within him Bob felt an emotion he had never known before. He'd always looked up to Sandra. She'd always been the leader, the dominant one ever since he could remember. Now, could it really be possible that she needed *him?* As well as flattering it was also worrying, because she had not yet been at Desmond a year and it looked as though the whole thing was getting her down.

Henri, who hated trouble, looked concerned too; his fine gray eyes clouded with anxiety.

"My dear Sandra," he spoke more gently than usual. "I told you Zac was a dangerous man because he is a disappointed one. He thinks he has been deprived of his birthright and he is like a wounded animal. This is just what makes him so dangerous. Georges *may* have been right to have been worried about Zac and his business, but the way he handled the whole thing was stupid. He should have made his wishes clear before he died and the reasons for them. As it is he did you a disservice. This is obviously some ruse on the part of Zac to discredit you, but it cannot possibly be laid at your door. . . ."

"All that loss . . . twenty-five million dollars. How am I going to justify that in my first annual report? Everyone will say it is incompetence."

"You'll have to have a long talk with Latour and, look here, my dear. You know we champagne producers try not to pry too much in the affairs of our competitors. We are interested, of course, but we wouldn't normally interfere. However, to my mind there *is* something strange going on. I can't recall a similar mistake at the House of Desmond since a famous instance during the First World War when, allegedly, the barrage of guns over the city of Reims caused a rockfall into the Desmond caves which made the hand of its then cellar master tremble in the middle of his calculations . . . they are still talking about it fifty years later. No there *is* something funny going on."

Henri rose and his elegantly clad form walked thoughtfully toward the window overlooking beautiful gardens in the center of the famous hotel. For a moment he gazed broodingly at them then, hand on chin, he turned to Sandra.

"Can you get me a bottle of the current *tirage* plus a photocopy of the order you signed to proceed with the bottling? I'll have it analyzed, under strict conditions of secrecy of course. My head cellarman has been with my firm for fifty years. He is to be trusted utterly." Henri paused and looked at Sandra slumped now rather dejectedly on the sofa by the side of Bob. Indeed she did look, momentarily, a shadow of her former, robust self; but the last weeks had been trying not only on account of this latest mishap but also because of Bob's injury.

It is said that every person has a breaking point and Henri wondered how near they were to Sandra's. For her own sake, and that of the House of Desmond, he hoped very far away.

"Can you trust Latour?" Henri said, continuing his walk back and forth after the pause. "Have you spoken to him? Do you think Zac got at him?"

"Seriously I don't know." Sandra gazed at him anxiously, running a hand through her hair. "I would have said he was such an honorable man that it would be impossible to corrupt him. My idea, the feeling I had was that he was as bewildered as I by the whole thing, also unprepared. He took a crumpled piece of paper from his pocket as though he had fished it out of the back of a drawer or the rubbish basket. Mind you, he is utterly devoted to the Desmond family and was at wine school with Zac. He obviously respects him enormously."

"Yes, but he's not a crook."

"Decidedly not. If there has been any skulduggery it would not be the fault of poor Latour. I'm sure of that."

"Then how?" Uncle Henri looked at the ceiling. "How did they do it?"

Sandra knew that everyone in the headquarters of the Desmond Group knew, and was talking, about the business of the disaster to the current *tirage*. She knew too that there was an unspoken assumption, unspoken because no one would dare accuse her of it, that, nevertheless, it was her fault; or some fault on her part or that of her staff. Sandra saw that this was Zac's first serious attempt to undermine her and it was very cleverly done. Champagne, it was true, was the part of the business she knew least, and he most, about. If anyone had made an error surely it would be the newcomer and not the man with champagne in his blood?

There was even the feeling that Zac had the right to be so annoyed and the balance of opinion subtly shifted from Sandra's side to Zac's.

But Sandra was determined that the harm done would not be irreparable. She quickly set in motion a detailed internal inquiry both at the Reims Headquarters and in Paris to see how the slip-up occurred, and she obtained the samples she needed for Henri to have analyzed. She knew she had to be absolutely discreet about this because Zac was Sophie's blood relation, and Henri did not want to be seen again too openly siding with Sandra. However, he had never been fond of his wife's eldest nephew. They were men of very different characters and temperaments and had crossed each other too often before. Zac knew, moreover, that Henri tacitly supported Sandra and preferred her to him in the running of the business.

Sandra was very careful what she told even someone as trusted as Agnès, although she knew that Agnès was loyal, hardworking and discreet. She never asked her boss personal questions, and was silent on the subject of her own private life. This impersonal but friendly relationship suited Sandra. They were new to each other, but so far so good; the person she had taken a risk in promoting seemed to have justified the risk.

Agnès was given the task of discovering all she could about how the mistake regarding the *tirage* came to be made, and promptly produced all the necessary documents which she had photocopied for Sandra, allegedly to study at home but in reality to give to Henri. Sandra never mentioned his involvement in this to her secretary.

Life meanwhile had to go on. The Desmond organization was a huge conglomerate and champagne, though at its heart, was only a part. There was the delicate political question of sales of aircraft to the Middle East; the attitude of French and British governments to be taken into account and the whole business of the build-up of hostilities in that part of the world. Sandra flew to London to have personal talks with the minister in charge of aviation on the subject and was unexpectedly entertained to lunch by the Prime Minister who, naturally, approved of a member of her own sex having achieved such eminence so young and closely questioned Sandra about her work.

Sandra flew back to France, her equilibrium almost completely restored by the success of her British visit. She had taken Bob with her for company and now gave him the task of finding an apartment, a town house or whatever, not too far from the office.

Bob hankered to go to Tourville but Sandra was reluctant to go there herself in the present climate, feeling the whole Desmond family ranged against her, remembering the cold disapproval in the eyes of Lady Elizabeth as she gazed at her across the boardroom table, the furtive glances of Claire. She was glad Tim hadn't been there to add to her isolation and feeling of misery. Tim . . . every time she even thought of him it rankled. She had trusted him and he had taken her in. Thank heaven, in a way, he had; an affair with one of the Desmonds at this moment would have been disastrous.

Sandra was, as usual, early at the office after her return from London and Agnès was, as always, there even before her. She greeted her secretary with a smile and Agnès, the mail already open and in her hands, preceded Sandra into her office where there were fresh flowers on the desk.

"Oh how nice, Agnès." Sandra leaned forward to smell them. "Who are these from?"

Agnès colored slightly, her eyes suddenly riveted by her highly polished shoes.

"Just a little gift from me, Mademoiselle. A flower-seller was selling them by the Métro and I thought they were so pretty."

"Oh *Agnès* . . ." Sandra was for a moment so moved by this gesture, which she also took to be a tacit one of support, that she nearly hugged her; but, just in time, she thought how odd it would appear if she were to be seen by a casual intruder or passerby embracing her secretary. Warmly repeating her thanks, she told her to sit down and began to recount her London trip and discuss in turn what had happened in the brief time she had been away.

"My visit to London was most successful. The Prime Minister and various government officials I met were most helpful. They are extremely interested in all our products, some of which they produce in common with us for the benefit of the EEC. As to the wisdom of selling to the Arabs at this time . . ." Sandra made a fluttering movement with her fingers to indicate equivocation. "Now, what has happened here . . . ?"

Agnès consulted a sheaf of notes. "Dr. Harcourt came and said he was sorry to have missed you."

"Dr. Harcourt?" Momentarily Sandra looked mystified.

"He runs the Foundation in Africa."

"Oh." Sandra snapped her fingers with irritation. "Oh damn. I so wanted to meet him."

"He is *very* handsome," Agnès said slyly. "I rather fancied him myself."

"Not because of that, silly!" Sandra shook a finger at her. "But I wanted to hear something about his job."

"He is going to New York, Mademoiselle." Agnès consulted her notes again. "He will be there for the big gala that is being organized at the end of March."

"Well I'm going to be there too. I'll see him then."

"He didn't seem very happy about funds for his work." Agnès lowered her voice. "He is really quite a *formidable* person, a bit frightening . . ."

"Really?" Sandra's lips twitched. "It gets more and more interesting. Now . . . is there any news from that arch-troublemaker in my life?"

"Monsieur Zac, Mademoiselle?" Agnès consulted her notes. "I don't think so."

"No more news about the *tirage?*"

"They have stopped bottling . . ."

"I should think so. Well, I *may* have some news on that front quite soon myself."

"Oh, Mademoiselle?" Agnès made encouraging noises, but Sandra was not to be drawn.

"All in good time," she said firmly. "Now could we do a few letters, Agnès?"

"Bien, Mademoiselle," Agnès said, dutifully crossing her legs and balancing her pad on her knee, poised for dictation.

Sandra ran through the morning's mail, made a few rapid notes then drew a file toward her.

"Here are some details of properties I'd like to look at."

"You're thinking of moving, Mademoiselle?"

"Yes. I can't live in a hotel forever, though some people do and the Ritz *is* very comfortable. But I am trying to persuade my brother to stay with me for a while . . . to get over his injuries mainly, so we do need a proper place to live. Also I want to keep an eye on him.

"I rather like the idea of avenue Foch."

"*Trop démodé,* Mademoiselle," Agnès said dismissively. "Also too near your office." She gazed across the place de L'Étoile from the window toward the entrance of the avenue. "The left bank is very chic . . ."

"Too near Monsieur Zac!" Sandra said with a smile and suddenly Agnès's heart froze. She was now regularly photocopying any item of news she thought Zac would find interesting and he, in his turn, had suggested that maybe the room she shared with her cousin near the Bastille was too tiny, too cramped. . . .

"The Île Saint-Louis." Sandra, who had been studying the brochures from the agents, threw one across to Agnès. "Does that please you more?"

"Oh that has *style,* Mademoiselle," Agnès said, recovering from the moment of shock that the mention of Zac's name had given her. "And there is water between you and Monsieur Zac!"

They both laughed at the joke but, as Sandra started dictation and Agnès bent earnestly to her task, she was aware of the tiny flickering in the region of her heart: danger. She was treading, had indeed already trodden, on very dangerous ground and Mademoiselle, if she found out, would be an implacable enemy.

Sandra dictated rapidly, leaning back in her chair, hands characteristically in her pockets, swiveling about as she talked. She wore a gray suit with a pearl-colored tie blouse, and her hair was tied at the nape of her neck with a small gray bow to match her suit. With her back to the window it was like a silhouette, the classical profile of someone who was at once beautiful and elegant: the straight nose, the firm chin, the mysterious recessed blue eyes with their opaque lids. The wintry sun glanced on her blonde hair as she moved around in her chair speaking quickly, her eyes on her ringless fingers with their neutral polished nails. Here was a woman of dynamism and energy, a very formidable opponent if one were not careful. . . .

At about ten o'clock Sandra finished dictation, gave Agnès some further instructions and then started to prepare for a meeting of the Foundation Board, at which Henri would also be present, at eleven.

"I'm sorry I missed Dr. Harcourt," Sandra said at lunch at the Brasserie Lipp which followed the meeting, held at the headquarters of the Foundation in place Saint-Sulpice. "I hear he's rather attractive."

"Really, Mademoiselle." Henri pretended to be shocked. "How *frivolous* of you."

"I intended to be frivolous; but it's been a hard day. He even impressed my secretary." Sandra put her hand lightly over Henri's. "But nice to be with you, Uncle Henri, and unwind."

"I wish you wouldn't call me 'uncle,' " Henri said, not attempting to remove his hand from beneath hers. "You rarely do, but it makes me feel so old."

"Oh dear!" As if conscious of a new *nuance* to their relationship, Sandra quickly removed her hand. "I didn't mean to offend you. I never think of you as old, or as an 'uncle' really. It's a term of endearment." She regarded him for a few moments and then smiled at him across the table. "It's because I love you. . . ."

Realizing immediately that she'd said the wrong thing again, put her foot right in it, she added hurriedly, "I love you, that is to say, as I'd love an uncle. . . ."

"I know what you mean," Henri said. "Of course I do. I don't at all misunderstand what you are trying to say, Sandra, and I love you too . . . as a niece. I am *very* fond of you and always have been. Now I admire you and I know the kind of strain you're undergoing. However, my dear, I believe I may have some good news for you."

"Oh?" Glad to drop that part of the conversation, Sandra joined her hands on the table, her manner alert and attentive.

"I've given a good deal of thought to this problem, my

dear, and I believe that the key to the mystery of the *tirage* is the programming of the computer. Are you listening?"

"You know I'm listening," Sandra said eagerly. "Now why didn't *I* think of that before?"

"Yes, why didn't we both think of it? Maybe I didn't because the House of Piper is not as automated as Desmond, and we don't use computers except for the accounts department. Technically now, as you know, the only way to change the composition of the *cuvée* is by modifying the computer program. Either an error has been made unconsciously, which I doubt, or—"

"Or?" Sandra encouraged him, beginning to feel excited.

"Or somebody tampered with the software."

"If that's what happened whoever did it isn't going to boast about it. It certainly lets Latour off the hook, as he's always telling me he knows nothing about computers at all and curses the day they were introduced and the old ways changed, 'gone forever, Mademoiselle,' he assures me ruefully. You'd think he was about eighty instead of thirty-five."

"Well," Henri said slowly, "we have tried to find out who that person is. *You* have to find out." Henri glanced at his watch.

"Look, if you have time, we could take the helicopter to Reims later this afternoon and talk to my cellarman, Pierre Jourdain. He will have finished the analysis and then we can decide what to do. I've alerted Sophie that you might be down to dinner and staying the night. Let's take Bob."

"What a nice idea," Sandra said, careful not to touch him again. "And how typical of you to think of it."

She looked at him thoughtfully as he called the waiter and paid the bill, checking it carefully with his usual thoroughness.

In many ways she did love him . . . and not just like a niece.

"I told Pierre that we would do it when everyone had gone home," Henri explained, ushering her through the green baize door that was the *chef des caves'* holy of holies, on the ground floor of the offices in Reims. Bob had gone on to Marsanne in the helicopter.

Pierre was a much older man than René Latour. He greeted them respectfully, shaking hands with Sandra whom he was meeting for the first time.

"Though I do remember you at the harvest, Mademoiselle, but you won't remember me."

"It was too dark if anything," Sandra said diplomatically. Her heart was drumming with a kind of repressed excitement. Pierre, still wearing his white overall, held up the unlabeled bottle from the new Desmond vintage which Henri had brought over to him in conditions of great secrecy.

"Now," Henri said, crossing his arms and examining the liquid by the light of the candle placed behind it. "Tell all."

"Well, Monsieur Henri, it all seems very normal." The wrinkles multiplied on the old man's forehead as he looked at the liquid as if searching for fresh clues. He then consulted a piece of paper on the desk in front of him and said: "The analysis shows: degree of acidity six, remaining sugar twenty-two grams, alcohol ten point eight degrees. In fact the composition of their blend is very close to ours. On paper it's all perfectly correct . . . and yet it seems not to have sparkled."

Henri, his face also showing how perplexed he was, turned to Sandra, who was studying the clear liquid too, though she knew less than either of them.

"So what in your opinion went wrong, Jourdain?"

The cellar master carefully put down the bottle, scratched his head, tickled his nose and then joined his arms across his chest in an attitude of great thought.

"Well it's quite unbelievable but it may be that . . . no yeast was added."

"No yeast at *all* was added?" Henri echoed. "But that is incredible."

"It is." Jourdain nodded again. "But it seems that somebody

has forgotten to add the yeast." He turned to Sandra as if in explanation though this was something that, by the fact of it being so frequently dinned into her, she knew quite well by now. "The enzymes in the added yeasts activate the sugar in the wine to form carbonic gas, Mademoiselle, which in turn—"

"Forms the *mousse.*" Sandra nodded vigorously. "The white froth which is an essential sign of good champagne."

"Essential to champagne, *bien sur,*" Jourdain said. "You see, Mademoiselle, here at Piper we still add the yeast by hand. It's slow and complicated but that way there is never any mistake."

A note of unctuousness crept into his voice. "Now, as you also know, Mademoiselle, at Desmond's it's all done by computer . . . the practice of which I believe you approve." He glanced slyly at Henri, who shook his head as if warning him not to aggravate Sandra too much.

"Well yes I do approve," Sandra said, "providing that the system is safe from crooks who can exploit any computer system. One, however, doesn't expect to find them in a close family organization."

"Exactly, Mademoiselle." Jourdain nodded deprecatingly. "But I am not keen on these newfangled methods myself, to tell you the truth. Now I have a nephew, Jerome, who works, incidentally, on the Desmond's computer and I tell him 'Jerome, wine is a living creature, it breathes like any human being, it catches disease like a human being. . . .' "

"Yes, yes, Jourdain, go on," Henri said, good-temperedly winking at Sandra who, however, was too engrossed in what the cellar master was saying to notice.

"Well I say, Mademoiselle, that wine can't be made by computer . . ."

"Do you mean to tell me that your nephew actually *works* at the Desmond HQ . . . ?" Sandra said excitedly, pausing to catch her breath. A look of apprehension immediately came on Jourdain's good-natured face.

"Oh I assure you, Mademoiselle, my nephew . . . would *never* do anything wrong. Never. He wanted, in fact, to be a monk. He goes to Mass every day. He—"

"I am not attempting for a *moment* to accuse your nephew of anything dishonest," Sandra said quickly, turning to Henri. "Nevertheless it is very useful, is it not? to have someone so strategically placed to help us there? We know that we can't approach Latour or any of the staff who, in this matter, have been inclined to support Zac Desmond. But Monsieur Jourdain's nephew, now . . ." She looked speculatively at the *chef des caves.*

"He's only a technician, Mademoiselle. . . ."

"Never mind. He knows about computers. He knows about software. If someone fiddled the disc your nephew Jerome will undoubtedly be able to detect it."

"I assure you he would never *dream* of doing . . ."

"I'm quite sure he didn't."

"You see," Jourdain was still studying the paper on which the order for the *tirage* had been given and recommenced scratching the bald pate in the middle of his head. "This composition isn't bad at all, but it has no pressure, no *mousse.* The *dosage* for the yeasts is correct. I don't understand. Normally it should have sparkled."

Jourdain filled his glass with the Desmond wine. He put it to his nose, then his mouth. Tasting a few drops, he swirled them around his mouth before spitting them out in a brass spitoon, followed by the rest of the contents of the glass.

He made a grimace of distaste and then wiped his mouth carefully on his sleeve.

"No sparkle," he said. "None at all. I simply don't understand it."

Sandra picked up her handbag and tucked it deliberately under her arm. Gone were the lines on her brow, the expression of anxiety that had transformed her features for many days now, ever since the emergency Board meeting at Reims.

"I think, Monsieur Jourdain," she said, "you will have to have a little word with your nephew. You'd better have it soon because, otherwise, my head will be on the block. Ask him to meet me in the offices in Reims as soon as possible, but, first of all, he must check the discs and, if one is suspect he is duty-bound to give that to me." She drew herself up, dwarfing the rather diminutive cellarman. "And remind him he is doing nothing dishonest. After all, I am the Head of Desmond, and I must find out the truth."

Despite her position Sandra still felt like a burglar as she let herself in by the main entrance to the Group's headquarters at about nine o'clock a few nights after the discussion with Pierre Jourdain. Earlier that day had come a guarded message from Henri to be in the computer room at nine where she would learn something to her advantage. He wouldn't say what and he had rung off leaving Sandra nearly breathless with excitement.

The conspiracy was about to reach its climax.

As soon as she entered the hall the night watchman, alerted by the noise, came running down the main stairs of the building, his face showing apprehension and concern.

Carefully Sandra locked the door behind her and greeted him with a reassuring smile, "Good evening Albert. It is I, Mademoiselle Desmond."

"Of course I recognized you, Mademoiselle. Your car in the courtyard. Is there something you have forgotten?"

"Not quite," Sandra said, turning to get her bearings. "Which way is the computer room?"

"Er, that way, Mademoiselle." Albert pointed up the stairs. "Can I assist you . . . ?"

"I think I'll be all right." Sandra began to walk briskly across the polished parquet floor to the hall with its reminders of the history of the Desmonds and their champagne; the softly illuminated bottles in their alcoves still standing like silent witnesses to the march of time. "Put on the lights would you, Albert? I think you have a master switch in the reception."

"Very well, Mademoiselle." Albert watched her as she approached the staircase. Then quickly he went into the reception off the hall, opposite the main doors, and switched on the second-floor lights. He stood where he was for a moment or two, his brow creased with the effort of thought, and then he went to the door to make sure that the hall was clear. He could hear Sandra's steps growing fainter in the distance as she walked purposefully along the first-floor corridor.

Then, with the air of one in possession of an exciting secret, he took the receiver off the telephone on the receptionist's desk and dialed a number, cradling the receiver closely to his ear, as if it were possible for Sandra to hear, as he spoke softly into it.

Sandra meanwhile reached the room at the side of the building, which was identifiable by the almost imperceptible whirr of machinery. Some computers would be kept running for twenty-four hours carrying out the complex activities to do with the making of champagne.

She pushed open the door which was unlocked. It should not have been, so she assumed that Jerome Jourdain was responsible for this and crept, rather timidly, into the room illuminated only by the red, yellow and green lights operating on the machinery. It was very eerie.

Suddenly a shadow intervened between her and the main computer and she jumped back in alarm.

"Oh," she said.

"I'm sorry, Mademoiselle. I didn't mean to disturb you; but Albert mustn't know I'm here."

"Of course not."

"He is trusted by the Desmond family," Jerome said with a note of reproof in his voice.

"So, I hope, am I," Sandra replied. "So, I'm sure, are you. We are doing nothing wrong. You must accept that I mean what I say. What we are on the trail of is someone who is *not* to be trusted by the family."

"Of course, Mademoiselle. I quite understand. Please come this way."

Sandra followed him to a filing cabinet in a corner of the room which was partly open. She put on her glasses and followed his actions carefully. They were only illuminated now by the light of a solitary desk lamp as Jerome's hands went rapidly through the files.

He drew out one of the soft discs that are used for computer work, examined it on both sides and put it into her hands.

"Here you are. This is the one. You will find—"

Suddenly they were both rooted to the spot by the sound of a car drawing up in front of the courtyard with a screech of brakes.

Jerome crossed rapidly to the window and looked out.

"It is Monsieur Desmond's car!" he hissed. "He must not know I am here."

"Of course not." Sandra quickly put the disc inside her bag. "And thank you. . . ."

"Here." Jerome flung a file at her before closing the cabinet and locking the drawer. "This has nothing important in it. Use it as an excuse, to put him off the scent. *Bonne chance,* Mademoiselle."

"I won't forget this, Jerome," Sandra said as he put out the light and disappeared by the door through which he had first come, leading to a fire escape at the back of the building.

Sandra rapidly left the computer room, leaving the door unlocked as she had no key, and started to walk toward her office. She could hear a commotion in the hall and then the noise of someone rushing up the stairs. Just as she reached the door of her office Zac, out of breath, appeared at the top.

For a moment the two confronted each other. Then Zac inquired with an air of facetiousness, "Have you come to erase your mistake from the records, Miss O'Neill?"

"I've simply tried to understand them, Monsieur Desmond," Sandra said coldly, pointing at the decoy file in her hands. "If *I* made a mistake I have offered to make good the damage. Twenty-five million dollars is a lot of money, so I have to be convinced before I would even attempt to find such a sum. Yet all the time I am hampered by the reluctance on the part of people, like René Latour and Albert, obviously briefed by you, to help me."

"Have you found someone to help you now?" Zac said, suspiciously looking around.

"Merely my nose." Sandra pointed to it then turned the handle of her office door and went in, closing it behind her. She removed the incriminating disc from her bag and popped it into a drawer in her desk before there was a rapid fusillade on the door and Zac shouted.

"Let me in please! This is very serious. You might have committed a criminal offense. Forcing your way into the building. . . ."

Sandra quickly crossed the floor to the door and threw it open, surprising Zac who had been leaning against it. He nearly fell on his face in front of her, righting himself only at the last minute.

"Criminal offense; *forcing* my way in?" Sandra observed coolly. "May I remind you, sir, that *I* have not resigned yet, nor, at this moment in time, have I any intention of so doing."

"Investigators will want to know what you were doing in the building at this hour of night. You asked your way to the computer room. Albert says it is unlocked. Trying to destroy evidence of professional mismanagement is an offense under French law, Miss O'Neill, something which doubtless you are unfamiliar with."

"I may be unfamiliar with French law, Monsieur," Sandra replied, "though, in fact, I have probably learned more quickly than you think.

"But I *do* know skulduggery when I come across it; threats and blackmail made against my staff to discredit me. Please come in."

She made an elaborate gesture with her arm and, reluctantly, as though the wind had abruptly been taken out of his sails, Zac ambled into the room and sat down heavily on the leather sofa facing his father's desk which, once again, Sandra ostentatiously took her seat behind.

"Now, Mr. Desmond, I believe you have declared war against me, am I right?"

"Not at all. . . ."

"The gloves are off." Sandra poked the file at him and he gazed at it as if affected by some kind of mesmerism. "I am on the track of a swindle here and, believe me, if the facts are right, and I suspect they are, I'll throw the book at you, Zac." She stood up and pointed the decoy file at him in such a way that he, instinctively, cringed. "And, believe me, I won't be the one to resign. It will be you. And if there's a jail sentence for *you* at the end of it, don't expect *me* to be among the visitors."

17

Zac carefully put a key in the latch of the door in front of them then, gently pushing it open, stood back as if to offer someone a gift. Hand outstretched he bowed, inviting Agnès Guyon to precede him into the room. She looked at him with a deceptive air of childish wonder and then she cautiously followed him into the room which was of a good size, well but not lavishly furnished and with a view onto the Parc Monceau behind.

"Go on," Zac encouraged her, giving her a little push. "Explore."

Agnès, hands on cheeks, stared at him as if unable to comprehend what was happening, but it is doubtful if someone as astute as she didn't know what was going on. However, the act was a good one. Zac found it charming and, as she walked through a door at the far end into an adjoining room, he walked behind her giving her little prods in the small of her back whenever she attempted to stop. "Go on, go on," he said. Zac in his way was as excited as she. Provided there was a reward in it for him too, he loved giving presents if only to see the gratitude, followed inevitably by an expression of subservience, on the face of the recipient.

The pretty little park set in the middle of tall apartment blocks as well as gracious houses and bounded on one side by the busy boulevard de Courcelles, was commissioned toward the end of the eighteenth century by Philippe Egalité, the cousin of Louis XVI. Then it was rich in game and bird life and, after the fashion of the time, the painter and writer Carmontelle designed a garden fit for *A Midsummer Night's Dream* with colonnades, arches, pyramids and statues, pagodas and ornate bridges.

In the twentieth century the park was still almost the garden of delights it was then. It had little streams, an attractive pond half surrounded by tall pillars and well stocked with fish, a tiny hump-backed bridge nestling in a wooded arbor, a waterfall and, inevitably, lovers entwined on the benches or on the grass, and pigeons perched on the heads of the many statues.

The only concession to modernity was a kiosk selling food and souvenirs and some of the newly built, large elegant apartment blocks surrounding it.

But it was the older houses leading onto the Parc Monceau that held the fascination for the area, much favored in the eighteenth and nineteenth centuries by wealthy men who wished to establish their mistresses not too far away for them to visit. Around the avenue van Dyke the rue Murillo and the avenue Ruysdael were numerous grand houses backing on to the park, many of which had been converted into flats for the well-off.

Such an apartment had Zac Desmond acquired for the girl he hoped to make his mistress; a small apartment on the third floor reached by a grand staircase leading from the marble entrance-hall below. Both the sitting room and the bedroom had views over the park, through the massive oaks and chestnuts that bordered the paths, across to the colonnaded lake on the far side. The view was charming, restful in all seasons and, some would have said, romantic too. For it was the air of romance, of illicit intrigue, rather than expense alone, that still gave the area much of its fascination, its desirability as a residential area.

The first room had been furnished as a sitting room, the one leading off it was a bedroom. It had a good-sized double bed, a wardrobe and chest of drawers. This was quite small and next to it was a bathroom.

Agnès ran to the window and once again looked out on to the same elegant view. Then she turned and gazed rather shyly at the large bed upon which Zac, too, had fixed his eyes.

Yes, there would be a price to pay. She knew it, but then . . . what did it matter if he was so rich, if he could release her from poverty and its limitations as the late Georges Desmond had the mother of Mademoiselle?

Carefully she rounded the bed and, as she passed through the door back into the sitting room, Zac gently encircled her waist and gave it a little squeeze.

"Like it?"

"*Like* it, Monsieur Desmond? I should say I do like it."

"It's yours. . . ."

Now it was harder to pretend, but she had known the moment would come, so she made an extra effort that would not have disgraced an actress at the Comédie-Française.

"*Mine* . . . Monsieur? Oh no!"

"Why did you think you were here then, you little minx?" he said with amusement, chucking her under the chin. "Don't think I'm taken in. Of course you knew it was for you."

"Well . . ." Agnès fluttered her eyelashes, contriving to look very provocative indeed. Had it not been for her lack of inches, Zac decided he would find her most desirable; but she certainly wasn't bad looking with a full but neat bosom, good hips and thighs. There was a pleasing candor and freshness about her face. But, it was true, he preferred tall women. His sister was tall, Tara even taller with the marvelously long legs and lithe body of the professional model. Sandra was tall . . . but the thought of her made him grind his teeth though rape had featured among the many fantasies he had had about that thorn in his side, especially the night he'd seen her naked in bed.

Maybe one day, as the final humiliation . . .

He shook his head to free himself of such lustful thoughts and concentrated instead on Agnès. These were lustful too, but of a more tender and, hopefully, rewarding nature. Yes, a little love nest in the Parc Monceau. Why not? Many men had done it before him and doubtless many would again, though not too many if the soaring rents were anything to go by.

His eyes narrowed . . . but to have an ally right in the enemy camp was the sort of bonus which only came to someone who had God on his side. It was worth a price. He didn't want to be ridiculously generous and he'd taken this on a six months' lease. After that if she didn't shape up she could be kicked out of it, back into a bed–sitting room with her cousin near the Bastille where she'd come from.

Agnès was now running about like an excited child exploring a doll's house. The kitchen, back into the sitting room, the bedroom—very quickly in and out—and the bathroom.

"It's absolutely beautiful," she said, hands still to her flushed cheeks. "And it's really all mine, Monsieur?"

"For the time being," Zac said, teasingly sitting on the sofa and holding out his arms. "As long as you behave yourself."

Agnès paused and looked at him. He really was making the running, or trying to. But he needn't think he was going to get her into bed that quickly. She had already betrayed a boss whom she actually liked, and she was going to have to go on doing it while being the mistress of this attractive, powerful and important man . . . well she didn't find him *all* that attractive though lots of girls in the office did. They said his power, a hint of cruelty, made him sexy: some of them liked that, apparently, but not Agnès. She thought he looked too mean. She would have preferred a younger lover who wouldn't leave her to go home to his wife but would, maybe, share the flat with her, cook and shop with her, take her to the movies . . . wishful thinking. A man like that wouldn't be able to afford a place like this in an elegant house that had once been someone's *hôtel particulier*—now divided into six flats.

Maybe the kind of lover she preferred would come. As long as Mademoiselle never found out that her confidential, private secretary was a wooden horse within the very walls of Troy, she could well end up winning—whatever the outcome of the war between Monsieur Desmond and her boss.

She came over and sat beside him, though he had patted his knee intending her to sit there.

"Oh, a minx," he said again, quite pleased by this show of coquetry.

"I didn't *think* the intention behind your generosity, Monsieur Desmond, was to seduce me," Agnès said primly, "but to thank me for such services I am able to perform for you . . . as a messenger."

"As a spy," Zac corrected her harshly, reminding her suddenly—as if she needed reminding—what kind of man he was.

"Well not as a *spy,* exactly, Monsieur." She gazed at his large powerful hand resting on her knee. The thought of that hand caressing her intimately wasn't immediately pleasing but, maybe, it was something one would get used to.

It was said that a woman with ambition and in need of money could get used to anything.

"Well if you're not going to spy for me I'm not going to give you this apartment," Zac said, folding his arms forbiddingly. "I'm not a philanthropist, Mademoiselle Guyon, nor a fool. I have other things to do with my money, believe me. Rents in this area aren't cheap. . . ."

"Oh, Monsieur, *please* don't misunderstand me," Agnès said. "My loyalty to you is unquestioned . . . as a matter of fact I have something for you."

"Ah." A pleased expression softened Zac's granitelike features as Agnès withdrew the copy of a letter from her bag and gave it to him. Typed on the top were the words "Private and Confidential" and the letter began: "Dear Prince Abdullah."

Rapidly Zac scanned the contents then he placed the letter to one side and placed a hand over that of Agnès's.

"Very good my dear little spy. My little wooden horse, I shall call you. Very good indeed."

"I *thought* it would interest you, Monsieur Desmond."

"It interests me very much." Zac got up and strolled to the window as if he had already lost interest in making love to Agnès. "Mademoiselle is so far ahead with the Arabs is she . . . ? *Very* interesting."

"Well it doesn't actually *say* that, Monsieur."

"No, but it implies it," Zac said, turning to her. "She is negotiating to sell the D-2000 to the Arabs. It is a very powerful fighter plane developed by Desmond Aeronautics that even the Americans, or certainly NATO, might be interested in. She has used her cunning and skill, her wiles to get there before our competitors."

Zac moodily stared out on the wintry scene in the park; a thin layer of snow covered the grass which made the pigeons huddle together for warmth.

"No wonder she has spent so much time in the Middle East. Yet she keeps it all to herself. Why?" Zac spun around and Agnès feared the expression on his face, the look in his eyes. She feared for herself, and for Mademoiselle. "I am still a director of the Desmond Group. Why am I not party to these negotiations? Why do I have to bribe her secretary to find out? Do you think that's fair?"

Agnès nervously studied the tops of her shoes regretting, not for the first time, everything that so far had led her to this well-furnished apartment in the 17th Arrondissement. It was a long long way from Clermont-Ferrand and she was not quite sure that this, even this, was worth it. Anxiously she looked around at her new abode. After all, most of one's life was spent at work. An apartment was just a place to sleep in.

Well . . . nervously she looked at Zac chewing away at a corner of his nail—was it? Just a place to sleep in? Not always, alas; not always.

"Is it *fair,* Agnès?" Zac repeated, raising a finger to the ceiling. "Tell me, do you think it's *fair?"*

"No . . . no, Monsieur," Agnès mumbled.

"You don't sound very convinced."

"I do think," Agnès twisted her hands, "that Mademoiselle *is* very clever. But so are you. I wish you could work together in harmony. . . ."

"Harmony!" Zac threw back his head and laughed, so loudly that Agnès fervently hoped the walls were thick. "That *is* a joke. Mademoiselle and I will never work in harmony. Never. It will be a fight to the death." Zac pretended to stab himself in the heart. "And I shall win. I will reduce her to the state of a pauper. Believe me.

"She will need to move out of the Ritz soon," he continued grimly, "because, if I have my way, she won't be President of the Group for very much longer. She won't be able to afford the Ritz. Mark my words."

"Really, Monsieur?" Agnès looked rather shocked and felt not a small amount of guilt. Had she already been so successful . . . ?

"This business of the ruin of the *tirage.* I intend to have her over it. I'm going to summon the special Council my father formed to monitor her performance. He specified in his will that if she showed herself professionally or socially incompetent to manage the company at *any* stage she could be dismissed."

Agnès looked apprehensive. "I didn't realize it was as serious as that."

"Of course it's serious. We have lost twenty-five million dollars for which she is directly responsible . . . such incompetence and inefficiency is stupefying. Oh yes she's floundering, but I know she can do nothing. . . ."

"If you'll pardon me, Monsieur Desmond," Agnès said in that prim voice that Zac found rather appealing. "Mademoiselle is very *active* at the moment."

"I know she's very active. She's very busy. Desmond is a huge group and as she's so incompetent it will make her task that much harder."

"Monsieur Desmond, I must tell you frankly," Agnès said with a note of reprimand in her voice, "that Mademoiselle O'Neill is *not* incompetent. Far from it. *You* may like to think it; you may even like to believe it, but she is not. She is an extremely competent and efficient woman and, believe me, I know because I have worked for a good many different people since I was seventeen.

"Mademoiselle misses nothing, and if you think that she is not doing anything about what happened to the *tirage* you are very much mistaken. She is most active."

"But what is she doing? What can she do?" Zac cried in alarm. "Why didn't you say something about this before?"

Agnès shrugged her shoulders and lit a Gauloise which she'd fished from a crumpled pack in her handbag.

"Because Mademoiselle is playing her cards very close to her chest. I had nothing to tell you. I believe she trusts me, but this is so important that she does not even confide in me."

"Then *how* do you know?" Zac felt both angry and perplexed.

"Because I *know,* Monsieur," Agnès said, tapping her nose as one who keeps it close to the ground. "Believe me I know. She is *very* busy; she is out a lot; she consults a great deal with Monsieur Piper. . . ."

"Henri is a villain," Zac said in a savage aside. "He should be shot . . . maybe one day he will be," he finished thoughtfully.

"Nevertheless he is her ally. I think you're in for a surprise soon, and you won't be very pleased about it." Agnès shook her head and, at the same time, noticing his expression of bewilderment, she realized that she got pleasure from it. Defeating Zac Desmond at his own game, acting as a kind of double agent might, after all, be a most agreeable occupation.

Sandra was at her place at the head of the table as the members of the Board trooped into the room. She was pretending to be busy writing, dispatching two secretaries on various tasks as she handed out piles of paper to them. In reality she was far too apprehensive to be seriously at work, but she felt it was important to put across the message that this Board meeting was, as far as she was concerned, not the be all and end all of her day. Important it might be, but not that important. As President of the Group she had many similar and just as urgent things to attend to.

As she sat there at the head of the table bowing her head with a graceful smile to those who came in she looked what she was: elegant, capable, important—a veritable female dynamo of the business world. She wore a beautifully tailored black suit with a high-collared red blouse underneath. Her stockings were very dark and the feet tucked under her chair were encased in black suede shoes.

Lady Elizabeth thought, as she punctiliously returned her smile, that she looked like a very capable funeral director come to bury them all. Why on earth had Zac ever imagined he or any of them could get rid of her so soon?

There was something in Sandra's air that had not been there two weeks before when Zac had accused her of altering the instructions for the *tirage,* at the worst out of incompetence, at the very least out of carelessness. Certainly she was not a person fit in any way to run a business as large and important as that of Desmond, besmirching its name as one of the most famous makers of champagne.

Zac, again, the last to enter—this time Philippe de Lassale had gotten there before him—noticed the difference at once and also the fact that everyone around the table except Sandra seemed to be shifting about uncomfortably. Even his mother looked worried, and normally her air of imperturbability scarcely varied, whatever the occasion. *Noblesse oblige.*

As soon as he sat down Zac began to ask rapid questions in the tone of someone seriously inconvenienced and annoyed about it but Sandra, who had provided herself with a small gavel, brought it down gently but firmly on the polished table, and called the meeting to order.

"*If* you would allow me to have my say, Monsieur Desmond," she said, politely looking directly at Zac, "I would be grateful. I, in my turn, have called this meeting according to Article Eleven of the statutes which permits us to call a meeting within twenty-four hours in cases of emergency; similar to the one you called two weeks ago."

She paused and looked around the faces, whose various expressions reminded her of those one saw on juries in films of courtroom trials: doubt, curiosity, wariness and, on some, anxiety. The one person who had been here last time and was absent now was Claire and, of course, Tim was still in America playing polo at Palm Beach. But Belle, sharp-nosed and suspicious, was there next to her mother who kept her eyes on the papers in front of her. De Lassale, Leriche, Dericourt, Vincent, le Blanc, Maître Laban registered mixed emotions, however bland they tried to appear.

"I am sorry to disappoint you, Monsieur Desmond, and perhaps some other members of the Board—I don't know, I hope not." She allowed herself a slightly malicious smile as if promising herself that retribution would quickly follow against those who were not loyal.

"But I see no reason for me to resign as President of the Desmond Group. On the contrary, since we last met here, I have had detailed and intensive investigations made and some new and most important facts have come to light which, I think, will be of interest to those who have been left in ignorance." She laid heavy emphasis on her words and cast a glance at de Lassale, whom she had hitherto regarded as an ally, but who had deserted her in her time of need. She would remember.

However, she was interrupted by Zac, who lolled back in his seat, his expression one of amusement.

"All this mumbo jumbo is an attempt to mislead the members of the Board, Miss O'Neill. Through your incompetence you have lost this Group *twenty-five million* dollars, a sum unparalleled in its history. . . ."

"Except for supermarkets . . ." Sandra said smoothly, but Zac refused to be halted.

"I repeat: twenty-five million dollars. A large sum. If you refuse to resign—I hoped today we were meeting to hear of your resignation—I shall summon the Council appointed by my father, in his wisdom, to monitor your performance, and have you dismissed."

"I think a *little* patience is called for, Monsieur Desmond, if you don't mind," Sandra continued in the gentle, courteous tone with which she had begun the proceedings. "You will soon be enlightened I can assure you." She paused for a moment, and looking in a friendly way at each member of the Board, continued:

"The last time we met Monsieur Desmond accused me of an extremely serious professional mistake that might, indeed, have led to my resignation. Though even at the time I would have thought it obvious to anyone it was something I could not directly be held responsible for, as I had no experience in the making of champagne. However . . ." she reached for a file in front of her and opened it, "happily I am now able to report to you today the facts behind the error that was made. For there is no doubt that an event of the gravest imaginable consequence has occurred, unknown since, I understand, the First World War: almost a whole *cuvée* of Desmond champagne has, indeed, been written off."

Sandra paused so that the full effect of the profound silence around the table could be felt by everyone present.

"Now." Sandra assumed her glasses and carefully consulted the document put together with such care by herself and Henri Piper.

"The order slip for the *tirage* for the new vintage that I signed did, indeed, correspond to the yeast additives chosen by the experts, and myself as President at the Tasting Committee last month. Thus it was logical to suppose that the mistake was made afterward, in subsequent operations, that is to say," she looked at them over the top of her glasses, "in the programming of the computer. Now I am glad, or rather, sorry to say that I have proof the software was changed. . . ."

Zac leaned forward and banged his fist on the table. "What rubbish!" he said. "Who could have done that?"

"Who indeed? It is easy enough for someone qualified and, in this case, the eyes of suspicion must be cast at our computer staff. But which one? And why?"

As Zac threatened to intervene again, Sandra tapped with her gavel on the table and said sternly, "Well it was brought to my notice that one of the staff did indeed notice something unusual at the time the *tirage* began. . . ."

"Who . . . who . . . ?" This time Belle, who hitherto had been silently trying to support her brother, leaned over the table threatening Sandra with a quivering finger. "Say who, Mademoiselle, and your proof, please."

"All in good time, Princess," Sandra said sweetly, "for you can be sure I shall reveal all in a moment."

Now she was beginning to relax and enjoy herself. Days, nights of hectic activity, secret meetings and investigations, tests in the cellars of the Piper organization were about to prove worthwhile. She took a sip of water as Zac said in the smooth, even tones of one who was trying to be reasonable:

"Before you go *on,* Miss O'Neill, why don't you be so good as to tell the Board, what *you* were doing in the Desmond headquarters in the dead of night, the door to the computer room unlocked? Were you not tampering with the evidence yourself? Are you not a clever woman, a self-proclaimed enthusiast of the computer, which you would introduce into all the activities concerned with the making of champagne? Were you not there by *yourself* at night breaking and entering the computer room to destroy the proof of your own incompetence . . . ?"

Sandra felt that her own patience was wearing thin, but she swallowed hard, determined to retain the firm grip she had had on herself since Zac's outbursts began.

"I can hardly break and enter my own property as I was, and remain, President and main shareholder in the Desmond Organization, as if you need any reminding. Besides, I am not such an expert that I am in a position to tamper with software or know how to do it. . . ."

"Then *who,"* Belle said again, trying hard to imitate the composure, the silken tones of Sandra, the deceptive sang-froid of her brother, *"do* you suppose was responsible? Who is this, er, informant who communicated his, or her, 'unusual' observations to you . . . ?" Belle contrived to make the word *unusual* sound like a sneer and Sandra felt almost more angry with her than her brother. Belle was clever and devious. It took a thief to catch one; a woman to outmaneuver another.

As Belle spoke Sandra reached for a cardboard box which had lain by her side unopened since the meeting began and now she undid it and drew from it a floppy computer disc such as were used in the Desmond computers. She waved it first at Zac then at Belle, then showed it to each individual member around the table, pausing in front of each one. Philippe de Lassale, she noticed, did not even glance at it, intent on avoiding eye contact with her.

Then she put the disc down in front of her and joined her arms on the table.

"This is the proof," she said. "Here, now, right in front

of us. This is the disc with all the modified instructions for the *tirage.*" She then opened another flat file and drew out a pile of photocopies which she proceeded to pass around.

"This is a photocopy of the typed order I signed for the *tirage.* Now," she lifted the floppy disc again and held it in her hand, "the instructions on this do not correspond with the ones you see before you. Someone has changed them. . . ."

"What a joke," Zac said, scarcely glancing at the photocopy Belle passed on to him. "What a farce. What are you trying to prove? Any little computer operator can cook up a phoney disc like that. . . ."

"I think not, Monsieur Desmond." A note of menace was discernible now in Sandra's voice. "Behind that door is a young man whose testimony I am sure will interest you all."

Dramatically Sandra rang the bell in front of her and a secretary came in.

"Antoinette, would you be good enough to tell Monsieur Pagés that the Board is ready for him now?"

"Bien, Mademoiselle."

Zac, whose head had sunk on his chest, looked up sharply and leaned forward as a slight man of about thirty sidled around the door and crept across the carpet with a crablike movement.

"Do come in, Mr. Pagés," Sandra said, turning to greet him, her tone pleasant and inviting. "Please sit down."

She pointed to the chair next to her which she had deliberately kept vacant, then, adjusting her position, turned to him.

"Would you be good enough to tell the members of the Board what exactly your functions are in the computer department, Monsieur Pagés?"

"I am the Head," Pagés said a little sullenly.

"The Head!" Sandra exclaimed, looking around at her fellow directors. "Monsieur Pagés is the Head of the computer section. Now, Monsieur Pagés, did you notice anything unusual at the time of the *tirage* of our last *cuvée?"*

"Nothing unusual, Mademoiselle." Pagés cast a surreptitious glance at Zac, who, avoiding his eyes, was frowning deeply.

"But you were in charge of the programming of that *tirage,* were you not?"

"You know I was, Mademoiselle O'Neill."

"Please just give me the facts, Monsieur Pagés, if you would be so kind. *I* may know but I want my fellow directors to know too and to hear the words from your mouth. Now . . . could you please tell me how it was that the instructions for the *tirage* as they appear on the order slip which were, in fact, perfectly correct were not, in fact, followed?"

"I really don't know, Mademoiselle." Pagés' voice was scarcely above a whisper. "I did the programming from the instructions on the slip signed by you. That is all I can say."

"Indeed." Sandra appeared, by the expression on her face, to doubt his word as she pointed to the disc beside her again. "How is it, then, that the disc I have here, which is the one *you* programmed—you have just admitted it—doesn't correspond with the order slip?" Her voice rose sharply as Pagés mumbled again, "I don't know, Mademoiselle."

Sandra twirled about in her chair, undid the jacket of her suit and put a hand on her hip. With the other she tapped the disc before her with a silver pencil.

"You don't seem to know a lot, Monsieur Pagés, for a man in such an important and *responsible* position. Let me try and refresh your memory."

Pagés didn't look at her, nor at Zac, who now kept on trying to catch his eye, maybe with the idea of signaling a message.

Sandra consulted her papers again.

"I have information based on an impeccable source that the week before the programming—that is, after our Tasting Committee met—you were called in to see Monsieur Strega, a personal assistant to Monsieur Zac Desmond at his office at the Banque Franco-Belges. Is that correct . . . ?"

When Pagés didn't reply, Sandra rapidly continued, "I believe it is. It was unusual enough for you to be in such a place for one of your old colleagues, who had previously worked at the Reims headquarters, to notice it. I don't think you are often consulted by Mr. Strega, are you . . . ?"

"No, Mademoiselle."

Suddenly Zac, like a dog straining at a leash, cut in. "This is once again absurd. I like Paul Strega to keep in touch with all the staff who, very shortly, will be under my jurisdiction, may I remind you, Mademoiselle. . . ."

"I think not." Philippe de Lassale spoke for the first time *sotto voce* but loud enough for everyone to hear him. Zac looked immediately mollified and signaled for Sandra to proceed.

"Thank you, Monsieur Desmond," she said, the strain in her voice beginning at last to show. "Whether that is the truth or not I personally find it very odd that your personal assistant, a person of little power, if any, in this organization now that he works for the Banque Franco-Belges, should ask to see Monsieur Pagés. I don't believe there was any friendship between you, was there, Monsieur Pagés? Could you tell us what you talked about?"

"Go on, Pagés," Zac said encouragingly. "Please do tell us."

"Er nothing . . ." Pagés replied, hesitating.

"Nothing? How interesting." Zac smiled at Sandra as if, now, they were conspirators.

"Well nothing important . . . just about my work."

"I see, and did Mr. Strega by any chance make you a proposal? A proposal," she went on, as Pagés didn't reply, "which would mean a considerable sum of money to you if you altered the programming of the *tirage?* Omitted the yeast altogether, for instance?"

"No!" Pagés shouted. "No, I would never—"

"Come, now, Mademoiselle O'Neill," Zac said in a more reasonable tone of voice. "Strega would never make himself responsible for something like this. He has no authority. . . ."

"Unless it was given by you," Sandra said.

"Certainly not!"

"Well then. So be it, Monsieur Desmond, but it has come to my knowledge that Monsieur Pagés has just bought himself a magnificent sports car, one expensive enough to make the colleague I referred to, and the source of all this interesting information, wonder where he got the money to pay for it. Though head of his department Monsieur Pagés has a wife and three small children and a modest home. One would have thought that such an expenditure on such a car extravagant by any standards. May I ask your monthly salary, Monsieur Pagés?"

"Twenty thousand," Pagés said sulkily.

"And may I ask the cost of the car?"

Pagés didn't reply. Large beads of sweat had formed on his forehead and he kept on twisting and untwisting his hands.

"I believe it cost you one hundred fifty thousand francs, Monsieur Pagés, paid in cash to Rochar's Garage. . . ."

"Monsieur." Pagés turned to Zac, but Zac stuck his head in the air, his attitude now one of rejection.

"You'd better answer, Pagés, and be careful what you say."

"No need to warn him, Monsieur Desmond," Sandra said. "I think he knows that already."

"I didn't want to do it, Mademoiselle," Pagés burst out when he realized that there would be no support from Zac. "Monsieur Strega told me it was at the command of Monsieur Desmond. That's why I expected him to help me today. . . ."

"Nonsense," Zac raised his voice at last, rising to his feet. "Do you think *I* would want to defraud my own company of twenty million dollars, to bring ignominy on the name of the House of Desmond?"

"I . . . no, I don't think so, sir." Pagés appeared close to tears.

"Quite right I don't." Zac, leaving the table, strolled around it until he came to rest between Sandra and the unfortunate head of the computer department whose job was certainly now in peril.

"What you and Strega cooked up between you—villains the pair of you—will be the subject of a very intense investigation, do you hear, an investigation in the course of which nothing and no one will be spared. Do you realize that you and Strega between you—and one of the first things I shall try and determine is *who* was responsible for this nefarious plot—could have ruined not only yourself but me as well? Maybe this is a plot to cause my downfall. . . ." Zac gazed speculatively at Sandra, who lowered her eyes, not wishing even him to see her contempt.

"Oh, Monsieur Desmond, I—" Pagés wiped a tear from his eye.

"I have accused Mademoiselle O'Neill most unjustly." Zac swept an arm in her direction, "and asked for her resignation. She would have returned to America, her reputation in tatters. Did *you* think of that you, you miserable, crawling little worm, when all you wanted was a car costing 150,000 francs and what else besides? For what reason?"

"Exactly *what* reason," Sandra intervened. "I don't see what there was in it for Pagés, *or* Strega. . . ."

"*That* we shall have to determine," Zac replied ominously. "I think quite a lot. As for you, Pagés, I don't need to be the President of this Group to order you to pack your bags and don't ever show your face here again, and if we do see you it may well be in the law courts!"

Zac pointed to the door and Pagés scrambled for it like a rabbit scurrying to its burrow at the sound of the farmer's gun, before Sandra could say another word.

"Well!" Lady Elizabeth said as the door closed. "What a

revolting little man. What an incredible, *horrible* story. . . ." She got to her feet and her eyes traveled slowly around the table, stopping momentarily to gaze at each face. "But those men seem so *small* to hatch such a plot. Who could be behind such a despicable scheme?"

"Who indeed?" Sandra said, a bitter smile playing on her lips, her eyes on René-Zachariah Desmond the Second.

18

Bob lay in his bed aware of the sound of birdsong in the park, conscious of the play of the morning sun through the branches of the trees, casting interweaving patterns in the intricate plasterwork ceiling of his room. Sometimes it was hard to realize that this house was a mere hundred years old, so perfectly had the Rococo and Baroque, the elegant neo-Classical style of the eighteenth century been recaptured in its wall mountings, the pillars and canopies above the doors, the rich varieties of plasterwork in the moldings. Above all the style of the priceless furniture was original and authentic whereas the Château de Tourville, despite its magnificent opulence, was not. It was a copy, a pastiche, an attempt to recapitulate a much grander and loftier age.

Bob was a contemporary young American who was more interested in sports and politics than art. But no one could help but be overawed by the grandeur, the sumptuousness, the style of living at Tourville. That was exactly what the Desmonds had set out to do when Sandra was asked to introduce him to the family at the extraordinary reconciliation following the revelations about the alleged machinations of Pagés and Strega.

For, of course, after that not enough could be done for Sandra; the family was at pains to disassociate themselves from such an impudent piece of trickery.

The unfortunate Strega was made to sign a document

which confessed to his own guilt and completely cleared Zac. Zac begged Sandra to bring charges against Strega; perhaps he knew she would refuse on the grounds that enough harm had been done to the image of the company already. Strega was quietly sacked and sent abroad whereas Pagés, dismissed ignominiously from his job, was probably punished enough by the certainty that he would never find another in the same field.

It was a great commotion played with typical Desmond panache and thoroughness and, in the circumstances, it went on for quite some time. Zac couldn't do enough to try and right things with the woman he had so nearly succeeded in defeating. The affair had frightened him for it made him realize once and for all the nature of his adversary. She was as strong as he.

Sandra was never for a moment taken in, convinced as she had been all the time of Zac's guilt. She did not know Strega who was fairly new to Zac's entourage at the bank, but she was sorry for Pagés who only did what many petty criminals had done before him: betrayed someone for gain, maybe insufficiently aware of what he was doing.

How much Lady Elizabeth knew of the truth, Sandra had never been able to determine because she was so anxious to make amends, to assure Sandra that bygones would be bygones and that she must take her place in the "bosom of the family."

Belle had used the same phrase at Burg-Farnbach. When said by the Desmonds it had a hollow ring. She was extremely glad to escape to New York, away from it all, leaving the capable Agnès in charge and her brother resident at Tourville where she was sure that, for once, he would come to no harm under the maternal eye of Lady Elizabeth. At least no one had anything against Bob.

Bob liked luxury. He had been spoiled as a boy and was sybaritic by nature. The way of life at Tourville appealed to him enormously and he told his sister he didn't know why she hadn't made more of her right to live there. She could live in great style and commute quite easily to Paris, only an hour away.

Sandra found it practically impossible to begin to tell Bob what she really felt about the Desmonds, and how she could never regard the house as truly home as long as any of them lived there.

There was a knock on Bob's door and he called out, *"Entrez."* Like Sandra he was bilingual, though his French wasn't as good as hers. The longer he stayed in France the more he warmed to Sandra's idea that he should make it his home: study at the Sorbonne or the University of Reims, a life of ease at Tourville. . . . He looked at the maid who came in with his morning coffee, placing it on the table beside his bed. He reached out to touch her bottom as he did every morning and she, as usual, neatly skipped sideways and went to open his curtains while he lay there, sheets up to his chin, grinning.

One day he would have her in his bed; but he wasn't in a hurry. This kind of teasing was a pleasant and undemanding occupation and he thought that the girl, Nadine, enjoyed it too. She always smiled at him provocatively as she stood by the door before leaving the room.

"Shall I run your bath, Monsieur Bob?"

"Yes and get into it with me," Bob said, but she laughed and firmly closed the door behind her. He listened to the sound of running water as he sipped his coffee and felt truly content.

It was midweek and they were alone in the house except for the usual cohorts of servants. Lunch later that day was taken with Lady Elizabeth. She liked to keep to the style of the grand house. When Georges had been alive it was his custom to lunch at home when he could. They ate in the main dining room each at one end of the oval table with acres of space between them, waited on by Pierre and two footmen.

It was archaic, slightly farcical, but Bob enjoyed it. It was like acting in a real life film. When Lady Elizabeth was alone she ate like that too—at the head of the long table with this huge polished space in front of her.

Bob had never known anyone quite like Lady Elizabeth. This elegant, rather overdressed, haughty, still beautiful woman dominated Tourville in a way she had never been able to dominate her husband. It was her domain and she ruled over it, and it was that power and determination that he knew made Sandra feel she had no place in the great house until the day Lady Elizabeth was no longer there.

Bob, however, amused Lady Elizabeth. He reminded her a little of Tim, her darling. He was natural, outgoing and uncomplicated—attributes he did not share with his sister. Lady Elizabeth, to her relief, found Bob much easier to get on with than Sandra and, indeed, in those days after Sandra's departure the two struck up a friendship that surprised almost everyone.

To begin with Bob was not the least in awe of Lady Elizabeth. He often abbreviated her name to "Lady E" and this act of *lèse-majesté* seemed to amuse her. With Bob it all appeared perfectly natural and what delighted her was this naturalness, his lack of affectation.

After lunch, which they ate comparatively in silence because of the distance between them, coffee was taken in the English way in Lady Elizabeth's pleasant sitting room which overlooked the rose garden, her special domain. In the summer coffee would be taken in the rose garden but, alas, Bob would probably no longer be with her. She gazed at him fondly as she stirred her coffee in some sort of wonderment that this uncomplicated, very American young man who stood for none of the things she was interested in, should prove to her such an engaging companion. He was extremely adaptable; friendly and sympathetic.

"And what are you going to do this afternoon, Bob?"

"I thought I'd go for a drive. See the countryside."

"What a good idea. The country is beginning to look so pretty, as it begins to recover from the winter. Have you heard from Sandra by the way?" Lady Elizabeth, who had kept her slim youthful figure, bit daintily into a macaroon which she always enjoyed with her coffee.

"She telephoned me last night. She sent her best to you, Lady Elizabeth. I think she thinks it's time I got on with something. I'm a bit lazy." Bob smiled engagingly. "But I know that."

"Your sister's not lazy." Lady Elizabeth wondered to herself if she should chance a second macaroon? Would it be greedy?

"Sandra's certainly not!"

"Has she always been like that?"

"Like what?"

"Well, as she is now. . . ."

Bob appeared seriously to consider the question. He was young and his appetite was good. He had no qualms at all about helping himself to a sixth macaroon.

"Sandra has always been as she is now, as far as I can remember. She has always been more a mother to me than a sister, you must remember that. She helped to rear me. I think that's what gave her the sense of responsibility. She takes life very seriously."

"Oh she does indeed." Lady Elizabeth drained her coffee cup which she put carefully down in its saucer to gaze at the young man. Oh to be young, she thought, young and carefree.

"I don't think you like Sandra very much, Lady E." Bob regarded her solemnly from under his long eyelashes.

"That's not quite true, Bob," Lady Elizabeth said quickly. "We didn't have much time to adjust."

"She knows that. She realizes far more than you think. Sandra is, in fact, very thoughtful. . . ."

"That . . . hadn't really occurred to me," Lady Elizabeth said slowly.

"You wouldn't see *that* side of her. She's very shy. I bet you didn't notice that did you, ma'am?"

"Not really." Lady Elizabeth laughed and looked at the clock on top of her *bureau à cylindre,* a rolltop desk that came into fashion at the end of the reign of Louis XV. "It's time for my rest," she said, comparing the time on her wrist with that of the clock on the desk and put her arms on her chair. "Have a nice drive, Bob. Are you going anywhere special?"

"Nowhere special," Bob said vaguely. "Here and there, you know."

"Take care then." Lady Elizabeth smiled at him.

"I'll take very great care, my lady." Bob accompanied her to the door which he opened for her.

She wanted to bend and kiss his cheek as a sign of affection but she didn't dare. It might reveal too much how lonely she really was in this great house, mostly by herself when she wasn't surrounded by her warring brood locked now in this awful mortal combat with Bob's sister. It was all highly unpleasant to a well-bred Englishwoman who felt rather betrayed, not for the first time, by her own husband.

She touched his hair and said in her nursery voice, "Dinner at eight."

"Dinner at eight, Lady E." Bob echoed, like an obedient son.

As she crossed the hall and began to climb the stairs to her room, Bob stood watching her. Then, when she was out of sight, he ran up after her, changed into jeans and a sweater and, very carefully stuffing something into his pocket, patting the flap to make sure it was safe, went out again to select a car in the garages at the back of the house. He chose a red Ferrari convertible.

Bob knew that the home of his mother was only a few miles from Tourville and for days he had been studying the map so that he could find it with ease. He had thought of telephoning but didn't dare. He feared a rebuff and it would also make it look more casual, less intentional as though he just happened on the house in the charming village of Crémy.

Despite his youth and his temperament nothing that Bob ever did was done without a reason. His one intention in staying at Tourville was so that he could make an attempt to see his mother, and his reasons for being so nice to Lady Elizabeth were that she should remain unsuspicious of this.

Bob had been impressed during his stay in France with the Desmonds' reticence about Hélène O'Neill. It was as if she didn't exist. No one ever mentioned her; Sandra scarcely referred to her and it never seemed to have dawned on anyone that he should wish to see her.

It was as if the mistress of the late Georges Desmond had disappeared from the earth with him. Why?

Bob's own feelings about his mother were complex: they were not as harsh as Sandra's because he had in his nature more forgiveness; also, in a way, he had been hurt less because Sandra had protected him.

Once out of the gates of the Château he took the road along the river bank and crossed the bridge leading into Épernay. He didn't linger but drove through the town in the direction of Avize. It was a new fast road cut through the chalky soil and on either side were the frosty fields sewn full of wheat or maize, or covered in vines, bare now of leaves and pruned close to the ground. It was a clear cold day on the Côte des Blancs and, as he took the direction of Crémy he began to climb very slowly until he was on an escarpment, with the whole plain of the Côte lying to one side, and the tree-covered slopes on the other.

Crémy. He knew the name very well. Crémy. It was so simple and straightforward and yet it had always held a special place in his heart. Crémy and the rue de Seine. When he was younger he had written quite often to his mother, but she hardly ever replied and it became one of those exercises where the sense of anticipation was finally eclipsed by a feeling of futility. In the end they exchanged Christmas cards and there was usually something for his birthday. Bob didn't understand how a mother could forget her son or treat him in this way. But Sandra had explained that it was because her mother had fallen in love with Georges Desmond to such an extent that she had become oblivious to her other responsibilities.

Yet the impact of the few visits to California still lingered in Bob's memory as he approached Crémy. There the excitement of anticipation actually became reality. Mother came with Georges and there was always a lot going on. Meals eaten in deluxe restaurants and long stays in grand hotels. Trips in Georges' jet with a drawing room and bathroom. Georges became to Bob like Santa Claus—some magical person who appeared about once or twice a year, out of the sky, with a sack full of goodies.

And Sandra, though she may not have been aware of it, had been transformed when Georges was there too; as though responding to someone she would like to have had for a father.

Bob couldn't completely understand why or how Sandra could have failed to contact Hélène since she had been in France. It was atypical of the warm, compassionate sister he knew. He thought something had happened to Sandra to change her nature.

Bob drove very slowly through the village and in the end he had to ask his way at a local shop. Quite a few people gathered idly on the steps helpfully pointing out the direction to him.

"La bas, c'est la maison de Madame O'Neill."

La maison de Madame O'Neill. . . .

It was a house just off the main square in the village approached through an arch, the door always left open. In summer he imagined there would be flowers everywhere, but now the gravel was hard with frost and traces of snow lingered in the corners where it had been blown into drifts. It was a very big house; too big for one woman. But Georges Desmond would hardly have had anything smaller even for himself.

It was large and it was attractive, freshly painted cream with red woodwork and open shutters. Smoke was coming from the chimney . . . Bob stopped outside and knew that he was very nervous. His mouth was dry and his heart was beating quickly. He kept on touching his pocket to be sure that the present he had brought for his mother was still safe.

He had bought it for her in Paris to try and charm—buy, steal—what was the word?—his way into her affections.

Very quickly he drove the car on to the terrace, shut and locked the door, got out and then he stood hesitating in front of the door before he found the strength to knock.

Immediately the door opened. A rather frail, elderly lady leaning on a stick and clutching the door frame for support was looking at him and he thought at first that it was the maid, or that he had come to the wrong place.

But as he studied her face he knew . . . and it was a strange feeling to realize that, in the space of a few years, his mother had grown old, yet he was not yet twenty and she was not yet sixty. . . .

Pain did this to a person, Bob said to himself, reaching out his arms as she let her stick fall to the floor. He caught her or she would have fallen. He cradled her in his arms, his face awash with tears as she clung to him, the heave of her bosom telling him that she was crying too.

"Mother . . ." he said, leading her gently inside. "Why didn't you tell us you were so ill?"

Later she looked better sitting in her chair by the fire, her feet on a stool. She had more color in her cheeks and her breathing was easier. She loved the little mother-of-pearl brooch he'd brought her and still held it in her hands. Bob had immediately made himself at home, forbidding her to do anything. In the trivial little chores he found an easier means of communication than by talking. He made tea and they sat together in front of the fire in companionable silence, his hand sometimes in hers; sometimes her hand on his head as in a blessing.

"There is so much to forgive," Hélène said. "It is as though God has been punishing me ever since Georges died for what I did to you. From that day onward my health got worse and who would have thought it, Bob?" She stopped and looked at him with surprise. "I am quite a young woman you know. Yet look at me now. I appear older than Lady Elizabeth. . . ."

It was true that she did appear older, much older than Lady Elizabeth. He looked puzzled.

"When did you see Lady Elizabeth?"

"She came to see me one day." Hélène spoke as if trying to remember. "I can't recall whether it was before Christmas or after . . . before I think. Do you know what she came to ask me?" Hélène chuckled and took a sip of the sweet tea Bob had made her. It was the maid's day off.

"What did she ask you, Mother?"

"If Sandra were Georges' daughter. . . ." Hélène smiled as if genuinely amused by the idea. "She can't understand why he left everything to her. Neither can I." Hélène shrugged as if at an unfathomable mystery. "It just shows, Bob," she gazed at him tenderly for a moment and then once again put her hand on his head, "you can never really know people. I loved Georges Desmond for over twenty years. I gave up everything for him . . . and yet, was it worth it? I think not.

"I forfeited your love," Hélène continued after a pause. "I deserved to. Sandra has never forgiven me. She was older, of course, when I left and had more to forgive. I think if it hadn't been for that resentment on her part, which was tangible, Bob, you could actually *feel* it, I wouldn't have done what I did. I would have kept more in touch. I hoped that Miss Wingate would make up for me because when I knew her she was a generous-hearted woman, but she seems to have changed too."

The look of a bewildered child came into Hélène's eyes.

"But you, Bob, you were always close to me in my heart. I pray you know, and I always prayed for you." Once again she touched the back of her hair, little sausagelike curls which sat neatly on top of one another.

She had a strangely old-fashioned appearance for a woman who had captured the lasting affection of such a famous man. She looked what, probably deep down, she was: a member of *la petite bourgeoisie,* the backbone of France, the people who, from underneath, gave power and prestige to men like Georges Desmond.

Hélène O'Neill had never been a beauty; but she had been ambitious, and had gained by her ambition what many more beautiful women want but often fail to achieve. She knew that to be essential to someone was of more importance than being beautiful and she had made herself, her support, so essential to Georges Desmond that he couldn't do without her.

Had Lady Elizabeth not been such a beauty, so aristocratic and well connected, she might have realized this a lot earlier and saved herself much pain.

But because she was ambitious Hélène was also single-minded and that meant a certain degree of ruthlessness, a certain amount of cruelty, the infliction of pain.

And yet Bob had forgiven her. He forgave her because now she was small and ill and old-looking. He forgave her because she was crushed and pathetic and no one could look on such a creature and still be angry; even Sandra, now almost as powerful as Georges Desmond.

"As soon as Sandra comes home I'll bring her to you, Mother," Bob said. "I know she'll want to see you, and you should see her. You'll be proud of her. . . ."

"I *am* proud of her," Hélène said. "I read the papers and I see a lot about her. If we haven't seen each other maybe the fault is as much mine as hers. I never contacted her either. I should have perhaps written to congratulate her, but I did nothing. I sat and waited and she waited too." Hélène shrugged her shoulders. "Two people who completely failed to understand each other. Maybe that's the problem. But now that she's older, maybe she too will fall in love one day; maybe then she will forgive me."

Hélène sighed. "Of course I'm proud of her; but I'm concerned for her too. Georges should never have done what he did. It was foolish and it was wrong. Sandra will never ever have peace of mind as long as Belle and Zac Desmond are left out in the cold. Believe you me. I know this . . . they will not let her rest."

That night when Bob got back to the Château he found that Zac and Tara had arrived and could hear them being entertained in the salon before dinner.

He hurried upstairs to get into his dinner jacket and just made it back to the hall as the gong sounded and Madame Desmond appeared followed by Zac and Tara.

Lady Elizabeth looked at Bob with some disapproval.

"I said dinner at eight, Bob. We're very punctual here. The staff needs to serve meals on time."

"Sorry, Lady Elizabeth. I went . . . I lost my way."

"I don't think you've met my wife Tara," Zac said affably, bringing Tara forward to introduce them. "Tara, this is Sandra's brother Bob."

"How do you do?" Tara said, pleased to see someone else to liven the tedium of an evening with Zac and his mother. Her face lit up and she shook him warmly by the hand. Bob, aware of the pressure, let his linger for a fraction longer than was necessary.

He didn't think he'd ever seen a more beautiful woman.

"I didn't know . . ." he began and then stopped, feeling foolish. He couldn't say, "I didn't know Zac had such a beautiful wife," so he said, "I didn't know I was so late."

"Do let us proceed into dinner," Lady Elizabeth said, as

though marshaling a cohort of guests for a dinner party. "I fear the soup will be cold."

The huge dinner table with four people around it was only a trifle less absurd than when there were two, or even one. Yet Zac knew that it was one of his mother's idiosyncracies to dine in this way and he was used to it. One day she would cease, but their father hadn't been dead a year. One day she would withdraw to one of the many smaller rooms, and the dining room would be saved, as it should be, for formal occasions. Lady Elizabeth liked to believe—or pretended to believe—that Georges was still alive.

But it was nice to dine in style; crisp dinner napkins on one's lap, the best silver and glass sparkling. Champagne in a silver bucket on the side. A servant stood at each end of the table supervised by Pierre at the door, a footman at the sideboard.

In many ways it was ridiculous; but there were few things like this left in life and, on the whole, Zac approved of it. Zac glanced around the table at his mother eating, his wife looking about her and young Bob clearly mesmerized by the beauty opposite him.

It was nice to have other men admire one's wife, especially when the man, scarcely out of boyhood, was the brother of a woman he hated. It would be nice for Bob to fall in love and suffer on account of Tara, and then be packed off home for misbehaving himself. Another humiliation for Mademoiselle!

He had gone out of his way to be nice to him. Someone so close to Sandra was, as far as Zac was concerned, an easy and vulnerable target.

It was quite certain that she hadn't realized the danger when she went to America, leaving him in the care of the Châtelaine of de Tourville.

* * *

Zac watched Bob surreptitiously but carefully all during dinner. It was the first chance he had had to study Sandra's young brother and he was immediately struck by the dissimilarities between them. Bob's hair was dark and Sandra's was blonde; both were tall but she was lithe, slim and graceful whereas Bob had the girth and gait of an American footballer. He was a chunky, beefy, all-American teenager and, in many ways, he seemed a simple, trusting kind of lad. Not simple in the sense of being simple-minded—obviously he was far from that—but, whereas Sandra was complex, Bob was the opposite. It seemed or, rather, to Zac it seemed that one could read his face like a book.

The friendly, outward-going, impressionable young American boy felt buoyed-up by all the show and appurtenances of gracious living. Besides, the Desmonds were a family, and as far as he was concerned, a friendly one. He had badly missed family life. He took to Lady Elizabeth and she took to him and now, in his turn, Bob was responding to the hands that reached out to welcome him.

He wanted to be loved.

Tara on the other hand wanted to be admired. The thing she most cared about in life was the admiration of men, be they young or old. She craved love in the same way that Bob did and, inevitably, it seemed to be drawing them together.

Zac was rather pleased to see the effect his wife had on their susceptible male guest and her response to him was interesting too. The ex-cover girl couldn't help being aroused by a young male who had the build of an athlete and a certain *savoir-faire* that was rather unexpected. One felt that Bob had been around, seen life. He looked older than he was.

"What did you do today?" Zac asked when they gathered after dinner for coffee in the main salon. Lady Elizabeth had put some Schubert on the stereo and she took up the embroidery of which she was so fond, and sat with her feet on a small stool which long ago she had embroidered too.

"Oh I went for a drive," Bob said.

"Anywhere interesting?" Lady Elizabeth looked across at him, snipping off a piece of thread with a pair of tiny scissors.

"Well . . ." Bob was nothing if not honest. He found dissembling difficult and it showed now in the healthy pink color of his skin. "I went to see my mother." Bob's skin turned puce.

There was a small silence during which the magnificent ormolu clock—one of the items that Zac had had to return—could be heard ticking on the marble mantelpiece. Then Lady Elizabeth said gently, "Perfectly commendable. I'm glad you did."

"I suppose I shouldn't have mentioned it." Bob looked around awkwardly.

"Why not?" Lady Elizabeth replied. "A mother is a mother, as I have pointed out to your sister. Believe me, I have suggested to Sandra that she should visit Madame O'Neill, but she told me very politely to mind my own business."

"When was that, Maman?" Zac said, lighting a cigar, his eyes on the flame as he puffed.

"Well . . . I wanted to see Madame O'Neill and ask her certain things. It is a private matter between her and myself. But I was upset to find her unwell and knew that she wished to see her children. I'm very glad, Bob, that you went. I was about to bring it up this afternoon but thought it was early days yet. I didn't want to appear to be interfering and I hope now that you will stay with us for some time, and see her often."

"That's very good of you, Lady Elizabeth," Bob said. "And very generous."

"What happened happened," Lady Elizabeth said simply, "and the man in question is now dead."

"Mother is overgenerous." Zac drew on his cigar. "Generous to a fault; but I won't say any more because this young man is a guest in our house."

"I can understand you don't like my mother," Bob said quietly.

"I don't dislike her. I hardly know her. As far as I was concerned she was a servant who—"

"Oh Zac," Tara exclaimed, "why *must* you be so unpleasant?"

Tara had been sitting on the sofa opposite Bob watching him as he spoke. One of her long elegant hands, with its lacquered nails, was spread beside her; the other rested on her knee. She wore a tight-fitting green dress with a bodice that left little to the imagination, displaying her full, prominent breasts. These in turn emphasized her tiny waist and the pleasing fullness of her hips which drew attention to the length of her legs, the elegance of the ankles.

As she addressed Zac, she was looking at Bob.

"Unpleasant?" Zac replied. "It's not unpleasant at all. It's true."

"Madame O'Neill was *not* a servant, whatever else she was."

"She was paid," Zac insisted. "Paid for services—"

"Zac, please stop," his mother said peremptorily.

"I didn't mean to upset Bob." Zac bowed in the direction of the young man, by this time rather confused. "And I apologize if I did. Maybe we shouldn't talk about your mother, in the circumstances. I apologize if I offended you. Maman, didn't you want to watch a film on the television?"

"Oh yes!" Lady Elizabeth put down her embroidery and looked at the clock. "Thanks for reminding me. Would you excuse me, everyone?"

As she rose Bob rose too.

"No, you stay here," Zac said, "and keep Tara company. I'll take a look at the film with Maman."

"What is it?" Tara said. "We might all like to see it."

"I think it's a little too intellectual for you, my love." Zac took his mother's arm and tucked her hand under his. "You stay and entertain Bob."

Tara raised her eyebrows again but said nothing more as Bob, with some discomfiture, stood first on one foot then on the other as the two went out of the door.

"Thank God for that," Tara said, kicking off her shoes and tucking her feet under her as she stretched out on the sofa. "The pretension of this place gets me, always dressing for dinner and I don't know what. My family was of the highest Italian nobility, but we never did this. I suppose, though, you find it rather quaint?"

"Sort of," Bob said, not knowing quite what to do with his eyes. To be alone with Tara so soon was almost overwhelming.

Tara went on. "I'm sorry he's so insufferable, Bob, but that's the way he is."

Bob, frowning, was looking at the door which was now shut.

"I see why Sandra doesn't like him." He scratched his head. "Yet he seems kinda nice to me."

"Nice?" Tara said with amazement. "Did you say *nice?"*

"Yes. He's been very nice to me since I came here. I believe it was his suggestion that I come. I guess he and Sandra just get across each other."

Bob smiled and, undoing his jacket, sat opposite Tara.

"I *can* understand it, you know. What Georges Desmond did wasn't very nice. Even my mother thinks it was an awful thing to do."

"Oh does she? That surprises me." Tara took a cigarette from her bag and popped it into her mouth. Bob bounded forward to light it.

"Thanks. . . ." Tara caught his wrist as he held the light in front of her. Then she exhaled and let it go. "I'm not supposed to do this." She exhaled again, luxuriously. "They hate it in Champagne because it spoils the palate. As the wife of a *champenois* I am supposed to abide by the rules." She laughed at him wickedly. "Do you?"

"What?" Bob looked embarrassed.

"Smoke?"

"Only . . ." he stopped awkwardly.

"Pot?" she asked quietly.

"Do you?"

"Doesn't everyone?" Tara said.

"My sister doesn't. She doesn't approve of it."

"Oh I smoke pot—the lot," Tara said nonchalantly. "In fact I can get you something stronger. . . ."

"Oh I wouldn't touch that," Bob said quickly.

"You never tried coke?" Tara looked surprised. "I don't think I could get through the day without coke, especially since my miscarriage. . . ."

"Oh . . ." Bob, still standing in front of her, dropped his lighter into his pocket. "I'm sorry."

"Didn't you *know* my husband raped me?" Tara put her hands behind her head and stretched, stretched until her breasts looked as though they would burst out of her dress. Bob was transfixed by the sight of her bare armpits, the swell of that astonishing bosom . . .

"Come and sit beside me," Tara said, indicating the sofa. "Or have I embarrassed you?"

"Not at all," Bob replied. "That is . . . well, I don't know what to say."

"I thought everyone knew. I certainly told the family and I was sure Sandra would know and maybe have passed it on. . . ."

"You mean your husband *raped* you and . . ."

"And I had a miscarriage. His violence brought it on. I nearly died."

"Oh my goodness." Bob put his hands to his face. "That is awful."

"I've only just got better. We try to keep up appearances in front of people. You see, Zac may seem very nice to you and when he makes an effort he can be. Some people find him charming but I hate him . . . and Sandra hates him too. He is a very evil man, no doubt about that." Tara took hold of the hand so near hers. "You can see that I need sympathy, can't you? I need it very much indeed."

19

The throng outside the Metropolitan Opera House in New York started to disperse as long, elegant limousines drew up to claim their passengers. Behind metal barriers a less elegantly dressed throng shouted and called as celebrities appeared, pausing to give those affected waves or smiles before they, too, were carried away into the brightly lit streets.

Sandra, together with Sophie and Henri Piper, took her leave of some people they'd been talking to and wandered out onto the pavement to look for their car, Sandra pausing to glance over her shoulder.

"Is there someone you want to see, dear?" Sophie Piper followed her gaze.

"I wanted to meet Dr. Harcourt. . . ."

"Oh don't worry about him." Sophie tucked an arm through hers. "He never attends this kind of thing."

"Oh dear, how disappointing! But I thought he was in New York just for this?"

"He will probably be at the reception," Henri said, waving his hand as their car came into sight. "I hear he wants to meet you too."

"Indeed," Sandra said, smiling to herself.

"Oh yes, he's a very determined man." Henri ushered them into their seats behind the chauffeur. "I'm afraid he'll buttonhole you for more money."

"He's very charming though." Sophie took hold of one of

the straps to steady herself as the car moved away from the curb, driven with exaggerated care to avoid jay walkers who rushed across the road after their favorite celebrities. "I don't think Henri likes him very much, but I do."

"Why do you say that, my dear?" Henri, looking momentarily annoyed, rubbed his hands.

"I just don't think you do. You're always criticizing him for one thing."

"Well he's always criticizing *me* for another," Henri said, tapping the driver on the shoulder. "Please go straight to the apartment of Mr. and Mrs. Porter."

"Yes sir," the chauffeur said. "But I was instructed to take Miss Desmond back to the Hotel Pierre first."

"Yes really, I'm very tired, if you'll excuse me," Sandra said. "It's been a heavy day."

"Oh that *is* disappointing." Sophie looked distressed. "The Porters so *wanted* to meet you. Besides they have one of the loveliest apartments in New York."

"I'd love to see it another time." Sandra smiled at her. "Do you know I have a breakfast meeting and it's already after midnight?"

"These galas go on for too long," Henri agreed. "But I believe we may have taken over five million dollars." He leaned toward her with a smile on his face, lightly putting his arm around her.

"Please, Sandra, stay half an hour or so. It really is very important for you just to be seen at the Porters."

"We may raise another million that way." Sophie smiled rather stiffly as her eyes followed the direction of her husband's arm. "Besides, you might also see Dr. Harcourt."

"I shall probably see him anyway. If he's after more money he's bound to find me. . . ." She paused and looked at the garishly bright cafés and movies, the gorgeously dressed shop windows as they flashed by. "Oh well, maybe it *is* rude to your friends. Just half an hour then."

"I know they'll be pleased," Sophie said and Henri instructed the chauffeur to take them all on to Park Avenue.

Scott and Nancy Porter were the leaders of a certain section of society that was bright, clever, witty, fashionable and rich. Scott was a writer: a critic, a playwright, a successful Hollywood scriptwriter. All the best people in society engaged Nancy to do their houses or apartments over, once they had seen hers.

They were the beautiful, not-so-young arbiters of New York, New England and Hollywood society. As well as their apartment on Park Avenue there was a house on Martha's Vineyard overlooking the breakers of the Atlantic, a cabin on Malibu beach and a villa outside Cannes.

Both Porters had money when they married each other and afterward they made even more. Now in their early forties they had everything in life they wanted except, like the Pipers, they were childless and, like the Pipers, they gave a lot of their considerable fortune to charity.

Nancy's charity parties were famous. Their apartment on two floors resembled more a gracious town house than a mere number in a block of apartments. One floor was joined to the next by a huge monumental staircase beyond which were windows with a spectacular view of New York.

The elevator from the lobby of the apartment led directly into the Porters' hall where the coats and cloaks of the guests were taken by a team of uniformed maids. Slowly the guests ascended the staircase to the next floor and, at the top, stood the Porters: handsome, very young looking, Nancy exquisitely gowned by the favorite dressmaker of Jacqueline Kennedy, the famous Galanos.

Nancy's hair was artificially blonde but so cleverly done that only the people who knew how often she changed the color could possibly know it wasn't real. Besides, what did it matter now? Everybody changed the color of their hair;

some hair styles were multicolored. Sandra didn't care what Nancy Porter did with her hair. She judged people immediately by what she saw and heard and by the pressure of their handclasp. She could tell a lot from the way people shook hands and, as hers lingered in Nancy's, she knew instinctively that she liked her.

"You don't know how I've *longed* to meet you," Nancy said in a mellow cultivated voice with just the slightest trace of a New York drawl.

"It's very kind of you to say that." Sandra remained clasping her hand, smiling.

"Already you're famous!" Nancy extended an arm to the throng who milled about them. "So many people asked me if you were coming."

"I can't think why." Sandra observed the press about her with some amusement. "I'm just a businesswoman."

"Yes but *what* a businesswoman! Well here's one of your admirers, my husband Scott."

Scott, who had been talking to Sophie and another well-known New York socialite, bowed over Sandra's hand.

"And every bit as beautiful as everyone has said. I am enchanted to meet you, Miss Desmond. As Henri told me—"

"Oh Henri's always talking about you," Nancy chimed in. "I think he's a little in love—" She stopped, hand to mouth, eyes seeking Sophie, who had heard her remark. She turned and laughed.

"Go ahead, say it! Henri is *very* susceptible. . . ."

"Henri is an old friend," Sandra said with a slightly gravelly tone to her voice. "He is a *very* old friend and mentor. Sophie too."

"Oh of *course,*" Scott said contritely. "And we didn't mean—"

"My wife will be divorcing me." Henri's suave Gallic charm immediately overlaid any awkwardness. "Sandra, my dear, I want you to meet—"

And so it went on. Adulation, in its way, could be seductive and Sandra soon began to lose her feelings of tiredness and to enjoy the admiring words and glances she received wherever she went. This was certainly the biggest, probably the most fashionable party held in New York that spring, and here she was the obvious center of attention. There were many famous people present: film stars, television personalities, the stars who had taken part in the gala, several English and American politicians, members of the diplomatic corps and yet . . . everyone wanted to meet the woman who had come from nowhere to inherit a fortune and not only inherit it, make it work. Her story was given an added attraction for some by what was known of the feud between her and the Desmonds and, especially, the latest episode concerning the *tirage.*

Those who knew Zac Desmond realized at once that he had met his match.

Sandra drank some champagne—naturally only Desmond and Piper were served—toyed with the buffet, talked to too many people to count and was on the verge of taking her departure when she saw the back of someone she thought she knew. A tall man, a long neck, a familiar head . . .

As she looked at him he turned suddenly and immediately she felt confused and the smile of welcome on her face died. At his unspoken question she said, "I'm awfully sorry, I thought you were someone I knew. I'm mistaken."

"Ah but I know *you,* Mademoiselle Desmond," the man said in French, extending a hand. "Michel Harcourt. How do you do?"

"Of course!" Sandra clasped his hand and shook it warmly. "Of course I recognized you and I felt, indeed, that I did know you. The film of your work was excellent. I'm very sorry I missed you in Paris."

"And I you, Mademoiselle." The charming doctor stopped a waiter to offer her a glass of champagne.

"No thank you." Sandra showed him her half glass. "I must

go soon. I have to have breakfast with someone at eight o'clock."

"How uncivilized." Dr. Harcourt smiled. "And just as I had the pleasure of meeting you for the first time. Maybe I could make an appointment to see you in your office while you're here, Mademoiselle?"

Sandra shook her head.

"Unfortunately there will not be time this visit. When will you be in Paris?"

The smile on Michel Harcourt's face gradually disappeared.

"I'm afraid I have no idea. I, too, am an extremely busy person."

"I know you are, Dr. Harcourt and, believe me, I'm sorry. But I have to leave tomorrow night for Canada, so you see. . . ."

"Then maybe I can talk to you here," Harcourt demanded, his tone hardening.

"Of course." Sandra looked around and saw that, beyond them, was a terrace with a few couples dancing. "How about there?"

"Do you dance?" Harcourt's engaging smile returned.

"Well . . . why don't you try me?" Sandra gave him her arm and they moved toward the couples gyrating on the terrace twenty floors above New York City.

His step was expert even in the cramped conditions, the feel of his arm about her waist secure. For a moment she felt a curious sense of security as she let herself be guided through the throng by him. Then, his face very close to her ear, he whispered, "Isn't it hell here?"

"It *is* hell," Sandra whispered back. "But that's just because there are so many people. I think we'd do far better to see each other again in Paris."

"But I'm off to Africa." He stepped back but maintained the ease of the rhythm. "Is there any chance of you coming there?"

"Of course, but not yet." Sandra neatly sidestepped a couple who had, perhaps, had a little too much to drink. "I have a lot on my plate in America and Europe."

"You're fortunate in that case," Harcourt said abruptly. "The plate in Africa is invariably empty."

"I know that, Dr. Harcourt, and, believe me—"

"But do you *really* know it, Mademoiselle Desmond?" Harcourt stopped dancing and looked at her, holding on to her hands. "Do you really, can you possibly, understand what it is to starve? I think not."

"No I don't know what it is to starve, Dr. Harcourt." Sandra suddenly felt tired and a little annoyed. The exhilaration of the previous moment had evaporated. "But I assure you that I am looking into the funds for the Foundation and as soon as I can I will let you have a report."

"Starving and dying people can't wait for *reports,* Mademoiselle Desmond," Harcourt said in a sudden display of temper and threw down Sandra's hands so that they fell to her side. She felt a sudden, ungovernable feeling of fury at his rudeness.

"Then I'm very sorry, Dr. Harcourt. If that's the case they'll have to go on as they are. Please don't blame me, though. I'm not the World Bank or the United Nations. I simply can't let you have money that we don't have. I can't make funds available that are not there. *Please* don't think that you have the monopoly of compassion for the suffering. I know the work you do is magnificent, but you are not the only ones making demands on our time or money. Believe me I *care. . . .*"

"I don't think you know anything about caring or compassion," Harcourt shouted at her above the music and, gradually, one or two of the couples stopped dancing to listen. "I think you are just what you seem: an ambitious, vain, grasping, egocentric woman and I wish you good night!" There were one or two gasps as Harcourt pushed roughly past the dancers toward the door; but soon those in the room remembered their manners and returned to the sensual, insinuating sounds of the stereo.

Sandra felt angry and humiliated and stood where he'd left her while Henri, who had been alerted by an observer of the scene, hurried through the door and over to her, seizing her by the arm.

"What on earth happened?" he said. "I hear you had words with Harcourt. . . ."

"What a terrible, horrible, *hateful* man he is," Sandra cried, stamping her foot regardless of the audience. "If you ask *me* I think he's ten times worse than Zac Desmond."

Henri Piper stood at the window of his hotel suite and watched the airplane cross the open expanse of sky above Manhattan. Which direction was it flying in? He didn't know: north, south, east, west? He turned from the window and came thoughtfully across the room watched by Sophie who had been answering a pile of letters at a bureau in the corner.

"She'll be on her way now," Sophie said.

Henri stopped and looked at her, then recommenced his walk.

"Oh I wasn't thinking of Sandra."

"Weren't you?" Sophie put down her pen and sat back in her chair. "Are you sure?"

"Of course I'm sure. *I* know what I was thinking about." Henri stopped again. *"What's* the matter with you, Sophie?"

"Isn't it true?" she insisted, twisting her cap back on her pen, a smile playing on her lips. "Aren't you just a *little* in love with her?"

Henri sat down in a chair, spread his long legs before him and threw his hands in the air.

"My dear Sophie, I am not the least bit in love with Sandra O'Neill, excuse me, Desmond. I don't know what makes you think or even say such an absurd thing."

Now Sophie got up, tucked her arms inside each other and walked across to her husband.

"Sometimes I think that very little else concerns you but Sandra—where she is, what she's doing, what's happening to her. If you ask me she *is* on your mind twenty-three out of twenty-four hours of the day."

Henri looked sharply up at her and waved a finger at her.

"That is utterly untrue. It is a stupid, wrong and very silly thing to say. Good God, my dear, don't tell me you're jealous of Sandra?"

"Not jealous." Sophie cocked her head on one side. "Maybe a little envious. I would like to be twenty-seven and beautiful and clever with the world at my feet, and men like Henri Piper, and younger, falling over themselves to do things for me."

"Then you are jealous." Henri got up, looked around and, for lack of anything better to do, sat down again. There were limits to what the circumference of the hotel room offered. "I cannot believe it, my dear Sophie. In any case what point would there be for me to fall in love with Sandra . . . ?"

"Does one *need* a point?" she persisted gently. "Doesn't it usually just happen?"

"No it does not. Not to me. My dear, I'd no idea you had brooded so much and obviously so long about this." Henri got up and this time stayed on his feet. He went over to the cabinet in the room and, producing a bottle of Bourbon, poured some into a glass, gesturing to her.

"No thanks." Sophie shook her head and smiled. "It *is* a little early."

"I don't call five o'clock in the evening early." Henri looked at her defiantly and downed his drink.

"Maybe that's because you need it. Maybe I hit a nerve. My dear Henri . . . believe me, I'm not going to make an issue of this."

"But you have," Henri said heatedly. "You *are* making an

issue of it and, incidentally, a fool of yourself into the bargain."

"Or a fool of you," she said quietly. "Old goat."

"I refuse to listen to any more of this." Henri glanced at his watch. "I am going to wait in the lobby until it is time for dinner."

"What good will that do you?" Sophie turned her back on him, her eyes on the view from the window. To see the expression on the face of a husband she knew to be lying was a painful experience. "Aren't you avoiding the issue? Seriously, Henri, the business about the yeast seemed to turn your head as far as Sandra was concerned."

"How do you mean 'turned my head'?"

"Made you soft. You were never away from that laboratory or her office. . . ."

"I wanted to help her. . . ."

"Why . . . ?"

"Because I knew she was a victim. . . ."

"How did you know?"

"My dear woman," Henri's voice was getting louder. "It was quite obvious that she was being victimized by Zac. . . ."

"Who happens to be my nephew."

"Who happens to be a villain." Again Henri shook his finger at her back. "And don't you forget that. He may be your brother's son, my dear Sophie, but he is a blackguard. You know it too. Of course I had to protect Sandra and help her. I was the only one there who could."

"And shall you *always* be the only one? Don't forget, Henri, this is merely the first of what I promise will be many crises. There will be many, many more like this . . . until, that is, Sandra is defeated by Zac. For believe me, my dear husband, I know my brother's son and he will win.

"And where will that leave you?" She turned to face him, but found she was now talking to a closed door. For Henri Piper had already gone.

* * *

Although one would hardly have dignified or elevated Zac Desmond with the title "philospher" he did, in a way, have a nature given to a kind of philosophical acceptance, though with none of the benignity associated with that word.

In fact Zac knew when he was beaten, but he always came up again. In a sense he cheerfully accepted the inevitable and then looked around for another way to achieve his end.

When Zac was younger this attitude had earned him a reputation for duplicity. He would accept a reprimand or a rebuff with a smile and then he would go to his room and either do the same thing again or something worse.

Whereas Claire got the reputation as a sneak Zac, in his way, was sneaky too; he went about what he had to do surreptitiously.

Zac now sat at his desk in his office on the avenue de l'Opéra listening to his younger sister who had arrived unexpectedly and insisted on seeing him.

They had never been close and he knew that she harbored feelings of animosity against him and Belle. It was true that they had not liked her lover Piero Borghi and that they had not helped him when he accidentally fell into the sea. Maybe they hoped he would survive and maybe they didn't. It was hard to remember now.

It was not the first bad thing they had perpetrated together, but it was one of the most serious. Belle and Zac had grown up together performing many little deeds that were thought of as merely naughty, except that one or two of their nursemaids used a much more sinister adjective to describe their behavior: evil.

In her heart of hearts Claire probably didn't really think they were evil, even though she had once said as much to Sandra. She too was a Desmond and she had their genes. It is more likely that she was a little afraid of them, a little jealous.

It was certain that when she wanted or needed something

she knew where to go to get it. She was just as ruthless as the others in this respect and, like the rest, she would use people for her own ends, maybe with a little more justification than either Zac or Belle.

To her surprise Zac had welcomed her, canceled all calls and given her his whole attention as she unfolded a sorry tale of marital misery and unrequited love.

She now wanted out. She wanted money and help.

"Do you mean a *divorce?*" Zac had said in tones that might have been used by a member of a strict Catholic family considering such an abhorrent idea.

The use of the very word shocked even Claire and she had paused a minute to consider it.

"Maybe just a separation," she said. "But legal, so that I don't have to go back to him."

"I wouldn't have thought Armand was the sort of person to force anyone to do anything against his or her will. This isn't the dark ages or even the nineteenth century, *ma petite soeur.*" Zac had spread his arms wide, perhaps hoping to imitate the soaring action of a bird. "You are as free as air."

Claire had explained that she had no money. Or insufficient to make the clean break she wanted.

"In fact," Zac had said, "you want to pay off Armand? Stop him causing trouble?" Claire had said that that was exactly what she meant. A settlement because the Saint-Aignans had married her for her money, and she . . . she never wanted a title, only happiness.

Claire also wanted Zac's help with the family, particularly their mother. Lady Elizabeth, born into the Church of England, had adopted with enthusiasm the Roman Catholic faith and, to her, divorce was and always had been out of the question.

There were many things to think about and Zac, gnawing the corner of a finger, ran over most of them; but, primarily in his mind, was what he could get out of this situation, how he could use it to his advantage and what he could do to turn Claire against Sandra.

He opened a drawer in his desk which he carefully unlocked with a key that he carried on his personal key ring. He extracted a sheet of paper from the drawer and gave Claire a peculiar look before passing it on to her.

As she studied it her expression underwent a slow change; a blush rose from her neck until it touched the roots of her hair.

"Not very nice is it?" Zac said when she'd finished reading, but her eyes still seemed mesmerized by it. "Not a very nice thing to say about your brothers and sister?"

Claire was about to screw the paper into a ball but Zac reached over and sharply took it from her.

"Oh no," he said. "This is a copy, sure, but I don't want people to find it in the wastepaper basket."

"How did you get it?" Claire asked, her pale, tired eyes swimming in tears as she looked at him.

"How do you think?"

"Sandra gave it to you?"

"Of course." Zac nodded vigorously. "Of course she gave it to me. Who else?"

"But why would she do such a thing?"

"Because she wanted to know if it was true. Of course I said it wasn't . . . and it isn't as a matter of fact." Zac gnawed again at the tiny bit of skin on his index finger that appeared to be troubling him. "Tim tried to make a running with Sandra and he got nowhere. Why do you think he has taken himself off to Florida?"

"He genuinely likes her?"

"He genuinely does. Don't ask me why," Zac added offhandedly. "I can't understand it myself. As you know I can't bear the woman, personally. All we, Belle and I, were trying to do at Burg-Farnbach was help him. . . ."

Claire looked confused. "But why did Sandra leave in that case? I don't understand."

Zac hunched his shoulders.

"Maybe there was a little slap and tickle. Who am I to ask?"

"I'm sorry then." Claire lowered her head, biting her lip. "But it was a despicable thing for Sandra to do, show you the letter."

"But she *is* despicable, my dear sister." Zac put the letter back in his drawer, locked it, returned the key ring to his pocket and sat down. "Why has it taken you so long to find that out? Didn't you see the way she behaved over the business of the *cuvée?* She was out to get me the whole time and nearly succeeded."

"I thought it was you. . . ."

"Ah!" Zac thumped the desk and then leaned back in his chair, his expression one of total exasperation. "*You* thought it was me. You were *meant* to think it was me. She was clever. She not only diddled the company out of twenty million . . . she nearly ruined our reputation as well. You see," Zac got up and strolled to the window, looking down, as he often did, at the traffic, the people jostling each other on the pavement—many of them tourists now that spring was here.

"You must realize, my dear, that Sandra is evil. I don't know how, or why, Father did what he did, but I feel he was under some sort of spell. . . ."

"But that's ridiculous." Claire burst out laughing as much with relief as anything else.

"No, I mean it seriously," Zac said. "I have never liked her mother who always seemed to me the reincarnation of a witch and, if you ask me, Sandra, though she in no sense resembles her physically, has something of that in her. Why should small, comparatively unattractive, completely undistinguished Hélène bamboozle our father—one of the most attractive and successful men in France—into making her his mistress when he had a beautiful, talented, distinguished wife of an ancient British line of nobility? Even if he needed a mistress there were far more beautiful women available than Hélène O'Neill. Why? Have you ever asked yourself that?"

Claire shook her head.

"Witchcraft if you ask me," Zac said firmly. "Believe me, it is not dead in France and Hélène is wholly French—Sandra half French. It may also be rife in America. Remember the witches of Salem?"

"But that was centuries ago. . . ."

"Mark my words." Zac held up a hand in warning. "A lot goes on these days that we know nothing about. However, now that I have succeeded, I hope, in opening your eyes to the true nature of Sandra maybe you will be able to help me defeat her."

"How can I do that?" Claire looked at him in surprise.

"If the whole family unites against her we can defeat her. We want to catch her out, destroy her reputation. Now, as a start and to help you get away from your family, you can go to Rome and see Falconetti for me."

"Falconetti?" Claire looked nonplussed.

"Marco, my brother-in-law. I have to send him money—he is always short of cash—and you may as well take it for me. If I send a check the bank immediately gets hold of it and tries to reduce his overdraft. I would like you to deliver it in person and, while you're there, why not take a little holiday as well?"

Zac smiled and seemed by his gesture to indicate that the meeting was at an end.

"But what do I tell Armand?"

"Do you have to tell him anything?"

"As long as he is my husband, yes."

"Then tell him that you're attending to some business for me and, in exchange, I myself will interview that little toad and ask him how much he wants for you to be free of him."

"Oh Zac." Claire leapt out of her chair and, all restraint

gone, leaned over her brother's desk and threw her arms around him.

It was the first time either of them could recall such a thing happening between them.

The embrace over, Zac was telling Claire how he would contact her and book the plane ticket to Rome when the intercom from outside his office buzzed and his secretary spoke into it.

"I'm sorry to interrupt you, Monsieur Desmond, but Monsieur Gomez is here to see you. He says it is very important."

Zac frowned but Claire, looking so happy, appeared scarcely to have heard.

"My sister, Madame de Saint-Aignan, is just about to go," he said. "Please put him in the small waiting-room next to yours. I won't be a moment."

Zac switched off the intercom button with an expression of annoyance. The very last thing he wanted was Gomez and his sister to meet, or for her even to be aware a man with such a name existed.

"This is very inconvenient, Gomez," Zac said a few moments later, closing the door firmly behind him. "I told you not to contact me unless—"

"It *is* important, Monsieur Zac. I have news for you," Gomez said unctuously, twisting the rim of his hat around and around in his hand.

"Then you should have telephoned for an appointment. I don't like to see people like you at my place of work. It's most unwise."

"I'm sorry, Monsieur. I won't do it again."

"You certainly won't or I won't use you," Zac said impatiently. "What is it now?"

"It is about your wife, sir."

"Well." Zac looked at his watch, calculating the time he needed to reach a lunch appointment. "My wife is staying at her sister-in-law's chalet in Gstaad. They are doing the very end of the season. I told you I had no need of your supervisory services just now."

Gomez shook his head, a pleased expression on his face. "I took the liberty of disregarding your advice, Monsieur Desmond, and I hope you will be pleased with me." He paused to catch his breath. "It is true your wife *is* in Switzerland, sir, but not with Principessa Ferrucini. She is with Monsieur Livio in a small *pension* on Lake Lugano. I believe they haven't come out of their chalet for several days, not even to take an airing on the slopes."

With all the agony of a Lear betrayed by his daughters, Zac put his hands to his temple, pressing so hard that the imprint of the soft parts of his thumbs remained visible for some minutes on either side of his head.

Even Gomez felt quite sorry for him.

20

Most of the men around the table were strangers to her except for Philippe de Lassale and Antoine Dericourt, who had come over especially from France for the negotiations. Sandra was the only woman present except for two stenographers who took down every word that was said. Yet she felt completely at home.

The world of aeronautics, defense equipment and the various aspects of advanced radar technology may not have been one with which Sandra was very familiar when she joined the Desmond Group, but one commodity she did know about was money. She had an instinct amounting almost to genius for a good deal and could do lightning sums in her head.

So, while Dericourt, the expert, was expounding to those around the table the virtues of the Desmond-2000 fighter bomber, Sandra was translating the facts into dollars and francs and then into fractions and percentages.

She realized that if they pulled this deal off, beating American, English and other French competitors, it could keep the Desmond works busy for four years and mean profits in the region of two hundred million, all of it underwritten by the Banque Franco-Belges with a consortium of American and Swiss banks.

Dericourt had brought three of his technical experts with him and the American Defense Department had at least six of theirs. The interested Arab state was a friendly power important to the Americans in the Gulf where the deadly war between Iraq and Iran was in progress. A fighter bomber that could swoop on an unsuspecting target almost with the speed of an Exocet missile was a tempting proposition, and Desmond was ahead in the field.

Yet, really, if one thought about the implications one might be tempted to abandon the arms business altogether. It wasn't something she'd chosen; she'd inherited it. She'd much rather be concentrating on champagne, on recouping the losses on the recent *cuvée* and paying attention to the preparation for this year's vintage. She'd much rather be planning with Henri Piper for an increase in allocation of funds to the Foundation . . . and, ironically, it was the sale of these deadly weapons which would help people like Michel Harcourt.

Harcourt . . . she jerked herself upright and realized she was daydreaming. His ideals were fine but what a detestable man he was. It was difficult to reconcile his abrasive personality with the stories she had heard about him; not only his medical skills and humanitarianism, but his flying—he was also a pilot who had introduced the flying doctor concept to remote areas of Africa.

What would Harcourt say now if he heard the plans for selling dive bombers whose only useful function was to kill and destroy?

Prince Abdullah, the chief Arab negotiator, flanked by his assistants, was looking at her with polite interest.

"Have we a deal, Miss Desmond?"

"I should say we have," Sandra said, rapidly turning her mind to the figures on the paper in front of her which she had been extrapolating with the aid of a calculator, even while she had been thinking about champagne and Harcourt.

The Prince got up and, coming around the table, extended his hand.

"You've got a very fine setup here." He turned to Dericourt, who joined them and put a hand on his shoulder. "And your boss is remarkable . . . for a woman."

"Now Your Highness," Sandra said with the chilly smile she kept for putting male chauvinists in their places. "You know we can't allow remarks like that even from someone from your country!"

"And you know that I was only joking. I hope you're going to have dinner with us tonight?"

"I'm looking forward to it."

"And Monsieur de Lassale and Monsieur Dericourt too of course. . . ." The Prince stopped and looked around the table.

"My colleagues will be working on their briefs for tomorrow, thank you very much Your Highness," Sandra said diplomatically. The best business was done when there were few people present.

"That's fine then," the Prince said, bowing and, surrounded by his robed minions, walked solemnly out of the room like a mother duck taking her chicks for a stroll.

"That's *that* then," Sandra echoed with a smile. "Well done, gentlemen."

"And well done to you, Mademoiselle." Philippe de Lassale and the Americans bowed deeply in her direction.

Later at the Hotel Pierre over drinks the three discussed the negotiations; the way they had gone and the prospects for the next day when delivery dates would be examined and, maybe, signatures appended to a draft contract which officials would have been up discussing all night. Sandra liked the Arabs and their style of doing business. The Pentagon officials had been helpful. She felt at home in the American ambience. There were times in France when she could have thrown not only a book at business colleagues but her desk and furniture as well, provoked by an air of chauvinism in French business negotiations that was absent here—despite the remark of

Prince Abdullah. Only, the French these days called it gallantry.

Philippe de Lassale perhaps best represented this type of businessman who seemed to find it very amusing to do hard business with a woman. That was why, maybe, he was giving too much power to Zac. He let Zac deal with many important matters while he concentrated on arms negotiations. Gradually, however, Sandra felt his respect for her was returning after the affair of the yeast that he had put down to her inexperience.

The negotiations in New York had been tough and Sandra had mastered her brief about all the financial details and implications. Philippe now was inclined to listen to her very carefully. In this case it was just as well because he had a great deal of money to find in order to adequately finance the deal.

"You're sure you can do it, Philippe?" Sandra said, their heads bent over the papers on the table in front of them in her suite. "We must be sure before we sign."

"Do what, Sandra?"

"Put the whole financial package together?"

"No doubt at all, providing we have the Americans' signatures. I have at least three Swiss banks, and the possibility of the NATO contract."

"NATO we'll come to later." Sandra looked thoughtful. "Did you mention any of this to Zac Desmond?"

"Well, he knew what I was coming for."

"Don't ever tell him too much about it, will you? It *is* top secret and on *no* account must the possibility of a big sale to NATO be mentioned to him. On that I insist."

"Agreed," Philippe said, freshening his drink.

Sandra gazed at him solemnly for a minute or two and Dericourt reached in his pocket for a handkerchief and blew his nose hard.

"I'm sorry, Antoine." Sandra turned to him. "I know you like Zac Desmond. . . ."

"Whoever said I liked him?" Dericourt finished wiping his nose and tucked his handkerchief back in his pocket. "I thought you did."

"It's not a question of like or dislike," de Lassale said, looking a little uncomfortable, "and, of course, I know this is hush hush. But sometimes I think you have got the wrong side of Zac, Sandra."

"Oh I don't think so at all. . . ." Sandra gave a brittle laugh.

"I don't want to interfere and it's nothing to do with me," de Lassale went on. "But I wouldn't let personal vendettas and personalities come between you and business."

"I certainly don't do that!" Sandra said with indignation. "And I resent the implication that I do."

"I didn't mean it like that for one moment."

"Then what did you mean, Philippe?" Sandra looked at her watch, wondering whether it was time to change for dinner.

"Zac's heart is in the right place . . ." he began lamely.

"Well that's good to know," Sandra said, getting up and straightening the slim leather belt around her dark blue dress. "Sometimes I thought it was in the seat of his pants." Then she rounded on him, a hand on her hip, her blonde hair swaying. "You do remember don't you, Philippe, that not long ago Monsieur Zac Desmond deliberately threw away nearly twenty-five million dollars of the Desmond money. . . ."

"We have no proof . . ." De Lassale spread his hands.

"We *know*. We know Strega would never have worked on his own."

"Well, until we have positive evidence . . ."

"We shall never know for sure," Sandra snapped at him. "In the meantime he is not someone I personally can trust and nor should you. In fact," she put a finger thoughtfully to her chin, "if I were you I'd try and ease him off the Board altogether. I won't stop you."

De Lassale turned away and lit a cigarette, feeling increasingly uneasy. He was already heavily involved in a deal with Zac that Sandra as yet knew nothing about. He'd been reluctant even to start it as it involved Desmond champagne; but Zac had said he knew what he was doing and they all knew how little Sandra knew about champagne. However, it was very unwise to underestimate this woman.

"I must be off to change." Dericourt stood up, placing his empty whisky glass on the table. Then he looked closely at de Lassale, having seen the way he turned to light a cigarette as though trying to hide the expression on his face.

"I agree with Sandra about Zac, Philippe. He is not to be trusted. Sometimes I think he would sell his own mother if he thought he could get a fair price for her."

Even Philippe de Lassale began to join in the laughter when the phone went and Sandra hurried over to it, thinking it might be Bob, who telephoned her every day.

"Hello," she said.

"Sandra." It was Carl's deep, attractive voice, sounding very far away as it crackled over the static.

"Carl! How lovely to hear you—just." Sandra talked loudly, thinking that as she could hardly hear him he must scarcely be able to hear her.

"I can hear you very well, Sandra," Carl called back. "But I'm speaking from my yacht *Rare II.* When are you coming to join us? The weather's lovely."

"You make me want to come at once." Sandra glanced out of the window where snow-laden clouds hung over New York City. "I do believe it's going to snow. But I can't. Too many important deals."

"Oh come on, just for a few days. You did promise."

"I promised to try and get away if I could. Well I can't. . . ."

"Yes you can," Dericourt hissed in her ear. "You know you can. It will take me a week to get everything together."

"We don't need you," Philippe de Lassale pointed to the phone and smiled at her, "and you need a break."

Sandra hesitated, looking at them, her hand over the mouthpiece. Then:

"Carl, Philippe and Antoine are here with me. They say I must go."

"Then come."

"I think I should keep an eye on them."

"Come. They're probably dying to get rid of you."

"I think you're right about that," Sandra said. "I'll call you back."

But there was really no need. It didn't take much to convince her that a few days in the Caribbean was just what she needed and the following morning her private jet was refueled on the tarmac at Kennedy Airport in preparation for her journey.

"It really *is* lovely, Belle," Sandra said, looking around the cabin with its teak furniture, brass fittings and wide panoramic view of the bay in which the *Rare II* was anchored.

"We've given you the best cabin, naturally." Belle ran a hand along the brass rail by the side of the double bed. Presumably in bad weather it was there for someone to hang on to; but on this balmy day anything but bad weather was forecast for the Bahamas, especially Harbour Island, now clearly visible on the port side.

It was a very big yacht. Much bigger than she'd expected. In fact it was huge and she commented on this fact to Belle as she also protested that the best cabin ought not to have been taken away from her host and hostess just for her.

"I'm only here for three days," she said, sitting on the bed and testing it for comfort. Perfect. She sighed deeply.

"I can see you need a rest." Belle looked at her sympathetically. "I guess you've been overdoing it, as usual."

Sandra yawned. "These negotiations take time. They are very complex. I . . ."

Sandra was going to tell her more about them and then she remembered to whom she was speaking. Belle interpreted her sudden silence quite accurately, as it happened, and sat on the bed beside Sandra so that the tips of their fingers nearly touched.

"I *know* how you feel about us, Sandra, and I want to say again that we're sorry. We gave you a bad start and Zac in particular has behaved very badly. The business of the yeast . . ." She shrugged her shoulders. "Who was to know . . . ?"

The moment had, to Sandra, a sense of *déjà vu* and she remembered vividly recalling something very similar as Belle had shown her her room at Burg-Farnbach, again the best in the castle, only three months before. The expression on her face must have betrayed her misgivings because Belle got up and went to the window, leaning on the brass rail, her eyes seemingly fixed on a spot in the far distance.

"You don't *really* trust us, do you, Sandra? You feel that you've heard all this before. . . ."

"As a matter of fact I was just thinking that, to be perfectly honest," Sandra said.

"We *tried* to give you the best time we could at Christmas. We meant what we said; but Tim . . ." She turned to Sandra and looked so miserable that Sandra almost felt tempted to sympathize with her. Almost, not quite. "Tim did behave badly. He's spoiled, you know . . . and Zac, well, Zac had no right to say what he did. I believe Tim wants to make that all right with you now."

Sandra leapt off the bed as though she'd been stung. "Tim! Here?"

"Yes . . ." Belle averted her eyes. "Tim *is* going to be here. He's on his way."

"Then I must go." Sandra suddenly felt furious with them,

with herself, with the whole charade, the long and now wasted journey. "I have *no* intention of sharing another holiday with Tim and being made to look a fool. I can assure you of that!"

"My dear . . ." Belle caught her arm and held on to it. "Please don't react like that. I assure you Tim was originally not one of this party. We had no idea he'd be here. But when he heard you were coming he said he wanted to see you. He's only in Palm Beach."

"Then he can go right back there. I won't see Tim. I refuse. I'm sorry, but I can't. . . ."

"I can well understand how you feel, my dear, and, believe me, as your hostess on that occasion I was deeply hurt and humiliated by what happened. . . ."

"*You* were hurt and humiliated? What about me?"

"Listen to me please." Belle held on to her arm, the pressure of her fingers increasing as if she were trying to imprint the message on Sandra physically as well as emotionally. "It was all a misunderstanding. My brother I believe does care for you. Tim, that is. Zac . . . well I know how you and he feel about each other. I was angry with Zac and, you see, we have taken good care that he does not know you are visiting us now."

"Thank God for that at least."

"Do please stay."

Belle felt Sandra relax and released her arm. Then she went and sat in one of the low, comfortably upholstered wicker chairs, inviting Sandra to do the same.

"I sincerely meant what I said at Burg-Farnbach, but I couldn't be held responsible for the behavior of my brothers. I knew nothing of what had occurred until you left so suddenly. Then I had the whole story out of them and they were left in no uncertain feelings about my displeasure. I tried to see you and apologize to you at that tiresome Board meeting, but I missed you. I had to return to Bavaria, as you know, for the funeral of Carl's uncle. Maybe I should have written. I did want you to know that that is all in the past. We accept you and we admire you . . . we like you and want you to like us."

It sounded so disarming, so sincere. Sandra looked intently at the woman she felt she trusted less than Zac. Yet what could one find beyond that apparent charm except more charm, more sincerity? Belle's beautiful velvet brown eyes positively blazed with it. Sandra wondered if her own paranoic feelings concerning the Desmonds had made her oversuspicious about someone who, after all, to her knowledge had done her no positive wrong.

In an uncanny way Belle seemed able to read her thoughts. Her eyes moved restlessly over Sandra's face as though she were reading from a book. Perhaps she too was searching for reassurance. Belle seemed so anxious to impress her with sincerity, so determined to try and win her friendship.

But could one trust a Desmond?

"I know what you're thinking." Belle broke the silence. "But you can't blame us, can you? You can't really *blame* Zac. . . ."

"What about Zac and the *tirage?*" Sandra hoped to trick Belle into betraying herself by the suddenness of her question.

Belle's expression became more perplexed.

"Oh Zac had *nothing* to do with that," she said, leaning forward. "How could he have? He was completely shocked. If you don't understand how Zac loves champagne you will never begin to understand Zac. He would do nothing to harm it. To him the Desmond reputation is sacred."

"I see," Sandra said quietly. "I still find it very hard to believe that a mere underling could hatch such a complex plot."

"Maybe there was someone behind Strega," Belle said suggestively. "*That* was Zac's opinion and it is something he means to find out."

"Who?"

"I can't tell you whom he suspects . . . oh well I might as well. It might make you trust us more." Belle sat back looking thoughtful. She had on tight-fitting blue shorts, a navy nautical top and a navy bandeau around her head. Her healthy suntanned face wore only lipstick, the color that was once known as a bright, Schiaparelli shocking pink. She looked vibrant, and very beautiful. Her long brown legs were bare, her feet with their painted toenails, encased in espadrilles.

"You've heard of the Tellier brothers," Belle said, with a conspiratorial air. "Luc and Rudy."

"I know the name *Tellier* but not the brothers. They are part of the same Group that owns the Banque Franco-Belges."

"Exactly. Well, there's not a very happy relationship between Desmond and Tellier. You see, as families, we were old friends and Luc and Zac were at school together. We were, how shall I put it without sounding boastful?" Belle studied the ceiling which had a bluish tint as though from the reflection of the water. "We were slightly better than the Tellier family. We were richer; we had a bigger house and our family brand of champagne was much better known. Theirs wasn't even considered among the *Grandes marques* like Desmond, Piper-Heidsieck or Krug. There was always a little envy among the Telliers, if you know what I mean, and they were anxious for their sister Marie to marry Zac. Frankly they were after our money and prestige. Zac, however, wasn't interested in Marie: she was pretty but nothing much else—he hadn't met Tara then, but he knew what he wanted—and the Telliers were affronted by it. From that day on they had it in for us, especially Zac."

"This is beginning to sound like an interesting story," Sandra said.

"Well it isn't. It stops there really." Belle stretched her arms above her head. "The Telliers were taken over by the Heurtey Group of America and Luc and Rudy are still there, paid executives. However, they haven't done too badly with all that money behind them, frankly; but they have always had their eyes on Desmond. . . ."

"You think *they* put Strega up to it?" Sandra said incredulously. "That sounds a tall story."

"Not really." Belle replied with a deceptive air of nonchalance. "Strega, don't forget, worked at our bank. The Tellier headquarters are close by. Zac thinks, and I agree, that it was a plot by the Telliers and as soon as he has evidence of this he will put it before Philippe de Lassale." Belle paused and her lip curled. "De Lassale is a bit of a fool, you know. He doesn't see things that are going on under his nose."

Sandra sighed but said nothing. In many ways she was beginning to agree with Belle. She had misjudged de Lassale and was beginning to realize it.

"As for my brother, Tim." Belle looked at her watch. "He will tell you in his own time. It was not as you think at Burg-Farnbach. He wants to make amends. We all do. Please."

Sandra shrugged her shoulders and held out both hands.

"What can I say?" she said. "Do you think *I* don't want to be friends too?"

Impulsively Belle got up and, leaning over Sandra, kissed her on the cheek, her arms around her shoulders.

Momentarily, but only momentarily, Sandra was reminded of the coil of a snake, and the sharp forked tongue of the viper as Belle's lips brushed her skin.

Tim was in the dining room alone as Sandra entered. She knew she had dressed especially for Tim and the look of admiration on his face as he turned to her was her reward. In his white tropical dinner jacket he looked almost too handsome, his face deeply bronzed by the sun. His thick brown hair was several tones lighter than it had been three months before.

"Oh," Sandra said, wishing she had known he was there.

"Don't go. . . ." Tim said, coming toward her. "Please don't go, Sandra." He stood in front of her, looking straight into her eyes.

"I do know how you feel; but it's nothing to how *I* felt. I felt very badly too."

"I should think you did," Sandra said, her anger suddenly rising again at the thought of that humiliating night in Bavaria.

"But it wasn't as you thought," Tim went on. "It wasn't at all as you thought. . . ."

"Then I'd be quite interested in your explanation." Sandra began to feel more relaxed and, moving away from him, started to examine the comfortable room with its long teak table, leather-covered chairs and a deep leather sofa with a view of the bay. It was a semiformal but pleasant room with brass sconces on the wall and a bar at one end with high stools. Sandra selected one facing a mirror in which she could see Tim and the admiration on his face. She knew that, in her casual white cotton dress with its low neckline she looked her best. Her long blonde hair swung over her face and she wore white thonged sandals on her feet.

"You do look incredibly lovely," Tim whispered, climbing onto a bar stool beside her. Cooling in an ice bucket in front of them was a bottle of vintage Desmond rosé champagne, which he removed and started to uncork.

"I didn't come here to hear flattery but the facts, Mr. Desmond Junior." Sandra gave him the briefest of smiles. "In fact had I known you were coming I shouldn't be here at all. I expect you understand that."

"Oh I do," Tim said, carefully prising the cork from the bottle.

His knees were almost touching hers. She knew then that, despite everything, she still desired him; even his proximity was unsettling and she was aware of the flush that slowly traveled from her neck and over her face. She earnestly hoped that the low lighting in the room helped to conceal it.

"There was no question of my sleeping with Corinne that

night," Tim said earnestly. "I had to take a call from America as it was only six o'clock in the evening in New York."

"But couldn't you have told me that? If true?"

"It was true," Tim protested. "I thought it was too unimportant and that I would explain when I got back. As it was the call took so long that when I was going back to your room I saw Zac. In fact he seemed to be waiting for me. I was about to pass him but he stopped me. He said you'd come out of your room and told him you wanted to go to sleep as you were leaving the next day. You sent your apologies. Naturally *I* felt a bit surprised."

"You felt surprised?" Sandra exploded. "But how, knowing your brother, could you possibly believe a story like that? Do you honestly imagine I would have told Zac, of all people, I was waiting for you? I'd even denied you were with me."

Tim frowned.

"The whole thing was a bungle. It sounds implausible when you say it now; but then I believed it. I truly did. In fact . . . I told him I'd see for myself, but he told me not to be such a fool. Why throw myself on you if you didn't want me? Anyway he said you'd locked your door.

"I felt extremely angry with you because I thought after all you'd pretended to want me so that you could make a fool of me, to get your own back."

"But I felt *exactly* the same about you," Sandra said. "Zac told me that you were with Corinne."

"That was an awful thing to say and completely untrue. Zac is malicious, you know that. There is no doubt of that. He has also always been jealous of me." Tim lowered his eyes. "My so-called success with women. I was so humiliated that I left Europe. . . ."

"Didn't you think to come after me and explain . . . if true?" The doubt in Sandra's mind was reflected in her voice.

"It *is* true, Sandra. I do wish you'd believe me. I didn't learn the truth for some time until Belle wormed it out of Zac and then told me. She also told me that Carl had invited you to the yacht and you said you'd come. Belle really has tried to help to make it up between us. She's played the good fairy."

Sandra looked over her shoulder across the bay toward the distant outline of the island with its tiny pinpoints of lights.

"I *would* like to believe she was a good fairy," she murmured. "I really would."

But that night she slept alone. He didn't offer to come to her and she didn't ask him. It really was as though the family were doing all in their power to prove that they were not what she thought, and that here in this peaceful, incredibly beautiful environment she wanted to believe it.

Sandra woke the next morning and lay for some time in bed, aware of the cool linen sheets next to her skin. She reminded herself that she had a reputation for being astute, perceptive, not letting her heart rule her head.

She must be very careful not to part from that image now; not to be seduced not only by the beauty of the islands, the sound of the calm sea lapping against the sides of the yacht riding majestically in the bay, but by that obvious master of seduction: Timothée Desmond.

When she got up and went on deck in her bathing suit Tim, Carl and Belle were already in the water and hailed her. Between them they had a huge ball and, from a dinghy anchored by the side of the ship, a sailor watched over them in case anything should happen.

Sandra sat on the edge of the yacht dangling her legs over the side. She was anxious to dive in and yet . . .

"Come on," Tim said, "Bet you can't swim."

"Can't *swim?"* Sandra shouted back indignantly. She stood up and flexed her body while pointing her hands above her head in the diving position. "I was nearly junior champion of California."

"Show us then!" Belle called and Sandra, bracing herself,

lowered her arms until the top of her head was just between them and dived expertly, slicing the water neatly in two.

For a moment she continued her dive and then she came out of it and struck out for the surface where the laughing faces of the three greeted her, clapping their hands above their heads in acclamation.

"Race you out to sea," Tim cried and, together, they struck out using the crawl until the boat was some distance behind them. Then they turned around and lolled on their backs treading water. Sandra, gazing at the sky, aware of the salt on her lips, felt that she had never been so free, so deliciously happy . . . so like a woman in love.

Belle said after breakfast, "Carl and I have chores to do on the island. We might be buying some property there. Would you like to come?"

"I had other plans," Tim said, passing Sandra a basket containing warm, freshly baked rolls. "I thought Sandra and I would go water-skiing, but if you need the boat—"

"We can send it back," Belle said. "Then we can ask Wesley to pick us up at a prearranged time."

"Wesley's a new member of the crew," Carl explained. "He's from Trinidad and seems quite good. The other West Indians are part of our regular crew."

"Where did you get him?" Tim inquired, thickly buttering his bread.

"Oh through an agency I suppose." Belle, deliberately vague, was consulting a list in her hand. She wore a pretty floral-patterned dress with a broderie-anglaise top which contrasted beautifully with her bronzed skin.

"He's a useful man," Carl said. "I need him to drive the motor boat."

"The yacht's much bigger than I thought it would be," Sandra said and Carl, as if sensing criticism, replied:

"And much bigger than we needed. But we charter it for

most of the year. It has all the latest electronic gadgets. I'll show you around later on."

"It has paid for itself," Belle said, "rented by wealthy Americans, like you."

Tim flushed and looked annoyed, but Sandra pretended to regard it as a compliment.

"I shall have to empty the piggy bank when I get home. Meanwhile," she glanced at Tim, "I like to think I'm family."

"Which you *are,"* Carl said emphatically. "Belle was just teasing . . . weren't you, darling?"

"Of course." Belle reached over and touched Sandra's hand. "Which my sister knows quite well."

"Sister?" Sandra could hardly believe her ears. It all seemed too good to be true, this harmony. Tim smiled with relief.

"Excellent idea about using your boat for water-skiing, Carl."

"That's fine, then," Carl said, looking pleased too. He was clearly in his element. The previous night he had warmly welcomed Sandra and she immediately felt at home with this amiable, genial host of whom, unlike the Desmonds, she felt no apprehension at all.

After breakfast Carl and Belle clambered into the speedboat which Wesley had skillfully brought alongside the yacht, promising to be back in an hour.

"Ever been water-skiing?" Tim said in an aside to Sandra as they watched the motorboat head for the harbor.

"Of course," Sandra said laughingly.

"Junior champion of California no doubt?"

"Not quite." Sandra stood on tiptoe and stretched her arms as far above her head as they could go.

"I think I'm going to love this holiday," she said as Tim put his arm around her waist and this time she didn't try to remove his hand.

* * *

The motorboat carefully approached the jetty and a willing hand leaned down to take the painter while another reached out to help Belle. Carl turned to wait for her but she said to him:

"You go ahead, darling. I just want to give some instructions to Wesley."

Carl frowned. "What kind of instructions?"

"I want to tell him what to do and when to pick us up. You know. I won't be a minute." She threw up at him a wicker basket she'd held over her arm, for all the world like a simple, ordinary housewife, her thick hair bound by a brightly colored scarf tied under her chin, a pair of large dark glasses on her nose.

"You could tick off the things on my shopping list, darling." She pointed to some stalls that stood by the water's edge. "See if you can get some lobster for dinner tonight."

"Right." Carl leaned down for the basket and nodded to the new member of the crew who, together with Belle, stood watching him amble over to the stalls laden with fish where he was immediately surrounded by a pack of interested, indigenous spectators.

"Now," Belle said briskly, turning to Wesley who was beginning to unfasten the painter and addressing him in a low voice: "You have your instructions?"

"Yes ma'am," Wesley said without looking at her.

"You must be very careful my brother is in the boat with you. We don't want anything to happen to him."

Wesley looked at her with an expression Belle immediately found insolent.

"I know what I'm doing, ma'am. Mr. Strega gave me full instructions."

"See that you pay attention to them then," Belle said sharply, waving to Carl who was looking interrogatively into the well of the boat holding a large lobster above his head.

"I'm coming," she called. "That looks wonderful. Get two."

"I like lobster too," the new member of the crew said.

"You're not paid to eat lobster," Belle said sharply. "You can buy it from the profits you make if you do your job well. . . ."

Wesley gave her that insolent look again as he helped her clamber onto the wooden jetty and she walked toward Carl. A sense of disquiet gnawed away at her, rather as it did the day she and Zac watched the distance between the yacht and Piero Borghi increasing and wondering if anyone would ever find them out.

FOUR

The Sands of Time

21

Tim drank the last of his wine and stretched himself out on the sand, letting it run between his fingers.

"This is bliss," he said. "Why don't we stay here always?"

Sandra, resting her head on her knees, glanced at him sideways. "Why don't we?"

"Are you serious?"

"Quite. Are you?"

Tim laughed. "I am *very* serious."

"Perhaps it's a little plot to get me to relinquish my interest in Desmond." Sandra's eyes were still on him. Though they gleamed with amusement, she was partly serious. Deep down she felt she could never be sure; that she was always on the lookout for clues, various signs that would indicate to her which way the wind blew. In a way, it was a kind of paranoia the Desmonds had managed to inflict on her.

Tim put up a hand and reached for hers. "You'll never believe us, will you? Never trust us?"

"It *is* hard."

"It's only because of Zac and he's not here."

Sandra sat up straight and shook her hair which hung shoulder length.

"It's not really just that. I wish it were. It's always with you Desmonds that things never seem what they are."

"How do you mean?"

"I don't really trust Belle either. I'd like to, but . . ."

"And me?"

"Well." She pressed her head between her knees again. "I really would like to trust you."

"Look, you can . . ." Tim leaned over on his stomach and as he gazed at her the grains of sand fell between his fingers as through an hourglass. Sandra watched them wishing she could hold this moment in her heart forever: the tiny cove they'd found at a part of the island which could only be approached by the sea; the gentle breeze that tempered the fierce heat of the sun which would otherwise have burned them; the motorboat lying at anchor some way ahead of them with Wesley's head bent over the controls . . . and Tim.

She and Tim alone.

"For all I know you could all be plotting against me," Sandra said abruptly. "Even you . . ."

"Never me. You must believe that. Once upon a time maybe, I didn't like you. I sided with the family. I didn't want the business but I didn't see why you should have it. But I'm not Zac."

"Maybe a love affair with me would suit you," Sandra said jokingly. "It could be part of the plot."

Tim sat up abruptly and threw a handful of sand over her knees.

"What a nasty thing to say, Sandra!" He jumped up and dusted the sand angrily from his trunks. Looking at him, she wondered why she said things like that when he attracted her. Why did she want to deprive herself of even a little happiness with Tim?

"I'm sorry," she said immediately. "It was childish."

"Besides it's not true." Tim was calmer too. "If I want you it's for what you are, nothing else."

"That's good." Sandra held out her hand. "So we can just be good friends. . . ."

Tim pulled her to her feet and kissed her. It was a long, passionate kiss that reminded her of the night she had first desired him. She desired him more than ever. His body trembled against hers and she knew he felt the same.

"Damn," he said, looking toward Wesley. "I wish he'd go away. He's messing around with that boat. We should never have brought him."

"We were *meant* to go water-skiing. . . ."

Reluctantly she looked at Tim and he smiled, as excited as she was by the prospect of intimacy.

"We could go back to the boat. . . ."

"It *does* seem a shame, now we're here, not to go water-skiing . . . and then we can maybe pack him off and have a sleep here."

"What a *brilliant* idea." Tim held her hand tightly. "Two minds with but a single thought. I say, Wesley—" He put his hand to his mouth and hailed the West Indian who acknowledged him with a wave.

Then he finished what he was doing, ducked into the cockpit and carefully drove toward them.

The bay was perfect for water-skiing. As they crossed it they met other couples indulging in the same sport and cheerful waves were exchanged as the motorboats ploughed across the bay. Wesley drove carefully and well, quite undecided as to what action he should take. He was not a killer and, as far as his brief had been concerned, he thought he was never engaged to be one. But he was a man with few scruples who loved money, and now he knew he would do almost anything for it. However, he felt a little nervous as Tim and Sandra climbed onto their skis.

Behind the wheel he began to hum the song "Island in the Sun" and as they shouted "Ready" he looked behind them and gently eased his boat into the bay. Very gently. Nothing must go wrong: just yet.

Sandra was an excellent skier, but Tim frequently lost his

balance and found himself floundering in the water while, laughingly, she sped on as they circled around to collect him.

"I bet you *were* junior champion of California," he said at last, clambering ruefully back into the boat. "You're better than me. I think I'll have a rest."

Next to him Wesley felt a spasm of fear and licked his lips.

"Shall we go back to the shore, sir, or the yacht?"

"Miss Desmond wants to practice the slalom, Wesley," Tim said, settling back beside him. "I'm here for the ride."

Sandra called out that she was ready and Wesley set off again, this time pressing hard on the accelerator. Tim turned and watched her admiringly as they went around the bay, faster and faster. Her poise was magnificent, her balance superb, she was perfectly controlled. They could go on like this all day. She waved to him and he waved back. She started to perform tricks, lifting one leg in the air, then a leg and an arm and finally, like this, she tried to slalom across the waves created by the boat, lost her balance and fell with a shriek of laughter into the water.

Tim laughed too but watched anxiously for a moment until she bobbed up again, still laughing.

"I think I've had enough," she called. "Better come and get me."

"Let's pick her up," Tim said, his eyes on Sandra, and slowly Wesley approached the figure in the water, stopping a few yards from her head.

"You're a bit near," Tim said, looking critically at the driver. "Reverse."

He didn't see the white fear in Wesley's eyes as, putting the gear lever into "reverse" he pressed the accelerator and shot forward in the direction of Sandra, who was wrestling with her skis.

"Go back you *fool,*" Tim cried but Wesley—as genuinely afraid now as Tim—appeared to wrestle desperately with the gear while, ahead, Sandra gazed at them like a mesmerized rabbit.

Without a second's hesitation Tim dived into the water and struck out strongly toward her and Wesley, the nightmare getting worse, quickly spun thc wheel to the right, missing both of them by inches but catching one of Sandra's skis which struck her in the face, causing her to submerge again.

This time, however, Tim had his arms around her and, strong swimmer that he was, went into the lifesaving routine, keeping her head above water, while boats in the bay, whose crews had seen the accident, began to come toward them.

Wesley, however, who knew quite well that his boat would only go forward and not into reverse, drew slowly up alongside them and reached out for the half-conscious woman as Tim held her afloat.

His anxiety was acute enough now to show real fear: there was no need for pretense. Dreams of a king's ransom vanished as, his own safety in jeopardy now, Wesley pulled her aboard.

Belle, perched on the high stool at the counter of the dockside bar in Harbour Island, looked nervously about her. It was not the sort of place in which she would like to be seen or should be seen and, even though it was after dark, large beads of perspiration stood out on her forehead.

"You really blew it, Strega," she hissed at the man across the table. "That Wesley was a *fool.* It was only because Sandra didn't want publicity that my husband was dissuaded from bringing charges."

"There's nothing they could charge him *with,*" Strega said calmly, though he felt uncomfortable beneath the Princess's gaze. "He is a first-class mechanic and easily reversed what hc had done to the gears before anyone could suspect him. No one could prove that it was anything but an accident."

"But I could and I *know,*" Belle said sharply. "My brother will not be pleased when he hears about this."

Strega swallowed and sipped his beer. The Princess always made him nervous; if anything he thought her worse than her brother. Between him and Belle von Burg-Farnbach there was a state of fixed hostility as though he never quite came up to scratch.

She rounded on him harshly after the bungling of the *tirage*—though God knows he was innocent enough—and now this.

"Anyway." He put his glass carefully on the table. "I came here to take photographs that would compromise Miss O'Neill, not to kill her. Your brother might not like *that* very much when he hears it."

It was only the fact that they were in a public place that prevented Belle from hitting him in the face. He was a man she had never liked, never trusted, despite all Zac had on him, and she felt even more strongly that way now.

"My brother will approve *everything* I do, do you hear?" she said, craning her neck.

"How is Miss Desmond, anyway?"

"O'Neill you mean," Belle said furiously. "Kindly never refer to her as 'Desmond' in front of me or anyone. For Desmond she decidedly is not. Anyway she's fine, thanks to you. She had concussion, a slight bruise but, being as hard as steel, she's otherwise OK."

"Wesley wants his money." Strega licked his lips again. "Two thousand pounds sterling was the deal."

"Deal?" Belle cried. "A deal *if* he was successful. . . ."

"He still wants his money. I promised it to him because he took a risk. He said if he doesn't get it he will go to the police. . . ."

"And who would believe *him* . . ." Belle began disparagingly.

"Still it wouldn't be nice, Madame." Nervously Strega lit a cigarette. "I might get it reduced to 1500 pounds."

"I suppose that includes your cut. . . ."

"I must have the money, Madame." There was a doggedness about Strega that was one of his qualities, a quality appreciated best by Zac. "I dare not see Wesley again without it. He mightn't be quite as delicate as we are in Europe. Besides he's no killer. He said he nearly killed two people not one when Mr. Tim unexpectedly dived into the sea. He said it affected his nerves badly."

"His *nerves!*" Belle said derisively. "I didn't know he had any." Then she thought swiftly and, opening her Gucci bag, took a wad of notes from an inside pocket and handed them to Strega.

"A thousand," she said firmly, "and no more. A thousand pounds wasted. You can give him that *without* your cut and if I so much as hear his name again—" she pointed a finger at Strega—"I'll get you, Strega. Don't forget what *we* know about you. If Wesley's not a killer you most certainly are and if you're not careful one day I'll tell."

Belle snapped the clasp of her bag and, rising, gazed contemptuously at him.

"What's more you'd better go straight back to Paris—let me do the photography. You'd probably fall off the cliff and I don't want any more 'accidents.' "

Then with a gesture of contempt she turned her back on him and swiftly left the bar, one or two faces turned curiously toward her.

Strega watched her departure before carefully counting the notes. Then he placed £500 in one pocket and £500 in another, smiling as he did so.

People in these parts didn't know the value of money and, as for the Princess . . . he looked craftily in the direction she'd taken and muttered a curse. If she knew something about him he knew plenty about her. The trouble was, there was no proof: yet.

* * *

Sandra and Tim lay on the beach, bodies close together. It was too public a place to make love but, surreptitiously, they had kissed and they knew that they would that night.

Sandra lay on her back, Tim on his stomach, letting the white sand run through his fingers. They looked steadily into each other's eyes seeing there that promise of fulfillment they each knew now was inevitable.

Tenderly his finger reached for the bruise on her forehead, the plaster that covered the wound just by her hairline, and he brushed it gently.

"You're *much* better today," he said.

"Much much better. Thanks to you. . . ."

Gently Tim kissed her lips, feeling the tremor that ran through her body. "Carl simply can't understand what happened to the boat. It goes perfectly into reverse now."

"It doesn't matter. I never liked that man Wesley much anyway. Somehow he didn't look like a sailor."

"Someone they picked up in the harbor looking for work." Tim shook his head. "I'm sure it was an accident, but he panicked. Can't have panicky people in charge of boats. The main thing is, I've got you and having got you I'm going to keep you," and then very gently his lips pressed down on hers for a long, long time.

Later that night Tim said, "I want to live with you."

Sandra whispered back, "You know that's impossible."

"Why?"

"Is that part of the Desmond plot?"

He tapped her on the bare behind and then let his palm linger and caress her buttocks.

"You know, if you talk about a Desmond plot in connection with the two of us I will smack you," Tim whispered. "It is quite cruel to taunt me like this as if you still didn't trust me."

"There is a sense," she murmured, reaching for him, "that I can never trust you."

But Tim appeared not to hear, or not to want to hear. He put his hands over her ears and drew her face to his, and finally she knew that the moment that had so many false starts had come.

Relax and enjoy, she told herself, trying not to think it was a Desmond, Zac and Belle's brother, who slowly possessed her, bringing at last to fruition all the false attempts they'd had before.

Somehow, inevitably, it was meant.

"*If* we go around the world," Tim said as they lay together afterward, "we can forget everything. . . . You don't *really* want to run Desmond."

"I do."

His body slid finally, reluctantly, off hers and he lay beside her staring into her eyes.

"You really *do,* don't you?"

"Yes and I'm doing it well."

Tim sat up but she grasped him by his head.

"That doesn't mean I can't love you too. I don't go to bed with Desmond, only 'a' Desmond."

"That's a very good pun," Tim said, "as long as you don't go to bed with any other Desmond."

"I swear never to do that," Sandra said, drawing him tightly to herself again.

As the sun slowly crept over the horizon Belle shivered and went back to her own cabin along the deck, next to the one where Sandra and Tim had spent the night. She gazed for a moment at their closed door with an expression of satisfaction on her face and then pushed open the door of the one she shared with Carl. She herself had also had a sleepless night.

Carl turned in his bed as she came in and said drowsily: "Where have you been?"

"Taking a stroll on deck. I couldn't sleep."

"You're very edgy this holiday." Carl settled back, his head on his arms. "I think something's wrong."

"Wrong?" Belle said nervously, going to the window and staring across the bay to where she could see activity in the little port as it began to come to life. "Whatever could be wrong?"

"I don't know. Ever since Sandra came into your life something's been the matter."

"Well can you blame me?" Belle spun around and gazed at him. "Stealing our birthright. . . ."

"Oh come!" Carl tried to sound reasonable. "She didn't *steal* anything. I don't think it would have made much difference if she took over or Zac. . . ."

"Of course it makes a *difference!"* Belle stamped her foot. "Even *you* can see that, Carl. . . ."

"What do you mean, even me . . . ?"

"Well . . ." Belle left the window and wandered over to the bed. "You don't *really* know much about what goes on outside your little world, *mon petit lapin."* Suddenly she leaned over and began to kiss his brow. "And *that's* what I like about you. You're one of the sanest, nicest people I know. . . . You are even nice to Sandra."

"Actually I quite like her." Carl tentatively put his arms around the slender body of his wife. They didn't make love often but when they did it was good, like an unexpected gift for which the recipient was grateful. They hadn't made love all this vacation and he wanted her.

But Carl never had the initiative with Belle—what she wanted she got. She was not a giver and if she wanted sex she got it; but she never thought about what Carl wanted in the times between.

However, he loved her. She was a mysterious woman and

part of the reason he loved her was because he didn't feel he really knew her. It was like being married to someone who was a permanent stranger. Beloved stranger.

He held up his arms to embrace her and, momentarily, he thought she responded. He wanted her, but he was concerned about her. Always figure-conscious, she had become almost gaunt.

He knew that she was obsessed about Sandra, who preyed on her mind. Why? That worried him too and the accident to Sandra worried him a lot more . . . as though it was an omen that boded ill for the future.

Hopefully he held on to Belle and she seemed undecided as to whether to respond to him or not. Suddenly she straightened up and he knew that her mind was not on love. Without another word she went into the bathroom and began to shower.

That day was the last that Sandra would remember with pure happiness for some time to come. There are few periods in life when days such as this occur. For lucky people they may come often or last longer; for a few there are seldom any. And Sandra certainly hadn't had many during her time as the Head of the Desmond Group.

Neither had she had such satisfaction from a man, not even Claudio Menendez, and when she and Tim joined Belle and Carl on the deck at about eleven it showed. They came out of the cabin holding hands and there was a glow, an aura that made that most practical and realistic of women, the Princess von Burg-Farnbach, experience a moment of primitive jealousy.

However, as is usually the case, everyone pretended that nothing untoward had happened and Belle suggested a picnic on a nearby island.

"It's practically uninhabited," she said, pointing in a direction away from Harbour Island. "After that we could have some water-skiing, oh," she clasped her hand to her mouth and looked at Sandra. "Sorry, maybe you don't fancy—"

"I didn't suffer anything water-skiing." Sandra's voice was light with happiness. "It was when I wasn't water-skiing."

"Anyway he's gone," Belle announced. "And that's that." There was a note of finality in her voice that made Sandra glance at her.

"I'll go and arrange for the picnic," Belle said and, getting to her feet, disappeared for a time. When she returned to lie on the deck beside Tim, Sandra rose, stood on the edge of the yacht, put out her arms and dived in, to the admiration of Tim, who sat up to watch her, unable to take his eyes from her long, lissome body.

As she surfaced she called out and waved.

"Come on in, the water's lovely."

"I will in a minute," Tim said and then he stretched out on deck beside Belle, his arms linked behind his head. "I am falling in love."

"Don't be absurd," Belle grunted as she began to smooth oil gently on the area of her body not covered by a skimpy bikini.

"No, I'm serious."

Belle stopped oiling herself and peered at him over the rim of her sunglasses.

"You'd better not be."

"How do you mean? How can you control love? She's simply fantastic. We made love all night. I don't think we had more than an hour's sleep."

"And it shows," Belle said as if she disapproved.

"We can rest this afternoon," Tim murmured. "I feel like a million dollars."

"Zac will be absolutely furious if this is true. . . ."

"It *is* true. I don't care what Zac says." He pointed a finger to his chest. "I, Tim Desmond, the most selfish, self-centered man on earth who has used many women, treated most abominably, do solemnly swear that I am losing my heart to Sandra O'Neill Desmond, my adopted sister. . . ."

"Your *half-sister* probably," Belle said wryly.

Tim sat up and stared at her.

"What do you mean?"

"You know what I mean."

"I most certainly don't."

"Forget it then."

"How can I forget something like that? Are you serious?"

"Oh put it out of your mind." Smilingly Belle waved in the direction of Sandra. "Go and enjoy yourself with your mistress . . . while you can."

An hour later they all set off in the motorboat driven by an Antiguan, with another member of the crew to carry the hampers and picnic baskets.

Sandra could see that Tim was preoccupied and she asked him what was the matter; but he said nothing.

"You're a moody man." Sandra tenderly touched his nose. "I can see that. Can we really have an affair that will last forever and ever?"

But Tim, to Sandra's consternation, did not answer.

Belle went swimming in the bay of the tiny cove they'd found and Carl snorkled deep underwater. Later the Antiguan cooked them a splendid lunch on a cleverly improvised barbecue, and then he too began to fish while the other crew member slept in the sun by the boat drawn up on the beach.

Tim and Sandra lay side by side in the shadow of a rock, their toes touching.

"I'll tell you what I'm moody about," Tim said suddenly. "It's something Belle said this morning. You should know. . . ."

"What's that?" Sandra put her head closer to his. He could see right down the top of her bikini bra to her nipples which not so long ago he had sucked and caressed until they were a deep cherry red. The blood throbbed in his head. Even if she were his half sister he could never ever lose her. He would say nothing.

"Belle said that you were going soon," Tim said on the spur of the moment. "I meant what *I* said about us going around the world."

"Not just yet." Sandra's eyes narrowed. Something about him made her feel he was sidetracking. "Come on, what is it? I want the truth. Why are you moody. It's not just about me going."

"You *do* know me, don't you?" Tim lay on his back and reached for her hand. "Are you sure that my father wasn't yours as well?"

For a moment Sandra stared at him, then she threw her head back and the laughter which seemed to come from deep inside her filled him with joy.

"Belle has been trying to frighten you again, hasn't she?"

"Well . . ."

"You know." Sandra lifted her head to make sure that Belle was still swimming around the bay. "Sometimes I think that sister of yours is pure mischief."

"Sometimes I do too." Tim nodded his head. "Is she this time?"

"Yes. She can't help intriguing. Your mother asked me the same thing. Georges Desmond was *not* my father. He couldn't be. He hadn't met my mother when I was born."

"Are you quite sure?"

"Yes."

"Did you ask her?"

Suddenly Sandra paused and realized that no, she had never actually asked her mother, for sure.

"Maybe they met before you knew it."

"I'm positive they didn't." Sandra turned on her side and faced him. Her breasts had nearly fallen out of their flimsy hold and he wanted to take her in his arms and crush her. "I am definitely *not* your sister," she said.

But, as he slipped his hand inside her bra and his mouth came down on hers she knew that now she would *have* to see Hélène and ask her, just to be sure.

Belle saw the couple behind the rock as she came out of the water and wished she'd had a camera. Tim was practically on top of Sandra, who looked as though she had removed her bikini trunks. Belle could hardly believe her luck. Completely unobserved by the people totally engrossed in each other she continued up the beach and stealthily retrieved her camera from her beach bag where she had it ever at the ready.

Chances had been few. In public, at least, the couple had hitherto behaved with complete decorum.

Belle was not an expert photographer but she was skilled. She had taken an interest in photography from quite a young age and especially liked pursuing her hobby in Bavaria among the high Alps.

Her fingers suddenly clumsy with nerves, she fitted her zoom lens to her Olympus, angling it on the amorous couple. Click . . . click . . . a few more just to be sure. She sat back and regarded them objectively; no one for a moment would think they were completely naked, but that small matter could soon be attended to in a skilled technician's darkroom. The main thing was to get the faces clear: Sandra . . . her fingers rapidly brought her face into close focus. Then Tim; poor Tim. She smiled wryly. But Tim wouldn't mind . . . not much.

Belle was not a *voyeuse* and, after a while, she removed the zoom and put her camera back into its bag. Done. The evidence. Stage two, or was it stage three?

Looking around, she saw that the beach was empty. The Antiguan had disappeared and the other crew member slumbered deeply in the shadow on the far side of the boat pulled up on the sand.

She undid the top of her bikini and slowly began to massage her breasts with oil, gently and tenderly, as though she were making love to herself.

They were all sitting around the dining table having eaten yet another meal. Sandra was laughing and pointing to her stomach, as if it were the size of a beach ball. There was a sudden rap on the door and the captain put his head around.

"There is an urgent message for Mademoiselle Desmond," he said. "Shore to ship. From France."

"Tell them to call tomorrow," Tim said langorously. "Or, better still, the day after. Miss Desmond is not at home."

"I'd better go," Sandra said, reluctantly getting up. "I asked them not to ring unless it was something urgent."

With a sense of foreboding she followed the captain into the wireless room, which was full of the most advanced and up-to-date kind of electronic gadgetry.

He handed her the cellular telephone, which she put to her ear and immediately recognized Bob's voice.

"Bob," she cried with joy, relieved that it was not the office. "This *is* a pleasure. How're things?"

"Sandra." Bob's voice sounded strained even from a distance. "I'm afraid there's awful bad news about Mother. She's dying. Do you think you could possibly come at once?"

22

The white face on the white pillow already looked like that of a corpse. There were tubes and supports of various kinds connected to and leading from her body. By the side was a machine monitoring her heart.

For a second it reminded Sandra of the first time she had seen Bob not so long ago in the hospital in Los Angeles and she groped behind her for his hand. He squeezed it hard and murmured in her ear:

"She doesn't look it, but she really is much better."

Sandra peeled off her gloves, removed her coat and put it over a chair. Then she perched on the edge of it and gazed at the face of that person it was very hard to feel affection for. Hélène O'Neill was someone she had seldom felt close to even when she was small. It was an indifference that was very hard to discard even now, when she could die at any moment from the stroke she'd suffered three days before.

"Trust you," Sandra thought, "to take me away from happiness." But then she banished it at once, glad that such an unworthy thought could not be read or interpreted by Bob, who clearly felt very differently. He'd met Sandra at the airport and had filled her in on his relations with their mother before her stroke. Bob clearly still felt a lot for her; loved her. She, Sandra O'Neill Desmond, certainly didn't. It was useless, and equally unworthy, to pretend.

Restlessly she got up from the chair and went to examine

some of the equipment in the room, one of the best at the American Hospital at Neuilly. She prowled around like someone inspecting a machine room rather than a sick room. She felt as detached and unemotional about the machines as she did about Hélène.

"She looks awfully sick to me," she said after a while, pausing to look at Bob, and letting her hand run down his cheek.

"But better than she was. She's just sleeping now. I don't think the doctors actually want her to see you if she wakes up. It might be too much of a shock."

"For me too," Sandra thought, again with a feeling of shame. She took up her coat and put it over her arm.

"I'll come back when they say I can," she said. "Anyway I'm here now."

"I'm glad to have you, Sis." Bob trustfully put his hand in hers. "I've missed you."

Lady Elizabeth greeted Sandra as Pierre showed her into the small sitting room, rising to shake her hand. Then, to Sandra's surprise, she warmly hugged Bob.

"I'm sorry about your mother, Sandra." Lady Elizabeth, dignified rather than effusive, gestured for her to sit down. "We did all we could."

"I know, and thank you. . . ."

Sandra sat down and, joining her hands in her lap, studied them.

"Oh Tim," she thought, "if only you were here." She looked up at his mother, her face showing signs of strain but not for the reason Lady Elizabeth thought.

"I believe she has a good chance of recovery, of regaining her speech and movement. She is still a relatively young woman, you know. Luckily Bob was there when it happened. Bob was very good." Lady Elizabeth smiled up at Bob who had remained standing behind his sister. "Do sit down and I'll have a nice pot of English tea sent in. The French never know how to make it, you know. I have it sent from Jacksons in Piccadilly and there is only one maid I allow to brew it."

"The tea here *is* wonderful," Sandra said, thinking how absurdly irrelevant such talk was in the crisis of Hélène's illness. How English, too. Leaning back, she began to feel the tiredness draining out of her, "Oh it *is* good to be back!"

"But you enjoyed Harbour Island, I hear."

Sandra looked at her sharply, wondering what she knew.

"Oh very much."

"Tim was there too."

"Yes, taking a break from polo. The water-skiing was marvelous. It's a lovely place."

"So I hear." But Sandra thought Lady Elizabeth looked worried; a worry that, surely, she wouldn't simply feel about Hélène O'Neill?

"Bob," Lady Elizabeth said, catching his hand. "Would you go and order tea personally, darling? Make sure Christiane is there to make it for me. Would you then run up to my bedroom and see if my reading glasses are beside my bed? Do you mind?"

"Not at all." Bob jumped up eagerly. "You know I said to treat me like a son."

"And I am doing so." Lady Elizabeth smiled at him warmly, watching him until he had closed the door behind him. Then she too joined her hands in her lap.

"I'm very fond of Bob, Sandra. In such a short time too. He is a lovely boy."

"I'm so glad," Sandra said. "He *is* a lovely boy and he deserved better of—"

Lady Elizabeth held up a hand.

"Don't say it my dear. I know *quite* well what you feel about your mother, natural feelings, believe me. . . ."

"But I don't wish her dead. . . ." Sandra felt inexplicably close to tears. She was going to lose her celebrated control and weep in front of Lady Elizabeth. She realized now that, in fact, her emotions were in a state of turmoil. This woman in front of her was her lover's mother . . . it was one of those intimate relationships that, when people are suddenly made aware of them, come as a shock.

"Of *course* you don't wish her dead." Lady Elizabeth leaned forward and, taking her hand, pressed it hard. "Believe me, I do know how you feel. I also know how she feels. . . ."

"Have you seen her?" Sandra looked up at her in surprise.

"Oh not since the time I told you about, when she told me she wanted to see you. I wish you had gone then."

"I couldn't," Sandra said. "I only came now because," she blew her nose and looked at Lady Elizabeth. "I know this sounds hard but there *is* something I must know and only she can tell me."

"I think I know what it is," Lady Elizabeth lowered her voice, "and I think I know why you want so badly to know now. It *is* Tim, isn't it?"

"I wondered if you knew." Sandra couldn't meet Lady Elizabeth's eyes as she got up and wandered over to a table to clear it for the tray, looking for something to do.

"I know my dear. There's very little that happens in this family that I don't know. I think Belle is a little surprised, but . . ."

"Belle threw us together," Sandra said, looking at her defiantly. "Sometimes I think the whole thing has been *planned* by Belle."

"Oh that's *quite* impossible," Lady Elizabeth said, firmly putting a plant pot on top of the bureau. "Belle would never plan a thing like that. Why should she? Tim was attracted to you from the start. Even *I* noticed that. But, like you, I too was aware of the danger. . . ."

"Aware . . ." Sandra opened her mouth to speak but Lady Elizabeth anticipated her.

"Well we both fear that you might be Georges' daughter,

dear. Isn't that the truth? Isn't that really why you came back to see Hélène before she dies?"

Claire de Saint-Aignan felt like a young girl again or, rather, she was capturing, maybe for the first time, that joyousness of youthful spirits that she had never really had. Her early life had been dominated by a sense of inadequacy. Then, when she met someone whom she loved and who cared for her, her family showed to her, not for the first time, the sharpness of their claws. Piero was whisked away out of her life.

She had told Piero Borghi that she would never forget him and she never had. What she could not understand was why he had never tried to get in touch with her again because she had kept her promise, her part of the bargain, even though for six years she had been married to a man she did not love.

Claire had always felt a victim: of the Desmonds, of the de Saint-Aignans, particularly her dominating and jealous mother-in-law. It was a wonder that she hadn't taken refuge in some neurotic or, perhaps, even psychotic illness such had been her unhappiness since her youth. But now at twenty-six and liberated by the last person she expected it from, her brother Zac, she was beginning to find that zest she had so lacked as a girl and young woman.

Claire loved Rome. She loved not only the architecture but the spirit of that ancient city. She had traveled there after all by train so as to prolong the journey. She had given Zac's bulky, heavily sealed envelope to Marco Falconetti, who had evidently been delighted by its contents and had invited her to stay on.

"Feel free," he had said rather as Zac had spoken to her in Paris.

Claire knew that most of the members of her family didn't like Marco Falconetti. It was not hard to see why. He was feckless, he was lazy, unambitious and as she had soon discovered, he was a homosexual. Every night he brought some different man home and they went to bed together.

What was extraordinary to Claire, nurtured in a convent and relatively inexperienced in the ways of the world, was how little she minded this.

She didn't mind at all what Marco did because he had given her her freedom. So, free as a bird, she wandered daily through the streets of Rome sightseeing, visiting churches and galleries but above all breathing the air, the atmosphere of the Eternal City.

Maybe one day, she thought, it would happen.

And then, one day, it did.

The Piazza Navona is one of those old, attractive Roman squares which the tourists delight in because of its antiquity but which is also patronized by the native Romans themselves. They gather there in the evening to stroll about, walk their dogs, gossip, see their children at play and, sometimes, to eat or drink in the many bars or trattorias with which the square abounds.

Around the area of the Piazza Navona are several churches, some of which are architecturally celebrated, and one of which was a particular favorite of Claire's, who had in her still a strong, instinctive air of piety and went often to Mass. In her unhappy life religion had been a great consolation.

Claire was one of those traditionalists who, with her mother, shared a horror of the reforms introduced into the church by the Vatican Council even though she was only a little girl when it had been held. Lady Elizabeth insisted on Mass still being said in Latin in the chapel at Tourville, with the priest fully robed in traditional vestments, celebrating at a conventional altar, his back to the congregation.

There was something dignified and beautiful about the ancient Tridentine rite which modern-day Catholicism had destroyed.

Off the Piazza Navona was a church belonging to a religious order where Mass was sometimes said in Latin. There was a quiet side altar where an elderly priest said a late Mass, probably unaware that the reforms had even taken place, and he mumbled away in the ancient tongue, taking no notice of any congregation he might or might not have. Claire knelt behind him mouthing the responses of the ancient Mass from an old Roman missal.

One day not long after she arrived in Rome Claire attended morning Mass at the church and then afterward she went to one of the cafés in the square for breakfast: *cappucino* with *pane* and jam. She sat there in the sun, although it was a little chilly, feeling utterly content. A few city sparrows and pigeons hopped hopefully about in front of her and she ordered extra bread so that she could feed them until quite a flock had formed.

This bucolic scene to Claire, Countess of Saint-Aignan, represented simple happiness. The kind of happiness she had craved all her life. Because it was the simple, solitary life that she loved and, not a few times, she had thought that if she could ever escape from her hateful marriage she might seek entry to a convent.

Opposite her was the splendid Baroque church of Saint Agnese. Now the early tourists were beginning to throng through its doors to take in the sights of this forerunner of the Italian Baroque which was copied not only in Italy but in many other countries.

By the door an artist had set up his easel and the tourists were pausing to look at the paintings he had already on display. Claire looked at him, still with a smile on her lips. What an easy, happy way to enjoy life. . . . Suddenly the painter, looking in her direction, took off his dark glasses to see her better . . . and their eyes met. For a moment it was as though iced water flowed through her veins to be followed by a red hot sensation of burning.

The painter put down his brush and got up . . . she half rose. The painter stretched out his hands. She started to run toward him, leaving her bag with her passport, money and all her credit cards, on the table. Happily no one was around or, maybe, if they were, their eyes were not on the recently vacated table but on the peculiar sight in the square: a couple, arms flung around each other, embracing and weeping. . . . Piero and Claire, together again.

Claire didn't know Livio's room, the attic where he and Tara made love; she didn't even know about the existence of Livio. But had she ever seen that room she would have been struck by its resemblance to the one where Piero Borghi lived. It too was over a garage; only it had been converted into a large studio which he shared with some other painters, who also earned their living mainly by painting scenes which would be of interest to tourists.

Happily, today, they were all out at work.

Claire lay on his bed with Piero beside her, her face awash with fresh tears. She had hardly stopped crying since she met him. Tears and laughter, pure joy alternating with the memory of so much sorrow. The sorrow of the futile, misspent years. She had been eighteen at the time. Now she was twenty-six. Eight unhappy, barren years.

"I didn't realize you were still a virgin," Piero said, whispering gently to her, though there was no one about to hear. "I'm sorry."

"That's not why I'm crying." Claire turned her head to him. "I'm happy. That's why I'm crying."

"I see." He bent to kiss her and his hands brushed across her stomach, tenderly resting on that place on which there was still a little blood.

"It didn't hurt," she said. "I wanted you because I've waited for you for so long."

"But your husband. . . ." Piero looked puzzled. "For *six* years. . . ."

Claire shook her head and her finger touched his mouth.

"Don't talk about him," she said. "We have all the time in the world to tell each other about our lost years."

Marco Falconetti was not a curious man or, even, an especially observant one but even he noticed that something had happened.

One morning a few days later Claire and Marco met in the vast decrepit hall with its dusty curtains and the gaps on the wall where once the grand pictures, masterpieces of Italian art, had hung. As he kept all hours of the day and night he never knew if she were there or not. In a way he was an ideal person for her to stay with at this critical moment in her life. Claire had begun to appreciate someone who lived his own life and let others live theirs in a way that none of her family would have approved of, especially if they knew what she was up to.

Marco was about to say *"Buongiorno"* and pass on when he paused and stared at her.

"You don't look like the same person," he said, examining her closely. "You look like someone to whom something has happened."

"It has." Claire enclosed her burning cheeks in both hands. "I'm in love. Does it show so much?"

"It very definitely does." Marco smiled and wagged a finger at her. "Don't let your husband find out or Zac will cut off my allowance. . . ."

"Is *that* what happens?" Claire said. "Does he give you an allowance? Is that the money he sent you?"

"He *is* my brother-in-law," Marco said, carefully rubbing his polished nails on the front of his coat. "We have business together. From time to time I do him a favor."

"What kind of favor?"

"Having you here, for instance," Marco said archly.

"He wouldn't pay you for that!"

"Don't you tell tales and I won't. Bye." Marco gave her a cheery wave and went to the door. "Oh by the way," he said, looking back, "take care, won't you? Don't get pregnant."

Claire went to the door and stood watching him walk busily up the street as though bent on a task of some urgency. He was a peculiar man, there was no doubt of that, but at least he left one alone.

During the day Piero went on with his work and Claire, at some stage, went to join him. She didn't want to interfere or put the tourists off so she sat near him, sometimes at a café just content to observe him, as if she could not drink in enough the sight of the man she loved.

The man she loved and adored, who should have been her husband. Who would one day be her husband legally as already he was in the sight of God. She was quite sure of that.

Soon after Marco left the Palazzo, Claire left too. Piero seldom painted in the same place each day and they always made a rendezvous to meet. This day he was painting by the Spanish Steps not far from the Palazzo Falconetti and, as always, she stood for a few moments gazing at him before he noticed her and removed his dark glasses and smiled.

For one thing she had forgotten he was so handsome. He was not very tall and his face was swarthy, a Neapolitan whose forebears, perhaps, came from Algeria or Morocco. He had dark eyes, brilliantly white teeth, a mouth that could instantly burst into laughter. If the years had not been kind to Piero financially, he had not been destroyed by them. It was as though he had spent all this time waiting for her, as she had waited for him. He had had many women, but had never married. Maybe he too had known that one day they would meet again.

Finally Claire went over to him and squatted down beside

him, watching the easy, graceful strokes he made with his brush. Behind him stood one or two tourists commenting to themselves in English about his work, unaware they were understood.

"They think you're quite good," she whispered.

"I am, very good," he whispered back, making a movement with his mouth as though he would kiss her.

"I think we can spend the night at the Palazzo. I'm sure Marco won't mind."

"Did you ask him?"

"He *asked* me." Claire made no attempt to hide her blush. "He said I looked as though I was in love."

For a moment Piero appeared concerned and put down his brush on his palette.

"Won't he tell your family?"

"What if he does?"

"I won't forget last time so easily." Piero humped his shoulders and gritted his teeth. "Don't forget your brother and sister left me to drown. What will they do now that you're a countess?"

"Only in name. You know I wasn't really married."

"But do *they?*"

Claire looked at the ground. Then she raised her eyes, squinting against the sun.

"I think my mother knows. My mother knows everything. She guesses, you don't have to say anything."

"Why didn't you tell her?"

"It's very hard to talk about something like that. You don't know how hard it is, in a family like ours with a person like my mother. I wouldn't know how to begin to tell her."

"But you said all the time the old countess, Armand's mother, blamed you."

"She doesn't know that her son's impotent. How could *he* tell her a thing like that. . . ."

"I think the whole affair is disgraceful," Piero said crossly, throwing down his brush again. "Cruel on you, and cruel on him. Come on, *cara,* let's go and eat. I don't feel like painting today."

"What about the money?"

"I'll work harder tomorrow."

He picked up the half-finished picture, stacked away his portable easel and put them in a large bag which he slung over his shoulder.

"I know a very good trattoria where the spaghetti is the best in Rome."

"If I eat any more spaghetti," Claire said, laughing, "people will think I *am* pregnant."

Suddenly Piero stopped and a strange, wild look came into his eyes reminding her that his ancestors were North African peasants. He seized her arm and roughly drew her to him.

"That is what I want more than anything in the world," he said. "To have a baby with you."

Claire knew then, for sure, that she would never go back to Armand; never return to the de Saint-Aignan residence again.

Zac paced up and down the floor of his office, the letter in his hand.

"My God," he said to Belle, who was sitting in a chair facing him, "that bloody girl is with that bloody painter again."

"What bloody girl? What bloody painter?" Belle asked with irritation. Zac was getting on her nerves. He seemed to be permanently in a state of temper verging on the manic: first about Tim and Sandra, then about Sandra's mother, and now about this letter which had just been delivered by hand.

Belle felt very tired and out of sorts herself. Once things were straightened out she would get herself off to a clinic in the mountains for a few days of peace. People expected a lot of her because she was a capable woman. She drove herself, but sometimes even she felt the need to recuperate from a life largely spent in machination and intrigue against other people—especially since the advent of Sandra.

Zac didn't answer her but went on reading the letter, so she repeated her question in a louder voice and then he thrust the letter at her saying: "Read that."

Belle read it through calmly, twice, and then put it down on his desk.

"Well, you can see why she wants him. Never slept with Armand! Did you know that?"

"I didn't but *you* should have."

"Why?" Belle gave him a sardonic smile and produced her cigarette case from her bag.

"Because you're her sister."

"We were never exactly close as sisters."

"Still you should have known. Someone should have known."

"We should have guessed," Belle said quietly with, perhaps, a note of contrition in her voice. "I knew she was terribly unhappy with him and we all knew they slept apart."

"Yes, but we didn't know they *never* slept together. That old countess used to go on to Mother about Claire's inability to conceive. The *nerve* of the woman! Well I shall have great pleasure—"

"Oh don't, Zac." Belle leaned over to him and shook his arm. "Please don't interfere in this too."

"What do you mean 'this too'?"

"Well you seem to interfere in everything."

"I *am* the head of the family," Zac said, then menacingly under his breath, "whatever anyone says. As for trying to kill Sandra—" he clenched his teeth and threw his hands in the air—"supposing it had succeeded? My God, it was a lunatic plot!"

"It was just an idea," Belle said vaguely as if discussing an item of fashion. It so infuriated Zac that he, in turn, seized her and thrust his face close to hers.

"Just an idea eh? Just a notion that suddenly came to you?"

"In a way, yes. I felt it would solve a lot of things, just like *that,*" she snapped her fingers in his face.

"And you, my dear," his face inched even closer, "kill people as easily as you shoot game."

Belle thrust her hand in his face and pushed him away. "That is a most offensive remark."

"It's true."

"I have never killed anybody, and you know it."

"Huh!" Zac put his hands in his pockets and recommenced his walk. "It was *your* idea to do nothing about Piero Borghi."

"That was just an experiment. We wanted to see if he could swim."

"Yes, but we didn't know, *and* the boat was going very fast."

"He came from Naples, it was reasonable to suppose that he could. Anyway you were quite happy to do it too. *I* did not instruct Gomez to push Sandra into a ditch."

"That was just . . ."

"It could have killed her too."

"As could tampering with the gears . . . eliminating reverse."

Belle stared at Zac. Then she, too, rose and slowly, with a hand on her hip, came toward him until her face was inches from his.

"Look, brother Zac, we're both into it up to the neck. We have never been particularly respectful toward people who crossed us. Let's admit it. Let's not be purer than we are. We have the killing instinct. . . ."

"Do shut up," Zac hissed at her, looking at the door. "Supposing someone heard?"

"We know it," Belle hissed back. "And one day we're going to use it."

"Now Strega knows it too." Zac shook his fist at her. "That's what annoys me."

"Strega should never have been there in the *first* place." Belle stuck a finger in his stomach. "You sent him. He wasn't necessary and his presence on the island was a danger to us."

"I thought you'd give him a job on the yacht!"

"And have Tim recognize him?"

"Tim doesn't know Strega."

"He's bound to have seen him once or twice, I'm sure, in your office. And then Sandra . . . she misses nothing. Later she may have met him in Paris. I had to leave Strega on the island and he couldn't take photographs from there."

"But the accident to the boat was *your* idea," Zac said sulkily. "He told me he thought it was idiotic."

"Oh *did* he?" Mentally Belle chalked up another black mark against Strega. "Well, he got a very idiotic fellow to do it."

"You bungled."

"He bungled . . . anyway let's not continue this mutual recrimination. You got the photographs and they're fine."

"Fine, no problem." Zac sat down at his desk and joined his hands into a church steeple. "Now look, Belle, we have some very serious business to attend to and we are squabbling." He tried to smile, but it was a halfhearted attempt which didn't come too easily to him.

Belle returned sulkily to her seat and stared moodily at her nails.

"Right then," she said, looking up at him, "let's stop squabbling. I don't want to. Now, what is the serious business?"

"First." Zac ticked them off on his fingers. "What do we do about Piero? What do we do about Sandra? What do we do about her mother?"

"Why not kill them all?" Belle suggested and then, as she saw the expression on Zac's face, started to laugh.

His voice was as clear as though he had been standing next to her and she could almost feel the warmth of his breath on her cheek.

"I'm taking the plane tomorrow," Tim repeated. "I must be with you at this time."

"I don't want you to, Tim," Sandra said again and, in the almost palpable pause, she could sense his hurt. *"Please* understand," she went on. "I'd like you to be here but the whole thing is too complicated. For one thing your mother is hostile. . . ."

She knew him so well, even after such a short time, that she could feel his shock.

"Mother is hostile?"

"Belle has told your mother about us. Your mother strongly disapproves."

"On what grounds . . . ?"

Now Sandra was silent.

"You don't mean she thinks we're brother and sister?"

"Your mother's not convinced we're not."

"Then ask Hélène, ask your mother. Get her to put it in writing."

Sandra sighed and, taking the phone to a chair sat down, cradling the receiver in her hand, speaking very low in case there were eavesdroppers. Not that anyone in the house couldn't pick up the phone and listen to their conversation. This house had no secrets or, if it did, it couldn't keep them.

"Mother is paralyzed, Tim. She can neither speak nor write. She hasn't made the recovery the doctors expected. Don't you think *I* want to know too?"

"Even if you are my sister I still want you," Tim said savagely into the phone and she could imagine his anger, his frustration. "I still want you," he went on, "and I'm sure we're not brother and sister."

"So am I. The facts are all against it. The dates are all wrong."

"Then that should be enough to convince anyone."

"Belle doesn't seem to think it is."

"Belle?"

"Belle sides with your mother. There's talk of incest . . . it's a horrible situation and I wish . . . I were with you," Sandra lowered her voice again. "I feel with you, Tim, I could withstand them. Without you—" She wanted to add "I'm broken" but she knew that if she did and anyone heard, any of the many ears that might be listening in that huge, cavernous house, she would be finished.

"I'm coming home anyway," Tim said.

"Please don't, Tim. I beg of you with all my heart. Not just yet, not now . . . not until . . . Mother can't really last very much longer. It's a matter of days."

Even then those days seemed to pass slowly. Hélène O'Neill had indicated that she wanted to be brought home to die and her wish was granted. An ambulance drove her slowly through the French countryside and deposited her in her house among the vines. There she was looked after by a team of nurses so that she was never alone.

Sandra sat for hours by her bedside willing with all her heart that she would speak. She had tried to explain to Hélène what she wanted, saying over and over again: "Please try and convey to me, once and for all, that I am not the daughter of Georges Desmond. It is very important to me. Please. . . ."

Sometimes Hélène's eyes opened and they seemed to mock her, but she never spoke, never said a word or made a sound except the painful, stertorous breathing. Occasionally they had to use a ventilator which had been rushed from the hospital, and oxygen was permanently at the head of the bed.

It was a terrible way to die, Sandra thought, a warning, perhaps, that age was no protection against death. Hélène O'Neill was only fifty-six, but her wrinkled, parchmentlike skin, her thin emaciated frame made her look ninety. They had discovered too late that she had cancer of the lung that had probably spread to her body.

Yet she was in no pain. The doctors assured Sandra that

Hélène's was a twilight, relatively happy world where images came and went and, maybe, the memories she had were sweet ones. Certainly her face looked tranquil.

Sandra and Bob alternated the bedside vigil and sometimes they sat together, one on each side, holding her hand. Difficult to imagine that this had once been a strong, vibrant woman who had won the love, the undying love, of Georges Desmond.

One day Lady Elizabeth came and stood by the bed looking down on her erstwhile rival. It was hard for her to believe that this was a woman she once hated.

"Thank you for coming," Sandra said as she saw her to the door.

"It's a terrible ordeal for you, my dear." Lady Elizabeth put a hand on her arm.

"It's worse for Bob. He cared more for her than I ever did. I only feel . . ." Sandra lowered her eyes, finding the words hard to say, "I only feel sorrow for what never was, a mother I never had, someone who never loved me."

Sandra was close to tears and when she felt that comforting hand tighten on hers, and another steal around her shoulder, she leaned against the warm, fragrant, motherly bosom of Lady Elizabeth and wept.

"There, there," Lady Elizabeth said in soft, soothing tones. "I'm sure she loved you. I know she wanted to see you and now you are doing for her everything a daughter could. I'm sure, in her way, that she has forgiven you and you, in your turn, must forgive her."

Somehow the words comforted Sandra and she felt stronger. That night she sat alone by the bedside and, taking Hélène's hand in hers, said:

"Mother, I don't know if you can hear me but I am sorry. I am sorry . . . that what has happened between us happened. I'm sorry that I was so unforgiving because I know, now, what it is to be so powerfully in love that any other emotion is cast aside. I think I love Tim Desmond, Mother, and I know how strongly you felt about his father.

"But please, if you can, let me know once and for all. Please press my hand, if you can, to confirm that he was *not* my father too. Please, Mother, please."

Sandra watched closely as Hélène's eyes slowly opened and she seemed for a moment to gaze enigmatically at the woman sitting by her side. But there was no movement, no pressure of her hand and a very short time later, she died.

23

Hélène O'Neill was buried not beside the body of Georges Desmond—the man for whom she had forsaken her family—in the cemetery at Reims, but in a little churchyard at Crémy.

The ceremony was strictly private; the only mourners Sandra, Bob and Hélène's maid Blanche who had looked after her well in her last years. There was no member of the Desmond family present and the photographers, for once, had resisted the bait to pursue their quarry, if bait there was. For Hélène O'Neill had died much as she had lived: quietly, anonymously, without fuss, as much in the background at the mortal end of her relationship with the Desmond family as she had been in the beginning.

On the hillside in the little churchyard overlooking the Côte des Blancs Hélène's coffin was lowered in the grave as the priest committed her soul to God. It was a moving and rather strange ritual because neither Bob nor Sandra had been brought up as Catholics. Hélène had abandoned the Church when she began her life with Georges Desmond—a state of mortal sin, of which she was well aware.

Maybe the priest, in order to give her a Catholic burial, thought she had made an act of contrition in her heart before she died. No one questioned his judgment and only a few curious onlookers had watched the hearse carrying the coffin drive through the village. Mostly people stayed respectfully and, perhaps, a little reprovingly, behind closed doors.

Sandra clutched Bob's hand as the coffin disappeared from view. Then she stepped forward after the priest and threw some earth on top of it. She was followed by Bob and, finally, a sobbing Blanche in deep mourning. Then, quickly and without ceremony, the gravediggers began to fill in the hole containing the remains of a woman who in death, as in life, had been something of an enigma.

Ashes to ashes, dust to dust . . .

During the brief ceremony and the subsequent committal Sandra felt no sadness, nor sorrow, only guilt . . . guilt that she had failed someone who had wanted her, had failed to provide that ultimate forgiveness that all men expect of God, however much they have sinned. Hélène had wanted her and she would not come; but in the end Hélène had won—because when Sandra needed her she couldn't, or wouldn't speak: only stare, with that hint of mockery in her eyes.

Now, alone except for the tiny remnant of Hélène's family and entourage, she stood on the hillside, the richest woman in France, a force in the world but, essentially alone, confused and uncertain as to what the future would bring.

For with her Hélène O'Neill had taken the secret of her own past and it would remain buried with her in the grave for all time.

It was a very strange time for Sandra; a strange, and rather frightening time. There were too many questions that Hélène had left unanswered. She hadn't even left a will which was odd for a woman who was such an efficient secretary. Perhaps she wanted her next of kin to have everything, but Sandra would take nothing and gave all that Hélène had left, which was very little considering the status she had occupied in Georges' life, to Bob. Perhaps the late Monsieur Desmond had been too aware of what his family's ultimate opinion of him would be.

As usual Sandra found Henri Piper of more comfort to her

than anyone else. Bob's behavior on the other hand was strange. He seemed to blame her for not going to see Hélène before she was dying and this did, still, sit uncomfortably on Sandra's conscience.

"It's the hardest thing to bear," she said to Henri on their way to a meeting of the Foundation shortly after the funeral. "I really feel guilty. I think she meant me to."

Henri took her hand and she let it remain in his until they stopped outside the building in the place Saint-Sulpice.

"You can always lean on me," he whispered and his lips briefly brushed against her cheek.

"Oh I wish I could," she said, turning to him but, suddenly, the look in his eyes disturbed her.

"You know I love you," Henri said, his hand still clasping hers.

"Yes I know . . . like an uncle."

"Exactly. Like an uncle. . . ." Henri paused as if trying to find the exact words. "More particularly as a friend." His hand tightened on hers. "And as a friend I must warn you about Tim, my dear. I have known Tim—"

"Oh please, Henri, not today," Sandra hastily tapped the glass to instruct the chauffeur to open the door for them. "I don't want to hear anything about *that* today."

"But you *must* listen to me, Sandra," Henri said urgently as the chauffeur, as if uncertain what to do, half turned in his seat. "Tim Desmond *is* dangerous. You have done an incredibly silly thing. . . ."

"You surely don't still think he's my brother. . . ."

"I think he's a dangerous man. He's a Desmond. He's incapable of true affection. Please, Sandra, come to your senses before something terrible happens."

"Nothing terrible can happen," Sandra said coldly as the chauffeur opened the door, holding out a hand to help her out of the car. "You can be sure I have everything under control, *Uncle* Henri."

*   *   *

Henri took the chair for the meeting and Sandra, her mind still preoccupied with their conversation—his unwarrantable intrusion in her personal affairs—took her place halfway down the table.

The meeting began formally with the condolences of the Board on the death of her mother which she accepted gracefully. But the main business was to consider funding a research project that Dr. Harcourt was especially interested in. Apparently Dr. Harcourt waited outside to tell them about it.

Sandra looked up with interest as the doctor was shown in and formally introduced to the Board. She inclined her head with a smile when her name was mentioned, but thought that he deliberately avoided her eyes.

Henri Piper invited Dr. Harcourt to explain the problem and he began to tell them about the disease which was now front page news on all the world's newspapers.

"You all know about AIDS," he said, looking sternly around the table, "and our anxiety to find either a cure for it, or a vaccine to prevent it. I don't think any of you doubt how serious it is."

They all nodded as though none of them had any doubt at all.

"The Acquired Immune Deficiency Syndrome attacks the body's ability to fight infection. In some parts of the U.S. where I have been studying it, the disease has reached major proportions. We in France claim it was first isolated here by Professor Mantagnier and I feel it is in France that we should try and find a cure.

"I propose that the entire funds of the Foundation should be used to find a cure for, or a vaccine against, the disease. In some underdeveloped countries it is epidemic; it exists on a huge scale. We would not be going against the principles of our Charter if we devoted most of our funds to this research."

Sandra had been listening, doodling.

"What exactly are you suggesting, Doctor?" she inquired gravely.

For once Harcourt smiled at her and Sandra was reminded that when she had first met him she found him attractive, or even before that, when she had first seen his picture.

"We want much more money, Mademoiselle. I know this is a point on which you and I have already had an argument but—"

"No argument, Doctor, I disagree with you," Sandra said with a polite cough. "When we had that very *slight* contretemps in New York I assured you that I was as anxious as you were to channel more money to the Foundation. Actually—" she smiled wryly across the table at him "—as a result of my visit to New York we have secured a highly profitable contract to supply the Desmond-2000 fighter-bomber to an Arab State, and I am glad to tell you today that funds to the Foundation *will* indeed be stepped up."

There was a round of applause but Dr. Harcourt, biting his lip, stared at the table and did not join in.

"Aren't you *pleased,* Dr. Harcourt?" Sandra inquired when the room was quiet again.

"I suppose, Mademoiselle, that death is just the same and just as painful whether it is from disease or bombs. For my part I wish this Foundation were wholly separate from the Desmond Group, which stands for everything I happen to detest. Excuse me please, messieurs, mesdames—"

Abruptly he rose, gathered his papers into his briefcase and left the room to what might accurately be called a stunned silence.

"There is really *no* pleasing that man," Henri Piper said, shaking his head. "Can't we get rid of him?"

"Well." Professor Jumet, a noted virologist, looked doubtful. *"Everyone* is in a sense expendable. I *suppose* we could find a way to terminate his contract."

"Then let's find one quickly," Émile Fourneau, a prominent businessman, said. "I've always found him arrogant. Let's find a way to kick him out . . . such ingratitude."

Sandra swung back in her chair from the table, hands in the pockets of her suit.

"Messieurs, mesdames," she said. "Dr. Harcourt may be terrible. He may be rude and ungrateful and I personally think he is *all* of these things. I regret to say I have not taken to him at all and my encounters with him so far have been unpleasant, but . . ." she paused for effect, "he *is* a great man. Please have no doubt of that, no doubt at all. He is perhaps among the great men and women of science and medicine of our age. None of them were easy to live with. I believe his research into diseases of the blood could help find a cure to this terrible disease and that would, in its turn, bring glory not only to our Foundation but to France. Glory in the name of humanity? Is that not what we all wish?"

Everyone murmured approval and one or two heads nodded agreement.

"So you see Dr. Harcourt may be difficult; but his is the kind of talent we want. I vote that we approve the funds he needs for his work and beg him to stay with us; then give him all the resources he requires. One day I'm sure he will be one of the great benefactors of mankind."

Lady Elizabeth sat bolt upright in her chair in the way that only Lady Elizabeth could; back ramrod straight, hands on the arms of her chair which seemed to resemble a throne. The expression on her face was severe, the severest Claire could ever recall having seen; but she was not afraid. In fact she thought her mother looked slightly ridiculous; like a caricature of what a disapproving old lady, startled by unpleasant news, should look like.

Beside Claire stood Piero Borghi, clutching her hand.

Maybe he was more frightened of Lady Elizabeth, whom he had never met before, than Claire was.

"I fail completely," Lady Elizabeth said at last, "to comprehend any of this ridiculous story. You must return at once to your husband, Claire, and dispatch this man back to where he came from."

Of course they'd done it badly, Claire realized that now. Sighing, she released Piero's hand and with an encouraging smile pushed him toward the door.

"Wait for me outside," she whispered. "I'll deal with Mother."

Piero was only too pleased to do as she said. As a Neapolitan he was used to formidable women; but Lady Elizabeth . . . gladly he hurried outside. Claire shut the door behind him and walked slowly back into the room to face a parent who for once, perhaps the first time, quite failed to frighten her. It was an extraordinary, a unique experience.

"I'm sorry, Maman," she said, brushing her hair back from her face. "I shouldn't have done it like that. . . ."

"You shouldn't have done it at *all,*" Lady Elizabeth said. "Do you realize you're a Catholic girl, the wife of—"

"I know quite well what I am, Mother." Claire quietly took a seat opposite her formidable parent. "But I don't think *you* do. You never made it easy for me to confide in you, Mother, and thus you do not know that the six years of my marriage to Armand have been a sham. I am not a wife, not in the eyes of God. Until I met Piero again in Rome I was a virgin. . . ."

"A—" Lady Elizabeth seemed incapable of pronouncing the awful word. "I don't believe it."

"Nevertheless it is true. . . ."

"But I thought once . . . you thought you were expecting a baby . . . ?"

"That was pretense, Mother. I was ashamed and Armand

was ashamed too. We wanted to pretend to make ourselves feel better."

"You mean he *never . . . ?"* Once again the image seemed too awful for Lady Elizabeth to conjecture.

"You must understand, Mother, that I felt sorry for Armand. He was an emotional cripple and I was too. In a way I loved him as I know he loved me, and probably still does love me. You know, Mother, about the relationship that John Ruskin had with his wife Effie? Well, ours was like that. Armand loved me, he embraced me but he could not make love to me in the proper way . . . and in time I didn't want him to. I was repelled. I was afraid too. So we lived like that until I went to Rome and . . ." she shrugged, "you know what happened. I am very happy now, Mother, and I want you to be happy for me too."

Suddenly, instinctively, Lady Elizabeth reached out her arms and Claire fled into them. For a while mother and daughter remained locked in an embrace, as if for the first time. It was certainly a very long time since either of them could recall such a thing happening between them. Physical contact had always been very rare.

"Oh my poor baby," Lady Elizabeth said at last. "What an ordeal. You should have told your mother. You should have told *someone. . . ."*

"Who was there to tell, Maman?" Claire said, breaking away. "I have never been very close to Belle. I tell you I loved Armand as one does a brother. I felt desperately sorry for him and I promised never to betray his secret. But you know, Mother, there was something wrong with me too. I was very afraid. I always had been. When I knew Piero when I was eighteen . . . he tried to make love to me . . . and I was afraid then too. In a way with Armand I was relieved that he couldn't make love. . . . Now I know better."

"Oh my child," Lady Elizabeth said again, dabbing at her eyes with her handkerchief. "I don't know what to say. All this suffering . . . too awful. But *what* can we say to Madame de Saint-Aignan?"

"You could probably say to my mother-in-law, if you had the courage, that it's all her fault anyway. She so dominates her son that he can't get an erection. . . ."

"Shh," Lady Elizabeth said in startled tones, looking around as if the walls had ears. "Don't say that *word.*"

"Oh *Mother . . .*" Claire, happy now and relaxed, laughed and sat down again. "In a way you are as unaware as I was. . . ."

"I am not indeed," Lady Elizabeth said indignantly. "May I remind you I have had *four* children. . . ."

"Yes, Mother . . . but did you enjoy it?"

"Really Claire." Lady Elizabeth got up and walked over to her bureau. There she fiddled with a few family photographs, repositioning them to try and calm her nerves, deprecating in her mind the frankness of the young. Then she turned to face her daughter.

"Don't forget, my dear child, we are very different generations, you and I. In my day it was never the thing to talk about sex, even with one's husband and, if you ask me now, I think we were wrong. But, also in my opinion, today people overdo it. And I cannot answer your question. My relations with your father were private, and I would never talk about them, or my feelings . . . even now."

"I'm sorry, Maman." Sensing she was the strong one, Claire also got up and came over to Lady Elizabeth. "I know I'm burbling a bit because I'm so happy. . . ."

"But, my dear, what does he *do?*" Lady Elizabeth wailed. "Did you say a *painter?*"

"He paints outside churches and places of interest for tourists. He is a very gifted artist, but Father destroyed his career. . . ."

"Your father would *never* have done a thing like that. . . ."

"But he did, Mother, though he might not have told you."

"I know he thought he was unsuitable. He convinced me the relationship was unimportant. He never even allowed me to meet him."

"He had his paintings declared worthless, there were some terrible reviews, and the gallery where Piero was exhibiting chucked him out. Before that . . ." Claire paused. How could she tell her mother about the "prank" played by Zac and Belle? At least she would spare her that. "Oh well, it doesn't matter."

"You can't possibly *marry* him, darling, someone like that."

"Someone like what, Mother?"

"Well." Lady Elizabeth abruptly sat down again. "No background, no money . . . an urchin from Naples. You do see it's impossible, don't you?"

"What do you want me to do? Go on being the Countess of Saint-Aignan?"

Lady Elizabeth twisted her handkerchief awkwardly in her hand.

"I do realize that is very difficult, in view of what you tell me; but in a way it *is* a relief, my darling. The marriage can be annulled and you can start again. There are many extremely nice, eligible young men around, or so I hear."

"I don't want to marry Piero, Mother," Claire said and, as Lady Elizabeth breathed with relief she added, "I want to live with him. I'm going to have his baby anyway. I conceived probably the first time we made love. You can see how thrilled and excited I am, Mother; but for the moment, we don't plan to do anything but enjoy each other and our baby. *And* we're going to live in Rome."

"But how?" Lady Elizabeth murmured weakly. "Oh, what a dreadful story. A *baby!*" Both hands clutching her head, she rocked from side to side.

"It's not dreadful at all, Mother," Claire said energetically. "It's happy; positive. I do so want you to try and like Piero, Mother. He is going to be around for an awful long time."

* * *

The reactions of the various members of the Desmond family to Claire's news varied but, on the whole, it was unfavorable. Piero Borghi was thought to be a rogue, a bounder and an opportunist who had corrupted an innocent and, understandably, tortured girl. Obviously he was after the Desmond money and Zac, in particular, began to draw up all kinds of plans to have Claire declared mentally unfit and incapable of looking after her own money. Belle was inclined to agree with him and even Henri and Sophie Piper had doubts about her mental health. It was all too sudden, too quick. Besides, his appearance they didn't find exactly pleasing: he was short and swarthy, attractive maybe, but in the way that no Desmond would have found desirable. He was also quick tempered and, if he loved Claire, it was soon obvious that he dominated her too.

"Soon she will find herself a hen-pecked Italian wife with ten children," Zac said darkly. "I know the type."

Zac, his mother and Belle went into little huddles to see what they could do, while Claire and Piero ignored them altogether and went on behaving in Tourville and Paris as they had in Rome. They spent a lot of time in bed but otherwise they enjoyed themselves like teenagers, eating in bistros, going to bars and discotheques.

Sandra for one approved and so did Tara, who liked to think of the Desmonds being upset. Tara and Bob formed what the family interpreted as a strange, but innocent, alliance and often made up a foursome with the lovers.

Zac, who didn't imagine his wife would stoop to an affair with a mere boy, didn't object. But Sandra was more suspicious. She saw more of them together and she knew that Bob was susceptible. She began to suggest that, now that Hélène was dead, maybe it was time to think of returning to Los Angeles. But Bob preferred to linger.

Bob, temporarily, was the least of Sandra's worries. There

was so much to see to in the weeks following Hélène O'Neill's death and the return home of Claire, which came shortly afterward. There was a huge company still to be run, and Sandra could never find enough hours in the day to do all she had to do.

She and Henri often met in her office or at his home and, gradually, Sandra began to realize that Sophie's attitude toward her was changing.

"Somehow I don't feel Sophie is so pleased to see me these days," she said to Henri one evening as they were catching up on the day's work together in the main bar of the Ritz. "Is it my imagination?"

"I expect so," Henri said offhandedly. Then he paused. "Well, to tell you the truth she and I had a bit of an argument over you in New York. She said she thought I paid you too much attention. She's getting on, you know."

"Oh dear," Sandra said thoughtfully. "I'm sorry about that. I must talk to her and ease her mind."

"I should just leave it," Henri said. "It will die away when she knows there is nothing in it. Now my dear, Tim. . . ."

"Tim is on his way over." Sandra's face was a curious mixture of happiness and apprehension. "We can't spend all our time avoiding each other. We've got to sort it out. We've got to *know.*"

Later that night Bob came in with Tara, Piero and Claire. Sandra was at her desk working and listening to them in the next room mixing drinks and putting music on the stereo. There was the happy, youthful sound of laughter and clinking glasses.

She leaned back in her chair listening for a moment. It was true Tara disturbed her. Bob could say it was just innocent fun, but Sandra wondered if it was and when Zac was going to do something about it. They were, anyway, an odd couple. Tara was fourteen years older than Bob, yet no one could pretend now that their relationship was anything other than flirtatious. How much farther it went than that Sandra didn't know, but what she didn't know she didn't like.

She was about to get up and go in and greet her guests when there was a knock at her door and Claire put her head around. Sandra immediately got up and beckoned to her.

"Come in and close the door," she said. "I was about to say 'hello.' I wanted to talk to you anyway." She bent down to embrace her and then showed her to a comfortable chair, taking a seat next to her.

"I haven't really had the chance, Claire, to tell you how happy I am for you. I—"

"If you're happy you're the only one," Claire said with a rueful laugh. "Apart from Tara and Bob. They're happy. The rest of the family is not."

"But honestly I'm *really* happy, and I want you to know that you always have my support and help. . . ."

"You know, I suppose, that Zac is trying to stop me getting my hands on all my inheritance? You could help there."

Sandra sighed.

"I did hear; but there's not much I can do about that. It's a personal family matter and he and I don't get on too well, as you know."

"I know." Claire bowed her head. "I'm sorry I wrote that letter, Sandra. I wanted to make that right with you as soon as I could. I'm sorry." She raised her head and there was an angry gleam in her eyes. "But I'm sorry too you showed it to Zac. I thought your attitude toward me this time had been funny, and I realize why." Claire looked up and held out her hand. "Friends?"

Sandra took her hand, but there was an expression of bewilderment on her face.

"Of course we're friends," she said. "And I'm sorry you thought my attitude toward you funny. I didn't intend it to be. But I haven't seen you alone and I have been very preoccupied, with Mother's death and so on. But a *letter* . . . what letter?"

"The letter about Tim." Claire got up and started to walk restlessly around the room. "I shouldn't have interfered."

"I didn't get any letter about Tim," Sandra said and suddenly she had a horrible sensation of *déjà vu.* All this had happened before.

"But you showed it to Zac."

"I didn't get a letter from you and I didn't show a letter to Zac." Sandra slowly stood up. "I've no idea what you're talking about."

Claire went to the door and made sure that it was shut. In any event the noise from the room next door was sufficient to drown any sounds made by them. She leaned against the door, her hands pressed to her sides.

"When I was at Burg-Farnbach after you'd gone I heard Belle, Zac and Tim discussing you in a very frank way. I didn't like what I heard and I wrote to warn you. . . ."

"What exactly did you hear . . . ?" Sandra felt as if her own voice were coming from very far away.

"I shouldn't repeat it now. It's a bit late, from what I hear."

"But still I would like to hear it. It may be important. The three of them were discussing me. . . . Do go on." Sandra sat down, her head to one side as if listening with interest.

"Tim said he felt ashamed of what he had done. I gathered that he'd been led on by Zac and Belle. They were teasing *him* and said he had the family to think of. He owed it, something—I don't know what—to them. I felt it had to do with you leaving so suddenly.

"I thought the best thing was to write and tell you to beware of Tim. He was up to something, something that Zac and Belle knew about. I felt you should suspect his sincerity. There was a kind of conspiracy to get you." Claire stopped, looked apologetically at Sandra and shrugged her shoulders.

"I guess now it's too late. It's happened, hasn't it?"

"Nothing is ever too late," Sandra said smoothly, recovering her composure. She rose, went over to Claire and put her hand on her shoulder. "Thank you for telling me. You may have just about saved my pride, if not my life."

Émile Livio turned to Tara and said, "Something's wrong with you. I don't know what it is."

"I'm tired," Tara said. "Can't you understand that?"

"You've never been tired like this before. Are you pregnant again, or something?"

"I hope to God not." Tara turned over on her stomach and lit a cigarette. "I just don't feel like it that's all."

"Is there someone else?"

"Of course not!" Tara began to get out of bed but Livio pulled her back, rather roughly.

"You can't force me to make love if I don't want to," she said sulkily.

"Oh can't I?" Livio had a sinister expression on his face.

"My husband raped me once before," Tara said. "Don't say *you're* a brute like him."

Livio suddenly let her go and jumped up, sitting on the edge of the bed, his head in his hands.

"I don't know what's happening to me," he said. "Maybe all this isn't enough for you. Why should it be? You're a lovely woman; you're rich and I'm nothing."

"You know that's not the point." Tara made as if to touch him, but he moved aside.

So, instead, she stubbed out her cigarette and reached for her brassière which she began to put on while sitting on the bed. It was a tiny wisp of a thing to contain her prominent breasts and Livio, because he felt frustrated, broke out into a sweat even watching her.

He knew that Tara was slipping away from him; out of sight, soon out of mind. She had never been so cold or so passionless in bed, never so impatient with him or nonchalant about not having a climax.

"Take it or leave it" seemed to be her attitude. It had been like this since Switzerland, when he had suddenly realized he bored her.

The way Tara put on her bra and briefs seemed designed to provoke him deliberately. Maybe she was inviting him to make love to her violently as Zac had? Maybe she really liked that? She was a curious woman who, now that she was slipping away, he wanted more than ever before.

He rubbed his head until he felt dizzy, then he got up to put on his jeans while she completed dressing at the far end of the room.

"When shall I see you again?" he said to her as she carefully applied her lipstick with the aid of her compact mirror.

"Who knows?" she said apathetically.

"When, then?" His voice was hoarse with anxiety.

"I'll telephone you." She went up to him and kissed him on the lips.

"But you *do* love me still?"

"You know I do." She backed away, her arms still around him. "But I can't pretend, can I, if I don't feel like making love?"

"You have in the past."

"It's since my miscarriage. The urge I had has gone. I never needed to pretend with you," Tara said, patting him on the cheek.

There was something maternal about the gesture and he noticed the tense she had used was in the past.

It was a warm spring evening and the days were getting longer. There was a spring in Tara's step as she walked away from the garage, and she never turned, as she usually did, to see if he was looking out of the window after her.

Yes, there was no doubt that she was tired of Livio.

She had come to realize during their sojourn together in

Switzerland, the longest time they had ever spent in each other's company, that Livio was rather boring. An affair was only exciting so long as it was brief, clandestine, dangerous. . . .

In Gstaad she had felt that she and Livio were like an old married couple. Like a married man too, and an Italian one at that, he expected her to do all the work in their isolated chalet on the mountains. Tara hadn't liked that at all. She wasn't used to it. Useless too to remind him that she was a contessa, one of the long noble line of Falconettis. It only made him laugh.

But now there was a younger, more desirable man in her life. It was something to be wanted, seriously wanted, by a man fourteen years her junior. It had a certain novelty and charm and that was enhanced by the fact that there were no financial problems, no dirty little garage room stinking of grease. There were endless possibilities at the prospect of an affair with Bob O'Neill. All she had to do was say "yes."

To Tara, perpetually in search of novelty, there was something almost alluring about teaching a much younger man the arts of love.

She thought she would pop in on Bob on her way home and walked eagerly to the Alfa-Romeo parked in its usual place. It was already like saying "goodbye" to Livio. Poor Livio.

She got into her car, backed into the street, turned and drove away. A few minutes after she had gone the doors of a car that had been parked nearby, and out of sight, opened and three men got out.

One by one they went toward the garage, where Livio lived above the shop.

24

Despite the eminence of his position, Philippe de Lassale was by nature a lazy man. He had got to where he was by inheritance and enjoyed the good things of life. He was not unintelligent; he had degrees from the Sorbonne and Harvard; but to Philippe everything did, and always had, come easy. He had a beautiful home, a charming wife, an alluring mistress, three interesting and intelligent children, a yacht, a holiday home in the Tyrol, and at the age of fifty-five, he was inclined to indulge himself.

Completely lacking the ruthlessness of the late Georges Desmond, he had perhaps more in common with Henri Piper in that he was laconic, charming, elegant, cultured. They were from a similar background of the French upper-middle class, the *haute bourgeoisie*.

His father had only died five years before, upon which Philippe had succeeded him as President of the family bank. It was a very big and successful bank and one thing had led effortlessly to the next. People simply approached Philippe and he merged with them or took them over, in the easiest, most delightful of ways, just as his father had done for years and his grandfather before that.

In a way Philippe de Lassale was an easy pushover for someone like Zac Desmond, a man obsessed by a grudge; no, not merely a grudge, but hatred, a thirst for revenge. Philippe de Lassale would have been a stranger to emotions of such intensity and complexity. He had never really felt very strongly about anything in his life. There had never been the need.

Zac had had a bad time since the death of his father. He had been deprived of his inheritance and the bank of which he was head had been merged with another, against his will. He was still on the Board of Desmond, a major shareholder and a power to be reckoned with, but he felt like an eagle shorn of its wings. He never had any intention of remaining too long in the position of number two at the Banque Franco-Belges, maybe, dancing to the tunes of both Sandra and Philippe, a man he considered his inferior the more he knew him.

He had, however, been very lucky in the affair of the yeast because de Lassale was at heart something of a male chauvinist who didn't really think women should be running major corporations. He was prepared to give Sandra the benefit of the doubt because her acumen, expertise and drive did at first seem impressive and remarkable; but the *tirage* débâcle had revealed that she had one Achilles heel. Maybe she had more?

It was obvious to de Lassale that Zac knew all there was to know about champagne and Sandra O'Neill Desmond knew nothing. Inevitably, a little unfairly perhaps, she had fallen in his estimation and even her skill in negotiating the supply of war planes to the Arabs did not make up for this major lapse. She was vulnerable.

Thus when Zac began to talk to Philippe about Desmond champagne: the advantages of it being part of the Heurtey Group, which already owned Tellier, Philippe listened to him with respect. The House of Desmond had lost a lot of money; there was simply not the supply available that there should be eventually to represent the recent *cuvée* in the markets of the world.

On the other hand Tellier, under the control of the Group, had flourished. Its products were everywhere. Never mind how much of it was not champagne from the first pressing, its name had become a household word. It made sense for Philippe as it made sense to Zac that as close associates of the Banque Franco-Belges, Heurtey should take over Desmond too and control the whole enterprise under one umbrella. There would be advantages in marketing, production and distribution, and yet each brand name would be distinct and separate.

There was one thing, however, that Philippe didn't know and he was such a gentleman that it would never have occurred to him to guess or suspect: in Zac's scheme of things it would be an inverse takeover when, finally, he would be in control of the Desmond Group and the usurper ousted. Desmond would control Tellier, the Banque Franco-Belges and maybe the Heurtey Group as well. In that event Philippe de Lassale would be expendable and Zac would not be half as charitable with him as he had been with Zac.

The rivalry between Tellier and Desmond went back a long way, as Belle had explained to Sandra. The families had superficially got on but, between Zac and the two Telliers who still ran the company, there was nothing but enmity. They hated one another with great cordiality and no one was more surprised than Rudy Tellier when Zac invited him and his brother to dinner, and started discussing a fusion between the two houses of champagne.

Tara was an asset at any dinner party. These days she looked particularly good; but she was too much of a risk. Zac knew she couldn't keep her pretty mouth shut, and she played about too much in these adolescent-style parties with young Bob O'Neill and his crazy sister Claire and her paramour.

Zac had nothing but contempt for such goings on, but it was useful both to know what Bob was up to and where and to keep Tara occupied and, if necessary, out of the way.

Belle stood in as his hostess the night he entertained the Telliers to dinner at one of the most exclusive restaurants in Paris, where the enormous bill would naturally be footed by the Banque Franco-Belges.

Both the Tellier brothers brought their wives and it was

an interesting if strained and, certainly, not an amusing evening. There was very little small talk because neither side liked to gossip; there was too much danger of inadvertently spilling confidential information.

Certainly the Telliers were very happy with Heurtey. They were both large, expansive men, both overweight, who had changed a great deal since their young adulthood.

It was a period of which neither had very happy memories of Zac or Belle. Zac had rather rudely turned down their sister as a prospective bride although some said that on the way he had seduced her; but there was no proof. Luc in turn had been rebuffed by Belle who much preferred the Prince of Burg-Farnbach for a number of compelling reasons: he had a title, as much money and, certainly, more charm.

They were unattractive then and they were unattractive now, as far as Belle was concerned: scheming, ambitious men but with little talent; none of the zest that compelled Zac or herself, onward, ever upward. She listened carefully but said little during the major part of the dinner, preoccupied with her own thoughts and schemes, her own ideas of ultimately sharing control of the company with Zac.

It was after dinner, over cigars and brandy, that Zac brought to the fore what was in his mind and the Telliers listened at first with boredom, increasing to respect and, finally, amazement.

"You mean *we* should take over Desmond?" Luc said at last with a sideways glance at his brother.

"No, no, you misunderstand me." Zac puffed thick cigar smoke into the air. "The Desmond bank has merged with the Banque Franco-Belges, yet it is still, separately, part of the Desmond Group. What I propose is that the Champagne House will merge in a similar manner and then—" He spread his arms wide as though to indicate anything could happen, a characteristic gesture of Zac, as if embracing the whole world.

"Does de Lassale know anything of this?" Luc Tellier said with a greedy glint in his eyes. For years the two men had dreamed of getting their own back on the Desmonds, for the many slights they had received from them, by controlling their champagne. Now Zac was, apparently, playing into their hands.

"Good heavens no!" Zac exclaimed. "This is confidential between you and ourselves. If a word gets out before we are ready, the deal is off."

"We?" Luc Tellier murmured. "You mean yourself and Mademoiselle Desmond O'Neill?"

"I mean myself and my sister Belle," Zac snapped. "By the time we are in control Mademoiselle O'Neill will be on the other side of the Atlantic. I am just telling you what may happen . . . but you must be *very* quiet about it."

"Of course," Rudy said with the air of a man who could hardly wait to get to the telephone and broadcast the news and, shortly after that, the meeting broke up and the couples went their respective ways.

Belle said later in the car taking them toward Zac's house, "That was very skillfully done. Now we are covered in case de Lassale ever *does* anything about the business of the yeast. I have already put the suspicion of the Telliers' guilt into Sandra's head."

"That was a clever idea," Zac said, smiling with satisfaction. "With any luck Philippe will sack Rudy and Luc and *then* we shall have not only Tellier but Desmond too." He put his hand over his sister's. "Well done, little Belle. I will make you Vice-President as soon as I take over control of the Group."

"Oh will you?" Belle said, but there was a faraway look in her eyes as though she had them set on something even higher.

"Let's stop for a drink," Zac suggested as they passed the Café Flore on their way along the boulevard Saint-Germain toward rue de Varenne. "I feel in an expansive mood tonight. Maybe I'll drop you back at the house and go and see my mistress."

"Oh?" Belle's eyes widened. "La petite Agnès is already your mistress?"

"Of course," Zac said with an air of satisfaction. "You don't think I'd pay all that money for an apartment and not get anything for it, do you? What she gives me from the office of *l'Irlandaise* is a mere trickle, not worth her upkeep. But in bed," Zac sucked his lips, "no complaints."

"You are a very busy man," Belle said reprovingly. "I don't know where you get the time."

"That is none of your business," Zac said, pulling the car into a side street off the brightly lit boulevard. "Besides, she is my little wooden horse."

He helped his sister out of the Rolls and then, linking arms, strolled around to the bar which was still patronized by *le tout Paris,* who like to sit staring at the passersby or the customers entering and leaving Brasserie Lipp opposite.

Zac felt relaxed in the company of his elder sister; perhaps with her more than anyone else in the world. It is true that they were very attached, perhaps attracted, to each other in the same way that myth, more than historical fact, alleges about Cesare and Lucrezia Borgia. But there was something mythical too about the relationship of Zac and Belle.

They had the ability of divining each other's thoughts, anticipating each other's actions. In many ways they could both intuit each other's next move.

It was a balmy spring evening still quite early and the boulevard was thronged with couples, tourists and inquisitive strollers. Next to Zac a man was reading the late edition of *France-Soir* and as they waited for their drinks, perfectly at ease with each other, Zac glanced casually at the front page, which was on a line with his nose.

He gave such a jump that Belle turned to him with concern.

"Are you all right?"

"I thought I saw something," Zac said, but even in the garish light his face had a deathly pallor.

"You look quite ill to me," Belle observed with sisterly concern. "Why don't you go home and lie down? Perhaps the *rognons* were too rich?"

"It's nothing to do with the *rognons,"* Zac said, getting up. "Excuse me a minute, Belle. I must get a paper." By the Métro of Saint-Germain des Prés, a newspaper kiosk was still open. Zac paid for a copy with a hand that shook though the vendor, thankful to have parted with one more copy so that he could soon shut his kiosk and go home, didn't notice. Zac paused under a street lamp, shook open the paper and studied the small paragraph in heavy type at the bottom of the first page, that had attracted his notice in the first place. It said:

Brutal Murder of a Garage Mechanic

Monsieur Émile Livio, the owner of a small garage in the Batignolles district of Paris, was found brutally battered to death when his men turned up for work early this morning. Monsieur Livio once had prospects as a Formula Two racing driver but failed, for lack of sponsors, to enter the Formula One and became instead owner of a garage specializing in racing cars. He was well known in the racing fraternity as a first-class mechanic. One of his employees has been detained for questioning.

Zac read the paragraph twice and then he threw it into a wastepaper basket before returning to the café where Belle observed that he looked better.

"It was just a touch of indigestion," Zac said and downed his double brandy in a single gulp. "They're out of the evening edition." He couldn't tell even her everything.

*   *   *

Sandra could feel his presence in the room even before she saw him. The door had quietly opened and she knew that he was standing there behind her, looking at her. She sat writing letters at the small desk by the window of one of the salons at Tourville which overlooked the lake. Mostly she dictated but she had one or two friends in the States to whom, from time to time, she wrote brief personal notes. Now, still in her riding clothes, she was writing to an old friend from Berkeley who had told her she was expecting a baby.

Sandra put her pen down and, as his steps drew nearer, waited. Then as his hand touched her shoulder, she half turned and said, "Don't."

The hand stayed where it was; the other was put on her other shoulder and, slightly turning her, he bent to kiss her cheek.

"I said 'don't,' Tim, and I mean it," Sandra said sharply, pushing him away and getting up.

The happy smile of anticipation on his face vanished and he held out his arms.

"Sandra . . . why?"

"I told you not to come."

"But that was weeks ago."

"A month. It's not so long."

"My dear," Tim said with an edge to his voice. "I have a perfect right to come to my own home . . . besides, I wanted to see you. Darling. . . ."

"Please don't call me that, Tim." Sandra, steeling herself, stared into his eyes. "Everything has changed."

"Oh *Sandra* . . . still not that absurd idea about brother and sister."

"No, a much more *absurd* idea." Sandra sat on the edge of a chair, her fist clenched on her knee.

"And tell me what that is, my darling." Tim's suave, easy manner never faltered and he joined his hands in front of him, smiling.

Sandra continued to stare stonily at him.

"I always told myself you should never trust a Desmond, and I know now that you never can."

"But you can trust *me.*"

"You least of all. I was a fool, Tim, and how I regret it."

"Regret what?"

"Harbour Island . . . all that."

"Well I don't," he said a little bitterly. "But then my memory isn't so short. . . ."

"Maybe it is and maybe it isn't," Sandra replied. "Can you remember Christmas?"

"Oh that . . . I said. . . ." A shadow finally crossed Tim's pleasant face.

"Not what you *said,* or to me anyway."

"You're talking to me in riddles," Tim insisted, looking around for a chair. "This is not the woman I knew in the Bahamas. I know your mother has died, Sandra, and you have a lot on your mind. I am very sorry. Maybe I should have come before, despite what you said. I have been through agonies to know how you were. In the end I couldn't wait any longer. . . ."

Sandra suddenly uncrossed her legs and got to her feet. She felt the need to stand above him, assume superiority over him. Tim remained sitting where he was looking up at her, a laconic expression on his face.

"Tim," she said. "I know, now, that it was always your intention, and Zac's and Belle's too, that you should try and seduce me. Of all the maneuvers which your family has tried this was the most despicable. I have no doubt about it; but what I don't yet know is quite *why* you did it. I believed you to be a cut above the other two. Now I'm not so sure. I've been very badly hurt, Tim." She paused and drew a deep breath. "I must tell you that I never want to have anything to do with you on a personal level again. Inevitably I must see you on family occasions, and you have as much right in this house as I have; but in the future, when I know you are here, I shall not come, and if you are here when I arrive, I shall leave. Is that understood?"

"It sounds very hard . . . and unnecessary." Slowly Tim's expression had changed as she spoke to him, in turn puzzled, bewildered and, finally, affronted.

"It is what I wish," Sandra said and pointed toward the door. "You or I . . . not both."

"If that is what you want." Tim gave a stiff bow and was about to turn his back on her to leave when he changed his mind.

"I am beginning to realize, alas, Sandra, that much of what my family feels about you may be justified. You have accused me without giving me any chance to defend myself. I admit, shamefully maybe, but I do admit my motives at first may have been unworthy; I was sorry then and I'm sorry now. Whoever told you this tale did a mischief for, as I have gotten to know you, my feelings about you, and myself, have profoundly changed. After the Bahamas everything was different. I felt, to my surprise, that I was falling in love with you. Now—" He stopped and looked at her as if he still clung to some hope.

"It is too late," Sandra said, turning toward the window. "Please go."

All she heard then was the click of the door and she knew that he was gone.

Lady Elizabeth said, "How very odd that Tim should come and yet leave so quickly." She looked searchingly at Sandra. "I suppose it was to do with you?"

"Yes." Sandra put her teacup down on the small table beside her. It was late afternoon and, although the shadows were lengthening on the grass, it was warm enough to sit under the tree near the greenhouse where they had first met nearly a year before. Lady Elizabeth even wore the curious, long, gray monastic robe which was her favorite gardening apparel, although the straw hat had apparently had its day. Instead she wore a colorful scarf bound around her gray-blonde hair.

Lady Elizabeth reached for one of those small, exquisite cucumber sandwiches without which no upper-class English tea is complete. Teatime was as much a ritual to Lady Elizabeth as breakfast in bed or dinner at eight. She was a creature of habit and now it was too late to change. She liked to boast, as though it were some kind of virtue, that she was set in her ways.

"Well it *is* best," she said, gazing sympathetically at Sandra above her half-moon glasses. "Don't you think?"

"Yes I do: but not for the reasons you think, Lady Elizabeth."

"Oh?" Lady Elizabeth paused, her sandwich halfway to her mouth.

"I don't believe we are brother and sister, even though my mother was never able to speak to me. I am quite sure we are not; that she told you the truth. I have told Tim that anything that was between us was over for another reason."

Sandra gazed fixedly at Lady Elizabeth as that curious, enigmatic, self-composed woman carefully finished her sandwich, taking tiny bites with fine white teeth, apparently unconcerned by what Sandra was saying; an attitude which Sandra found mildly irritating.

"I think Tim was set up by Zac and Belle to humiliate me."

"What a farfetched idea." Lady Elizabeth, at last, registered surprise. "My son, you know, Sandra, has always been fond of women. He is, I'm afraid, what is known as a philanderer. He means no harm; but he can't resist them. I'm distressed of course that you've been hurt. . . ."

"I don't think *hurt* is the right word, Lady Elizabeth," Sandra said with a trace of a smile. "I must admit to some amusement at the idea. As if something as trivial as *that* would make me forsake the Desmond Group."

"I think it's simply in your mind." Lady Elizabeth studied the sandwich plate with her customary sangfroid. "My children are not the monsters you take them for. Understandably they were hurt by what their father did; but I don't honestly think they would stoop quite as low as you suggest." She selected her sandwich and put it daintily on her plate.

"Tim is not a cynic. He has genuine enthusiasm. You are a pretty girl. . . ." She shrugged and popped the sandwich into her mouth, a suggestion of laughter in her eyes.

Maybe she was pleased that Tim, after all, was not to be aligned with Sandra against Zac and Belle, and herself. . . . Sandra eyed her keenly but could discover no real clue to the truth. One could never *really* tell with this odd woman, she thought, and decided to say nothing more for the moment. Tim was now against her, and the last person she wished to make into an enemy was his mother.

Suddenly she looked up as Pierre came at what seemed to her precipitate speed around the corner of the greenhouse. His face was flushed and a hand was on his chin as though he scarcely knew what to say or how to say it.

Lady Elizabeth looked up at him sharply.

"What on earth is the matter, Pierre? Have you been stung by a wasp?"

"Oh My Lady, oh Madame," the servant said. "I hardly know how to tell you this but—"

"What *is* it?"

As Lady Elizabeth half rose from her chair Sandra caught her arm to steady her, sensing that something really terrible had happened . . . an accident . . . an accident to Tim? Her own heart lurched at the thought.

"Do compose yourself, Pierre," she said, "there's a good man, and tell us what it is you have to say."

"Well My Lady, Mademoiselle." Pierre looked from one to the other. "It was just on the television news and I came at once."

"What was?" There was now a note of impatience in Lady Elizabeth's voice. Clearly she didn't have Sandra's premonition of disaster.

"My Lady . . . Madame Tara has just been arrested for murder. It concerns a man found battered to death in a garage. . . ."

To say that the arrest of Tara Desmond for the murder of Émile Livio was a national scandal was to simplify the matter. It involved not only her relations with her husband, her affair with a garage mechanic, but the whole ramifications of the Desmond inheritance as well.

It is the custom in France, much to Lady Elizabeth's disapproval, not to hush up crimes as in England after an arrest is made. There the silence of the accused is protected by law until he or she appears at the magistrate's court for arraignment. In France the system is not quite the same and Tara Desmond was immediately deemed to be a woman who had sinned and who, to cover her sin, had killed her lover in a fit of fury.

The facts fitted perfectly. She had been seen coming from the garage shortly after dark. A neighbor happened to be looking for her black-and-white cat, who habitually was fed by the men working at the garage, and saw her come down from Livio's room, walk nonchalantly away and get into her red Alfa-Romeo car. It was a distinctive car and the lady in question had seen it there often. Everyone in the neighborhood knew about the rich woman who came to sleep with Monsieur Livio. It was the talk of the locality, certainly the gossip among his employees.

Madame had found her cat, taken him home—no doubt administered a scolding—and the next thing she knew was when, the following morning, first of all the workmen arrived, then the police, and Monsieur Livio's body was taken out of the garage under a white sheet.

Really she was quite sad to think that a little bit of interesting tittle-tattle in her otherwise humdrum life was over. But maybe her greatest glory, and that of the cat, was to come. Maybe she would be called as a witness in the trial.

For Zac Desmond, who knew the truth, the whole thing was a nightmare. Just when he felt that he was sitting pretty, in control of himself, his affairs and his destiny, this happened. What was more, Gomez had gone to ground and could not be found. Realizing how big his blunder had been, he didn't even rendezvous with Zac to collect payment.

Zac knew that it was very serious when Gomez failed to turn up. Gomez knew a lot about him and could be a dangerous opponent. In justification he could spill the beans about the attempt to get Sandra's car off the motorway and, if Gomez told all he knew, it would probably be the end of Zac and his ambitions to reign over the affairs of Desmond for good. Zac would very much like to have gotten his hands on Gomez to keep him under control, if not to silence him completely.

In his extremity, while the reporters bayed at his door and his mother had the police to guard the gates at Tourville, Zac turned to the one person he knew who would do anything for money and explained the situation to him.

He told Strega, now back in France and living under an assumed name, all about Gomez and how Gomez had been hired to have Livio beaten up.

"Just beaten up," Zac said furiously. "Nothing more."

"That *is* unfortunate, Monsieur," Strega said smoothly, aware how large was the account with him now. How much Zac owed him.

"Such a *bad* time, Strega," Zac bleated, biting his favorite fingernail where that little bit of flesh was always at just the right length to gnaw at. "The pictures are all ready. I have the newspaper primed with the scandal about Mademoiselle O'Neill and now all *this.* Gomez *must* be found."

"And what then, Monsieur?" Strega's mean little eyes narrowed. "A little accident perhaps? *Another?*"

"Good heavens no," Zac said. "Gomez must be found and accused of Livio's murder. I want to get my wife out of prison just as soon as can be. It's *very* bad for my business."

"Leave it to me, Monsieur," Strega said, hiding a smile of satisfaction. "Though, of course, it will cost you."

"Anything you like," Zac said expansively. "I want this matter taken off my hands and settled once and for all."

And he made a gesture with his finger—slicing it right across his throat.

If the whole thing was a nightmare for Zac it was doubly so for Tara who, incarcerated in a women's prison, was innocent. It was a nightmare too for Bob, her would-be lover, who was unable to give her an alibi for the night in question, much as he would have loved to, because he hadn't been at home when Tara said she called. She'd gone straight to Sandra's suite; but no one at the Ritz remembered seeing her at the crucial time, which would be around the time of Livio's death according to forensic evidence: eight or so in the evening.

Sandra couldn't help knowing now, by the scale of Bob's anxiety on Tara's behalf, exactly how he felt about her. The depth of his feeling shocked her. Something she'd assumed to be innocent was now seen to be full of threats.

"I wish you'd *told* me," she said, gazing from the window of her suite into the tranquil square. "I could have saved you from much hurt. Bob, she is so much *older* than you. I never imagined. . . ."

"You still think of me as a kid, that's why," Bob said angrily. "A child, too young for sex."

"But she's fourteen years older than you."

"I don't care how old she is. I love her. . . ."

"But it's hopeless, futile and dangerous. My God, she's married to Zac. . . . If Zac knew he'd have you killed too!"

Sandra stopped abruptly, hand to mouth, aware that Bob was looking at her with interest.

" 'Too'?" he said. "What do you mean 'too'?"

"Zac *is* a very dangerous man," Sandra said in a low voice. "I become more and more convinced of it now. I wouldn't be surprised if he was behind what happened to Livio. I can't see Tara battering a chicken to death, never mind a grown man."

"She swears to me she didn't and I believe her."

"I do too." Sandra nodded. "You see. . . ." She ran her hands through her hair and, going over to Bob, sat beside him as if reluctant to take him into her confidence.

"You see, darling, this is a very difficult thing for someone like you, as nice as you are, to realize. It is for me, too, but I am older than you and, well, let's say it, maybe harder. But I do think the whole Desmond family, possibly with the exception of Claire and Lady Elizabeth, is evil."

"Evil?" Bob gave a shaky laugh. "Isn't that rather an old-fashioned word, Sis?"

"Yes it is," Sandra agreed, nodding her head. "Very old-fashioned and I would never have used it a year ago. I'd have laughed at the notion. I was very simple when I came over here and imagined everyone would go out of their way to help me or, at least, if I was nice to them they would be nice to me. I didn't know the can of worms I would open when I unintentionally deprived the Desmonds of what they considered their birthright."

"It was a silly thing of Georges to do," Bob said, absent-mindedly rubbing his chin. "The more I think of it, the more I wonder that he didn't know what would happen."

"The more I'm inclined to agree," Sandra said. "The point is, he did it. Maybe I was clumsy, brash, trying to be too clever. Anyway I think that from the moment they knew what had happened, the three Desmonds mainly affected—Zac, Belle and Tim—conspired to get rid of me . . . and I don't just mean out of the Group. I mean out of the way, Bob. For good."

"You mean . . . ?" The expression on Bob's face was one of an incredulity that was almost comical.

"Yes. I do. Just before Christmas I was nearly killed by a car following me. I turned over, escaped with scratches. . . ."

"You never said—" Bob said reproachfully.

"I didn't want to worry you. Anyway I wasn't sure. Well." Sandra took a deep breath. "When I was in the Bahamas, foolish enough to accept an invitation to holiday with them, something went wrong with the boat that was taking us water-skiing. I had fallen in and it was coming to pick me up, and it didn't stop but just kept on going. . . . It was a horrible sensation, I can tell you. Tim Desmond was sitting beside the driver and he dived in just as I was hit on the head by one of the water skis. The driver was sacked immediately for carelessness, but Tim afterward made an inspection and thought the gears had been tampered with so that the boat couldn't reverse. Tim knows quite a lot about engines."

"Didn't Tim tell anyone?"

"Tim told Carl and Belle, but I wanted the whole thing dropped. The man who'd driven the boat left the same day. It wasn't very fair, perhaps, but that's how it happened. Only later did anyone think it might have been deliberate." Sandra laughed ruefully. "All I got was a bump on the head, and a nasty shock . . . but the real shock came later.

"It was suggested to me by a member of the family that Zac and Belle deliberately tried to push Tim into having an affair with me . . . to be dropped and humiliated, as he does with all his women."

"A member of the family. . . ." Bob's voice trailed off. "Tara I bet. She hates them all."

"Not Tara as a matter-of-fact, but Claire. When she was

in Burg-Farnbach she overheard a conversation suggesting that Tim had been set up to seduce me. She wrote and warned me but I never got the letter. I only learned this a short while ago." She paused and abruptly covered her face with her hands. "You can imagine how I feel now, knowing all this."

For a long time there was silence and then Bob's arm slowly stole around her shoulders.

"Is it worth it, Sis?" he said quietly. "Is it worth it? Why not quit?"

"Quit?" Sandra looked up, staring at him in amazement. "Quit?" she repeated. "Don't you know me better? The last thing I'd ever do is quit."

25

Belle sat in a dark corner of the saloon bar of a pub off Fleet Street that had seen better times. "The Street" was in the process of breaking up as newspapers started moving out to print elsewhere. *The Times* had gone to Wapping and the *Daily Telegraph* to the Isle of Dogs. Some said that the City of London business and financial institutions would gradually encroach on Fleet Street and there would be no printers' ink left there at all. No bales of paper would be loaded off lorries which jammed small roads, never constructed for such operations anyway.

The advent of the new technology and the decline of the traditional power of the print unions would see to all that.

Belle knew very little about the English Press and had gone by taxi to Fleet Street from Waterloo Station. Ostensibly she was visiting her mother's relations at Farley Hall in Hampshire, the country seat of the Earls of Broughton; but in fact she had a much more sinister reason for being in England.

The reason was a bulky packet lying safely in her large leather handbag which she clutched compulsively as she looked toward the door.

Belle was uncomfortable about her mission. It had never been intended that she would be the person to carry it out; but events had overtaken them. The French Press, *the Journaux des Concierges,* were full of Tara Desmond. Zac couldn't come himself and his henchman Paul Strega was scouring the streets and environs of Paris for Ignacio Gomez, perpetrator of a murder.

Belle wore a dark blue suit, a red blouse with a thick blue stripe and a large pair of tinted glasses concealing her eyes. She looked out of place, and many curious glances were cast her way as she nervously sipped a gin and tonic and waited for the person with whom she was to rendezvous to show up.

She felt annoyed and anxious about the situation she was in. She also felt vulnerable and conspicuous and knew that the task she was engaged in was a dangerous one. If she were caught she could be sent to prison, and prison was a subject that made her shudder at the moment, having visited Tara in Fleury-Mérogis. It was a horrible place for a woman of breeding, wealth and refinement to be mixing with prostitutes, thieves, drug addicts and petty or notorious criminals of various kinds.

The Farleys had been extremely surprised to see Belle at all in view of what was happening to Tara; but Belle had said there was so little she could do that she wanted to be out of the way. The strain was bringing on a nervous breakdown.

Belle looked, for the fourth or fifth time, at her watch and the polished toe of her right shoe played a little tattoo on the floor. People kept on coming and going and she had no idea what the man she was supposed to be meeting looked like; but she had identified herself over the telephone—dark glasses, red and blue striped shirt. She didn't add that she was considered by some of the very chic French magazines to be one of the most beautiful and best-dressed women in France.

She looked nervously at her watch again, wondered whether to get a fresh drink and a voice by her elbow said, "Mrs. Farley . . . ?"

Belle looked up and saw a youngish man of nondescript appearance. He had a round bald head, glasses with tortoise-shell frames and a lounge suit of an indeterminate color. In his hand he carried a copy of the *Daily Enquirer* which was one of the lower, if not the lowest, of the Fleet Street tabloids recently launched by a multinational conglomerate.

"How do you do?" Belle put out her hand, which was taken by the man who said politely:

"Would you like a drink?"

"No thank you, I haven't got a lot of time. You must be Mr. Smith."

"Yes." The man gave a nervous laugh and sat beside her. "It actually *is* Smith too. Don Smith. Do you mind if I get myself a beer?"

"Please do," Belle said, beginning to relax. Mr. Smith seemed perfectly presentable; presentable compared, say, to someone like Gomez, or Strega with his blackmailing propensities.

Mr. Smith came back with his beer, calling out cheerily to some colleagues drinking at the various tables dotted around. He seemed proud to be seen with a woman as stylish as Belle.

"Sorry about this," Mr. Smith said. "I can see it's not the sort of thing you're used to; but they do a very decent Ploughman's Lunch."

"Really?" Belle said without the least interest in what a lunch so described might be.

"Now Mrs. Farley." Mr. Smith sipped his beer and, with the froth still clinging to his upper lip, said to her, "I think you've something interesting for my editor."

Belle, suddenly feeling very nervous and unsure of herself, slowly opened her bag and, with an air of reluctance, extracted the large envelope from it.

"Everything is here," she said. "You'll find everything quite authentic."

"And it is . . . er." Mr. Smith sipped his beer again and Belle imagined, in the gloom, that his cherubic face went rather pink. "It is *the* Miss Desmond in the nude? The one who met recently with the Prime Minister?"

"Oh yes. She lunched with the Prime Minister not long ago."

"And it is *the* Miss Desmond actually making love?" Mr. Smith inquired a trifle lasciviously.

"Undoubtedly," Belle said. "On the beach . . . and there are other details besides, not too savory, I'm afraid. All here." She patted the packet.

"I don't suppose I should take a peep at them?" Smith suggested, glancing around, but all his colleagues seemed intent on their own affairs.

"You can if you like," Belle said. "But we're not expecting any money you know."

"Oh I *know* that, Mrs. Farley. It's just that we have to be careful."

"You are also indemnified for libel," Belle said, "so I don't know what you're worried about. In fact this whole operation has cost the party I represent quite a lot of money. You won't lose a penny, but will gain through the publicity." She was going to add: "for your awful paper" but decided not to. Zac had had enough difficulty getting anyone to cooperate with him, so doubtful was the project felt to be . . . almost too much even for the notorious British tabloid Press.

"I know what you mean, Mrs. Farley, and my editor *is* grateful. You see we're very much against the Government and we thought this kind of thing would discredit it."

"Oh *that's* your interest is it?" Belle said, thinking of the friendship of the Broughton family with various members of the Government. "Well, make sure that you don't identify *anyone* from this side. . . ."

"I *quite* understand." Mr. Smith paused. "Mrs. Farley isn't even your real name. I can tell you're French, or German or something."

"There's no need to go into that." Belle began firmly to

pull on her gloves over her fine, white hands with their glistening parade of rings. "Just do your job and we will do ours."

"Right, Mrs. Farley." Mr. Smith, suddenly brisk, slipped the packet into his pocket. "They'll be safe here."

"I hope so."

"I'm taking them right back to the office now. I do wonder though," Mr. Smith finished his beer and looked at her curiously, "what *your* interest in this is. One can't help wondering from the human point of view, you know."

"My interest," Belle said, standing up and straightening her slim-fitting skirt, "is to see justice done. Good day, Mr. Smith."

"Good day, er—"

Mr. Smith stood up and watched Belle walk quickly across the bare boards of the pub and out onto the street. He whistled softly and, his hands on the packet in his pocket, walked slowly after her.

She was someone he decided he wouldn't like to cross; someone who had a touch of malice, possibly evil in her. Those eyes glinting behind the tinted glasses had looked very, very mean.

Farley? Well it wasn't Farley to be sure. He shrugged his shoulders and went out onto the street; but there was no sign anywhere of Mrs. Farley or of anyone like her . . . as though she'd disappeared in a puff of smoke, like an apparition from the Devil.

Sandra gazed out of the window of the apartment and was pleased with what she saw, both inside and outside. The idea of an apartment on the Île Saint-Louis had been given to her by Agnès. It was a lovely part of Paris; central, old, yet one actually had the impression of space, of being, somehow, in the country. The only irritation was the lights of the *bateaux mouches* which turned at the end of the island lighting up one's windows at night.

The origins of the City of Paris lay on the largest island on the Seine which the Parisii tribe, who discovered it, called Lutetia. The island was not called the Cité until the sixth century when Clovis made it his capital.

In the reign of Louis XIII the Île de la Cité was joined by a bridge to the neighboring small Île aux Vaches, which was subsequently renamed after Saint Louis of France.

Building began on the island in the seventeenth century and many of the great classical houses, the *hôtels particuliers,* still remained with their lovely views over Paris.

Sandra's top-floor apartment had a balcony which ran the whole length of the house and from which trailed nasturtiums, geraniums, petunias, lobelia and a host of summer flowers from boxes and hanging baskets. There were retractable blinds across the windows to give shade from the afternoon sun which sank each day below the cupola of the Pantheon which, together with Notre Dame Cathedral, dominated the skyline.

The apartment was duplex, on two floors, and had four bedrooms with bathrooms *en suite,* quarters for servants, two magnificent salons and a dining room.

Sandra felt immediately at home there. It was a refuge from the place de L'Étoile, the Ritz and, it had to be faced, even Tourville. Most weekends Sandra would have liked to stay in her apartment with its view over the trees and the river, its peace and its elegance. But Tourville was home too.

Bob was also pleased with it and it was Bob, who had been so destroyed by Tara's imprisonment and arraignment, she thought about most.

For once in her life Sandra had felt almost sorry for Zac. He was pestered on all sides, and yet stoutly maintained his wife's innocence. If only Bob had been at the Ritz the night Tara allegedly came to see him. But the curious and unfortunate thing was that no one remembered her; not one person could recall a beautiful, striking woman coming through those doors, which were always manned by a porter, crossing the busy foyer and going into the lift. That had been unusual enough in itself and, so far, had helped to condemn Tara in the minds of the public. That, and the evidence of the woman with the cat who practically kept a twenty-four-hour surveillance on the garage from the sound of it. What a pest *she* was. Nosey women with cats and not enough to do were the bane of some people's lives and this had been the truth here, no doubt about that. Her evidence alone might condemn Tara.

Sandra felt an instinctive pity for a proud man, now down on his luck and so, in a spirit of goodwill, she had asked him to lunch at her apartment.

Now from the fourth-floor window on the quai d'Orléans she looked down into the street for a sign of his car, hoping against hope that he wouldn't be followed by reporters. Her own whereabouts were a secret too, which was why she still kept a suite at the Ritz.

She stepped back into the room and looked at the table at which lunch was to be served. From the kitchen she could hear the sounds of her chef making further preparations.

There was a ring at the door and Sandra went hurriedly across the room into the hall to open it. Zac stood outside the door.

"I was looking out for you," Sandra said with surprise, stepping back into the small hall to usher him in. "No sign of your car. Welcome anyway."

Zac came in looking around and nodding with approval at what he saw.

"Very nice," he said. "Furnished, I suppose?" He looked around at the good but mock antiques with a slight sneer on his face.

"It's only for a while until I find something more permanent." Sandra immediately felt on the defensive. "I've taken it for six months. But I like the Île and shall look for a *hôtel particulier* of my own here."

"Couldn't stand the Ritz any longer I suppose?"

"I love it, of course, and it's very convenient, but it is too noisy and, after this. . . ."

Zac nodded understandingly and turned as the butler came in.

"Monsieur?"

"Champagne, please," Zac said, turning back to Sandra. "Have you a bottle of Desmond in your refrigerator? I suppose you've only Piper."

"Of course we have Piper," Sandra said with the merest trace of a smile. "But the Desmond *brut Centennaire* is waiting for you in the fridge." She nodded to the butler and led Zac into the salon with its spectacular views; then she turned and looked frankly at her antagonist.

"It *would* be nice to be friends, Zac, at last. Maybe it takes something like this to bring us together. I mean about Tara."

"It *was* a terrible blow," Zac said, sitting down and mopping his brow. "I came by taxi and left it outside the Hôtel de Ville. Then I walked." His expression changed to one of self-approval. "Not often I walk. Not often I have the time. There are too many people around."

The butler entered with the champagne in a silver bucket, two tall glasses beside it. With due solemnity he uncorked the bottle of vintage champagne and poured. The thick mousse rose sparkling to the surface watched with approval by Zac and Sandra who handed his glass to Zac. Then she took her own and held it up.

"To the prosperity of the Desmond Group."

"To Desmond," Zac said, admiring the color of the liquid, the depth of the *mousse* before taking a sip. "And to my wife."

"Of course."

Sandra sat down opposite him and carefully crossed her legs, looking at him as she did. She had on a dark green suede suit from Ungaro with a matching green and beige striped silk blouse. Like everything she wore it enhanced her natural good looks, which was always a source of annoyance to Belle because so far Sandra had avoided patronizing the House of Marvoine.

Her thick fair hair had been cut and one swath hung across her face almost obscuring her right eye. She flicked her hair back and with that movement, the tilt of her chin, Zac thought what a very attractive woman she was, and how stylish. Sandra had style, no doubt about that. It was instinctive style . . . something she was born with. Suddenly he remembered her lying nude on the bed.

She, as if divining his thoughts, pulled her skirt severely over her knee.

"You were about to say something?" Zac raised his eyes from her knees and looked at her with a bland incurious expression on his face that continued to be vaguely insulting.

"I do want us to be friends," she said.

"I do too."

"But you haven't played fair with me."

"Or you with me."

Sandra shook her head. *"That's* what you think. Granted that I was at a disadvantage in the first place, I think I did what I could to placate you."

"You could never placate me, Sandra, you know that. If that's what this lunch is in aid of we might as well say goodbye now."

"I'm sorry, then." Sandra briskly uncrossed her legs. She felt suddenly angry; slightly foolish. She was glad the staff was in the kitchen close by, otherwise Zac might have put it about she had tried to seduce him.

Why *did* one ever attempt to trust a Desmond?

"I really wanted to talk to you about champagne," Sandra said matter-of-factly. "But first, shall we eat?"

"If you like," Zac said, rising. "That would be a good idea. I have to see Tara's lawyer at three."

"And my plane is ordered for four but, what *is* the news of Tara?" Sandra took her place opposite him and shook out her napkin as the butler entered with a dish of cold fish mousse.

"The news is not good." Zac nodded his thanks to the butler. "There is *no* doubt my wife is innocent of murdering Livio. I know that, but I cannot prove it, yet."

"How are you so sure?"

"I know it because I believe her." Zac took another sip of champagne. "Also I know Tara. Why would *she* set about someone and kill him in such a bloodthirsty way? She is incapable of it. She had no need to kill him. She was sick of him, anyway. If anything he might have killed *her* because he knew she was sick of him. . . ." He looked askance at Sandra. "Anyway I thought you wanted to talk to me about something else."

Sandra, who was about to speak, paused as the butler removed the empty *hors d'oeuvres* dishes and reentered with the entrée. This was quails with wild mushrooms, which he deftly and skillfully served.

"Excellent," Zac said, taking a bite. "Your own chef?"

"Naturally, I lured him from the Ritz. But seriously, I wanted to talk to you about reconciliation."

"That's good," Zac said. "I thought you said it was about champagne."

"Champagne certainly enters into it, but I am not, you will be sorry to hear, thinking of relinquishing control. I am, however, prepared to make you President of the Champagne House and float it as a separate entity."

"From the Group? How can you do that?"

"No, *not* from the Group. You have complete control *within* the Group."

"It's not the same thing is it?" Zac said, picking his teeth.

"Well, it's a bit like Tellier, isn't it . . . ?"

"Tellier?"

"You must know all about Tellier. I understand there is

even a suspicion they were behind Strega and the affair of the yeasts."

"Oh yes, that," Zac said hurriedly. "There is no doubt they were, in my mind. Who told you? Belle I suppose."

"We can sue them if we can prove it."

"I wouldn't want to do that," Zac said hurriedly. "I have my own way of dealing with the Tellier brothers. . . . As for your suggestion, well certainly I'll think about it. . . ." He looked at his watch. "Now I really must go."

"Won't you have dessert? Or cheese. It's all been very rushed."

"I'm in a hurry you see," Zac said as he stood up. "I'm worried about my wife too, needless to say." He looked at her with an expression on his face that was almost benign. "It's *very* good of you to have invited me, Sandra, and, like you, I hope for better relations. We need them, you'll soon see. We must all stick together."

She was still wondering what he meant by "you'll soon see" as, from the window, she watched him emerge from the door on to the pavement and hail another cab to take him across the Seine.

She was thanking the butler and getting her things together when the telephone rang. Agnès was on the line.

"Oh Mademoiselle," she said. "I wondered if I'd catch you."

"I'm just off to the airport, Agnès. I'm due in Geneva by five. Can I . . . ?"

"Please, Mademoiselle, I think you should come to the office . . . or I can come to you. There is something you should see. You may wish to cancel your plane."

"But what *is* it, Agnès?"

"Something not very pleasant, I'm sorry to say, Mademoiselle. I can't possibly tell you on the phone."

"Won't it wait until tomorrow? I'll be back by lunchtime."

"I think you should see it at once, Mademoiselle. It's the kind of thing that could change your life."

Sandra sensed that everyone in the office was awaiting her with bated breath, as twenty minutes later, she hurried through the swing doors and across the secretariat to her office. Whatever it was everyone knew, except her.

Agnès was waiting by her desk, head bowed, a newspaper in her hand which she silently handed to Sandra who, tossing her briefcase on the couch, sat down and started to read.

"GUEST OF PRIME MINISTER ENJOYS HOLIDAY WITH LOVER ON BEACH," screamed the banner headline and, sure enough, there she was with Tim, both of them apparently naked as they nearly had been only two months before. . . .

She stared at it for several seconds, various emotions registering on her face until she realized something else and looked at the photograph even more closely.

"But . . . it's not true," she said eventually to Agnès, who was looking over her shoulder. "Tim and I never made love on the beach in the nude."

Agnès merely grimaced—an expression that meant neither belief nor disbelief.

"It is not true, I tell you," Sandra said, getting up and thumping the paper with her fist. "These are fakes."

"It looks so real, Mademoiselle. It *is* you. . . ."

"Oh it's *me* all right," Sandra said. "It is my face. But it's not my body and . . ." She scrutinized it, a half smile on her face despite the circumstances. "I don't think it's Tim either. Really, I don't know that this was enough to call me to the office for, although I know you meant well. Tell my pilot to prepare my plane."

"But Mademoiselle," Agnès wailed, "I'm afraid there is more. It gets worse." She flicked through the pages of the *Daily Enquirer* and held it away from her as if she could hardly bear to look at it. Sandra, snatching it from her, spread it on her desk, staring at it with an open mouth.

"Well, I don't believe it," she said. "How on earth did they get *these?*"

In front of her was a double-page spread of photographs in various suggestive poses of a woman taken in the nude. The poses were clearly deliberate; those of a professional model. The face was undoubtedly hers. Beneath them was the legend:

"Before taking up her position as head of the Desmond Group Mademoiselle Sandra Desmond O'Neill took time off to model for an agency that specialized in supplying pictures of a pornographic nature to girlie magazines. Lovely Sandra is clearly a talented, versatile lady, as these photographs show.

Mademoiselle Desmond was at the center of a family storm when she inherited the Desmond empire from the late Georges Desmond, who thus disinherited the rest of his legitimate children.

It has always been supposed that this charming young lady was a natural daughter of the late Georges Desmond. If that is the case she is seen on another page with her half-brother Mr. Timothée Desmond . . .

Compromising circumstances. No?"

"My God," Sandra said, standing upright and firmly shutting the pages containing such damning and offensive material. "Cancel the plane and get me my lawyer."

Tim, ashen faced, stood together with Zac and Belle gazing at the same pictures that were preoccupying Sandra on the other side of Paris.

"That's going much too far," Tim said, crossing the room to the telephone. "I'm going to tell her."

Zac, moving surprisingly quickly, got to the phone before his more athletic brother and slapped his hand across the receiver.

"Don't be such a fool! Can't you see we've got her?"

"But you've got *me* too." He pointed angrily to the photos.

"Yes, but that doesn't matter," Belle said nonchalantly. "You're a man. Besides, you didn't have lunch recently with the British Prime Minister." Belle giggled. "Nor, I think now, is it ever *likely* you'll get an invitation."

"It *is* absolutely scandalous," Tim said.

"But remember how she treated you. . . ." Belle lay back against the sofa in Zac's drawing room with the air of a woman utterly and completely at peace with herself and the world.

In fact Belle von Burg-Farnbach was the sort of person who only seemed completely alive and at ease when she *was* engaged in some sort of trouble, especially at the expense of someone else. She thrived on danger, uncertainty and, in a sense, insecurity. "Didn't she kick you out of the house . . . the house where you were born?" she added slowly.

Tim straightened up and folded his arms. The memory of that encounter with Sandra still brought a feeling of bile to his throat.

Having loved, or thought he was falling in love, he now disliked her in equal measure. In some people love turns quickly to hatred and Tim, prey to violent emotions from his childhood, was one of these.

Maybe, he thought, he had fooled himself in the Bahamas, as Belle had suggested.

Zac was standing by the phone, as if to keep an eye on his younger brother and Belle continued to lounge on the sofa with all the ease and elegance of a leopard.

Tim suddenly realized that his brother and sister were an evil pair and he should have had nothing to do with them.

By concentrating on his vanity and Sandra's vulnerability, they had enmeshed them both in their wrongdoing.

He moistened his lips, feeling suddenly like a fly trapped between two fat, bloodsucking spiders, if such things existed.

"What will happen when you finally *destroy* Sandra?" he said, slipping into the seat beside Belle. "Will you think of something else?"

"What do you *mean?*" Belle said, looking at him curiously. " 'Something else.' "

"You're a nasty pair," Tim said. "I suppose you know that."

Belle parted her lips in that sweet smile that reminded Tim of his sister when, much younger, he really had believed she was the quintessence of beauty and innocence.

"We're nothing of the kind," she said. "You know that. If *anyone* is nasty it is that person who has usurped our inheritance, and I hope you understand that." She leaned forward, pointing a finger at him. "You *see,* Tim, if we get what we want *you* will get what you want too."

"Well I don't want her," Tim said savagely. "I'm over that episode."

"Quite." Belle nodded approvingly. "You've now seen her for what she is; grasping and arrogant. Throwing you out of your own home—you, a true Desmond. Either you, or her, indeed. What cheek! *We* felt anything was justified to get rid of her . . . *anything.*"

"You might have told me." Tim studied the paper again. Then his face broke into a smile. "Actually I look rather good, don't I?"

"You look very good." Belle stroked his back approvingly. "You look *very* good . . . and you *are* very good. Much, much too good for her."

Sometimes Lady Elizabeth thought there was no end to the tears she was capable of shedding. Alone of course. There wasn't a member of her family, including her late husband Georges, who could ever have claimed to have seen her weep in public. Then she was the strong, quintessential Englishwoman; epitome of the stiff upper lip.

But alone she cried quite frequently, and then she wished she had a cat or a dog to stroke and give her the sort of comfort that only dumb animals can give, silent, unreproachful friends.

Lady Elizabeth was born an Englishwoman and, naturally, like most upper-class women of her kind, she loved animals. She shared a passion with the English Royal Family for horses and one of her brothers had been a trainer to Royalty.

However, the animals she had at Tourville were not the kind that one could readily stroke, and there were no cats. Lady Elizabeth had quite a thing about cats—silent, enigmatic creatures—and wouldn't allow them in the house.

Thus she sat in front of her window with its view of the rose garden; or at her bureau writing letters to her sister or sister-in-law, while the tears pouring down her face would have stained the pages were she not careful. Her pride took care of that.

For now, on top of the scandal about Tara, there was this atrocious article about Tim and Sandra . . . an article that said all the things that she had dreaded and which, once again, implicated the whole family.

Tim and Sandra . . . lovers . . . brother and sister. Incredible! If only she knew . . . if only she knew the whole truth.

She sighed and, once again, she dried her eyes and resumed the letter to Laetitia Broughton, who was so steadfast in times of trouble. Not, Lady Elizabeth felt, that the Broughton family had ever had troubles like these. They had the troubles that customarily concerned the English gentry from time immemorial: homosexuality, debt, and heterosexual adultery—not murder and the suggestion of incest.

"If only my dear Georges had known what a hornet's nest

he would stir up when he did what he did," she wrote and then paused as there was a knock on the door. She glanced into the mirror to make sure that there were no traces of tears on her face.

"Come in," she called, knowing quite well who it was as Pierre's tap was a singular blend of respect and authority. He entered with a silver tray on which there was a thick parchment envelope and bowed.

"This came for you by hand, My Lady. . . ."

"Oh great heavens," Lady Elizabeth said with a sigh, shortsightedly gazing at the address on the envelope as she took it. "Not *more* trouble I hope?"

"I hope not, Madame," Pierre echoed sympathetically and bowed his way out.

For some reason, she did not know what, Lady Elizabeth remained for some moments studying her name and address neatly handwritten:

Madame Georges Desmond
Château de Tourville
Tourville
Reims.

It was a quaint copperplate style of handwriting such as young people in France were taught before the War. Finally she took up her silver paperknife and slit through the flat of the envelope, extracting from it several sheets, closely written.

She frowned, then turned to the last page to read the signature whereupon her frown turned to an expression of intense surprise. Getting up from the bureau, she took the pages over to her chair by the window, adjusted her glasses and began to read a letter dated six months before.

Chemin de la vigne, Crémy

My dear Madame Desmond, [it began in French and continued:]

I am writing this letter to you because I feel I am very close to death, and that I cannot depart this life without entrusting a burden I have carried for a long long time to someone whom I can trust and respect.

Recently you came to visit me, Madame, and asked me certain questions. I had the feeling you were not satisfied with what you were told, thinking, maybe, that I was withholding some information that might be important.

You were quite right, Madame, I was. . . .

Hurriedly Lady Elizabeth scanned the letter and then she read more slowly through it again, digesting every word, until she came to the last paragraph.

I would beg you never *to divulge this information, Madame, unless it is absolutely vital. A matter, if you like, of life and death. For this reason too I have instructed that the letter should not be passed on to you until some time after my own death. When that will be I know not; but I hope that, at the end, God will be with me.*

Thank you, dear Madame, for your kindness,

Yours respectfully,
Hélène Marie O'Neill

Lady Elizabeth let the letter fall on her lap and, for a long time, it lay there while the darkness gathered around the vast house and she stared uncomprehendingly out of the window.

26

Throughout the summer, the scandals surrounding the various members of the Desmond family continued to titillate that vast readership of popular newspapers that flourishes not only in Europe but also on the other side of the Atlantic.

The fact that two prominent members of the family were involved naturally failed to impress the various stock exchanges of the world. With the news of the bottling disaster to the vintage, a few minor reverses in companies allied to the Group and doubt about the future, Desmond shares began to fall. It was no time to take a vacation and Sandra had a considerable amount of juggling to do in which she required the help and support of the Franco-Belges Bank and Philippe de Lassale.

Philippe knew if Desmond went he'd go, and Zac knew that if the Banque went they'd all go. Accordingly he stopped his machinations for a while and became a responsible member of the Board, momentarily the true ally that Sandra had so desperately sought.

The predicament of Tara continued to be a matter of great interest. A lot of ferreting around was done by journalistic sleuths and some skeletons were dug out of the family cupboard of the Falconetti. At least one murderer was discovered in the past, if not more. Zac had publicly stated that he was on the track of Livio's real killer, which involved sordid illegalities in the used-car industry, and declared that when he had news it would be released to the police. Tara was let out of jail into his custody on payment of a substantial sum of bail money.

In England the *Daily Enquirer,* on secret instructions from Zac, announced it would defend a suit of libel and slander slapped on it by Sandra, whose lawyers were instructed to try and get an early hearing, the wheels of justice being notoriously slow.

Tim Desmond, again on instructions from his elder brother, deduced it was the opportune moment to take a trip to the Far East and disappeared. He had the ability to forget.

Strega, meanwhile, was a very busy man. He had made himself indispensable to Zac but, seeing that he was supposed to be in exile and disgraced, he slipped about under a variety of aliases as he either crossed the Channel to instruct the *Enquirer,* or flew down to Marseilles on the track of Gomez.

Strega and René-Zachariah Desmond seemed destined to meet at some time in their lives. Except that one had money and the other had none they were very similar characters. They were both insecure, inclined to violence and did things by stealth. Evasion and distortion of the truth came to both of them with consummate ease.

Strega was always called simply that: Strega. It had long been forgotten whether it was his first name or his second, though when he worked for the Desmond Group he was listed in the personnel department STREGA, Paul.

His relationship with Zac had a curious, slightly sinister, history. He had been Zac's batman when he did his national service in the 501 Regiment of Cavalry, and remained with him until he left for the United States to study at Harvard. Then Strega had worked for a time for Desmond Champagne in Reims.

When Zac returned to France he made Strega his personal assistant and found him lodgings at Épernay at the home of a wealthy old lady known to the Desmonds, who didn't like to be alone.

A few months after he went to live with her, the landlady, Madame Meunier, was found murdered, her belongings scattered throughout the house as if by the act of a thief.

Strega was arrested immediately; but Zac at once provided an alibi for him, saying that on the night of the murder he had been at Tourville on the other side of the river. None would question the word of a Desmond.

Strega never denied his guilt to Zac and Zac knew that his employee had the soul of a killer. He had been reduced to the ranks in the army, after becoming a sergeant, on account of his aptitude for violence. There had been a nasty scandal when several of the new recruits had been seriously beaten upon his orders.

Strega's true feelings for Zac were ambivalent and became more so as he saw the depths to which his master could sink, especially since his ambitions had been thwarted by Sandra O'Neill. He had never imagined that such a grand man who had birth, wealth and talent at his command could be in the grip of so much hatred; and he felt that in this strong and strange emotion there could only be something of benefit for him.

Strega was afraid of Zac and his power over him, but he was even more afraid of the Princess because he felt that Zac had an odd kind of affection for him whereas she had none. He sensed she was a vengeful, vindictive woman; that she was ruthless and that she would use him for whatever purpose she wished and discard him if she wished too. She had no liking for him, no loyalty toward him.

Strega was anxious to build up as much evidence as he could against the Desmond brother and sister so that, should they ever use what they knew about him he, in his turn, could turn the tables on them.

Like Zac, Strega was greedy. He would do anything for

money and Zac always saw that he had enough: just a little more than was needed. His greed made Strega keen to better himself, to accumulate enough wealth one day to disappear: to be free from Zac, change his name and be his own man.

He knew that, one day, his chance would come.

Strega was a loner; he liked to live dangerously and, since the business with the yeast, he had had his fill. Trips to the United States, the Caribbean, Marseilles, London . . . he was Zac's right-hand man and he made the most of this.

Strega soon discovered his suspicion that Gomez was connected with the underworld of the used-car business was right. He was proving a very good detective. He found out the name of the man who had hired the car to Gomez in which he nearly killed Sandra, and this led him to the sleazy substrata of Marseilles where drug-trafficking and prostitution were rife. It transpired that Ignacio Gomez had been born here to an itinerant Spanish worker and a French mother and so, finally, it was in Marseilles that Strega ran him to earth.

Gomez and Strega had never met; but Strega knew that his quarry had a large uneven scar on his cheek, the consequence of an encounter with the police in his youth. He finally found Gomez outside a café in the hinterland of Marseilles engaged in an innocent game of boule, his cap on his head, a cigarette permanently wedged in the corner of his mouth. It was as innocuous a sight on a balmy summer evening as you could ever wish to see.

Strega joined some other members of the local community on a bench. He too wore the customary cap and was sipping from a glass of Pastis. He really seemed to be enjoying the game, admiring the skill of Gomez and applauding when, finally, he was declared the winner.

He got up as if they were old friends and, holding out his hand, shook that of Gomez and invited him for a drink. Gomez at first seemed to think he knew Strega as his cronies gathered around him and were treated to free drinks as well.

Finally, when some time had passed and many glasses of beer or Pastis had been consumed, Gomez found himself almost alone in the bar with this friendly chap whom he now looked at out of the corner of his eye, as one hand touched the still sensitive scar on his cheek.

"Do I know you, Monsieur?" he inquired politely.

"I think so," Strega said in an equally pleasant way. "Certainly you know *of* me."

"I think you're a friend of my brother Pedro? Did he send you to see me?"

"That's it," Strega said, whereupon Gomez seized him by the throat at the back of the dark café where they were sitting and pinioned him against the wall.

"I have no brother Pedro, Monsieur."

"Ah I thought you hadn't," Strega said with a change of tone and at that moment Gomez felt something hard pressed against his thighbone.

"A gun, Monsieur," Strega whispered. "Let's go outside."

"And be killed?" Gomez hissed. "Are you mad? Do it here if you have to. At least there is a witness." He looked at the bar owner inconsequentially polishing glasses in the far end of the bar.

"But I don't *wish* to kill you, Monsieur Gomez," Strega hissed back. "I just want a little talk. You may find in the end it is to your advantage to do business with me . . . *and* Monsieur Desmond!"

Even in the gloom of the bar it was easy to see Gomez's face change color as his eyes took on the yellowy tinge of fear.

"Yes, Monsieur Desmond," Strega repeated with a good-natured smile, continuing to jab Gomez in the ribs. "Your crime has caught up with you, my son."

"I tell you, I never meant. . . ."

"Let's go outside." Strega gestured brusquely toward the door. "I want to talk to you. I promise you I haven't come to kill you. At the moment I think you are too valuable for that. You may even find our little discussion to your advantage—who knows?"

Gomez looked imploringly at his friend the barman and proprietor of the café who was clearing up after his night's work; but the gentleman in question had been for much too long on the wrong side of the law to come to the aid of a fellow malefactor. To him Strega looked like an important man, maybe a "flic" and he gave him an ingratiating smile as he passed, with his concealed gun pressed close into Gomez's side, and a polite: *"Salut,* Monsieur Ignacio!"

After they left he quickly ran from behind the bar and hurriedly closed the shutters of the café before he could hear the muffled sound of a pistol shot.

Once inside he wiped his brow, gave a sigh of relief and helped himself to a large cognac.

Meanwhile Strega and Gomez walked together for some time in the dark, the latter breathing heavily, the former whistling a tune. Finally Gomez stopped but he felt that hard object again, this time in the small of his back.

"Don't run for it, Gomez. It would be foolish. I said I just wanted to talk."

"But where?"

"Have you a car?"

"We're not far from where I live."

"Then let's go there . . . oh I know you have a woman. But she'll have to shut her ears if she knows what's good for her. Don't worry, I know a lot about you, Ignacio Gomez, because you led me and Monsieur Zac a merry dance for quite some time. But," he clapped a friendly hand on his shoulder, "no hard feelings. In fact I admire you, to tell you the truth." Gomez looked at him warily, guessing, probably accurately, that Strega had seldom told the truth in his life.

Gomez lived in one of those tall apartment blocks that had been built on the edge of Marseilles for the teeming working population shortly after the War. The walls were covered in graffiti both inside and out, there was an elevator which seldom worked. But this night it did and they went to the tenth floor glaring at each other in the gloom of the flickering naked light bulb inside.

"What a depressing place," Strega remarked, wrinkling his nose at the stench of urine, the marks of damp in the corners of the elevator. "Why are you roosting in a hole like this, Gomez? I would have thought working for Monsieur Desmond would pay you better, but he said you never even came to collect the money. That would have made you quite rich, I understand."

"I was never meant to *kill* him," Gomez said, the sweat breaking out on his forehead. "Beat him up, were Monsieur Zac's instructions. Mark him a little. That sort of thing. When I saw Madame Desmond had been arrested I thought her husband would kill *me.*"

"And *well* he might, Gomez," Strega said with a sinister chuckle. "And well he might; but not me. I have other ideas for you."

"Really?" For the first time since Strega had identified himself, hope briefly flickered in Gomez' bilious-colored eyes.

"Ah yes." As the elevator stopped they got out and walked together along another dreary ill-lit corridor stinking from pools of urine and what occasionally looked like vomit, until Gomez put the key in the lock of a door. However, the door was wrenched open from the inside by a woman whose own colorless features were marked by fear. When she saw Gomez she clutched at the lapel of his coat and shook him.

"Where have you been? Horace from the bar phoned to say—" Then she saw Strega standing behind, in the shadow of Gomez, and she put both hands to her face.

"Oh no. . . ." she cried, shrinking back.

"There's nothing to fear, Maria," Gomez said in Spanish, putting a brave face on it. "This is a friend of mine, Monsieur

Strega. He has come all the way from Paris about a job he wants me to do. . . ."

"Oh. . . ." The woman lowered her hands, the fear in her eyes momentarily replaced by a look of hope.

"This is Maria," Gomez said briefly to Strega, who nodded his head. "Get us some brandy, Maria, and then leave us alone."

"Coffee for me, if you have it, Madame," Strega said politely. "If I drink too late at night it gives me heartburn." He touched his heart with a look of pain.

They went into a poorly furnished room whose evident poverty was only relieved by a splendid view of Marseilles and the bay. The twinkling lights of any city can make it look beautiful at night and Marseilles was no exception, but during the day it was a different story. Few came to Marseilles for its scenic attractions, though it was surrounded by beautiful countryside. To it came the flotsam and jetsam of the world, the down-at-heel, bedraggled and dispossessed and, consequently, the city was a cesspit of crime to which these deadbeats were attracted.

Strega paused briefly by the window to admire the view but was too conscious of the steep drop down from the tenth floor to the concrete earth below, and hastily stepped back as Maria entered with a bottle and two glasses.

"Just in case you change your mind, Monsieur. The coffee will be ready in a moment."

Gomez, who had taken off his jacket, quickly poured some liquid into the two glasses and handed one to Strega, who shook his head noting the spreading stains under Gomez' armpits. He could even smell his fear. He wondered why Zac had engaged such an obviously frightened and incompetent fellow to do his work and, to try and ease the tension, he began to encourage him to tell him about how he knew Monsieur Zac and how long he had worked for him.

"I did, in fact, once work in the garage where Monsieur

and Madame Desmond had their cars serviced. From time to time I would come around to the house to wash their cars, and then I began to do little jobs for Monsieur. I hoped he would take me on permanently as a handyman. . . ."

"And so he might have done had you not been such an idiot as to knock out the brains of Monsieur Livio! Even *that* might not have been such a bad thing had Madame Desmond not been arrested for the murder. That is something I think Monsieur Desmond finds it hard to forgive."

"I know, I know." Gomez anxiously wiped his face so that two streaks appeared down each cheek as if he'd been crying. "Believe me I was terrified. I took with me two men who knew just what to do, as Monsieur Desmond had said. 'Just rough Livio over, so that he leaves Madame Desmond alone,' that was what he said. Believe me I *liked* working for Monsieur Desmond. I had some pleasant jobs to do. I was able to drive his car. . . . Believe me I never meant that Livio shouldn't recover. Never, never." Gomez, still sweating, put his face in his hands.

Strega watched him, sipping the hot black coffee which Gomez' unattractive female companion had brought in.

Gomez really was a man down on his luck, Strega thought without pity; but someone like this, unscrupulous as well as poor, could be useful. It might be an error to give him over to the police as Zac wanted.

Besides, Gomez undoubtedly knew too much and when cornered would certainly not hesitate to squeal, bringing to Monsieur Zac more harm than he had already.

As Gomez prattled on, drinking a second and yet a third brandy, Strega still listened, but, as Gomez went for a fourth, he put his hand out and deftly removed the bottle.

"That is *quite* enough," he said. "I want you to talk sense."

"There was this man called the Gorilla," Gomez said as if unable to stop. "We should *never* have brought him. He's an animal. I didn't know he was a killer. Once he started hitting

Monsieur Livio he couldn't stop. I never touched him. Honestly. I simply stood at the door and watched the Gorilla do his work. I begged him to stop. I tried to *make* him stop, but he went on hitting him. In the end I, and the other bloke, pulled him off and ran for it. I didn't know until I read it in the papers that Livio was dead. My God, I was scared." Gomez covered his face again.

"That *was* a very big mistake," Strega said, lighting a small cigar. "But Monsieur Desmond would, I think, overlook your part in all this if you could deliver the Gorilla to the police. Now, could you do that?"

"You mean accuse *him* of Livio's murder?"

"Of course. You know he did it. He was the culprit. Poor Madame Desmond, whatever her faults, and indiscretion is certainly one of them, is not a murderess. All Monsieur Desmond wants is to clear the name of Madame Desmond because he has other fish to fry. Also it is very bad for business, for his reputation. Now . . ." Strega put a hand on his knee and with his other pointed at Gomez.

"I think there is a lot of work for you, and me, to do for Monsieur Desmond, Gomez. I think we could work well together and we should be kept in employment and, incidentally, in clover for years if we play our cards properly. Now . . . where does the Gorilla live? Do you know?"

Gomez shook his head and that look of fear which had never left him appeared to intensify.

"If I fingered the Gorilla he would kill *me*. He would probably kill Madame Desmond as well. He did not get his name for nothing. I can promise you that. He is a sadist."

Suddenly a shifty look came into his eyes and, running lightly to the door, he opened it swiftly and looked outside to make sure Maria didn't have her ear at the keyhole. Shutting it again, he crossed the room and sat on the threadbare sofa next to Strega who, repelled by the smell of perspiration that came from him, tried unsuccessfully to move out of his way.

"Now look." Gomez clutched his arm and Strega resigned himself to the inevitable. "The Gorilla is no good. The other guy who was with me has disappeared. The Gorilla, however, *does* want his cut and I am hiding as much from him as anyone else. He is after me; he'll be after you, Monsieur Desmond, anyone, until he gets his money. He doesn't stand on ceremony, you know. He's not a nice man."

"Then *if* we hand him over to the police we shall all be safe."

"Impossible." Gomez shook his head. "He is a blabbermouth. He will talk. He knows too much but," the crafty look returned, "the man who drove the car is a half-wit. He had nothing at all to do with the crime and he would be perfect to finger for this job. He knows no one and nothing. . . ."

"Then how can *he* be arrested for the murder?"

"We will tell the police where the car used for the job is hidden and you will find that the fingerprints of the man who drove the car—a small-time crook called Mourad Aziz—are all over the wheel."

Sandra stopped by the laboratory bench and, for a few seconds, looked at the man peering intently into the microscope. She was about to pass on when he lifted his eyes and, with an air of surprise, saw who was standing next to him.

"Mademoiselle Desmond," he said, getting up and removing his glasses. "No one told me you were coming."

"I didn't want to disturb you, Dr. Harcourt," Sandra replied. "I know how hard you're working."

She was about to smile and pass on; but he took her arm and led her over to the bench, indicating a tall stool for her to sit on. "Please sit down, Mademoiselle, at least for a moment."

Perching rather uncomfortably on the stool, she gazed at him as he sat opposite her pointing to the microscope.

"These are the cells of the AIDS virus," he said. "Would you care to look?"

Sandra screwed up her face.

"Isn't it dangerous?" she said half jokingly.

"Not like this I assure you, Mademoiselle. You are perfectly safe."

Sandra smiled and, as the doctor showed her how to adjust the lens of the powerful microscope, she peered into it but could see nothing.

"It's just a blur," she said but, as his hand continued to twiddle a knob beside her, clearly in view she suddenly saw a lot of activity on the slide beneath the lens.

"Those are the microbes," he said. "You can see how the structure of the cell has changed. . . ." He continued to give her a lecture on the ability of the virus to invade human cells and change them.

Sandra listened attentively. When he finished she said, "You must forgive me; I know nothing about biochemistry but I am fascinated by what you're doing and the vital nature of your work."

Sandra got down from her perch and prepared to continue her tour of the laboratory, which was supported now primarily by funds from the Desmond Foundation. "I won't detain you any longer, Dr. Harcourt. I am *very* glad to know the work is going well."

Harcourt held up his glasses and proceeded to clean them on the sleeve of his white coat. Sandra was surprised to see that a man she had only ever had conflict with, whom she was sure hated her and all she stood for, looked embarrassed. He even had a shy smile on his face as he raised his eyes from their apparently futile task and looked at her.

"Mademoiselle Desmond, I *do* feel I owe you an apology. I have not been very nice to you. I have been rude, unintentionally so, I assure you. Sometimes my feelings get the better of me. . . ."

"Oh I quite understand, Dr. Harcourt," Sandra replied to spare him further embarrassment. "I know you have your principles and I respect them."

"Yes, but you have given me a lot of money and I know that at the moment things are not very easy for you."

"That's *very* kind of you." She bowed her head in acknowledgment. "I must tell you that things have *never* been easy for me since I took charge of the Desmond Group. They are no better and no worse. Unfortunately, due to one or two matters beyond our control, the price of our shares is depressed but now that the real, or alleged murderer of Madame Desmond's friend has been found, I think that will help; the market will start to recover again."

"Why do you say 'alleged'?" Harcourt inquired curiously, proving to Sandra that he was not above a spot of gossip; maybe he was quite human after all.

"Because I am not the only one to find it extraordinary that a man who is apparently almost half-witted found the strength, the resources, or the motive to murder single-handedly someone not only much more intelligent than he was, but bigger and more powerful too."

"But the motive was the money. Don't people murder for that?"

"I'm really not an expert on the subject, Dr. Harcourt. All I can say is I'm glad the charges against Tara Desmond have been dropped, though I am not convinced the police have found the true assassin."

Dr. Harcourt glanced at his watch and then at Sandra. "It is nearly a quarter to one. I don't suppose I might take you to lunch . . . ?"

"Why . . ." Momentarily and uncharacteristically Sandra was lost for words.

"I feel I owe it to you to say 'thank you,' Mademoiselle. There's a little bistro around the corner. Nothing much. . . ."

"I can't think of anything I'd like better," Sandra said. "I didn't have time for breakfast."

Somehow it was like being at college again. The small sort of bistro she rarely patronized these days, with an attractive man opposite her, surprisingly youthful looking though she knew he was nearly forty. She also found that she had an engaging and articulate companion and not the morose, intense, aggressive foe she had thought him to be.

When she first met Michel Harcourt she had found him attractive, but this soon faded when she got to know him, even remotely. But she recalled how she had looked at his picture for a while longer than was strictly necessary, and how amused Agnès had been by it. "I fancy him myself," Agnès had said.

They ate simply, a cold *ratatouille niçoise* followed by *tartare de Sauman* and both drank Perrier water. For dessert they ate strawberries. For a long time they talked about America, where Harcourt had worked and which he knew well. They spoke partly in English and partly in French and, for some reason, the time flew by. There was a lot of laughter. By the end of the meal there was a bond.

Sandra had avoided talking about herself until coffee when Harcourt said, "I was very sorry to hear about this libel case you're bringing in England."

Sandra couldn't resist a smile. "My, you *are* up to date, aren't you? I wouldn't have thought that sort of thing would interest someone like you."

"Why 'someone like me'?" Harcourt looked a little hurt. "I am quite an ordinary guy, I assure you."

"I didn't mean to be offensive," Sandra said immediately. "But you *do* strike me as extremely devoted to your cause. Tittle tattle I shouldn't have thought of much interest to you."

"Ah, but my boss is suing someone, a newspaper. I don't think *that's* tittle tattle. It must be very distressing to have your parentage in question."

"It is," Sandra said, bowing her head. "You see, *I* know, but I don't think that," she paused before she mentioned his name, "that Tim Desmond does. He has gone away, very distressed about the whole thing."

"Let you down in fact."

"No." Sandra again paused before continuing, wondering how much she could and should say. "He didn't let me down. I know Tim has a reputation as a womanizer, but I think he was genuinely fond of me. . . ."

"I'm sure he was," Harcourt murmured and it was at that precise moment that the personal element entered into a relationship that, hitherto, had been purely formal and businesslike. It was the tone Harcourt used, and the way he looked at her. Sandra found herself at first staring at and then avoiding that deep, penetrating gaze.

It was then too that she was aware of what she had sensed the time she first saw his photograph: his fascination. He was a very compelling and fascinating man.

"Tim was . . ." Sandra faltered again. "Yes, very fond of me, and I him; but there was an element of doubt. We can't know for sure, now that my mother is dead."

"There are blood tests," Harcourt said. "You can't be one hundred percent sure but at least you could know if he wasn't."

"Really?" Sandra looked at him.

"Oh yes, they're becoming better and more advanced all the time. We can identify genes. It's called blood printing. It's a pity he's gone away. It could have saved you a lot of misery."

"I never thought of that," Sandra said slowly. "Just because I myself was so *sure* he was not my brother."

"Why are you so sure?"

"Hélène O'Neill told Madame Elizabeth Desmond, Tim's mother, that Georges Desmond was not my father. I believe her. As for those photographs . . ." she flushed slightly, "they are completely false. Tim and I did make love, but not on the beach. Never. And the studio poses . . . never in my life have I worked nude for a professional photographer. Anyone who knows me at all knows it is quite out of character."

"I'm sure of that," Harcourt said, "but how did they get the photographs?"

"They are all fakes! My face could easily be superimposed over any nude model. Someone took a picture of me and Tim lying on the beach, but we wore bathing suits; Tim trunks and me a bikini; not much, but we were respectably clad for the Caribbean. It is my face and his face but not our bodies."

"Then that can be proved too," Harcourt said, signaling for more coffee to the waiter. "You must get the originals. . . ."

"Unfortunately we have thought of that and we can't. We don't know where they came from and in British law a newspaper can respect its sources. It is an inviolable principle. They have delivered to my lawyers the copies of the photos they received. But that's what they are: copies. You need the originals to work out the fine details of where the cuts were made and so on."

"I don't think they've got much of a case," Harcourt said, leaning back and fingering his spoon. "But it is all very distressing for you."

"Very."

"Don't you think you should drop the case?"

"No."

"I was thinking of your peace of mind."

"Would it give *you* peace of mind, Dr. Harcourt, to be accused by the world's Press of incest, of posing in the nude for money?"

"No it wouldn't." Now it was Harcourt's turn to lower his eyes and when he raised them his expression had changed.

"I hope you will call me Michel. I feel you could use a friend . . . Sandra. I feel you are a pretty lonely woman and that the burden you are carrying is almost overwhelming."

"It is and I am," Sandra said, realizing to her dismay that she was not very far from tears. It was rare these days that someone was really kind to her, or seemed to care about her as a person and not as the head of Desmond. She was surrounded either by enemies or sycophants, except for Henri Piper, and now there was the complication of Sophie's jealousy.

She opened her handbag and, producing a handkerchief, gave her nose a hearty blow.

"You must excuse me," she said. "I think it's a touch of the hay fever."

"You'd better not go near the harvest, in that case," Michel said, smiling, and called for the bill.

It didn't seem a year since the last harvest when Tim had intervened to stop her dancing with an attractive young man. She remembered how carefree she'd felt then, how full of confidence and brimming over with hope for the future.

It had been a very difficult year and now the wine year was beginning all over again with the harvest of the grapes. There had been no talk, no mention of time-and-motion experts this year. She had learned something; she hoped she was always learning and always would. But this time they would be very careful indeed when the important moment came to select the blend for the *cuvée*.

Once again the festival was at the Château de Marsanne; but this time there was no Claire, who was living happily in Rome with Piero, her baby nearly due. Nor was there Tim; but Bob and Lady Elizabeth had driven over, and Zac and Tara were there.

Zac and Tara were seen everywhere together these days, in the manner of the happy couple reunited after a near catastrophe. Zac refused to let her out of his sight, unless she was accompanied by a bodyguard; a tough, nasty-looking man with a scar who, apparently, used to clean his car. His name was Gomez, Tara's bodyguard. There would be no danger at all, everyone felt, of her falling in love with him.

Bob had been banished since Tara had been released on bail, and Tara took care to be as offhand with him as she could. The very last thing she wanted at this time was to excite Zac's jealousy again. She was afraid of Gomez and she was afraid of Zac. She also shared a general suspicion that the real murderer had not been caught, though the examining magistrate had found the case against Mourad Aziz overwhelming. He lived alone, had no dependents, and no witnesses to his movements on the night Livio was killed. Also his fingerprints were, indeed, all over the wheel of the Renault car which had been found abandoned in a run-down garage outside Paris.

The guilt of Aziz seemed proven to the satisfaction of everyone. All that remained was the sentence.

Sandra thought Tara a much subdued woman these days and it was not hard to understand why. A spell of imprisonment did no one any good, especially a woman used, as Tara was, to a life of luxury. It made some people bitter.

Belle and Carl were staying at Tourville, and had also joined the family party gathered at the Pipers for the harvest.

Sandra would have liked to ask Michel; but she felt it was too early to show the family that their relationship had changed. Even that was premature. They were hardly friends, they were certainly not lovers; but Sandra felt that it was a relationship full of possibilities, something that had to be treasured and gently nurtured along, not open to inspection by the Desmonds.

Philippe de Lassale was also one of the party with his wife

Barbara whose father had been a rich merchant in Lyons. Sandra had never met Barbara de Lassale and spent a lot of time talking to her.

She was a well-known socialite; an espouser of good causes, charity balls and functions that put her in the limelight. She had that rather brittle kind of beauty, a hard-eyed elegance that some women have who are unsure of their husband, his fidelity, their place in his affections and, ultimately, their security. Any moment it may be banishment to a country house, or a flat on one's own on the wrong side of Paris.

"I really know nothing about champagne," Barbara said when they were gathered in the drawing room at the end of the *cochelet,* after the dancing in the fields was over and the fires had all been put out. "Do you?"

"I know more than I did," Sandra said pleasantly. "But not as much as Belle or Zac."

"And I hear Zac is going to take over your champagne business," Barbara said chattily.

"Oh really?" Sandra looked startled, wondering if there was something this social butterfly knew that the Head of the House didn't.

"That's what I heard."

"Well it was suggested but nothing is fixed. It has been a very busy, rather difficult summer for all of us."

"I heard it *was* fixed," Barbara said, looking around for her husband. "That Tellier and Desmond are to merge. . . ."

Sandra literally felt her face change color. Her limbs stiffened and her heart began to beat faster. She looked around for Zac, but neither he nor Philippe de Lassale had yet come in from the vineyards.

"Probably it's just a rumor," Barbara said nervously, sensing that she had made a *faux pas.*

"Well we'll soon find out," Sandra murmured. "Please excuse me." She strode rapidly to the door.

On the terrace Uncle Henri was standing talking to a group

of fellow *négociants.* As Sandra passed him he caught her arm and drew her into the group.

"Sandra, I want you to meet—"

One by one he introduced them, one by one, they smiled, shook hands, said a few words and drifted away.

"You seem very tense," Henri said to her, his hand still on her arm.

"I *feel* very tense," Sandra replied. "Have *you* heard anything about a merger between Desmond and Tellier?"

"No I have not." Henri threw back his head and laughed. "But I would be the last to know and you, presumably, would be the first. Who told you that?"

"Barbara de Lassale." Sandra glanced back to the salon. "Oh quite innocently. She had no idea of the *gaffe* she made. I am on my way to find Zac. . . ."

"He's showing Philippe the place." Henri looked around vaguely. "By the way, you'd think he owned it."

"You'd better look out or he probably will one day," Sandra said and savagely wrenched her arm from Henri's tender grasp.

"Now my dear," Henri chided, putting his hands on her shoulders. "Please, I do beg of you, *don't* make a fuss here tonight. It is neither the time nor the place."

"But I *must* find out—"

"What can you do?" Henri looked into her eyes. By the soft lights from the Château she looked so beautiful he could feel his heart melt. If he could only protect her, help her.

"Look," he continued. "Say nothing tonight, sleep on it and then tomorrow make inquiries . . . act by stealth. You should know that by now when it comes to dealing with the Desmonds."

Sandra, feeling the pressure of his steady hands on her shoulders, seeing the light in his eyes, the determination of his chin, knew he was right. He was such a comfort; so wise. A rock.

Impulsively she threw her own arms around him and kissed his cheek, hugging him to her for a moment or two.

"Oh *Henri,*" she cried. "You're right as always. I *do* love you."

Just behind the door leading to the terrace Sophie Piper, who had been on the verge of stepping out, heard the last words, saw the final gesture and remained where she was, as if rooted to the spot.

27

"Of course the merger with Tellier isn't fixed," Philippe de Lassale said, looking awkwardly from one antagonist to the other. For they were antagonists, Sandra and Zac and, through the stupidity of his wife, he had fallen into the very middle of them like a referee trying unsuccessfully to stop a fight.

"I should think it isn't," Sandra said, glaring at him from behind her desk. These days it was a delicate point of etiquette about who went to see whom. Technically she and de Lassale were equal, Zac the inferior partner. Accordingly, one day she would go to de Lassale's office, the next occasion they would meet at hers.

Zac had insisted that, on this occasion, since Sandra was the one in search of information, they met at the avenue de l'Opéra; but she had flatly refused. So far she was the one in charge and as long as that was the situation she would give the orders.

Orders?

Both Philippe de Lassale and Zac were hardly men to take orders. They were showing her that now, their expressions aloof and hostile. Neither of them felt like being treated as schoolboys summoned to the study of the head teacher. Yet that was exactly what seemed to be happening.

"The very fact," Sandra went on in view of their silence, "that you could *presume* to discuss a merger with Tellier in my absence. Well." She sat back in her chair and stuck her hands firmly in her pockets. "Frankly I find it amazing."

"Zac said that *you* had approached him about running Desmond." Stiffly de Lassale looked for confirmation to Zac, who nodded.

"Mademoiselle invited me for lunch in her apartment."

Sandra spoke slowly so as to choose her words carefully, knowing that Zac was waiting to pounce on any mistake. "I did suggest that as you knew so much about the champagne business compared to myself, strictly as a gesture of reconciliation between us, there *was* a possibility that I might offer you the sole running of the Champagne House of Desmond as an entity within the Desmond Group. I know you love it and are very knowledgeable."

"Tellier was mentioned," Zac said petulantly.

"Tellier *was* mentioned, but only as an example if I recall." Sandra pressed the intercom buzzer to summon her secretary. "Luckily I made some notes about it afterward. The facts are all there."

"Without witnesses," de Lassale said blandly.

"Philippe," Sandra found she was keeping her temper with difficulty, "do I take it you doubt my word?"

"One of you has clearly got the wrong end of the stick," de Lassale said equably. "I wouldn't, naturally, go so far as to call it lying."

"Well thank you for that. . . ." Sandra began with some heat but de Lassale put out a hand:

"A moment please, Sandra. Let me try and establish the facts as I know them."

He joined his arms, raised his eyes to the ceiling and sat back in his chair in the attitude of one deep in thought.

"I understood from Zac that you had asked him to lunch to discuss a merger with Tellier and Desmond, rather as here we had an amicable merger between the Desmond Bank and the Banque Franco-Belges."

"That is quite untrue. It *is* the wrong end of the stick. I—"

Sandra paused as Agnès came in hesitantly, looking nervously first at her then at Zac.

"Yes, Mademoiselle?"

"Please get me the notes I made the day I had lunch with Monsieur Desmond." Sandra began to go through her diary. "I can't recall exactly when it was. Yes." She came to a place and put her finger firmly on it. "It was the day we had the news from England about that scandalous report and I canceled my trip to Geneva. See if you can find them for me, Agnès."

"Bien, Mademoiselle," Agnès said, sidling out of the room without another look at Zac, who had his eyes fixed firmly on the view from the window.

"That should be proof enough for you," Sandra said coldly to de Lassale. "I would hardly make them up in retrospect."

"Well there is obviously a misunderstanding." De Lassale had modified his tone of hostility. "Zac?"

"Evidently," Zac said, "I was under one impression and Miss O'Neill under another."

"Ah thank you, Agnès." Sandra decided to ignore the "Miss O'Neill" which Zac only used when he felt like being offensive, reached for the file as Agnès returned and put it on her desk. Hurriedly she riffled through the papers. "Here it is." She withdrew a typed sheet and gave it to Agnès:

"Would you have this photocopied for me please? Two copies."

Once again Agnès departed while Sandra began to read quickly from the notes.

"I have written here a brief account of meeting with Zac on that day at my apartment. I invited him for lunch because I felt it would be a nice gesture in view of the misunderstanding between us. I said," Sandra peered closely through her glasses, "that I was not relinquishing control of Desmond as a Group, but that I was prepared to make him President of the House of Champagne and treat it as a separate entity *within* the Group."

She looked over the rim of her glasses at Zac. "Within *this* Group that is to say. You were a bit doubtful about it and I said it was rather like the situation with Tellier and Heurtey."

"Ah that's where the misunderstanding occurred." De Lassale looked relieved. "I can see it now."

"Well I didn't think it much of a misunderstanding," Sandra said bluntly. "I thought it was quite clear. We even went on to discuss a suspicion Zac had apparently had in his mind that Tellier were responsible for the doctoring of the software concerning our *cuvée. . . .*"

"That *is* a monstrous idea," de Lassale said, looking at Zac with alarm. "Surely you didn't say that?"

"Of course I didn't," Zac protested. "There Mademoiselle's memory *is* at fault. I don't care what she wrote down. Maybe she had this other business on her mind. It was she who suggested they may have been responsible. It was certainly not I. She even offered to sue them. . . ."

As Sandra gazed at him incredulously the photocopies arrived and each man began studying his intently. Unfortunately Sandra noted as she read further that nowhere had she mentioned the fact that Zac *had* referred to Tellier. Clearly now she could recall the phrase he had used: "There is no doubt they were, in my mind," but she hadn't written it down. What was on record was her offer to sue them and Zac's reply that it shouldn't be done.

This seemed to indicate that Zac's version was the correct one and she was at fault. In future she would tape-record any conversation with him.

De Lassale glanced at his watch.

"I can see no reason to prolong this meeting, Sandra. It is clearly a misunderstanding which I hope has now been cleared up. However, why *don't* you consider it? The Franco-Belges

Bank and Tellier have done very well under the umbrella of Heurtey. Why shouldn't Desmond?"

"Unthinkable," Sandra said. "Quite contrary to the wishes of Georges Desmond. I'm sure Zac will agree with that."

"No, I am not so sure," Zac said, rubbing his chin thoughtfully. "We could have a vast dynamic organization like the Groupe Nicolas, but retaining our own identity. I, of course, would like to control the whole thing, as I have in my little finger as much knowledge as the Tellier brothers have in their two thick heads."

De Lassale laughed uncomfortably and rose.

"I'm afraid I must go, Zac. May I give you a lift?"

"That would be very nice," Zac said, also rising to his feet and looking at Sandra.

"So, Sandra, how shall we leave it now?"

"Well, the whole thing is off as far as I'm concerned." Sandra carefully put the papers back into the file.

"You mean you withdraw your invitation to me?"

"I mean exactly that," Sandra said. "If you can't trust your own memory from one day to the next, I certainly don't want you to take on any further responsibility for me just now. Thank you and good day."

She put out her hand, politely shook those of each of her visitors, and asked Agnès to show them out.

Then, still feeling very angry, she returned to some work on her desk.

The two men sat at the back of the firm's Mercedes which took them back to the avenue de l'Opéra. They both had their eyes on the road in front of them and after a few moments of silence as the large car drew away from the Étoile and made its way along the Champs Élysées Zac was first to speak:

"I think Mademoiselle is losing her grip, Philippe."

"Do you really?" de Lassale replied as if considering a point of interest.

"Decidedly. Don't you?"

"Perhaps."

"She was a very different woman a year ago. She has not nearly as much self-confidence now and," Zac shook his head, "her memory is extremely unreliable."

"I must say," Philippe glanced out of the window as they passed rapidly across the place de la Concorde, "I thought the whole episode distinctly odd. You would hardly tell me that she approved of a merger with Tellier if she hadn't."

"Of course I wouldn't. And the Telliers confirmed I spoke to them?"

Philippe nodded. "They did. I asked them before our meeting. They were surprised, but they told me you broached it to them only a short time ago at dinner."

"It was actually quite a long time ago." Zac could recall the day vividly. "It was the evening I found out about the murder of Livio. . . ."

"You've had a lot on your mind, poor chap." De Lassale put a hand on his arm. "Why not take a break with Tara. A second honeymoon eh?"

"It's kind of you," Zac said, stiffly resenting the implication that maybe his nerve was going too, "but I would first like to see 'Miss O'Neill' put firmly in her place."

"And how do you propose to do that?" Philippe looked at him inquiringly.

"I have a little plan that is not without its interest." Zac glanced at his watch. "Care for a spot of lunch?"

"Why not?" De Lassale gave orders to the chauffeur who changed direction toward La Tour d'Argent on the Left Bank. "I'm always interested to hear new plans."

As Zac, using his key, entered the apartment, Agnès, who had been waiting for him, got up to welcome him. She was surprised when, rather brutally, he pushed her out of the way.

"Whatever is the matter?" she said as he went over to the sideboard and poured himself a large drink.

"You should know." He looked at her over his shoulder.

"I hope it's nothing to do with what happened this morning. That was completely out of my control."

"You could have *told* me that she kept a careful account of every meeting."

"Why should I?" Agnès replied sulkily. "I thought you would know it. She's very thorough."

"Because it's your job." Zac stomped back to the center of the floor and sat on the sofa, his legs spread out before him. "That's what I pay you for; keep this expensive apartment for. I was made a fool of and it was completely unnecessary. You could have pretended it was lost."

"Look." Agnès stood in front of him, hands on hips. "How do *you* imagine Mademoiselle would have responded if I'd said I couldn't find the vital file?"

"I don't know, frankly," Zac said harshly. "But it's your job to do these things and I must say you don't do them very well."

"Oh really?"

"Yes really."

"Then maybe I should stop."

"Maybe you should and get another apartment . . . *if* you can afford one. The six months' lease I took on this is nearly running out anyway."

"Thank you very much, *Monsieur* Zac," Agnès said, going over to the door and throwing it open. "I'll post the key through the mail when I've moved out."

Zac hurriedly put down his glass, clambered to his feet and came over to her. "Now don't be so silly," he said, attempting to put his arm around her. "Just a little bit of temper on my part, and I apologize. I had a hard day."

"So did I. Mademoiselle wasn't very pleased after your

visit." Agnès cast her eyes to the ceiling. "And the things she said about *you!*"

"Oh yes?"

"She called you a liar. She hasn't got a very high opinion of you, that's for sure."

"And I haven't got a very high opinion of her." Zac's anger quickly returned. "Making notes about a meeting with *me. Me!* I ask you."

"She said you were never to be trusted and that, in future, all meetings with you would take place in front of a witness and be tape-recorded."

"Oh *did* she?" Zac smiled. "Hopefully, you."

"I would have to be honest, Zac," Agnès said a trifle maliciously. "Mademoiselle is so sharp she would know quite well if I had made an error."

"Well, she flipped badly over this one." Zac smiled with satisfaction. "And I think I have evolved a way of getting rid of her altogether . . . with the help of Philippe de Lassale, who is fed up with her too. He's not too keen on women in top positions in business. Really, emotionally they're not up to it. It's still a man's world. No, she'll soon be on the way out."

"Oh?" Agnès's eyes gleamed with interest. "How is that?"

"I can't tell you yet my little wooden horse." Zac chucked her playfully under the chin. "But one day, quite soon, you will find yourself working again for me and not her . . . so come now and earn your nice apartment. Make up for this morning. Come to bed."

Agnès was a miner's daughter who had had a hard life. She was ambitious and, to a certain degree, she was capable of deviousness and disloyalty; but she hated to be used and abused and now she realized Zac was doing both.

He was a selfish man, a clumsy lover. His happiness, his fulfillment, certainly came before hers. She resented having to fall into bed whenever he wanted it, whenever it suited him, but she had done it . . . because it had suited her too.

But recently she had begun to long for the time when she could free herself of this bully . . . a bully in bed and the boardroom. When she did she thought she knew of someone who would reward her.

That day, however, was not yet. Obediently, concealing her rebelliousness, she took off her robe and climbed docilely into bed to wait for him.

As the plane took off from the small airstrip, nothing more than a rough track, really, before tilting into the air at what looked like a dangerous angle, the pilot leaned out the cockpit, gave a cheery wave and then set his sights toward . . . what?

Michel Harcourt had spent his life in dangerous missions, and the investigations of the HIV virus was only one of them. He had helped to pioneer the flying doctor services in remote parts of Africa, just one aspect of his personal war against poverty, fear and disease.

The showing of the film in Paris about his work and the work of the Foundation in Africa was a very low-key affair; lounge suits, short dresses. Informality the key word. Sandra knew that Harcourt hated the sort of show that these charity occasions often produced and either he left early or didn't come at all. This time she had wanted him to be present.

She didn't know him very well but what she did know, or was slowly learning, was that he was a very private person, possessed by a vision of the future that very little would deflect him from. He hated all kinds of show and superficiality, displays of obvious wealth.

Michel Harcourt had been born in Arras in northern France; his father had been a clerk at a local factory and the family of five children were not well-to-do.

He had gone to the local school, got a scholarship to the Lycée, then the Faculté de Médicine de Lyon, then the Institut

Pasteur and the Schweitzer Foundation. Now he was one of the most brilliant virologists in the world, internationally renowned for his research in the field of rare viral diseases.

Naturally the challenge posed by HIV would interest him as it also frightened him, and others who knew the enormity of the problem facing medical researchers in the world.

He only slipped into the showing of the film when it had begun, and the seat next to Sandra which had been reserved for him remained vacant. The only time his face had been seen was the brief shot of him from the cockpit of the tiny plane. All the rest were of his back, his head or of his co-workers.

The more one knew about Michel Harcourt the more one could not help becoming intrigued, and Sandra realized she was dangerously near to hero-worship herself. To be in the proximity of such a person was a privilege and, yet, it was a strangely asexual attraction as if one were in the presence of one of those great people who transcend mere humanity.

She was aware all during the performance that he was there somewhere behind her and, as soon as the lights went up and polite applause broke out, she swiftly turned to make sure that he would not disappear beyond the doors before the reception had begun.

She leaned over to Henri Piper, sitting next to her, and said: "Do make sure Dr. Harcourt doesn't go, there's a dear. You know he hates this kind of thing."

Henri smiled understandingly if a little sadly and, as Harcourt got up with, it seemed, just that intention of disappearing, Henri rose too and waylaid him by the door. Sandra, satisfied her prey wouldn't go away, was thus able to greet other people around her without showing any undue curiosity about the chief guest, who was being drawn into conversation with a variety of people by Henri Piper.

As it was low-key, the evening at the Institute itself was a success. The food was plentiful but not lavish; naturally there was champagne but provided by Desmond and Piper free of charge.

Sandra felt all evening that she and Harcourt were gravitating toward each other without actually meeting. Maybe they were intentionally staying apart, and yet there was a sense in which she felt as if an invisible thread were drawing her in his direction.

Eventually they met in the middle of the room and, as sometimes happens on occasions like this, they found they were alone. Or, rather, maybe it *seemed* as though they were alone. He was actually smiling, looking at her, and she held her glass up to him, eyes laughing:

"We do seem to keep on meeting like this."

Michel made a pretense of looking around him. "No balcony with dancing couples I see, Mademoiselle."

"Thank heaven," she said. "I recall it was not too successful last time. Tell me, do you *still* fly those small planes?"

"Well, not as in the film." He looked rueful. "That was shot about seven years ago and of course the whole aspect of what was called the Flying Doctor Service has extended and magnified many times over."

"How's AIDS?" Sandra whispered, leaning toward him.

Harcourt looked grim.

"Not too good I'm afraid. It might be years before we find a vaccine, never mind a cure. There *is* hope in some of the measures to stem the advance of the disease but," he shrugged, "I must return, anyway, to my field laboratory in Africa and put some of these things to the test."

"Oh? Soon?"

"Quite soon," Harcourt said. "Just one or two final experiments in Paris and then I'm off."

"We shall miss you." Sandra's voice was deliberately casual. "I hope you will come and have dinner with my brother and myself before you leave."

"That would be nice, Sandra," Dr. Harcourt bowed, "and

I shall look forward to hearing from you. Before that, however, you must come and have another look around the laboratory."

"I'll make sure I do that." Sandra was aware that inside her was a feeling of desolation, as though she were saying "goodbye" to someone or something before she had properly said "hello."

Henri Piper had been hovering on the edge while they were talking and now, as Harcourt was led off by an American research scientist to meet a colleague from Peru, he said to Sandra:

"I feel you don't dislike this young man as much as you did."

"Dislike is not the right word," Sandra said slowly. "I thought he was rather rude and probably he still is. But, as I've said, he is very clever. We must help him all we can." She looked around her. "Where's Sophie?"

"Sophie has one of her migraines," Henri replied, taking a glance at his watch. "I mustn't be too long."

Sandra paused for a moment and then gave Henri her familiar, frank look. "Henri, Sophie has been *very* odd with me recently. I don't like it."

"I don't like it either," Henri said. "She is being ridiculous."

"Then please let's do something. She *is* a Desmond you know and if she starts whispering about you and me there would be a lot of trouble."

"Oh she would *never* do that!"

"Wouldn't she?" Sandra continued to stare at him with her penetrating gaze. "I think she might, quite easily. I believe she has already hinted something to Lady Elizabeth who is, after all, her sister-in-law. I am not in very good favor in those quarters, so please be careful."

"I don't think you need disturb yourself too much, my dear," Henri said casually. "I am going back to California quite soon. I have a lot to do there. We both like the climate.

Already I've stayed too long in France . . . more to be of help to you than anything else." As he gazed fondly at her she impulsively took his arm.

"I know you'd stay for me and I'll miss you; but yes . . . perhaps it's the right thing. I'm interfering with your business. Besides, I'm much stronger now. I have . . ." She was about to say "Michel," but the announcement suddenly struck her as premature. All she had had was an interest in Michel, a sign from him that he was interested too. Perhaps Henri, dear "Uncle" Henri, had already read those signals. If so he would bow out gracefully and with charm and, at the same time, give confidence and comfort to the wife whom he adored.

"However, I do wish you'd drop the court case," Henri said pleadingly. "It will only bring it all to the surface again and the matter is just beginning to die down."

"But not lie down. It is too damaging to me. If we don't prove it *is* a lie it can resurface again at any time. The English lawyers are doing all they can to get a quick hearing. They hope for one in the spring."

"That is still six months away . . . *plenty* of time to arrange a settlement."

"But the *Daily Enquirer* won't settle. They won't retract or apologize." Sandra looked angry. "Do you think we haven't tried? They want a fight. Let them have one."

"My dear." Henri put a hand on her arm as, from the corner of his eye, he saw the Director of the lab approaching him. "You have too much on your plate, you are too belligerent. You know you are about to have a fight with Zac on account of Tellier. You will lose friends if you carry on like this."

"And make them too. Confidentially, some NATO countries are talking of buying as many of the Desmond-2000 as the Arabs. Imagine what a coup that will be! There will be more of our fighter-planes than in any other air force in the world. The Foundation will never again have to worry about funds or, at least, not until the next generation of aircraft

comes along. I was in Italy last week and I'm going to Germany tomorrow. . . . Ah!" She turned as Professor Jumet came up with a Dr. Martens from Holland, who was also on the trail of a vaccine for the elusive HIV. She put out a hand to Henri, who was saying good night.

"Can't I give you a lift home?" Henri looked worried. "I know you haven't your car."

"No, you go." Sandra gave him a friendly wave. "Who knows, I might even take a stroll. Paris in autumn, falling leaves. . . ."

"Don't you *dare* go out by yourself," Henri replied in alarm. "You'd be a ready subject for a kidnapper. A wealthy, famous woman like you. Promise me now?"

"Of course I won't, don't be silly. I'll take a taxi. I—"

"I'd be delighted to give you a lift home," Michel Harcourt said in her ear. "In fact it would be a privilege as well as an honor. The only thing is I am going quite soon. . . ."

"So am I," Sandra replied, her face involuntarily lighting up. "Shall we say in about half an hour?"

Michel nodded and went off with an English doctor who was making a specialty of counseling the victims of AIDS.

Sandra linked her arm in Henri's and escorted him down the staircase that led to the vestibule.

"He's very nice," Henri said. "Very suitable. I know you hate him, but I think you like him too."

He looked at Sandra slyly, catching her out as she blushed.

"I've never felt quite so strongly that I disliked someone and now . . ." she paused briefly, "quite so strongly that I like them."

"Perhaps one day you'll feel that way about Zac," Henri teased.

"Unlikely." Sandra pretended to smack his arm. "But seriously . . ." She stopped and looked earnestly at him. "Do you *really* think *he* likes me? Can you tell?"

"I think he finds you extremely fascinating . . . as we all

do." By now they were at the door leading out into place Saint-Sulpice, the twin turrets of the ancient chuch looming in front of them.

Henri stopped and took both her arms, looking at her solemnly. "If he gets you he's a very lucky man," he said, quickly embracing her on both cheeks then striding swiftly to his car.

Michel Harcourt said with a suspicion of irony in his voice: "I'm very honored that you should deign to step inside my little Citroën."

"Please." Sandra looked across at him in the light of the street lamps, the brightly lit shop windows. "I am quite an ordinary person you know."

"But whenever I see you now you're getting out of a dark blue Bentley."

"That just comes with the job." Sandra's voice was light. "It's not really *me* any more than this pretense of total modesty is really you."

The car swerved slightly as Harcourt gripped the wheel, and Sandra thought he was going to stop and turn her out into the street. She could see his jaw working as he struggled to control himself and she realized that beneath his bland, tightly disciplined exterior, he was a creature of very violent impulses indeed.

"Isn't that a little provocative, Sandra?"

"No more provocative than what you said about me. I happen to think, Michel, by what I know and what I've read about you that you are indeed a great man. Why should you be a modest one too?"

Suddenly Harcourt laughed and briefly his hand touched her arm.

"I think you've hit the nail on the head, Mademoiselle. And here we are at your address." He stopped by the side of the pavement and looked up at the tall apartment building which had once been a grand *hôtel particulier.*

"Would you like to come up for a nightcap and see if we can call a truce?" Sandra smiled at him in the dark and saw him gazing at the dial of his illuminated watch.

"Well . . . I can't say no can I? Besides I'm quite curious to see how the very, very rich live."

Later, with a glass of whisky in his hand, Michel stood looking out at the river where the *bateaux mouches* with their crowds of tourists and sightseers plied quite late into the night. He put his nose against the window pane and, for a moment, she thought she saw the young boy whose father worked in a clothing factory and whose mother had had quite a struggle to bring up five children. Maybe Harcourt was so ambitious because, like her, he had been deprived. But had he been deprived of love? You could be very poor and yet have a lot of love. She had been relatively affluent and yet had had none.

"It's really very nice," he said finally, turning to face her. "It's more modest than I expected. Someone told me you lived at the Ritz."

"I still have a suite there." Sandra lit a cigarette and perched on the arm of a chair.

"You shouldn't smoke, you know," he said, frowning.

"I shouldn't but I do, and there are too many tensions at the moment for me to give it up. You know, Michel . . . I feel that you and I should *try* and understand each other a little better. Have fewer arguments. In fact," she paused rather warily because she didn't want to be misunderstood. "In fact we need each other."

"*You* need me?" Harcourt looked at her incredulously. "How do you need me? You are one of the richest women in France I understand, certainly one of the most powerful, if not *the* most powerful."

"That's why I need you," Sandra said quietly. "I need a critic. Someone who can see through me, like you. I have plenty of sycophants and enemies, but few real friends."

"Henri Piper is a very good friend."

"Very good," Sandra agreed. "But unfortunately his wife is a little bit jealous of me. . . ."

"I can see why. . . ."

Sandra ignored the compliment and continued.

"There is no reason for it at all. I am only twenty-seven. Henri is thirty years older. Apart from the difference in our ages he is actually very happily married. I regard him as a relative, though he is not a proper one. He's one of the few people over here who have known me since I was quite small. I've always thought of him as an uncle. You see . . . rich I might be, but I have not had a very happy life."

"Tell me about it." Michel sank slowly into one of the deep armchairs, his whisky glass clasped in his right hand. He still had on the glasses that he'd worn for driving and a lock of thick black hair hung over his forehead.

He was a tall, intense-looking man with skin deeply tanned, dark hair and blue eyes. He looked as though his origins were Semitic but, as far as she knew, they weren't—neither Arab nor Jew. He seldom smiled and she liked this, because when he did it was as though the sun shone. She knew now that he was one of the most interesting, most important men she had ever met—and beside him Tim Desmond and Claudio Menendez and the other less important ones seemed to lack luster.

Sandra felt too that she was in the presence of someone who not only cared about her personally but who had a professional interest in her, like a good psychiatrist. Maybe he really was the complete, rounded doctor who was not only an excellent diagnostician and technician in the laboratory, but a gifted counselor and friend to his patients as well.

She found herself, to her surprise, beginning at the beginning. She did tell him the story of her life; not just the story but her feelings and emotions toward her mother, her brother, and particularly toward Georges Desmond and his surviving family. Finally she told him all about Tim.

When she finished there was a very long pause and, as Michel's head had sunk on his chest, she thought that, perhaps, he had fallen asleep.

Slowly, however, he raised his head, drained his glass, and put it on the small table beside him.

"That tells me a great deal about you, Sandra, and I thank you for the privilege. I think I, too, am in the presence of a great person, as you were kind enough to say about me." He got up and held out his hand which, rather numbly, she took.

"Please do me the honor of thinking of me as a friend, a real friend."

Strega was one of those people who, fortunately or unfortunately, had the gift of adaptation. At one moment he could look like a businessman; at another a gangster or, perhaps, an ordinary law-abiding member of the public.

For someone whose instincts were those of the criminal classes he was able to merge like a chameleon into his surroundings, while retaining enough personality to impress people with confidence in his ability, his *savoir faire,* if need be. Mr. Ronald Epstein of Epstein and Co., brokers of New York, looked up with surprise when a new client was announced and, as he came into his room and over to his desk to shake hands, Epstein said, "Mr. Strega, isn't it?"

"That's right, Mr. Epstein," Strega replied. "It's good to see you again."

Epstein looked as though he wasn't too sure about that and also whether or not he should invite Strega to take a seat. In the end Strega decided for him and, flicking his hat into a chair, sat down in the one next to it and undid the top button of his well-cut jacket.

"There's one thing I'm a bit uncertain about, Mr. Strega,"

Epstein said, "and I'll come out with it straightaway. When we were in contact before, you were the representative of Mr. Zac Desmond. Am I to understand that's all changed?"

"Completely," Strega said with easy confidence, crossing one leg over the other. "I fell out with the Desmonds and I'm on my own now. I've come into a little money and I want you to use it for me."

"Oh?" Epstein said curiously. "And how much is that?"

"About fifty million dollars . . . not all on my own account, of course," he added, pleased to see the astonishment on Epstein's face. "I represent a number of important financial interests who, at the moment, have one thing in common."

Epstein sat up straight and made sure that the knot in his tie was in the right place as he strove to smarten himself up for, possibly, a rich and important client.

"What is that may I ask, Mr. Strega?" he inquired politely.

"We wish to buy about two million Desmond shares . . . in small amounts at a time. Rates are to stay where they are. We don't want to frighten the market."

"Well." Epstein looked at him with amazement. "Two million? That represents about ten percent of the Group's capital."

Strega, instead of answering, sat there with an arrogant expression on his face while, hastily, Epstein began to punch the keyboard of his computer and, after taking a look at what he saw, jotted down some figures on a piece of paper.

When he began to speak again his tone had changed considerably to one of studied politeness, even deference. He had become someone with a distinct desire to please.

"The Desmond shares are priced at twenty-eight dollars this morning for a market of one hundred seventy thousand shares. Recently they have been down a bit. We know that the champagne had a disastrous year due to some fault in the bottling, and the frosts of this past winter point to a poor harvest in the autumn. The market isn't too impressed with Desmond at the moment."

"The people whose interests I represent would like to buy the shares at a price of about thirty to thirty-two dollars. It mustn't exceed thirty-five."

"And how do you propose to pay for this?" Epstein could not resist a note of skepticism creeping into his voice—after all Strega had been a mere PA, a functionary, who had formerly spoken to him on the telephone. At that Strega fastened the jacket of his expensive suit and reached for his hat.

"I don't like your tone, Mr. Epstein."

"Please." Epstein shot out of his chair as Strega rose to go. "Don't misunderstand me, Mr. Strega; but we are talking of around fifty six million dollars."

"And I told you I have the money. Later today when the banks open in Hong Kong you will receive an important credit transfer in my name. Others will follow. You will find a money order on standby in my name at the New York branch of the Saint Louis Bank." He gazed rather insolently at the bemused broker. "You have no need to worry, Mr. Epstein. Everything is in order."

"Oh I'm sure of that, Mr. Strega," Epstein said earnestly. "I wouldn't for a *moment* doubt—"

"You'd better not, Epstein." Strega's voice was brusque as he assumed the air and manner of the practiced bully. "And no telling tales. Zac Desmond trusted you, and I expect to be able to trust you too. Complete confidentiality is the key word . . . not a word of this must get out or the price will shoot through the roof. Do you understand me?"

"I understand you completely, Mr. Strega," Epstein said, rising and going to a cupboard in the wall to try and conceal his dislike of his visitor. "Maybe a drink before you go?"

"I never drink while I'm conducting business," Strega said curtly. "Five million dollars on deposit in New York, so please begin your purchases today. And don't forget, small quantities." He took a sheaf of papers out of his breast pocket and put them in front of the astonished Epstein. "Here is the order of payment, together with fiscal guarantees. You should have no trouble.

"You can contact me at the Waldorf."

Then he put his hat on his head and went to the door without even a farewell nod, letting himself out.

For a long time after he'd gone Ronnie Epstein remained where he was as if in a state of bemusement.

Epstein was a young, creative and dynamic man who had taken over the main part of the highly respected business of Epstein and Co. from his father who was now in semiretirement in West Palm Beach. His father had known Georges Desmond well and retained a business relationship with him for over twenty years. He had also been responsible for the introduction of Desmond shares on the New York Stock Exchange in the late sixties.

Ronald Epstein Junior's first reaction was to ring Zac Desmond and check Strega out with him; but it was against the ethical code of business. He hadn't taken to Strega and disliked his manner, but slowly he walked back to his desk and picked up the phone.

"Could you get me my father please?" he said to his secretary, still staring at the documentation Strega had left on his desk. When he heard the voice of Ronald Epstein Senior on the end of the phone he said:

"Dad? Dammit if I haven't had the darnedest request. Just listen to this. . . ."

28

"Dr. Harcourt on line two, Mademoiselle," Agnès said, noting how Sandra, who had been standing by the filing cabinet in her office, leapt to the phone as she made her announcement. Once back at her own desk she kept the switch to line two open so that she could hear the conversation.

"Hello, Michel." Sandra's voice was warm and vibrant. "This *is* a pleasure."

"I'm glad to hear you say that, Sandra." Agnès thought the voice of Dr. Harcourt too had overtones she had not heard before. "Any chance I can show you something interesting in the lab," there was a pause before he added, "and then take you out to dinner?"

"Nothing I'd like more," Sandra said, then there was silence during which Agnès imagined her casting her eyes over the packed pages of her diary. "Except that unfortunately I'm not free tonight. Certainly though I could pop into the lab about five."

"That would be fine." Michel sounded disappointed. "Will you take a rain check on the dinner?"

"I certainly will," Sandra said. "See you later. Bye."

"Bye."

Agnès quickly closed the switch before Sandra replaced the phone and was tapping busily at her typewriter when the door opened and Sandra came out, a frown on her face.

"Have you seen the Banque Franco-Belges file, Agnès?"

"Isn't it in your personal filing cabinet, Mademoiselle?" Agnès said innocently, hoping that her confusion would hide the blush that immediately stole up her cheeks. She jumped to her feet and began to make a big play of searching for the file while knowing all the time exactly where, or rather with whom, it was.

Sandra returned to her room and Agnès followed her. Together they explored Sandra's personal filing cabinet and then the various trays of documents scattered around the room, though Sandra was a tidy person and her filing was meticulous.

"How strange!" Sandra said at last, sitting down in her chair, hands in her pockets. "Very, very strange. It's gone."

Suddenly she looked directly at Agnès, whose blush went even deeper. But it was a warm autumn day and close indoors, and Agnès hoped Mademoiselle would attribute this to the lack of efficient air-conditioning.

"I can't understand why or how that file could have disappeared, Agnès, can you?"

"Certainly not, Mademoiselle," Agnès said with an air of mystification. "Is there any particular reason you wish for it today, Mademoiselle? I could search extensively and definitely produce it for tomorrow."

The significance of her words appeared to escape the normally astute Sandra, her mind on another even more worrying mystery.

"Someone has been buying our shares at a great rate," she said slowly. "And I'm anxious to try and find out *why* before I meet Monsieur de Lassale this evening. He may have some clues."

"Is that so serious, Mademoiselle?" Agnès continued to feel not only extremely nervous, but sick as well as the reason for Zac's wishing to see the file dawned on her.

"It is very serious, Agnès." Sandra looked at her absent-mindedly. "You see if the deal with NATO does come off the price of the shares will shoot up and the only one who really knows about that deal with, possibly, the exception of yourself and Monsieur Dericourt, people whom I trust implicitly, is Monsieur de Lassale. It's what's known as "insider trading," that is, people who have privileged information being able to profit by it. It is forbidden by law. For instance if I, knowing that we were on the verge of making a large and important deal, bought Desmond shares for my own gain even through an intermediary, I could be prosecuted. So could any of the directors . . . there *may* have been a leak which I have to check on. See if you can get me Monsieur Piper on the phone in California, will you? I may have to ask him to go to New York."

Agnès felt that her legs were weak as, thankfully back at her own desk, she dialed the international code for California.

"I should never have given you the file," Agnès said to Zac, whom she had summoned hurriedly to meet her in the Tuileries Gardens in her lunch hour. "You *must* get it back by this afternoon."

"But it is in Tourville," Zac said petulantly.

"Then you must go and *get* it." Agnès's tone, no longer that of the docile mistress, was peremptory. "I think Mademoiselle already suspects me and, if she does, I've had it."

"But *why* does she want the blasted file?" Zac bit the bit of loose skin on his finger angrily.

"It's something to do with the Desmond shares. Someone is buying them in New York. . . ."

"But there's *nothing* in the file about the Desmond shares—" Zac broke off and looked at her anxiously. "Forget I said that."

"Is that something you know about, Zac?" Agnès began to feel the ground tilting beneath her. "Mademoiselle told me today that it was a crime . . . if you, as a Director—"

"Now just cool it, will you?" Zac looked angrily at her. "Just shut up and keep your mouth shut."

"Then *when* will I have the file?"

"You'll have it by the morning, better, later tonight. I'll drop it at your flat." He gave her a suggestive wink.

"I *must* have it this afternoon. I *must* find it or . . . Mademoiselle will suspect me. Don't you see? She trusts me and I will be the first person she suspects. She is so thorough. She won't rest until she gets at the truth."

"But if you do suddenly find it she'll think that funny too."

"She is organizing a search for it in the building. I think I know a way I can make it appear quite feasible to find it. I will say it was in the photocopying room. Even then she will be angry. Some documents she keeps in her personal filing cabinet. That was one of them. I should never, *ever,* have let you have it."

"Too late for that now, my poppet," Zac said patronizingly. *"And* very useful it was. That swine Lassale had told me nothing at all about the potential deal with NATO. In fact he has pretended there was no chance of it coming off in the foreseeable future. No chance of inside information from him. They have deliberately falsified information on the deal. . . ."

"But that's not a crime. Insider trading is," Agnès said tearfully, "and *you* have used me to do something criminal. Oh . . . oh dear, what *will* I do?"

She began to cry and Zac, anxious about the scene she was making in a public place, seized her by the arm and shook her.

"Now look here you silly little thing. Since I got you this apartment and made you my mistress you have done scarcely *anything* for me at all. At all. One or two tiny things. *You* never even mentioned to me about the deal with NATO, which is something *really* important, yet you must have known about it. . . ." She tried to break away from his clasp but he held on to her, a wild gleam in his eyes. "It is *really* big. If I can get the Irishwoman in a big financial mess she will be able to do nothing else but resign and then I . . ." he held her tightly to him, "I will be occupying the desk on the first floor of the place de L'Étoile to which I am entitled and you," he pulled her even closer despite her struggle, "and you will be sitting opposite me."

"Please, Zac," she said, struggling, banging against his chest with her fist. "Let me go or—"

"Or what?" Zac asked as if suddenly coming to his senses, realizing who he was and where, and what he was doing.

"Or I'll leave you!" she said. "I'll leave you and I'll take the consequences. . . ."

As she broke away from him he saw an expression on her face he had never seen before:

Fear . . . fear and defiance. Rebellion.

"Look," he said, glancing quickly at his watch. "Belle is at Tourville. I shall ring her now and ask her to drive up straightaway. She will do it, I know."

"Oh thank heaven!" Agnès said prayerfully, clasping her hands to her bosom. "Please tell her to be quick—and careful. Address it to me, personally. Mark it urgent."

Zac, thankful to see her expression change, grasped her wrist tightly.

"She will leave it in the foyer not later than, say, four, and you have simply to go down, collect it and pretend you found it in the photocopying room. No problem, is there, my little kitten?"

Agnès continued to look doubtful but, slowly, the fear seemed to evaporate and a little color returned to her face. But the fear was soon replaced by another expression: stubbornness.

"And," Zac said quickly as her willful silence continued. "Once I am in the seat of power, who knows, I might make you Madame Desmond . . . you don't think I want to continue to be married to that harlot for the rest of my life. Do you?"

Belle looked at her watch and tapped her foot on the floor with irritation. She had a meeting with Tara at Jean Marvoine and had already changed from casual into town clothes.

"You've just caught me as I was leaving," she said to Zac. "In fact I should have gone already. I really *can't* possibly go out of my way."

"It's *terribly* urgent," Zac said also impatiently. "That little idiot, whom I shall get rid of as soon as I possibly can, gave me the entire file instead of photocopying it as I asked. Of course the Irishwoman *would* want it just at that moment. . . ."

"It was very careless of *you* if you ask me," Belle retorted. "You say her control is slipping. I think *yours* is too. Well, where is it?"

"It is in the drawer in my bureau. Now be a good girl, put it in an envelope and slip it into the office for me."

"You mean for her."

"Of course for her! For *Agnès.* Address it clearly to *Agnès,* for God's sake, not to Sandra . . . and take care you're not seen."

"You take care *you're* not caught," Belle said angrily and crashed the phone down.

She ran along the corridor to Zac's room and, without difficulty, found the file in the place where he said it would be. As she was coming out she bumped into her mother who was on her way to her room.

"Why my dear." Lady Elizabeth stepped back, surprise registering on her face. "I thought you'd have gone by now."

"I should have. I had to get something for Zac. Something he wants urgently."

She bent over and kissed her mother on the cheek.

"Bye, Mama," she said. "Take care."

"You take care, darling." Lady Elizabeth, both arms around

her shoulders, pressed her mouth warmly against her daughter's fragrant cheek. Then she stepped back and looked at her anxiously. "I think you're overdoing things. You don't look too well to me."

"I'm perfectly well thank you, Mama, just in a hurry . . . also, well to be truthful, Tara *does* get on my nerves. She has no business sense at all. Yet as Zac's wife how am I to get rid of her?"

"Rid?" Lady Elizabeth looked shocked. "How do you mean 'get rid,' Belle, dear?"

"Out of the business completely. I'd like to run it on my own in preparation for the time when Sandra is forced out and Zac and I have the reins in our hands, as we were always meant to."

"Sandra forced out?" Lady Elizabeth repeated with some astonishment.

"You know, Mama, that's what we always intended. She will have to be forced out for sure. But we have ways of doing it. We have plans. You'll see."

Belle lightly and cheerfully kissed her mother again and, with a farewell wave, sped along the corridor clutching the file under her arm.

Lady Elizabeth watched her go and then slowly went along to her room where she was in the habit of taking an afternoon nap, or maybe doing some embroidery or watching TV. It was her quiet time; a precious time of the day for her.

But it could also be, like today, a time of worry. Things magnified so when you were on your own. So, instead of getting on her bed she sat in a deep comfy armchair beside the fire and, as her delicate fingers wove in and out of the complex tapestry she was making, she let her mind drift; but all it came up with were perplexities: perplexities and worry.

Zac and Belle were plotting something, she knew that. She had, at last, been forced to admit that, in her heart of hearts, she knew they were up to no good.

Sadly she let her needlework drop onto her knee and gazed into the fire. They had always been an odd couple; children one never felt completely comfortable with. There was a "knowing" about them that had been disturbing from their early youth. They had always seemed older than their years, a silent, secretive couple although Belle, in particular, had always loved sport.

Their nannies were forever complaining about them in a way they did not complain about the other two. Yet you could never believe something like that about your child, the insinuations the nannies made: they were more than naughty; they were evil.

What an awful word to use about young children: *evil!* She had dismissed the idea immediately and usually the nanny too who had dared to perpetrate such an outrageous suggestion. Yet she was not the only one. . . .

Of *course* one's children weren't evil . . . they were naughty, obstreperous, difficult . . . and then had come the time when one of the nannies had been found floating in the lake. Someone said Belle had woven a spell about her. What ridiculous rubbish! That person was immediately dismissed too, of course, and the verdict was clearly one of suicide. The nursemaid in question had been of unstable temperament and should never have been engaged.

She had no one to confide in, no one to whom to tell one's darkest thoughts, one's innermost apprehensions. Georges would have laughed at any idea that either of his children were evil . . . one would never dare to say a thing like that to Georges.

She found herself nodding by the fire and shook herself. The image of Tim somewhere in the Far East then came vividly to mind.

Tim, her darling, her baby. Oh Tim, what had he done . . . and, she sighed deeply to herself, what *could* they do about Sandra?

In her heart she couldn't help feeling that if Sandra O'Neill were somehow to disappear from the scene forever all would, in fact, be well. Because, maybe, there was something inherently destructive and evil about *her.* She had taken over the business, seduced her son, killed her own mother with neglect and now . . . well there was no end of trouble with Sandra and, knowing what she knew from Hélène's secret letter, somehow it was easier to understand why.

The premises of the fashion house of Jean Marvoine were among the most sumptuous in the avenue Montaigne, which was full of elegant buildings housing world-famous names: Ungaro, Caron, Chanel, Vuitton, Nina Ricci, Guy Laroche, Givenchy and many more. The fashionable tree-lined avenue ran from the place de l'Alma, with its view of the Eiffel Tower, to the Rond Point des Champs Élysées where it became the avenue Matignon.

Jean Marvoine had been killed in a car crash shortly after selling his business to the Desmond Group when he was short of capital. He had been a young and gifted designer; but his equally young and gifted assistant, Maurice Raison, had stepped easily into the breach becoming, in time, even more famous than the founder of the fashion house which still traded under the original name.

The premises now occupied by Jean Marvoine had once been a *hôtel particulier,* but the great wooden door that had formerly led into a cobbled courtyard was now made of glass, the courtyard tiled in marble, and a fountain in the shape of a golden caryatid with water spouting from its mouth played in the middle. The sandstone walls of the original *hôtel* were lit by hidden lights, and a stone staircase with a wrought-iron railing led up to the first floor where the fashion shows were held.

The Directrice of the House was an accomplished woman called Louise Reboux. She was no relation to the famous pre-war milliner Caroline Reboux, but she had the same sort of flair and she and Maurice Raison between them controlled the House to such an extent that there was little work for Tara or Belle to do, and they rather got in the way.

Madame Reboux was not an especially tactful person when it came to dealing with her employers. She put Maurice Raison first and that was that. There were frequent outbursts and jealous scenes, especially from Tara who liked to think she knew as much, if not more, about taste and fashion as anyone in the House of Marvoine, or the avenue Montaigne if it came to that.

Consequently Belle was constantly being called upon to make peace between the arrogant Directrice, the temperamental designer and the spoiled and flamboyant Italian who was co-owner with her. It was an unsatisfactory situation exacerbated by the fact that Sandra, who was dressed by Ungaro across the road, declined to be dressed by Raison or to take any interest in the business which was such a tiny part of the Group. It was galling to be patronized; even more so to be neglected, and it added to the sense of grievance both women had about the President of the Group.

Tara had been at the House for half an hour delivering a tirade to Madame Reboux when Belle arrived, bad tempered and out of breath, having experienced heavy traffic on the *périphérique*.

Madame Riboux chose the moment of the arrival to make her excuses and disappear for a few moments while the sisters-in-law effusively greeted each other.

"And at the last minute!" Belle held up a packet after the explanations. "Zac had to telephone and ask me to get something. Do you think there is anybody who could deliver this to the Étoile for me? Where is Madame?" She looked around.

"Gone for reinforcements," Tara said, making a face. "There are days I would really like to sack that woman."

"Then Maurice would go too. Look, this really is urgent,"

Belle said impatiently. "I do wish Louise wouldn't disappear like that!"

"Why not send a cab?" Tara still looked perplexed.

"Because it's something *terribly* important. It has to be delivered personally."

"Oh!" Tara suddenly laughed. "In that case let's send my minder. Señor Gomez has *nothing* to do. He never has but that's not the point."

"Where is he?" Belle inquired, looking around.

"He's always outside in the car in case I try and slip away."

"Oh don't be *silly*, Tara," Belle reprimanded her. She tugged off her gloves and threw them onto a gilt chair in the elegant salon. "You know that Gomez is only there to protect you."

"Protect me from what exactly?"

"Revenge. You know that. Zac is afraid that the colleagues of Mourad Aziz will be after you. . . ."

"Oh yeah . . ." Tara said derisively, "*that* little man? Do you think I believe that? I never saw anyone so frightened in my life as when he was in the dock."

"Yet he confessed everything."

"Well, I didn't believe it for one. And I'm sure you don't either. Police 'persuasion' if you ask me."

Tara looked at Belle who returned her gaze.

"What do you mean? Look, could we first get rid of this and get on with our meeting? Maybe Madame will then deign to return."

"Of course." Tara snatched the envelope from Belle before she could say a word and, striding to the door, called for Gomez, who got hurriedly out of the car parked just outside and came running. As Tara gave him his instructions he looked doubtful.

"I don't have any authority, Madame, you know that. I am not a messenger. I have to be always by *you* to protect *you.*"

"Don't be absurd. *Spy* on me you mean. Well, the Princess von Burg-Farnbach is here and she will 'protect' me while you are away. Besides it is on the orders of Monsieur Desmond." Tara looked at the name on the envelope.

Mlle. Agnès Guyon. It was marked "Private and Confidential." Agnès Guyon. The name rang a bell.

"Anyway see this is delivered to Mademoiselle Guyon at the Desmond offices immediately, do you understand?"

"Very well, Madame," Gomez said, reluctantly taking the envelope and saluting. "I will be back in half an hour."

Tara stood for a moment on the pavement watching him drive off. Agnès Guyon . . . of course. She was the personal secretary of Sandra O'Neill. Well, well.

Now what would Zac and Sandra's personal secretary be hatching now?

With a smile on her face she went back into the marble hall for yet another confrontation with the Directrice and, probably, Raison as well.

Tara Desmond was a frustrated and unhappy woman. It was easy to see why. She knew that Gomez was not her protector but her keeper, and there was something about him that frightened her. It was the way he watched her; the way he observed her. He was always there, outside or inside, wherever she was; driving the car, standing at a corner, a few steps behind while she walked her dog in the park or the Bois. He never attempted intimacy, was never intrusive. Yet she couldn't stand him. How long could this kind of thing go on?

More and more she longed for escape and more and more she thought of Bob, her youthful admirer. It seemed the only way to do it.

Michel looked at Sandra across the table and said, "I'm awfully glad you were able to make dinner."

"So am I," Sandra replied. "It was quite unexpected, besides," she paused and fiddled with the bread roll beside her on the plate, "I'd rather be with you."

"I take that as a great compliment." Michel pretended to study the menu. Then he put it down, removed his glasses and gazed at her.

"You know, Sandra, I'd ask to date you if you weren't who you were. . . ."

"Who *I* am?" Sandra replied in amazement aware that her heart had given an unseemly flutter, like a Victorian maiden being propositioned.

"You know—Head of Desmond."

"Why should that make any difference? I'm a woman too."

"You know it does."

He picked up the menu again, but didn't look at it.

"I'm a bit scared of you, to be truthful, a bit intimidated. . . ."

"You intimidated." Sandra leaned back and her laughter reverberated around the small bistro where they had eaten before. One or two heads were curiously raised.

"Honestly I am."

"But my dear Michel." Sandra leaned toward him speaking quietly. "You are a *far* more important person than I am. I so much admire what you do. You maybe have in you the key to a better life for millions of people. I . . ." She shrugged. "I have nothing but problems and difficulties. I do not spread happiness or bring health, as you can."

She looked down at the table where Michel had his palm outstretched in invitation. She put her hand into his and let it stay there for some moments.

"Thank you for that," he said, smiling at her. "I feel better already. Now let's order, shall we?"

To her surprise Sandra discovered that, after all, she wasn't hungry.

As they finished the meal, Michel asked, "Now why has it been such a bad day?"

Sandra wiped her mouth on her napkin and pulling a packet of cigarettes from her handbag looked at him for his permission to smoke. He grimaced and reluctantly gave it.

"Someone is trying to put the price of our shares up on the New York Exchange."

"Is that so terrible? I don't really understand these things."

"Well, we don't know why; but it *is* serious when shares are bought on such a large scale. There's usually a reason. You see," like the professional she was she warmed to her subject, "according to the latest news, four million Desmond shares have changed hands. They've been bought at an average of thirty to thirty-two dollars each and that is an awful lot of money."

"A hundred and twenty million dollars." Michel whistled. "Wheeooo."

"Yes it *is* a lot of money. Now two things might happen: either we'll be subject to blackmail on repurchase or else someone is trying to buy out the family control of the Group."

"Do you have any idea who is behind it?"

Sandra shook her head, blowing smoke into the air away from him.

"I *may* have a shrewd suspicion but no, officially we haven't. The only thing we do know is that the transaction is being done through the brokers Desmond have always used in New York. They, of course, are not allowed to tell us what is going on or who their client is."

"So, what are you going to do?"

"Well tonight, officially, I was going to have a talk with Zac Desmond and Philippe de Lassale, our bankers. But something worried me. . . ." She hesitated and stubbed her cigarette out half smoked.

"I'm sorry. I know you hate these things. I'll stop it one day. I promise."

"For *your* sake." Michel smiled encouragingly.

"For yours too," Sandra said then, catching the look in his

eyes, went on hurriedly, "You see . . . and I am treating you as a friend rather than a colleague."

"Of course," he put a finger to his mouth. "And my lips are sealed."

"Yes I knew I could trust you. Well, today I couldn't find a very important file that I keep locked up in my own filing cabinet in my office. It was to do with the Banque Franco-Belges of which Zac and Philippe de Lassale are directors. Zac is head of Desmond and Philippe of Franco-Belges."

"And did you find it?" Michel leaned forward.

"I did, eventually, but in a very funny way. My secretary simply produced it at about four-thirty in the afternoon, shortly before I was leaving for our meeting in the lab."

"Well then . . ."

"*She* said she'd left it in the photocopying room."

"I see, and is that so very mysterious? I don't quite understand."

"Nor did I then. I had never asked her to photocopy anything from this file, but she insisted I had. Now," Sandra permitted herself a brief, sardonic smile, "as you may imagine I am not a person who easily forgets things. If I say I did a thing or didn't do it you can be pretty sure it's true. *I* know that I never asked Agnès to photocopy anything, so, you see . . . a secretary whom I trusted and promoted to my personal office is clearly lying. Why?"

Michel shrugged. "I don't know. Office politics are beyond me. Although, unfortunately, from time to time we have them too."

"I think I have a *glimmer* of an idea," Sandra went on. "That's all it is, but, if true, it's horrible, disturbing. . . . I think my secretary *may* be spying for Zac Desmond."

Now Michel threw back his head.

"Isn't that too absurd?"

"It's neither absurd nor is it too unlikely. She did once work for him. My last secretary was reluctant for me to promote her; but I thought she was jealous. You see I *may* have a spy in my camp who reports to Zac everything that goes on, has gone on for months . . . so that is why tonight instead of seeing him I'm seeing you, so that I can clarify my mind and decide what to do."

"I'm deeply honored," Michel said. Then he leaned back, crossed his arms and frowned. "But I'm very worried too in case what you say is true. You think that *Zac* may be buying shares in his own company?"

"It's not impossible. . . . We have a deal going on that Zac is not supposed to know about. *If* it comes off Desmond shares which are low at the moment will shoot up and he, or someone, might make a very handsome profit. It's what's called insider trading and it's illegal. I *may* have a criminal case on my hands. . . ."

"Involving your adoptive brother. . . ."

"Exactly. But not only him. One of the few people who knows about the deal because he is helping to finance it—and whom I swore to secrecy because I've never trusted Zac—is Philippe de Lassale and if he and Zac are in this together I'm sunk."

"Why?" Michel gazed at her, his eyes deeply sympathetic.

"Because they're a very powerful duo. How can I possibly get the money to buy back our shares, which is what we must do, if they are against me? I couldn't *possibly* raise such a large sum without them.

"Zac has always tried to get rid of me and now, I think, he might succeed."

"That would be disastrous," Michel said quietly. "For now I know in you I have a real friend, not only to my work but to me."

"You have a real friend." Sandra stretched out her hand across the table. "And if you do ever want to 'date me,' I'd be the happiest woman in the world."

Once again his hand closed over hers and held it for several moments.

This time there was no question as to where to meet. Sandra sought a meeting with de Lassale and Zac in the avenue de l'Opéra, and the way she was welcomed made her feel that what had amounted to a suspicion was a certainty. She was sure now that Philippe de Lassale and Zac Desmond were consorting in a highly suspect way to get rid of her. Whether or not Zac had all the time been prey to her inmost secrets via her secretary she did not as yet know.

One step at a time.

When she put to them the point that Desmond shares were being purchased on the New York Stock Market at such a rate they, naturally, professed surprise; but when she told them that she intended to buy them back with their help they shook their heads.

"Impossible, Sandra," Philippe said with his exquisitely charming, ineffably polite smile. "For one thing we would have to call a meeting of the full Board to authorize funds for such a huge sum of money. That would take at least a couple of weeks. . . ."

"It can be done in twenty-four hours if you really want to," Sandra said.

"It can, but is it necessary?" Philippe de Lassale equivocated again. "I, personally, think it isn't and that the shares will find their own level. Also getting hold of one hundred million in a few hours doesn't produce too many problems, except that Zac and I have to agree."

As they exchanged glances Sandra already knew the answer.

"And you refuse. . . ."

"Well . . ." Philippe de Lassale shrugged again, his pained expression indicating infinite regret.

"Let's be blunt, Sandra," Zac said, speaking for the first time. "Neither Philippe nor I have too high a regard for the way you are managing the affairs of Desmond. In fact it is probably your *mis*management that has led to this raid against our Group, for that's undoubtedly what it is. We don't really feel like launching a rescue operation just for you."

"So the cards are on the table," Sandra declared, feeling suddenly chilled . . . cold and alone. Then she remembered Michel and his warmth, maybe his love, certainly his support, and the chill left her.

"The cards, in a way, *are* on the table." Philippe offered her a cigarette which she refused. "You know that one or two things have made us unhappy. . . ."

"And one or two things have made *me* unhappy," Sandra snapped back. "Things that I'd like to discuss with you when Zac Desmond is not present. Things that he should not have known, dealings he should not be party to but which undoubtedly he does and is. Now if you, Monsieur de Lassale," here she paused to point a finger at him, "if you are personally engaged in dealings which are contrary to the law, have no doubt that I will expose you. I'll have you investigated by the Bourse and also the U.S. Securities Exchange Commission. . . ."

"Please, please, *please,* Mademoiselle." De Lassale put out a hand in an effort to stop the flow of words. "You are distressing yourself quite unnecessarily, and I can assure you that matters which have been confidential between us, and I know what you mean, are so still. It is simply that," he spread his hands and studied his well-manicured nails, "I feel, as Zac Desmond I know does, that you have taken on too much. After all it was an enormous task for a young woman of your age, despite your considerable ability and, in the circumstances, you have managed reasonably well, but," he held up a hand, "there *have* been mistakes. . . ."

"Big mistakes," Zac corrected, not attempting to conceal his satisfaction at his complete domination of a man technically his superior. "Your blackmail threats mean nothing to us. You have become a subject of scandal . . . my brother has had to flee the country to avoid you and the Press . . . you know nothing about the champagne business and little, it appears now, of the financial markets of the world. I can tell you that if you do not consider resigning immediately as President of the Desmond Group, I shall shortly be calling a meeting of the Council my father set up, to have you removed."

Zac, who had remained standing throughout the entire interview, put both hands on his hips and stared at her.

"In my view you are a liability and I have no doubt that the Council will agree with me."

Henri Piper said, "I can't hear you too well."

"Can you hear me better now?" Sandra raised her voice. It was mid-afternoon in Paris and seven o'clock in the morning in San Francisco.

"That's better," Henri said. "What is it, Sandra?"

"I want you to listen very carefully," Sandra replied and then, after a brief pause, "and I want you to promise *not* to pass on to Sophie what I'm going to tell you now. Is that a promise?"

"It sounds very scarey," Henri said with a chuckle. "Actually she's out of the house. She's staying a few days with her friend Emmeline de la Berendière in Malibu."

"That's excellent news then," Sandra replied, "because if we are to succeed this must remain totally confidential. Are you listening, Henri?"

"Fire away," Henri said cheerfully, and Sandra sat back, using her phone in the flat, for reasons of privacy, and explained to Henri exactly what had happened and her suspicions.

It took quite a long time and when she'd finished there was a deep silence. Finally, thinking that the explanation had been lost in the airwaves, she cried, "Are you there, Henri?"

"I'm here my dear." Henri's voice sounded decidedly shaky.

"I can't believe what you're telling me. There must be a mistake."

"Can't you? I think it's all very simple. There's no mistake. It *is* a final maneuver to get me out. Zac has made of an honest man someone as crooked as himself."

"But it's illegal."

"That doesn't stop either of them. If you ask me Zac doesn't stop at murder either . . . but I have less proof of that."

"You should be more careful. You shouldn't say such things, Sandra."

"Maybe I shouldn't," Sandra replied. "But, nevertheless, I am saying them. I think he is a thoroughly evil and unscrupulous man and he is out to destroy me. Do you know I even think he might be behind the story about me and Tim?"

"Oh surely that's impossible! Look, he wasn't even there."

"But Belle was. Do you really believe she's not in cahoots with him?"

"But if so, it's a monstrous plot."

"But one I'm going to defeat," Sandra declared, "with your help." She paused and cleared her throat. "And now I must ask you, Henri, in view of your relationship with Sophie who was, after all, born a Desmond: are you with me or against me? Think carefully please."

As the seconds ticked by and he didn't answer, Sandra had a sickening sensation in the pit of her stomach.

Maybe they *were* all against her; Henri too and, if so, she had lost her best and perhaps last friend (except for Michel but he was no help here), and she might as well throw in the sponge.

"You know I'm with you, Sandra," Henri said at last, so quietly that she could hardly hear him. Then more loudly he continued: "Whether you're right or whether you're wrong I know you're not wicked and you're not incompetent and I support you. How can I help you?"

Sandra took in a large breath and said, "By lending me fifty million dollars plus. Can you do it?"

"Fifty million!" Henri whistled.

"It has to be done urgently. By tomorrow at the latest, as soon as the markets open. And you have to go to New York as soon as you can."

"It is a hell of a lot of money."

"I actually need a hundred million, but I myself can raise half. I'm depending on you to raise the rest."

Henri paused for a moment as if in thought; then he said:

"My dear, of course I can do it if you insist; but I think you would be wrong to borrow such a sum to buy back your own shares. I *can* see why you're worried," he went on, "but my informants in the market, and I keep closely in touch with them every day as you know, tell me that the Security Exchange Commission is investigating the potential of insider trading in the mass purchase of Desmond shares."

"When did you hear that?" Sandra's voice sounded excited.

"Only an hour or so before you rang. For you to buy back the shares, or consider taking Desmond privately, would be a disaster, and you would make people lose faith in you. By behaving as I advise everyone will think you show good judgment. You don't want to become overburdened with debt, my dear, at a time when you should be concentrating on consolidating the business around mainstream activities such as champagne.

"Believe me, the SEC is very powerful. It has a nose for irregularities and gets onto them very quickly. I'll go and see Ronald Epstein, a young man full of integrity, and be sure that he knows what is going on."

"Where would I be without you?" Sandra's voice had a note of humility Henri had seldom heard. "You're so *wise,* Henri."

"Call it the advantage of years," Henri said lightly, and replaced the receiver.

* * *

Ronnie Epstein put out his hand.

"Very glad to welcome you, Mr. Piper. I think we had dealings with you before."

"Not with me," Henri said pleasantly, "but with my brother-in-law Georges Desmond."

"Oh yes, of course. . . ." Epstein indicated a chair.

"Do take a seat Mr. Piper. Coffee? Something stronger?"

"Coffee would be fine," Henri said briskly. "I've had a very busy morning in New York." He flicked a speck of dust off his immaculate jacket and gazed at Ronald Epstein, Jr.

"It's about the recent large purchase of Desmond shares, Mr. Epstein."

"Yes?" Epstein said, pencil poised. "Do you wish to make a purchase too, sir?"

"Not on your life!" Henri laughed. "The SEC are investigating insider trading. . . ."

"With *Desmond* shares?" Epstein looked aghast. "But nothing has happened. They're depressed. . . ."

"It is just possible that something may be about to happen very soon. I've no idea what it is, I'm glad to say, nor do I wish to. But I had a phone conversation last night with the Group President, Miss Sandra O'Neill Desmond, and I have come to see you on her behalf. A highly confidential file in her office disappeared. Shortly after that this large purchase of shares was made. I don't need to emphasize the trouble you'd be in with the SEC if you refuse to cooperate and tell her, through me, who placed that order."

"I'm afraid I really can't, Mr. Piper." Epstein primly joined his hands in front of him. "You know that kind of information is *strictly* confidential."

"Nevertheless for years you have been on friendly terms with the Desmond Group acting as one of its brokers . . . how can you suddenly turn and act *against* its best interests?"

Epstein gave a wry smile and threw his hands in the air.

"What can I do, Mr. Piper? We are stockbrokers. Anyone can purchase through us."

"Naturally." Henri nodded his head "In that case, I shall have to get in touch immediately with the SEC and tell them what I have just told you. Insider trading as you know is an offense. . . ."

"Never in my life, or the lifetime of my father, has this firm been accused of such an act," Epstein said indignantly.

"Quite. But it might happen *this* time, Mr. Epstein." Henri continued to look the soul of affability. "Believe me, I know what I'm talking about, and if you value the reputation of your firm—"

Slowly Epstein stood up and gazed out of the window at the skyscrapers silhouetted against the Manhattan skyline. It was a sight he loved and valued, and a scandal. . . . He cracked his fingers one by one and when he turned he appeared to have reached his decision.

"I'll level with you, Mr. Piper," he said, sitting down slowly and drawing a file toward him. "As long as you'll level with the SEC and say we cooperated. . . ."

"You can trust me," Henri said with a reassuring smile.

Epstein turned over the papers in his folder and then slowly looked up.

"Does the name *Strega* mean anything to you . . . ?"

FIVE

Voice from the Dead

29

"He's such a horrible man I can't bear to have him near me," Tara said, nose pressed to the window of Sandra's apartment as she looked at the car waiting for her in the street below. "He's always there; always waiting."

"Why don't you sack him then?"

Bob approached from behind her, tentatively put a hand on her arm and looked down past her to the road where Tara's car was parked by the side of the curb.

"I can't. You know I can't." Violently she shook her head and, as she turned, Bob caught her to him and, for the very first time, held her tight.

"Oh Bob . . ." she sighed, looking up at him. "Oh *Bob* . . ."

"You know . . ." Bob said hesitantly, looking at her. "You know I'd do anything . . ."

"I know you would." The moment passed, she moved away. "But what can *you* do? Besides . . ." Her hands fell helplessly to her side. "You're much too young."

"Who cares about that?"

"People care. They talk. Your sister would absolutely hate it, if . . . anything happened between us."

"My sister's not one to talk, the mess she's got herself into."

"Has she?" Tara looked up, her self-preoccupation diverted by a momentary interest in something else. "*I* understood she was knocking Zac all over the place. He's in such a foul mood you can hardly speak to him. Something about shares . . . he claims he's lost a lot of money."

"*She* claims he diddled her." Bob gave a wry smile. "She is after his guts."

"They hate each other; but I hate him too." Tara clenched her fist and banged it against her side. "I hate him. Gomez *is* my jailer not my protector. Do you think I don't know why he follows me everywhere? It isn't to protect me at all, it's to keep an eye on me. He's such a hateful man . . . Do you know," she looked past Bob through the window, "I could imagine him more involved in poor Livio's murder than that man they finally sent to prison for life. Now Gomez . . . there *is* a killer."

Bob rapidly crossed the room of Sandra's salon overlooking the river and took her again in his arms.

"I can't bear to have him near you. Tara . . ."

"Yes?" As she looked up at him, so vulnerable, so alone, he yearned to kiss her but until she gave the signal he didn't dare.

"Let's go away."

"Go away?" Still she clung on to him.

"Run away."

"Don't be silly. I've got two children."

"Yes, but they'd be all right. . . ."

"Are you thinking of the future, my dear boy?" Tara gazed at him tenderly. "If so you can forget it. You have no money and neither have I. Besides there is too much difference in age between us."

"What does it matter so long . . . as we love each other?"

"Oh Bob . . ." Tara stood in the middle of the room, her expression a compound of tenderness and pity. "Oh Bob, you are so sweet." She went up to him and, as she touched his cheek, he grabbed her mouth and planted on it a clumsy, harsh, almost adolescent kiss. But she didn't break from him. She clung to him and then, very gently, encircled his face with her hand and showed him how loving and lingering a proper adult kiss could be.

Finally she broke away and strolled over to the window to gaze down again at the stationary car.

"What time is your sister coming back?" she asked, looking at her watch.

"I don't know. I think the plane took off from Rome about noon. I don't know if she's going to come here or to the office."

"She mustn't find us here anyway."

"I don't care."

"I do." Tara got out a compact from her bag and, looking carefully at herself in the mirror, began to touch up her face. Gazing at her, Bob thought he had never seen anyone so beautiful or, in his wildest dreams, hoped he would aspire to the love of a woman like her. He also knew, at that moment, that now there was another woman in his life more important even than his sister.

"Better go." The brilliance of Tara's smile made his heart turn right over. "Don't let my minder see you."

"What does he think you're doing here?"

"Oh he's not intelligent enough to 'think.' I told him I was visiting a friend. There is only one entrance and he saw me go through it. I very much doubt if he even knows it's Sandra's home. Don't forget, to many people she still lives at the Ritz. Incidentally . . ." Tara paused thoughtfully. "Zac sent a package to your sister the other day, or rather to her confidential secretary. It is Agnès, isn't it?"

"Agnès?" For a moment Bob looked puzzled. "Agnès Guyon. Yes. Why should Zac send a package to *her?*"

"It was something awfully important," Tara said as Bob reluctantly helped her into her coat. "Belle had brought it from Tourville and it had to go to Sandra's office in a great hurry. What interested me, though, was that Belle said specifically to make sure it went to Agnès first, before Sandra saw it. Do you suppose that Agnès is having an affair with my husband? Wouldn't it be a *scream* if she were?"

"I doubt it." Bob shook his head. "Any man with a wife like you having an affair with someone like Agnès must be out of his mind. She's nobody."

"Oh Zac wouldn't mind that," Tara said with an edge to her voice. "As long as he got something out of it, he wouldn't mind who she was . . . and Sandra's secretary? It's an idea isn't it? Typical Zac, that kind of ploy."

"An absurd idea," Bob said reaching for the door. "Besides, Sandra trusts her implicitly."

"Please close the door, Agnès, and sit down." Sandra nodded in the direction of the chair in front of her desk.

"Shall I get my book, Mademoiselle?"

"Not yet." Sandra was flicking through a sheaf of papers. "I want to have a little chat with you."

Agnès looked desperately at the door, wishing that somehow she could be spirited through it and vanish. But it was too late. Docilely she sat down, covering her knees with the hem of her plain woollen skirt.

"Yes, Mademoiselle." She bowed her head and waited. For a moment or two Sandra looked at the bent head unable to believe that the suspicions she had only slowly arrived at, and which Bob's story now seemed to confirm, were possibly true. Was she after all such a poor judge of character? Had she entrusted secrets of the most important kind to someone who was betraying her? She hoped the answer would be "no."

"I wanted to ask you something, Agnès," she said after the pause. "How did you come upon that file regarding the Banque Franco-Belges which you unexpectedly returned to me the other day?"

Crisply, as if repeating something she had carefully rehearsed before, Agnès said, "I found it in the photocopying room, Mademoiselle, as I told you."

"But I had *never* asked you to photocopy anything in it, Agnès. It is confidential."

"I *think* you'd forgotten, Mademoiselle. You have so much on your mind," Agnès suggested helpfully.

"No, Agnès," Sandra said slowly. "I did *not* forget. I have a particularly good and clear memory, as you know quite well. That is a personal file kept in my personal cabinet. There was nothing in it that needed photocopying . . . unless you wanted it for someone else."

"How do you mean, Mademoiselle?" Slowly Agnès lifted her head while a telltale blush stole up her cheeks. But no, she could not meet those clear blue eyes with that curiously mesmeric quality. Not yet.

"I'll come to the point, Agnès." Sandra glanced at her watch. "I'm expecting a call from Bonn at any moment and I don't want to play cat and mouse with you. What I'm suggesting, backed by some evidence that has just come to me, is that that file came from Zac Desmond via his sister Belle. It was delivered here by Monsieur Gomez, who Monsieur Zac Desmond has engaged to protect his wife in case she is attacked. I don't think that even *he* thinks they found the real killer of Monsieur Livio."

As Agnès didn't answer Sandra went on:

"I would also like to know what happened to a letter that was sent to me here, marked 'personal' by the Countess de Saint-Aignan? It was a long time ago. It would have been sent shortly before you became my secretary. . . ."

"That I know nothing about, Mademoiselle!" Quickly she lifted her head and gazed defiantly at her tormentor.

"I think you do. Certainly Edith Huelin knows nothing about it because I asked her. I went to see her yesterday, Agnès, I think I should tell you this. I wanted to know how she and the baby were; but I also wanted to ask her why she was so opposed to my appointing you my secretary. At the time I supposed her to be jealous. She said," Sandra paused to give full effect to her words, "that she didn't think you could be trusted. That you had worked for some time with Monsieur Zac Desmond and had a very good relationship with him. I would also like to know, Agnès," here Sandra turned to another document, "how on what you earn you manage to pay fourteen thousand francs a month for a flat in the Parc Monceau? It is almost your entire salary."

"May I leave the room please, Mademoiselle?" Agnès begged.

"No you may not until I have had the answers to my questions. I'm sorry I appear to have done some snooping, Agnès, but I had to. The details I received made me very unhappy indeed, particularly in view of my relationship with Zac Desmond and the recent scandal about the shares. Was it *you* who tipped him off . . . ?"

"No, no Mademoiselle," Agnès cried, in evident terror. "I *swear* I never told Monsieur Zac anything about you . . . well, not for a long time. . . ."

As she burst into tears burying her face in her hands Sandra felt almost a sense of relief. She hated mysteries and this one had been quite easily solved. The thing was, however, that this girl had been passing on to Zac everything that happened in her office for nearly a year. Casually she handed her a Kleenex.

"Here blow your nose," she said, "and tell me everything. I have to know you see. It is the only way I can undo the harm you have done me."

"Mademoiselle . . ." Agnès began after a few seconds during which she blew her nose and dried her eyes, and then went through the whole routine all over again.

When she had finished she started once more to sob, head held in her hands. It was a heart-rending sight and Sandra almost felt pity for her.

"You see, Mademoiselle . . . it was *very* hard for me to resist. Monsieur Zac, well, he was the son of the great Monsieur Desmond. It was not just *only* for the prestige; but I always admired you, Mademoiselle, I honestly did. I *told* him I admired you and I told him, not long ago, that I would do nothing more. . . ."

"Do you love him, Agnès?" Sandra said in a voice so full of compassion that Agnès wanted to howl all over again. "Because, you know, I too know something about how foolishly one can fall in love . . . that is not a sin. Betraying an employer in my opinion is."

"I do *not love* him, Mademoiselle," Agnès burst out. "I am afraid of him. He is always threatening to take the apartment away unless I help him. You've no idea what it is, Mademoiselle, to live in a place like that after what I am used to. Recently Monsieur Zac," she bowed her head again and continued in a whisper, "said he would divorce his wife and marry me."

"And did you believe that?" Sandra inquired gently.

"No, I never believed it." Agnès again blew her nose which, by this time, was very red indeed. "I knew he would never marry me. Me? Can you see *me* in charge of the *hôtel* in the rue de Varenne? Never. He may not love Madame Desmond or be loyal to her, but he would never marry me. Never. I tell you, Mademoiselle, and you need not believe this if you don't want to; but I *hate* myself for what I have done to you. I respect you and I admire you. Him . . ." She made a gesture of the streets of which Lady Elizabeth would certainly have disapproved, even had she understood it. "I tell you I hate him, Mademoiselle, for the way he has treated me. And *if* I can do anything, at any time, to help *you* in any way . . ." Hopefully she looked at her employer with the expression of a dog who, after a good hiding, hopes to be given at least a bone.

Sandra's smile continued to be kind but there was steel in her voice.

"I think you know you'll have to go, Agnès. I can't keep you here and I don't want to."

She rose and, turning her back on the crouching woman, gazed out of the window.

"I can't have someone working for me whom I can't trust. . . ."

"But never again, Mademoiselle." Agnès began to snivel.

"I'm sorry, Agnès." Slowly Sandra turned round again. "I've thought about it and, believe me, I'm sorry for you. You have gotten yourself into a mess and you showed such promise."

Sandra sat down again and began to fiddle with her gold Cartier pencil.

"If I fire you you're absolutely finished in every way. I could quite easily ensure you never got a decent job again. I think it goes without saying that Monsieur Desmond won't keep you on in the rue de Monceau once you're no longer of any use to him. You're doubly punished I'm afraid. However . . ." All she could see now of Agnès was her bowed head, her shoulders convulsed with sobs. "I am prepared to let you work for a company within the Group. We have many scattered round Europe and as long as I don't personally see you again, I don't care where you go or what you do."

As Sandra lowered her voice, Agnès raised her tearstained face, handkerchief crushed pathetically in her hand.

"Yes, I'm giving you a little hope, Agnès, and also I want you to learn this lesson and never forget it: Never, ever betray someone who puts such great trust in you. Goodbye, Agnès."

Agnès rose and, mumbling something Sandra couldn't make out, began to shuffle toward the door. Watching her, Sandra felt a momentary sense of pity; but it was a lesson for her too. Her next secretary would be someone who was plain, middle-aged and happily married . . . and hopefully, out of the clutches of Zac.

Edith Huelin? Why not try her again?

Her face brightened at the thought as the intercom buzzed and Agnès's temporary replacement said:

"A personal call for you, Mademoiselle, from NATO headquarters. Shall I put them through?"

"Of course," Sandra said, taking the phone and pressing a button that automatically recorded all incoming calls.

"Good afternoon, Herr Strauss. I hope you have good news for me. . . ."

"Excellent news, Mademoiselle." The diplomat began to speak and Sandra, listening carefully, put all thoughts of her banished, disgraced secretary from her mind.

Philippe de Lassale, from being a very contented man, had become a very unhappy one. He realized, too late, that he had been more than influenced by Zac. Against his better judgment he had committed a criminal offense and all for the sake of greed.

Like others before him and, doubtless, many after, he wanted to be richer than he was already, accumulate more wealth than he needed.

"But what," he wondered mournfully to himself as he waited in the anteroom of Sandra's office, "did it profit a man if he gained the whole world . . . and ended up in disgrace?"

"Mademoiselle will see you now," the temporary secretary said.

It was already seven in the evening, but the lights burned brightly in the Desmond offices in the place de L'Étoile.

Philippe de Lassale had an ancestor who had perished on the guillotine in the first days of the Republic. As he entered Mademoiselle Desmond's office suddenly the years seemed to roll back into that singular moment when his ancestor, Comte André de Lassale, had placed his head upon the block. . . .

"Good evening, Mademoiselle," he said with a formal bow.

"Good evening, Philippe," Sandra replied with a reassuring smile. "Please do sit down. I have good news."

"Good news, Sandra?" Philippe's eyes lit up as the prospect of a reprieve seemed a possibility.

"I heard this afternoon from Herr Strauss of the NATO Secretariat that they have agreed to take as many of the Desmond-2000 as the Arabs. Already," she looked at the computer screen at the side of her desk, "the price of the Desmond shares has leapt on foreign markets to forty-eight dollars . . . and rising."

"That is *excellent* news, Sandra." Philippe crossed his legs and in his relief drew a cigarette case from his pocket which he held out to her. As she declined he put one in his mouth and said:

"Congratulations. That was a lot of hard work on your part."

"And yours," she said.

"Oh my part was quite small." He attempted a modest smile.

"No your part was quite big," Sandra said, switching off the computer. "Zac Desmond would never have attempted such a huge *coup* involving so much money without your help and support. . . ."

"But I . . ."

"I know quite well you were behind the attempt to have me ousted, Philippe, and please don't deny it. My lawyers in America have already had depositions from Epstein, and the case could well become a Federal matter involving vast sums in insider trading. Only you knew that the deal with NATO was more than likely to come off. Everyone else thought it would not; that the Desmond shares were in decline because we had a bad year. The 2000 was expensive to develop. We needed a big new sale to turn in real profits. Britain had said 'no.' It all depended on NATO. Profits were down all round, and the vintage had been a fiasco. There were rumors that the Group as a whole would be taken over by Heurtey, rumors which, I have no doubt, you and Zac fueled." Sandra got up and, folding her arms, slowly walked round her desk until she stood in front of him.

He realized then, at that instance, that he had never felt so small in his life.

"You, Philippe de Lassale, are a man with a rich and proud tradition of honor in the field of business. Yours is a family with a long and distinguished past. I have had some inquiries made and I have heard nothing but good of you, your father or your grandfather. So how could you have let Zac Desmond undo all that? You stand accused of fraud . . . of conspiring with him to buy shares when they were low knowing that a deal was in the offing which would immediately raise the price, as it already has by ten dollars and we have only just begun. The news has only just started to get around.

"Only *you* had that knowledge, Philippe de Lassale, and only *you* could have passed it on to Zac Desmond. . . ."

"Mademoiselle . . . Sandra . . ." Philippe took his unlit cigarette from his mouth and his bowed head and dejected attitude reminded Sandra of Agnès only a few hours before.

She sighed. It had been a hard and tiring day; a day when one wondered who one's friends really were, and where?

She had only been back from Bonn for forty-eight hours and a hornet's nest of deceit and intrigue had already revealed itself.

"Sandra," de Lassale said again. "I don't know *what* to say."

"It *is* all true then?"

"Partly . . ." Momentarily he raised his eyes and met her frank gaze. He seemed to capitulate. "Yes, it is all true. I admit I was corrupted. I shall resign at once."

"I think you have no option," Sandra said, "but I am telling you that *I* shall make a bid for the Heurtey Group. We have sufficient funds and we are poised to do it."

"The whole of the Group?" de Lassale said in amazement.

"All of it. We are actively engaged in conversations in New York with Ebenezer Heurtey III in the hope of a friendly takeover. With the Heurtey Group we shall control not only Tellier *but* the Banque Franco-Belges as well. In charge I propose to put Antoine Dericourt, who has been not only a staunch friend and ally but has shown remarkably good judgment in all this. Moreover," she looked at him sternly, "he is a man of integrity. A man I can trust."

"And Zac Desmond?"

"Zac Desmond, if I have anything to do with it, will be kicked out, on his backside, to put it crudely. I intend to show no mercy there. None at all."

Michel Harcourt had little interest in possessions. In a way he was like the tortoise who carried its house about on its back. He claimed that everything he needed could be fitted into a small suitcase: a change of clothes, washing and shaving gear, some books . . . oh and a stethoscope because as a doctor one always had to be ready for emergencies.

Accordingly his modest home in Paris was not far from his old stomping grounds in Saint-Germaine-des-Prés, and the medical faculty in rue des Saintes Pères where he had been a postgraduate student. It was a small but not unattractive apartment at the top of a house in rue de Lille which, many years before, had been the *hôtel particulier* of a wealthy antique dealer. This quarter of Paris was still full of antique shops which were visited by discerning patrons and dealers from all over the world. Now, however, the once large and gracious house had been converted into apartments but, gradually, even they had the air of having seen better days. A coat of paint was badly needed, some renovation work to the walls and courtyard, and there was no elevator to the fifth floor.

However, there was a balcony from which it was possible to see the spire of the Sainte Chapelle and the huge cranes that were poised at the other side of the Louvre in extensive reconstruction work.

Michel had never in his life expected to entertain Sandra

Desmond in his apartment. In fact he had never even wanted to invite Sandra there; but she insisted.

"Where do you live?" she had asked him. "You know about me. I want to know about you."

Of his five brothers and sisters Michel was particularly close to his eldest sister, Anique, a widow in her forties with two grown-up children. One was in America and one was a student in Lyons, and she herself taught at a school in Montparnasse.

Brother and sister shared a disdain for worldly things, and Anique was more troubled than she cared to reveal to Michel about his burgeoning relationship with the richest woman in France.

Anique, however, need not have worried. Like everyone who met Sandra for the first time, and who was honest and well disposed toward her, she found her the quintessence of charm. She possessed the instinctive ability of the great to make people relax. Anique had been brought in to cook for Michel, who claimed the proverbial male ability to boil an egg and not much more.

Sandra's chauffeur left her by the street door not long after her talk with Philippe de Lassale and she was tired. She would much rather have gone home to bed, but the date was a longstanding one and Michel someone she preferred not to let down.

Michel noticed her pallor as soon as she arrived at the door.

"Too many stairs?" he asked, sympathetically, drawing her in.

"Too long a day. Too much to do. Too little time in which to do it . . . or has someone said that before?"

"It does ring a bell," Michel said, taking her arm and leading her from the small hall into the main room with its balcony over rue de Lille.

"This is charming," Sandra said, looking round. The furniture was plain but not cheap; the walls were lined with books and there was a deep armchair by the stove which was obviously regularly used. Over it was a reading lamp, and at once she could imagine Michel sitting there night after night reading his journals and scientific books in search of a cure for AIDS or, maybe, watching TV in the corner.

"You've a balcony just like me," she said.

"Not *quite* like you, Mademoiselle," Michel said with meaning and as a woman came into the room through the door from the kitchen he said:

"This is my eldest sister, Anique. The one I told you was a teacher."

"How do you do, Anique?" Sandra said warmly, and Michel's sister felt immediately drawn to this beautiful, but natural and friendly woman who took her hand, smiling into her eyes.

She knew then why her brother loved Sandra Desmond. Anique made a *blanquette de veau* with fresh vegetables and cheese and salad to follow. The dessert was *oeufs à la neige* with a delicious vanilla cream. They ate at a table by the window covered with a check cloth, with a view of the rooftops opposite through the frosted glass because it was very cold.

After the meal Sandra said, "I haven't enjoyed an evening like this for . . . many years," she added swiftly. "Truly. I mean that."

"It was nothing much," Anique said deprecatingly. "And as for you, Mademoiselle . . ."

"Please call me Sandra," Sandra said at once. She had noticed that for the entire evening Anique, with the reserve of the nervously disposed, hadn't referred to her by name at all.

Anique was a woman she instinctively found sympathetic. She was tall with curly hair like Michel, a little gray at the sides. Her husband, whom she had nursed for a long time before he died, had been a victim of cancer. After his death she resumed her career as a schoolteacher.

Sandra knew in that instance that she envied Michel. He

had something she hadn't gotten, and never could have, and whose absence she would miss all her life: a large family and the close bonds such security gave.

"I hope you feel privileged," she said to him as Anique went into the kitchen to prepare coffee.

"Dining with you? Of course." Briefly his hand closed over hers.

"No, having Anique as a sister. Do you know that's the main thing I've missed in my life? Brothers and sisters, mother and father, cats and dogs. . . ."

"It's not too late," Michel murmured.

"It's too late for that. . . ."

"I mean for the future . . . to *make* a large family."

"I know what you mean," Sandra lowered her voice. "But, perhaps, in a way, it's too late for that too. Have you heard of the Heurtey Group?"

Michel frowned but Anique coming in with a tray on which were the cups with the *café filtre* said:

"I have. I read something in the papers about it the other day."

"It is a very large American corporation. It has links with the Banque Franco-Belges and owns Tellier Champagne. It is a bit like Desmond used to be before I rationalized. A conglomerate, but larger than Desmond. If I bought it I should rationalize that too; strip the assets we couldn't use; hive sections off profitably. . . ." Michel, watching her closely, saw the enthusiasm positively glow from her. It was industrial power she was thinking of . . . not the patter of tiny feet. To her they were incompatible. "Well," Sandra, flushed, paused and gazed at him. "*We* are going to try and take it over. It will make us, if we do, the twenty-third largest company on the U.S. list of 500."

"Well?" Michel looked at her with a wry smile.

"Well. I'll be too busy to have a family."

"I can see that." Michel lowered his head.

"But do you *want* the Heurtey Group?" Anique, looking puzzled, sat down at the table, passing them their cups.

Sandra took hers and looked with some astonishment at Michel's sister.

"Of course I do."

"Why?"

"Why?" Sandra searched for the right words. "Because it is there. That's why I'm in business. . . ."

"To get richer and bigger . . ." Michel lifted the lid of his *filtre*. "To have more and more problems. . . ."

"To give *you* more money for research," Sandra retorted with a wink to Anique. "To rid the world of AIDS. I bet *you'd* do anything for money."

"No I wouldn't." Michel removed the lid and put the cup of hot coffee to his lips. "In fact I'm not. I have been offered the Professorship of Virology at Lorimer College in the States with all the funds I need; a house, a car . . . probably a boat." He smiled in a self-mocking way.

"Oh!" Sandra clapped her hands together. "But that's *wonderful*. The Lorimer College is very prestigious and I commute to the States so often. . . ."

"Only I'm not going," Michel said. "I turned it down today."

"But *why . . . ?"* Sandra thumped her fist helplessly on the table, conscious of a personal sense of anger that he should turn down such an opportunity.

"Because I want to do what I want to do. I want to continue my researches into the HIV virus and that is *not* the speciality I would be expected to pursue at Lorimer at all. They have quite different plans for me. You see we are on the track of a vaccine that could help stop the spread of the disease. It's not a cure but it is an important step, and I want to try that soon . . . in the field. In Africa."

"Africa?" Sandra gazed at him, aware of a curious thud in her chest. "Africa did you say?"

"I always wanted to go back to Africa. You know that, Sandra. I'd like the Foundation to put in a lot of money for an Institute there."

"And you'd live there?"

"Maybe for a few years . . ."

Sandra wanted to say: "But what about me?" but she was too aware of the curious, kind eyes of Anique on her. Instead she said:

"I've had a heck of a day. Would you mind if we call it quits?"

"Of course not. I'll take you home." Michel was about to get up but Sandra put a hand on his arm.

"I did ask my car to come for me at eleven. Forgive me, but I have to be in Reims first thing in the morning so it's taking me to Tourville tonight. It will be downstairs waiting for me now."

"I'll see you to your car then," Michel said rather stiffly.

"Thank you so much." Sandra turned and instinctively embraced Anique. "Do you know that I'm quite a good cook too?"

Anique's look was a little unnerving to Sandra, who felt as though she were under a microscope, every bit as powerful as those used by Michel in his laboratory. Her appearance and behavior were being closely inspected and analyzed by Michel's sister. What would the verdict be?

All at once her eyes crinkled into a smile. "I can guess it. I think you must be good at most things."

"I wish I were," Sandra said with a sad look in her eyes, though glad of the tacit approval of Michel's sister. "I only wish I were."

Michel took his time seeing Sandra to her car and when he returned Anique had washed up and was ready to go herself as her brother only had one small bedroom with a single bed.

"Sandra could have given you a lift, I didn't think of it."

Michel clicked his fingers with dismay. "It's practically on her way."

"No thank you. I'll get the Métro. I prefer not to take a lift with Sandra."

"Didn't you like her?" Michel asked anxiously.

"On the contrary." Anique sat at the table and reached for a Gauloise—a legacy from years of nursing her husband. "I liked her very much. I liked her almost too much. . . ."

"Why do you say that?"

"Because it frightens me." Anique lit her cigarette and slowly waved out the match. "She is so suitable for you. I feel you have such a rapport."

"We have." Michel nodded. "I feel it too, and so does she. But we are at the moment both fighting it."

"Why?"

"Why do you think? That I want to be the husband, or lover if you like, of the wealthiest woman in France, maybe soon one of the richest in the world? Not a day passes that someone writes an article on her. Every move she makes is recorded. She is off to America next week to appear on a talk show. I'd be like her poodle."

"You know you wouldn't. You'd be someone in your own right. Is that why you didn't take the professorship so that you could be near her?"

"It had nothing to do with it." Michel got up and looked out of the window across the rainsoaked roofs. "That was purely a professional matter. As she said, Lorimer is near New York. She's there practically every few weeks. If they take over Heurtey she said she might go and live there for a while . . . no that had nothing to do with it at all. You see, Anique," Michel turned and his large blue eyes wore a melancholy expression, "Sandra and I might want each other and I believe we do, but our worlds are too far apart.

"Why even start something you know has no future?"

*   *   *

Zac Desmond was a man who didn't know when he was beaten. He refused to acknowledge defeat. The moment he heard that Philippe de Lassale had resigned as President of the Banque Franco-Belges he plotted to succeed him by climbing unmercifully and energetically over the back of someone he had helped to bring down.

If Phillipe de Lassale was a gentleman, a man of honor, Zac, emphatically, was not. He traded on the misfortunes of others, and he knew that on the Board of the Bank were enough people cast in his own mold who could be swayed by him.

He had a number of cronies, some of whom he had zealously cultivated. They were allies rather than friends; people who could see that their advantage ultimately might lie not in the courtly, quaint world of a gentleman's agreement and words of honor, but in the rough and tumble of the marketplace. This was the kind of world typified by Zac, whose only idea of trust was that they could be relied upon to put his, and their, corrupt notions into practice.

The three men who, with himself, were ultimately to be crucial to the success of his plan were Luc and Rudy Tellier and Auguste de Lassale, the son of Philippe and, at thirty-two, the youngest director of the Bank for which he had always been groomed to succeed his father.

But when? Philippe was a fit and athletic man of fifty-five and Auguste, like Zac, was ambitious. Yet Auguste had no intention of being eclipsed by his father as Zac had been eclipsed by his. Although Auguste had been educated at the best schools and had the same kind of upbringing, he was not the man his father was and when he resigned as President of the Board for an unspecified reason—vaguely connected with his health, it was diplomatically put about—his son despised him.

Zac lost no time when he heard of Philippe's resignation to distance himself from him. He didn't return calls or answer urgent letters, delivered by hand. To him Philippe had become a nonperson and he knew that his own future depended on maintaining this distance and then profiting by it.

For once in her life Sandra slipped up about Zac. Her mistake was fundamental. So relieved was she to have secured the deal with NATO, to have stopped the drain on Desmond shares and see them plunge then rise again, that she almost forgot about Zac and went back to Bonn, Brussels and Rome as soon as she could to tie up the deal.

During the time she was gone, Zac swiftly but carefully prepared his attack. Surprise was crucial. Luc and Rudy Tellier, Auguste de Lassale and Baron Gustave Martens, a very old man whose Belgian grandfather had been one of the original founders of the bank and who was a longtime enemy of Philippe de Lassale, because he felt he should have been President, were invited to his office. There they were presented with a set of completely illusory and inaccurate facts and figures which Zac had cobbled together with the aid of his new assistant who had succeeded Strega, a clever, ambitious and unscrupulous accountant called Hubert Jeantet.

Zac had a facility for attracting to him like-minded people; those who combined greed with a lack of scruple and who were not averse to double dealing.

Hubert Jeantet was, like Auguste de Lassale, thirty-two years of age and had had a successful if unremarkable career in the money markets before being spotted and called in by Zac who knew that Hubert liked the things all men of his age liked: a house, a flashy car, plenty of loose change in his pocket. There were also girls if Hubert should be tired of his pretty wife, Monique, which he sometimes was.

Zac knew that he must get his four members of the Board to vote for him and, perhaps, persuade one or two of those who were above obvious corruption. Here the Baron would be a suitable influence because everyone believed that he was a gentleman not only by birth but by breeding. Zac knew better. He knew the Baron to be short of funds and not above a bribe; even a few cases of vintage champagne and one or two invitations to Tourville were frequently a help in getting things done.

Accordingly armed with his phoney figures—none of them were financial experts—Zac called his coterie into his office within a day or two of Philippe's resignation and within hours of the departure of Sandra for Bonn. Solemnly he asked them to sit down around the circular table in his office while Hubert, his face suitably grave, circulated the figures that he had spent two days cooking up and only a few minutes photocopying.

Zac took his seat authoritatively at the head of the table and asked Hubert to stand near the door.

"Occasionally pop your head outside and be sure that no one is lurking there."

"Come, my dear fellow," the Baron said with a chuckle, "things can't be as bad as that."

"Oh but they *are* my dear Baron," Zac said earnestly. "Things are very bad indeed. We are surrounded by spies, saboteurs and fifth columnists to use the jargon of war."

"You're joking of course," the Baron laughed pleasantly.

"Not at all, Gustave." Zac put a hand on his arm. "That truly is the reason for this clandestine meeting." He looked solemnly around. "You see we are among friends."

"But why . . . ?" Martens began to look uncomfortable, never having numbered the Tellier brothers among his friends, or particularly liked young de Lassale.

"Read the figures." Zac stubbed a finger at the sheaf of papers in front of the Baron. "See what a bad way we are in. How much money has been squandered by Mademoiselle O'Neill in her desperate need to cover herself with glory and supply fighter-planes to NATO as well as the Arabs. All these figures were kept hidden from us. . . ."

"And that is the reason . . ." The Baron, not troubling to study the papers, looked from one colleague to another.

Solemnly Zac nodded his head.

"That *is* the reason why Philippe went. It had nothing to do with his health. He was as fit as a fiddle."

"Is it true, Auguste?" the Baron whispered, a hand on his heart. "He *did* seem so fit."

"Can't tell you the truth," Auguste murmured. "Doesn't want it to be known."

"Oh dear me, I am sorry." The Baron screwed a monocle into his eye and stared blindly at the pages of figures before him.

They did, indeed, paint a very black picture. According to them the Banque Franco-Belges was on the way to ruin and would leave several directors, whose own considerable assets guaranteed the Bank's funds, in ruins too.

"It would be the end of the House of Tellier," Zac said offhandedly. "Everything like that would have to be sold."

"All assets stripped willy-nilly," Auguste agreed.

"But does Mademoiselle know this?" The Baron looked frightened. "I can't believe . . ."

"My dear Baron," Zac said harshly. "You are unwilling to believe *anything* about that Irishwoman. She's at the root of it all."

"But she always *seems* so capable. . . ."

"Huh!" Luc Tellier took up his cue. "Is that what you think? It is she alone who is responsible for the poor financial results of the House of Desmond due to the ruined *cuvée* which had to be scrapped. The supermarkets *Maumes,* which she sold off, are now profitable. The Immobilière Lacroix is making a fortune out of real estate in the West Indies and Spain where time-sharing has become big business. All these assets Mademoiselle got rid of. She is a liability . . . and yet . . ." He looked at his brother as if they were doing a double act.

"And yet she continued to fool people," Rudy Tellier affirmed. "It is only a matter of time before the whole of the Desmond empire crumbles and that is why. . . ."

"We propose Monsieur Zac Desmond, true heir to the Desmond empire, shall be elected President of the Banque Franco-Belges."

"With the intention of, one day, bringing the whole of the Desmond Group into its orbit," Auguste de Lassale intoned with satisfaction. "You can *see* it makes sense."

The Baron Martens spent a lot of time at his villa in the South of France. His position at the Bank and the few other directorships he still maintained were sinecures and he knew very little about either finance, business or the accumulation and retention of wealth. He did, however, like living well and his house on the Côte d'Azur was a particularly pleasant place in a beautiful position and expensive to maintain. Besides, he was getting old. What did he care, really care, what happened to the Banque Franco-Belges or the House of Desmond? Quite frankly he didn't really care two hoots.

"Of course I will give you my support," he said. "The matter looks exceedingly grave."

A few minutes later Zac ushered his fellow conspirators out knowing that even if Ebenezer Heurtey III, who was on his way over, disapproved and, of course, Sandra would, they would be outvoted on the Board.

And he, René-Zachariah Desmond, would already be halfway up the ladder towards the achievement of his life's ambition.

Not only President of the Banque Franco-Belges, President of the Desmond Bank, but soon President of the whole of the Desmond Group. It might take him time but it would happen.

What price Miss Sandra O'Neill now?

As he was on his way out he put a hand on the Baron's arm and drew him aside from the rest.

"Your help and business ability are *invaluable,* Baron. You *will* let me know if you need anything, won't you? I understand that a nice yacht in the harbor of Cannes has caught your eye. . . ."

30

"You'll be on screen in thirty seconds, Miss Desmond," the voice of the producer said into her ear and Sandra gave a brief, nervous pat to her hair and smiled to the camera. Opposite her Mortimer Hatch was glancing at the clipboard he had on his lap while the technicians on the studio floor made some adjustments to the light and the floor manager began to count.

Briefly Sandra glanced at Henri Piper as an assistant said softly to him:

"You'll have to go now, Mr. Piper. We shall be on the air any second."

Henri gave Sandra the thumb-ups sign and left through the door just as the red light above it came on and he could hear from the TV screen in the room, to which he was ushered, her interviewer Hatch making his preliminary announcement.

"Good evening, ladies and gentlemen. Our guest this evening is making one of her rare appearances in an interview on American television. Her achievements since becoming President of the International Desmond Group only eighteen months ago have been acknowledged by the specialist Press as among some of the most astonishing ever to be witnessed in her field.

"I'm delighted to welcome here a young lady whose striking looks would make most people mistake her for a model or a movie star. But no! Sandra O'Neill Desmond is a businesswoman, and by general consensus one of the best there is."

Here the camera focused on Sandra, who made a deprecating gesture, which Henri knew to be sincere, as Hatch prattled on.

She hated being compared to a film star or a model. It offended her feminist instincts and she showed it as Hatch hurriedly drew his eulogy to a close, saying, "Sandra O'Neill Desmond, good evening."

"Good evening." Sandra had already replaced her frown with a pleasant smile.

"I can see the introduction upset you a little, Miss Desmond. Was it my remarks about your looks . . . ?"

"If you like, yes," Sandra said, her friendly tone preempting any criticism. "If I were a man you wouldn't start talking about looks in an introduction, would you?"

Mr. Hatch laughed nervously as Sandra continued:

"Well, I feel the same. Take certain politicians, for example. You don't talk about *their* film-star good looks, but about their prowess as politicians. . . ."

"You're quite right of course."

"I like to be taken for what I am and, as you say, in that field I like to think I am a successful person. Not just a woman."

"You are, *very* . . ."

Hatch went on to enumerate some of Sandra's successes including the recent sales of the Desmond-2000 and questioned her about some technical details concerning the plane, its speed, firepower and so on, all of which she was able to answer with remarkable competence.

Henri, leaning forward in his chair, watched, fascinated. No nuance of expression, no gesture or glance escaped him.

Was he in love with her, as Sophie taunted? Perhaps, at last, he had to admit he was. She fascinated him and the call to New York had been instantly obeyed, even though Sophie when she found out had tried to stop it.

"My dear," he had said, "it's a business trip. I rendered Sandra a real service in what I did for her in New York. It was essential that I helped her when I did. A run on the shares could have meant their suspension from the Stock Exchange. Disaster would surely have followed. Happily a few days later the deal with the Gulf State was announced. Sandra owed a lot to me and we have many things to finalize, above all what to do about the brokers, who benefited illegally and whether to sue them or not."

Sophie had sat upright in her chair listening to him intently but with an expression of disbelief on her face. Then he had stopped, realizing, suddenly, how futile it was; but the last words she flung at him as he went out of the front door still reverberated in his ears:

"You're in *love* with her. Don't try to deceive yourself, Henri Piper."

No, he didn't deceive himself. He *was* in love with her. There was nothing avuncular in the passion he had suppressed so long for her. And if he wanted to help her as a friend, and he did, maybe he also hoped that one day she might need him. One day she might realize she loved him too. What then?

Henri sighed as the interviewer got on to a more difficult subject.

"That really *is* a success story Miss Desmond, but I hear that everything has not been exactly going your way in Paris. An attempt to impose your own choice of President on the Banque Franco-Belges was defeated."

"Narrowly," Sandra acknowledged, biting her lip.

"And I believe the person who was elected President is the Vice-President of your own company, Mr. Zac Desmond himself."

"That is correct." Uncle Henri observed her fist curl tightly in her lap. Certainly, even though she must have been expecting this question, it made her very tense.

"Would you like to tell us more about it, Miss Desmond, or is it a secret?"

"There's nothing at all secretive about it," Sandra said, choosing her words carefully. "Mr. Zac Desmond has been elected President of the Bank and that is all there is to it."

"In effect it was a 'coup'?"

Sandra appeared to consider the question and then said with an engaging smile:

"If you like, yes. My fellow Board members obviously considered him very very capable and I welcome Mr. Desmond, who is my adoptive brother, to the highest echelons of the organization, the bulk of which was founded by his father. . . ."

"But I believe that the relationship is made more difficult by your unsuccessful bid for the Heurtey Corporation, who have links with the Banque Franco-Belges—"

"Oh!" Sandra held up a hand to stop the flow. "The battle isn't over yet! It *is* true we would prefer a friendly takeover of Heurtey, whose shares are even more depressed than ours were on the American market before our arms deal. We think we can improve their performance. However, they have been bolstered up by enormous loans, a second attempt at reconstruction, and we don't feel the price is the right one for us at this moment. However, we shall be keeping an eye on them. For the time being the battle may be lost, but the war is by no means over."

Mr. Hatch consulted his notes and then leaned forward:

"Now could you tell us, Miss Desmond, the reason for your strange inheritance. . . ."

Sophie Piper, watching three thousand miles away on the other side of the continent, didn't try to suppress a smile. She felt now that she was one of the many people who had been deceived by Sandra O'Neill: so "nice," so eager to appear to do the right thing. Yet slowly, imperceptibly, she had been trying to seduce Henri, there was no doubt about that. A man who crossed the Atlantic and the continent of America at her beck and call was clearly besotted. She should long ago have seen it coming.

"Uncle" Henri indeed! Well she, Sophie Piper, born Desmond, no longer considered herself an "aunt"; but an enemy . . . determined as much as any other Desmond to deprive Sandra once and for all of her position of power . . . a position that enabled her to prey all too easily on the susceptible husbands of other women.

And she had trusted Sandra, loved her, wanted her to succeed. But now, by any means in her power, she would continue to help Zac regain what was rightfully his . . . and, in the struggle, keep her husband for herself.

Sophie felt the bile rise in her throat as she lifted the remote control and firmly flicked to another channel.

Sandra had just finished explaining about the inheritance, which Henri thought she handled well.

"Now I understand there is a court case coming up, Miss Desmond."

"That is correct."

"And your defense is that the accusations made against you are complete fabrications."

"They are complete fabrications, but I'm afraid that, as the matter is *sub judice,* I am unable to comment any further except to say that I will be very glad of the chance I shall have in the English courts to scotch, once and for all, the calumnies that have been spread about me. . . ."

Hatch consulted his notes again and then raised his head with that reassuring smile with which the practiced interviewer tries to trap the unwary.

"But yet, are your relations with the Desmond family, and especially Mr. Zac Desmond, currently completely friendly?"

"Oh completely," Sandra said. "Why shouldn't they be?"

"I just wondered . . . one hears rumors. Tell me, Miss Desmond, to change the subject; as your company is multinational, why do you choose to live in France?"

"The Desmond Group is essentially a French Group," Sandra said at once. "Its origins are in France. At its heart is champagne, on which I intend to concentrate a lot more time. I am half French and I love France. I speak the language. . . ."

Behind him the door opened and closed very softly and Henri, still spellbound by the sight on the screen, the skill with which Sandra dealt with a rather awkward interviewer, turned round.

Michel Harcourt stood by the door, his hand still on the knob, his finger on his lips.

"Sorry," he whispered. "Have I missed it all?"

"Most of it," Henri replied.

"I won't disturb you," Michel whispered. "I hope someone got it on video."

"There's sure to be a tape."

Henri spoke briefly and irritably, ashamed of himself but still unable to conceal the irrational sense of dislike he always had when he saw Harcourt.

If he was honest with himself he knew why . . . because Harcourt was in love with Sandra too.

Michel put another log on the fire, which leapt into life, illuminating the woman stretched out on the sofa in front of it. Outside the wind howled, sending flurries of snow over Sugarbush Valley in Vermont which, with any luck, might keep them snowbound for days. Or so Michel hoped as he went back to the couch and curled up beside Sandra, who was still dreamily gazing into the fire.

"How do you feel the interview went, darling?" He put his arms around her.

"I thought it went well. They were out to trap me over Zac, but I think I answered the questions correctly. I tried to avoid the obvious pitfalls. Did you think it was OK?" She put a hand on his wrist and looked at his face, half obscured by the shadows.

"I missed most of it to be truthful. I came late."

"Trust you." Still she nuzzled her cheek against his.

"Henri said I could probably get a video of it."

There was another pause while Sandra appeared once more lost in thought. She was in a reflective mood after the drive from New York.

"Did Henri seem all right to you?"

"His usual self." Michel tried to make the cushion behind his head more comfortable. "He's never particularly nice to me."

"I wonder why that is?" Sandra looked at him curiously, reaching out to touch the lock of hair that fell over his face.

"He's jealous, I think."

"Jealous of what? Who?" Sandra struggled to sit upright, her look of tiredness vanishing.

"Of me. . . ." He returned her gaze, touching her forehead with his thumb as though to ease out the lines of tension which furrowed her brow. "Didn't you know that Henri was in love with you?" he said gently.

"Oh that." Sandra tossed her cigarette toward the fire and put her head in Michel's lap snuggling comfortably against him. "I think he *thinks* he's in love with me, or Sophie has made him think so. She's the jealous one."

"Oh, so it has all come up?"

"Let's say it's surfaced." She slowly brought his hand to her lips. "It started last summer or maybe a bit before. Henri always used to joke. You know the sort of thing; he'd do anything for me and I'd do anything for him. He used to say:

'I love you' and I always added 'like an uncle' because ever since I was a small girl I used to call him 'Uncle' Henri and her 'Aunt' Sophie though, of course, they're not relations. Then, last summer for some reason, he asked me to stop calling him 'uncle' and I think he did get a bit amorous, but I deflected it. Then afterward . . . I got to know you. Since then you've been constantly in my thoughts, believe it or not."

"Constantly?" He leaned over to look in her eyes.

"Always . . . somewhere there in the background."

"Even while you were struggling with Zac?"

"Yes."

"And fighting with Heurtey?"

"Yes. I need the thought of you to keep me sane." She sighed, passing her hand across her brow. "They've been very difficult months. If I'd thought that Zac would have done a dirty deed like that . . ."

Yet, to his surprise, she chuckled.

"You seem to find it amusing."

"I take my hat off to him, you know. I do. He is a dirty swine and a dirty fighter. To keep even with him you have to sink to his level. We'll get Heurtey one day because they can't go on borrowing enormous sums to prop themselves up as they are at the moment. They're overborrowing. Dericourt is monitoring every move and he's very shrewd. I'm going to make him my number two—Vice-President—as soon as Zac makes another wrong move, which he's sure to. I might even take Heurtey to court," she added as if as an afterthought. "The lawyers are working on that now. But for Zac to sail so easily, so skillfully, into the Presidency of the Banque Franco-Belges . . ." She whistled.

"That *is* something. It's a maneuver I never considered. He is an opponent I underestimated. I think if his father knew what Zac was capable of he might not so readily have left the business to me. Unless . . ." She paused and stared at the fire again.

"What?"

"Unless he knew what a dirty dealer he really was, and there's too much evidence he did. You see," she gazed into Michel's eyes, "he's not just clever in the business sense; he's dishonest. I don't think I ever knew such a swine. He is a really evil man. I wouldn't put it past him to have had Livio killed to get even with his wife."

"That's a pretty awful thing to say."

"But why does he have her followed everywhere by that minder? She surely doesn't *need* protection if Aziz, who was convicted, is the real killer. And if he isn't how does Zac *know?"*

"He wants to keep his eye on her, I think."

"I wouldn't put anything past Zac Desmond . . . anyway don't let's talk about him. We might have nightmares."

The soft fall of snow outside was almost palpable, Michel thought, as he lay beside Sandra in the deep warm bed, a fire glowing in the grate. They had rented a shack on the slopes of Mount Abraham. It had a bedroom, a living room and a kitchen and it was about as inaccessible as any place in the world could be. No cameramen, no journalists to follow them there, not even a telephone. Michel had insisted on that. Mademoiselle Desmond was unavailable and, for a few precious days, would remain so.

Immediately after the interview he had spirited her away while the Press thronged about poor old Henri Piper, who had unwittingly been made into a decoy. Now, for a few days, they were cut off from the world. Or were they? How long would Sandra be able to resist tracking to the nearest phone? How long could she really stand this isolation?

Some time before Christmas, while still in France, they had become lovers: a meeting of minds and bodies that was every bit as satisfactory as they had hoped it would be. Sandra had been reluctant at first, and he knew that she had Tim in mind;

not that she loved him anymore, but because she was the sort of woman who did not sleep around. She wanted that to be clear.

Michel had assured her that he knew that; but also that, this time, their bond would be for good.

And, for a time it seemed that the bond would last; that their lives and work were deeply compatible and harmonious. He the busy research doctor at work in his laboratory, addressing conferences, writing papers, being interviewed on TV about the advances in the fight against AIDS. Sandra was his counterpart in the business world: traveling abroad, buying businesses, interviews, newspaper articles, meetings, oh the endless meetings of the business tycoon. When they met, each time was like the first time; a honeymoon that seemed to renew itself over and over again.

But what of the future? Soon he must go to Africa. Soon her court case would be coming up in London when she would need him. But could he be there and what would happen after that?

He put his arm round her; her delicious, silken, naked body vibrant with life against his. Most of the time he could hardly believe he was in the real world but that, somehow, without knowing it, without passing the barrier of pain or death, he had been taken into heaven.

The days that followed were, maybe, the best of any time either of them had ever spent; a time of harmony, fulfillment and fun. For two days they were completely cut off and they skied from one valley to the next to get extra supplies.

Now the sky was clear and the only car parked outside the cabin and covered with snow was an old Chevy which had, with difficulty, made it to the spot on which the chalet stood.

There were waffles with honey and plenty of coffee for breakfast, hamburgers for lunch and broiled steaks with a bottle of California wine for dinner. Like a truly modern, enlightened couple they shared the cooking, made their bed together and as for the rest of the housework, that could wait.

They both loved the outdoors and though Michel was a better skier than Sandra she was a good pupil and an adept one. They made long journeys, sometimes as far as Sugarbush North and Stark Mountain, or they raced down the slopes of Mount Abraham or Lincoln Gap, often ending with a tumble in the snow, laughter and excitement and . . . passion. Yes, always passion.

For the evenings ended early, deep in the downy mattress when a couple who had never expected to end up in each other's arms found that they couldn't get away; couldn't break it; wanted nothing else except that special feeling of being alone with each other, surrounded by the sky and the vastness of the snow which kept out all other predators.

But then it was time to think of departure. Michel spent a whole afternoon scraping the Chevy and testing the engine while Sandra inside made a desultory attempt to pack her things and tidy up.

But her heart wasn't in it. She kept on coming onto the porch to look at him, jeering at him in a good-natured way to egg him on.

"Need any help?" she called. "I'm not much of a mechanic, but I could possibly be better than you."

He emerged from inside the hood of the car, his face and hands covered with grease, and made a dive toward her.

"Don't you dare!" she screamed as he threatened to smear his hands over her thick white cashmere jersey.

"Well, you come and do it then. Come on, 'women's lib.' "

"I don't want to make you feel inadequate, don't you understand?" she said smiling at him but, already, he could see in her the signs of strain and tension.

"I think you don't really want to go back," he announced suddenly.

"Back where?" She averted her eyes and started shifting some of the thick snow from the porch with her bare hands.

"To the world."

"We can't stay here."

"Would you like it if we could?"

"Yes I would."

"If you stayed here, threw it all up, I might reconsider the job at Lorimer."

"Oh?" A glint came into Sandra's eyes. "But how about you giving up *your* trials in Africa to stay in France with me?"

"You know I can't."

"And you know *I* can't." Sandra leaned against the wall of the house while, despite the freezing temperatures, Michel perched on the now closed hood of the car.

"You see, I know I have a vocation. It's a calling. Something I must do. I'm not religious, but it's the only way I can explain it."

"I have a vocation too," Sandra said, "which I can quite easily explain without the aid of religion: I want to work; I enjoy business. Now that I am with Desmond I want it to be the greatest, best-run company in the world."

"But it's not exactly a vocation. . . ." Michel's tone was patient.

"It is," Sandra insisted. "Yours is the same old story of male chauvinism only in another form."

"It isn't at all." Michel began to show his anger.

"Yes it *is.* You may not realize it, but it is. You think, as men have through the centuries, that I should in a sense subordinate myself to you. . . ."

"I don't."

"You do."

For a moment they gazed at each other as enemies and Sandra, her heart sinking, had a familiar feeling of having been here before. She knew that, maybe, this was how it would always be between them; how it would end. But not now.

She got up and walked toward him, banging her feet, which were beginning to freeze, hard on the ground. "It is a very new phenomenon we're dealing with, Michel. The woman who wants, who needs to work, however much she is in love. Men don't really appreciate it. It is a thing women have to fight for; as well as against all the prejudice they encounter. I know people say I am hard, tough, unfeminine. This is invariably the fate of any successful woman. The British like to attack Mrs. Thatcher in that way. They say things about her they wouldn't dream of saying about a man. It *is* chauvinism and it *is* prejudice. If you were in my position and not a doctor I would never dream of asking you to give it up. Say if you were President of a Corporation—as I am."

Michel stared at her and, slowly, reluctantly, he realized that she was indeed teaching him something. It was a lesson he thought he knew already but obviously he didn't. He had always considered himself enlightened in his attitude toward women but, maybe, in many ways he was cavalier: as long as they didn't impinge on his working life he was tolerant toward them. Would he give up Africa for her? Well, no, he wouldn't.

Now here at last was someone he had at first been afraid of. She had made him nervous just because she was so important. He had felt she couldn't possibly be womanly. He admired her, but he was wary of her too.

Sandra had changed that. Now *he* must change. He went over to her and, putting a hand on her shoulder, gently kissed her.

"I do love you," he said.

For an answer she put her arms round his neck and hugged him.

"I wish you'd throw out the court case. I think it's worrying you too much."

"Why do you say that?" She lowered her arms and continued with aimlessly pushing back the snow.

"It's made a difference to you. It's on your mind. Is it Tim?"

"No." She shook her head and, starting to feel herself trem-ble, joined her arms as though to keep herself warm. "It's not Tim. It's something else. I don't know what. It's such a long time ago now, over a year. . . ."

"Then forget it. Throw it up. I may not be able to be with you to support you, darling."

"I know that, but I can't throw it up or forget it. It's too important. While that rumor, that suggestion is there it will never go; besides," she pushed a final handful of snow onto the ground from the car and then began to dust her hands vigorously. "I *must* know the truth you know. Somehow I feel that in court, whether I like it or not, I'll find out the truth . . . about me."

Claire's baby was three months old. He was a boy called Guili-ano and, according to Italian law, he was illegitimate. But he was loved as no baby, in Claire's mind, had ever been loved; loved and wanted, an essential bond, a part of her and Piero. They had a flat in a side street in the Trastevere and Guiliano was christened at the church where she was first reunited with Piero, by the old priest whose Latin Mass she always heard.

The apartment was small, rented, sparsely furnished but, for a time, until Piero did better, Claire knew that nothing would change. He was a stubborn Italian of peasant extraction and he refused to live on her money. This stubbornness of his could have caused problems between them had she not been prepared to compromise. Constantly to compromise.

Compromise in fact meant giving up her freedom because, as Zac had prophesied, however attractive Piero was he had a Latin way of thinking about women. Claire was already pregnant with another child by the time Guiliano was three months old.

And what would happen then?

But Claire was too happy, too contented to live at any time

other than in the immediate present: herself, Piero, Guiliano and the unborn child she carried inside her.

For a woman who had never known much happiness she felt she could hardly ask for more. She was in love, she was wanted, she was a mother and, although in the eyes of the world she had had many enviable things, acquisitions, a title, wealth, she had never had these.

Maybe like Sandra in another part of the world she, Claire de Saint-Aignan, was making her own adjustment to domesticity; the prospect of a future with another human being. But whereas Claire had made her choice Sandra had not yet made hers or, rather, she had not yet decided how the choice she wanted to make could be fitted into the kind of life she already led. Being happy in a snowbound cottage for a few days was one thing. Being happy in a confined space without money, perhaps for life, was another.

Claire was just bathing baby Guiliano, contentedly humming a tune to him, when there was a sharp rap at the door. She looked at the clock and saw it was only ten-thirty in the morning. Piero, who liked his spaghetti lunch, his glass or two of wine, his siesta, was not due home for two or three hours yet.

Before she reached the door the sharp peremptory rap sounded again and, apprehensively, she stood by the door and listened.

"Who's there?" she asked quietly in her hesitant Italian.

"It is I, Tara," the voice whispered back in the same language. "Let me in."

Quickly Claire drew back the bolt, which Piero insisted she fastened every time he went out, and threw open the door. In front of her was Tara, looking tired and disheveled for a former world-famous model. She wore traveling clothes, a beret pulled tightly over her head. She was carrying a small suitcase fastened with a strap.

"Good heavens," Claire cried. "What on earth . . . come in."

She stood back as, slowly, Tara entered the small apartment looking around as if she hadn't quite known what to expect.

"It's very small," Claire said almost in apology and then Tara's attitude suddenly changed and, her face wreathed in smiles, she rushed toward the crib where the newly bathed baby lay gurgling.

"Oh Guiliano!" Tara squealed with delight, picking him up and cuddling him to her. "Oh Claire, he is *adorable.*"

"He is," Claire said with unabashed pride and, together, the two women looked foolishly at the small scrap of humanity who had for a moment captured their complete attention.

"Where's Piero?" Tara suddenly inquired.

"He's at work." Claire straightened up. "He still does the same thing; but I am hoping that when the matter is settled with Armand and I have the annulment, things will be better. I want him to paint seriously as an artist because he has a *great* talent. A really great one but, for the moment . . ."

"The same thing?" Tara nodded sympathetically and, removing her beret, shook out her beautiful, lustrous hair, as she looked around the apartment. It was small but it was appealing, rather like a setting for the first act of *La Bohème.* Its attic walls, freshly distempered, were covered with Piero's paintings and on the bare floorboards were colorful rugs, comfortable armchairs of bleached calico and books and art magazines piled high on the small tables scattered about.

In one corner was a large easel with an unfinished canvas still in it by the enormous window through which could be seen the church at the top of the Spanish Steps, the Trinita dei Monti.

There were flowers everywhere, a small TV and a stereo with two loudspeakers in opposite corners. It was simple, pretty, cozy and the last place in which she expected to find a Desmond at home. But then Claire had never really been a Desmond, not in the way her family was.

"We're happy here," Claire said a little defensively, watching Tara's eyes and probably guessing what she was thinking.

"I can see that," Tara said, hugging her. "But I can see there's no room for me."

"You . . . ?" Claire stared at her as Tara removed her coat and sat in one of the deep canvas-covered armchairs.

"I've left Zac. He doesn't know where I am and I hoped you could put me up, for a while."

"Of course we can put you up." Claire appeared at a loss for words. "You can sleep on the couch in the corner . . . but what will Zac say?"

"Who cares *what* Zac says," Tara said. She put her hand on her forehead and momentarily closed her eyes. Then, opening them, she flung her head back and gazed at her sister-in-law with those huge brown eyes. Half of Tara's appeal lay in the air of tragedy, of unhappiness that haunted her beautiful face. Claire knew she was the sort of woman who Piero would love to paint. "I've had enough, Claire. Also I was pursued by Bob. I had enough of him too. He's sweet; but he's a child. He got terribly serious. What with him, Zac and Gomez, my minder, I felt I wasn't my own person. I could never for a *moment* be myself or by myself . . . In the end I just went, and do you know what?"

"What?" Claire finished pinning Guiliano's diaper, put a cotton top on him and then laid him in his crib, sitting for a minute gazing at him.

"I'm happy too. For the first time for years I'm simply, basically *happy*. I don't want to have anything to do with Jean Marvoine, Bob O'Neill, Zac or the Desmond family. And as for Belle . . . Her attempts to dominate my life, my work, never cease. She is so close to Zac it is like a conspiracy. I felt that together, they're spying on me. She wants to run the business herself. Let her. I don't want it. She is a good businesswoman but I am the one with the flair, the eye for fashion . . . let her see how *she* gets on by herself."

"And the children?" Claire's eyes strayed to Guiliano and rested on him with an expression of tenderness.

Tara shrugged.

"Well they are no longer young, like Guiliano. They do not need a mother so much. Giada is twelve and Roberto eleven. Giada has always been the apple of Zac's eye, Daddy's girl. Roberto . . ." Again she shrugged. "Maybe when we are settled Zac will let him come and visit me."

"But *where* will you settle, what will you do? How will you live? Zac will think of me immediately."

"Why should he think of you?"

"He will wonder where you've gone. You'd go to people who could help you. You're Italian. I shouldn't be surprised if he didn't telephone within hours . . . luckily we have no phone, so he will telephone your brother Marco."

"Marco," Tara said, hand to her mouth, eyes thoughtful. "Of course! I should have gone to my brother, Marco. Moreover, though it is not very comfortable, there is plenty of room there."

Claire got up, gently tilting the crib of the sleeping baby to peep at him. Then she covered him with a shawl and, putting a finger to her mouth, pushed his crib into the bedroom where she left him, shutting the door behind her. There was still the smile of maternal happiness as she crept back into the main room, but her eyes looked worried.

She went over to the dresser and began to gather together the baby things that she'd used for Guiliano's bath. Then she turned to Tara, who seemed to be watching her every move.

"You must not tell your brother Marco you are here," Claire said with exaggerated quietness, as if she expected someone to overhear her. "You must be very careful he doesn't know. Because I tell you your brother Marco is a very unscrupulous man . . . and, if he could sell you back to Zac, or blackmail Zac to reveal your whereabouts, he would do that too. He is a man without any principles whatsoever, and you must have nothing to do with him."

"Believe me, I know."

31

Bob seemed to have spent the days gazing out of the window, yet seeing nothing. He'd had little to eat or drink; he just sat and stood there, looking.

Sandra had never known Bob like this and his wretchedness had deeply affected her, busy though she was going over the details of the case for the prosecution in the forthcoming libel trial in London. They'd been lucky to get it brought forward early in the English courts: nine months, whereas sometimes it took two years.

One couldn't utter platitudes like "cheer up" or "it will soon pass" because Sandra knew that things like that never did. Hurt took a long time to heal. Instead she said:

"I saw a beautiful house today. It's just past the Pont Saint-Louis, near the little garden at the end. It's eighteenth century and incredibly well preserved. The last owner, who has just died, was a member of the original family who built it in the time of Louis XV. I think you—"

"I'm going back to the States, Sandra," Bob said, interrupting her. "I guess I decided."

With a sigh he stood up, hands deep in his pockets, a day or two's growth of beard on his chin, his eyes bloodshot. Sandra's heart went out to him in love and sympathy and, going over to him, she put her arms round his neck.

"Oh *Bob* . . . I can't persuade you to stay if you want to go; but I'll miss you."

"I'll miss you too," Bob said. "But I'll miss . . . her more." Even after a week he couldn't say her name; not after the note had come:

"Dear Bob, I'm running away—from Zac, from Gomez, from you, from everything. I have to live my own life, be my own person. Besides I'm too old for you. Be happy.

Love, Tara."

It was all he had to remember her by—no snaps of them together, no presents from her, nothing. Just a kiss, this note, and the memories of precious times alone with her: meals shared, little bistros on the Left Bank where Zac would never dream of going; moments alone in Sandra's flat—very few of them because of Gomez and his car. He was quite sure it was really because of Gomez she had gone.

If he hadn't always been there hovering, Bob was convinced Tara would not have left without him. Ironically it was he who had put the idea of flight in her mind . . . and now she'd gone, alone.

All he had were memories . . . not much really to hang on to.

Bob had mooned about, increasingly silent after the first shock nearly a week ago, and Sandra busy with her own worries had been at a loss as to what to do.

"Maybe going back *is* best," she said at last, hugging him.

"She'll never come back, not to me. Maybe to Zac because he has the money; but not to me. She thinks I'm a baby . . . you do too."

"I don't think *you're* a baby, Bob, but you were much too young for Tara. Tara is a woman of the world, married, a mother. She's had lovers; why she's even been in jail!"

"I loved her," Bob said stubbornly. "I really loved her and I *know* I would have made her happy."

"Well," Sandra removed her arms and shrugged, "personally I feel it is for the best. Only I wish you could come to London with me for the trial. I've got no one you know, but you."

"I can't, Sis. I just can't face *anything* at the moment. I'd be no help to you. I'm not much help to myself. I want to go home; back to where I belong."

"I'll wire Maria," Sandra said.

In a way she envied him. If only life could be that simple for her.

Springtime, early summer, in London sometimes finds the capital at its best, sometimes at its worst with rain-soaked streets and sodden foliage clinging to the trees. The weather on the occasion of Sandra's case brought against the *Daily Enquirer* was middling; not the sort of weather that made one wish to be lounging in the parks, but bright enough to encourage a display of fashionable wear made for her by the top Paris couturiers.

Not that she wanted people to write about what she wore; that in her eyes would be sexist. But she thought counsel looked very impressive and authoritative in their gowns and wigs, clutching their briefs as they earnestly made their way along the Strand from the Law Courts to their chambers in the various Inns of which they were members: Lincoln's Inn, Gray's Inn, Middle Temple, Inner Temple. It was all very timeless and old worldly and Sandra, knowing the eyes of the news media were upon her, wanted to look the part of a woman more sinned against than sinning; someone who refused to allow her future to be ruined by what had happened in the past.

But on some days during the trial she bitterly regretted bringing it as much of her life was laid bare, however hard her counsel, Jeremy Harte, QC, tried to stop it.

On the whole it had gone well but the court had been told

of a girl uncertain about her origins, maybe insecure despite a life of comfort. Yes she had been deserted by her mother—well, deserted in a manner of speaking, and yes, she had been a brilliant student and had achieved the highest honors at school and university.

And yet . . . what sort of person *was* Sandra O'Neill Desmond *really?* That was what the lawyers sought to find out and Sandra, who protested that it was irrelevant to the issue, was told that it was not. So out it all came and she had to stand there in the box and answer, glad at least that the Desmonds had not thought it worth their while to come.

However careful and considerate he was, the counsel for the defense was out to probe. He wanted to prove her a liar: why should not a beautiful woman *wish* to flaunt her body? Would it not be natural?

No, Sandra had replied firmly. Not for her, never. And, being Sandra, after three days of examination and cross-examination in the box, she had not cracked; lost her temper occasionally, been reprimanded once or twice by the judge, but she'd never given in, insisting that she had not posed nude, never could and never would! Why should she? She had a career, money . . .

In the end most people thought she'd proved her point. She was eventually allowed to stand down and resume her seat next to her solicitor, in front of counsel, to the left of the jury.

It was amazing, though she was getting used to it, how intimate the atmosphere in the small court was; how cozily, almost chattily, counsel spoke. Addressing, examining and cross-examining witnesses in voices that scarcely rose and sometimes could hardly be heard.

In front of the court the robed, bewigged judge seldom stopped writing except to interpose a question of one of the witnesses or, maybe, utter a witticism or two. The barristers were very deferential. Everyone was exceedingly polite; the judge positively solicitous, frequently ordering breaks for cups of tea. Sandra had at first been astonished that the court's day was so brief. Ten until about four with an hour for lunch. But, really, despite the courtesy, the air of timelessness, the sense of English law, evolved over centuries, slowly taking its course, the day was a strain. Hours in the witness box trying to remember tiny details were hard on the nerves.

Sometimes she had felt it was she who was on trial under the watchful eyes of the judge, the stares of the jury, the curious gaze of the entire court packed for every day of the trial which was nightly sensationalized by the evening papers: "BEAUTY NEVER POSED IN THE NUDE. LOVELY SANDRA SAYS SHE'S A VICTIM OF FRAUD."

That was personal; that she hated.

After her evidence the first week of the trial had been devoted to the authenticity of the photographs. Her counsel was quite sure that the case against the photographs would be thrown out. Then he would try for a settlement on the other issue to save Tim Desmond and Lady Elizabeth being brought to court as they would have to, to try and establish the truth of Sandra's paternity.

A photographic expert had been flown from the Kodak laboratories in America in order to demonstrate that the photos were a montage: the heads of Sandra and Tim superimposed on the bodies of two other people. All they had to go on were copies but even then by enlargement it was possible to show . . . or *was* it?

Another equally renowned photographic expert came from the Agfa laboratories in Germany to try and prove the opposite, and the argument continued back and forth for days.

Then there was a breakthrough. Due to the publicity the case had been receiving a New York model phoned an American television station to say that she thought the body of the woman in the photo was hers.

Now here she was in the witness box and Sandra watched

her with fascination, tempered with unease, as nude photographs of the girl, who was a professional model known as Jay, were passed to the jury and shown to the judge, counsel and, of course, Sandra herself. Together with Jeremy Harte she examined them in the barristers' room.

The case was proved. Sensation. The papers had their customary field days: "HEIRESS VICTIM OF FALSIFICATION." "SANDRA DESMOND WINS HER CASE." "FRENCH TYCOON BEAUTY NOT THE WOMAN IN THE NUDE PICTURES."

"Thank God it's all over," Sandra said as she kicked off her shoes in her suite at Claridges and toasted the verdict with a bottle of Desmond Rare champagne. On the floor around her were the newspapers while an English secretary, who was engaged to help her, fended off a flood of telephone calls for interviews, to appear on TV, to go to the hotel lobby to make a statement.

But not yet.

"It's not over," her solicitor, Randall Harper of the eminent legal firm Harper, Low and Threshfield of Lincoln's Inn, said.

"But *surely* the *Enquirer* will back down?"

"I understand they won't," Randall Harper said. "I spoke to their solicitor before coming to see you. They think they can prove a case of incest. . . ."

"That's what I was dreading," Sandra said. "Maybe we'd better call it off."

"Then you would look guilty. You don't really have the option to back out now."

Randall Harper was a man of about fifty who had reached eminence in his profession solely on the grounds of competence. He did not correspond to the stereotype of the prosperous lawyer with a country house and a Rolls Royce though, undoubtedly, he had the means. He had been recommended to Sandra by a legal colleague of Henri Piper's and, so far, Sandra approved of what he'd done.

The Pipers were not there either. Henri dared not make the journey to be with her, though he called her daily from California. As for Michel . . . already he'd been in Africa for six weeks. It was clear where his priorities lay. He called her too, but not so often.

Harper was tall, slim and ascetic looking. He could have been a monk, or a cleric in the Church of England; maybe a bishop. He now turned and looked gravely at Sandra who lay back in her chair, glass in one hand, her eyes closed.

"You have had an ordeal, Miss Desmond; but you had no choice."

"I'm glad you think so."

"I do. If I were asked to donate my entire fee to charity to prove that I believed this, I would."

"Oh I'm not asking you to do that!" Sandra said with a wry smile. "How are you on commercial law? We could do with a good English lawyer for some of our operations over here."

Harper smiled with pleasure and, picking up his glass, toasted her.

"I do regard that as a compliment, Miss Desmond. But first things first. I'm afraid we shall have to call Lady Elizabeth. . . ."

"Oh but I couldn't. . . ."

"Oh but you must. Her word will carry great weight. She, I believe, is as convinced as you that you are not the daughter of her late husband. . . ."

"It will be very painful for her."

"It is inevitable, I'm afraid. Do you mind if I call her tomorrow?"

Zac switched off the television bulletin and swung back to his desk.

"Would you like a drink?" he inquired of Belle, who had been anxiously watching him.

Belle glanced at her watch.

"If we've time."

"There's always time for champagne." Zac, in an attempt at jocularity, pressed the intercom on his desk and Belle was glad to see him smile because she knew how long it was since Zac had felt happy.

Every day he had pored over the English and French newspapers about the trial, seen every TV bulletin and listened to every radio broadcast.

Maybe, although he had been very careful to keep away, out of earshot and out of sight, he was afraid something would emerge about his own involvement. Maybe he was still angry about Tara but, whatever it was, Zac was an anxious and unhappy man and Belle, who loved him as she loved no one else, grieved for him.

His secretary appeared with a tray on which there was the usual bottle of Desmond champagne in a bucket, and two glasses.

"Could I go now, Monsieur Desmond?" she inquired.

"Of course Henriette, but leave the phone switched through. I am expecting an important call."

"Bien, Monsieur Desmond. *Bonne nuit,* Monsieur, *bonne nuit,* Princess."

Belle smiled at her and Zac waved as he rose to pour the champagne.

"Pretty girl," Belle said as Henriette closed the door.

"I like her. After that little shit, Agnès, she is careful and sensible."

"I don't know why you must always sleep with your secretaries. . . ."

"Agnès wasn't my secretary."

"Well, any secretary. Surely there are plenty of bored housewives looking for a bit of fun?"

"Yes, and a bit of fun I'd have with their husbands. No thank you." Zac passed Belle her glass. "But no apartment for Henriette. Anyway she lives with her mother. Occasionally I send her flowers."

Zac toasted Belle and sipped his drink appreciating, as he always did, that first encounter between the palate and the sharp excellence of the wine.

"Bon," he said, smacking his lips. "Well, what are we to do? Do we go on—or do we stop? They want instructions."

"I think it will cost many thousands of francs. Do you have that kind of money?"

"I have it at my command, shall we say?" Zac said with a smirk.

"Well don't add embezzlement to your woes," Belle snapped at him. "You've been lucky to have gotten away with what you have. I never for a moment thought you'd persuade the Board to make you President of Franco-Belges. It just goes to show how corrupt the banking fraternity can be."

"Belle, please . . ." Zac hissed, looking nervously at the door. "Walls have ears. It's nonsense to say that anyway. The Board trusts me. They know I have their interests at heart. The Baron has a very nice new yacht, and I have promised the Telliers Desmond when we get hold of it. . . ."

"What?" Belle cried, thumping her glass dangerously down upon the table next to her.

"Under my control, of course. Don't worry, we'll soon get it back; but I hoped by this stage . . . the *Enquirer* thinks we will lose."

"That was the person on the phone when I came in?"

Zac nodded.

"They are quite happy to settle. But I . . ."

"You *could* lose a fortune and your reputation. I'd like to know how they found that girl who modeled for the photos."

"It was a fluke. I have it on the authority of Blake, my English attorney. He swears that Sandra has no detectives on the prowl." He finished his wine and, getting up, went over to pour himself and Belle fresh glasses. Then he stood moodily in front of the window, looking on to the busy rush hour traffic in the avenue.

"What do you say, Belle? I'll take your advice."

He swung around and gazed at her. Sometimes she felt sorry for Zac and this was one of those times. Many people would have laughed at the notion but, to her, he was still the small wounded boy who always so badly wanted the love and trust of his father. A love and trust hideously betrayed when he disinherited his eldest son.

Ever since then Zac had been like a man in purgatory, and she knew that she was with him there, suffering the pains of the damned, or almost damned.

Just then the sharp ring of the telephone sent Zac striding across to his desk where he rapidly lifted the receiver, his face tense as he rasped into it:

"Oui?"

Belle watched him closely, seeing his face change; registering first surprise, then dismay and, finally, anger. He said a few sharp words during which Tourville was mentioned several times, then he put the phone down with a respectful:

"Adieu Maman, merci."

For a long time he let his hand rest on the receiver, his head bent in thought.

"That was Mother," he said eventually to Belle, raising his head to stare into her eyes. "As I suppose you realized. She has been subpoenaed to appear in defense of Sandra."

"And if she refuses?"

"There will be one hell of a fuss." Slowly Zac sat down, his face thoughtful. "The strange thing is that she seems to *want* to appear. She says she has something to say and that, ultimately, it will be for our benefit."

Zac rose from his desk again and, reaching for a book containing telephone numbers, hastily riffled through the pages. Then he lifted the phone and started to dial, a long thirteen-digit number.

"I'm calling the English lawyer," he said to his sister, his hand over the mouthpiece. "I think we'll have to intervene."

Pierre said with a bow, "The car is at the door, Madame."

Lady Elizabeth, dressed in gray, rose to leave. One last look round the room, a slow walk along the corridor, down the main stairs, across the great hall and through the rear door of the Phantom IV Rolls held open by a footman.

On the steps Pierre stood bowing and, at several of the windows, she glimpsed the heads of the maids taking furtive peeps before hastily withdrawing their heads.

It was as though they were all saying goodbye.

As the car bore her down the drive she took a look at the place she loved, almost as if seeing it for the last time. Perhaps she was.

In her bag lying safely on her lap was the letter; the one she had hoped she would never have to use. It had been locked in a box in the safe in her bedroom.

Whatever happened in London would mark either the end, or a new beginning.

Sandra shifted uncomfortably in her seat as Zac solemnly took his place in the witness box and raised his right hand as he repeated the oath.

"I, René-Zachariah Desmond, do solemnly swear that I shall tell the truth, the whole truth and nothing but the truth. So help me God."

With that he bowed to the judge, cleared his throat and joined his hands in front of his neatly buttoned jacket while awaiting the examination of counsel for the defense.

His was a distinguished presence in the box and no doubt he would be a convincing one. He was tall, upright, grave of demeanor, impeccably dressed, with just that cosmopolitan air that made him out to be the man of the world he undoubtedly was.

Convincing, sincere, truthful.

How many people would he deceive?

For she, Sandra O'Neill Desmond, knew him, without a shadow of a doubt, to be a liar, a swindler and possibly, a murderer. Between her and Zac Desmond there was now fixed a gulf so wide it could never be breached. That she knew for sure.

Whatever happened, from now on it was war to the death: each ranged against the other. Behind her back he had made himself President of the Banque Franco-Belges which, with his Presidency of the Desmond Bank and Vice-Presidency of the Desmond Group, made him a powerful and feared force in the French business world, a real rival to herself.

But not only that. His influence had been felt in America where she knew he had advised the Heurtey Group in resisting the takeover attempt by Desmond; surely an irregularity in itself, yet no one could pin him down as having actually done anything wrong. That was the trouble. He left no traces, no marks, nothing in writing. He was undetectable and indestructible.

As counsel adjusted his wig, fiddled with his papers, consulted with his junior and prepared to question him, Zac looked at her. Momentarily their eyes became locked in mutual hatred.

Then Zac turned his face to Sir Arnold Parker, QC, whose fees, although no one knew it, even the learned lawyer himself, were being paid by the witness in the box.

"You are Mr. René-Zachariah Desmond, known I believe as Zac Desmond?"

"That is right, sir."

"And you are the eldest son of the late Georges Desmond. . . . ?"

"I am."

The voice droned on, the answers became repetitious.

"That is correct." "I am." "I did." "I did not." "Not to

my knowledge" and so on and so forth. Polite, correct, firm, truthful. . . .

Eloquently, gracefully, counsel took him through his life, his studies, his ambitions, his position in his father's firm.

What was this leading up to? Even the judge wondered at one point.

"I am coming to that in a moment, my Lord," Sir Arnold said with a sweeping bow to the bench.

"Now Mr. Desmond, may I ask you if you expected to inherit the Presidency of the Desmond Group from your father?"

"I did, sir."

"I see." Sir Arnold glanced at the papers on the table before him. "An honest answer." He looked at the jury to make sure they understood. "And at no time did he give you any hint otherwise?"

"No, sir. The first time I learned that my father had disinherited me was when the will was read on the day he died."

"And of course you had a terrible shock."

"I did, sir."

Sir Arnold glanced behind him to the public benches at the back of the court which was now, since Zac's decision to take part, full of Desmonds. Belle sat there with Carl; her aunt, Lady Broughton, and Sophie Piper who had clearly, by her appearance, allied herself to the Desmonds. Henri, Sandra knew, remained in California.

"But I believe," counsel for the defense said, "that you and your brother and sisters bore your father no ill will?"

"None at all, sir."

"None at *all?*" repeated the judge with a slight note of incredulity as he leaned across the bench, pen poised in his hand.

"None at all, my Lord," Zac assured him respectfully. "We all venerated our father, and thought he must have the best reasons in the world for his bequest. . . ."

"And what was that, may I ask?" Sir Arnold raised his arm

in a flourish, as a showman demonstrates his latest trick producing, perhaps, a rabbit from his hat.

"My family—at least my mother and I—were convinced that Miss O'Neill was my father's illegitimate daughter by his mistress Hélène O'Neill, with whom he had a relationship that was known and acknowledged by everyone for over twenty years. In fact our father had decided, in his wisdom, that his own flesh and blood should still inherit."

"I believe that the prosecution will seek to show that such a relationship was impossible." Sir Arnold consulted his junior again in a hurried whisper. "Mrs. O'Neill and your father, Monsieur Desmond, did not meet until Sandra O'Neill was six years old."

"I believe that is not true, sir. I believe they did meet and there is evidence to show that they did."

"Evidence that he will have manufactured!" Sandra hissed angrily to her solicitor, who put a finger to his lips. "This is the master of counterfeit."

The judge looked disapprovingly in Sandra's direction and she bowed her head. He was the last person she wanted to prejudice against herself.

"And you will no doubt have evidence of that nature?"

"I believe it is before you, sir."

"Oh yes." Sir Arnold took a document from his junior and perused it carefully through his half-moon glasses.

"There is evidence, my Lord, that Mrs. O'Neill worked in the typing pool of the Desmond organization, in fact, for a year before Sandra O'Neill was born."

At that, Jeremy Harte rose to lodge an objection but the judge told him that he could have his say in his own good time. The clerk of the court took from Sir Arnold the document which he placed before Mr. Justice Goodsire, one of the senior High Court judges, who proceeded to read it.

"I see," he said, eventually returning it to the clerk. "This is a testimony of a Madame Marie Benoit who worked in the typing pool at the same time."

"And doubtless she is also in the pay of Zac," Sandra whispered to Randall Harper who whispered back:

"All in good time." He raised his head as a pupil from his chambers crept over to him and put a piece of paper in his hand. Scarcely attending to what was going on in the witness box, Harper put on his reading glasses, unfolded the paper and read the neatly typed message two or three times. Then, removing his spectacles and putting them in his breast pocket, he quietly handed the paper to Sandra. It read:

"Madame Georges Desmond agrees to testify in favor of Miss Desmond. She is making a deposition to this office."

It was signed by a junior partner of his law firm.

Sandra handed the paper back to Harper and realized that her fingers were trembling.

After the lunch break, Jeremy Harte, QC, rose to address the judge in a manner that was as restrained as that of Sir Arnold. He too rustled his papers, clasped his wig as though he were unsure of the fit, and fiddled with his pen. But when he rose to speak his voice was firm and clear.

"My Lord, as a result of the widespread publicity concerning this case, certain evidence has come to our notice that is a complete rebuttal of the evidence we heard this morning. I have informed my learned colleague," Mr. Harte bowed deeply to Sir Arnold, "of the nature of that evidence, and he and his clients wish to have time to consider it, as do my client and those who are instructing me. We ask for an adjournment, my Lord, until tomorrow morning."

"Very well, Mr. Harte," said the judge, "the court will adjourn until ten A.M. tomorrow morning." And as the usher told everyone to rise he left the bench while a frantic buzz broke out behind him.

* * *

Sandra watched Lady Elizabeth go into the witness box in very much the same frame of mind as she had watched Zac only the day before. Yet her emotion now was very different from what it had been twenty-four hours ago. She still felt the effects of the tension of the previous day, long talks with her solicitor and counsel, and an examination of Lady Elizabeth's testimony. In legal terms this is known as the "Discovery" and in a civil case must be made available to both parties before it comes to court.

Sandra, on hearing the nature of the evidence the previous afternoon, had wished to suppress it and call off the case.

In which event, both Mr. Harte and Mr. Randall had explained to her, she would not only have to pay all the costs of both sides amounting to thousands and thousands of pounds, but it was tantamount to an admission of guilt. Her resignation from the Desmond Group would thereafter be inevitable.

Yet all night long she had lain awake wondering if it were not better to drop the case, resign from the Group and disappear . . . rather than let all the world know what she now knew:

Bitterness, humiliation, incomprehension and, finally, defeat.

For the incongruity was that even though she knew she must now win her case, in another way she would lose it.

Yet she was not Sandra O'Neill for nothing. She had not gotten where she had and held onto power in the Desmond Group for two years to be deprived of it for a life of anonymity and, if she had dropped the case, shame. She would have been known forever as the person who had failed, lost. and as she had told Doug Hammerson two years before, she couldn't live with failure.

As Lady Elizabeth raised her right hand and took the oath, she and Sandra too locked eyes, like a pair of antagonists well matched.

"This is my revenge," Lady Elizabeth seemed silently to be saying to her, "this is my revenge on you for what you have done."

Lady Elizabeth looked away as in a firm, authoritative English voice she vowed to tell the truth.

"You are Lady Elizabeth Desmond, widow of the late Georges Desmond?"

"I am."

In a way it was marvelous theater. A packed house pressed forward in their seats. Even the judge had lost his air of detachment and sat back in his chair as if enjoying a good show. Jeremy Harte, QC, rose to examine her.

"Lady Elizabeth, although you were subpoenaed, I believe you have come here today quite willingly to testify for the prosecution in this case."

"I have sir," Lady Elizabeth said, glancing not at Sandra, but at her family.

"And would you tell the court why that is, Madame?"

"It is on account of a letter I received nearly a year ago." Lady Elizabeth carefully took something from her bag, which stood on the ledge of the witness box. Slowly she unfolded it with one hand, placing on her nose her reading glasses with the other. "I think the best thing is for me to read this letter to the court."

"Please do, Lady Elizabeth." Jeremy Harte, a pleased look on his face, sat down again.

"The letter is dated September last year and is as follows," Lady Elizabeth said in a low clear voice drained of emotion. "I am translating it into English as I go along, my Lord," she observed directly to the judge who nodded his head and asked her to continue.

"My dear Madame," [Lady Elizabeth began]

"I am writing this letter to you because I feel I am very close to death. . . ."

The silence in the court was absolute, though Sandra was quite sure that it must reverberate with the pounding of her heartbeat as, with the rest, she listened to this voice from the dead.

"You asked me, Madame, if Sandra O'Neill were the daughter of your late husband and I said she was not. I had the feeling you did not believe me and, in a sense, you were right. I was withholding something from you that has been withheld all her life from Sandra herself, and it is because I am a sick woman that I cannot bear to entrust this information now to anyone except you in a confidential letter, Madame Desmond, which will not be delivered until after my death.

"For Sandra I know this will be painful and I wish I had the courage to tell her to her face. But as you know, Madame, Sandra, perhaps rightly, has never forgiven me for leaving her when she was a small girl, and I felt I was beyond her pity or forgiveness.

"Had I been her mother I would *have been a bad mother, but I was not. For as Georges Desmond, most certainly, was not her father, neither was I her mother; and for this she may reproach me for withholding the truth from her, as she will reproach me anyway, for the rest of her life.*

"The story, Madame, is this. . . ."

Lady Elizabeth continued to read the letter in the same monotonous tone she had begun, as if taking no part in it except as an intermediary, as a medium in contact with the spirit world.

At the end there was a profound silence, followed by a stampede in the court as the journalists in the reporters' gallery rushed headlong for the doors, to be the first to telephone the astonishing news to a waiting world.

EPILOGUE

More Sinned Against Than Sinning . . .

32

Sandra put down the paper on top of all the others in various languages—French, English, German, Italian—that lay at her feet on the floor. It was only now that she could bring herself to read all the accounts of the sensational Desmond libel trial that had finished so dramatically in the English law courts two weeks before, leaving her, technically, the victor but, most emphatically, the loser. For she had lost not only her precious anonymity but any sense she had of belonging: she had lost her past.

It was only now that, with Hélène O'Neill's last letter in her possession, she could look at the whole matter with any kind of objectivity and try and find, in her heart, forgiveness.

It was very hard. First she had to forgive Hélène for concealing the truth for so many years; then she had to forgive Lady Elizabeth who with, perhaps, no small amount of venom, acted in the interests of her disinherited children, rather than Sandra, and deprived her of any sweetness in her victory.

But most of all she had to forgive her real mother, who had consistently and persistently deceived her throughout her life, and even now had not tried to come forward. Maybe she was too ashamed.

The incredible story [the newspaper at Sandra's feet repeated] *is that the famous film star of the post-war years, Virginia Wingate, had a baby by a man who has never been named and asked her then secretary, Hélène O'Neill, to adopt her and bring her up as her own. Mrs. O'Neill, married to a fickle, inconstant husband who was permanently in debt and, consequently desperately short of cash, agreed. She went to France, taking the baby with her and, in a sense, the evidence produced by Mr. Zac Desmond at the trial was right. Mrs. O'Neill* had *met Georges Desmond many years before she became his mistress, but little Sandra had already been born. The exact recollection of that date escaped Madame Benoit who gave evidence on behalf of Mr. Desmond.*

It appears that, unhappily, Hélène O'Neill never took to the young Sandra for some reason that is unknown. Eventually she was reunited with her husband and had a son, Bob, who is now a student at the University of California. By this time, however, the restless Mrs. O'Neill once again got employment with the Desmond Organization and, eventually, she told Miss Wingate that she no longer wished to look after her daughter. Miss Wingate, fearing the effect on her declining screen career if the story were known, begged Hélène O'Neill to continue the pretense but agreed to keep an eye on her natural daughter as well as little Bob as long as the truth were not revealed.

It is a sad, even tragic tale, and the effect on the Desmond empire is unknown, for Miss Desmond has declined to be interviewed and left London immediately after the end of the case. The Desmond press office has issued a statement saying that Miss Desmond is taking a short holiday, has no intention of relinquishing her presidency, and will soon be returning.

But would she?

Restlessly Sandra got up and walked slowly to the window which overlooked the perfectly kept lawn that sloped down to the still lake. Beyond that was woodland and beyond that the acres upon acres of vineyards which had given Tourville its meaning, its reason for existing and the reason she was here.

For now, at last, it was hers. Set amid a hundred acres of

gardens and parkland with its fifty bedrooms, its many state and reception rooms, its extensive servants' quarters, its famous marble staircase and painted hall, its minarets, turrets, gables and crenellated towers—everything belonged to her and here she was, by herself, in this huge place: silent and alone.

It was not, she reflected, what Lady Elizabeth or any of the Desmonds had anticipated when Georges Desmond had been so unexpectedly and precipitously taken from them. Certainly not what she, Sandra, the reluctant legatee, had expected or wished.

Lady Elizabeth wanted it to be, as it always had been, the family home, the center of the Desmond world; and so had Sandra who, having adopted the Desmond name, so badly wanted a family too.

So, in a sense, everyone had been let down, disappointed, and now they were all scattered while she found herself alone in a huge house in a way she had never thought she would be.

It was noon, not the time of day that usually saw Sandra by herself with little to do. She was taking a break, but one that had been enforced on her. In a way she was afraid to show her face until the hubbub had died down: requests for interviews, TV appearances, explanations . . . a publishing company had offered her an advance of over one million dollars for her memoirs, and she was not yet twenty-eight!

She realized now that she was something she hated: a celebrity. She was celebrated for being celebrated and because, from obscurity, she had in two years become one of the best known and, now, most controversial, women in the world.

On the lawn under the disapproving eyes of a majestic swan who had solemnly waddled up from the lake to bask in the sun, a flock of tiny sparrows fought over some morsel they had gathered, probably from the kitchen door where crumbs were sometimes thrown to the birds. In front of her was frantic activity and elsewhere, she knew, the servants were going about their tasks as they always did whether or not the family was in residence. There was an orderliness about the place, a solemn, half-monastic routine that never varied. One almost expected bells to ring out at intervals to denote the passing of time.

She had already consulted with the cook over her solitary menus for the day, and in an hour or so Pierre would announce lunch as he did when any of them were in residence. Lady Elizabeth was quite used to lunching and dining alone and, always, the routine was adhered to: one o'clock for lunch, four-thirty for tea, eight o'clock for dinner, and nothing and no one altered it.

Would she, could she in time become a lonely eccentric in this vast house afraid to face the world? More importantly would the Desmonds, in their thirst for revenge, ever let her?

From the corner of her eye, beyond the hedge that screened the drive from the side of the house she was in, she saw the top of a car approach and, as it passed out of sight, she realized who it must contain and ran to the door. Flinging it open, she rushed across the hall before the servant on duty had time to react and then wrenching open the main door, she ran out onto the portico and down the steps even before the car door was properly open.

"Uncle Henri!" she cried, flinging herself into his arms as he tried to alight. "Oh I *knew* you would come!"

"Sandra . . ." His hands caressed her cheek but his eyes, raking the windows of the hall, looked worried. "Don't let the servants see. . . ."

As she stepped back he could see that her eyes gleamed with tears.

"I'm so relieved to see you," she murmured. "I feel like a . . . an outcast in this huge place."

"Then *why* did you come here?" He took her hand as she tucked her arm through his and patted it.

"Let's go around the back," she said. "Lady Elizabeth had a favorite little spot near the greenhouse which is a favorite of mine too. I know why now. No one can see you from the house. It is one of the few places at Tourville where you can be completely alone. Oh I *am* glad to see you." She looked up at him with shining eyes. "I'm more pleased to see you than anyone else in the world. *Dear,* dear Henri." She pressed his arm close to her body and he fancied he could feel the beating of her heart. Wishful thinking. He wanted to put his arms around her and caress her as if they were lovers, but, of course, he didn't dare. . . .

"I saw Virginia Wingate," he said quietly. "She confirms everything. She said to tell you . . ."

"I don't care what she said to tell me," Sandra interrupted him, her voice rising.

"Nevertheless," Henri stopped and continued gently, "she is very sorry. She said she would do anything to undo the harm . . . and she *was* fond of you."

"Well, I was never fond of her!" Sandra flopped down in one of the cane chairs as they reached the spot under the oak. "And to think she is my *mother. . . ."* She buried her face in her hands and, momentarily, her shoulders contracted so that Henri thought she was going to cry like a small girl. But, after a few seconds, she lowered her hands and her eyes were dry. "It was such a terrible shock."

"I can imagine." Henri nodded sympathetically. "I wish I'd been there, but what help could I have been?"

"You were more help where you were and also to go and see her and have her confirm the story is, I suppose, in its way a help." Sandra took a cigarette from a case in her bag and leaned forward while Henri lit it.

"I must stop these," she said as if to herself with a shaky laugh, holding up the smoldering cigarette in front of her. "It makes Michel very cross. . . ."

"He's still on your mind then?" Henri inquired.

"Of course. He's on my mind the whole time."

"Then why don't you go to him?"

"Go?" Sandra gazed at him in astonishment. "To Africa?"

"Why not? Why stay here in this huge empty house grieving about the past?"

"I couldn't go for *good,"* Sandra said quickly. "I'm not finished you know. Bloody and bowed, but not finished."

"I'm sure you're not, my dear." Henri smiled as Pierre appeared from the direction of the house with a bucket on a silver tray in which there was a bottle and, beside it, two tall glasses. "I know you're not; but a holiday in Africa wouldn't do you any harm. It would also take you out of the way. The Press will wait for you for a long time, you know. It could be announced you are visiting the Foundation in Zimbabwe. Much harder for them to get to you there."

"I don't want them to think I'm scared." Sandra nodded her thanks as Pierre put the tray on the table. "How thoughtful of you, Pierre, thank you."

"I know Monsieur Piper always enjoys a glass of champagne at about noon, Mademoiselle."

She smiled as he uncorked the bottle and watched as the white frothy mousse slowly rose to the top. Henri watched too and suddenly their thoughts seemed to converge.

"To champagne," Sandra said as she raised her glass.

"To champagne," Henri echoed, taking his. "And never let us forget it."

"We are not likely to, or at least I'm not." Sandra settled back, her glass still in her hand. "Maybe I didn't remember it *enough* and, if I had, we shouldn't have had all the trouble we've had."

"What do you mean exactly?" Henri frowned, acknowledging Pierre's bow as he prepared to go back to the house.

"Well, champagne was at the heart of Desmond. It was at the heart of *Georges* Desmond."

"True."

"Tourville and the Desmonds are about champagne. If I had made my home here or in Reims, or somewhere near as I should have done, constantly to be reminded of my heritage by the sight of the vineyards surrounding me, maybe I would not have let myself be so carried away by the intrigues and machinations of big business."

"That you could hardly help," Henri said. "Zac made it impossible."

"Well, Zac's not here now and nor is Lady Elizabeth. Belle and Carl are back in Austria, and Claire is in Rome. Tim is still in the Far East and Bob . . ." Sandra shrugged. "Well, Bob's back in L.A."

"You'll miss him."

"Very much. I still can't believe he's not my real brother! I'm not related to him at all! Think of the shock of that."

"A terrible shock." Henri nodded sympathetically.

"Bob was my one bond—flesh and blood. Now he's not even that." She paused for a minute. "I still love him, though."

"I'm sure you do," Henri murmured. "How's Zac taken the whole thing, I wonder?"

"Who could *ever* know the mind of Zac Desmond?" Sandra said with a cynical smile. "Who can wonder what he feels about his wife running away, or about losing the case in court? Losing, yet winning. I bet he thought it worth the terrible publicity to the family."

"But what does Zac actually do now?"

"As far as I know he's doing what he normally does, apart from making mischief. He's back at his bank, living in the rue de Varenne and hunting for his elusive wife."

"She'll come back." Henri nodded wisely. "When she's short of money."

"But won't she be too frightened? I would."

"*You're* not frightened of Zac surely!"

"Not me." Sandra shook her head vigorously. "But I would if I were an erring wife, if I were Tara. God knows what he'll do to her. No, I'm not afraid of Zac now, and I'm not afraid of Belle. All the world knows who I am and what I am and do you know?" She folded her arms behind her head and gazed at him. "Now it's not so important." She looked around her at the shadows cast on the lawn by the fabulous trees planted over a hundred years ago by Jean-Timothée; aware of the peace, quiet, serenity and hope that was Tourville.

"And this, *this* is all mine, for a time. I'm mistress here because they have all sworn to stay away until I go. I won't go; not I, not Sandra O'Neill Desmond."

Henri looked at her with admiration and some pride. In the past two years he had helped her; he had given her courage when even her formidable strength failed, and upheld her when she was weak. To him she was the most interesting woman he had ever known, and yet his place would always be in her shadow.

"And Elizabeth?" he murmured. "She can't be too happy the way things have turned out."

"They've turned out as she herself made them," Sandra said firmly. "I wanted to like Lady Elizabeth and trust her; but for the sake of her family she has decided to make an enemy of me. So be it." Sandra folded her hands in her lap. "If she wants a reconciliation I'll be ready, maybe, one day. Right now she's staying on at Farley Hall with her brother, Lord Broughton. She can stay in England as long as she likes. I," Sandra's lips curled, "I can't help blaming Lady Elizabeth in full for the mischief of what was done. She should have told *me* a long time ago and spared me all this—spared me and the Desmonds, none of whom have relished the publicity."

"I agree." Henri screwed up his eyes. "I find it incredible she didn't."

"I can guess now what was on her mind. She hoped it would never have to come out. Then when she was subpoenaed she saw how she could humiliate me—and help Zac. I would never have believed she could be so devious; but by broadcasting it to the world she has made me an object of ridicule or, maybe, pity in the eyes of everyone. Have you seen some of the papers: "BUT WHO IS THE *FATHER* OF SANDRA DESMOND?" And I believe there are actually detectives looking for him."

"Oh there are," Henri said. "Poor Virginia has gone completely to ground. It's a terrible shock for her too, don't forget, to have this secret from the past suddenly exposed. If she hoped for graceful retirement she's had it."

Suddenly Sandra had a vision of the tall, elegant, vain, rather flamboyant woman who, she had constantly to remind herself, was her mother. Yet it *would* be a shock for her, the legendary Hollywood beauty. Hopefully the chance of publicity would not provoke her into announcing a comeback!

"Luckily," Henri went on as Sandra, lost in thought, didn't reply, "she has a friend who has a house in the mountains, and as soon as the news broke she closed her own house and went there. . . ."

"She didn't say anything about . . . my father?" Sandra said hesitantly and her expression was hard to judge as Henri shook his head.

"She refused to talk about it. I'm not sure she knows herself, to be honest. She's had, inevitably, many lovers. She is a beautiful woman . . . like you." Henri looked at her closely. "It's a wonder *you* never saw the likeness during the years you knew her. . . ."

"She was always changing the color of her hair," Sandra said defensively, "and with all the makeup she wore it was hard to tell what she really *was* like."

"Still beautiful, and proud . . . again like you. Frankly I liked her. Maybe she never felt at ease with you. One day I hope you will forgive her—go and see her. She only wants to see you if you wish it. However," Henri shrugged, "I'm sure she will understand why if you don't. She's quite dignified; unhappy, but resigned." He sighed. "Many things, my dear, many decisions to be made. I wondered . . ." He paused and fiddled with his now empty glass as Sandra looked at him.

"Yes?"

"If you'd like to come away on holiday with me? We could go anywhere you liked. I would ask nothing of course . . . just as a friend. But you do know, don't you, that I love you?"

Sandra put out her hand and affectionately took his.

"You are in love with love, 'Uncle' Henri. You're not really 'in love' with me. It happens to lots of men even if, like you, they've been happily married for years. Did you notice that I've started to call you 'uncle' again?"

"I did notice." Henri gave a rueful smile. "To remind me of my age, I suppose?"

"It's not just your *age,"* Sandra said. "That is not the question; but it is because you are my friend, my real friend. You have been of so much help to me. That *is* love too, though not the kind, maybe, you have in mind. You have given up so much for me, even perhaps your wife for a time. Sophie was in the court. She never glanced at me. She was allying herself firmly with the Desmonds. None of them spoke to me afterward . . . I don't think I ever felt so alone in my life as when my lawyer hustled me into a taxi to escape the waiting crowd of reporters. The Desmonds went one way and I another."

"Sophie has asked me if I want a divorce." Henri leaned over to pour more champagne. "Of course I don't."

"Of course you *don't* and of course she doesn't. You are very suited. The whole thing is so absurd. It will pass. She'll come back in time and the Château de Marsanne will be what it was."

"Do you know." Henri firmly put down his glass and got up. "I don't think anything will ever be what it was again." He shaded his eyes and looked past the house to the lawn, to the forest beyond. He couldn't see the twin towers of Reims Cathedral but he knew, approximately, in what direction they lay. They were like beacons that give a bearing to a traveler who is alone and lost—rather as he and Sandra were. One always came home to Reims, from whatever part of the world one happened to be, rather as the Muhammadans went home to Mecca. He turned to Sandra and continued: "This place won't be what it was, and you won't be. The Château de Marsanne certainly won't. Things might be different; they might even be better; but they will never be the same."

From the house the gong sounded for lunch and Henri held out his hand.

"Actually I'm quite hungry," he said. "This talk has helped clear the air. I hope they've laid a place for me."

The voice announcing the plane for Harare came over the airport P.A. and Sandra, her face concealed by dark glasses, prepared to go through passport control, taking her place in the line of fellow travelers: a preponderance of black faces, but many white as well. None, happily, that she knew. No one who recognized her. Anonymity, at last.

The passport officer took her passport, glanced through it at her picture, which he studied for a few seconds, then at her face. She thought he smiled, but immediately he returned it and began examining the passport of the person who came behind her.

She walked along the corridor to the plane, which stood on the tarmac being loaded with food supplies, refueled because it had flown in from New York.

The stewardess welcomed her aboard and, as though she'd been expected, a steward immediately stepped forward to take her small case and led her to her seat in the first-class compartment by the window.

"I think you'll be comfortable here, Miss Desmond," he whispered. "We have instructions that you do not wish to be disturbed. Please let me know immediately if you need anything. Anything at all."

Sandra smiled. Even here it was difficult, after all, to be completely anonymous. She was still who she was and that would never change. It was impossible to escape fame and sometimes, to be honest, it was useful.

She had also booked the seat beside her so that it would remain empty throughout the journey. On it she put her handbag and a traveling case containing her wash things, a change of clothes, and some magazines and then looked out of the window, where the lorries and trucks were driving away from her plane, which soon afterward started taxiing slowly toward the point of takeoff.

She had decided not to use her own jet. She wanted to arrive at Harare just like anyone else, a passenger transported for thousands of miles in a large plane. She knew Michel would like that. He hated show and privilege and she wanted to prove to him that she was what she said she was: the sort of person she'd been in Vermont. Just an ordinary woman who, despite money and power, could love and wanted to be loved; who wanted to move about an ordinary house and do ordinary things. But what then? That was, indeed, the question.

The large plane reached the point for takeoff; the engines roared; then it began its sprint along the runway before arching itself like a bird and leaping into the air. Up, up through the clouds, toward the sun, to blue skies that gave a sense of everlasting peace. For a time at least.

Sandra closed her eyes; the tension drained slowly away. Her journey had at last begun; a journey toward the unknown.

Nicola Thorne was born in South Africa but grew up and was educated in England. She has a degree in sociology from the London School of Economics, and worked as an editor before deciding to write full-time. She lives in Dorset, England.